D0893935

# The social reality of ethics

The comparative analysis
of moral codes

**International Library of Sociology**

Founded by Karl Mannheim

Editor: John Rex, University of Warwick

A catalogue of the books available in the **International Library of Sociology,** and new books in preparation for the Library, will be found at the end of this volume.

# The social reality of ethics
# The comparative analysis
# of moral codes

**John H. Barnsley**

*Industrial Administration Research Unit,*
*The University of Aston in Birmingham*

Routledge & Kegan Paul
London and Boston

*First published 1972*
*by Routledge & Kegan Paul Ltd,*
*Broadway House,*
*68–74 Carter Lane,*
*London EC4V 5EL and*
*9 Park Street,*
*Boston, Mass. 02108, U.S.A.*
*Printed in Great Britain*
*by Cox & Wyman Ltd,*
*London, Reading and Fakenham*
*© John H. Barnsley 1972*

ISBN  0 7100 7286 4

# Contents

v

# Tables

A*

**Figures**

# Acknowledgments

This study began life as a research thesis. For the present publication in book form a number of changes have, naturally, been necessary. But for any remaining infelicities of style or format, the reader's indulgence must be requested.

Thanks are due to all who, in one way or another, helped me with this research. I am indebted firstly to Professor Alasdair MacIntyre, from whose tuition I benefited greatly, for his supervision and encouragement of this research. And secondly, I am indebted to the Social Science Research Council, under whose extended postgraduate studentship it was carried out. I am grateful, too, for the advice and suggestions of various colleagues. In addition, my own research experience abroad, in Spain and Canada, suggested many fruitful lines of inquiry. Gratitude is therefore owed to those who made these occasions profitable ones. In the case of Spain, special mention should be made of the assistance of Professor Salustiano del Campo and Srta Guillermina Santana; and in the case of Canada, to that of Dr Robert A. Stebbins. Acknowledgment is also due to Roland Robertson for his supervision of the early stages of this research.

# Introduction

We live in an age in which new levels of technical achievement impose new requirements of responsibility, corresponding to the ever-broadening scope of man's power. Much of what was once settled by chance or ineluctable circumstance has become now a matter of decision, a matter of choice. Many of the moral issues of our time are novel ones—birth control, prosthetic surgery, ecological conservation. . . . And there are other, perhaps less striking, examples; the imminence of the data-bank society, the growing availability of new techniques of surveillance and control, the emerging possibility of lifelong education, and so on. Essentially these are problems that have emerged from our advances in technology. Yet beside such advances, the development of shared principles for their use and control seems to have lagged behind, as has the development of an adequate sensitivity to their likely social consequences. As Dr Brock Chisholm, for example, former Director-General of the World Health Organization, has said: 'We have been slow to recognize that we are the first generation that holds the veto power over the continuation of humanity.'

But the advances in technology do not only give rise to questions involving the prevention of destruction, in its various forms, or such issues as the limitation of pollution and the production of waste. They imply also a positive freedom: a freedom *to* realize previously inaccessible goals.[1] And indeed it is here that the rationale for such advances must finally lie.

The social sciences have a contribution to make to such questions of principle by helping to ensure that whatever choices are made are *informed* choices. A substantial part of this contribution should derive from the development of an empirically-based 'sociology of ethics', however innately imprecise this last term might be.[2]

1

The nature of this contribution may in the long run prove to be a modest one. Our own view, however, would be that its potential significance cannot be wholly determined *a priori*.

The present study, then, seeks to review some of the conceptual and empirical issues raised by a sociology of moral codes, and, most especially, attempts to locate these issues within the comparative context provided by the sociological perspective.

The two principal disciplines being drawn upon are those of sociology and moral philosophy. Although once interwoven, each is now an independent field of inquiry, with its own traditions and its own distinctive style of approaching its subject-matter. The separation between the two arose out of the growing fidelity, over the nineteenth and twentieth centuries, to the canons of empirical science. And on these grounds alone one cannot but applaud it.

In terms of the transfer of ideas, however, the distinctness, and separateness, of the two disciplines seems to have been overdrawn. Each has considerable relevance to the other. And to recognize, and pursue this fact is not *ipso facto* to surrender one's claims to scientific 'objectivity'. Thus, the principal feedback from moral philosophy, for the sociologist, is one of conceptual clarification. And this is not only much needed, but can take many forms. Certainly, it is not to be restricted to such traditional issues as the alleged value-neutrality of sociology, but may be much more directly practical, as when moral philosophy suggests a range of possible models of ethical justification, or develops a calculus appropriate to prescriptive discourse.[3] In short, moral philosophy can directly assist the development of theory in sociology, and in ways that largely await to be explored.

The gain to moral philosophy from an acquaintance with sociology, on the other hand, is likely to be of a more empirical kind. Systematic evidence about the moral codes of other societies may make us more aware of our own presuppositions about ethics, and call into question their generality, as well as indicating novel ways of approaching and resolving moral problems. A degree of ethnocentrism persists in moral philosophy. There is still a tendency for the philosopher to underrate the subtlety and coherence of the ethical systems of even preliterate peoples. As one philosopher wrote of his experience doing fieldwork among an Amerindian group: 'From my experience in talking to a Navaho moralist, I am convinced that his ideas are as rationally coherent and systematic as any of those to be found in the moral codes of our own culture, although before I visited the Southwest I had no preconceptions one way or the other. The evidence seems to confirm the Greek conception of man as a rational animal.'[4] Empirical sociology, then, can have a useful role to fulfil here.

But if sociology and moral philosophy have this mutual relevance, one must also acknowledge the applicability of the philosophy of sociology to normative philosophy, since there is a considerable overlap in their respective concerns. As one writer puts it: 'The philosophical analysis of ethics invites coordination with philosophical findings about social science since social science describes and explains the same human activities which ethics appraises and seeks to direct.'[5] The conceptual analysis of social action, and of the relationship between attitudes and actions, are particularly important examples of this potential co-ordination.[6]

Moral philosophy may be broadly divided into its analytic and normative components, the former being concerned with the analysis of moral reasoning and moral theories, whilst the latter is concerned with the construction and application of such theories. Of the two, analytic moral philosophy holds the greater interest to the sociologist. Also, it has been the development of this aspect of the subject that has most characterized moral philosophy in the twentieth century, a substantial impetus to such development coming from advances in the analysis of language.

The relevance of normative philosophy, on the other hand, is both less great and of a different kind. Thus, the sociologist, *qua* sociologist, is interested in those moral codes that are institutionalized in societies, and give meaning to the everyday activities of their members. He is less interested in the artificial theories of individual philosophers, except in those cases where, as significant contributions to the intellectual history of a society, they prove amenable to a sociology of knowledge perspective: that is, where they can be comprehended in terms of the social reality from which they emerged, and which, in turn, they serve to illuminate. None the less, one allows also the possibility that such philosophical theories may, under certain historical circumstances, become appropriated by broad sections of a society, or at least by an élite able to impose its own interpretations upon society. Marxism and Christianity form the most important examples of such theories in Western history. In both cases, from being the preserve of marginal groups, they became the 'natural' vehicles of self-interpretation for whole societies.

With regard to the data that, directly or indirectly, can be considered to have relevance to the sociology of ethics, one immediately encounters an *embarras de richesse*. Although public recognition of this has yet to be fully achieved, it is clear that the range of pertinent information supplied by the social (and psychological) sciences is very extensive. As a result, considerable selection is necessary. We shall outline, therefore, the principal ways in which we have chosen to delimit the field.

In his book *Sociology and Philosophy* (1953), Emile Durkheim

3

states that the fundamental questions to be asked of *choses morales* are threefold. First, what are their distinctive characteristics? Second, how is their existence to be explained? And third, how are they to be evaluated? Of these questions, we have given little attention to the second and the third. The third question is properly one for normative philosophy, and so outside our present terms of reference. The second, however, constitutes a particularly important field of inquiry in sociology. This is concerned with the social *determination* of moral codes, and as such forms part of the broader sociology of knowledge. A few comments may be offered on it here.

The fundamental assumption underlying sociology of knowledge approaches is that certain (or all) social theories present in a given society have not been arrived at by purely rational methods, but are the product of causal factors, identified usually in terms of the society's social structure. This intellectual perspective, although its relative popularity is of recent origin, can none the less be traced back at least to the *philosophes* of the Enlightenment, by whom it was used principally as a means of attacking the presence of religious and political privilege in their societies.

The sociology of knowledge attained its classic theoretical formulation, however, in the nineteenth century in the works of Karl Marx. He interpreted moral codes, like other idea-systems, as ideologies protective of vested class interests. As he stated, 'It is not the consciousness of man that determines his existence—rather, it is his social existence that determines his consciousness.' Most of the subsequent work in this field has, like Marx's, been mainly conceptual and theoretical in nature, as Mannheim's *Wissenssoziologie* well exemplifies. Although some recent approaches to the subject have attempted to utilize correlational analysis; Gouldner and Peterson's *Technology and the Moral Order* (1962) illustrates this.[7]

We have not devoted attention to this field in the present study, in part because of the attention it has received already, and in part also because we do not feel that the sociology of moral codes should be restricted to this particular type of inquiry. Nevertheless, there seems no reason why moral ideas should not be subject to the same kind of social determination, and have similar social and psychological functions, as other cultural ideas. That is, there seems to be no *a priori* reason for affording them a privileged status in this respect.

If one allows this, then it is important also to note that this form of sociological understanding does not, as often seems supposed, lead to a simple invalidation of the claims of normative philosophies. For to explain the *origin* of an idea, whether in terms of the social environment in which it was produced or in terms of an individual's biography, is not thereby to discount the truth-value of this idea. Nor does it discount its value in, say, a moral or aesthetic sense.

4

What it does do is aid our comprehension of the idea and of the social—or psychological—function which it fulfils. The distinction here is that between *explanation* and *justification*, and is one that is often not sufficiently insisted upon.

In addition to which, it should be noted that sociology-of-knowledge accounts usually provide explanations of why a particular *type* of ideology—such as one protecting bourgeois class interests—should emerge. They do not usually tell us why the specific beliefs in question should arise. That is, the scope of determination involved in such accounts is far from complete. Millenarian movements, for instance, might all be treated under the same rubric, and as though caused by the same social conditions, despite considerable variation in the actual content of their beliefs.

It is probably true to say that the most significant theoretical contributions thus far to the sociology of moral codes have been constructed within the general framework of the sociology of knowledge, not least among these being the contribution of Marxism itself. Sociology forms part of the knowledge of modern societies. Hence the possibility arises of a sociology of sociology, as a branch of the more general sociology of knowledge. However, this would not only be of theoretical interest, but has a potential practical importance. Thus, a comparative, empirically-based sociology of sociology could help elucidate some of the conditions that facilitate or hinder the development of the more objective forms of social scientific knowledge. In this way, it could provide firmer evidential grounds for future discussions of the relationships between values (and especially social values) and social science.[8]

In the present inquiry, however, it has not been our concern to present a theory of moral codes, either in the above sense of their social determinants and consequences, or in a more general one. This is not because of any particular distaste for theory on our part, or any doubts concerning its necessity. Rather, the reasons for its omission are twofold. Firstly, it derives from the simple pragmatic motive of wishing to delineate the field to manageable proportions. And secondly, and more importantly, it derives from the fact that we would tend to view such attempts at theorizing as premature. That is, we would maintain that a consideration of the conceptual and empirical issues which this field raises is both pragmatically advisable, and also a very necessary prolegomenon to any adequate theoretical enterprise. It is suggested further that the inadequacy of several of the theories that are currently available derives from a failure to give such issues adequate prior consideration. The history of sociology indicates also that such theories can easily become constrictive, since the desire to preserve an analytic symmetry is often pursued at the cost of comprehending adequately the complexities of the data.[9]

5

This does not imply, and we would not claim, that our account is 'theory-free' in a broader sense, although, wherever possible, we have attempted to make our assumptions explicit. This leads naturally on to a second question: namely, that of whether, and how, values enter into sociological inquiries. This has been a continuing topic of debate and might be thought particularly relevant to the present subject-matter. The most obvious aspect of this concerns the selection of a problem-area for study. On this, few would question that the overall concerns of the social sciences are, in the last analysis, dictated as much by value-criteria as by scientific principles. And this as a matter of necessity, for the pursuit of science is itself ultimately the expression of such choice.

It would be misleading, however, to claim that such preferences are solely matters *de gustibus*, of taste. The overall concerns exhibited by the social sciences are themselves matters for empirical inquiry, and such inquiries as exist have helped to clarify the degree to which these concerns are in fact socially structured. That is, they have brought our attention to the fact that science, social as well as natural, is a social enterprise undertaken within a societal context, and that social considerations, as well as ones of a logical and theoretical nature, will enter into the selection and formulation of problems, as into the utilization of the results.

The most apparent aspect of this, and the one which has received the most attention, concerns the sponsorship of social research, and the deployment of social-science information by the sponsoring organization. A number of recent reports and case-studies, such as those by Baritz (1960), Bramson (1961), Horowitz (1967), Sjoberg (1969) and Boalt (1969), have contributed to our knowledge of this process.[10] Also, on the basis of such reports, we may say that although, as modern government and business practice both testify, the sociologist has ceased to be involved solely in the investigation and interpretation of social phenomena but has become also an adviser on these phenomena, in relatively few cases has he been party to the decisions taken on the basis of his information or advice. And it is within this type of social context that contemporary discussions of value-freedom in social science should be viewed.

The selection of problem-area and the utilization of results provide, as we have said, the most apparent examples of the operation of values and vested interests in sociological inquiry. If it is taken as a descriptive thesis, then, few would deny the inapplicability of the doctrine of value-freedom in these respects. Less obvious, however, is the possible operation of values in the definition of more methodological questions, such as the selection of research technique, an emphasis upon explanation or prediction, or, more broadly, upon an holistic or analytic sociology. Yet it seems that the social organization of science must be taken into account in order to understand the decisions made on these issues too. And this we would suggest as a fruitful area of inquiry for the sociology of sociology, although one that lies outside our own immediate concerns.[11]

The above point may be put more generally. Thus this debate upon the possible ideological elements that enter into social research has been perhaps marked by a surfeit of polemic and an absence of facts. In consequence, we would share the view of Curtis (1970)[12] that

> It would seem desirable to have, in the future, systematic studies of the values, interests, and opinions of various social scientists as compared with those of other groups. If it is found that social scientists do have characteristic values, it would be important to study both the precise causes of these distinctive attitudes and their consequences for research activity.

Considerable discussion exists on the possibility, and desirability, of Max Weber's doctrine of *wertfrei* sociology, and the issue is related to various aspects of the philosophy of social science.[13] A perceptive paper by Gouldner, however, treats the doctrine not in logical terms, but as an *ideology* appropriate to the social environment in which Weber wrote, although, as he argues, inappropriate to the contemporary context.[14] This draws attention not so much to the truth or falsity of the doctrine, as to its consequences. We would point to one such consequence as having a particular importance to the present thesis. This concerns the tendency of the doctrine of *wertfrei* social science, by drawing a sharp distinction between the processes of 'science' and 'evaluation', to neglect the mutual interconnectedness of facts and values. One consequence of this, in turn, has been that investigations of values and investigations of beliefs in social science have been treated as autonomous, mutually exclusive domains of inquiry, or at best as contingently related. And this has led, not only to an impoverished understanding of moral codes, but also to a systematic neglect of the processes by which these codes are justified and made plausible. This is perhaps better appreciated, however, if some outline is given of our usage of the term moral code.

Conceptions of what is right and wrong, and valuations of what is desirable and what is not, whether characteristic of an individual or held in common by a social group, are not normally apprehended as constituting part of *a* moral code. Rather, they are typically perceived as constituting components of a broader viewpoint on the nature of things. They form part of a community's, and an individual's 'knowledge'. That is, within this *nomos* what is recognized to be right and desirable is usually perceived in the same manner, and frequently expressed in the same language, as what is recognized to be true in a broadly factual and descriptive sense. Institutionalized in the society at large, such ideas are mediated to the individual through his particular group-memberships. The world so created is thus apprehended as objectively real. Its fundamental assumptions go normally unquestioned. Its possible relativity is typically unrecognized. Rather, it is taken to constitute *the* world *tout court*. The need for its justification is perceived to exist but rarely.

As separate from such world views, therefore, moralities have always a status which is to some degree analytic. The term 'moral code' is preferred for their description, however, since it draws attention to certain of their basic functions. Thus, firstly, such a 'code' has a broadly interpretative function, of making meaningful the individual's experiences, both in regard to his own actions and to those of others, by providing criteria for their discrimination and evaluation. Secondly, it serves as a code to live by: that is, it possesses a practical function as a guide to behaviour, again both for the individual and for others. And thirdly, the term draws attention to the fact that moralities consist normally of more or less integrated *systems* of precepts and values.

From these three aspects, we may say that the principal psychological function of moral codes is to free the individual from a continuous reassessment of the meaning and significance of his experiences and activities. Internalized and taken-for-granted by the individual, such codes become institutionalized in society, and order the activities of its members accordingly. The codes which are internalized and institutionalized in this way may, according to circumstance, be more or less complete and determinate.[15] In any event, it seems that a certain degree of *mauvaise foi* will be involved, and that existentialist choice will enter more at the stage of the application of moral principles than at that of their continuous reformulation.[16]

Finally, the term 'code' suggests comparisons with analyses of language. The analogy is, we would suggest, an appropriate one. Thus, Humboldt's remark about language to the effect that it uses finite means for infinite ends, draws attention to the fact that in order to speak a language one must have a system of general rules by which an unlimited number of sentences can be constructed. In the same way, since neither individuals nor social institutions can deal uniquely with all the contingencies of everyday life, one must have another such system to distinguish right from wrong, the desirable from the undesirable. And, like language, such a system may be employed with a degree of creativity.

The analogy, between linguistic and moral codes, leads to two further points. These concern the degree of self-consciousness with which such a code is held and applied, and the question of the conditions under which it becomes explicated and justified. We may deal briefly with each of these in turn.

Most of the time we are able to use language, in speech and in writing, correctly, but without being aware of the rules for its legitimate use. That is, we can produce well-formed sentences, and recognize incorrect English in ourselves and others, instinctively, without the need to consciously explicate the principles we are putting into practice. Indeed, should the occasion arise, most of us would be unable to give a complete account of the rules of English grammar. Our 'theoretical' knowledge of this is limited and rudimentary, even though we may faithfully avoid grammatical errors and infelicities in our practice. The point is even more clear with respect to language learning. We have every evidence that, as children develop their vocabulary, they acquire also the ability to utilize syntax long before they can make explicit the rules of such a syntax to themselves. This appears to be true also of the internalization and use of other cognitive codes, such as those embodying the fundamental principles of logic. For instance, Piaget has shown that children operate as if space were Euclidean well before they can make Euclidean representations of objects in space.[17] Speculation has therefore followed as to the natural logical propensities of the human mind.[18]

Perhaps much the same, however, may be said of the development and habitual use of moral codes. We draw distinctions between right and wrong, good and bad, all the time, without being cognizant of the criteria we are employing. Again, faced with the necessity, we would probably find it difficult to explicate these principles. Even less are we aware of the more formal aspects of our moral codes, and of the structure of our moral reasoning. Like language, they are mainly used instinctively, despite, in this case, the emotional importance that may be attached to them.

In a similar way, for the sociologist the explication of empirically available moral codes can be at varying levels of abstractness and of accessibility to the agents' own frames of reference. For instance, some of the more recent theoretical approaches to the analysis of moral, and other, codes have depicted them by means of models which focus upon their more latent, genotypic aspects. The *anthropologie structurale* of Lévi-Strauss and others may be taken to illustrate this, and as such it is analogous, at least in certain respects, to the analysis of linguistic codes in terms of their 'deep structures', associated with the work of such linguists as Chomsky.

But although one may allow that certain latent models of such cultural codes have established their pragmatic utility from the point of view of developing fruitful theory, it is none the less also clear that a privileged status must be claimed for the agent's articulation of his moral code 'in his own terms'. The reasons for this are threefold.

First, since actions are distinguished from mere behaviour by virtue of the fact that they embody meanings (intentions, purposes, etc.) and since they do not thereby interpret themselves (except in the important sense that they are only describable, and so identifiable, with reference to a repertoire of socially-available descriptions), a *prima facie* validity must always be ascribed to the agent's own interpretation of his actions, and so account of his moral opinions.[19] Second, it is evident that we cannot fully investigate the occurrence of apparent inconsistencies between attitudes and actions unless we have acceptable evidence from the agent as to what (i.e. what behaviour) he would consider a violation of his standards. Finally, since to understand a moral code is to understand the way in which it is normally justified, as well as the manner in which it is to be explained, recourse to the agent's own accounts would again seem necessary. Although it is to be noted here that the agent may be taken to refer, not only to the single individual, but also to representatives of social collectivities of various kinds, representatives whose adherence to the moral code they profess derives principally from the office they hold or the role they occupy.[20]

The second point we wish to consider concerns the conditions under which individuals become self-conscious of their moral views and attempt to justify them. Such occasions will be of importance to the sociologist since, as we have seen, moral codes are usually held and applied unreflectively, and are not, therefore, subject to a continuous justification. Under what circumstances, then, do they become self-conscious? What conditions lead to their justification?

These are empirical questions, and in answer to them we will suggest that it is situations of perceived crisis that most typically elicit self-awareness about moral principles and the need to justify them.[21] The term is being used here in the broadest sense to denote that class of circumstances in which the integrity, consistency, or applicability of standards is called into question. These circumstances may occur at the level of the individual, the collectivity, or the total society. In each case, their source may be either internal or external. The point is perhaps best clarified, however, by considering some examples.

At the societal level, external threats in the form of wars, or the likelihood of wars, provide a conspicuous incentive for the explication and justification of a society's values and beliefs, activities which noticeably diminish in times of peace. Of course, the threat may be more ideological than physical, although the two are usually present in some form of combination. A salient example in the modern world would be the adoption of a series of ideological *prises de position* that has characterized American-Soviet relations since the Second World War, at least until relatively recently. Similar postures have, of course, characterized Sino-Soviet and Sino-American relations in recent years.

A good example of response to threat that is internal to a society would be the period of the Spanish *Reconquista*, which involved the adoption of a militant Catholicism in response to the Moorish occupation, and which was sufficiently successful to have persisted until the present day as one of the principal bases of justification for the Spanish social order, a basis which the Civil War of 1936-9 served only to strengthen.[22]

More institutional illustrations of the justification and elaboration of moral codes under conditions of social and ideological threat would be both the Counter-Reformation, and also the periodic summoning of Vatican Councils and issuing of encyclicals by the Catholic Church, of which the recent and important *Humanae Vitae* (1968) is but the latest example.[23]

All this finds its analogy in the individual's biography, where crisis-situations may force him to reconsider and rejustify (or simply consider and justify) the moral code he has adopted, or where he finds himself in a situation where basic *choice* is required, in which case he may have to develop new principles that he can justify to himself. An important class of such situations in sociology fall under the rubric of role-conflict, cross-pressures, and the like.[24]

The examples could be multiplied, and indeed it can be argued that moral philosophy itself developed under conditions essentially similar to those of the category we have been describing.[25] It is worth noting also that a stress on justification, and the delineation of defensible moral principles, is characteristic of our own times. The reasons for this are various. One fairly evident reason concerns the diffusion of scientific reasoning throughout many areas of social life, together with the fact, alluded to earlier, that our technical advances have increasingly provided us with novel problems, for which traditional rules are either inapplicable or in need of careful reinterpretation. Another set of reasons derives from the fact that modern societies tend to be pluralistic, in the cultural as well as social-structural sense of this term. This means that a series of different ideologies exist in a state of competition for the individual's allegiances, even though, as modern Protestantism well illustrates, the differences between them may be relatively marginal.[26]

In summary, we may say that moral codes become consciously adopted and justified under specific social conditions. At other times they have a taken-for-granted status, comparable to people's factual assumptions. Indeed, the separation of empirical knowledge from moral 'truths', both culturally and institutionally, is itself a recent phenomenon, and one that finds its parallel in the similarly recent division of moral philosophy into its analytic and normative components. Several continuing debates in modern society testify to one consequence of this specialization. This may be expressed by saying that in a society such as ours where the cognitive aspect of culture looms so large, there may be a kind of imbalance between this and the normative aspects, the latter finding it difficult to, so to speak, 'keep up' with the former. Christianity, for instance, might be thought to be incompatible with a psychological (or, for that matter, sociological) view of motivation.[27] However, the dilemmas which this may give rise to for certain social groups, and even the *carpe diem* philosophies which it might encourage, can be taken to be relatively exceptional. Various social and psychological mechanisms are usually available for protecting social groups against interpretations and empirical information that would create inconsistency within their moral codes, whether with respect to their descriptive assumptions or to their specifically moral elements.[28]

It is rarely the case, then, that a social group under study can fully articulate its moral 'theory'. But from what they say, and what we observe, it may be possible to reconstruct such a theory, within which their attitudes and actions become plausible. The individual may not be wholly aware of the system he has adopted, in the same way that we are not usually aware of the rules of grammar when we employ language, or of the rules of logic in a discussion. Reconstruction of the moral code is usually necessary because actual ethical discourse, like any other reasonable discourse, develops arguments in enthymemes: that is, by typically omitting certain premises, and sometimes the conclusion.

Such an interpretive activity is central to sociology. Among the founders of the discipline, Weber was perhaps most influential in establishing a perspective on society as a network of meanings. And since his work one of the main concerns, and achievements, of sociology has been to make explicit the institutional programmes which social groups, and whole communities, effectively put into practice, although with varying degrees of self-awareness. The philosophical parallel to this activity is the explication of the theoretical assumptions which lie behind the thought of those scholars, such as positivists, who specifically deny any theoretical assumptions. As Isaiah Berlin (1964) states in response to those who would reduce political theory to political science:[29]

> To suppose, then, that there have been or could be ages without political philosophy, is like supposing that as there are ages of faith, so there are or could be ages of total disbelief. But this is an absurd notion: there is no human activity without some kind of general outlook: scepticism, cynicism, refusal to dabble in abstract issues or to question values, hard boiled opportunism, contempt for theorizing, all the varieties of nihilism, are, of course, themselves metaphysical and ethical positions, committal attitudes.

It is salutary to remember in this connection that science itself operates according to a system of assumptions which are themselves outside the arena of scientific investigation, although presupposed by such investigation, and that they are normative as well as cognitive in character.[30] The philosophy of science has the task of making these assumptions explicit, whereas in the case of normal science, as Kuhn has shown, the dominant paradigm is consensually accepted, and put into practice in a largely unreflexive manner. It is worth recalling this since, at another level, science is also concerned with the pursuit of novelty and with the rejection of closed (i.e. self-validating) systems of thought. What it indicates is the importance, pragmatically as well as descriptively, of a shared, largely unquestioned frame of reference within which to work.

Moral codes, along with other aspects of culture, provide one such framework. And the more one becomes acquainted with the literature, the more difficult it is to specify criteria, applicable in every case, to demarcate specifically *moral* codes from the rest of culture. Whereas sociologists, at least in recent years, have given little attention to this problem, definitions derived from moral philosophy help little because of their lack of universality, and frequently because of their covertly prescriptive content.[31] The difference, it seems, is largely one of emphasis: there is no clear-cut and universally applicable line of demarcation. And, in the last analysis, the epistemological status of moral codes, at least within the sociological universe of discourse, is the same as that of the rest of culture. *In nuce*, they are treated as cultural artifacts. For this reason, we have devoted a chapter in the first part of this study specifically to the concept of culture.

At this point we may give a brief schematic overview of the text which follows. At the most general level, the present study is written in the conviction that sociology, both as perspective, as substantive theory, and as a repertoire of methods of empirical inquiry, can contribute to the clarification of ethical problems, including those ethical problems we face today. As such, it is our belief that sociology can have a pragmatic, and wholly contemporary relevance.

Our discussion, then, is concerned with a range of issues, both conceptual and empirical (or methodological) in nature, which have central importance to the idea of a sociology of ethics. We have attempted to elucidate these issues for two main reasons. Firstly, in order to provide a framework for the evaluation of available theory and research in this field. And secondly, to supply a basis upon which future developments in the sociology of ethics might build.

We have organized our discussion into three main sections. In the first of these, we examine a number of conceptual problems raised by the comparative sociological study of ethical systems. We examine also a number of definitions of morality and, on the basis of this, put forward a definition that seems best suited to sociological inquiry. And finally, we relate the study of ethical systems to the broader field of the sociology of culture.

In the second section, we review the available research in this area, with particular reference to alternative techniques of data-collection. A content analysis of the literature is provided and discussed in terms of patterns of content and method. The relative merits and demerits of a range of empirical techniques are then considered, special attention being given to non-survey methods of social investigation.

In the final section, we raise the question of ethical relativism. A classification of types of relativism is given and this is followed by a consideration of the relationship between these and sociological information. In this way, we examine the possible ethical implications of sociology itself, both as a substantive discipline and as an organizing perspective.

Broadly speaking, then, we may say that parts one and three are concerned with conceptual problems, whilst part two is directed towards more empirical matters. Thus each section has a degree of autonomy and independence from the others. However, it has also been our intention to produce a reasonably unified study, and not an overly compartmentalized one. Hence certain themes recur throughout the text and, wherever possible, the attempt has been made to interrelate the conceptual and empirical elements in our inquiry, and to demonstrate some of their mutual dependencies.

To this we add the proviso that although the specification of the term 'moral' is examined in part one, and a tentative definition proposed, this definition could not be consistently applied in our review of the empirical materials in the next section. This is simply due to the fact that few researchers have offered explicit and appropriate designations of specifically 'moral' phenomena in their investigations. However, as we shall see, the definition proposed is sufficiently flexible to mitigate this as a possible limitation.

**part one**

**Ethics and sociology**

# 1 The sociology of ethics

## Ethics and sociology

All men, in all societies, *evaluate*. In all societies evaluations exist which, to a greater or lesser extent, are shared, and this is an important part of their culture. Sharedness presupposes communicability and the notion of culture implies that these evaluations have a certain consistency over time. Culture is a summary word for social meanings; it is the key for interpreting those codes of behaviour which form social structure.

So moral standards are important in understanding any society. Yet explicit theory in this field is rare—for example, if one compares it with the work done on aspects of social structure, such as organizations or kinship systems. That this aspect of sociology has received little attention relative to its importance is due, we believe, to at least four reasons.

Firstly, the subject straddles several disciplines. Of these, moral philosophy, jurisprudence, and theology are perhaps traditionally the most important ones though a variety of emerging disciplines—like linguistics, prescriptive logics, and decision theory—must now be added to these. Thus sociologists have tended to leave the analytical problems which the subject raises to the practitioners of these fields and content themselves with descriptions of moral codes as between different societies.

Secondly, it seems that such a practice may also follow from our current tendency to disguise moral decisions as technical decisions. Overawed by science, we perhaps see its canons as superseding questions of value and moral choice, however logically naïve this may be. One finds this evident in many issues that are raised for public debate. For example, architectural designs, for housing developments, office blocks, city centres, and so on, are not merely the resultants of a series of discrete technical decisions. They involve also conceptions

17

of how people ought to live and hence, ultimately, moral choices.[1] The contemporary functionalist view of buildings as designed for pre-existing purposes reflects neatly the utilitarianism of the modern world. The danger is not so much that alternative conceptions are rejected, as that they are not recognized to exist.

This tendency is we believe true both of the general public and of intellectuals. In his 1967 Reith Lectures, Dr Edmund Leach characterized the outlook of intellectuals on moral questions as follows:[2]

> Beware of moral principles. A zeal to do right leads to the segregation of saints from sinners, and the sinners can then be shut away out of sight and subjected to violence. Other creatures and other people besides ourselves have a right to exist, and we must somehow or other try to see where they fit in. . . . So long as we allow our perception to be guided by morality we shall see evil where there is none, or shining virtue even when evil is staring us in the face, but what we find impossible to see are the facts as they really are.

This seems a fair picture. There are of course exceptions. And it is also true that such attitudes do exist within a moral framework, in this case that of a liberal-humanism. But the point we wish to establish is merely that being consciously moralistic is viewed as undesirable.

The result, of course, is not that value-judgments disappear, but rather that they become covert. In a similar way, we should remember that modern techniques of decision-making—such as operational research or 'cost-effectiveness' thinking—always operate within certain value parameters, whether these be implicit or explicit. They cannot themselves serve as the source of these parameters.

Without labouring this point, we may note that if such an attitude is, at least in the West, linked to the influence of scientific technology, we would expect it to be less true for those people who are little influenced by this development. What little data there are seem to support this. Thus within industrial society, the degree to which attitudes are held in a moralistic way consistently correlates negatively with centrality of social position.[3] Research also demonstrates that our expectation is fulfilled for non-industrial societies and, interestingly enough, for the type of sociology produced in such countries.[4] The cult of objective detachment is not a universal one, even for established traditions of social science.

However, it is understandable that a discipline which aspires to scientific status should have reasons to avoid studies of morality as such, since, on the face of it, it is precisely here that its objectivity would appear to be most in peril. But for a community which consensually accepts a certain set of moral beliefs, which are both clear

18

and unquestioned, these beliefs themselves acquire a kind of taken-for-granted objectivity. And this leads to our third point. The current position of our own culture is not only one of a diversity of moral opinions, alongside a broad area of uncertainty. The problem runs deeper than that. It is rather that we lack a common moral vocabulary for discussing, and potentially reconciling, these diverse opinions. As Professor MacIntyre has observed:[5]

> In our society the acids of individualism have for four centuries eaten into our moral structures, for both good and ill. But not only this: we live with the inheritance of not only one, but of a number of well-integrated moralities. Aristotelianism, primitive Christian simplicity, the puritan ethic, the aristocratic ethic of consumption, and the traditions of democracy and socialism have all left their mark on our moral vocabulary. . . . Between the adherents of rival moralities and between the adherents of one morality and the adherents of none there exists no court of appeal, no impersonal neutral standard. . . . [As a result] we cannot expect to find in our society a single set of moral concepts, a shared interpretation of the vocabulary. Conceptual conflict is endemic in our situation, because of the depth of our moral conflicts.

This confusion is likely to be reflected in sociological accounts, and hardly favours the clear-cut categorizations which could provide a basis for theory, and a motive for research. It is not unlikely that this situation would also be projected on to other cultures, so that the moral becomes synonymous with indeterminacy and vagueness, an area to be avoided. But if the current situation appears to militate against effective sociology, it also offers a challenge to it, and a reason for its potential value.

A fourth reason why the sociology of morality has received little attention is undoubtedly to be found in the intrinsic difficulties of the field. Clear thinking on the subject is difficult and rare. So it tends to be left to the discipline traditionally concerned with conceptual clarification, philosophy. The most immediate problem is one of language: what do predicates of the type 'good' and 'bad', 'right' and 'wrong' mean? This is a central question of moral philosophy. But it is also relevant to ask what type of predicates these are. The language of morals is normally not only a language of evaluations and preferences but also one of prescriptions of various kinds. Traditional logic gives us little help here because it has traditionally concerned itself with descriptive propositions and its methods are not directly translatable into this new field. Modern philosophy has begun to give attention to the kind of problems involved here, but, for instance, the development of prescriptive logics of various types is still in its earliest stages.[6]

19

It is secondly, however, a question of the social contexts in which this sort of language is used. One principal need is for a socially-based classification of the various types of imperatives. The implications of this kind of study would extend to various fields, including law and general sociology. But as yet sociology gives us few cues, because its concerns have in the past been elsewhere.

The history of moral philosophy has been characterized as a history of succeeding orthodoxies and the logical status of moral terms and moral propositions is still as disputed as it ever was, so we should not expect consensus in sociology. But it is in fact the case that sociologists have worked out their own approaches to social morality in remarkable independence from the efforts of philosophers. Some of the shortcomings of this will become apparent in this study.

However, the sociological perspective is a comparative one. And when moral terms come from other societies and cultures there is the additional problem of translation. This is partly a simple linguistic problem which follows from the fact that moral terms seem to be especially subtle in their meanings and, for instance, allow few accurate synonyms even in their own language; but it is also a result of the systemic nature of moral attitudes, which must thus be understood with reference to the whole of which they are a part.[7]

In his book K. M. Sen gives some examples (*Hinduism*, p. 14, 1970).

To explain the principles of Hinduism to people unfamiliar with its frame of reference is a difficult task. For one thing, some of the terms used do not have exact synonyms in the European languages. Almost every writer on Hinduism is forced to point out that *dharma* and religion are not the same thing; a *mandira* is not a Hindu church; *jati* has been translated as caste, but it is an unhappy rendering. A word so important to Hindu philosophy as *sadhana* has no equivalent in English. This is comparable with the difficulty in finding exact synonyms for such words and ideas as 'cross' and 'charity' in non-Christian cultures and languages.

However, despite the problems, descriptions of the moral codes of various societies are available, and authors are increasingly aware of the need to view these in systemic terms. Since the nineteenth century the amount of such reasonably reliable material has gradually accumulated. In this century particularly, such evidence in anthropology and sociology has had a distinct influence on moral thinking, both of professional philosophers and of the general public. This has been so far in excess of the numerical and fiscal strength of these disciplines that one might argue that this is *the* influence they have had on popular thinking.

What has been the nature of this influence? Fundamentally, it has led to an awareness of cultural relativism. Rephrasing Pascal, we may say that it has led to the recognition that what is good on one side of the Pyrenees is bad on the other. That is, people have become more and more aware that the content of moral codes varies widely both as between various societies and historically within any society, and, to some extent, as between the different social groups of any particular society. The ethical implications of this are to be considered later.

The spread of the awareness of cultural relativism has been buttressed by another idea derived from sociology; this is the notion, which lies at the root of the sociology of knowledge, that ideas—including moral ideas—are socially determined. It has also been supported by the scientific canons of questioning everything and of only accepting those propositions which have objective validity. Empirically, this cultural relativism has encouraged an ethical relativism: that is, a sort of moral thinking which denies the universalizability of one's own values.

Ethical relativism is a challenging subject in itself. But the fact that the diffusion of the social sciences has, along with certain other factors, served to encourage its acceptance makes it doubly important. Yet it has received scant attention from the present generation of sociologists, or, for that matter, from the philosophers. It is for this reason that the final part of this book is devoted to the question of relativism in ethics. For the present let us return to the very basic questions of definition raised by a study like this.

## Values and beliefs

'What are values?' 'What are rules?' 'What does it mean to say that they exist?' We will be concerned throughout the study with the answers that sociologists have given to questions of this type, whether by explicit definition or by implication, and we shall relate them to some major traditions of analysis in philosophy. But for the moment we should like to make two points.

Firstly, although answers to these general questions would for most people seem elusive, it is also true that most people could cite examples of morality, of values and rules, were they asked to do so. Few people would reject that in general the preservation of human life is a value, or that it is morally wrong to commit murder; similarly most people know some legal rules, if only those which affect them most directly, just as they know the rules of some sport. One could go further and say that most people recognize that our rules and values have some kind of coherence about them, that they form some sort of system, at least in the sense that either contradictions or gross inconsistencies are discouraged. Yet precise definitions remain elusive.

It is evident that the distinction between clear standard cases, such as those given, and challengeable border-line cases must be made for almost every general term that we use to classify facts of human life and of the world in which we live. Sometimes the difference is one of degree: as in the distinction, familiar to census-compilers, between an unskilled and semi-skilled worker. At other times the deviation arises when the standard case is a complex of normally concomitant but none the less distinct elements, some one or more of which may be lacking in the cases open to challenge. Is a hovercraft a vessel? Should suicide be (as it usually is) classed as deviancy when no direct sanctions can be brought to bear on the offender? Can we talk of international law in the absence of a centrally organized system of sanctions? And so on. Such cases encourage us to reflect upon, and make more explicit, our conception of the composition of the standard case. But this problem of specifying general terms is by no means peculiar to moral terms.

The second point is that the evaluative aspect of social life is usually introduced by contrast with what it is not. Thus most sociology textbooks of recent years have contrasted 'values' with 'beliefs' about the world. The sociological distinction follows from the familiar philosophical one. Hume demonstrated in his *A Treatise of Human Nature* as long ago as 1740, that no 'is' proposition can provide a logically conclusive ground for an 'ought' proposition. You cannot prove value-judgments by deriving them from what are claimed to be statements of fact. Thus the forerunners of sociology, the classical political philosophers—Plato, Hobbes, Locke, Rousseau, Mill, and the rest—were not really trying to give an objective answer to a single moral question, namely, 'What are the grounds of political obligation?' at all: they were each prescribing a particular political system.

Clearly it is restrictive to consider the relations between 'is' and 'ought' solely within the framework of a deductive model and the examination of other ways in which they may be related would permit the old question of the moral implications of sociology to be reopened. The fact that cognitive propositions and prescriptive or evaluative ones have been treated as so logically exclusive since Hume has led many to ignore the simple fact that the typical normative theory does make certain assumptions of a factual kind. To take one instance: any social theory of conduct must contain an implicit conception of man's nature, if only in the sense of excluding certain historically available 'philosophical anthropologies'. Similarly, theories of culture have often misconstrued the relationships between these two components, usually by understating the role of beliefs.

American sociology in particular has tended to regard values as the analytic terminus in the understanding of culture. Such a tendency is especially evident in the conceptions of society offered by the Parsonian school.[8] This approach has called forth a continuing debate between its proponents and critics. But the essence of the critics' attack has been to call into question the extent to which values are indeed shared and to draw attention to the elements of power, coercion, and conflict in social life.[9] Few have questioned the subordinate role which such a stress on values leaves to beliefs and knowledge of the world. A very clear example of the latter is provided by the scheme of 'components of social action' put forward by Neil Smelser, following Parsons, in his book *The Theory of Collective Behaviour* (1962).

The four components in question are ordered in terms of generality and centrality with respect to societal integration and are listed as values, norms, mobilization into organized roles, and situational facilities. These components are then further specified in terms of levels of generality. But the overall relationship between the components is, it is argued, such that any change in a higher component necessarily involves a change in all the lower components, but not necessarily vice versa. This is typical of much sociological theory. Again it is values which form the analytic terminus. While beliefs and knowledge are hardly recognized, except very partially in the facilities component, which includes as its first two, most general elements, preconceptions concerning causality and codification of knowledge.

It should be clear, however, that this is an inadequate conceptualization of beliefs, excluding such crucial items as the cultural view of human nature, both as to what it is like and the extent to which it is malleable. Secondly, and importantly, it is also evident that the relationship of determination which Smelser argues to exist between the components does not in fact exist. For example, a change in values, however radical, does not necessarily involve a change in conceptions of causality. In fact, the logical relationship between values and beliefs is much more the other way round: that is, values always imply certain beliefs, and part of the task of understanding any set of values is to understand the beliefs which lie behind them and give them meaning, but beliefs by themselves do not imply values.[10] Thus the value put upon 'progress' in the West presupposes a Judaeo-Christian conception of time as unilinear; but a unilinear conception of time does not commit one to value progress, however this is specifically conceived.

A further example might be drawn from Hinduism. When this religion is discussed in sociology texts tolerance is frequently cited as one of its characteristic virtues. But much more central is their belief that, to put it simply, 'There are many ways to God', and the value put upon tolerance is something which surely follows from this rather than vice versa. If there is no supremely valid way to God, of being a good Hindu, then it is clearly difficult to justify an outlook of religious intolerance. It is also this basic belief which accounts primarily for the oft-mentioned absorbent and syncretic nature of Hindu religion.[11]

It follows from our argument that, in the above sense, any study of values must necessarily be a logically secondary procedure in the understanding of any culture. But this is only from the point of view of logic. It might still be argued that in order to construct useful theories a more heuristic approach would be to ignore beliefs and start off with moral codes. One might justify this, for instance, by arguing that values are more easily detected and categorized than beliefs are. And in fact this is the procedure adopted by most currently available theoretical approaches to culture.[12] But this can never provide more than a partial view of culture. And secondly the apparent self-evidence of the meaning of certain values may well be deceptive, and in the absence of knowledge of the relevant underlying beliefs one is all too prone to assign meanings to the values on the basis of one's own conceptions of the world. For example, the meaning of tolerance to certain primitive band communities can only mean tolerance to one's relatives since all relationships, actual and conceivable, are phrased in kinship terms; whereas to the educated man in the advanced society all the world is a potential recipient of tolerance or intolerance, simply because he is aware of the world.[13] Clearly the two can only be said to share the same value in a highly qualified sense.

The above example is of course an extreme one. But the danger it illustrates is present whenever values are abstracted from culture and treated separately. And, as one may conclude from observing many discussions, what often appear at first to be differences in values are in reality differences of belief, and it is simply that many people are both more explicit and conscious of the former than the latter. Many social contexts call for an interchange of 'opinions' rather than basic beliefs. It follows that one way of altering the values of a person or group is to try and change the beliefs which they presuppose, or at least to make their beliefs explicit.

Thus a programme designed to improve race relations might well take as one of its tasks that of elucidating and educating people out of their existing concepts of race and its significance.[14] A similar issue often arises in relations with preliterate groups. For instance, there was widespread opposition in the primitive parts of Melanesia to Government regulations designed to prevent the spread of infectious diseases. It was assumed that this was a result of divergent values. The real reason, however, lay with the fact that the natives' theories of the causes of illness differed radically from those of Europeans. Given their epidemiological views, the actions of the Government were at best useless, and at worst positively harmful.[15]

24

We might allow, then, that many, perhaps most disagreements in attitude rest on, or are due to, disagreements in belief. However, a practical point arises here. Thus it would probably be conceded also that it is often exceedingly difficult to show that disagreements in attitude did *not* thus rest on disagreement in belief; for how could one be sure that one had established agreement in belief on *all* matters which either party might take to be relevant, however remotely, to the point at issue? Nevertheless, the distinction is perfectly clear in theory, however difficult it may be to apply in certain actual cases of disagreement.

Thus when we talk of beliefs we are referring to what is usually termed the cognitive aspect of culture; that is, those conceptions, descriptive and explanatory, empirical or non-empirical, about which it would make sense to say that they were true or false, real or unreal. In the case of values one can usually say merely that one approves or disapproves.[16] The distinction between cognitive and evaluative, between beliefs and values, is of course an analytic one, and as such does not necessarily match the perceptions of the individuals we may be studying. Thus, in some tribal societies, 'cause', for us a cognitive term, is a moral category. Similarly, Western thought throughout the Middle Ages was dominated by the Thomist tradition of natural law which claimed that values had the same epistemological status as facts about the natural world.[17]

The utility of the distinction, however, both in theoretical and practical terms, suggests that it ought to be retained. A simple illustration of its comparative application may be given. It is a truism in anthropology to say that the content of the cognitive and evaluative varies between different societies. Less attention, however, is paid to the formal aspects of relativism. Thus, most obviously, it is also true that the scope of the evaluative and cognitive may vary as between different societies, and also as between different historical stages of any single society. The contrast between primitive bands and modern civilization is particularly striking here. A specialist on the analysis of primitive band societies sums up the differences as follows:[18]

In very primitive societies, normative ideology bulks large and the existential is very limited; and, of course, the existential ideology in modern society is not only enormously large and complex but part of it is even institutionalized separately as science. . . .

The expression and organization of naturalistic knowledge is minute and simple in primitive society; and supernaturalism, proportionately great. But it seems that as naturalistic knowledge grows during the evolution of a culture it diminishes supernaturalism, encroaches on its territory. . . .

Furthermore, even the amount of purely pragmatic information is bound to be limited simply because of the rudimentary technology of hunting-gathering societies. Another aspect of this is a lack of specialization; nobody is at work discovering things to be imparted at large for the good of the society. Perhaps this lack of specialization is the reason for the lack of abstraction and generalization, as well as the absence of philosophizing about nature. . . . [For example] Most hunting-gathering societies numerate to four or five only. After that comes 'many' and 'very many'.

So far we have distinguished values and beliefs, and the different possible degrees of elaboration of each, but we have drawn no distinction between values of a moral kind and those of a non-moral kind, and it is to this that we shall turn now. Western society has long drawn a distinction between those values and rules which are moral ones and those which are not. Western philosophy, for its part, has devoted attention to describing, or in some cases prescribing, the criteria according to which the distinction might be made. None the less, the distinction in question, though an enduring one in our everyday language, is still far from clear, and philosophers have yet to come to a common interpretation of its nature. Again we can think of the standard cases: murder is morally wrong (except in times of war), whereas a preference for physical fitness is, for most people, a value of the non-moral kind. But a mere list of examples which fall into one or the other category would be an inadequate account of the distinction, even though it might seem the only feasible one. What we would really like to know are the criteria which, singly or in combination, are both necessary and sufficient to delineate non-moral values and rules from moral ones, and vice versa.

This is important to philosophy if only in the sense that it brings into question whether different moral theories are really talking about the same subject. In several cases they are not:[19]

Kant, for instance, takes it for granted that the 'moral law' imposes upon all rational beings unconditional, categorical demands to do and forbear—demands that are binding without any regard to human inclinations, purposes, desires, or interests, that have nothing essentially to do with human happiness, and call only for the absolute obedience of 'the good will'; his problem is to explain how there can be demands of that kind. But for Hume, for example, this problem does not arise at all. For it does not enter his head that there *are* any demands of that kind; on the contrary, he takes it entirely for granted that moral views give direct expression to human preferences and desires, and that it is the essence of a moral system to promote the interests, the general harmony and well-being, of human communities. That being so, it is of course entirely inevitable that their accounts of 'moral discourse' should be widely divergent; for it is not really the same thing that they are seeking to give an account of.

A similar dissensus is reflected in the literature of sociology and anthropology. Thus, on the one hand, authors such as Raymond Firth make morality virtually coextensive with a society's framework of values and rules, and on the other hand, authors such as Richard Brandt prefer to restrict the term to particular types of actions, such as those involving truth-telling or sexual relations.[20] Nowhere is an agreed interpretation of the term to be found, whether in fieldwork or social theory. In so far as the question is raised, authors often excuse this by pointing to the dissensus in philosophy; as one anthropologist humbly observes, 'Philosophers are not agreed on the definition of morality, and no sensible anthropologist will want to intrude into a debate in which the best brains of the past fifty or sixty generations have been engaged without reaching a definite conclusion.'[21]

It seems to us that this attitude is mistaken, and that one can pay too much attention to waiting for cues from philosophy. This is because the aims of the two disciplines—philosophy and comparative sociology or anthropology—are different ones. And if the definition is to be geared to the subject's aims we should not necessarily expect the definitions which best meet the demands of each subject to coincide. In the absence of a clear indication of the concept's meaning, intuitive criteria are chosen, and these are *not* the most useful ones for a social science, partly because the intuitions of different authors seem to vary so widely.

Before discussing the various approaches to the problem, we may outline the type of characteristics required by a definition which is to be appropriate to the interests of comparative sociology. First and foremost, it must have, as it were, an open-ended nature; that is, it must be sufficiently general and flexible to apply to the ethics of a wide variety of other cultures. Several philosophical definitions will prove to be ethnocentric in this sense. Secondly, it must be reasonably compatible with current ordinary usage of the term under consideration. Thirdly, the definition should be formulated with a view to its pragmatic use as a guide to useful research and a basis for sound theory. It is with these considerations in mind that we turn to a consideration of the criteria of morality.

# 2   Criteria of morality

## Review of criteria

In both philosophy and sociology there are a variety of theories to, respectively, justify and explain moral data. But in both disciplines, as we have noted, it is frequently uncertain as to what criteria are being employed to distinguish the pre-analytic data of ethics from that of other inquiries. Yet it is clear that conclusions about morality will differ radically according to the way in which 'moral facts' are distinguished from other kinds of available information. This has not been a central problem in social anthropology, or even in theoretical sociology, since these disciplines have been concerned with the wider ramifications of these facts, with their social origins, and with their consequences for social structures and motivations. But for the purpose of discussing ethical systems as such we must plainly adopt some clear-cut differentia of ethical and moral data.

If we wish to describe the standards of an informant that are peculiarly ethical, we must look at morality from his point of view rather than ours. In this way, we can avoid ethical evaluations of our own and the circularity involved in, for instance, defining morality in the functionalist or psychological terms of the spectator.[1]

Secondly, we should take care not to over-extend the range of morality. It is characteristic of Western moral philosophy to see moral choice implicit in every action, and this model has clearly influenced sociology.[2] It is a misleading model, however, because, although the range of morality can, as we shall see, vary widely, it is invariably more narrowly demarcated than this.[3] Thus moral codes are usually separated into *values* on the one hand, and rules or *norms* on the other. But not all values are moral ones—as in the case of aesthetic values; nor are all rules moral rules—as in the case of rules of etiquette.

28

For Durkheim, morality consisted of rules of conduct percei
both obligatory and desirable. The obligatory character of the
derived from the moral authority behind them (God or society
violation of them entailed a sanction (blame, punishment).
anthropologists have in general followed this account, either by
laying stress on the desirability of morality with the notion of moral
'values', or by emphasizing the constraining influence of morality in
the form of moral rules or norms. The authoritarian conception of
morality, implicit in Durkheim, has also been generally adopted,
with the result that rules have been conceived of as, in some sense,
commands. We shall argue presently that this conception is not
necessarily a universal one.

Within the field of ethics a logical distinction exists between
evaluative and prescriptive discourse. The validity of the distinction
will be discussed later. For our present purposes it will serve as a
useful framework for presenting various accounts of the criteria of
morality.

## Evaluative criteria

The process of evaluation involves both cognition and cathexis in the
sense that if an object is valued it has at least to be perceived and
desired. Most accounts would also say that 'values' are more 'objective' than mere objects of arbitrary and fleeting preferences.

There is reasonable consensus in philosophy that the objects of
moral judgments (or moral values) are distinguished from other
types of valued objects by their being intimately connected with
human conduct, where it involves intentional, *voluntary* action.[4]
Thus moralists think of moral values as attaching to such objects as
goals, ideals, motives, or character, and all of these relate in some
way to voluntary action or choice. Such valued objects as good
weather by virtue of being (at present) beyond human choice are not
the subjects of moral judgment. Actions may be either prescribed or
evaluated by moral codes and, it is argued, the criterion of voluntariness is required in both cases. A person is not considered to have
acted wrongly if he could not have acted otherwise. Similarly, a
person cannot be obliged to do what is beyond his ability.

A variety of philosophical accounts are available to demonstrate
the implausibility entailed by neglecting this criterion. It is embodied
in the majority of natural and artificial moral codes of Western
culture. If these alone are under consideration, then the sociologist
must clearly include it in his definition of moral facts. The problem is
raised, however, as to whether such a notion can do justice to cultures
with a more determinist view of the world. Are we to say that cultures
presenting, at the extreme, a completely determinist picture of man

contain no moral standards at all? This is a special case of the more general possibility that cultures may define their most important rules in such a way that intentionality is not normally associated with their transgression. The problem is illustrated in the case of certain tribal societies, as the following passage shows:[5]

> Most of the pre-literate tribal languages have no word for 'sin', but loan words such as the Hindi word *pap* are widely used, and with the word the concept of 'sin', i.e. an action of inherently negative moral value, has spread even to societies to which it had originally been foreign. The belief held by many tribes, according to which actions capable of attracting supernatural punishment may be committed unknowingly shows that not the intention but the completed deed, irrespective of motive, is thought to bring about such retribution. The agent's ignorance of his offence does not save him from misfortune, and there is hence often no element of moral choice such as Western moralists consider essential for the commission of sins.

One might say of deterministic cultures that they present a false picture, and that their members are wrong to deny that a wide range of their behaviour has an ultimately voluntary character.[6] But this raises the question as to whether we should be prepared to accept a definition of morality which, in the case of cultures such as these, would be basically at variance with the categories used by the actors themselves. The dichotomy at stake here is a basic one with respect to our present subject. It is that between, on the one hand, philosophical plausibility, and on the other, generality: one gains in philosophical merit at the price of cutting down on cross-cultural reference. And since generality was an important requirement for an adequate definition, we shall for the present leave open the question 'as to whether or not voluntariness is a necessary condition of morality.[7]

Any attempt to define morality as involving particular kinds of values commits us, in one sense, to regard conduct from the point of view of the spectator. Evaluation involves standing aside from what is evaluated. Actions are considered apart from their character as actions-in-view and the moral evaluation of actions does not always aim at directing and guiding conduct itself. Thus we can morally evaluate actions committed in the past or by people other than ourselves.

The spectator approach has been commonly used in social anthropology and sociological theory.[8] In both cases moralities have been described by appealing to socially shared standards of approval and disapproval. These standards have usually been distinguished from expressions of mere preferences. Thus, it is argued, approving and disapproving, unlike liking and disliking, connote some sort of impersonality and objectivity. To allow for this, reference has been made either to the disinterested or impartial spectator, or to the reaction of the community at large. In general, philosophers have chosen the first of these approaches, and anthropologists the second.[9] In the case of anthropology, however, it is often difficult to decide who is to be considered 'disinterested', for it can obviously not be the individual free of cultural prejudices because it is moral reactions within the context of the culture which he wishes to study. And the intellectual detachment of which the élite may be capable has usually to be weighed against their obvious vested interests. Similarly, although to interpret the term literally—i.e. to elicit from the informant opinions of actions which he does not perceive as immediately affecting his own welfare—may be plausible in certain contexts, it does not apply to a range of small societies where every violation of the moral order is deemed to affect the welfare of all.[10]

The notion of disinterestedness, therefore, as a criterion of the moral seems virtually impossible to apply in the full range of anthropological investigations. Added to this, the notion is not an unambiguous one for philosophical purposes.[11]

To substitute the community at large in order to account for the objectivity involved in moral evaluation raises its own problems. The first of these is that it is an empirical question as to the extent to which shared evaluations, and in this sense culture, genuinely exist.[12] Secondly, it commits one to a kind of conventionalism. Thus, one must allow that critics and reformers who think that the favourable or unfavourable reactions of the community are morally wrong have been crucially important to at least the development of Western ethics. Even primitive man has been known to criticize actions of which his society approved, and to act on the basis of 'conscience'.[13]

If the moral rightness or wrongness of acts were defined solely in terms of the public's reactions, then it would be logically impossible for a reformer to criticize public opinion on moral grounds. A community condoning racial discrimination, or even lynching, would by definition be right. It is clear, however, that to talk of moral criticism of public opinion is quite compatible with ordinary usage.

A final criticism of the criterion of impartiality, made by John Ladd,[14] is that it fails to distinguish the peculiarly moral character of virtuous actions and tends to reduce them to a species of aesthetic value, because impartiality seems to amount to what, in the field of art, is known as aesthetic distance or aesthetic disinterestedness.

We must conclude that 'moral facts' can be defined evaluatively, in terms of approval and disapproval, only if a more satisfactory explication of the difference between moral and other kinds of reaction is forthcoming. However, many social scientists who have approached moral codes through an analysis of the values they contain, have not recognized the above as a problem. For these, the definition of morality is self-evident. It is these views that we shall now discuss.

## Intuitive criteria

Writing of his colleagues, one philosopher has observed: 'Almost the only method of identifying moral and ethical data which has been employed in Western philosophical literature on ethics is an intuitive one. It is assumed that everyone knows what a moral judgment is, and that consequently there is no need for a criterion by which to decide whether a judgment is ethical or not.'[15] But whereas most philosophers have openly espoused this view, anthropologists have tended to be unaware that they have used it, especially with regard to the proper content of moral rules.

Within social anthropology the usual form taken by the intuitionists' argument is that although the scientific and ethical opinions of non-literate cultures may differ radically from our own, we can none the less expect them to be about the same problems and therefore to have the same subject matter. Thus ethics has been defined as those ideas concerned with actions involving sexual relations, homicide, theft, the destruction of property, truth-telling, and promise-keeping. This, for instance, is the approach of Richard Brandt in his *Hopi Ethics* (1954).

The danger of this line of argument is clearly the implicit ethnocentrism that it entails. The empirical question as to whether the spectrum of different moral codes does in fact exhibit this common content is prejudged. And it is only when we have a criterion which is unbiased with respect to the content of morality that we can have some degree of confidence that such lists as the above one accurately reflect the informant's moral code. More subtle versions of this view in sociology have offered *a priori* grounds for expecting moralities to have a shared subject-matter. Thus some functionalist theorists have assumed that a society's ethics have always and exclusively been concerned with those actions conducive to social order or disorder. For instance, it is frequently argued, or supposed, that we should regard as ethically relevant only those rules involving lines of conduct which serve a social function. One must allow, however, that not all informants are functionalists themselves, and that although a bias in favour of social welfare characterizes, particularly modern, Western morality, this is not necessarily true of other cultures.[16]

Another approach, not dissimilar to this one, is contained in Kluckhohn and Strodbeck's work, *Variations in Value Orientations* (1961). The principal aim of this book is to provide a general typology of values, rather than to delineate moral values from non-moral ones.

But the authors' argument for supposing their typology to be applicable to all societies is a relevant one. It rests on the view that each society faces a number of distinct 'conceptual' problems which are inherent in the very nature of the social, and natural, world as such. The problems in question essentially involve answers to certain dilemmas—namely, the attitude towards human nature, the natural world, time, activity, and social relationships. Each dilemma is seen to have three solutions, and these, it is argued, are all to be found in all societies, though with different relative emphases (hence 'dominant and variant value profiles').

We shall consider this theory in detail later. For our current purposes, we may note merely that, even if true, it leads to no definitive conclusions about the character of moral codes. For, even if these items are cultural universals, there is still no reason why moral codes should centre upon them, unless they do so by functionalist definition. The approach to society in terms of 'functional prerequisites' makes similar claims and is open to the same objections. This argument outlines a number of functions—socialization and recruitment, for example—the fulfilment of which is a necessary condition of any viable society. But these are usually very general, at times truistic, categories. And they leave open the question of the actual structural and cultural forms—such as the nuclear family—by which they might be fulfilled.[17]

Another approach, also essentially intuitionist, is a linguistic one. Increasing attention has been given by modern philosophy to the study of language as a means of solving its problems. But this tendency has not been without its critics. Ernest Gellner, for instance, in *Words and Things* (1966), has accused several linguistic philosophers of ethnocentrism, of being tied down to the protocols of a particular language.[18] We may, to a certain extent, see an example of this in its approach to ethics.

Linguistic philosophy regards as ethical those statements (or sentences) which use so-called 'ethical expressions'—that is, words like 'duty', 'ought', 'good', and so on. But how do we produce parallel lists in other languages? It seems that we cannot do so without relying on someone's intuition of synonymy with certain English expressions. Also, even in English none of these terms is used exclusively with moral connotation. Such common phrases as 'It ought to rain today' or 'It's a good day today' exemplify this point. So one must add that we are using words like 'good' *in their ethical sense*— and this has to be determined intuitively. It is thus also inadequate for a discussion of ethical standards in ordinary English. Similarly evident is the fact that a great many ethical discussions are held, again even in English, without using so-called 'ethical expressions' at all. In general we may say that the language of moral codes in cultures is

33

usually considerably richer than that of the moral philosopher.

Since the actual words used seem to be neither a necessary nor sufficient characteristic of distinctively ethical statements, it appears that we must check the respondent's statements against other criteria, which are more reliable. None the less, the usage of language will continue to provide an important clue in fieldwork.

Instead of proceeding through particular words or intuitions, a more subtle linguistic approach would examine the way statements are used. Indeed, even the other methods are likely implicitly to employ this one. Thus, analytic philosophy frequently takes as a criterion of ethical judgment 'universalizability'.[19] In general form, this means that the evaluation or prescription is intended to refer to all men, in all places, at all times, including the speaker. Whatever its philosophical merit, however, considerable difficulties arise in the application of this to anthropology, since so many moral codes would have to be ruled out.

It is not uncommon for preliterate groups to restrict the extension of their morality to their own community. For example:[20]

> Mankind (to the Siuai people) consists of relatives and strangers. Relatives are usually interlinked by both blood and marital ties; most of them live nearby, and persons who live nearby are all relatives. . . . Transactions among them should be carried out in a spirit devoid of commerciality—preferably consisting of sharing, non-reciprocable giving, and bequeathing, among closest relatives, or of lending among more distantly related ones. . . . Except for a few very distantly related sib-mates (i.e. clansmen), persons who live far away are not relatives and can only be enemies. Most of their customs are unsuitable for the Siuai, but a few of their goods and techniques are desirable. One interacts with them only to buy and sell—utilizing hard bargaining and deceit to make as much profit from such transactions as possible.

This seems to be the rule rather than the exception among tribal and band societies.[21] In some cases—such as the Bantu of South Africa—the moral code may be restricted only to immediate relatives in the extended family. In *The Moral Basis of a Backward Society* Edward Banfield holds essentially the same principle to be true of the village he studied in southern Italy. Here the essential motive was *interesse*—'Maximize the material, short-run advantage of the nuclear family; assume that all others will do likewise'—and the resultant culture he sums up as one of 'amoral familism'. He describes this as follows:[22]

In the Montegrano mind, any advantage that may be given to

another is necessarily at the expense of one's own family. Therefore, one cannot afford the luxury of charity, which is giving others more than their due, or even of justice, which is giving them their due. The world being what it is, all those who stand outside of the small circle of the family are at least potential competitors and therefore also potential enemies. Toward those who are not of the family the reasonable attitude is suspicion.

This situation, of course, does not hold true of all peasant societies; in some, such as several Spanish *pueblos*, civic attitudes are well-developed, and outsiders are afforded privileged treatment.[23] But it draws attention to the general point: that is, the scope, as well as content, of moral codes is to a large extent relative.

However, as John Ladd has pointed out, it is important to draw some distinctions here. We may distinguish universalizability from three basic viewpoints: those of the patient, the agent, and the spectator.[24]

The universal aspect of our own code which we usually emphasize refers to the patient, as in 'Treat all men as equal' and the provisions of the United Nations Charter. It seems an axiom of Western Christian morality that we should consider the claims of all men as equal in some sense, or perhaps more exactly that we should recognize that every man has at least some moral claim, however slight, upon each of us. This outlook is of course shared by a variety of other ethical positions, such as that of humanism; the distinctiveness of Christianity lies not so much in its moral code as in its supporting system of beliefs. However, where to draw the line on this issue is not always certain: many cultures, including such religions as Hinduism and Buddhism, extend the application of morality beyond humanity, whilst, as we have seen, others restrict it to some section of humanity. And since the extension of patients of a moral act varies so greatly and would require considerable preliminary definition, it does not offer a very reliable criterion of moral judgment.

Universalizability from the viewpoint of the agent raises similar problems. In its simplest form, it asserts that under certain circumstances everyone ought to do so-and-so. The moral law is often thought to be binding on all men, irrespective of race and culture, whether or not they recognize it to be binding. It was in this sense that Kant defined moral obligations as categorical as distinct from hypothetical obligations. Thus the judgment that it is wrong to commit incest seems to apply to all people, even though certain circumstances, such as ignorance, may excuse a person who does. But again the issue is more complex. Moral codes differ in terms of their criteria of *ethical competence*, that is, in terms of how potential moral agents are specified. It is obvious to us in the West that animals cannot break moral rules and we usually do not think that babies or the severely retarded have duties. Related to the latter is the legal system's, essentially factual, assumptions as to appropriate ages for legal responsibilities. Some cultures do not conceive of 'right' and 'wrong' in general as applying to the acts of children or slaves. Such agents are 'beyond the pale of morality'. Even for adults, certain actions may render them, according to society's judgment, permanently outside the moral community: the position of the *sinvergüenza* in Spanish pueblos and the *adiantropos* of Greek village communities are examples of this.[25]

Characteristic of the moral prescriptions of many traditional cultures is that they specify the behaviour required by particular roles and statuses, and especially those defined in kinship terms. The generalized notion of the 'good man' as central to moral reasoning is of comparatively recent origin. Professor MacIntyre makes the point as follows:[26]

> The history of ἀγαθός in Greek and of *duty* in English (or German) are of course as different as the history of the break-down of traditional Greek society is from the history of the transformations of preindustrial England. But in both cases we get a move from the well-defined simplicities of the morality of role fulfillment, where we judge a man *as* farmer, *as* king, *as* father, to the point at which evaluation has become detached, both in the vocabulary and in practice, from roles, and we ask not what it is to be good at or for this or that role or skill, but just what it is to be 'a good man'; not what it is to do one's duty as clergyman or landowner, but as 'a man'. The notion of norms for man emerges as the natural sequel to this process, and opens new possibilities and new dangers.

A different kind of universalizability would be that from the viewpoint of the spectator. This would involve judging the actions of others completely free of any partiality on one's own part. Unlike the two previous types, however, this refers not to prescriptions but to moral evaluations, and as such has been discussed in the section on evaluative criteria.

It seems, in conclusion, that 'universalizability' is unsatisfactory for descriptive ethics, mainly because of the difficulty in defining how universal a judgment should be. On the other hand, it is a characteristic of moral judgments in most cultures that they are 'impersonal' in the sense that they are thought not merely to reflect the personal bias of the individual making the judgment. Generality in this sense applies to the patients of actions, to agents, and to those who evaluate actions disinterestedly.

In summary, intuitive approaches to the specification of 'moral facts' have all been found more or less inadequate for our purposes. However, we recognized the general importance of studies of language, and from one branch of this came to accept generality, in a qualified sense, as a criterion of the moral. Several sociologists, and philosophers such as Peter Winch, have stressed the notion of rule-following as the basis of social life. For these, moral codes should be examined as sets of moral rules. It is to this approach that we now turn.

## Prescriptive criteria

Many philosophers and anthropologists have agreed with Durkheim that one distinctive characteristic of moral rules (prescriptions) as opposed to mores and customs in general is that they constrain; that is, they frequently conflict with the desires and wishes of the person concerned. This point has been made by writers as diverse as Hobbes, Locke, Kant, Malinowski, Freud, and Parsons. But opinions differ as to the source of the constraint which characterizes morality.

The notion of constraint has led to definitions of moral rules in terms of the *sanctions* which attach to them. It is argued, therefore, that moral rules are those rules to which sanctions in general are attached, or to which particular types of sanctions are attached. At first glance this seems a plausible way of answering the question we have posed. The difficulty arises with the heterogeneity of the notion of a sanction. Various kinds have been delineated: physical, political, social, religious; external and internal (guilt and shame); diffuse, organized; conscious, unconscious, and so on. Perhaps a basic typology would be that between internal and external and positive and negative sanctions. The heuristic value of such an approach can be seen by working out some of its implications. Thus, in general the negative aspect of sanctions has been overstressed in the literature. Yet a moral code in which the only legitimate sanctions were positive ones is quite conceivable. In this case deterrence would consist merely in the absence of rewards etc. Certain modern child-rearing theories seem to be of this kind. And the anthropological evidence suggests that this principle is embodied in the socialization practices of certain societies.[27]

The difficulty of specifying the ethical meaning of sanction, how-ever, remains. In fact, like the other examples we encountered earlier, this is a general term for which we can think of clear-cut standard cases, but which also has such diverse applications that it is difficult to see how they can all be grouped under the same genus. Following Ladd's account, we may distinguish a strict sense of the term from a more general one.[28] In its strict sense, sanction refers to a punishment due to the violator of a law and administered by the authority originating the law. Hence 'the precise use of "sanction" in connection with ethics presupposes an authoritarian conception of morality'.[29] That is, an authority commands the performance or non-performance of an action, and attaches penalties to the violation of these commands. The rightfulness of punishment rests in the authority, and the application of punishment involves some concept of 'desert': punishment is an unpleasant consequence of one's acts which is deserved. Thus, in its strict usage the concept of 'sanction' entails a connotation of propriety or fittingness.

However, if the notion of sanction involves the violation of a moral rule together with the morally justifiable consequences which such violation entails, then it can hardly be used as a differentia of the moral without circularity, for moral conceptions are already presupposed by the concept. Of course, it might still have an indicative usage. Thus, although it cannot be employed to define a 'moral rule', the seriousness with which breaches of those rules are regarded and treated might help us to recognize certain rules as moral ones. This is common practice in anthropology, where severity of reaction is taken as one (usually implicit) criterion of the 'moral'.

But a focus upon sanctions in this sense involves other problems. The authoritarian presupposition entails an ethnocentric perspective. And, secondly, sanctions of this kind are identifiable with punishments and rewards, and this supposes that every moral code includes the idea of punishment and reward. The evidence is that this is not the case. In support of this, we may cite a passage used earlier in this chapter. Thus, after studying a series of Asian societies one anthropologist concludes:[30]

> The belief in supernatural sanctions does not necessarily presuppose a sense of 'sin' in terms of Christian or Buddhist doctrine. The wrath of gods and spirits as understood by a tribe such as the Saoras is not necessarily directed against the person who offended against the accepted moral code, but may be the result of the disregard of a minor, almost trivial taboo. . . . The belief held by many tribes, according to which actions capable of attracting supernatural punishment may be committed unknowingly shows that not the intention but the completed deed, irrespective of motive, is thought to bring about such retribution. The agent's ignorance of his offence does not save him from misfortune, and there is hence often no element of moral choice such as Western moralists consider essential for the commission of sins.

For cultures such as these the present concept of sanction, with its implication of desert, is clearly an inappropriate one. Other societies call into question the whole idea of ethically justified punishment. For example:[31]

> The Navahos have no conception of punishment similar to ours —at least in the retributive sense which involves the notion of desert. Punishment and blame are frowned upon by the Navaho moralist as forms of aggression, although he admits that they may have to be taken into account as inevitable (though perhaps unjustifiable) consequences of one's crimes. Sanctions, as morally approved aggression, are not condoned in the Navaho culture.

It is perhaps also worth recalling Lévi-Strauss's point in *Tristes Tropiques* that whereas we punish those guilty of infractions against the moral order by segregating them from society, many primitive societies practise the reverse of this, involving them more intimately in their society. The Plains Indians, for instance, achieved this by instituting an elaborate series of gifts between the offender and the police, with each side being assisted to meet its obligations by the community.[32]

In summary, it seems that little is to be gained by using the concept of sanction, at least in its strict sense, as a distinguishing criterion of moral rules. However, the term can also be used more broadly to denote a large class of social and psychological conditions which tend to induce an individual to conform to some social usage or other, or some rule of conduct. This meaning is frequent in sociology. For instance, Margaret Mead defines 'sanction' as 'the term . . . used to denote the mechanisms by which conformity is obtained, by which desired behaviour is induced and undesired behaviour prevented'.[33]

From the agent's viewpoint, then, sanctions in the present sense are those conscious anticipations of pleasant or unpleasant consequences which are effective in inducing conduct in conformity with certain rules. As such, they are open to direct investigation, for instance by interview. But we must still distinguish those rules which are adopted to enable us to avoid certain unpleasant consequences, and those for which the unpleasant consequences act as incentives to conformity. Which comes first in the informant's mind, the unpleasant consequences or the rule? It seems that only in the case where the rule begets the consequences can we properly use the notion of sanction, since its meaning seems to depend on a rule or precept which is prior to it.

The above suggests that behind the usage of the term 'sanction' lies an implicit assumption to the effect that rules, or social norms, must have sanctions to enforce them. But it is not necessary to assume the informant looks at rules and unpleasant consequences in this order of logical priority. The rules in question may be conceptualized more like medical prescriptions, which help one avoid being sick, but sickness is hardly a sanction enforcing conformity. Again, it is clear that the term 'sanction' typically presupposes an authoritarian and command interpretation of moral prescriptions. Sociologists have frequently adopted such a view with, following Durkheim, society being viewed as the usual source of moral authority. In general, however, it seems best to use the notion of sanctions only with respect to authoritarian moral codes.

The most inclusive use of the term sanction is that which makes it coextensive with mechanisms of social control as perceived by the social scientist. Of these mechanisms, the agent may or may not be conscious. But its generality undermines its usefulness as a criterion of morality. For instance, the principle of reciprocity has been proposed as a criterion of moral rules. Malinowski argued that the principle of the mutuality of obligations was a universal one, and certainly its broad generality has been well established. Lying behind this principle seems to be the fact that, as Leach notes, social rules tend to specify relationships between pairs—husband/wife, doctor/patient, teacher/student, and so on. However, the obligation to reciprocate is not always an ethical one—it may be merely 'good manners' to do so. And secondly, several ethical systems would deny that reciprocity was a basis of obligation. Most Christians, for example, would reject the idea that the source of obligations to one's neighbour lies in what he or others will do in return.

Finally, *internal* sanctions of the present type have commonly been used to define the morality of an individual or group. Thus in our society morality and guilt feelings have long been thought to be inextricably related. But although one might contest the validity of the evidence that in some cultures guilt plays no role at all, there can be little doubt that there are many societies in which its role is a far from central one.[34] In some of these societies, shame is a far more important reaction. For instance, it is central to the moral codes of the Spanish *pueblo* and comparable communities throughout the Mediterranean area.[35] An essential condition for the importance of shame as a moral 'sanction' is that a person's actions possesses a high visibility before a community. This condition is realized in small-scale peasant communities such as those mentioned, but not in the context of an urban, highly mobile, industrial society. To define morality in terms of feelings of shame would thus be too narrow. Though, in another sense, it would also be too broad-ranging: thus, in our own society, a sense of shame can be invoked by a variety of non-moral contexts, such as breaches of etiquette. In short, neither guilt nor shame, despite their undoubted importance in some societies, seems to offer an adequate criterion of morality. Further, in view of its ambiguity, authoritarian connotations, and explanatory

status, it is questionable as to whether the most fruitful specif
of morality will come from an analysis of the nature of sancti

## Morality: towards a formal definition

Our survey of different approaches to the specification of moral facts
has of necessity been selective. It should have served to make clear,
however, that the problem at stake here is a genuine one, and that its
solution is far from self-evident. None of the above accounts sufficiently met our criteria of a satisfactory definition—namely, generality, consistency with ordinary usage, and pragmatic value. Lack of
generality, followed by low pragmatic value, were the most common
deficiencies. It seems that any definition which involves commitments
as to the necessary content of morality is likely to be ethnocentric,
whilst one with elaborate philosophical commitments is likely to be
of little pragmatic use. The need appears to be for an essentially
formal definition which is at the same time not over-philosophical.
We would naturally expect any solution to be more persuasive than
definitive, and the relevant context for its evaluation will be that of
the needs of the social sciences.

In view of this, it seems important to define morality in a way
which gives due recognition of its centrality. G. Warnock has drawn
our attention to this—

It has been held—less often, perhaps, explicitly than by
implication—that, for any person, his moral principles and
standards are to be identified as those which are in fact
dominant in the conduct of his life. This is the view which is at
least implicit in Hare's prescriptivism—'A man's moral
principles, in this sense, are those which, in the end, he
accepts to guide his life by.'

So far we would agree. Warnock, however, holds that, in its
unqualified form, this view involves a paradox. He argues as
follows:[36]

It is true, no doubt, that there are many good people whose
lives are ultimately guided by their moral principles; but, on
this view, we should be obliged to say that this was true, and
even necessarily true, of everybody, or at least of everybody
who has any moral principles at all, and surely that is wrong.
Surely there have been individuals, and even whole societies, of
whom or of which we should want to say that moral
principles did not play any large part in their lives—that,
perhaps, both their ideals of conduct were shaped in
accordance with standards that were not *moral* standards at all.

41

Homer, in approving the ferocity, guile, and panache of the warrior chieftain, might well be said to have been employing moral standards different from our own; but he might just as well, or better, be said not to have been employing moral standards at all.

Our own approach is the reverse of this, which we would view as employing too narrow a notion of morality. The quotation well illustrates, however, how the characteristic interests of sociology and philosophy can diverge on this subject. The fact that many philosophers, as well as people outside philosophy, approach the subject this way does indicate that the term 'moral' not only connotes a kind of rightness, but also, and perhaps more basically, a kind of importance and autonomy. The American philosopher, John Ladd, has usefully drawn our attention to these formal aspects of morality and, with certain reservations, it is mainly his account which we shall use as an overall framework for the following discussion.[37]

Like many writers before him, Durkheim included, Ladd holds that moral considerations are essentially ones which claim a special authority. This becomes evident in the contrast with what have been termed hypothetical obligations. Thus, the binding quality of hypothetical obligations is contingent upon a particular end-in-view. For instance, a technical prescription such as 'You ought to take your car for a check-up' or a point of etiquette, such as one ordering places around a dinner-table according to the seniority of the guests, are justified, respectively, in terms of having a safe and efficient car and in terms of social acceptability. However, we can also ask of these grounds whether they ought to be desired, or whether they ought to be accepted as ends-in-view. In such cases, our answer is no longer hypothetical, but categorical. In this sense moral considerations are superior to hypothetical obligations, and have a special authority over them.

Following Ladd's account, and taking care not to restrict ourselves to authoritarian ethics, we may explicate this special authority of moral considerations in terms of their supposed superiority and legitimacy. We say supposed because the viewpoint being adopted here is that of the informant. For the purpose of descriptive ethics, our interest is with the characteristics that moral values and prescriptions are *thought* to possess. Whether or not a particular moral code, or some aspect of it, does in fact possess these qualities is properly a question for philosophy and normative ethics, and not for sociology. The sociologist strives merely to provide a description of the code in question which is as faithful as possible to the evidence. This description may in turn be employed in explanations, either as subject or object, as causal agent or explicandum. But at no stage of the process is the sociologist involved in philosophical or moral adjudication.

The superiority of morality may be usefully subdivided into its autonomy and priority. Thus moral prescriptions claim the kind of autonomy which makes them independent of other reasons for action. That is, morality is autonomous in the sense that once a moral prescription has been accepted, no further justification of it is considered necessary. Hence the recognition that one is obliged to perform a certain act is thought to provide a sufficient reason for doing it. No other reasons need be added. Indeed, morality is autonomous also in the sense that it cannot be justified non-morally. To insist on extra-moral reasons for doing an act morally prescribed is to deny in effect that it is morally prescribed. The consequence of this is that any reasons which are adduced to justify a moral prescription *ipso facto* become moral reasons. Similarly, as one might say, any values invoked to justify moral values become themselves moral values.

It is therefore equivocal to give apparently non-moral reasons to the question, often posed in philosophy texts, 'Why should I be moral?' For example, a theological moralist might say, 'If you are not virtuous, God will punish you in the next life, but if you are good, then he will reward you.' But this is merely to abandon a theological ethics for a prudentialist ethics, which states, in effect, that one is morally obliged to avoid being punished and seek being rewarded. The social reality of religion may well be typically an uneasy mixture of these two emphases, but the logical point remains—and this is that attempts to buttress moral principles by appeal to other principles of conduct amount only to the substitution of a new basic moral principle for the old one.

The sufficiency and ultimacy of moral prescriptions does not exhaust their special claim over us, since there may be other considerations of this type. For example, an innocent pleasure may be both sufficient and ultimate in that the enjoyment of it requires no justification beyond itself. However, it is not always a moral end since it may be overridden by moral considerations. This characteristic of morality, namely its demand for precedence over other lines of conduct, may be called its *priority*. We pay recognition to this, for instance, when we say that duty comes 'before' pleasure. Similarly, all hypothetical obligations are subject to being outweighed by moral considerations.

The priority of moral principles over non-moral ones appears in both a strong form and a weak one. In the strong form, moral prescriptions always demand precedence over conflicting lines of conduct. Thus if an act is thought to be morally wrong, this consideration should overrule all other considerations, such as its utility,

43

pleasantness, social acceptability, and so on. In this sense, a moral prescription is mandatory. There may, of course, be situations in which moral rules themselves conflict, such as the rule against lying and the rule against hurting others, but if a moral prescription conflicts with a non-moral one, the non-moral prescription (or value) should give way.

It is evident, however, that although some moral prescriptions are mandatory there are others which are not quite so exacting. Different degrees of rightness and wrongness are ascribed to actions. We recognize this in our language when we say that such-and-such an action is 'right' but not 'obligatory' or one's 'duty'. Some obligations demand immediate and undeferrable actions, whereas others merely demand occasional fulfilment. These weaker moral prescriptions permit themselves to be overruled at times, although perhaps not always. I may, for instance, have a duty to give to charity, or to take part in voluntary service, but this cannot be taken to override the use of my money or time for other, non-moral purposes. This illustrates that there are, in Ladd's phrase, 'degrees of stringency' among moral prescriptions. Some make absolute demands on us, whilst others merely claim some consideration. The neglect of this in ethical theory encourages unrealistic models of natural moral codes. Thus, it is often more appropriate to view sets of prescriptions in terms of a continuum of moral preferableness, rather than as simply categorizing acts as right, wrong, or indifferent, although the latter approach is implicit in several types of prescriptive logic.[38]

The less stringent moral prescriptions may be said to demand priority in a weak sense. Although they may sometimes be neglected, and this permitted neglect varies considerably, every moral prescription (even the weakest) has the modicum of priority which stipulates that it should not always be neglected and that no justification is needed for following the morally prescribed line of conduct.

In summary, in its weak form, the priority of moral rules or values means that they are unassailable; in its strong form it means that they are never to be neglected. We should expect both types to occur in any natural moral code.

Granted that moral considerations are those which demand superior consideration in the above sense, it is clear that they must also be thought to involve legitimate demands, for there are many demands upon us which claim superiority but which do so unjustifiably. The claims of any moral prescription must be recognized as rightful claims before we are bound by them.

The legitimacy of moral codes can be seen to involve three interrelated aspects. Firstly, to regard a claim as legitimate is to regard it as well-grounded, which in turn involves the possibility of some kind of proof or argument. In general, it should be possible to specify the *criterion* which lies behind any moral evaluation or prescription and which justifies it. This is not to imply that argument from more basic premisses is always possible, but only that if it is not, then some reason for there being no such argument must be given. The clearest example of the latter type of theory in philosophy is, of course, intuitionism.

The second element in legitimacy is the requirement of inter-subjective reference; that is, *ceteris paribus*, moral prescriptions must be considered equally binding upon oneself and others. In this sense, they may be said to be impersonal or social. Thus a person honestly commending a moral value or prescription must be able to assume that if he were in the same position as the listener he would try to fulfil it. We noted earlier that ethical discourse is to be distinguished from a mere expression of the speaker's wishes or preferences, and this element of intersubjective validity accomplishes at least part of this differentiation. This accounts also for the obvious fact that in order to be successful a speaker commending certain precepts or values must be thought by the listener to accept them himself.

Intersubjective reference of the present type is a less rigorous requirement than some of those discussed earlier. It assures us of some sort of disinterestedness without involving a spectator approach to morality. Again, it provides a kind of generalizability but does not insist on universalizability. The concept of intersubjective validity is neutral *vis-à-vis* an ethics of disinterestedness, of egoism, of altruism, of social welfare, of universal laws, and so on, whilst at the same time it makes possible some type of genuine consensus or dissensus over moral principles. If this element were denied, ethical disputes would be transformed into disputes about private tastes over which there can proverbially be no argument; hence, the element of intersubjective validity is a necessary condition of public ethical discussion as well as of moral instruction and advice. Again, the way in which it is assured varies with different ethical systems.

The third element in legitimacy is the requirement that moral principles be in a sense founded on the nature of things. This requires that they be in some way derived from man's basic *beliefs*, his conception of human nature, or of the world, or of reality in general. We have already given some examples of relationships between cognitive and evaluative attitudes. In some cases the relationship is a very intimate one. For instance, ethical hedonism is founded on psychological hedonism, and most 'aristocratic' ethics rest upon an élitist conception of human nature. Of existentialist ethics, one might say that the only main prescription is that of putting the basic conception of man's nature into practice. The existentialist says simply that man should exploit his indeterminacy. Any commitment to a general set of rules is usually rejected.[39]

45

Of course, moral prescriptions cannot be strictly deduced from cognitive premisses of this kind without committing the so-called 'naturalistic fallacy' (that is, of deriving an 'ought' statement from an 'is' statement).

What has been termed anti-naturalism has, at least until recently, been so generally accepted as self-evidently true that the doctrine (or doctrines) being rejected has been afforded little systematic consideration. Part of the reason for this, as Warnock points out, no doubt lies in the fact that there do not actually appear to be any self-confessed naturalists among moral philosophers. Clearly the topic is too complicated a one for full discussion at present, but at least a few comments may be offered.

The phrase 'naturalistic fallacy' derives from G. E. Moore's *Principia Ethica*, published in 1903, but, as noted earlier, the issue at stake is popularly dated back to David Hume. In its usual form the thesis draws attention to the distinctiveness of the processes of describing on the one hand and evaluating and prescribing on the other. These processes are seen to be independent in the sense that any given description of the world cannot commit us logically to any particular evaluations or prescriptions. It might be granted that in general this is true, although rather obviously so. None the less, even here one might in some cases question whether natural languages can ever provide us with such 'pure', value-free descriptions. Description and evaluation are not clearly distinguished in our everyday language, with the result that it is often easier to distinguish between the two in principle than in practice.

On the other hand, there are several common contexts in which at least a conscious effort is made to keep these activities distinct. The usual form of legal proceedings and, say, of a governmental report which aims not only to supply information about a particular subject but also to put forward recommendations are examples of this.

What is misleading, however, is the converse of the above position. Thus, it is sometimes held that the anti-naturalistic thesis really means that we can value anything, or have *any* kind of rules. In this form, however, it is open to some objections. Firstly, we do not have absolute freedom either to describe or evaluate the world because we have to use a language with predetermined meanings, some of which, of course, will provide more leeway for interpretation than others. To put it another way, everyone lives in a personal world, but no one can live in a world which is entirely personal. Secondly, any evaluation or prescription presupposes descriptive premisses, the acceptance of which imposes limits on the potential variability of these evaluations and prescriptions. We mean this in the sense, for instance, that a person with an existentialist conception of man's nature could not seriously commit himself to an ethic of fatalism. We argued earlier for the logical priority of descriptive premisses, and would reassert this here. Thus, people must act on what they take to be the case in a broadly factual sense, whereas they need not, of course, act in accordance with what they take to be the right thing to do.

This close relationship which moral codes have with fundamental perceptions of reality explains why moral attitudes are typically proposed with the same kind of certainty as factual statements. Usually it is not a question of 'my opinion' or of what 'I believe', it just *is* the case that such-and-such is right or wrong. The factor which essentially reinforces this is that descriptive and moral beliefs become institutionalized and are then experienced as 'objectively' real.[40] But the relevancy of descriptive assumptions also renders moral viewpoints more susceptible to discussion and debate. It might also, as Ladd suggests, be primarily this intimate relationship with a fundamental part of reality, social and individual, which lends to (at least some) moral codes the quality of sacredness mentioned by Durkheim.

These three elements of legitimacy outlined—justifiability, intersubjective reference, and a foundation in reality—are obviously interrelated. For instance, the possibility of ethical argumentation already entails that it be communicable to others, and its realistic foundation gives it a kind of ground which is intersubjectively valid and justifies the moral principle in question.

In summary, we would define moral prescriptions and values formally in terms of the superiority and legitimacy which is claimed for them. In so doing, we have tried to eliminate the term's evaluative connotations of rightness, which we have tried to illustrate as culturebound and therefore inappropriate for a descriptive sociology. We have tried also to locate moral codes as central in the lives of societies and of the individuals who live in them.

Our definition is a tentative one, and is open to refinement in the context of research. For the present, we may indicate one or two of the methodological implications. Firstly, as a general principle it seems best to exploit as many methods as are available. This would include the standard methods of interview, questionnaire, and observation (participant and non-participant), together with the less common techniques of content analysis, experiment, simulation, and projective methods. In this way, the advantages of each method could complement the others, and the results of each be used to check the results of the others. There is no reason, for instance, why the criteria cited above could not be fitted into the questionnaire format, or in the interviewer's instructions. The aim will be to discover which standards and principles the respondent regards as having the required superiority and legitimacy. As noted above, one of the clues will lie in the informant's language. Thus words like 'duty', 'right',

47

'wrong', 'obligation', as well as 'good', 'bad', 'virtuous', and so on, and their correlates in other languages, serve conveniently to distinguish ethical as opposed to non-ethical discourse. Grammatical structure may also serve as a clue. But although these are the means most available to the investigator, they must be used with care. All these English words can be used in non-ethical contexts as well as ethical ones. Similarly, their usage is not necessary for genuine ethical discourse. In ordinary English, we distinguish ethical and non-ethical usages intuitively—this amounts to taking account of the way these expressions are used as well as the contexts in which they occur —we note who is doing the talking, his manner, the listeners, and his purposes. The relevance of these factors is entailed by the analysis above. But what is central is, ultimately, the kind of *justification* the respondent employs; in this sense, mere lists of values and rules approved by the respondent are inadequate.

However, our general knowledge of a particular society should also indicate to us the kind of contexts in which we would expect ethical discussion and advice to occur. Relatively formal discussions given by leaders to their people, or by heads of organizations to their members, or by parents to their children often form examples of these. Situations of crisis, or at least of perceived moral dilemma, are another useful type of context. Such situations, of course, may be hypothetical; that is, they may be simulated in verbal or written form, with the respondent then being questioned about his attitudes or probable actions. These are, in fact, a kind of projective technique, another example of which would be to ask the informant to describe certain selected pictures, or visual stimuli of one kind or another.[41]

We may turn now to a broad description of the constituents of a moral code, and to a question which has so far remained unexamined: that of the relationship between prescriptions and evaluations.

# 3　Elements of a moral code

## Values and precepts

One finds in ethical philosophy two opposed tendencies. Some moralists are mainly concerned with values and ideals; others with judgments that can be applied to concrete situations in human life. It is our contention that both types of judgment are of central importance to any philosophical ethics, and to any common-sense moral code. We shall identify these two elements as the evaluative and prescriptive aspects of a moral code.

Firstly, the prescriptive aspect. It seems self-evident that a moral code which does not include directives for conduct is no moral code at all, and certainly not one of interest to the sociologist. One essential element in any ethical system consists of answers to the question, 'What ought one to do?' Such answers may be called prescriptions, rules of action, norms of conduct, moral counsels, or moral precepts—but in each case one of their characteristic functions is to guide conduct. Linguistically, such prescriptions are usually expressed in a normative language, that is, in statements using words like 'ought', 'duty', 'right', or 'wrong'.

Moral evaluations, on the other hand, consist of assessments of the worthiness or unworthiness of an action (or agent) often without any reference to guiding possible actions in accordance with them.[1] This type of judgment involves words like 'good', 'evil', 'virtuous', 'morally desirable', 'praiseworthy', 'blameworthy', and so on. In summary, prescriptions are concerned with the *right*, whereas evaluations are concerned with the *good*.

The argument here is that, for sociological purposes at least, these two types of elements should be kept logically distinct. In practice, however, many sociologists who have used moral categories—values, norms, sanctions—as central to their accounts of society have allied

49

themselves with a different view. The view in question is known in philosophy as approbationism. Approbationists maintain that judgments about the rightness or wrongness of actions (or moral prescriptions) can be derived from judgments about the goodness or badness of actions or people (or moral evaluations). The usual sociological form of this argument is that norms are in some sense derivable from values; or at least that moral norms are derivable from moral values. Hence, the centrality of values in these accounts.[2] Some remarks may be made on this standpoint.

Firstly, it is clear that the objects of a moral evaluation are frequently not the same as those of a moral prescription, nor are the criteria of a good or evil (i.e. praiseworthy or blameworthy) action the same as those of a right or wrong act.

Within the Western conception, many moralists would argue that in the moral evaluation of an action we should take into account not only its rightness or wrongness but also the motives of the agent, the state of his knowledge, and the conditions under which he acted. In other words, an action is evaluated in its relevant context, and it is considered unreasonable to ignore the context. A right action committed under circumstances which made it easy is usually thought to have less moral value than one done in the face of great obstacles or temptations. The commission of a wrong action may be forgiven if it is done by reason of ignorance; this is one respect in which moral codes differ from legal codes, at least in so far as the latter give rise to 'absolute offences'.[3] Also we usually place a higher value on an action done from a worthy motive than on one done from an unworthy one, even though the former be wrong and the latter right.[4]

On the other hand, when telling someone how he ought to act, the question of his motives and extenuating circumstances are irrelevant. We simply say, for example, that 'You ought to tell the truth', or 'You ought to keep your promises'. The act is right or wrong independent of whether or not one is tempted to do the contrary. Indeed, one might well argue that an implausibility is involved in suggesting that one ought to do a certain act from one motive rather than another. The prescription to keep our promises does not say we ought to do so from, say, a Kantian sense of duty rather than for strictly prudential reasons; it simply says that we ought to keep them.[5] Although these specific differences may not occur in all ethical systems, they are quite apparent in our own culture, and there is evidence that they also find their analogues in cultures radically dissimilar to our own.[6]

Secondly, there are some difficulties in explaining how an evaluation, *per se*, can entail a prescription. How can we deduce the statement 'such-and-such ought to be done' from the statement that 'such-and-such is a good action' (in the sense that it is worthy of reward or praise)? It cannot be done, it seems, unless we intervene the premiss that 'one ought to do those actions which are good' (i.e. worthy of reward or praise). Without this addition, we would have to interpret the evaluative statement as also being prescriptive. For instance, we would have to say that the statement 'Lying is evil' contains the implicit prescription 'Do not lie'. In any event, it seems that a mere evaluation in itself is not sufficient to tell the agent what to do.

This difficulty is particularly evident where the moral evaluation is identified with social approval or disapproval or even with that of a disinterested spectator. The fact of approval or disapproval, whether it consists in the statement of it or the expression of it, cannot of itself tell anyone what to do.

Thirdly, and finally, although several sociologists have stressed evaluative standards, or simply 'values', as the primary elements of any moral code, one can, as John Ladd has argued,[7] object to this on methodological grounds. Thus, in trying to delimit the field of moral facts it seems that one should employ those data which are most readily and precisely identifiable. Given this, a focus upon moral prescriptions seems preferable, because 'the standards of right and wrong action are usually much more explicitly formulated and "objective" than those by which people evaluate actions.'[8] In ordinary discourse, the statement 'That's the right (or wrong) thing to do' is much stronger and less open to dispute than the evaluative statement 'That was a good (or bad) thing for him to have done'. This is no doubt partly because the same prescription can be justified according to widely different values; both Machiavellian and Christian grounds, for instance, could be invoked to justify politicians keeping their promises. But it is partly also because many of our evaluations are non-moral, and we are faced with the difficulty of providing some criterion by which to distinguish moral from non-moral evaluations. It is suggested that this is more difficult in the case of evaluations than moral prescriptions, since the considerations upon which they are based are more complicated and subtle. In general, the questions are more likely to be meaningful to the respondent if one is asking which actions they consider right, and which wrong, than if one is asking about what they value. The result of this is that 'values' are often secondary, theoretical constructs, derived from the data by inference.

Furthermore, evaluations are generally *post factum*, and it does not make as much difference how we evaluate as how we prescribe for future behaviour. For practical reasons people tend to be more careful when telling someone what to do than when merely expressing their approval or disapproval afterwards. Anthropological evidence suggests that an informant is much more clearly aware in general of the rules for action to which he subscribes than of vaguer and less exactly formulated evaluations of actions and personalities. Prescriptions by their very nature, even allowing for varying degrees of stringency, tend to be definite and precise, and hence more methodologically accessible; whereas evaluations are more indefinite and subtle—and probably more subjective.

A second methodological advantage is to be gained from a focus upon prescriptions rather than evaluations. This concerns the fact that sets of rules (or precepts) can exhibit systemic qualities in a far more rigorous sense than can sets of values. Further, as we shall see in the next part, such rule-systems may, at least in principle, be translated into a variety of formal languages for purposes of description, comparison, and further exegesis. In short, a focus upon prescriptions invites insight into the more *codal* attributes of moral systems.

It is no accident that most systematic studies of values have been carried out on students in colleges. These, by virtue of their position, are likely to be atypically explicit on the subject of the values of which they approve, if not to which they adhere, and possibly less explicit on particular rules of conduct.[9] Similarly, one of the most useful applications of the concept of values in sociology has been to provide overall categorizations of total societies. Thus one can usefully speak of the individualist, *laissez-faire* economic values of early capitalist society changing towards the social-welfare values of postcapitalist industrial society. Similarly, international comparisons of budgetary priorities, or of the overall utilization of GNPs, would seem well worth undertaking. Also, for instance, it seems plausible to analyse international relations within the framework of a stratification system based on the values of political power, prestige, and economic success, to which the various nation-states direct themselves.[10]

In summary, conceptions of the desirable, or values, and rules of conduct, or prescriptions, have been argued to be the basic elements of a moral code. Thus far, we agree with the usual sociological division of moral codes into values and norms. What we have questioned, however, is the extent to which the two may be related and the degree to which values should be treated as primary. For many sociological purposes, it was argued, general rules of conduct, or specific prescriptions, can provide a much more reliable and accessible means to the understanding of any particular moral code.

We wish to argue now that, although acceptable for general, comparative purposes, the division between values and norms may also oversimplify the nature of some moral codes. Firstly, within the morality of any particular society, there may exist, alongside the set of prescribed obligations and duties, certain moral *ideals*. The realization of these is not taken, as duties are, as a matter of course, but as an achievement deserving praise. The hero and the saint are the extreme types of those who do more than their duty; and the specific way in which they are conceptualized is pertinent to the sociology of moral codes.[11] What they do is not like the actions defined by obligations and duties, something which can be demanded, or, in non-authoritarian codes, expected of them, and failure to do so is not regarded as wrong, or as a matter for censure. On a different scale from the saint or hero are those who are recognized as deserving praise for the virtues they manifest in everyday life, such as bravery, benevolence, and charity. Such behaviour may be given specific recognition; soldiers are decorated for acts of bravery 'beyond the line of duty', outstanding contributors to the national welfare are recognized in the New Year Honours List. In other societies—such as China and Russia—this is even more clearly institutionalized.[12]

To extend our sociological language for discussing these matters, the anthropologist Walter Goldschmidt (1959) has suggested the Greek term *arete* to designate 'those qualities of person, circumstance, and position that distinguish an individual of honor from the run of the mill, and hence those qualities which are the desiderata, the goals, the hopes and expectations of every proper person within a culture'. The author argues further that the concept is applicable to all societies, since 'culture must provide a form of conduct which its members consider ideal; must provide with a special status those that fulfill this behavioral pattern, and must symbolize this ideal quality with honors, possessions or special privileges'.[13]

This approach has the advantage of leading us away from a simple conceptual dichotomy between actions which are forbidden and actions which are obligatory, and as such permits a more valid description of the social reality of certain societies. Indeed, it is probably applicable to the majority of available societies, and the moral codes which they encompass. However, despite its familiarity in the Western world, mention must also be made that our own notion of the morally exceptional individual as a subject for emulation is not to be found in all cultures. In some, such as the Pueblo Indians, virtue appears to reside in unexceptional behaviour and qualities.[14] In other cultures, such as that of traditional Hinduism, an emphasis on the personal attributes embodied in heroism in its various forms expresses an individualism which is incompatible with certain religious assumptions, in virtue of which personal idealism is not so much wrong as lacking in meaning.[15]

To digress slightly, we may note that literature in general, and the novel in particular, has been an important vehicle for conceptions of the heroic in Western culture, conceptions which have varied, often quite subtly, over time. And, as is well known, the rise of the novel as a central art form was itself closely related to the rise of individualism and to the development of a market economy (Ian Watt, 1957).[16] The decline in such conceptions in recent years, which has been remarked upon by various scholars, raises interesting interpretive problems for the sociology of literature. The results of examining these issues may well illuminate aspects of our present subject. The recent research of Lucien Goldmann (1964) is of special interest here. He has argued for a direct relationship between the different phases of industrial capitalism and of the novel.[17] From the close of the nineteenth century to the First World War—the period of cartels, monopolies, and colonial expansion—the novel exhibits a progressive weakening in the notion of 'hero'. The period between the wars—during which capitalism experienced a series of economic crises—completes the eclipse of the hero. Since 1945, he argues, the period of organized, consumer-directed capitalism, literature has acquired new central concerns; in particular, it has focused its attention upon failures of interpersonal communication, expressed most severely in the French *nouveau roman*.[18] The thesis is an interesting one, and awaits the evidence of comparative research and careful content analyses. It raises questions, however, which primarily concern the sociology of knowledge, that is, regarding the social determination of cultural ideas, and, as such, these lie outside our present terms of reference.

Our main point here is that conceptions of the ideal are acknowledged in a wide number of moral codes and that to recognize this is to draw attention also to the more general fact that the stipulations for conduct, both positive and negative, which these codes designate are typically associated with varying degrees of stringency. They are not, as many accounts imply, to be reduced to the homogeneous categories of obligatory, indifferent, or morally neutral actions. Rather, in any particular case, the number and type of degrees of moral stringency which are recognized, as the actions which fall under them, will be matters for empirical investigation.

A second, and very obvious, basic attribute of values and norms is that they may be positively or negatively accented. Thus, rules may prescribe or proscribe a class of activities, again with varying degrees of stringency. Sociologists and ethnographers have frequently either argued or assumed that rules are normally most explicit about what is bad; the good is then residual. Analogy is drawn with legal systems, which are seen to be concerned exclusively with prohibiting certain types of behaviour.[19] But this is to oversimplify. In a classic study, H. L. A. Hart (1961), for example, has demonstrated that there exist different types of legal rules, with different social functions.[20] Some of these are not to be conceived as orders backed by the threat of sanctions, since they essentially confer legal powers. Illustrations of such rules would be those which permit the individual to make legally binding contracts, or to get married, divorced, etc. Of similar status are the rules which lay down the powers of jurisdiction possessed by the courts. Hart suggests a comparison between the legal system and the rules of any complex game. In such a context, some rules (analogous to the criminal law) prohibit certain types of behaviour under penalty, such as fouling or disrespect to the referee; others define the authority of an official of the game (the referee, umpire, or scorer); others specify what is to be positively done to score. To reduce all these to one type, Hart argues, would be to obscure their different character and functions. However, perhaps a basic distinction, in terms of function, exists here between context rules and primary rules. The first of these would supply legitimations and limitations to the framework within which either moral behaviour, or activities in a game occur; thus, criteria of 'ethical competency' and criteria for participation in a game (e.g. acceptance of the rules, being a non-professional, etc.) could be included in this category on a similar basis. Primary, or positive rules, on the other hand, would define the achievement of desired ends, either within the moral code, or within the game. It is perhaps in times of dissensus over ends that moralities become focused more on the context than the content of men's activities. Thus, Professor MacIntyre (1967) has argued that as a result of class-polarization 'the moral concepts central to modern English life have been of the secondary kind' and that since the mid-nineteenth century there has been increasing emphasis on the 'secondary virtues' involved in the notions of pragmatism, co-operation, 'fair play', tolerance, a gift for compromise, and so on.[21] A functional distinction such as this may prove useful to other analyses. Careful discrimination, however, needs to be made between rules which are 'positive' in this functional sense and rules which are positive in the sense of specifying what is right, obligatory, commendable, etc.

It is rules and prescriptions which are positive in the latter sense, together with rules which are context-defining, that have been under-emphasized in the accounts of many sociologists. A particular reason may be suggested for the first of these omissions. Thus, we have already noted that rules, or prescriptions, tend to be more definite than criteria of evaluation (or values). There appear also to be differences between types of rules in this respect. Characteristically, negative prescriptions for conduct are determinate and allow little freedom of choice; whereas positive prescriptions are more vague and allow some latitude in fulfilment, if only to time and place. Thus the latter are more amenable to 'degrees of stringency', but the former are more easily identified.

But if sociological theory has tended, understandably, to overstate the extent to which rules are negative in character, then it has also tended to under-estimate the degree to which values may be of this kind. Thus, Sjoberg and Cain (1959) have argued that the Parsonian 'action frame of reference' scheme is limited in part because no explicit consideration is given to the distinctive role of positive and negative values.[22] The latter, they argue, may become particularly important under certain social conditions; during periods of reform and revolution, for example, negative values may serve to unify groups who share negative, but no positive, values in common. However, recognition of this is to be found in a few social theories. Thus, it is one of the virtues of Milton Rokeach's model of the 'open and closed mind' that explicit consideration is given to the existence of systems of *dis*beliefs and *dis*values, as well as to their counterparts and that these are viewed as having their own formal organization, the nature of which is systematically associated with certain social conditions (e.g. perceived threat) and psychological attributes.[23]

It was noted above that negative prescriptions are typically more determinate than positive ones. Somewhat analogously with this, there is some evidence that people tend to have a more elaborate code of language referring to negative evaluations than to positive ones. The study by Johnson, Thompson, and Frincke (1960) indicated that children may find it easier to develop a more diversified vocabulary of unfavourable than of favourable evaluative terms.[24] They found that only a small number of good or pleasant words are in frequent use when compared with the larger number of unpleasant ones used in English, suggesting that, at least in English, children may have a more diversified vocabulary of unpleasant or unfavourable descriptive terms. The research of Lambert and Klineberg (1967) on the development of stereotypes of foreign peoples found further that diversity of evaluations for various language-groups was consistently higher for unfriendly groups of children than for friendly groups when their attitudes towards foreign peoples were elicited.[25] Further research should improve our knowledge on this subject. However, it is important to distinguish here between frequency and diversity of usage. On the former, Johnson *et al.* (1960), as we noted, observed greater usage of positive evaluations, associated in part with their greater rigidity. Research has confirmed, however, that there is a tendency for people at least to express positive values more readily than negative ones. In his work in various countries on individuals' personal and national hopes and fears, Cantril (1965) recorded a consistent excess of hopes over fears.[26]

To conclude the present section, some of the foregoing may be summarized in the form of two polar 'ideal types' of ethical systems; namely, those of a positively-oriented 'ethics of direction' and a negatively-oriented 'ethics of constraint'.[27]

Thus in the ideal type of an ethics of direction, which comprises only positive prescriptions, the moral directives tend to be general and vague. Directives to be charitable and humanitarian exemplify this: no particular action is enjoined since there are various alternative actions of equal adequacy (giving to the poor, doing voluntary service, pressing for reforms, etc.). Hence no sharp line exists between what is morally prescribed and what is not. As a result, there is a tendency for positively-directed moralities gradually to encompass almost the whole of conduct, although perhaps to designate no one particular act with absolute stringency. Greek ethics (e.g. of Aristotle)[28] and much of Christianity, especially in its modern liberal forms,[29] exemplify this type of moral system.

In the ideal type of a negatively-directed ethics of constraint, on the other hand, the prescriptions which it includes tend to be more determinate and a sharp distinction exists between permitted and proscribed actions, with the latter usually being unconditionally prohibited. But such a code tends also to restrict its jurisdiction so that an appreciable area of behaviour is deemed morally neutral, outside its aegis, and purely an expression of personal taste, etc. Orthodox Judaism[30] and the moral codes of certain preliterate groups, such as the Navaho,[31] both illustrate this type of ethical code.

The transition from systems of negative prescriptions to systems of positive ones, which classically occurred in the development of Hebraic ethics, raises important questions for the sociology of knowledge in so far as it is systematically related to certain changes in the economy and social structure as well. However, we have mentioned only the ideal types; actual moral systems will partake of both positive and negative elements, even though they may veer mainly to one side or the other. None the less, the empirical investigation of these two types is to be encouraged since they are probably correlated with certain other 'ideological' features, such as distinctive conceptions of human nature and modes of ethical argumentation.[32]

## Typological approaches

It is a considerable limitation on the development of sociological theory in this field that there exists no adequate and generally accepted classification of basic types of values and norms. The best-known taxonomy of norms is, of course, the pattern-variable schema of Talcott Parsons.[33] Various applications have been found for this, particularly with regard to the overall categorization of total societies and of their major institutions (e.g. the military, the economy) and the discrimination of traditional from modern social forms.[34] However, since this scheme has been well discussed in the literature, little further attention need be given to it here.[35] Suffice it to say that criticism has usually been directed at the generality and abstractness of these variables, which, although they may clarify some issues for conceptual analysis, considerably restricts their descriptive value and their operational utility in hypothesis-testing research. Blau (1962), Scarr (1964), and Park (1967), for example, have all reported on the difficulties involved in attempting to operationalize these variables adequately, particularly with respect to the universalism–particularism dimension, which together with that of achievement–ascription forms also an important basis for the characterization of value-systems.[36] The fact that these variables are now conceived as continua, rather than dichotomies, imposes new problems of measurement, although Park (1967) has proposed Guttman-type scales as one solution to this.[37]

The pattern-variables were derived from an explication of Tonnies's *Gemeinschaft-Gesellschaft* pair into what seemed to be its more elementary components, and they still serve to summarize a number of distinctions which have been central to the sociological tradition, and particularly associated with the understanding of modernization. As Parsons's work has evolved, they have been theoretically integrated with a number of aspects of his general taxonomy of society, for instance with his functional approach to social systems in terms of the phase-cycle and with his theory of social stratification.[38] None the less, there is evidence that they do not permit unambiguous characterizations of certain important empirical instances of institutionalized relationships,[39] and secondly they have the defect from our point of view of not delineating moral norms from norms of other types effectively.

Similar limitations would seem to be shared by many other available classifications of norms in sociology, such as those suggested by Davis (1949) and, more recently, Barton (1955), Morris (1956), and Gibbs (1965).[40] These provide sociological typologies of varying degrees of usefulness, but little direction for the analysis of specifically *moral* terms. Rather, they serve as convenient shorthands for various fundamental distinctions to be found in the history of sociology (status-contract, folk-urban, *Gemeinschaft-Gesellschaft*, etc.). In addition, it has been common for many authors, since W. G. Sumner's *Folkways* (1906), to classify social norms in terms of the kind of sanctions imposed, or at least in terms of the severity of negative sanctions imposed to secure conformity, an approach which we have discussed previously.[41]

A review of the research literature, which is to be reported in a later chapter, indicates that the two most frequently employed typologies of values are those, respectively, of Allport, Vernon, and Lindzey, as contained in their *A Study of Values* (1951), and Kluckhohn and Strodbeck in their *Variations in Value Orientations* (1961).[42] Neither of these, however, is entirely satisfactory for our purposes.

The Allport-Vernon Scale consists essentially of a questionnaire designed to measure a respondent's relative acceptance of the following six 'values': theoretical, economic, aesthetic, political, social, and religious. Forced-choice questions are used which require a selection between two or more of the values listed. Thus one question asks, 'Do you think that a good government should aim chiefly at (1) more aid for the poor, sick and old; (2) the development of manufacturing and trade; (3) introducing more ethical principles into its policies and diplomacy; (4) establishing a position of prestige and respect among nations?'

Questions of this type are intended to gauge a person's relative concern for social, economic, religious, and political considerations. How effectively it does so, however, is questionable, since the categories are not necessarily logically or, for any particular moral ideology, empirically exclusive, although they are treated as such. Thus, although it may delineate categories familiar to a Western (or American) audience, its comparative applicability seems limited. Similarly, because of the general nature of its categories, the content of which may vary considerably, and crucially, the inventory has restricted value for a sociology of moral codes. In the second place, it can be seen that the 'values' listed have little utility for the analysis of types of societies and social institutions, or for interpersonal relationships. Rather, they serve to discriminate broadly between types of *individuals* (or personality-types). And they do so in a way which certainly has a social reference, and social implications, but not in the sense that they throw new light on social institutions, or on types of moral ideology. In short, their primary application as an instrument of research seems not to sociology, nor to individual psychology, but rather to *social* psychology. And, as we shall see, most of the studies which have made use of them are to be found in this last field.

The approach of Kluckhohn and Strodbeck (1961) is more sophisticated and given more support of a theoretical kind. They begin with the three premisses: firstly, that there is a limited number of human problems for which all people at all times must find solutions; secondly, that while there is variability in the solutions to these problems, it is neither limitless nor random, but variable within a limited range of possible solutions; and thirdly, that *all* the alternatives are always present in all societies, but are differentially preferred, resulting in ordered patterns of dominant and variant value-orientations.

The five problems the authors delineate concern (i) the character of innate human nature; (ii) the relationship of man to the natural world; (iii) the general orientation adopted to time; (iv) man's activity; and (v) man's relationships to other men. With the exception of the category describing human nature, each of these problems is given three basic solutions. The resulting matrix of categories may be represented as in Table 3.1.

TABLE 3.1 *Variations in value-orientations**

| Category | | Possible solutions | |
|---|---|---|---|
| Human nature | Evil | Good and evil (or neutral) | Good† |
| Nature/Super-nature | Subjugation to | Harmony with | Mastery over |
| Time | Past | Present | Future |
| Activity | Being | Being-and-becoming | Doing |
| Social relations | Lineal | Collateral | Individualistic |

* After F. R. Kluckhohn and F. L. Strodbeck, *Variations in Value Orientations* (1961).
† Note. Each of the solutions to the first category, 'human nature', is further subdivided into 'mutable' and 'immutable'.

To investigate the preferential ordering of the possible solutions in the culture of any particular society, Kluckhohn and Strodbeck have constructed a detailed questionnaire in which a series of items tap each of the five major categories in turn. Several of these items describe hypothetical situations in which basic choice is required, and the respondent is asked to select between a number of possible courses of action. This operationalization of the typology is, in our view, an effective one, and has been applied by the authors during fieldwork in the American South-West,[43] and, in suitably modified form, by other scholars in contexts as diverse as Hong Kong and Japan.[44] In the majority of these studies, appreciable and systematic variations have been discovered between different societies, or, for example, between different generations of the same society. Further, the typology has been related to various aspects of sociological theory, including role theory and the analysis of deviance, and particular use has been found for it in the understanding and characterization of social change. The process of modernization, for example, is broadly conceived as involving a shift in the emphases of a culture from the left-hand categories in the above table to those on the right. In a similar way, the scheme has been used to characterize particular moral ideologies: the Protestant Ethic, for instance, has been defined as involving emphasis on individualism, future-orientation, mastery-over-nature, doing, and a view of man initially as evil-but-malleable (even perfectible) and then becoming more that of neutral-and-malleable.[45]

Notwithstanding these points, a number of reservations need also to be made. It is to be acknowledged, however, that, whatever the shortcomings of Kluckhohn and Strodbeck's scheme, it at least serves to focus attention on some of the more important questions and problems which a typological approach to values both raises and must attempt to solve. We shall illustrate some of these.

The first point to be made concerns their use of the term value-orientations. The authors' definition is as follows:[46]

> Value orientations are complex but definitely patterned (rank-ordered) principles, resulting from the transactional interplay of three analytically distinguishable elements of the evaluative process—the cognitive, the affective, and the directive elements—which give order and direction to the ever-flowing stream of human acts and thoughts as these relate to the solution of 'common human' problems.

But this is to compound a number of elements which might more usefully be kept distinct. Although the authors talk of studying cultural value-systems, it is evident that not all of their categories can be conceived as unambiguously designating values as such. The clearest example of this is the first category, concerning the conception of human nature, the proposed solutions to which can hardly be viewed as specifying alternative values. These do not indicate desirable characteristics of human nature, nor do they classify views as to what human being ought to be like. Rather, they designate general *beliefs*, expressing conceptions of what innate human nature *is* like, and the degree to which it is malleable.

This is the only clear-cut example of this type. In at least two other cases, however, it is particularly difficult to separate the evaluative components of the category from the cognitive ones. These are the categories referring to attitudes towards nature and towards time. Thus, although 'mastery over nature' and 'harmony with nature' might be taken as roughly expressive of value-attitudes, it would be misleading to conceive of 'subjugation to nature' in this way, since, at least in Kluckhohn and Strodbeck's usage, this either reflects an empirical necessity faced by primitive economies, or an injunction following almost directly from a specific set of beliefs concerning the powers of the supernatural and their relation to man, an injunction which would be virtually without meaning in the absence of such beliefs. Similarly, with respect to the dimension of time, a choice between an emphasis on, respectively, past, present, or future is itself closely related to certain presuppositions of a cognitive kind regarding the nature of time: in particular, in any culture in which all three alternatives can be meaningfully and comparably rank-ordered, as the present account requires, time must be conceived as essentially linear.

C*

61

To charges such as these, the authors might reply that we have, in effect, misconstrued their purpose. Granted, they may say, that the categories listed in the typology encompass cognitive as well as evaluative issues, and that no sharp analytic distinction has been drawn between the two, none the less they are similarly conjoined in the empirical world and the typology is offered as a social classification, not a logical one. That is, it is a simple classification of basic themes universal to human cultures to be justified by its empirical and conceptual uses in social scientific inquiry. Arguments of this type are implicit at various points in their work.

However, to make the items inclusive in this way serves only to underline a second problem: namely, that of their completeness. This may be applied firstly to the five basic problem categories themselves, and secondly to the series of triads of possible solutions with which they are associated. The second of these aspects may be taken first, and here a number of omissions will deserve mention.

Consider the attitude to time, for example. As we have noted, any meaningful ordering of past-, present-, and future-orientations presupposes a broadly linear conception of time. Such a conception will be obvious to us and need no further comment; yet it is not, as we shall see, universally held. None the less, it has been the dominant conception in the Western world since at least Hebraic times. However the Judaeo-Christian tradition established more than the linearity of time; it ascribed also a general *intelligibility*, even a moral significance, to history. As one writer has expressed it:[47]

> Unlike some other great religions, Christianity was indissolubly tied to time, for the incarnation, which gave meaning and a pattern to the whole of history, occurred at a definite point in time. Moreover Christianity was rooted in Israel, a culture which, with its great prophetic tradition, had always been one for which time was real, and the medium of real change. The Hebrews were the first Westerners to give a value to time, the first to see a theophany, an epiphany, in time's record of events. For Christian thought the whole of history was structured around a center, a temporal midpoint, the historicity of the life of Christ, and extended from the creation through the *berith* or covenant of Abraham to the *parousia* . . . the messianic millenium and the end of the world. . . . In this world outlook the recurring present was always unique, unrepeatable, decisive, with an open future before it, which could and would be affected by the action of the individual who might assist or hinder the irreversible meaningful directedness of the whole.

In this way, history ceased to be a mere succession of contingencies; it acquired moral purpose and direction. This conception of time, as a continuous, linear, redemptive process, has, of course, had enormous consequences up to the present day. Various facets of its influence have been ably examined by historians and philosophers of history. For example, it has found dramatized expression at various stages in history in the form of millenarian movements;[48] then, during the Enlightenment, it became transformed into a secular belief in progress which has remained with us up to the present day.[49] The Judaeo-Christian concept of time has also been proposed as a contributing factor to the rise of science and technology at the Renaissance,[50] and, as an important element presupposed by the Protestant Ethic, to the Industrial Revolution also.[51]

In sum, the Judaeo-Christian conception of time has had an important and pervasive influence on Western consciousness. And even a minimal understanding of this conception requires an appeal to more than knowledge of the relative rank-ordering of past, present, and future. Indeed, its axioms are best understood comparatively; that is, by reference to other, non-linear conceptions. Of these, the historically most significant competitor has probably been the cyclical conception of time in its various forms. Such a view was particularly associated with the cultures of classical Greece and Rome, especially the former.[52] It also formed an important element in the Hindu and Buddhist traditions of India,[53] and in the cultures of a number of preliterate societies, some of which, of course, still survive.[54] If, therefore, time forms not only an inevitable parameter of human action, as of the physical world, but also, as Kluckhohn and Strodbeck argue, a basic conceptual problem common to all societies, then surely recognition needs to be made of the fact that, at least outside the West, cyclical conceptions have supplied one of the major types of solution to this problem. But within the cyclical framework, a rank-ordering of past-, present-, and future-orientations ceases to have the meaning it has within a linear context, and as a result the rank-order loses value as a tool for cross-cultural analysis.

Attention may be drawn here to some of the implications of the Indo-Hellenic conception. Firstly, the theory of cyclical recurrence precluded all genuine novelty. The future was closed and determined, the present not unique, and all time essentially past time. In consequence, time could not possess the value ascribed to it in the Christian tradition. The *realissimum*, the focus of value, was outside the constraints of time. And the consequences of this theory may well have been intellectual as well as moral. As Needham writes: 'Salvation . . . could only be thought of as escape from the world of time, and this was partly what led, as some suppose, to the Greek fascination with the timeless patterns of deductive geometry and the formulation of the theory of Platonic "ideas", as well as to the "mystery-religions".'[55]

Similarly, it can be seen that various implications of the cyclical view are not, for example, conducive to changes such as those associated with the rise of science in the West. Thus, the depreciation of the empirical, temporal world (as *maya*, for instance, in Hindu thought) does not encourage emphasis on the careful acquisition of natural knowledge. Nor does the cyclical view of history permit the belief in, and so value of, a continuous, cumulative, never-completed natural knowledge, the idea of scientific progress, which remains an important element in our culture and in the motivation for scientific activity. Thus 'it is probably reasonable to believe that in sociological terms, for the scientific revolution, where the co-operation of so many men together (unlike the individualism of Greek science) was part of the very essence, a prevalence of cyclical time would have been severely inhibitory, and linear time was the obvious background'.[56]

Further implications could be drawn, and other aspects of the conceptualization of time discussed, but perhaps sufficient has already been said to demonstrate the incompleteness of the solutions to this problem proposed within Kluckhohn and Strodbeck's scheme. Its inclusion as a problem, however, is understandable. As we have indicated above, the category is an important one for the understanding of cultures and their systems of ethics and well illustrates the mutual interconnectedness of cognitive and moral conceptions. Also Kluckhohn and Strodbeck's notion of dominant and variant solutions would appear relevant to the characterization of time-perceptions. Although linear-consciousness may have been the dominant conception in Western culture, it has not been the exclusive one, and cyclical models have been proposed also at various times, and occasionally accepted by sections of the population, just as linear conceptions persisted within the Indo-Hellenic civilizations.[57]

In summary, however, we would think a more useful typological approach would first treat time as a purely cognitive category, and include recognition of the linear and cyclical models, together with some of their local variants, and then introduce the evaluative elements on this basis: recognition here, for instance, could be made of whether history was conceived within a framework of social progress or social regress,[58] and so on. It is perhaps at this last stage also that the inclusion of rank-orders of past-, present-, and future-orientations would also be appropriate. Such an enterprise, however conducted, will necessarily involve considerable simplification. But in this way it might prove possible to construct a more valid, in the sense of more complete and less ethnocentric, schema, and one in which cognitive-evaluative elements would be more clearly separated and their interrelationships more easily diagnosed.

The other categories in Kluckhohn and Strodbeck's typology, of course, await similar scrutiny of their relative completeness, and, although the other proposed sets of solutions may appear less immediately vulnerable to criticism on this score, a number of deficiencies do exist. For example, although the first problem-category has the virtue of permitting a distinction between, on the one hand, a *tabula rasa* conception of 'human nature' and, on the other, an emphasis on innate characteristics, which is important for ethical thinking, a number of other distinctions would still appear almost equally basic. One illustration would be the cultural conception of the social distribution of these (moral and non-moral) characteristics of individuals, for which an *élitist-egalitarian* dimension might be suggested as a basic axis of variation. The early doctrines of pre-destined salvation in the Reformation exemplify well the élitist conception in its moral sense. But its connotations may be less strongly evaluative, as perhaps in the beliefs of modern societies regarding the fixed proportions of the population capable of benefiting from particular types of education (university, technical, etc.). Naturally, conceptions regarding the distribution of characteristics may also be related in various ways to the innate/learned and (not exactly the same) mutable/immutable distinctions. In the interest of space, however, further discussion of the completeness of this and the other proposed 'solutions' will, for the present, be put aside.

Instead, attention may be directed briefly to the question of the completeness of the five basic categories of 'common human problems'. Here at least two points deserve mention. Firstly, Kluckhohn and Strodbeck do not make the grounds of their selection of these particular items very clear. Why these and no more? Why are they universal? In particular, are they argued to be universal in a logical sense, as being implicit in the concept of human society? Or are they claimed to be universal on theoretical grounds, as derivable from the framework of sociological theory? Or, finally, are they considered universal for inductive reasons, from a review of the comparative empirical data? Whichever of these is chosen, further evidence will be needed to permit the authors' case to be properly assessed. In fact, Kluckhohn and Strodbeck seem, at various times, to imply an admixture of all three reasons, although with varying degrees of emphasis.

The question involved here is not a trivial one, since it concerns the grounds for rejecting a doctrine of cultural relativism, which would oppose their typological method either on the grounds of the extreme relativity of cultural standards and reasoning, and of the importance of comprehending these in their own terms, or by an appeal to the relativity imposed upon our ability to reliably understand them. Either way the claim for the universality of their categories is open to criticism. Indeed, relativist arguments of this type, which we shall examine in chapter 9, constitute the principal dilemma faced by any classification of values (and norms, etc.) which claims a degree of generality. Kluckhohn and Strodbeck propose their three 'axioms'—(i) a limited number of 'common human problems', (ii) a limited range of solutions, and (iii) the presence of all the solutions in all societies, though in varying rank-orders—in (largely tacit) recognition of the limitations imposed by relativism. But what they do not do is adequately justify these axioms, and hence, ultimately, effectively answer possible relativist criticisms.

Up to this point, the argument of Kluckhohn and Strodbeck is analogous to that of proponents of the analysis of social systems in terms of their functional prerequisites.[59] However, in this type of analysis theoretical reasons are usually provided to justify the inclusion of specific items as functionally necessary to the operation of any viable society, and the categories included are relatively formal and amenable to various structural interpretations: the prerequisites of adequate recruitment and socialization procedures, for example, may be empirically fulfilled within the context of the nuclear family, the extended family, or some arrangement of the kibbutz type, and so on. But the problem with this type of analysis is to decide the relevance of knowledge of these prerequisites for understanding the structure and central concerns of any particular society.

A similar question is raised by the common problems approach of Kluckhohn and Strodbeck. If one accepted the universality of these problems, would their solutions indicate thereby the central concerns of a society? Put differently, would they designate those precepts with the required legitimacy and superiority to qualify as moral precepts? Again, Kluckhohn and Strodbeck offer us no convincing grounds for thinking that they would, and proof of their universality alone, were it available, would not suffice. A demonstration that a set of problems, whether functional or conceptual, is faced in common by all societies does not itself entail that the principal concerns of the culture will focus upon these problems and their solutions. Thus, even if a particular importance and centrality were granted to Kluckhohn and Strodbeck's set of value-orientations, their significance would be a construct of the observer's frame of reference, and not necessarily matched by the views of the participant in any particular culture. This is not to deny that such matching may, in point of fact, at least sometimes occur. Rather it is to note the absence, within Kluckhohn and Strodbeck's account, of any special grounds for expecting the authors' criteria of significance to be paralleled by those of the members of the particular culture under study. Without such grounds, the typology loses some of its potential value as a conceptual tool for a comparative sociology of moral codes.

None the less, it is to be acknowledged that further analysis might suggest reasons which could be added to Kluckhohn and Strodbeck's account at least to justify the general relevancy of the items in their typology to the moral, or primary, value-system of any society. The most apparent example concerns the category of human nature. Thus, with respect to this, it could be argued that any social or moral theory which assesses or prescribes for human conduct must necessarily presuppose some philosophical anthropology, however minimal, which at some level will play a role in the self-justification or explication of the theory. In consequence, it would be necessary to include a category of basic alternative conceptions of human nature within one's typology. Perhaps their account could be further strengthened by other considerations of this kind.

In summary, our main point has been that any general typology of, at least moral, values should attempt to reconcile the positions of, so to speak, agent and spectator with regard to what are to be considered basic categories, and that, wherever possible, reasoned grounds should be provided to indicate that one's own criteria of relative importance and centrality will be generally shared by the cultures which are to be studied.[60] To this end, some appeal to the processes of ethical reasoning would seem necessary, and it is one of the more important limitations of the typological approaches available at present that little or no attention is given to the types of argumentation and justification which lie behind the lists of prescriptions and desiderata which are presented and render them plausible.[61]

The work of Kluckhohn and Strodbeck and Allport and Vernon was chosen above for discussion since these accounts have so far been responsible for generating the most empirical research based on general classifications of values. It seemed important, therefore, to be aware of some of their more salient strengths and weaknesses, and the Kluckhohn-Strodbeck scheme was given some additional attention here becaue of the general significance of some of the issues which it raises. Other classifications do, of course, exist, but the majority of these have been constructed *ad hoc* for use within a particular research-design, or for the analysis of a limited range of cultural types.

Perhaps the only other research of which brief mention need be made in the present context is that of Charles Morris (1956).[62] He has designed a questionnaire schedule to measure thirteen alternative conceptions of the good life, under the general rubric of 'ways to live', and has applied it in cross-national research on the attitudes of university students in ten different countries, the main samples being drawn from the United States, India, and China (in 1948).[63] A factor analysis of the results indicated that a common frame of reference was operating in the various countries and the following five factors were extracted: self-control, progress in action, self-sufficiency, sympathetic concern for others, and self-indulgence.

67

Systematic variations by nationality were discovered in the responses to conceptions of the good life, and intercultural differences were generally judged more substantial than intracultural ones. One conclusion drawn by Morris was that no simple distinction between East and West could be drawn in terms of preferred ways of life, except that Asiatic students were on average more social-centred than Western students, and showed more tolerance for cultural diversity. A major limitation of this research, however, concerns the content of the alternative ways of life: these are drawn largely from what appear, at least to Western eyes, to be some of the major themes to be found in the world's great religions and traditions of ethical theory, and in consequence they are of more philosophical, than sociological, interest. Secondly, these items (in questionnaire form) presuppose a relatively high degree of literacy and education on the part of the respondent. Thus, although they may have been intelligible to students of the humanities, from which the majority of Morris's samples were drawn, they could not be applied to the larger part of any national population. The philosophical nature of the questions also involved problems of translation, some subtle and possibly undetectable, but others quite apparent. As Fearing (1957), for instance, comments in a review of Morris:[64] 'In the Chinese translation of Way Thirteen (the Way widely preferred by Chinese students), the opening sentence had become: "A person should make himself useful." In the English original this sentence was: "A person should let himself be used." This suggests difficulty that deserves more than passing reference.'

It is perhaps in view of these limitations that Morris's work has generated relatively few subsequent empirical studies. It is noteworthy also, however, that, despite the 'philosophical' content of his questions and of his approach generally, very little explicit attention is given to the issue of the justifications offered for the alternative conceptions of the good life. All he notes is the affinity between these conceptions and a number of philosophical beliefs such as philosophical idealism, and so on.[65]

We observed earlier in this chapter that the lack of adequate typologies of values and norms has been restrictive to the development of sociological theory in this field. We have now considered a number of such typologies. One general conclusion we would draw would be to emphasize the benefits to be gained from, firstly, a closer association with moral philosophy, and particularly with some of its more recent advances, and secondly, from the development of more adequate and controlled methodologies. Various aspects of these two points will be considered later in the study. It is to be recalled also, however, that it was noted as well that the development of such generally-applicable typologies, except when phrased in the most abstract terms, could be argued to be a virtually impossible task, either in view of the extreme relativism of cultural standards, or of epistemological limitations upon our capacity to comprehend them without ethnocentrism. It was a virtue of the Kluckhohn and Strodbeck approach that at least recognition was given of this. And the inadequacy of their typology, together with the limitations of the others, might at least make us more aware of the difficulties to be encountered in such an enterprise.

### Ethical justification: some comments

We argued at the beginning of this chapter for a logical distinction between standards of *evaluation* and norms embodying *prescriptions* as the basic elements of a moral code. We pointed out that each is characteristically associated with a distinctive set of predicates, and that prescriptions cannot be deduced from evaluations without an appeal to additional assumptions. The sociological accounts, we suggested, had overstressed the centrality of values and the extent to which specific or general prescriptions (norms) could be derived from them. Because this relationship of derivation is thought to exist, sociological accounts tend to conceive of a society's values as more stable and enduring than its norms. The normative order, it is often argued, is more flexible and may change radically without a corresponding change in a society's values.[66] Yet it is also fairly evident that, as in the case of the Indian caste system, the same set of norms may be regarded as legitimate by quite different traditions which propound different values. As Birdwell (1966) noted in his discussion of the integration of complex societies, a single value-system can serve to legitimate different normative structures, and a plurality of value-systems can legitimate the same set of norms.[67]

To clarify conceptual questions such as these, and to avoid limiting preconceptions, more sociological attention needs to be directed towards analysis of the kind of *reasoning* involved in the adoption and defence of moral codes. Why are particular actions prescribed or prohibited? What dictates standards of evaluation? Naturally, an understanding of the processes by which particular moral standards are derived and justified will help us to predict their occurrence. And, as we suggested in the Introduction, these processes characteristically become self-conscious and explicit to the agent (and hence potentially to the observer) under the circumstances of perceived moral crisis and challenge to his unreflexive habits of opinion.

Full treatment of the issues of ethical argumentation and moral justification would require a substantial volume to themselves. The fact that the number of available analyses on this subject is few and of apparently limited interest to the concerns of the sociologist appears to be mainly due to the view that logical analysis is largely inapplicable to this field. We have already seen, with regard to relations between evaluations and prescriptions, that an over-extension of such analysis can be misleading. In a similar way, one can only examine the internal logical structure of value-systems in a metaphorical sense of the term.

However, the logical approach does seem applicable to the analysis of prescriptive discourse. In a later chapter we shall discuss the application of more complex prescriptive logics to this field,[68] but for the present we may note the relevance of conventional logical formulations to this subject. Models appropriate to the characterization of different types of ethical discourse may be derived not only from reliable and sufficiently detailed ethnographies, but also from the artificial theories constructed by moral philosophers, and this applies equally to the prescriptive aspects of such discourse. It is partly on the basis of evidence from philosophical ethics, for example, that John Ladd outlines four modes of validation for prescriptions, as follows:[69]

(1) Every particular prescription is self-validating (*mode of extreme particularism*);

(2) Every particular prescription is derived from one of a plurality of basic prescriptions, but there is no prescribed way of deciding which of these basic prescriptions applies in the case of conflict (*mode of selection*);

(3) Every particular prescription is validated by simple application of a single basic prescription (*mode of applications*);

(4) Every particular prescription is validated by creative interpretation of a basic schematic prescription (*mode of interpretation*).

This is a useful account of alternative relationships between basic precepts and the particular prescriptions (counsels, etc.) demanded by concrete situations, and further analysis might reveal other possibilities.[70] Thus the present classification may be expressed as a $2 \times 2$ typology, which discriminates firstly between those systems which assume only one basic prescription (e.g. Bentham's principle of majority happiness) and those which assume more than one (e.g. liberal-humanist philosophy), and secondly, between those which maintain that one or more basic prescriptions are necessary and sufficient to validate any particular prescription, and those which deny this. The latter category, however, may be further discriminated into those systems which deny only the sufficiency of the basic prescription(s) to validate the derived prescription, and those which deny any appeal to basic prescriptions for this purpose (as in existentialism, intuitionism, etc.). Ladd illustrates these types with reference to legal codes, ethical systems, and anthropological data,[71] but it is sufficient for us to note that the scheme seems to demonstrate successfully the possibility of using syllogistic models to summarize basic types of reasoning in relation to prescriptions. As such it should help to clarify and compare some of the sociological evidence and have a directing influence on future research, although it is only a relatively preliminary attempt and more sophisticated analyses may follow. In particular, it is to be noted that these four types of, as it were, decision rules may be translated into the formal language of deontic logic for more rigorous investigation. Further discussion of the latter, however, is to be reserved until later.[72]

Instead, two more common-sense observations may be made. Thus, firstly, and most simply, the above classification demonstrates that the structures of different moral codes will vary in their degree of complexity, and the simplicity with which they may be described. Secondly, and related to this, it is noteworthy also that the above scheme makes allowance for the varying significance of individual choice and judgment: type (1), for instance, is likely to involve the greatest reliance on individual judgment, and type (3) the least, with the other two occupying intermediate positions. By the use of such explicit models, one can avoid using implicit models which lack flexibility and ascribe too great a degree of determinacy to moral codes, faults which have characterized a great deal of the sociological, and surely the ethnographic, literature. The insufficient attention given to the flexibility and openness of rules has been noted, for example, by Oliver (1965) in his discussion of the Kamba tribe in Kenya.[73] He suggests that anthropologists have put too much stress on the tightly-knit nature of culture. In terms of selecting tribes for fieldwork, as well as for textbook illustrations, he argues that a choice has perhaps been made 'in favor of the more dramatic cultures which exhibit a firm kind of unity of the Benedictian sort'. Kamba society, which he cites as a counter-example, is loosely structured and susceptible to change. Their rules, he argues, are often vague and open-ended, and individuals are expected to make their own interpretations of them. Oliver's view is that flexibility belongs to the essence of culture, and that cultures analogous to the Kamba have perhaps been more widespread than has been assumed.

But if the determinacy of cultural standards is itself an empirical issue, open to the evidence, then the use of classifications such as the one cited above will be to direct attention to some of the leading characteristics of moral reasoning even in relatively indeterminate cultures. In a similar manner, the development of prescriptive logical systems holds the promise of providing us with formal languages which would permit rigorous and concise descriptions of structures of ethical reasoning irrespective of the culture in which they occurred.

More adequate recognition of the structural features of moral codes would have several advantages; it should, for instance, make possible more detailed understanding of the processes of basic cultural change which are being experienced today, in some degree, by virtually all traditional societies. In short, the development of conceptual tools appropriate to studying the relationships between the elements of a moral code would be an appreciable step forward from mere classifications of values and norms, however widespread the applicability of the latter might be.

But the issue of ethical argumentation raises broader questions than those covered by the alternative modes of validation and other accounts of internal relations among prescriptions. In particular, it raises the question of the justification of the 'basic prescriptions' themselves and also of the leading values. The answers to these questions will be to a certain extent interchangeable and will involve, at least in the case of moral attitudes, reference at some stage to underlying cognitive assumptions which serve to validate and give meaning to a system of values and prescriptions. But to investigate the sense in which they do 'validate and give meaning to' such systems is to raise, of course, the dichotomy of 'is/ought', facts and values. In a sense, this is a dilemma which, from a moral point of view, it can be deleterious to belittle and, within the present sociological terms of reference, to over-emphasize. Either way, it cannot be given here the lengthy attention that it deserves. Instead, we shall confine ourselves to two comments.

Firstly, our interest as sociologists is in attaining a valid description of ethical reasoning as it empirically exists in the variety of social contexts which are available to us, and not in philosophically assessing the logical propriety of the arguments so discovered. Given this, it surely seems possible, if not highly probable, that at least some of such naturally occurring moral codes will be found to embody arguments of a naturalistic type in their structure, in much the same way as many historically available ethical theories have done. That is, attempts may well be made to base ethical recommendations upon generalizations of an empirical kind, and, in particular, upon appeals to the nature of man as supplying conclusive evidence for the legitimacy of such recommendations. Indeed, in the case of different moral codes, or variants of any single one, the same factual assumptions may be appealed to in order to support different, and possibly incompatible, moral conclusions which are claimed to be inferred from them. In an analogous way, for instance, Rousseau accepted rationality as a distinguishing characteristic of man but, unlike most philosophers who shared this view, did not consider that this warranted the conclusion that activities which promoted or expressed rationality best were the most desirable; rather, he thought of reason as divorcing man from nature, which was undesirable, and he spoke of thinking man as a 'depraved animal'. The fact that incompatible conclusions can claim origin in the same premisses in this way serves to demonstrate, of course, the weakness of many naturalistic arguments. But such arguments do not seem uncommon, and they have the understandable motivation of wishing to remove morality from the realm of opinion and to assimilate it with descriptive accounts of what simply 'is the case'. And one of the simplest ways of apparently achieving this is to present the moral code as a natural expression of man's empirical nature, in the same way that Mill, for instance, attempted to infer to the desirability of happiness from man's allegedly universal tendency to desire it. In general, then, it seems that the ethnographer may restrict himself to recording arguments of this type as validly as possible, whilst leaving their logical evaluation to others.

It is not quite as simple as this, partly because our observation, what we decide to look for and how we conceptualize the results, will, in cases such as these, obviously be influenced by the model of logically possible relationships between cognitions and evaluations that we hold. In particular, a strong emphasis on the logical incompatibilities between 'is' and 'ought' propositions may encourage an approach to moral codes which fails to note, or recognize, the relevance of factual assumptions to their adequate comprehension. And this leads to our second point, which is that it is important to be clear about what the anti-naturalist thesis maintains. In its usual form it draws our attention to the principle of inference which requires of a strict deductive argument that nothing should be drawn out by way of a conclusion that is not already contained, explicitly or implicitly, in the premisses. It then applies this principle to ethical discourse, with the result that no moral argument (whether prescriptive or evaluative) can be deduced from any set of premisses not in themselves containing a moral principle or judgment. And, from our earlier discussion of the distinction between prescriptions and evaluations,[74] we may add to this the requirement that prescriptions may only be deduced from premisses containing a prescriptive principle, and evaluations only from premisses containing an evaluative principle. The main conclusion, however, is that statements about what is the case cannot provide logically conclusive grounds for statements regarding what *ought* to be done, or regarding what is desirable, worth while, etc. The failure of the naturalist argument, therefore, is that of not respecting the autonomy of ethics.

But this autonomy, though, it surely exists, can also be over-stated, especially if attention is restricted to the deductive aspects of the 'is/ought' question. We have already remarked upon the priority of descriptive premisses over evaluative ones, in two senses, firstly, in the sense that it is a minimum condition of intelligibility that people act on what they take to be the case in a broadly factual sense, although they need not, of course, act in accordance with their views of what is right or worth while in a moral sense; and secondly, in the logical sense that any meaningful evaluative or prescriptive statement will presuppose descriptive premisses, the acceptance of which imposes limitations upon the range of values and prescriptions which may be reasonably adopted.[75] But if this is so, then cognitive presuppositions will be entailed by any moral code. Indeed, it is from the latter of these two points that moral views acquire the 'objectivity' and 'legitimacy'[76] which is characteristically ascribed to them and which renders them susceptible to discussion and debate. These attributes of morality, and the absurdity entailed by conceiving of the processes of cognition and evaluation (or prescription) as wholly independent of each other, are correctly recognized in naturalist theories. But their response to this recognition involves proposing a connection to exist between these two realms of discourse which is too strict to be logically acceptable. But this failure should not lead us to ignore such lesser relationships as may exist. What is needed, therefore, is the exploration, in logical and philosophical terms, of possible non-deductive forms of relationship between cognitive, prescriptive, and evaluative formulations. Such an investigation would have considerable potential value for future analyses of ideological systems, in logic[77] as in sociology, and it may also permit a reconsideration of such issues as that of value-freedom in natural and social science. As Edel (1966) concluded on the alleged gap between facts and values in respect of this last issue:[78]

> The philosophical arguments for maintaining the gap pose the issue of the relation of science and value in a deductive model: how to deduce value conclusions from scientific premises. What is thus demonstrated by the arguments is really not that science and value have no relation but that such a model oversimplifies their relation to the point of irrelevance, that the relations are much more varyingly and complexly patterned.

Some of the kind of elements which will be relevant to these broader issues of ethical argumentation and justification were cited in our discussion of typological approaches—the categories of 'time' and 'human nature' in Kluckhohn and Strodbeck's scheme, for example—but the lack of insightful categorizations of different types of beliefs and cognitive assumptions relevant to the present subject is as important an omission as the presence of similar lacunae with respect to values and norms. However, we will not consider the general analysis of ethical justification further here. Rather, we will examine one particular aspect of this, concerning the distinction between two important types of justifying argument. In this way we would hope to give more specific content to our general argument above, which has been in favour of taking fuller account of the issues of moral reasoning in both theoretical and empirical studies in sociology.

## Two types of justification

We may introduce our discussion of the distinction between two types of justification in moral thinking by considering first a hypothetical example. Imagine a manager of a bureaucracy has to promote two people to higher posts in a month's time. If the organization measures up to Weber's ideal type of bureaucracy then our manager will have only two criteria in mind, seniority and merit.[79] According to these criteria, then, the manager selects two employees and tells them they are to be promoted in a month's time. Suppose that in the meantime the manager acquires new information to the effect that these two persons are either not the most senior or the most meritorious. What does he then do? If he were an 'ideal' bureaucrat, in Weber's sense, he would have to revise his decision and promote instead those candidates who were the most qualified in terms of these two criteria. But in the empirical case, a different sort of moral consideration is likely to enter at this stage. This is the kind that says 'One should always keep one's promises', or, more generally, that 'One should always tell the truth'.

The manager would thus be faced with a dilemma. But this dilemma is not solely one between two sets of prescriptions which differ in content. They differ also in form. Thus the justification for the original criteria, seniority and merit, is in terms of their consequences: they are right principally in the sense that they embody the most efficient means of serving the organization's goals. The second criteria, however, are not normally to be justified in the same way, although they in fact could be. Thus one need not extend the statements that 'One should always keep one's promises' or 'One should always tell the truth' any further. It is quite reasonable to maintain that the consequences of these actions are irrelevant to their rightness or wrongness as moral prescriptions. Indeed, to specify the good consequences they will lead to, or the bad consequences they will avert, is to alter the moral criterion. Thus to say, for instance, that 'One should always tell the truth because people dislike liars' is to alter completely the tone of the sentence.

Our main interest here is with the form, rather than the content, of these criteria. The first type, where the justification is principally a question of the good or bad consequences which can reasonably be expected to follow from the application of the principle, we may term

75

an *extrinsic* type of moral argument. The second type, where to be morally prescribed an action has merely to embody or exemplify the chosen criterion of rightness, can be called the *intrinsic* type. The distinction finds its parallel in moral philosophy and provides a useful basis for discriminating between different types of ethical theory. In his book *Ethics* (1963), for instance, William Frankena draws a distinction between two sets of such theories, the teleological and the deontological, which he characterizes as follows:[80]

A *teleological theory* says that the basic or ultimate criterion or standard of what is morally right, wrong, obligatory etc. is the nonmoral value that is brought into being. The final appeal, directly or indirectly, must be to the comparative balance of good over evil produced.

*Deontological theories* [say that there are] other considerations which may make an action or rule right or obligatory besides the goodness or badness of its consequences—certain features of the act itself other than the *value* it brings into existence, for example, the fact that it keeps a promise, is just, or is commanded by God or the State.

Further distinctions may also be drawn. Thus teleological theories differ firstly as to the choice of what is 'good'. A basic distinction here is that between hedonism, which, broadly speaking, identifies good and evil with pleasure and pain, and non-hedonism, which may define good in a variety of ways, such as in terms of knowledge, power, self-realization, perfection, and so on. Teleological theories differ secondly according to whose good one should promote, or as to how potential recipients should be preferentially ordered. The egoistic forms of this type of theory maintain that the agent himself should be either the sole or the primary beneficiary. The universalistic forms may argue that one should promote the good of the majority, as in utilitarianism, or of mankind, of the State, and so on.

Deontological theories vary also according to the definition of 'good'. But they vary secondly according to the role afforded to general rules. Thus, '*Act-deontological* theories maintain that the basic judgments of obligation are all purely particular ones like "In this situation I should do so and so," and that general ones like "We ought always to keep our promises" are unavailable, useless, or at best derivative from particular judgments.'[81] Existentialist ethics would form a good example of this type of theory, where any acceptance of general rules of conduct may itself be taken to be an instance of *mauvaise foi*.[82]

On the other hand, '*Rule-deontologists* hold that the standard of right and wrong consists of one or more rules—either fairly concrete ones like "We ought always to tell the truth" or very abstract ones like Henry Sidgwick's Principle of Justice.'[83] This classification invites comparison with the list of modes of validation given above[84] and it is also evident that, if one interprets teleological as extrinsic and deontological as intrinsic, Frankena's basic distinction is very similar to the one we have drawn. And it is, we believe, a particularly important distinction to be borne in mind for the analysis of types of ethical justification. This importance has both a general reference and a specific application to sociology. In our discussion, therefore, we will take each of these aspects in turn.

Firstly, it is to be observed that, at least within the Western world, many of the situations which are thought to involve basic moral dilemmas embody, in fact, a distinction between these two types of justification. A fuller awareness of this distinction, then, should help to clarify the nature of these dilemmas. For example, a great deal of theoretical writing, and public debate, has examined the question: 'Under what conditions does a desirable end justify undesirable means for its attainment?' This is a question appropriate to many classes of conduct for which a plausible distinction may be drawn between 'means' and 'ends', not only conceptually, but also in an empirical sense. And it is particularly clear in those cases where the ends in question enjoy consensual backing. Scientific activity, for instance, although it has not always done so,[85] would fall into this category today. Thus, despite general acceptance of the goals of science, certain of the means which scientists, both natural and social, have adopted for their achievement have been the subject of criticism on ethical grounds. Arguments against the use of vivisection in biology and biophysics,[86] and the use of concealed recording devices, and other intrusions on privacy, by social scientists may illustrate this.[87] Our point here is not to adjudicate these issues, but rather to observe that in many cases of this type clarity would be enhanced if the principle involved were not conceived as merely, or even primarily, a matter of 'weighing the respective consequences', but as involving also appeals to two different forms of justification, the intrinsic and the extrinsic.

A further, and equally familiar, example may be drawn from the field of social action. Here, for example, the question is often asked, 'When is violence justified as a legitimate means for the attainment of political and social reforms?' On this issue, the proponents of violence have tended not to reject its illegitimacy *tout court*, but to advocate it rather as a necessary, if unfortunate, means to the end at stake. Franz Fanon, for instance, has argued that 'liberation can only be achieved by force' in the context of the colonial situation on the grounds that (i) colonialism had been imposed by force and could only be maintained by force, and (ii) only violence could restore a necessary self-respect to the oppressed.[88] Similar arguments regarding the necessity of violence as an instrument of effective change are also employed by a number of current advocates of Black Power in the United States.[89]

Opponents of violence, on the other hand, have drawn attention not only to its intrinsic undesirability, but also the the presence of alternative means of effective change. Gandhian ethics, and the various forms of non-violent protest and civic action which his ideas gave rise to, serve to exemplify this.[90] And, in part, their argument may be phrased in extrinsic terms too; but whilst, for instance, Fanon's account emphasizes the debilitating consequences implicit in the *status quo*, and the value of the goals to be achieved, that of Gandhi stresses the debilitating consequences of the employment of violence as an instrument of reform. Not uncharacteristically, the dilemma involves issues of fact—do viable alternative means exist?— as well as principle: does the positive content of the end outweigh the negative content of the means? Each is relevant, although, in this case, advocates of violence frequently leave the question of principle tacit, by overstating the necessity of their policy.

Adequate assessment, and analysis, of issues of this type, then, requires that a number of contributing elements in the proposed arguments be distinguished. Again, the moral components involved are not reducible to a process of just 'weighing the consequences'. This would misrepresent the arguments at stake. On the other hand, these may be conceived as involving a relative assessment of alternative moral precepts, the one intrinsically justified (e.g. non-violence), the other enjoined on extrinsic grounds (e.g. insurgency).[91] But if one grants this, then under certain conditions intrinsic considerations might effectively proscribe any action, or at least appear to. As Galtung (1969), for instance, has written:[92]

> If we are interested in e.g. social justice but also in the avoidance of personal violence, does this not constrain our choice of means so much that it becomes meaningful only in certain societies? And particularly in societies that have already realized many social-liberal values, so that there is considerable freedom of speech and assembly, and organizations for effective articulation of political interests? Whereas we are literally immobilized in highly repressive societies, or 'more openly repressive societies' as modern critics of liberalism might say? Thus, if our choice of means in the fight against structural violence is so limited by the non-use of personal violence that we are left without anything to do in highly repressive societies, whether the repression is latent or manifest, then how valuable is this recipe for peace?

Secondly, then, and compatible with the above, it is to be observed that an emphasis on one or the other of these types of justification is related to certain types of social conditions. This constitutes part of the more general question of the social determination of the formal aspects of moral codes, and not only of their content. As such, it constitutes also a challenging subject of inquiry for the sociology of knowledge. But here we will restrict ourselves to noting that an emphasis on the extrinsic, or instrumental approach is often demanded in situations of special urgency. Isaiah Berlin (1964) effectively draws attention to this when, in a somewhat different context, he remarks:[93]

> In critical situations where deviation from the norm may involve disastrous consequences—in battles, surgical operating rooms, revolutions, the end is wholly concrete, varying interpretations of it are out of place and all action is conceived as a means towards it alone. It is one of the stratagems of totalitarian regimes to represent all situations as critical emergencies, demanding ruthless elimination of all goals, interpretations, forms of behaviour save for one absolutely specific, concrete, immediate end, binding on everyone, which calls for ends and means so narrow and clearly definable that it is easy to impose sanctions for failing to pursue them.

The kind of social conditions which can arise from such a thorough-going instrumentalism in politics, and the ethical problems which they embody, have been depicted, for instance, in Koestler's novel on the Russian Revolution, *Darkness at Noon* (1940). In this he depicts a situation in which the criteria of validity itself have become extrinsically defined, such that 'truth' is what is beneficial to the revolutionary cause, and falsehood what is detrimental. Such a reversal of ordinary assumptions provides a dramatic expression of our present point. However, a situation not dissimilar in form, although less severe in content, is to some degree being currently faced by those developing countries that wish to industrialize their economies, and heighten their productivity, as rapidly as possible, whilst, at the same time, promoting rather than salvaging the development of liberal-democratic procedures. The dilemma involved here is reflected, for instance, in Gunnar Myrdal's (1968) detailed review of the economic prospects of South Asian countries, and leads him to alternate between advocacy of a policy of *laissez-faire*, with its protection of individual freedom, and a policy of more totalitarian central planning, with its arguably greater economic efficiency in this area.[94]

Thirdly, attention may also be drawn to the utility of the distinction between intrinsic and extrinsic forms of justification within the context of modern societies. In particular, mention should be made of the contemporary emphasis, especially in regard to political

79

decisions, upon economic growth as *the* national goal, at least in many Western industrial societies. Such an instrumental policy of 'economism' necessarily involves the assignment of a lesser status to certain other possible injunctions. Thus, Mishan (1969), for example, has argued that such growth is achieved at the cost of an equitable distribution of the enlarged product, both socially and geographically.[95] The main theme of his thesis is to the effect that the realization of less quantifiable, although not less real, desiderata—political and industrial participation, leisure and recreation, the conservation of the natural environment—is equally significant as a moral precept and may be impaired by undirected growth.

It is of interest to compare this analysis with recent changes in the structure of our legal system. Thus it has been observed that[96]

> On the one hand, the law has become increasingly more liberal in its treatment of certain moral offences that have lain traditionally within its scope. . . . Not only have the penalties imposed on offenders been made less severe; in so far as the criminal law relates to the enforcement of morals, its scope has been gradually restricted. Many actions, including many expressions of opinion that would have led to prosecution in an earlier period, do not do so today. . . . Economic policy, on the other hand, presents a sharp contrast. The role of the state has enormously increased and the restrictions on private behaviour have been extended and strengthened.

The author, Professor Wilson, sums up these two divergent trends as involving a 'contradiction in our attitudes to law'. But this apparent contradiction, we would submit, is better understood as a shift of emphasis in the law from intrinsic to extrinsic types of justification. That is, we interpret these changes in the content of the legal system as, on the one hand involving a decreasing vigilance over a number of traditional moral issues, the rightness or wrongness of which was determined primarily by considerations of an intrinsic kind, and, on the other hand, as involving an extension of legal sanctions to cover a new range of actions the consequences of which—and particularly the collective consequences which no individual can control or even adequately foresee—can be regarded as socially harmful. Many of the latter sanctions have focused upon aspects of the national economy, and this new emphasis upon the priority of consequences for the justification of laws serves, in our view, to express both a lack of moral consensus over certain 'traditional' moral issues, and also the utilitarian reasoning which emerges from the new technocratic ethos of economic growth. But, again, the problems raised by such an ethos concern the lower status which tends to be ascribed to other plausible injunctions, such as those expressed in Mill's classic defence of liberty.[97] In such a situation, then, it is not to be unexpected that, as we noted at the beginning of this study, many issues of moral principle become treated as matters of technical decision.

Finally, therefore, it is to be observed that a specious necessity is ascribed to the choices implicit in the above situation. As it is assumed that there exists an inevitable correlation between economic growth and social welfare, so the disamenities produced by this growth are conceived as part of the 'inevitable costs of progress'. This habitual mode of thought, as Mishan has pointed out, helps preclude realization that there are critical social choices yet to be debated, and that 'policies radically different from those we habitually pursue are actually open to us all the time'.[98]

We have examined above three aspects of the general utility of drawing a distinction between two types of justification; namely, the intrinsic and the extrinsic. Attention was drawn to its applicability to a number of familiar moral dilemmas and to the analysis of certain aspects of modern society. Brief mention was also given of the social conditions which facilitate an emphasis on one or other of these forms of justification. Our concern now will be to apply this distinction within a more sociological frame of reference.

## Utilitarianism and sociology

In the first place, the present distinction invites some comparison with other discriminations which have been made in social theory, and in particular with Weber's distinction, in his typology of action, between *Wertrationalitat* and *Zweckrationalitat*.[99] Weber's conception of the progressive rationalization of Western culture involved a continuing extension of the norms of instrumental reasoning, freed of traditional limitations, which, we would suggest, were largely justified in intrinsic terms. Marx too spoke of the instrumentalism which characterized capitalist society. However, it is our impression that current theories, and empirical research, tend to produce inadequate descriptions of moral codes in society, in part because they give insufficient attention to the presence of *intrinsic* types of justification, as well as to the issue of ethical justification in general.

This may be illustrated with reference to Parsons' theory of social action. This theory, or classification system, comprises a number of assumptions[100] which prescribe a mode of analysis for explaining the action or conduct of typical individuals ('actors') in typical situations. A central assumption in this microcosm of the 'action frame of reference' is that of goal-directedness; indeed, this would appear logically implicit in the term action. However, it is on the basis of this model that Parsons develops his more general account of the nature of social order. An important problem raised by this type of enterprise, and one which has empirical as well as analytic significance,[101] is that of how one can move from a consideration of ends and means at the level of the individual to a consideration of social ends and means. More generally, how does one translate a concept and explanation of *individual* behaviour into a concept and explanation of collective behaviour?[102] It is more germane to our immediate concerns, however, to look at the way in which the basic concepts— those of values and norms—become conceptualized in the resulting taxonomy of social order. And in fact they extend the original model of individual action, with the result that 'values' are principally conceived as criteria which determine the selection of appropriate ends of social action, and norms are conceived as legitimate means to these ends.[103] Criticisms can be made of this, but from an external, functionalist viewpoint, this simple model can claim some plausibility. The problem enters when prescriptions and valuations tend also to be assumed to be *justified* in terms of their consequences for the realization of certain social goals. Although this usually appears more implicit than explicit in Parsons' work, it becomes more apparent in the work of some of his followers, and in particular in the simplified account of the 'action frame of reference' given by Neil Smelser (1962).[104] What is involved here may be termed a 'category mistake': the concepts which are applicable to the analysis of the structure of action, individual and social, are assumed to be analogously applicable to the structure of moral justification for action. In part, this mistake involves a compounding of the viewpoints of agent and observer, and its consequence is to omit recognition of intrinsic types of justification for an agent's actions. But justifications of this kind may be as much a part of culture, may be as fully institutionalized as instrumental rationales.

This limitation of the means-ends schema for the analysis of moral codes can be seen in various of its applications. One such illustration would be Merton's (1938, 1968) well-known typology of deviance and *anomie* according to the actor's orientation towards the prescribed norms (means) and goals (values) of a culture.[105] This, it will be recalled, generated four categories: those who reject the culturally prescribed means for illegitimate methods of attaining the goals (delinquency); those who stress scrupulous adherence to the norms whilst de-emphasizing the goals they lead to (ritualism); those who reject both the culturally-defined goals and the means of achieving them (retreatism) or assert new values (rebellion); and finally those who accept the legitimacy of both the goals and the approved means of their achievement (conformism). It can be seen now that this model is applicable only in the case of those moral precepts for which an instrumental rationale is supplied. It is inapplicable to those cases where the justification, which, again, may be institutional-ized, is of an intrinsic type. At least, this is true in so far as one is employing an internal approach, in terms of the agent's orientations to the situation, whether the agent is taken to be an archetypal representative of the culture in question or not. But Merton's typology still has value as an external model imposed on the evidence for the purpose of explanation and clarification. However, viewed in this way, it expresses little more than the conventional functionalist outlook, even though appeals could be made, for instance, to latent motivations as well as latent functions or consequences.

But awareness of distinctions such as the present one helps to avoid also limiting preconceptions in empirical research as well as theory. Thus, in view of the comments on modern society given earlier, there may be a tendency for us to expect instrumental replies to questions which seek to elicit justifying grounds for conduct. To the question 'Why are you doing this?' or 'Why is this the right thing to do?' the typical reply is an instrumental one—'In order to ...' or 'Because it will have the consequence that ...', and so on. Were the reply to be of the kind which said, for instance, 'Because it's right to keep promises' or 'Because it's wrong not to do it', then we would probably feel cheated of an answer. That is, we would assume the reply to be an ellipsis, and would then ask further questions designed to establish the goals actually at stake, even to make the respondent aware of the goals which he is 'unconsciously' pursuing.

But in so far as the morality of an individual or social group characteristically assumes a deontological form, the reply 'Because it's right in itself' is a perfectly valid one. To impose an instrumental perspective upon such cases would provide no understanding at all, merely a mirror-image of our own bias and preconceptions. On the other hand, we acknowledge that there is no necessary reason that these two types of morality should be mutually exclusive. Arguments of both types may be contained within a moral code, and particular moral injunctions or prohibitions may also be, as it were, 'over-determined', in the sense of being prescribed on both grounds. For instance, both intrinsic and extrinsic reasons may be given for keep-ing one's promises, telling the truth, fairness, non-violence, and so on. But further empirical detail on this awaits the collection of appropriate evidence by comparative research.

To approach the matter from a different perspective, we may say that, if the above conclusions are valid, then the pervasive model of morality in sociological theory and research is open to the same type of criticism as a thorough-going doctrine of utilitarianism. Thus, the central thesis of utilitarian theory, namely, that actions are made right or wrong to the degree that their consequences are good or bad, has recently come under criticism by philosophers, such as Rawls

(1955, 1958) and Urmson (1953),[106] for failing to provide an adequate account of a number of moral injunctions familiar to our society. These philosophers have brought attention to bear on the non-utilitarian elements in the justification of our concepts of, for example, justice and punishment. Similar considerations apply to such prescriptions as those concerned with promise-keeping in its various social forms and truth-telling. That is, for instance, we usually consider that there is some obligation to keep promises which does not depend on the *utility* of doing so. And, although under certain circumstances the breaking of a promise may be justified on the grounds of the harmful consequences which it may avert, we do not normally consider ourselves freed of the obligation to keep our promises merely by virtue of the fact that it would result in no good, or that breaking them would do more good than harm.

Similar considerations apply to other injunctions, such as those concerned with veracity. Moreover, it is not uncommon for moral codes, including our own, to designate certain actions that no good consequences could justify. E. F. Caritt, for instance, cited the example of hanging an innocent man who is publicly believed to be guilty in this category.[107] But it would seem that many objections to capital punishment in general, as well as to other, less severe, types of punishment, fall into the same class.[108] To arguments which rest on considerations of an intrinsic kind, then, statistical evidence regarding the relative efficacy of capital and other types of punishment is strictly irrelevant. However, in the discussions which attended Britain's decision in 1970 to make permanent, after the trial period, the abolition of capital punishment, the general tendency of all parties, both those for and those against, to neglect this and accept an extrinsic framework as an appropriate one to the assessment of the issue is both worthy of note and compatible with some of the observations given on modern society above.

But objections such as the ones we have mentioned serve, in our view, to demonstrate the possible cogency of intrinsic types of justification for ethical decisions. For the present argument, however, it is sufficient to draw attention to the fact that rationales of this kind are empirically available in both traditional and modern societies, and are therefore to be accounted for in any adequate description of social moralities. We have suggested also that the extrinsic approach is probably more characteristic of modern societies. But if one allows this, then we may regard the instrumental model in sociological theory to be both a reflection of the broader concerns of the society in which it arose, and, *ipso facto*, also an appropriate model for the analysis of at least appreciable parts of the moral life of these societies.

Somewhat parenthetically, but related to this last point, we may note also that utilitarian theory is allied with an individualistic con-

84

ception of society, which, as we shall argue later,[109] finds implicit recognition as well in much of the sociological research on moral codes. Thus Professor MacIntyre (1967) has written,[110] 'The utilitarian picture of society is of a collection of individuals, each with his own determinate desires and his consequent goals. The shared aims and norms of society are a product of the compromises and agreements of individuals: the public good is a sum total of private goods.'

He observes that although the set of practices which constitute justice may be justified as a whole by utilitarian considerations, in certain cases the principles of justice are waived on the grounds of (for example) human happiness,[111] and he comments:[112]

> Thus the attempt to shore up utilitarianism in this way is itself a misconceived attempt to give a false unity to our values. That such an attempt should be made is easily understood. The individualism of modern society and the increasingly rapid and disruptive rate of social change brings about a situation in which for increasing numbers there is no over-all shape to the moral life but only a set of apparently arbitrary principles inherited from a variety of sources. In such circumstances the need for a public criterion for use in settling moral and evaluative disagreements and conflicts becomes ever more urgent and ever more difficult to meet. The utilitarian criterion, which appears to embody the liberal ideal of happiness, is apparently without rivals, and the fact that the concept of happiness which it embodies is so amorphous and so adaptable makes it not less but more welcome to those who look for a court of appeal on evaluative questions which they can be assured will decide in their own favor.

This draws attention to a relationship between utilitarianism and the development of a society which is increasingly pluralistic, in the moral sense of the term. This pluralism is, of course, itself to be explicated in terms of changes in the social structure, and to chart this relationship over time is a problem for the sociology of knowledge. However, the concept of the plural society, in a broadly cultural sense, has obvious relevance to the sociology of ethics, and so we shall examine it more closely in the next chapter. For the present, let us note that although an extrinsic type of justification may be appropriate, and hence likely to be dominant, under social conditions of this type, it should not be thought of as the exclusive type. Not to recognize this is to impose a false unity upon moral precepts, both in sociology and philosophy.

## Further applications

But if, as we have argued, there can be other elements of an act, apart from its consequences, relevant to its characterization and justification in prescriptive discourse, then an analogous argument holds for moral evaluation. However, suffice it to say with respect to this that D'Arcy (1963) has provided one of the few accounts, from the viewpoint of analytic philosophy, of the diverse attributes of an action which could be relevant to its moral assessment.[113] Here again the sociologist's ability to characterize adequately particular moral codes would be enhanced by an awareness of these various elements potentially relevant to evaluation, and his tendency to biased observation—for instance, by over-stating the importance of motives or circumstances[114]—would be lessened.

It is to be acknowledged that in the case of certain classes of actions analytic or empirical difficulties prevent drawing distinctions which may have proven application and utility for other cases. Here, a distinction between, for example, means and ends may confuse rather than enhance analysis. R. S. Peters (1963, 1966) supplies a good example of this when he argues that much of the confusion about the aims of education comes about through treating the concept of education as embodying an extrinsic end, as in the sense of providing qualified people for the labour market and so raising a community's productivity.[115] As he writes,[116]

> Given that 'education' suggests the intentional bringing about of a desirable state of mind in a morally unobjectionable manner, it is only too easy to conceive of education as a neutral process that is instrumental to something that is worthwhile which is extrinsic to it. . . . But there is something inappropriate about this way of speaking; for we would normally use the word 'train' when we had such a specifiable extrinsic objective in mind. If, however, we do specify an appropriate 'aim' such as the development of individual potentialities or the development of intellect and character, then the aim would be intrinsic to what we consider education to be. For we would not call a person 'educated' who had not developed along such lines. It would be like saying the aim of reform is to develop an individual's sense of responsibility. This would give content to our understanding of making a man better, which is what it means to reform him, just as the development of intellect and character gives content to the notion of developing what is worth while, which is what it means to educate someone. If a dispute started about such 'aims'—e.g. whether a sense of responsibility was more important than respect for others or

whether the development of intellect was more important than the development of character—this would not be a dispute about ends which were extrinsic to reform or education; rather it would be a dispute about what was the most important characteristic of a reformed or educated man. Such aims mark out specific achievements and states of mind that give content to the formal notion of 'the educated man'.

Before concluding this chapter, we may consider briefly an example where the consequences of a distinction between extrinsic and intrinsic justifications may not only be theoretical in kind, but also distinctly practical. Thus, one *leitmotiv* running through current attempts to reform our legal system concerns the task of making the law conform to what the social sciences, and sociology and psychology in particular, are alleged to have demonstrated about human behaviour, and hence indirectly about 'human nature'. The image of man enshrined in our present laws is much more that of a voluntary, and so responsible agent than the image offered by either of these two disciplines, each of which has come to adopt a more determinist view of human conduct.[117] The assumptions from which reformers in this field start, then, are as much factual as ethical, as much questions of applying our knowledge as of modernizing our morality. Central to these concerns are the concepts of punishment and treatment, and it is these that we should now like briefly to consider.

There has been considerable debate on these topics in recent years[118] and in a recent review by Honderich (1971) diverse justifications for punishment have been examined, and largely dismissed. However, a degree of confusion has been caused in many of these debates by treating punishment as a special kind of treatment. On the basis of this, some reformers have argued that current forms of punishment—particularly imprisonment—are inadequate or unjustifiable as treatments.[119] But there is a conceptual confusion here, the clarification of which is important for our understanding of the rationales for those forms of punishment which are empirically available in modern societies.

Certain *prima facie* similarities between punishment and treatment do exist. Both are frequently painful (although perhaps not necessarily so) and both are undertaken in virtue of something that has already happened, whether a crime or an injury (at least when the treatment involved is not prophylactic). However, important differences also exist. Thus, treatment is an instrumental activity. It is always *for* some state of the person treated, and *in order to* produce some intended state or to forestall some undesirable state. Without the notion of a goal, even though the goal may vary in specificity, the concept of treatment is without meaning. Punishment, in contrast, is always inflicted or imposed *because of* some (usually voluntary)[120] violation of an established rule. There is no logical necessity in having any future state (e.g. reformation) as a goal of punishment and hence as a criterion for its justification. Whereas, as we have seen, treatment would not only be unjustified but also unintelligible without reference to such a goal.

To treat these two concepts as logically interchangeable in the sense that each must necessarily be understood, and justified, extrinsically, in means-ends terms, is to prejudge the issues at stake. Thus, a form of punishment may be justified in utilitarian terms, either with respect to its reformative consequences for the individual, or its deterrent value and (as in Durkheim's analysis) integrative functions for the wider society. But it need not be. The question is a matter of choice for those with the requisite authority. It should be noted, however, that a change of moral opinion in favour of treating offenders, and justifying punishment only as a special type of treatment, is usually preceded by a corresponding change in beliefs regarding the voluntary character of actions. When, for example, an action that was previously conceived as an infraction of a rule and so deserving punishment (e.g. attempted suicide) becomes viewed instead as requiring treatment, such change tends to imply the presence of a new set of beliefs according to which the action in question is more validly perceived as determined, at least in large part, by factors which are outside the individual's control. It is perhaps, then, a consequence of the perspective of the social sciences that such a change of attitude is perceptibly occurring today.

## Summary

In this chapter we have discussed some of the basic components of a moral code. These components may be divided into the elements of a moral code and the relations which pertain between these elements. With regard to the elements of a moral code, we distinguished primarily between the processes of evaluation and prescription. Prescriptions, we argued, both positive and negative, were afforded too residual a position in sociological accounts, and also could be more realistically characterized as embodying varying 'degrees of stringency'. The limitations of available typological approaches to values and norms were examined, and mention was made of the need for an appropriate classification of beliefs. The central problem of any *general* theory of morality, we observed, is that it has both to face the facts of cultural relativity adequately, and at the same time attempt to transcend them.

But relativism applied not only to the content of the elements of a moral code, but also to the kind of relations which held between them. The importance of analysis for avoiding limiting preconceptions on this matter was exemplified by the tacit adherence of many sociological accounts to a doctrine of approbationism, in which values are treated as the primary constituents of a moral code and prescriptions are conceived as derivative from them. The primary sense in which moral codes were systemic, we argued, was in the fact that they comprised characteristic modes of ethical reasoning and justification. Comment was made on the lack of attention which this central aspect of moral codes had received in the sociological literature, and extended discussion was given of one of the issues which it encompassed: that between intrinsic and extrinsic modes of justification.

Fuller account of these issues must await both the gathering of more refined ethnographic and sociological data and also further developments in analytic moral philosophy. Any adequate theoretical sociology of ethics will need to derive material from both these sources. More valid descriptions of moral codes will also, of course, constitute more challenging explicanda for the sociology of knowledge. Further attention to the more formal aspects of ethics, as expressed, for instance, in types of ethical justification, interrelationships between cognitive and evaluative assumptions, and underlying logics of classification, would also invite closer co-ordination with modern analyses of language and culture.

Certainly, the *sociological* understanding of moral codes will continue to be distinguished from the activities of moral philosophy by constituting a part of the sociology of culture, and hence by treating moral codes primarily as cultural products. In the next chapter, then, we are concerned with the concept of culture in a more general sense, without restricting ourselves exclusively to its moral ramifications. As such, this forms both a background chapter and a convenient introduction to the more distinctively sociological chapters to follow.

# 4  The concept of culture

## Consensus and pluralism

It is convenient to talk of sociologists as a single category of persons. Few things, however, appear to unite them. Except, perhaps, the presence of a common language, and the distinctive outlook that this entails, in spite of the wide variety of uses to which this language is in fact harnessed.

Central to this shared language is the notion of culture. Its pervasiveness, however, has yet to ensure consensus over its meaning. In 1952, two American anthropologists, Clyde Kluckhohn and Alfred Kroeber, assembled one hundred and sixty different definitions of the term in their book, *Culture, A Critical Review*, and themselves declined to offer a definitive solution. It is clear that we are dealing here with a general classificatory term, similar in status to the examples we discussed earlier (Chapter 1, pp. 21–2) and, like them, not open to the kind of rigorous definition to which certain other terms are amenable. Our concern, therefore, will be to indicate one, in our view central, interpretation of the concept, applicable to our present purposes, and to mention some of its implications.

Historically, the term comes to us from anthropology, where it has continued to have an almost all-embracing usage, synonymous with such common metaphors as 'ways of life' or 'patterns of thinking and behaving'. The classic definition was perhaps the one offered by E. B. Tylor, who saw it as 'that complex whole which includes knowledge, belief, art, morals, law, custom and other capabilities acquired by man as a member of society'.[1]

Having taken over the term, however, sociologists have tended to narrow down its usage. With few exceptions, the material aspects of culture—such artifacts as houses, tools, works of art, and personal possessions—have been excluded. Furthermore, the uniformities

included within the concept have been phrased at a more a[
level than one finds in anthropology; Parsons' pattern va[
which we discussed briefly in chapter 3, afford an extreme exa[
this tendency.

So much we might well expect, for sociology is a more self-
consciously analytic discipline than anthropology, although the
differences have grown less in recent years. The term still tends,
however, to be used uncritically: different authors vary widely in the
empirical scope and degree of abstractness they claim for it, and few
offer clear, substantive definitions of the concept.

But common elements may be diagnosed: at the least, 'culture'
connotes meanings which are not idiosyncratic to particular individuals, but both shared and communicable. In short, it refers to
social meanings. Given this, it is clearly misleading to contrast it with
structure, as though the two were related in the form of a dichotomy.
Structure refers to patterns of behaviour which reveal consistency
over time. But this behaviour is meaningful behaviour and the patterns
that it produces are meaningful configurations. (That is, for example,
that the criterion of identity between two or more actions is simply
that they mean the same thing, and not that they are identical as
physical movements in space.) Culture, then, is not in any true sense
an alternative to structure, but rather an abstraction from it.[2]

But this process of abstraction involves two principal dangers. The
first is that of reifying the concept, to treat it as a thing outside of
individuals. It may well, as Durkheim suggested, be experienced as
such in certain societies, that is, as an external, coercive force, but
this is a kind of false consciousness which the sociologist should be
best equipped to avoid.[3]

The second danger is the general one of moving from the existence
of a word to the existence of what it denotes: that is, in this case, to
ignore that the concept is an empirically problematic one—the
question of the sharedness of meanings is almost invariably a matter
of degree. The opposite position to this, the one which seeks to
impose a theoretical uniformity upon empirical diversity, and is
frequently associated, rightly or wrongly, with normative functionalism, has been aptly dubbed the 'cookie-cutter' approach by one
author.[4] This approach appears to be based upon an idea which,
though implicit, is none the less surprisingly common in sociological
literature. The argument is, in effect, that once you have located a
social group, most usually defined by economic, social, and ecological indices, then you have also discovered a common culture. It
needs to be recognized that this is always an empirical question, and
that the cultural requisites for *any* sort of interaction are of the most
minimal kind.[5] It might be mentioned on the other hand that in the
case of such ecologically scattered groups as the Jews, a common

culture may persist in the absence of the usual indices of group membership. But the question as to the conditions under which social groups do *not* develop a common culture remains to be asked.[6]

Given this, we would consider the study of consensus to be central to the sociology of culture. However, consensus may be either actual or perceived, and if we relate the two, four possibilities become evident, as shown in Figure 4.1.

FIGURE 4.1    *Types of consensus*

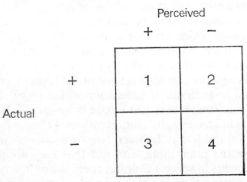

Thus, with respect to any particular group on any given issue, the members of the group may be in agreement and recognize themselves to be in agreement; or be in agreement but be unaware of this; or be individually in disagreement but think that agreement is general amongst the others; or, finally, be in disagreement and correctly recognize this.[7] We would normally speak of 'culture' only in cases (1) and (2). And the distinction between the two types is consequential. For instance, in order to take common action, consensus must not only factually exist, but also be perceived to exist.

Sociological theory has given due recognition to the importance of consensus for the integration of social systems. But it seems that in certain cases this importance can be overstated. By *defining* societies in terms of shared culture, such writers as Talcott Parsons appear to put to one side the problems and nature of the pluralistic society. Yet there may be societies which are both pluralistic and highly integrated, in which, as it were, the various groups have agreed to disagree, or in which other (political, economic) bases of integration are available, for which only minimal consensus is required. Switzerland, with its French, Italian, and German sub-cultures, and South Africa, with its official policy of ethnic pluralism, are, respectively, cases in point.[8] Other pluralistic societies may, of course, be characterized by dissensus and social cleavage; here Nigeria and Pakistan both provide recent and tragic examples. In such societies, the process of *polariza-*

*tion* may be described as both a heightening of consensus within groups and a growth of dissensus between them. Protestant-Catholic tensions in Northern Ireland, Turkish-Greek conflicts in Cyprus, and race relations in the United States illustrate this process.[9]

It is suggested then, firstly, that societies can be integrated on the basis of (as one author puts it) a 'pluralistic consensus', and secondly that the degree of pluralism within a society is useful both as a descriptive and explanatory variable.[10] Evidence for the last point would require some systematic collection and examination of cross-cultural data, in a study designed to reveal the characteristics and dynamics of plural societies. Unfortunately, no research of this type seems to have been conducted. However, an indication of the kind of direction it might take is shown in a recent article by Marie Haug.[11] In this, the author reanalyses the data in Banks and Textor's *A Cross Polity Survey* (1963), which presents relationships between 57 variables for the 115 independent polities in the world as of 1963. The variables involved were mainly political, but five of them are chosen for a preliminary index of pluralism among nations. This is constructed as shown in Table 4.1.

By summing the appropriate numerical values assigned to each polity, a scale with a theoretical range from 0 (non-plural) to 8 (highly plural) is possible. A polity with a score of 0 is homogeneous in language, race, and religion, has minimum sectional sentiment, and negligible or limited interest articulation by kinship, ethnic, or other non-associational groups. On the other hand, a score of 8 indicates a polity which is heterogeneous in language, race, and religion, with extreme sectional feelings and significant interest articulation by non-associational groups. In the study, of the 115 world polities (in 1963) only one, Mainland China, was omitted for lack of data. Contingency tables were prepared, comparing level of pluralism with a series of 16 demographic, communication, economic, and political variables.

In summary, when pluralism was taken as the dependent variable, significant linear correlations were found between degree of pluralism and geographic size ($+0.87$), population density ($-0.38$), urbanization ($-0.96$), literacy rates ($-0.95$), and newspaper circulation rates ($-0.86$). With pluralism level as the independent variable, the association with economic variables was as shown in Table 4.2.

Again taken as the independent variable, linear relationships were found with a series of political variables. Thus, the more extremely plural a nation, the more likely it was to have achieved independence after 1945; two-thirds were new nations since the Second World War. Of course, several ex-colonial nations have since been added to the 1963 figures, most of which we would expect to fall within the plural category. Further, extreme pluralism was found to be associated with a low level of political enculturation, defined by Banks

D*                                                                    93

TABLE 4.1   *An index of pluralism\**

| Variable | Coding category | Numerical value |
|---|---|---|
| Language | A Homogeneous (majority of 85% or more, no significant single majority) | 0 |
| | B Weakly heterogeneous (majority of 85% or more, significant minority of 15% or less) | 1 |
| | C Strongly heterogeneous (no single group of 85% or more) | 2 |
| Race | A Homogeneous (90% or more of one race) | 0 |
| | B Heterogeneous (less than 90% of one race) | 1 |
| Religion | A Homogeneous (80 to 85% predominance of one religion) | 0 |
| | B Heterogeneous (no religion 80 to 85% predominant) | 1 |
| Sectionalism | A Extreme (one or more groups with extreme sectional feeling) | 2 |
| | B Moderate (one group with strong sectional feeling or several with moderate sectional feeling) | 1 |
| | C Negligible (no significant sectional feeling) | 0 |
| Interest articulation by non-associational groups | A Significant | 2 |
| | B Moderate | 1 |
| | C Limited | 0 |
| | D Negligible | 0 |

\* This scheme gives greater weighting to language, sectionalism, and interest articulation by non-associational groups than to race and religion as indicators of pluralism. In part, this is a consequence of the insufficient differentiation of the race and religion variables, since categories of extreme heterogeneity are not specified. However, the fact that religious differences rather than incompatibilities have been coded, as well as the fact that racial variation may well be only indirectly related to pluralism, justifies the lesser weight.

and Textor as a relatively non-integrated polity with near majorities in active opposition, and in addition with negligible interest articulation by associational groups (e.g. unions, business organizations, ethnic or religious associations, or civil groupings). Also, nations with a significant horizontal power distribution were more likely to have a low pluralism level, while those with negligible horizontal power distribution were more likely to be extremely plural.[12]

In short, significant relationships seem to have been demonstrated between pluralism and a series of other structural variables, suggesting that the concept has explanatory as well as descriptive value. In many cases we would expect the true relationship between pluralism and these other variables to be circular. But the overall impression is one of a negative association between degree of pluralism and the level of development of a nation.[13]

This seemed a suggestive conclusion and in order to provide some supporting evidence for it, we rated each nation in terms of the five socio-economic 'stages of development' developed by Bruce Russett *et al.* in their *World Handbook of Political and Social Indicators* (1964).[14] These tables are based primarily on GNP *per capita* statistics, but a series of other social variables (on urbanization, literacy, education, etc.) which correlate with these is also presented, allowing

TABLE 4.2   *Association between pluralism and economic variables**

| Economic Variable | Pluralism level | | Chi square | | Proportion of chi square due to linear regression |
|---|---|---|---|---|---|
| | Negligible % (N base) | Extreme % (N base) | Total | Due to linear regression | |
| Propn of population in agriculture: | | | | | |
| High: over 66% | 3·8 (26) | 72·7 (33) | 35·10 | 29·06 | 0·83 |
| Low: 33% or below | 50·0 (26) | 9·1 (33) | (d.f. 6) | (d.f. 1) | |
| | | | p 0·001 | p 0·001 | |
| Per capita GNP: | | | | | |
| High: $600 and above | 50·0 (26) | 6·1 (33) | 42·08 | 34·81 | 0·83 |
| Low: under $150 | 3·8 (26) | 75·8 (33) | (d.f. 9) | (d.f. 1) | |
| | | | p 0·001 | p 0·001 | |

* This table reports only the 'four corners' of larger tables, ranging in size from $4 \times 4$ to $3 \times 4$, depending on the number of categories in the economic variable; $x^2$ values are for the complete table.

a division of nations by degree of development from a score of 1 (least developed) to 5 (highly developed). The results, together with the full list of nations by level of pluralism, are presented in Table 4.3. Some nations, such as Cuba, Senegal, and Sierra Leone, were not included in Russett's tables since economic data were not available for them. Other statistics, however, also included in the developmental tables, were available for them and provided a basis for assessing their score. Since these nations, apart from the ones excluded for political reasons, were by and large the poorest ones (hence the lack of data) we should not expect a great deal of error to be involved here.

The results lend support to our expectation and confirm Marie

TABLE 4.3   Distribution of 114 world polities by index of pluralism and degree of development

| Level of development (1–5) | Pluralism score 0 | 1 | 2 | 3 | 4 | 5 | 6 | 7 | 8 |
|---|---|---|---|---|---|---|---|---|---|
| | Denmark<br>Luxembourg<br>5 Norway<br>Sweden<br>Argentina<br>Austria<br>Chile<br>Costa Rica<br>4 Greece<br>Iceland<br>Ireland<br>Poland<br>Uruguay<br>Paraguay<br>3 Portugal<br>Tunisia<br>U.A.R. | 5 France<br>New Zealand<br>Finland<br>Germany E.<br>4 Hungary<br>Italy<br>Venezuela<br>3 Cuba<br>Dominican R. | Australia<br>5 Germany W.<br>Netherlands<br>Bulgaria<br>Japan<br>4 Mexico<br>Panama<br>Rumania<br>El Salvador<br>Honduras<br>Korea N.<br>Korea S.<br>3 Mongolia<br>Nicaragua<br>Saudi Arabia<br>Turkey<br>1 Burundi<br>Rwanda | 5 U.K.<br>U.S.<br>Colombia<br>Israel<br>4 Jamaica<br>Spain<br>3 Albania<br>Vietnam N.<br>2 Vietnam S.<br>1 Libya | Brazil<br>Lebanon<br>4 Trinidad<br>Algeria<br>Jordan<br>3 Syria<br>Cambodia<br>2 Haiti<br>Thailand<br>Cent. Afr. R.<br>1 Somalia<br>Yemen | 5 Belgium<br>Cyprus<br>4 Czech'kia<br>U.S.S.R.<br>Guatemala<br>Morocco<br>3 Philippines<br>Bolivia<br>Liberia<br>Malagasy<br>2 Senegal<br>Ivory Coast<br>Nepal<br>1 Tanganyika<br>Upper Volta | Canada<br>5 Switzerland<br>4 Yugoslavia<br>Ceylon<br>Ghana<br>Indonesia<br>3 Iran<br>Iraq<br>Peru<br>Congo (Bra.)<br>Gabon<br>2 India<br>Pakistan<br>Afghanistan<br>Burma<br>Cameroun<br>Dahomey<br>Guinea<br>1 Mali<br>Mauritania<br>Niger<br>Sierra Leone<br>Togo | Malaya<br>4 S. Africa<br>3 Ecuador<br>2 Congo (Leo.)<br>Nigeria<br>Chad<br>1 Ethiopia<br>Laos<br>Uganda | 1 Sudan |
| | N=17 | N=9 | N=18 | N=10 | N=12 | N=15 | N=23 | N=9 | N=1 |
| Mean development score (Overall mean = 3·0) | 4 | 4 | 3·4 | 3·4 | 2·5 | 2·5 | 2·2 | 2·1 | 1 |
| Standard deviation | 0·68 | 0·67 | 1·11 | 1·28 | 1·50 | 1·25 | 1·27 | 1·19 | 0 |

Haug's data. Thus a gradual decrease in average level of development is found with increasing pluralism. This suggests that pluralism is a relevant variable for characterizing nations. For example, for the purpose of research one might group together atypically homogeneous undeveloped societies—like Portugal and Tunisia—or heterogeneous developed societies—Canada, Switzerland, South Africa—to see their common characteristics and the extent to which they share common problems. It is suggested that, with a more refined index of pluralism, there is considerable scope for research on this subject.

Having drawn attention to the relevance of the notions of consensus and degree of pluralism for the sociology of culture, a few more general points may be made before concluding this section.

### The politics of culture

Firstly, it is clear that the study of culture, though central to the sociological perspective, is but part of the total picture: to comprehend fully any particular culture, whether of factory or nation-state, we must also be aware of the social distribution of power which lies behind it. Only this way will we understand the possibilities of change occurring. Yet it is just this part of the perspective which so many studies on the subject lack. Many would do well to take Marx's proposition, still largely untested, that the ruling ideas are the ideas of the ruling group, as their first, heuristic principle.[15]

There is a kind of unreality, a reification, about the approaches which deal with particular cultures *per se*, apart from their institutional and historical context. The fact that behind culture lies the social distribution of power and influence obliges one to consider what might be termed the politics of culture. Berger and Luckman make the point as follows:[16]

> Reality is socially defined. But the definitions are always *embodied*, that is, concrete individuals and groups of individuals serve as definers of reality. . . . To understand the state of the socially constructed universe at any given time, or its change over time, one must understand the social organization that permits the definers to do their defining. Put a little crudely, it is essential to keep pushing questions about the historically available conceptualizations of reality from the abstract 'What?' to the sociologically concrete 'Says who?'

The various mechanisms of the politics of culture—both conceptual and social (destruction, inclusion, segregation, etc.)—which they delineate may be seen to operate not only within society but also between societies. The colonial situation provides many examples of

97

this. And this is not only with regard to political and economic structures, as, in suitably polemical terms, the following passage indicates:[17]

> All other non-western people have been stripped of their own culture. They have been forced to accept a culture that does not belong to them. And so messed up are the minds of people of colour around the world, that in certain sections of Vietnam today, and in Japan certainly, women who have slanted eyes are cutting their eyes so that they can get round eyes to look like the West. Needless to say what black people have been doing to their hair, especially females: they have been putting hot combs in their hair, straightening it, attempting to look like white people, because the West has defined beauty as that which was theirs—the White woman, who was supposed to be taboo.

In the contemporary world, the most important examples of the operation of the politics of culture are obviously those which concern the relations of Russia and America with their respective allies.[18] Here, despite their 'wholly different concepts of the world, its freedom, its future', there is evidence that the two major power blocs are facing increasingly similar problems, with not radically dissimilar strategies.[19]

Thus the dominant culture of a society may be either that which is dominant in a purely political sense or that which enjoys consensual acceptance, or, most usually, some stage in between these. The conscious use of Christianity as a unifying force during the Spanish *Reconquista* may be cited as an example of the former, and the general position of Christianity in medieval Europe as an example of the latter. Thus, with respect to medieval Christianity, Berger and Luckman point out that Catholicism could hardly be considered the ideology of the Middle Ages—simply because everyone in medieval society participated in the Christian universe, serfs as much as their lords. They continue:[20]

> In the period following the Industrial Revolution, however, there is a certain justification in calling Christianity a bourgeois ideology, because the bourgeoisie used the Christian tradition and its personnel in its struggle against the new industrial working class, which in most European countries could no longer be regarded as 'inhabiting' the Christian universe. . . . The distinctiveness of ideology is rather that the *same* overall universe is interpreted in different ways, depending upon concrete vested interests within the society in question.

## Culture and 'theory'

Hence, the concept of culture is generally broader than that of ideology. But this is also true in other senses. Sociological theory has tended to interpret culture—like ideology—as a theoretical view of the world, and hence has examined it in terms of its system of values and beliefs, and, more peripherally, its distinctive aesthetic styles.[21] Writing of such theorists as Parsons, Edward Shils has observed:[22]

Sociologists and anthropologists might make it appear as if every man is implicitly a philosopher and a theologian with a coherent image of the cosmos and society and a hierarchy of standards of preference. This is, however, very far from the truth. Man is more concerned with what is near at hand, with what is present and concrete than with what is remote and abstract. He is more responsive on the whole to persons, to the status of those who surround him and the justice which he sees in his own situation than he is with the symbols of remote persons, with the total status system in the society and with the global system of justice . . . [Modern society is] held together by an infinity of personal attachments, moral obligations in concrete contexts, professional and creative pride, individual ambition, primordial affinities and a civil sense which is low in many, high in some, and moderate in most persons.

We would be in part agreement, and part disagreement with Shils's view. On the one hand, it is a valuable corrective to over-intellectualizing culture, and overstating the extent to which, for instance, general values can lead us to an understanding of particular social events. As Johan Galtung has remarked, '*most* human inter-action is not institutionalized and takes place on the basis of cues of a more evasive and ephemeral nature'.[23]

On the other hand, an awareness of the dangers of abstraction does not seem to rule out the possibility of a sociology of culture which takes as its starting point the actor's own frame of reference, shifting and inconsistent though it may be, and the standards and background understandings[24] which a community employs in its everyday affairs. In our view, then, there is a sense in which every man is, so to speak, both philosopher, sociologist, and moralist; and in which a society's institutions can be said to rest upon, and to put into practice, dis-tinctive social theories. Further, anthropology indicates that some societies, at all levels of material development, are more 'philosophical' than others in that they are concerned to develop belief systems which are both complete and consistent, and in that they value knowledge for its own sake. Again, the categories employed may be highly concrete ones, and not abstractions in our sense of the term; thus

99

Lévi-Strauss writes of the false antinomy between a logical and pre-logical mentality: 'The savage mind is logical in the same sense and the same fashion as ours, though as our own is when it is applied to knowledge of a universe in which it recognizes physical and semantic properties simultaneously.'[25]

A sociology of culture, therefore, should not preoccupy itself solely with intellectualized social theories, but with those everyday assumptions, categories, and frames of reference which might be reconstructed as partial social theories by the observer. Berger and Luckman put the point succinctly:[26]

> Theoretical thought, 'ideas', *Weltanschauungen* are not *that* important in society. Although every society contains these phenomena, they are only part of the sum of what passes for 'knowledge'. Only a very limited group of people in any society engages in theorizing, in the business of 'ideas', and the construction of *Weltanschauungen*. But everyone in society participates in its 'knowledge' in one way or another. Put differently, only a few are concerned with the theoretical interpretation of the world, but everybody lives in a world of some sort.

## Knowledge and justification

To exaggerate the importance of theoretical thought in society and history is, as they point out, a natural failing of theorizers. For this reason, we define culture not as socially shared ideas but as socially shared meanings. This draws attention to the fact that we are as much interested in common-sense 'knowledge' as in articulate world-views. Part of this knowledge is simple empirical information, as opposed to generalized beliefs. This is usually given little attention in the literature. Yet it is evident that any understanding of modern society must include reference to the exponential growth of knowledge within it, and the kind of informed society that this is producing.[27] This knowledge is socially distributed, and the nature of this distribution is relevant to the characterization and comparison of social systems. Figure 4.2 summarizes a basic aspect of this distribution.

This is the general relationship between social position and knowledge which social research has established. Of course, the slope of the graph may be more or less steep, depending on leading social characteristics of the society: the process of modernization, for instance, typically involves a progressive, though never complete, levelling out of this curve.[28] But the units being ranked here need not be individuals within a society. Societies themselves may be taken as the object of study. The few social inquiries which have examined this demonstrate that knowledge is also rank-distributed as between nations: the more developed, the more informed.[29] This, again, is rather self-evident. But it is also consequential. It has been observed, for example, that in the modern world the developed countries often know more about the developing countries than they know about themselves. The asymmetry which this expresses has been described as a form of 'scientific imperialism'.[30]

FIGURE 4.2 *The social distribution of knowledge*

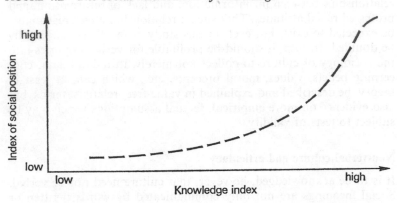

Other implications of the differential distribution of knowledge will be apparent; the point here is merely that this topic is highly relevant to a sociology of culture, and thereby to the sociology of ethics. That is, approaches to culture should not restrict themselves to sets of values and generalized beliefs, but take account also of available empirical knowledge. The special advantage to be gained from this inclusion is that such factual knowledge, unlike general beliefs, can be directly verified. The attribute of *validity* can therefore be employed to characterize expressed statements without falling into the usual dangers of attitude research: namely, ethnocentrism and concealed value-judgment. For these last reasons, the validity of people's attitudes has been treated perhaps overcautiously in research up to the present. The advantage of taking it into account, however, can be seen in various ways. In particular, it is clear that empirical knowledge, as well as general cognitive assumptions, enters into many processes of judgment and opinion-formation.

In their survey of racial attitudes in Britain, for example, Rose and his associates (1969) encountered many simple errors of misinformation.[31] Thus, almost a quarter of their sample believed that there were already 5 million coloured people in Britain; and nearly 50 per cent thought that there were 2 million. The actual figure was about 1,250,000. Secondly, a significant proportion of the respondents believed that the immigrant sector of the population benefited unduly from the social services, whereas the evidence is that they receive proportionately less (about −20 per cent) from these services than the 'natural' population, mainly because immigrants make little demand on pension benefits. Thirdly, it is noteworthy that many people interviewed greatly exaggerated the degree of racial intolerance present in the rest of the community.[32] Other misconceptions were revealed, but Rose *et al.* did not examine in any detail the interrelationships between misinformation, and lack of information, and professed racial attitudes. That such a relationship might reasonably be expected to exist, however, in this study as in others, can hardly be doubted. In sum, it should be profitable for verbal inquiries into the sociology of culture to collect not merely attitudinal data, concerning beliefs, values, moral precepts, etc., which can, at least in theory, be described and explained in value-free, relativist terms, but also evidence on more empirical, factual assumptions which may be subject to tests of validity.

### Non-verbal culture and articulacy

It is to be acknowledged, however, that culture need not be verbal. Social meanings are not only communicated by words, written or spoken, but also non-verbally, by gesture, facial expression, tone of voice, etc. As Galtung has pointed out, the methodology of sociology, with the survey method as its central technique, has biased us towards the examination of verbal cultures, and, one might add, towards those aspects of any particular culture that may be more readily verbalized.[33] Yet most behaviour is not verbalizable; much of culture is inarticulate. In Hall's phrase, it is a 'silent language'. Literature has long been concerned with the use of non-verbal cues as indicators of intention, character, and milieu. And in so far as sociology has attempted to reconstruct, in words, the meanings of non-verbal systems of communication, comparison with literature is appropriate, and especially with the genre of realistic social fiction, the main aim of which is to typify, often for didactic purposes, a distinctive sector of the existing social reality.[34]

It may be that the sociologist's emphasis on verbal culture reflects in part the characteristic social role, and milieu, of the academic, in which words are perhaps more salient than deeds as a standard of judgment between individuals. But if this is so, then it would seem particularly important to be sensitive to the biased observation and interpretation this may give rise to. Thus, it is evident that readiness to verbalize, and articulacy, will vary with type of content. The subjects which are given greater or lesser verbal attention will vary between different cultures. And we should take care not to assume that those subjects which are most readily articulated necessarily comprise those which are most salient to the community or individual in question. That sensitive subjects may be given little verbal attention has, of course, been given recognition in social science and, as in the Kinsey Reports (1948, 1953), various techniques have been proposed to resolve this problem. In a similar way, anthropologists have developed special methods of inquiring into subjects which are designated as taboo, whether in the context of discussion or observation. But secondly, and less well recognized, verbal methods encounter not only content restrictions, but also social limitations. A growing body of research literature exists on the differential ability of the various social groups within a society to use language as an effective instrument of communication. In Britain, this work has received much theoretical impetus from Bernstein's discussions of restricted and elaborated language codes, mainly in the context of the sociology of education.[35] A great deal of the research which this has led to has been concerned with demonstrating the divergent linguistic styles, and relative articulacy, associated with middle-class and working-class schoolchildren in Britain.[36] From the point of view of our concerns in this study, however, special mention should be made of the research of Robinson and Rackstraw (1967), which, again following some of Bernstein's ideas, showed characteristic differences of response by working-class and middle-class mothers when asked how they would answer certain questions from their children of an explanation-seeking or justification-requesting type.[37] Here middle-class mothers were more likely to answer the actual questions, and the information which they gave was more complete and accurate and less likely to be surrounded by confused or unrelated information. It is an implication of this study that any research into, for instance, accepted moral precepts, using verbal methods, would elicit far more complete and adequate justifications from middle-class than from working-class respondents. In short a sensitivity to such variations in the relative efficiencies of methods eliciting verbal responses is obviously necessary for their proper use, and for reliable interpretation of the results they yield. Where social or content limitations are encountered, verbal techniques may need to be supplemented by other methods, such as controlled observation or projective tests, or suitably modified, for example by using a relatively simple structured schedule rather than open-ended questions.

Midway, as it were, between the verbal and non-verbal aspects of culture are the metalinguistic attributes of spoken language: stress, pitch, intonation, and accent are all potentially meaningful cues in communication. But their meaning, and saliency, will vary both

103

between different language communities and also between different cultural traditions. In English, for example, one of the common ways of indicating that one is asking a question is by ending with a rising inflection. Such a procedure seems natural to us, not artifactual. The possibility does not normally occur to us that other inflections may serve the same purpose, or that, in other linguistic contexts, this particular type of inflection would have a quite different significance.[38]

Similarly, a notation system for the description of culturally-patterned posture and gesture (kinesics) has been proposed by Birdwhistell (1952, 1971).[39] Other aspects of non-verbal culture have been studied and attention has been given to a society's characteristic treatment of time and space. The anthropologist E. T. Hall (1959, 1969), for instance, has written popular introductions on each of these topics.[40] Hall's approach, however, is mainly informal and microsociological: little consideration is given to the principal alternative conceptions of time and space available in the major cultures of the world, as in the distinction between linear and cyclical conceptions discussed earlier. Yet, as we have observed, conceptions such as these are important to the understanding of a society's morality in comparative terms and, in view of their generality and taken-for-granted status, they are largely implicit. In order to articulate them it is often necessary to employ terms which may be part of a broader technical language, and which would be unfamiliar to the bearers of the culture in question. Such terms may serve either as secondary inductive constructs, summing up shared characteristics of concepts held by the respondents, or they may be derived from more theoretical sources. In either case, their characteristic function is to express in words certain inferred constituents of the 'implicit culture' under review. One way of achieving this is to search for general themes in the idioms of a language;[41] Hall (1959), for example, shares the view of other observers that Western industrial societies treat time as if it were a commodity: that is, we speak of it as something that can be 'bought, sold, saved, spent, wasted, lost, made up, and measured'.[42]

Proxemic behaviour (the structuring of space in interpersonal relations) also forms a non-linguistic aspect of culture. And just as the timing of interaction may indicate the importance of the occasion, so may spatial features have a communicative function. The positioning of guests at a table, for instance, can serve as a clear expression of relative status. Similarly, alterations of distance between people during a conversation may itself constitute a part of the process of communication, and, here again, the significance of particular spatial relations will vary as between different cultures.[43] Mention should also be made of recent research interests in the interpersonal psychology of non-verbal communication by such social psychologists as Michael Argyle (1967, 1969).[44]

## Culture as classification

The anthropological studies of non-verbal systems of communication so far, however, have concerned themselves with establishing the units of the 'code' under review, and to some extent with discovering categories of meaning, but have also tended to turn to rather anecdotal cross-cultural comparisons, often of an oversimplified kind, before attempting to work out the structure of any one system. Social psychologists too have focused upon relatively discrete and unrelated aspects of non-verbal communication. In sum, the studies so far have not offered adequate descriptions of non-verbal communication *systems*. As such, they contrast with the most recent anthropological approaches which have attempted to apply the notion of structural analysis not to the traditional field of social structure, but to the realm of cultural ideas. It is difficult to point to an unambiguous meaning of the structuralist method, as Runciman (1969) has observed in a recent review of the subject, and it has become used in description of a wide variety of types of social theory and research.[45] But, for present purposes, we may use the term to designate those ethnographic approaches to the analysis of culture which provide either relatively overt transcriptions of cultural principles of classification, or else rather abstract and latent models of such principles. The former of these, which has been especially influential in American anthropological fieldwork, has been termed, rather misleadingly, ethnoscientific analysis.[46] Useful overviews of its aims and methods have been provided by Conklin (1962), Frake (1962), and Sturtevant (1964).[47] Briefly, the method rests on two major premisses. The first concerns the importance of providing accounts of the outlook of the bearers of a particular culture in their own terms, without the introduction of extraneous descriptive categories. In the second place, it claims that processes of categorization, and the principles by which people classify their world, constitute an important, general characteristic of cultures, and that reliable evidence of the variability of such principles should provide a fruitful basis for theoretical developments.

These principles have long been suggested, but only recently have they been systematically put into practice in fieldwork. The idea of the importance of understanding the distinctive ways in which cultures classify the worlds which they inhabit may be traced back at least to Durkheim and Mauss's *Primitive Classification* (1963)[48] and is also to be found in the writing of later anthropologists. More recently, however, the approach received a new impetus from the application of linguistic analysis to anthropology, beginning with the pioneering studies of kinship terminologies in these terms by Goodenough (1951, 1956) and Lounsbury (1956).[49] Most subsequent work has focused both upon native terminologies and specifically upon kinship usages. Classificatory principles characteristic of a culture have thus been largely derived from an examination of the native language, and the main evidence for the existence of a category has been simply the fact that it is named. As Frake (1962) has written in justification of this:[50]

> The analysis of a culture's terminological systems will not, of course, exhaustively reveal the cognitive world of its members, but it will certainly tap a central portion of it. Culturally significant cognitive features must be communicable between persons in one of the standard symbolic systems of the culture. A major share of these features will undoubtedly be codable in a society's most flexible and productive communication device, its language.

Cultural classification systems have been investigated for various domains, including those of (ethno-) biology, botany, zoology, and also, less frequently, for such fields as colour terminology[51] and native aetiologies.[52] Future research will almost certainly extend the number of domains for which we have reliable ethnographic accounts, and also the range of cultures sampled. The most immediate benefits will be the production of more complete and systematic, and potentially more valid and replicable, sets of data on the intellectual framework, or frameworks, which particular cultures comprise. This will permit more adequate knowledge of different types of specifically cognitive systems. And by focusing upon the differentiating features, or principal axes, of a classificatory scheme, rather than on its categories or pigeon-holes, more basic and reliable evidence of the relativity of such systems will be provided. Studies of ethnobiology, for example, have provided ample demonstrations of the ways in which the species and genus categorizations of other cultures can diverge from those of Western science. A possible side-benefit from knowledge of this type, of course, is the greater self-awareness regarding our own criteria of discrimination in various fields that it may allow. Finally, this structural, or ethnoscientific, approach to culture promises to provide information which, although cognitive, is of obvious relevance to the cross-cultural analysis of moral codes, in the same way that our own scientific knowledge and assumptions are of considerable relevance to our own ethics.

But if this method has provided good evidence for the logicality, rigour, and consistency of (so-called) primitive thought, then its over-emphasis is also in some danger of reducing the cognitive, or intellectual aspects of culture to the processes of classification. In this way, modes of reasoning and justifications for particular cultural categories and precepts, which we argued above to be central to the analysis of moral codes, become understated and under-investigated.

To some degree, moral codes may themselves, of course, prove amenable to analysis as systems of classification. However, little evidence exists on this and so one must await the findings of future research. As it is, the classificatory approach would seem largely restricted to a synchronic perspective. In sum, it would be misleading if, through over-emphasis, the above approaches led to a conception of culture as nothing but a series of systems of classification.

Much of the above may, in our view, be also applied to the *anthropologie structurale* of Lévi-Strauss. Although this has enjoyed a greater *succès d'estime*, the approach seems essentially analogous to the ethnoscientific inquiries, except that it is set within the context of a more general, theoretical, even philosophical,[53] account of the nature of culture. Thus, Lévi-Strauss constantly stresses the rationality of primitive thought, and he seems to accept Rousseau's dictum that it is the possession of language which differentiates cultural man from the other animals.[54] Thus he too conceives of culture essentially as a system of communication; comprised of a series of interlocking 'languages', behavioural as well as spoken, all of which (he adds) are ultimately based on the same binary principles characteristic of all human thought. In practice, he analyses any particular culture, or at least its mythologies, in terms of various 'levels' of classification conceived as being formally analogous with each other. Thus he writes: 'On the theoretical as well as the practical plane, the existence of differentiating features is of much greater importance [for the analysis of culture] than their content. ... Once in evidence, they form a system which can be used as a grid is used to decipher a text.'[55]

In Lévi-Strauss's account, then, myths are to be understood in terms of a latent conceptual structure which comprises a series of binary opposites, by means of which 'Myths serve to provide an apparent resolution, or "mediation", of problems which by their very nature are incapable of any final solution',[56] these problems being contradictions present in a particular social structure, or possibly in the nature of society itself. The question is of course raised as to how Lévi-Strauss's interpretations are to be verified since, unlike many ethnoscientific approaches, they do not appeal to categories which are necessarily cognitively salient to the members of a culture and do not normally lead to testable predictions. Lévi-Strauss's main answer to this question seems to be to appeal to the simplicity and coherence of his reconstructions, but this still leaves open the question as to why only one interpretation should be considered valid.

A full discussion of Lévi-Strauss's mythography cannot be attempted here. Suffice it to say that his method of cultural analysis appears to have the consequence of leading attention away from the processes of argumentation and justification which are at least as important as systems of classification as subjects of inquiry for a

107

comparative sociology of moral codes. By way of conclusion, however, brief mention may be made of the importance Lévi-Strauss has ascribed to the 'opposition between nature and culture' and the theoretical attempts which societies have made to overcome this opposition and to conceive of the two domains as part of a unity. Totemism, it will be recalled, was, in his view, principally an attempt to achieve just this. And here at least many of Lévi-Strauss's points can provide insights for the analysis of moral codes, since the way in which the culture/nature dichotomy is conceived by a society will obviously have a fundamental significance for the structuring of its morality. We may conclude, then, with a few brief comments on this issue in relation to modern societies.

## Culture and nature

No one would doubt today that culture is ultimately a biosocial phenomenon. But the extent of its biological basis remains a complex and undecided question. The tendency of some modern sociological accounts, in reaction to a once-fashionable reductionism, has been to discount, or ignore, the biological factor almost completely. But this is to replace one one-sided determinism by another; the question of the interrelationships between the two still needs to be kept open to the evidence of research. Two aspects of such research may be indicated, both of them of relevance to moral concerns. Thus, in the first place, ethology is beginning to supply some useful clues—as in the recent debate on the spontaneous or learned character of human aggression. And the answers which research supplies to questions of this type, and to this question specifically, are highly relevant both to the particular content of moral codes, and to our evaluation of them. Thus, an influential contribution to this debate has been Konrad Lorenz's *On Aggression* (1966), in which the views are put forward that aggression is instinctive and spontaneous and hence virtually unmodifiable, and that intra-species aggression, as fighting between species, in fact possesses species-preserving functions. But these views are opposed by the more consensual doctrine in science which conceptualizes aggression, at least in man, as primarily a *response* to external factors, which may in large degree be learned.[57]

Each of these theories has some evidential backing, and their separate 'moral' implications are clear to see. Thus, if human aggression is primarily reactive in nature, the possibilities, and responsibilities, for appropriate 'social engineering' are immediately enhanced, particularly in regard to child-rearing practices. As one advocate of this point of view puts it: 'We are not yet in a position to specify conditions of rearing which minimize anti-social aggression. But at least we can help reduce rewards for aggressiveness, such as social approbation, and be aware of the influence which certain types of leader or of mass entertainment may exert. It is surely through the control of individual experience that man's aggressiveness can be tamed.'[58]

But on Lorenz's account, new methods of education, however enlightened, would be largely without effect, since man's aggressiveness is not in the main to be modified by experience. All that Lorenz can realistically advocate is the redirection or sublimation of aggressive drives in competitive games and, for instance, in sporting contests between nations. From the point of view of learning theory, on the other hand, such games might be conceived as enhancing and arousing aggression rather than dispelling it. And so on. In questions such as these, of course, intermediate positions could also be adopted. That is, the ascription of aggression on the one hand, to nature, and on the other, to culture, are not mutually exclusive choices, and most comparative biologists accept that even very basic and general behaviour patterns often contain a variable element that is more or less adapted to the particular situation, in addition to the fixed, inherited aspects.[59]

However, a comparative sociology of moral codes needs to take account of what, for any given society, are conceived of primarily as products of culture, or individual choice, and what are considered to be more or less immutable facets of nature. Such issues are important since, as we observed earlier, every morality must posit a more or less distinct anthropology, which, amongst other things, will determine the extent of the domain to which moral precepts are potentially applicable. Some of the conceptions proposed here will be, in effect, causal propositions, and some of these will, in turn, be amenable to further empirical evidence. One clear example of such a causal account concerns what Roger Brown (1967) describes as 'one of the best-established propositions' in the field of research into child-training practices. As he writes:[60]

> Parents who beat their children for aggression intend to 'stamp out' the aggression. The fact that the treatment does not work as intended suggests that the implicit learning theory is wrong. A beating may be regarded as an instance of the behaviour it is supposed to stamp out. If children are more disposed to learn by imitation or example than by 'stamping out' they ought to learn from a beating to beat. That seems to be roughly what happens.

Individuals, then, put implicitly causal, as well as moral, theories into practice in the upbringing of their young, and these two elements may be variously related. But where, as in the above case, the causal theory merely specifies the means to the end at stake then the

109

possibility exists of showing that the means is not only inefficient in relation to the avowed goals, but even counter-productive.

The question of the relation between theory and practice, and some of the research evidence available in this field, is discussed in the next and subsequent chapters. Here, we may note in conclusion that although difficulties exist in the extrapolation from ethology to sociology, the emergence of the discipline of ethology has at least led to the reopening of many of the issues concerning the interrelationships between nature and culture, and to a renewed awareness of man as a biosocial animal, whose behaviour is not to be understood almost exclusively within the terms of reference comprised by the notion of 'culture'. A second discipline which is also establishing the need for a complementary biological perspective, by pointing out the adverse consequences entailed by its neglect, is ecology. By examining the application of natural laws not only to man's immediate nature, but also to the relationships which hold between the massive behaviours of whole communities and their environments, ecology may contribute not only to the conservation of nature but also to the diffusion of a less one-sided conception of man and society, a change which could have many social as well as intellectual consequences.[61]

This last point deserves a little more elaboration. Thus, dissemination of an ecological perspective would no doubt have various consequences. But three of these may be singled out for special attention here. The first two of these have a particular relevance to the foregoing chapter.

The first is, quite simply, that the perspective of ecology is more inclusive than that of culture, since it embraces within it the complex and reciprocal interplay between man's culture and the realm of nature. As such, it can help put the findings of sociology, and of macrosociology in particular, in context. And this has the value—pragmatically as well as intellectually—of militating against an excessive 'sociologism' in our viewpoints upon society. That is, a full understanding of any given culture, of its causes and consequences, is essentially a subject for interdisciplinary inquiry. And to neglect this fact is likely to invite deleterious practical consequences. Or, as one author expresses it: 'Human society, with its complex environmental dependencies and manipulations, recognizes no arbitrary intellectual boundaries' (Watt *et al.*, 1970).[62]

The second point derives from this. Namely, that one lesson the ecological perspective can help underscore is our lack of knowledge regarding these culture-nature transactions. Our understanding of natural ecosystems and major ecological processes is severely limited, perhaps of necessity.[63] The causal chains involved are known to exhibit high levels of complexity and in ecosystems, as in social systems, causes and effects are often widely separated in both time

110

and space. This means that the full consequences of major social decisions, whether these be implicit or explicit, are commonly either unexpected or unknown, and that in order to even approximate such knowledge, new kinds of research methods will be required.[64]

This, in turn, leads to our final point, which is that the ecological perspective may accordingly have the practical consequence of suggesting that the popular equation, alluded to in Chapter 3, between economic growth and progress is in many cases somewhat facile.

In the present chapter we have tried to outline, albeit in a simplified, and perhaps occasionally truistic, fashion, the main ideas associated with the concept of culture. In the process we have digressed somewhat from our main theme. However, the sociology of ethics is in a rather obvious sense a sub-discipline of the sociology of culture and so influenced by the prevailing approaches taken towards culture, and its relative importance, in the social sciences. In the light of this, a brief introduction to some current approaches to the subject does not seem wholly out of place. Further, it may serve as an introduction to the next section, which is both more empirical and more sociological in focus, and is concerned with the available sociological research on moral codes.

# part two

# Review of research

# 5 Theory and practice

## Attitudes, thoughts and deeds

The fact that groups of individuals, and societies, unlike the objects of natural scientific study, provide interpretations of themselves, gives rise to an epistemological distinction unique to the social sciences. It is the distinction between, as we may term it, *social* theory and sociological theory: between people's interpretations of themselves and our interpretations of them. Since each is justified in different ways, and perhaps according to different types of argument, it is important that they be kept distinct.

It is evident that, at least ideally, sociological accounts are 'theories' in a much more rigorous and explicit sense than most social theories, and that the relevant criteria for their evaluation are shared with the natural sciences. Since, as we have seen, the content of social theories and the type of reasoning employed varies widely, both comparatively and historically, it seems best not to define social 'theories' too strictly: the sense in which they *are* theories (consistent, well-defined, etc.) is an empirical question depending upon the particular case under review. The recent evidence of anthropology— and in particular the structural anthropology associated with Lévi-Strauss—has been to the effect that, for preliterate societies at least, their institutions rest upon a framework of meanings which, given their basic premises, possess a considerably greater logical rigour than was at first supposed.[1] Primitive ethnoscience, for example, has been frequently demonstrated to consist of classificatory and explanatory systems which achieve a degree of internal consistency and completeness comparable to our own analogous endeavours.[2] Similarly, we 'make sense' of the various institutional sectors of our own society—education, medicine, government—by understanding the framework of ideas upon which they are predicated, ideas which, of course, are never wholly moral or factual, but always both. A clear example would be the institutionalization of certain political theories by modern democracies.

But the fact of social theory raises a further distinction; namely, that between theory and practice. That is, unlike the theories of the natural sciences, social theories are not just true or false, consistent or otherwise, they can also be put into practice. And it is here that the concern of sociology lies: not with social theory in the abstract, but, first and foremost, with social theory as *practised*.

To understand the nature of the theory we need philosophy, to understand the nature of the practice we need sociology, to understand the two we need both. To see social theory as socially practised, and social practice as practised social theory is, in our view, the essence of the sociological perspective. And since we understand social theories by a process of contrast and comparison, this perspective is also a comparative one.

Part of the sociologist's task, then, is to make explicit the social theories by which societies are ordered and individuals live. At least with regard to moral codes, the primary source of empirical information for the sociologist will be the expressed attitudes of his respondents. His second source will be the observed behaviour of his respondents. It will be evident that the two are not always congruent with each other. This raises the principal methodological issue entailed by a sociology of ethics, and we may offer some comments on it.

Firstly, with regard to the validity we should ascribe to expressed attitudes, we are concerned with the question of truth, not in the ordinary objective, scientific sense, but in respect of a person's relationship to what he says and does (in Greek, ἀλήθεια). We can never be sure of a person's relationship either to his expressed opinions or to his overt actions. Hence the possibility of being an actor, impostor, hypocrite; that is, of deceiving by actions or words. We gauge a person's veracity by a variety of subtle interpersonal cues: in part based on general expectations, and in part on our personal experience, both of ourselves and others. Also certain social contexts may be delineated in which truth-telling is to be expected: the confessional, and the situation of being under oath are examples in our own society. Other societies supply other instances.[3] In Bantu society truth-telling is largely restricted to relations within the family rather than outside it; the Navaho are prepared to divulge many of their secrets in the winter months but not in the summer.[4]

Research by social survey is obliged to postulate an identity between latent and manifest attitudes, as illustrated in Table 5.1.

Various techniques are available to effect this situation: by maximizing trust in the interview situation; by asking third-party questions about what the respondent thinks other people ought to do or to value, or what he thinks the consensus on these matters is; by asking logically interrelated but randomly ordered questions so that any inconsistencies soon become apparent; by having a number of questions that refer to verifiable facts, to past and present actions, or pure knowledge, so as to induce the interviewee into a pattern of speaking the truth, in the hope that this will be carried over to the value-questions; by carrying on interviews informally, over dinner, etc.

TABLE 5.1  *Relations between objects, values, and evaluations*[5]

|  | Stimulus | Intervening variable | Response |
|---|---|---|---|
| Manifest level (phenotype) | Psychological objects* | | Evaluations of objects |
| Latent level (genotype) | | Values held by the respondent | |

* The relevant 'psychological objects' may be of various kinds: questionnaire items, picture cards, an interviewer's questions, written stories, and so on.

In general the best principle to ensure veracity seems to be to remove any grounds for concealment. Assurances of anonymity and reasonably complete explanations of the aims and purposes of the research serve partly to achieve this. Even where this is not achieved, the results may still be of value. Thus Professor Galtung has argued:[6]

> In surveys, e.g. of how people react to certain policy measures, it may be socially much more important how people say they would react than how they 'really' (meaning when they are alone with themselves) do react. If the ordinary Frenchman polled says he is in favor of the *force de frappe*, then this is more important than his inner reservations. They may be important for a personal analysis, not for an analysis of attitudes here and now. The spoken word is a social act, the inner thought is not, and the sociologist has good reasons to be most interested and concerned with the former, the psychologist perhaps with the latter. . . . In short: the problem of expressions vs. thoughts depends very much on the analytical purpose of the interviewing.

Added to which, some questions propose novel issues, about which the subject does not have preconceived attitudes, and so to which the problem of correspondence in this sense is inappropriate. However, it is important to know which issues are novel ones in this sense, and so a certain amount of background information on the respondent's cognitive framework is always desirable. It is here that the pilot survey can be of value.

Distinct from the question of the validity of expressed attitudes in terms of whether or not they reflect the respondent's real thoughts, is the question, particularly important for a sociology of ethics, of the correspondence between words and deeds, between expressions and behaviour. Firstly, the way the two spheres are normally conceptualized, and the degree of consistency demanded, will depend on a cultural component, on the individual, and on the issue at stake. In our own society we tend to ascribe priority to actions; hence the phrase 'actions speak louder than words'. But we should not expect all cultures to be exact replicas of our own in this respect. It is our impression, for instance, that traditional Spanish culture demands, on several issues, less consistency between words and deeds than we do, though it is difficult to produce reliable data on this.[7]

Secondly, the relationship between attitudes and overt behaviour is not a simple one in logical terms, allowing direct inference from the one to the other. Thus, even conduct contrary to an avowed value or moral prescription is not conclusive evidence that the agent does not have a disposition to act in accordance with it—though it may be a fairly reliable indication of this. Thus, his action could be interpreted either as a conscious violation of the principle, or as being due to forgetting it, or as being due to mitigating external pressures, or as being due possibly to a conflict of principles.

Similarly, the fact that a person or society does not practise a certain value or rule does not necessarily indicate non-adherence to it, since the situation may not yet have arisen to which it was applicable. Thus a person may intend always to pay his debts, yet never incur any; on the other hand, a nation-state may make a pledge of neutrality in the event of any international war not directly involving its own territory, but still not have had its commitment put to the test by the emergence of a relevant situation. Similarly, socialist countries, whose adherence to Marxist principles is questioned, may claim that communism can only be introduced in their societies in the absence of a bloc of imperialist capitalist nations.

Galtung has pointed out that, in survey research, if the respondent describes his own behaviour in specific terms, and the reference is to the present, or very recent past or close future, we should have good reason to expect consistency between attitudes and actions. But, on the other hand, if he expresses values in general terms, applying to the distant past or remote future, there are so many very acceptable reasons for inconsistency that a process of validation on that basis would be out of place. He continues:[8]

Then, of course, it may be objected: what is the value of analyzing complex value-patterns if they do not serve as predictors of overt behaviour? We have three answers to this important question. (1) They may predict *verbal* behaviour, i.e. future value-assertions quite well, as shown by the relatively high degree of consistency over time in panel analyses (except when external events have changed the perceptual field of the respondent drastically). (2) They serve as signals from the depths of the person, giving us a synchronic cut in time both in the life of the person and the life of the system, valuable for the analysis of both (if not for the prediction) up till the date of the data-collection. And (3), even if the value-patterns do not predict behaviour or outcomes in a general sense, this only serves to indicate that a simplified model of consistency fails, and should lead to an analysis of *why*, not to mention the collection of behavioural data.

Finally, the relationship between expressed moral opinions and actual behaviour is itself open to empirical study. Here we find the degree of correlation depends in part on the value chosen: that is, some value choices are better predictors of behaviour than others. This is exemplified in Table 5.2, drawn from a survey of student attitudes at an American university.

TABLE 5.2    *Correlations between values and reported behaviours*[9]
(University Cross-Section: $n=218$)

| Value | |
| --- | --- |
| Intellectualism | 0·40* |
| Kindness | 0·12† |
| Social skills | 0·20* |
| Loyalty | 0·25* |
| Academic achievement | 0·17* |
| Physical development | 0·31* |
| Status | 0·21* |
| Honesty | 0·20* |
| Religiousness | 0·55* |
| Self-control | 0·16* |
| Creativity | 0·13† |
| Independence | 0·10 |

*$\propto$ <0·01.
†$\propto$ <0·05.

Much of sociological theory postulates a 'strain towards consistency', both with regard to the interrelationships of an individual's attitudes, and as between his attitudes and behaviour. A popular technique for studying this, particularly with respect to political attitudes, has been the panel analysis.[10] However, in terms of the relationship between expressions and actions, at least two distinct models are available. Thus, on the one hand, values inconsistent with present behaviour may none the less predict future behaviour, in so far as the individual is undergoing a learning process of which they are, respectively, the first and second stages. On the other hand, present behaviour may well serve to predict future attitudes, in so far as the latter are altered to rationalize, i.e. to provide reasons for, his actions. Given these alternatives, an exploration of the conditions under which the one or the other occurs is of sociological interest. Though, in the empirical situation, it will often be difficult to control for all the variables that could account for the change: that is, the person's knowledge or beliefs may have changed, or the conditions to practise his values may have altered, and so on.[11]

## Two studies of veracity

Even the changing relations between an individual's public and private attitudes do not seem wholly closed to empirical inquiry. This can to some extent be explored by employing different types of methods together. For example, one type of test requires subjects to complete partial statements such as 'My chief aim in life is . . .'. This is, of course, a direct statement which puts the individual on record as having a particular attitude, or value. In the study we will consider, statements of this type were regarded as *direct* rather than *projective*. A parallel statement, but on a projective basis, would be, 'If a Negro moved on to his street, Bill would . . .'. The latter statement did not so obviously implicate the person who completed it. His own involvement was even less evident when he filled out a series of similar statements in the belief that he was taking a speed test of verbal intelligence. The assumption here was that since the subject does not have to state what *he* would do, and since his attention is diverted from the true purpose of the test, he will seek the readiest possible completion and this will represent his personal attitude on the issue involved. The real purpose of the test was further disguised by mixing in several items on non-controversial topics, such as, 'When he has an opportunity to do so, John likes to . . .' or 'John often feels that he should . . .'.

A group comprising 48 freshmen and sophomores in a New England women's college filled out as quickly as possible a 'Verbal Intelligence Test' containing 59 projective items such as we have outlined. These dealt with attitudes towards their parents, religion, racial groups, and non-controversial and impersonal issues. The investiga-

120

tors felt that, for instance, although absence of prejudice towards Negroes is expected and expressed in such a community, there is a possibility that 'covert feelings to the contrary' might exist.

Some two weeks after doing the 'Verbal Intelligence Test' the same students were asked to fill in a Personal and Social Attitudes Record which they were led to assume would be filed along with their other records. The items on this questionnaire were comparable with those of the other test but each was framed directly. That is, in each case, the student said what *she* would do under the stated circumstances. There was no time limit.

One interesting result of this study is illustrated in Figure 5.1. The first histogram represents the frequency of completions on the ten projective Negro items. It can be seen that here there is a wide distribution of negative attitudes—two of the group gave no negative reactions, three gave one negative reaction, and so on. At the other extreme were three who reacted negatively to all ten items. We see, then, that the private attitudes of this group differed widely.

The outcome, however, was very different with respect to the attitudes which were to go on record and be identified with the person who expressed them. Instead of a wide distribution, suggesting a normal curve, there was a markedly skewed distribution, approximating a reversed J-curve. Most reactions were in a direction favourable to Negroes. Fifteen students, for instance, gave no negative reactions, nine only gave one negative reaction, and so on. No subjects expressed prejudice to the extent that they gave negative completions for all ten items. On non-controversial items the distribution was similar regardless of whether the projective or the direct form of the test was used.

FIGURE 5.1   *Comparison of projective and direct attitude scores*[12]
(N = 48)

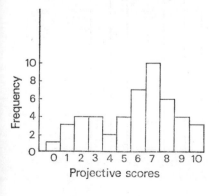
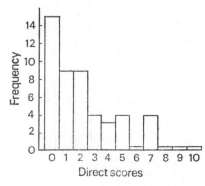

A skewed, J-curve distribution, like that obtained for the Negro items, is commonly found when individuals react openly to controversial issues. It represents the trend towards conformity and consensus which so many opinion surveys evidence. But, as we have seen, it may also conceal a certain degree of latent dissensus. However, as we shall see, the discrepancy between apparent and latent consensus, between 'real' attitudes and expressed attitudes, is itself in part a function of certain familiar sociological variables.

The investigators who conducted the above study, made also an extensive survey of children's attitudes.[13] More than 900 children ranging in age from 8 to 13 years were tested. The method was similar to that described except that the items were simpler and the instructions modified to adapt them to children. In the direct type of test, the children were asked to say how they would behave if certain things happened to them. Corresponding projective items were given as part of a test 'to see how fast you can make sentences'. In each projective item, however, the behaviour was attributed to Jane, Mary, or some other person named in the item. The items referred to such issues as cheating, religion, race, belief in God, honesty, and helping others.

In this study an index of differentiation (ID) was derived from the direct and projective responses. It represented the discrepancy between the personal attitude (as revealed by projective responses) and the overtly expressed attitude (as revealed by direct responses). It was predicted, on the basis of what is known about the socialization of children, that the ID would increase with age. This expectation proved correct, as Figure 5.2 indicates.

FIGURE 5.2  *Mean ID scores for children from 8 to 13 years of age* (N = 200)

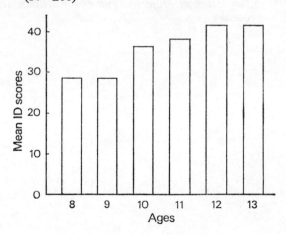

The increase in the ID score with age came about because the children's personal attitudes underwent greater suppression as they grew older. Their personal attitudes, as indicated by the projective reactions, did not change appreciably. Thus, the main projective scores, at successive yearly intervals representing age levels from 8 to 13, were 18·04, 17·33, 18·62, 18·73, 18·83, and 18·73—a difference between the lower and upper age levels of only 0·69 points. The direct scores, however, decreased between the 8th and 13th years as follows: 13·23, 12·40, 11·71, 11·12, 10·99, and 10·83.

It is significant also that the tendency to suppress overt expressions of personal attitudes was considerably more marked in girls than boys, in only children than in those with siblings, and in children from homes of high socio-economic status than in those from homes of low socio-economic status. These outcomes had been predicted on the basis of other information concerning the relative degree of socialization of these groups.

To sum up, we have argued that, by the careful use of two or more methods, the problem of latent v. manifest attitudes can itself be subjected to empirical scrutiny. And that, on the evidence of existing research, the degree of discrepancy between latent and manifest attitudes appears to be, at least in part, a function of such variables as age, sex, and socio-economic status. Parallel research could be conducted into the relationship between attitudes and behaviour over time, again by utilizing more than one research method. To a limited extent, research has already been carried out in this field.[14] One proviso, however, may be offered, and this is that, at least in our view, it is usually very important in research of this kind to elicit from the respondent the kind of actions which *he* considers to be relevant to the practice or otherwise of his value-choices.

### Behavioural dimensions: an illustration

This last point is perhaps best illustrated with an example. Very few of the studies on values, attitudes, and ideals include questions on the behavioural dimensions of these items. Exceptional in this respect, then, is the recent study of the ideals of Israeli youth by Hans and Shulamith Kreitler (1967).[15]

In this study, the authors included the variables of 'readiness to act for the realization of ideals' and 'knowledge about personal courses of action for the realization of ideals' in order to bridge the apparent gap, common to so many empirical surveys, between attitudes and actions. Their hypothesis was that the variable of *emotional relation to ideals* would prove to be correlated with the variable of *knowledge about personal courses of action for the realization of ideals*, but not with the further variable of *relative importance attributed to*

123

*the ideals*. The rationale of the hypothesis was first that degree of emotional relation to ideals is a function of action for their attainment and not of the importance evaluation set upon them, and secondly that acting demands knowledge about how to act.

Personal interviews were conducted according to a fixed questionnaire, and the sample of twelve Israeli and twelve general ideals was drawn from lists of ideals constructed by eighteen judges. The population sampled comprised 200 Israeli students: 100 in the age range of 17–25/6 years, and 100 in the age range of 25/6–32 years. The sample was selected so that it was ecologically, ethnically, and economically representative of the Israeli population.

We may summarize the results of this research in two tables. Of these, Table 5.3 presents the ideals in rank order, both in terms of the

TABLE 5.3   *Israeli and general ideals ranked according to*
      (a) *order of relative importance* and
      (b) *percentage of students who expressed their readiness to act in order to realize them*[16]
      $(N=200)$

| | (a) | | (b) | |
|---|---|---|---|---|
| Israeli ideals | Mean rank | SD | % of Ss | Rank |
| 1 Peace with the Arabs | 3·84 | 2·65 | 32 | 4 |
| 2 Guaranteeing Israel's security | 4·25 | 3·15 | 35·5 | 3 |
| 3 Achieving economic independence | 4·62 | 2·42 | 20·5 | 7 |
| 4 Guaranteeing democracy | 4·88 | 3·02 | 25·5 | 6 |
| 5 Educating underprivileged strata | 5·02 | 2·40 | 50 | 1 |
| 6 Integrating the various immigrant communities | 5·61 | 2·89 | 42·5 | 2 |
| 7 Assembling in Israel all Jewish communities | 5·67 | 3·32 | 16 | 8 |
| 8 Populating the Negev desert | 6·75 | 2·26 | 30 | 5 |
| 9 Raising standard of living in Israel | 8·38 | 2·94 | 6·5 | 10 |
| 10 Guaranteeing socialism | 8·69 | 2·86 | 7·5 | 9 |
| 11 Turning Israel into a spiritual centre | 9·62 | 2·45 | 4·5 | 11 |
| 12 Turning Israel into a biblically religious state | 11·63 | 1·57 | 2 | 12 |

| | (a) | | (b) | |
|---|---|---|---|---|
| General ideals | Mean rank | SD | % of Ss | Rank |
| 1 World peace | 2·05 | 1·58 | 32 | 2 |
| 2 Nuclear disarmament | 3·33 | 2·45 | 21 | 4 |
| 3 Guaranteeing human rights | 3·35 | 1·84 | 23 | 3 |
| 4 Promoting underdeveloped countries | 4·46 | 1·93 | 39 | 1 |
| 5 Raising standard of living in the world | 6·01 | 3·23 | 7·5 | 7 |
| 6 Coexistence between East and West | 6·18 | 3·14 | 7 | 8 |
| 7 Intercultural exchange | 6·82 | 1·92 | 20 | 5 |
| 8 Rule of the Western way of life in the world | 8·73 | 3·04 | 4 | 11 |
| 9 Conquest of space | 8·77 | 2·30 | 6 | 10 |
| 10 Making people more artistic | 8·96 | 2·44 | 8·5 | 6 |
| 11 Making people cleverer | 9·30 | 2·57 | 7 | 9 |
| 12 Rule of the communist way of life in the world | 11·28 | 1·90 | 2 | 12 |

relative importance attributed to them by the students, and also with regard to the number of students who expressed their readiness to act in order to realize them. The ideals are divided into those of specific relevance to the Israeli national context and those of general applicability. The second table, Table 5.4 gives the percentage distribution of replies to questions asking the respondents what action they could take in order to realize the ideals. The results are categorized according to the twelve Israeli and general ideals respectively, and according to nine possible courses of action.

For the purposes of interpretation, we may consider the two tables

TABLE 5.4 *Percentage distribution of answers by 200 students to the question 'What could you do in order to achieve actual realization of the ideal . . . ?'*
(*N* = 200)

| | Real personal action | Activating others | Joining an organization | Occasional action in daily milieu | Public propaganda | Actions of the 'good citizen' | Proposals to institutions | Proposal of no action | Helplessness and ignorance |
|---|---|---|---|---|---|---|---|---|---|
| *Israeli ideals* | | | | | | | | | |
| Underprivileged strata | 41·5 | 1·5 | 3 | 4·5 | 1 | 3 | 30·5 | 1·5 | 18·5 |
| Integrating communities | 16 | 6 | 3 | 27·5 | 6 | 0 | 20 | 2 | 18·5 |
| Israel's security | 10·5 | 1·5 | 2 | 2 | 0 | 35 | 30 | 8·5 | 10·5 |
| Peace with Arabs | 5·5 | 5 | 4 | 8 | 3·5 | 4 | 31 | 1·5 | 37·5 |
| Populating Negev | 40 | 1·5 | 2 | 1·5 | 2·5 | 2 | 21·5 | 9 | 20 |
| Democracy | 5 | 4·5 | 5·5 | 7·5 | 6 | 23 | 19·5 | 8 | 21 |
| Economic independence | 2·5 | 2 | 1·5 | 17·5 | 1 | 3 | 34·5 | 2 | 36 |
| Assembling communities | 14 | 4 | 1 | 8·5 | 7 | 7 | 19·5 | 8 | 31 |
| Socialism | 2 | 3 | 9 | 4·5 | 1·5 | 9 | 16 | 20 | 35 |
| Standard of living | 4·5 | 1 | 3 | 14 | 1·5 | 2 | 31 | 14·5 | 28·5 |
| Spiritual centre | 3·5 | 3·5 | 0·5 | 8 | 3 | 0·5 | 21·5 | 24 | 35·5 |
| Religious state | 0·5 | 0 | 1 | 1 | 1·5 | 0 | 2·5 | 38 | 55·5 |
| *General ideals* | | | | | | | | | |
| Underdeveloped countries | 35·5 | 0·5 | 2·5 | 3 | 0·5 | 1 | 34·5 | 1 | 21·5 |
| World peace | 2·5 | 2 | 7 | 4 | 7 | 7 | 25·5 | 1 | 45 |
| Human rights | 8 | 1·5 | 4·5 | 7·5 | 5·5 | 8·5 | 20 | 3·5 | 41 |
| Nuclear disarmament | 8·5 | 1 | 3 | 1·5 | 6 | 12·5 | 11 | 2·5 | 54 |
| Intercult. exchange | 7·5 | 3 | 1 | 23 | 4·5 | 1 | 23·5 | 3·5 | 33 |
| People more artistic | 3 | 7·5 | 2 | 7·5 | 4 | 0 | 22·5 | 9·5 | 39 |
| Standard of living | 7·5 | 1·5 | 1·5 | 3 | 1 | 0·5 | 28 | 3·5 | 53·5 |
| Coexistence | 1 | 2·5 | 2 | 4·5 | 7 | 1·5 | 11·5 | 6·5 | 63·5 |
| People cleverer | 4 | 4 | 1·5 | 8·5 | 2 | 0 | 13·5 | 14 | 52·5 |
| Space conquest | 4·5 | 0·5 | 1·5 | 1 | 2·5 | 2·5 | 10 | 13 | 64·5 |
| Western way of life | 0·5 | 1·5 | 3 | 11 | 4·5 | 5 | 8 | 23 | 43·5 |
| Communist way of life | 1 | 0 | 2·5 | 0·5 | 1 | 1·5 | 2 | 38 | 53·5 |

together. The most apparent finding that emerges from them is the ranking of the ideal of peace at the top of both the Israeli and general lists of ideals, and of the low ranking of such socio-political ideals as rule of the communist way of life, and also of the Western way of life, in the world, and of socialism and religiousness in the Israeli context. Notable also is the location of the item most directly associated with 'materialism', namely the ideal of raising the standard of living: for the Israeli context, this was ranked 9th, and for the world context it was ranked as 5th. In neither case was its evaluation outstandingly high. In both cases it was surpassed by such items as those involving educational ideals, guaranteeing human rights, and political security.

The majority of students (73 per cent) expressed also their readiness to act in order to realize their ideals; a further 18 per cent gave a qualified positive response, and only 9 per cent replied clearly in the negative. With reference to particular ideals, a total of 94 per cent of the students responded to the questions, mentioning each on average 4·9 ideals (the respective averages for the younger and older groups were 5·1 and 4·6), the range for the younger group being 1–12 and for the older 1–20. However, the response rate for Israeli ideals (2·9 per student) was higher than that for general ideals (1·9 per student).

There was some tendency for those ideals which were evaluated highly in terms of importance to be also rated highly on appeal for action. The correspondence, however, is an imperfect one: thus, although the Israeli ideals of 'Educating underprivileged strata' and 'Integrating the various immigrant communities' ranked 1st and 2nd on appeal for action, they were rated, respectively, 5th and 6th in terms of importance. In fact, the rank correlations between the ideals in the two lists (Table 5.3) are 0·75 for Israeli ideals and 0·82 for general ideals.

Particularly important to our purposes, however, is the finding that, when asked 'What could *you* do to realize the ideal . . .?', only 22 per cent of the responses could be interpreted as denoting courses of action available to the individual, whilst the largest percentage of replies (38 per cent) were in the category of 'helplessness'. The authors consider that answers in the three categories (in Table 5.4) prior to the latter one have similar practical implications and so conclude that '74 per cent of the answers can be interpreted as denoting the subjective feeling of the individual that he personally could not promote the realization of ideals'.[17] They note also that the distribution of answers in the categories shows no significant differences either in line with the age of the students or with the nature of the ideals, but for the expected greater 'helplessness' ($t=3·80$, $p=0·01$) in respect to general rather than Israeli ideals. Further, if we compare the rankings of evaluated importance (Table 5.3) with the first column of 'Personal action' in Table 5.4, we find

126

that for Israeli ideals the rank correlation is only 0·41, and for general ideals only 0·42. The relationship between perceived relative importance and readiness for personal action with respect to these ideals is thus one of approximate independence.

The authors interpret these responses in the light of the great centralization of power in the modern welfare state: the result of this, as they see it, has been both to give the individual a feeling of impotency with regard to what he personally is able to accomplish, and to transfer responsibility for society's welfare to the great institutions which the student often even fails to name, and on which he relies to the point of relinquishing any personal action. It is noteworthy, then, that 26 per cent of the students could not give even one answer in the categories denoting courses of action available to the individual.

In sum, the principal merit of Kreitler and Kreitler's research is that the authors included within their attitude schedule questions regarding the respondents' willingness to act on their expressed ideals, their knowledge of possible courses of action, and the degree to which they believed that they personally were able to effect the realization of their ideals. This provides a more detailed background of attitudinal data upon which predictions of behaviour may be based, and it also supplies a number of possible reasons to account for any discrepancies between attitudes and actions, between theory and practice, that might be observed to occur.

One such reason, as we saw, concerned the relatively widespread belief in the impotency of the individual as such to effect the realization of his ideals. This lack of an individual sense of efficacy within modern industrial society has been commented on by other researchers. In political science, for example, a number of studies have demonstrated the importance of a sense of personal efficacy for participation in routine politics.[18] Evidence has also been provided that feelings of political efficacy are considerably lower among those towards the bottom of the stratification system.[19]

But if a sense of personal ineffectiveness accounts for some of the discrepancy that may exist between attitudes and actions, then this is largely restricted to those cases involving the realization of some *ideal* or general value, such as the ideals of peace and human rights in the Israeli study. But, as we saw earlier, ideals are by definition difficult of attainment; hence they often refer to items which constitute relatively distant 'hopes' within an individual's value-system.

Specific moral prescriptions, in contrast, are both more immediately tied to action, and in consequence also more concrete. In view of their practical content, and allowing for their varying degrees of stringency, prescriptions tend to be more definite and precise than less exactly formulated evaluations and social ideals.[20] As such, we

127

would expect these to form more appropriate and effective predictors of behaviour. It should be fruitful, therefore, for a sociology of ethics concerned to investigate the relationship between moral theory and moral practice to concentrate initial attention upon prescriptive attitudes, which should serve as more valid indices of moral theory for this purpose.

## Résumé

At this stage in the argument it will be useful to reconsider some of the points made so far. Briefly, we have distinguished, and discussed in turn, two issues raised by social science research: firstly, that of the relationship between latent (or 'real') attitudes and verbally expressed attitudes; and secondly, that of the relationship between expressed attitudes and overt action or behaviour. These may be presented in simple graphic form, as in Table 5.5.

TABLE 5.5  *Relations between latent attitudes, expressed attitudes, and overt actions*

| Manifest level (phenotype) | | Expressed/verbal →attitudes ─────→ | Overt actions |
| Latent level (genotype) | Attitudes held by respondent | (a) ┐ | (b) |

(a) Problem of validity
(b) Problem of prediction

We have noted that the relationships (a) and (b) are problematic: that is, we should not expect, and the evidence does not support, a necessary and simple transition from latent to expressed attitudes, or from expressed attitudes to actions. Social research which assumes an identity in these two cases, then, is making an assumption that is unwarranted on both theoretical and empirical grounds. The usual format of modern attitude research, of course, is to take some explicit measures to both estimate and control for validity and reliability, but to avoid detailed consideration of either the veracity of the expressed attitudes or their reliability as predictors of behaviour. Most social research, then, restricts itself to the analysis of expressed attitudinal data: that is, it deals with verbal responses to entirely symbolic stimuli, whether in the form of an interviewer's question or, perhaps more commonly, a written item in a questionnaire.

For many purposes, however, such attitudinal data is insufficient; we also want to know how under certain conditions individuals typically behave. Certainly in the study of moral codes it is relevant to take account of the behavioural correlates of attitudes; as we noted earlier, all moral codes offer directives for action (prescriptions) as part of their content and demand not only, or even primarily, that these be given verbal acceptance, but also that they be practised. Secondly, there is the methodological point that it is generally considered to be an important criterion of the 'validity' of an elicited attitude that it effectively predicts a certain type of behaviour, this being taken as an index of the fact that the individual 'really' holds the attitude in question (i.e. of its validity in the sense used in our diagram). Finally, as we shall see, in some ethical systems, in contrast to our own assumptions, it appears to be far more important that an individual perform the correct ritual actions than that he adequately internalize the principles which supply the rationale for these actions.[21]

It is important, therefore, to conceptualize and explain the relationship between an individual's 'real' attitudes and his expressed attitudes and between his expressed attitudes and his overt actions, and this importance derives from both pragmatic and theoretical reasons. Our main point so far has been to indicate that both these questions are in some degree amenable to empirical investigation, and secondly to illustrate some of the intervening variables that may influence these two relationships of, respectively, validity and prediction. It will be evident that, although some reduction may be possible in certain cases, there are no theoretical or empirical grounds for reducing all these possible variables to a single type. Rather, both relations appear to be in part a function of psychological factors (e.g. individual veracity, sense of efficacy, etc.) and sociological factors (e.g. role-conflict, age, class, etc.), as well as factors related to the issue in question (e.g. generality, prescription/evaluation, etc.), to the situation and method used (familiar/unfamiliar conditions, structured/unstructured instrument, etc.), and finally to factors derived from general features of the culture and of the broader ethical system in question (e.g. norms of truth-telling, an emphasis on actions/intentions, etc.).

Some examples of these factors have been cited already, and some further ones will be given below. It will be evident that a similar range in types of intervening variables is applicable to both these questions, and not solely to that of the relation between attitudes and overt actions. For example, it is obviously important for an anthropologist gathering data on attitudes to be sensitive to a particular society's norms of truth-telling and the content or population restrictions which these may imply. It is clearly unwarranted to assume of other societies, as indeed of our own, that all sectors of the population, over all types of subject-matter, will express their attitudes, whether

129

elicited or not, with an equal readiness or veracity. For the purpose of efficient and valid research, then, it is important to be informed of whatever (patterned) deviations from this purely hypothetical norm may exist in a particular society.[22]

Similarly, it is important to be aware that we normally postulate a symmetry between the questions of validity and predictability in attitude research: that is, we assume that those expressed attitudes which most adequately represent an individual's true opinions or beliefs also constitute the most reliable predictors of their behaviour; and, on the other hand, the greater the ability of an elicited attitude to predict the respondent's behaviour, then the greater the confidence we can have in its status as a valid expression of their 'inner' convictions. In short, predictive value is taken as an index of validity, as validity is taken as an indicator of predictive value.

Yet, although commonly assumed, it is clear that this symmetry will not always hold true. The relation is not a necessary one since people can lie with actions as with words; that is, overt behaviour also may neglect, or even contradict, inner convictions. In particular, certain forms of role behaviour may determine both actions and public attitudes to which the individual conforms but has little or no personal commitment.[23]

What this example suggests, however, is the lesser importance of veracity, or of a congruence between latent and manifest attitudes, at least for sociological purposes. As we observed earlier, in the case of social surveys it may be more important to be concerned with expressed attitudes as social acts. Inner thoughts are not social acts, and, ultimately, they are closed to investigation, for how can one ever be certain that one has ascertained what an individual 'really' thinks or believes? This uncertainty derives from the fact that theoretical and philosophical considerations are involved. Thus, the way in which one answers this type of question will depend in large part on the psychological model one has adopted. Such a model will determine both the degree and the kind of validity to be ascribed to verbal behaviour. For example, an existentialist-oriented psychology would appear to give more *prima facie* validity to an individual's words than one deriving from, say, psychoanalysis. For, as one author puts it:[24]

> After Freud it became common to think of man as a being who existed on a number of different levels at once. . . . Freud also relied heavily on the communicative significance of man's acts rather than his words. He distrusted the spoken word, and a good deal of his thinking was based on the assumption that words hid much more than they revealed. He depended more on communication in the larger context; on the symbols of dreams

and the meaning of insignificant events which would ordinarily go unnoticed and were therefore not subject to the censors that we all have within us.

In this tradition of analysis, non-verbal cues and peripheral verbal acts become more salient as indicators of real thoughts and feelings. However, sociologists are not obliged to accept this model, and the issue of veracity in general seems more a question for the psychologist than for the sociologist as such. Both for sociology, and for most ethical traditions, the question of the relationship between attitudes and actions seems the more relevant of the two issues. And from now on we shall restrict ourselves to this question.

## Attitudes v. actions: research findings

Beside an ever-growing abundance of attitude surveys in social science, the paucity of studies on the behavioural correlates of these attitudes is particularly marked. Also, such evidence as does exist on the relationship between verbal attitudes and overt acts provides a limited basis for generalization. This is largely because of often considerable restrictions in the nature of the methods, samples, and issues chosen in this research. Virtually none of these studies provide comparative evidence, either across the dimensions of time, subject-matter, methods, or substantially different populations. Thus, most of these empirical inquiries have been carried out in the field of race prejudice and discrimination.

## LaPiere

One such study, well-known by virtue of its pioneering status, is reported in a paper by Richard LaPiere (1934) entitled 'Attitudes vs. Actions'.[25] In this, the author describes an extensive tour which he made of the Pacific Coast and transcontinental United States in the company of a Chinese couple. During this tour, they were accommodated by over 250 restaurants, hotels, and similar establishments, and refusal of service because of the 'racial' characteristics of the Chinese occurred only once. On the basis of the service they received, then, the author found no indication of intense prejudice towards the Chinese; often they were treated with more than ordinary consideration. As he sums up his experience:[26]

Factors entirely unassociated with race were, in the main, the determinant of significant variations in our reception. It would appear reasonable to conclude that the 'attitude' of the American people, as reflected in the behavior of those who are for

131

pecuniary reasons presumably most sensitive to the antipathies of their white clientele, is anything but negative towards the Chinese.

However, when LaPiere later sent each establishment a letter and questionnaire requesting a statement of its policy regarding accommodating Chinese clients, over 90 per cent of the replies noted that they adhered to a policy of non-acceptance of such minority group members. To control for the possible effects of experience of his two colleagues, responses were also secured from 32 hotels and 96 restaurants located in the same regions but which had not been visited. But the evidence from this served only to confirm the previous response. LaPiere concluded, therefore, that at least for this aspect of minority groups relations, virtually no relationship appeared to exist between a person's expressed attitude and the way in which he actually behaved. On the basis of his study, he advocated also the greater use of qualitative observation in social science, in place of the more common quantitative attitude measurements.

LaPiere's study, although interesting and perhaps the first of its kind, provides a limited basis for generalization since it derives from the experience of only one group of travellers. Yet few more broadly-based inquiries have followed up the questions that it raises. In part, this lack of attention is due to the methodological difficulties of constructing adequately standardized situations or instruments to record actions that would indicate, unambiguously, and preferably on a quantifiable scale, the acceptance or rejection of an attitude (precept, etc.). The fact that the field of race relations would appear to offer more opportunities for the development of this kind of measure than most other areas of sociological concern would at least explain in part the concentration of research attention on this subject.

## DeFleur and Westie

An ingenious example of such an attempt to construct a controlled measure of behaviour is provided by the study of DeFleur and Westie (1958).[27] In this, a group of students were given a structured interview to determine their attitudes to Negroes. From the distribution of total scores, 23 subjects were selected from the top quartile (indicating the greatest verbal rejection of Negroes) and matched with an equal number of subjects scoring in the lowest quartile (indicating the least verbal rejection of Negroes). The matching of these groups was based on eight relevant characteristics of their social background.[28]

The individuals in these two groups were then tested on their physiological ('autonomic') responses to race-relations stimuli in the form of photographic slides which portrayed Negroes and whites both singly and in pairs.[29] They were then questioned further about their feeling towards Negroes, and shortly before the end of this last interview session the subjects were told that a new set of the photographic slides used previously would be needed for further research. Each subject was asked, therefore, if they would be willing to be photographed with a Negro of the opposite sex. A 'photograph release agreement' was presented to them containing a graded series of uses to which the photograph would be put. These ranged from laboratory experiments, such as they had just experienced, where it would be seen only by professional sociologists, to a nationwide publicity campaign advocating racial integration. The subjects were asked to sign their name to any of the uses they would permit. The purpose was thus to give an action opportunity for subjects to provide overt testimony of their acceptance or rejection of Negroes.

The results showed this time that there was a correlation between attitudes and actions regarding Negroes. A significantly greater tendency to avoid being photographed with a Negro was shown for prejudiced than for unprejudiced respondents. However, the relationship did not constitute a simple one-to-one correspondence: one-third of the respondents behaved in a manner inconsistent with what might have been predicted from their verbally expressed attitudes. Whatever the direction of this inconsistency, however, further questioning indicated that it was a *peer-directed* decision for the majority, with the subjects making significant use of their beliefs concerning the possible approval or disapproval of reference groups as guides to behaviour. Thus, in most cases of inconsistency it was argued that the factor of social constraint intervened between the verbal attitudes and the overt acts corresponding to them. The authors therefore concluded that normative influences deriving from an individual's social context should be taken into account in attempts to predict behaviour on the basis of attitudinal data.

This conclusion has been arrived at by other studies (e.g. Lohman and Reitzes, 1954)[30] and clearly constitutes a sociological principle applicable to cases of inconsistency in a number of other areas of behaviour. Also, the authors rightly indicate the need to develop other overt 'action opportunities' for controlled inquiries into other examples of the relationship between attitudes and actions. But their own choice of an indicator of overt action has several limitations. In particular, it relates only indirectly, and rather peripherally, to the usual connotations of racial discrimination. Also, it would appear sensitive to the influence of other factors, such as an unwillingness or reticence to allow oneself to be photographed for such uses in general, irrespective of the racial element. The authors made no attempt to control for this. Finally, although signing a document connotes, as the authors observe, a sense of binding obligation in Western society,

133

it is still in a sense a symbolic act, and in this case also one carried out under atypical social conditions. In view of this, it would have been useful if the authors had provided information on the degree of subjects' commitment, or seriousness, towards the particular actions they had volunteered for by signing the form. One should also, of course, allow the possibility that at least some of the subjects, all of whom were drawn from introductory sociology classes, might have been able to diagnose correctly the true function of the 'photograph agreement'.

## Methodological considerations

We have discussed this study in some detail to illustrate some of the problems involved in the development of adequate methods for controlled inquiry into the behavioural correlates of expressed attitudes. To the familiar limitations of verbal methods are added the problems of constructing adequate indices of behaviour.[31] Many types of behaviour are not easily observed; in other cases, the visibility of a certain category of naturally-occurring behaviour is a function of social factors, as in the case of white-collar crime.[32] In so far as these acts can be observed under experimental conditions, the very atypicality of the circumstances often limits severely the extent to which the findings may be generalized. Indeed, as LaPiere has noted, it is only when we cannot easily observe what people do in certain types of situations that the questionnaire is resorted to. But it is also just here that the shortcomings of this technique arise.[33]

It is not to be unexpected, therefore, that most of the studies carried out in this field so far have serious methodological limitations. Good evidence for the effect that such limitations of method have on the results has been provided by Tittle and Hill (1967) in a useful review of the attitude/action literature in terms of selected characteristics of the techniques employed.[34] The authors maintain that adequate investigation of this problem-area requires that two main methodological criteria be met. Firstly, they draw attention to the fact that the general superiority of multi-item instruments over single-item ones and introspective orderings of data has been well established in attitude research. Hence they advocate that particular attitudes should be measured by this type of instrument, constructed according to a replicable set of procedures and resulting in at least the objective ordering of respondents. Secondly, it is suggested that an appropriate index of non-attitudinal behaviour requires consideration of action taking place under *typical* social circumstances, and that, preferably, such an index would designate sets of acts indicative of consistent or patterned behaviour. The justification for this is to the effect that if an attitude structure is taken to be derived from normal socialization

experiences, then it would seem reasonable to expect that the correspondence between attitude and other behaviour will be highest in
those situations which the individual has come to define as normal
and common. On the other hand, the individual is unlikely to have
a well-structured set of attitudes relevant to behaviour in situations
characterized by unfamiliar contingencies.

With these criteria as terms of reference, the authors examined
previous research work specifically designed to assess the relationship
between measured attitude and other behaviour. The studies chosen
were those most frequently cited in this connection and usually considered to constitute the crucial investigations of the problem. From
this, it was evident that the degree of discrepancy observed could be
considered a function in part of the methodological strategy adopted.
Table 5.6 summarizes the evidence from the fifteen studies carried out
between 1934 (LaPiere) and 1964.[35] As the table indicates, research
was classified by the measurement instrument adopted, the type of
behaviour criterion, and the kind of circumstances under which the
behaviour occurred. Several behaviours occurring over time, or the
same behaviour repetitively engaged in, were classed as patterned
behaviour. With regard to behavioural circumstances, the studies
were divided into two groups: namely, those that used an index of
behaviour representing 'normal action alternatives' and those that
employed atypical or unusual options. Where detailed information
was lacking, the authors used their own judgment—'following the
general prescription that laboratory situations represented unusual
behavior contexts or options'.[36] Finally, it was also noted whether the
relationship discovered between attitude and behaviour was high,
moderate, or low.

The table suggests the conclusion that a number of methodological
factors appear to influence the correlation between attitudes and
behaviour in these studies. Specifically, the degree of correspondence
observed is at least a function of (i) the measurement techniques
employed; (ii) the degree to which the index of behaviour comprises
action within the individual's common range of experience; and (iii)
the degree to which the criterion of behaviour represents a repetitive
configuration of behaviour.

Tittle and Hill (1967) also carried out an investigation of their own
into the relation between measured attitude and other behaviour,
using procedures designed to meet the methodological strictures
listed earlier. In this, five commonly-used types of attitude measure
were compared in terms of predictive efficiencies: viz. the Thurstone
successive-interval technique; the semantic differential; a summated-
rating (Likert) technique; and a Guttman scale. In addition a simple
self-rating attitude measure was examined.

The object of measurement was the respondent's attitude towards

TABLE 5.6 *Summary of studies of correspondence between measured attitudes and actions*

| Study | Attitude measure | Index of behaviour | Circumstances | Correspondence* |
|---|---|---|---|---|
| LaPiere† | Hypothetical single question | Single act | Atypical | Low |
| Kutner | Single question | Single act | Atypical | Low |
| LaPiere | Stereotypical single question | Patterned behaviour | Normal | Low |
| Bray | Summated rating scale | Single set of acts | Atypical | Low |
| Corey | Thurstone-Likert scale | Patterned behaviour | Normal | Low |
| Zunich | Summated rating scale | Single set of acts | Atypical | Low |
| DeFleur† | Summated differences scale | Single act | Atypical | Moderate |
| Linn | Intuitive scale | Single act | Atypical | Moderate |
| Pace | No indication | Patterned behaviour | Normal | Low to moderate |
| Rogers | Battery of single questions | Patterned behaviour | Normal | High |
| Murphy (1) | Thurstone scale | Patterned behaviour | Normal | High |
| Murphy (2) | No indication | Patterned behaviour | Normal | High |
| Murphy (3) | No indication | Patterned behaviour | Normal | High |
| Nettler | Thurstone scale | Patterned behaviour | Normal | High |
| Nettler | Thurstone scale | Patterned behaviour | Normal | High |
| Poppleton | Thurstone, scored 4 ways | Patterned behaviour | Normal | High |

* Where measures of association given:
  Low = <0·35
  Moderate = 0·35 to 0·59
  High = >0·59
† Previously discussed.

personal participation in student political activity. The five attitude measures designed to assess this were constructed according to standard procedures and incorporated in a questionnaire which, together with some items of background information, was administered to a sample of 301 students. A number of indices of behaviour were chosen. Firstly, the voting behaviour of each respondent was noted from student-voting records in an election held one week prior to the study. This objective measure was then supplemented by four indicators based on a series of reported activities.

Reported behaviour, of course, does not always adequately represent actual behaviour, and research has shown that the extent of error varies with the type of information being reported, and with personality differences.[37] But in the present study it was possible to compare reported behaviour and actual behaviour on the issue of voting at the last student election: here, 11 per cent of the cases revealed a discrepancy between report and record. The authors consider this instances a 'fairly close' approximation to actual behaviour, and they note that the validity of the self-reported data appears reinforced by the finding of a relatively high correlation between recorded vote and four other indices of reported behaviour which are related to this. At least, all the indices of behaviour referred to actions occurring under normal social conditions.

The results of relating the five measures of attitude to the five measures of other behaviour indicated only a moderate degree of correspondence between attitudes and actions. They also indicated that the degree of correspondence was, again, partially a function of the methodological conditions. Thus, the highest correlations were found where the criterion of behaviour encompassed a wide range of activity with respect to the attitude object in question. Wide variation was also shown in the relative predictive efficiencies of the various attitude scales. The Likert scale was the most highly associated with each of the five indices of behaviour; the Thurstone scale showed the poorest correspondence—indeed, in four out of five instances a simple self-rating of attitude provided better results than the elaborate Thurstone procedure. This is an interesting finding in view of the fact that a number of researchers have treated the Thurstone scale as a standard by which other attitude measures are to be compared.

The authors sum up the significance of their results as follows:[38]

It could be argued that these findings strengthen the indictment against attitude measures as predictive tools. It is clear that attitude measurement alone, as examined herein, is not totally adequate as a predictor of behavior. However, when it is possible to obtain an average association of ·543 using a Likert scale in its crude form, it seems entirely possible that

137

technical refinements and additional methodological considerations could increase predictive efficiency. Investigation of the performance of the various measuring instruments suggests certain refinements and considerations meriting further attention.

It is necessary, then, to delineate those attributes of the various attitude scales which appear most closely related to their relative predictive values. In fact, three such features emerge. Firstly, the difference in *reliability* coefficients appears to account in part for the different performances of the Thurstone and Likert scales. Secondly, those scales seemed to have greater predictive value which comprised items of greater *specificity*, in the sense of embodying self-referential statements (e.g. 'I think . . .'). Thirdly, the Likert technique also seemed to possess the advantage of providing for a factor of attitudinal *intensity*; that is, the summated-rating procedure allows not only a favourable-unfavourable response category but also a ranking factor influenced by how strongly the subject feels about the item in question.

In sum, the development of efficient means for handling such components as intensity, specificity, and reliability should permit the predictive value of existing attitude-scales to be enhanced. Of course, full confidence in the generalizability of their findings would require additional evidence from several similar studies. As the authors conclude:[39]

> The data presented here and the results of previous research with attitude measures strongly suggest that the error factors accounting for the differential predictability are to some extent intrinsic to the several measurement procedures. This conclusion, of course, cannot be advanced as compelling since any particular instance of the application of a given measuring technique or instrument represents only one of many possible applications. As such it is subject to various random errors. The crucial questions concerning these measurement procedures can only be answered convincingly when the results of numerous applications are available.

Tittle and Hill have usefully drawn our attention both to the possibility that observed discrepancies between attitudes and actions are artifacts of the methods used, and to the specific components of method which appear to affect the predictive efficiency of an attitude scale. As such, their study is one of the few in this field which has compared the effects and relative values of different methods. The only major limitation seems to be their utilization of somewhat inadequate indices of behaviour: four out of five of their indicators referred to *reported* behaviour and this, as we have noted, is a procedure sensitive to various kinds of error.

## Further considerations: the context of attitudes

However, the issue of method is not the only factor involved in determining the degree of congruency between attitude and action, and by concentrating exclusively upon it, these authors effectively neglect other relevant considerations of a less technical kind. For instance, they pay insufficient attention to the type of issue involved, for the measurement of which the attitudinal and behavioural instruments are designed. Yet it is clear that there are grounds, theoretical as well as empirical, to expect differences in the predictive value of expressed attitudes according to their content or subject-matter. We have already cited (in Table 5.2) examples of the differential predictive efficiencies of a number of familiar elicited values. And the pursuit of this question within the specific context of what we have designated as moral attitudes and behaviour should have considerable heuristic merit as a task for future research.

Clearly, a research programme of this kind would need to consider the demonstrable effects of certain methodological variables involved in the construction of indices of attitudes and actions. But methodological factors, however assiduously examined and corrected for, would not exhaust the type of problems deserving consideration. Instead, it would appear necessary also to take account of the broader intellectual context of particular moral views. That is, an adequate assessment would need to think in terms of the moral *code* of the subjects in question, whether these are taken to be individuals, groups, or whole societies. Most research to the present has focused upon the behavioural correlates of certain discrete attitudes held by individuals. But the connection between moral attitudes and actions cannot be properly examined without some reference to the structure of reasoning, and the modes of justification associated with the attitudes under consideration.

In particular, it is evident that in order to understand the extent to which a specific action constitutes a violation of an expressed precept, or to understand the importance of non-performance of the precept, it is necessary to know the degree of stringency that is attached to the precept in question. Hence, more information will be required regarding the status of the prescription within the broader moral code of which it forms part. Thus an evident difference in significance exists between, on the one hand, non-fulfilment of a precept (such as charity) which demands only occasional recognition, and, on the other, the non-fulfilment of one which demands constant and unconditional acceptance (e.g. honesty). Between these two types a number

139

of intermediate positions will exist, comprising actions which are 'commendable', 'preferable', and so on. As we observed earlier, the non-fulfilment of positive prescriptions is typically a less reprehensible and less readily identifiable matter than the violation of negative prescriptions, which are both characteristically more specific, and so more easily identified, and more absolute in stringency.[40] Distinctions of this kind are certainly to be found in the relatively formalized ethical and religious traditions, but would also seem applicable to less explicitly formulated moral codes too.

Research so far, then, has tended to neglect the importance of taking into consideration the processes of reasoning and justification associated with particular moral attitudes. The result has been an oversimplified model of the relationships to be expected between attitudes and actions. As we have seen, the correspondence that is required by particular moral views may be of different kinds. But recognition of this will also affect our selection of behavioural indices as well as indicators of attitude. In sum, these 'intellectual' aspects of moral codes must be taken into consideration in any examination of the relation between moral theory and moral practice which lays claim to comprehensiveness.

Moreover, such an examination is preferably to be conducted within a comparative perspective. In our Western traditions, for instance, much emphasis is placed on the moral significance of intentions, of internalizing the right motives for action. This derives both from Judaeo-Christian ethics and the traditions of Roman jurisprudence.[41] We ordinarily associate the concept of guilt with intentions rather than, say, consequences. But the relative emphasis we place on the internalization of moral principles, and thereby the adoption of prescribed attitudes, should not be generalized to all societies. Hinduism, for instance, might almost be said to offer a degree of choice in its ethics between an emphasis on attitudes (internalized beliefs, correct understanding, etc.) and on actions (i.e. various forms of service) in its tripartite doctrine of the alternative prescribed ways of devotion (*bhakti*), action (*karma*), and knowledge (*jnana*).[42] Islam, on the other hand, would seem to place more emphasis upon the performance of certain ritually prescribed behaviours, and less emphasis on the necessity of internalizing the system of values and beliefs which provides a rationale for these behaviours. This has been proposed as one factor contributing to the greater missionary success of Islam in a continent such as Africa, in comparison with the more intellectually demanding religion of Christianity.[43]

In sum, the fact that different ethical traditions ascribe varying degrees of relative importance to actions and attitudes needs to be taken into account as does the more general point that the way in which the attitude/action relationship is conceptualized will be in a number of respects culturally-specific. Comparative research in this subject, then, would need to examine these factors, and in doing so will probably serve the additional purpose of highlighting our own assumptions.

Having drawn attention to the need to consider the issue of moral theory v. moral practice within the broader framework of the sociology of moral codes, taking account of ethical reasoning, justification, degrees of stringency, etc., it will be apparent that many of the subjects discussed (in parts one and three) have a direct bearing on the theme of the present chapter. In the interests of space, however, a detailed reconsideration of the attitude/action dichotomy within these terms cannot be attempted here.

## *Steinitz*

Instead, we may draw attention to one piece of research which has some relevance in its findings to the foregoing argument. Victoria Steinitz (1969) has reported on a programme of carefully-executed research into the validity of those theories, associated with such writers as Heider (1946, 1958), Festinger (1957), and Abelson and Rosenberg (1958, 1960),[44] which postulate a tendency towards 'balance' in the structuring of an individual's attitudes.[45] Her inquiry examined individual differences in the content, structure, and degree of balance of attitudes towards United States foreign policy in a sample of 264 college students. The research was initiated in the conviction that 'cognitive imbalances were not necessarily random, unstable, and ill-conceived as the prevailing theory would have it, but that they sometimes represented a considered response to a complicated situation'.[46] By means of questionnaires, simulated debates, and a final interview, data were gathered on whether subjects liked/disliked 12 different countries and whether they would favour/ oppose a range of relationships (from, e.g. 'tourism' to 'political alliance') between these countries and the United States. Positions were defined as imbalanced where either (a) the country was liked and the relation opposed, or (b) the country was disliked and the relation favoured.

The results showed that a sizeable minority—28 per cent—of the combinations of responses represented imbalanced positions. And the frequent adoption of imbalanced positions appeared to be largely a function of the complexity of the individual's cognitive structure concerning international affairs, 'complexity' being broadly defined as the number of reasons given for a proposal. The author concludes that attitude theorists have placed undue emphasis on the universality of the need for congruency between attitudes; and that, since they

141

have relied upon studies of simplified, experimentally-induced beliefs and have rarely examined actual positions on complex social and political issues, they have under-estimated the capacity of individuals to take a number of different factors into account when arriving at positions.

Steinitz's research was concerned with relations and comparisons between attitudes, but in our view her conclusions could be transposed to the issue of congruency between attitudes and actions as well. Thus, the observed effect of the reasons offered in the case of attitudinal imbalance would also seem applicable, *mutatis mutandis*, to cases of imbalance between expressed attitudes and observed or reported actions. That is, it should be fruitful to consider whether instances of discrepancy between attitudes and actions, occurring under relatively natural conditions, do not themselves represent 'a considered response to a complicated situation', to elucidate which attention would have to be directed to the kind and complexity of the reasons proposed for the attitude and behaviour. Also Steinitz's research design is a suggestive one for these purposes, since it incorporates, alongside the familiar questionnaire and interview, a debating procedure designed to provide data on the justification of attitudes, and on the complexity of the arguments offered, under relatively 'natural' social conditions.[47]

## Attitudes and actions: conceptual relations

As a concluding point, attention needs to be drawn to one important respect in which the relationship between attitudes and actions has tended to be misconstrued as a purely empirical question, rather than one of a conceptual kind. That is, the nature of the relation between beliefs, or attitudes, and actions is not external and contingent, but rather internal and logical.[48] Because it is a condition of the intelligibility of an action that it actualizes some belief or set of beliefs we can never strictly talk of 'actions' as distinct from corresponding beliefs. We may, however, talk of beliefs which are distinct from actions—as, for instance, in the theoretical notion of 'uninstitutionalized culture'. Thus, from any action an attendant belief may be inferred, which renders it intelligible, and to describe an action is to explicate the beliefs and purposes upon which it was premissed.

The fact of this intimate connection with communicable ideas distinguishes actions epistemologically from mere physical movements. Thus the criterion of identity between two or more actions involves an appeal to their shared *meaning*, and not to their attributes as physical behaviour. Hence, the same action may be expressed by different physical movements, just as different actions may be expressed by the same set of physical movements. A handshake, for

142

instance, might symbolize greeting or welcome in one context, but departure in another, and perhaps formal agreement in yet a third.

However, the fact that an individual's actions, properly so called, are always indicative of some attitude or belief does not, of course, imply that they will express the attitudes, and especially the moral attitudes, to which he has committed himself verbally. The cases in which such coincidence does not occur have been the subject of the present chapter. But the very fact that we designate these as instances of inconsistency draws attention to the fact that the relation between belief and action is not contingent, but logical. As MacIntyre (1964) has commented:[49]

> When Humeans ask rhetorically how an action could possibly be logically related to a belief, since only one belief can be logically related to another, they are in a way right. It is because actions express beliefs, because actions are a vehicle for our beliefs that they can be described as consistent or inconsistent with beliefs expressed in avowals.

In cases of inconsistency, then, we have to make additional assumptions about the agent's intentions: most usually we presume that he did not *really* hold the views that he expressed; that is, that his manifest, recorded attitudes did not adequately reflect his latent or true attitudes about the subject in question. But this does not exhaust the issue. Thus, we have also observed in this chapter that instances of this kind can be expected to exhibit some form of ordered distribution across population and subject-matter, and that the nature of this distribution, which will vary from society to society, will both require and be amenable to analysis in sociological terms. In addition, we have pointed out that many observed discrepancies between attitudes and actions may be more apparent than real, or at least more complex than a simple model of them might suggest. At least three types of consideration were noted as relevant here. First, for example, a particular precept may require only occasional realization in behaviour, or its realization in a particular instance may be overridden by considerations of a more stringent or immediate kind: in either case it is clear that some attention must be given to the reasoning processes with which particular expressed attitudes or behaviours are associated. Also, for example, in cases where the ideals or precepts expressed are relatively unspecific in content, it will be important to know what actions the individual considers relevant to their realization, how effective these would be, and which of them are available to him personally.

Secondly, we have seen that the failure to implement previously avowed attitudes may be explicable in terms of the characteristics of particular social settings. Explanations here, for example, might refer to the competing demands embodied in the notion of role-conflict (e.g. Lohman and Reitzes, 1954) or to the social pressures deriving from the individual's reference groups (e.g. DeFleur and Westie, 1958). Thirdly, it has been noted that some instances of inconsistency may be considered to be artifacts of the methods adopted to identify the attitudes and corresponding behaviours in question. Thus a review of the research literature suggested that an appeal to factors of this kind might serve to explain some of the variation in the findings. To the extent that methodologies can be improved upon, then, apparent inconsistencies of this type should prove to be corrigible.

In more general terms, the conceptual link between communicable ideas and actions implies that in order to comprehend the characteristic forms of social action present in a particular society we must appeal to the concepts and forms of self-interpretation which are available in that society. That is, we must turn to the social theories present in the society—and thereby to its culture—which the actions of its members serve to express. Such 'theories', of course, will always be to some degree in a state of flux and mutual inconsistency, and will not exhibit completely determinate and clear-cut features of content and structure. But at least it can be seen from this that the conceptual analysis of a society's 'culture' forms an integral part of the sociologist's task.

The foregoing is not to be taken to imply that sociology should restrict itself to the analysis of social action or to the attitudes and purposes which inform such action. Nor do we believe that all social states of affairs will be reducible to such action-descriptions: those involving ecological and demographic variables, for example, will not normally be so.[50] But it would appear to be largely true to say that a society's self-descriptions of its characteristic actions will supply the initial *explicanda* for social science.

# 6 Review of research

## A content analysis

The pattern of references in social science literature on the various aspects of moral codes is both extensive and extremely diversified. It seemed useful, therefore, to try and obtain some overall descriptive account of the kind of material available. To achieve this systematically, though on a limited scale, we conducted a content analysis of the references falling under the rubric of 'Values' contained in the *Sociological Abstracts* journal from its inception in 1953 through to 1966. Values, of course, do not exhaust the content of a moral code. However, they form a principal part of it, and, as we noted earlier,[1] have tended to provide a focus of sociological attention in this field.[1] Such references were thus both more easily identified and also better represented than, for example, those under the headings of 'rules', 'prescriptions', or even 'morality' as such. Certainly, we have gained a much fuller sample of empirical studies by following this procedure. It is to be acknowledged also, however, that no consistently applied distinction between the processes of prescription and evaluation is to be found in the literature under review.[2] In consequence, empirical studies, or discussions, of what one might strictly term prescriptions are frequently subsumed under the protean concept of values.

The *Sociological Abstracts* journal was chosen because, as the only publication of its kind in sociology, it seemed to offer the most complete and representative selection of the sources of sociological information available to the social scientist, at least within the Western world. Thus, all the major sociological journals are fully abstracted, and an extensive range of other journals are partially abstracted.[3] In addition to this, a comprehensive selection of social science literature in book form is also summarized.

For the first part of our analysis, we examined all the references

145

on 'Values' over the fourteen-year period from 1953 to 1966, including within our survey all books or articles in which the content was primarily sociological.[4] Needless to say, most of the material reviewed fulfilled this last requirement, the only significant exception being a few references on values in a primarily economic sense, referring to such topics as land values over time, and so on.

Our analysis fell into two distinct parts. In the first part we sought to provide an overall description of all the references, between 1953 and 1966, according to their content and the trends in content revealed over time. In the second part, we chose references from regular intervals of time for more detailed examination, particular attention being paid here to the empirical studies. We will begin our discussion with the first part of the analysis.

At first, all the references were coded according to 23 categories of content. These, in turn, were subdivided into a total of 50 sub-categories, intended to represent the major distinguishable foci of interest in sociology. The coding scheme employed was a modified version of the one used in the *Sociological Abstracts* after the mid-1960s to present its own abstracts. This facilitated the analysis of later editions of the journal, but meant that considerable reclassification was necessary for the earlier volumes.

In a few cases, the classification was equivocal, mainly because some references comprised more than one category of content. For example, one study of the respective content of Soviet and American popular magazines could have been included under either of the categories of communications or mass culture. The only guideline in such cases was an assessment of the author's main intentions, which a rereading of the publication usually revealed.

## Patterns of Content

The complete distribution of references, by year and subject-matter, in terms of totals, percentages, and rank-orders over the 1953–66 period is presented in Table 6.1. To determine the trends in subject-matter over time we took the percentage of references in each of the 21 major subject-categories for the three four-year periods, 1955–8, 1959–62, and 1963–6. The results for this are given in Table 6.2. Taken together, these two tables may be said to summarize the first part of our analysis.

To a large degree we would trust that these tables are self-explanatory. However, some explanation of a number of the points they give rise to may be given. Table 6.1 indicates the very broad distribution, across the various sub-disciplines of sociology, of the concept of values. One can think of few other sociological concepts

146

TABLE 6.1 *References on values, 1953–66: totals, percentages, and rank orders by subject-matter* (Source: *Sociological Abstracts*)

| Rank | Content category | % | No. of cases | Rank | Quar-tiles |
|---|---|---|---|---|---|
| I | *Sociology: history and theory* | 16·7 | 107 | | |
| | a theories, ideas and systems | 11·5 | 74 | 1 | |
| | b history and present state of sociology | 3·6 | 23 | 7 | |
| | c of professional interest | 1·6 | 10 | 15·3 | |
| II | *Culture and social structure* | 10·3 | 66 | | I |
| | a social organization | 4·8 | 31 | 3 | |
| | b culture (evolution) | 3·4 | 22 | 8 | |
| | c social anthropology | 2·0 | 13 | 13·5 | |
| III | *The family and socialization* | 8·7 | 56 | | |
| | a sociology of the family | 3·9 | 25 | 6·3 | |
| | b adolescence and youth | 2·8 | 18 | 10 | |
| | c sociology of the child/socialization | 1·1 | 7 | 17·25 | |
| | d sociology of sexual behaviour | 0·9 | 6 | 18·25 | |
| IV | *Social differentiation* | 7·8 | 50 | | |
| | a social stratification | 3·9 | 25 | 6·3 | |
| | b sociology of occupations and professions | 3·9 | 25 | 6·3 | |
| V | *Methodology and research techniques* | 6·7 | 43 | | |
| | a methodology (general) | 5·1 | 33 | 2·5 | |
| | b research techniques | 1·2 | 8 | 16·3 | |
| | c statistical methods | 0·3 | 2 | 22·3 | |
| VI | *Social change and economic development* | 5·6 | 36 | | II |
| | a social change and economic development | 5·1 | 33 | 2·5 | |
| | b market structures and consumer behaviour | 0·5 | 3 | 21·3 | |
| VII | *Social psychology* | 5·6 | 36 | | |
| | a personality and culture | 4·4 | 28 | 5 | |
| | b interaction within (small) groups | 0·9 | 6 | 18·25 | |
| | c leadership | 0·3 | 2 | 22·3 | |

147

TABLE 6.1—*continued*

| Rank | Content category | % | No. of cases | Rank | Quar-tiles |
|------|------------------|-----|-------|------|--------|
| VIII | *Social problems and social welfare* | 5·1 | 33 | | |
| | *a* social disorganization (crime) | 2·2 | 14 | 12 | |
| | *b* applied sociology (social work) | 1·9 | 12 | 14·5 | |
| | *c* social gerontology | 0·6 | 4 | 20·2 | |
| | *d* delinquency | 0·5 | 3 | 21·3 | |
| IX | *Sociology of education* | 4·5 | 29 | | |
| | *a* sociology of education | 4·5 | 29 | 4 | |
| X | *Sociology of health and medicine* | 3·7 | 24 | | |
| | *a* social psychiatry (mental health) | 2·5 | 16 | 11 | |
| | *b* sociology of medicine (public health) | 1·2 | 8 | 16·3 | |
| XI | *Sociology of religion* | 3·6 | 23 | | |
| | *a* sociology of religion | 3·6 | 23 | 7·5 | |
| XII | *Political interactions* | 3·6 | 23 | | III |
| | *a* political sociology | 3·0 | 19 | 9 | |
| | *b* interactions between societies, nations and states | 0·6 | 4 | 20·2 | |
| XIII | *Mass phenomena* | 2·8 | 18 | | |
| | *a* communication | 0·8 | 5 | 19·5 | |
| | *b* mass culture | 0·8 | 5 | 19·5 | |
| | *c* public opinion | 0·6 | 4 | 20·2 | |
| | *d* collective behaviour | 0·3 | 2 | 22·3 | |
| | *e* social movements | 0·2 | 1 | 23·3 | |
| | *f* sociology of leisure | 0·2 | 1 | 23·3 | |
| XIV | *Complex organizations (management)* | 2·5 | 16 | | |
| | *a* industrial sociology (labour) | 1·1 | 7 | 17·25 | |
| | *b* bureaucratic structures | 0·9 | 6 | 18·25 | |
| | *c* military sociology | 0·5 | 3 | 21·3 | |
| XV | *Sociology of knowledge* | 2·0 | 13 | | |
| | *a* sociology of knowledge (and history of ideas) | 2·0 | 13 | 13·5 | |

TABLE 6.—1 *continued*

| Rank | Content Category | % | No. of cases | Rank | Quar-tiles |
|------|------------------|---|--------------|------|------------|
| XVI | *Community development* | 1·9 | 12 | | |
| | a sociology of communities and regions | 1·9 | 12 | 14·5 | |
| XVII | *Demography and human biology* | 1·7 | 11 | | |
| | a demography | 1·6 | 10 | 15·3 | |
| | b human biology | 0·2 | 1 | 23·3 | |
| XVIII | *Rural sociology* | 1·6 | 10 | | |
| | a rural sociology (village, agriculture) | 1·6 | 10 | 15·3 | |
| XIX | *Sociology of science* | 1·2 | 8 | | |
| | a sociology of science and technology | 1·2 | 8 | 16·3 | |
| XX | *Sociology of the arts* | 1·2 | 8 | | |
| | a sociology of language and literature | 0·6 | 4 | 20·2 | |
| | b sociology of art | 0·6 | 4 | 20·2 | |
| XXI | *Group interactions* | 1·1 | 7 | | |
| | a interactions between (large) groups (race relations, group relations, etc.) | 1·1 | 7 | 17·25 | |
| XXII | *Urban structures and ecology* | 1·1 | 7 | | |
| | a urban sociology and ecology | 1·1 | 7 | 17·25 | |
| XXIII | *Social control* | 0·9 | 6 | | IV |
| | a sociology of law (penology, correction problems) | 0·9 | 6 | 18·25 | |

| | | | |
|---|---|---|---|
| Total | 100 | 642 | |
| Major categories: | Mean = 27·9 | | |
| (N=23) | SD = 23·7 | | |
| Sub-categories: | Mean = 12·8 | | |
| (N=50) | SD = 12·8 | | |

TABLE 6.2   *References on values: trends in content over time*

| Content category | Time period | | | | | | | |
|---|---|---|---|---|---|---|---|---|
| | 1<br>1955–58 | | 2<br>1959–62 | | 3<br>1963–66 | | Total | |
| | N | % | N | % | N | % | N | % |
| 1 Methodology and research techniques | 6 | (15·4) | 16 | (6·5) | 20 | (6·0) | 42 | 6·8 |
| 2 Sociology: history and theory | 10 | (25·6) | 44 | (17·9) | 45 | (13·4) | 99 | 15·9 |
| 3 Social psychology | 1 | (2·6) | 14 | (5·7) | 20 | (6·0) | 35 | 5·6 |
| 4 Group interactions | — | — | 2 | (0·8) | 4 | (1·2) | 6 | 1·0 |
| 5 Culture and social structure | 3 | (7·7) | 32 | (13·0) | 30 | (8·9) | 65 | 10·5 |
| 6 Complex organizations | 1 | (2·6) | 8 | (3·3) | 7 | (2·1) | 16 | 2·6 |
| 7 Social change and economic development | 1 | (2·6) | 9 | (3·7) | 26 | (7·7) | 36 | 5·8 |
| 8 Mass phenomena | 2 | (5·1) | 8 | (3·3) | 8 | (2·4) | 18 | 2·9 |
| 9 Political interactions | 1 | (2·6) | 10 | (4·1) | 12 | (3·6) | 23 | 3·7 |
| 10 Social differentiation | 3 | (7·7) | 22 | (8·9) | 25 | (7·4) | 50 | 8·1 |
| 11 Rural sociology | — | — | 5 | (2·0) | 5 | (1·5) | 10 | 1·6 |
| 12 Urban structures and ecology | — | — | 3 | (1·2) | 4 | (1·2) | 7 | 1·1 |
| 13 Sociology of the arts | 2 | (5·1) | 2 | (0·8) | 4 | (1·2) | 8 | 1·3 |
| 14 Sociology of education | 1 | (2·6) | 12 | (4·9) | 16 | (4·8) | 29 | 4·7 |
| 15 Sociology of religion | 1 | (2·6) | 13 | (5·3) | 9 | (2·7) | 23 | 3·7 |
| 16 Social control | — | — | 6 | (2·4) | — | — | 6 | 1·0 |
| 17 Sociology of science | 1 | (2·6) | — | — | 4 | (1·2) | 5 | 0·8 |
| 18 Demography and human biology | — | — | 7 | (2·9) | 4 | (1·2) | 11 | 1·8 |
| 19 The family and socialization | 1 | (2·6) | 13 | (5·3) | 40 | (11·9) | 54 | 8·7 |
| 20 Sociology of health and medicine | — | — | 9 | (3·7) | 14 | (4·2) | 23 | 3·7 |
| 21 Social problems and social welfare | 3 | (7·7) | 5 | (2·0) | 23 | (6·9) | 31 | 5·0 |
| 22 Sociology of knowledge | — | — | 3 | (1·2) | 10 | (3·0) | 13 | 2·1 |
| 23 Community development | 2 | (5·1) | 3 | (1·2) | 6 | (1·8) | 11 | 1·8 |
| Total | 39 | (100) | 246 | (100) | 336 | (100) | 621 | (100) |

Chi-square, with 34 degrees of freedom,* equals 49·72, which is significant at the 0·05 level.

* 5 rows were omitted to avoid bias owing to low cell values.

with so wide a scope of application, both conceptual and empirical. The distribution, none the less, is distinctly patterned.

In terms of our major categories, the most represented fields of inquiry were, in order, those of 'sociology: history and theory';

'culture and social structure'; 'the family and socialization'; and 'social differentiation'. The first two of these categories accounted together for over one quarter (27 per cent) of the total number of references on values. As these are the most general categories, summing up the field of sociology as a whole, we may take this to indicate the centrality of the concept of values to the overall perspective of sociology. It indicates also that the foremost attention to values in sociology has been a conceptual and theoretical one. As we observed earlier, American sociology in particular, though not exclusively, has tended to stress the theoretical importance of social values both for the integration of social systems and for our understanding of them.[5] And it is this which is mainly represented here.

In contrast, 'the family and socialization' and 'social differentiation' the categories which rank respectively third and fourth, represent the first substantive fields of inquiry. The larger part of these studies were empirical rather than conceptual. Together they accounted for approximately one-sixth (16·5 per cent) of the total sample. 'Social differentiation', which includes the familiar concepts of class, status, and power, as well as the sociology of occupations, encompasses a field of research that has traditionally been an important one in sociology, as also in the societies from which this discipline emerged. Hence perhaps its relative constancy over time (Table 6.2).

The 'family and socialization' studies, on the other hand, are perhaps relatively more significant than one might have predicted. This is also the category which has increased most rapidly in importance over time, showing a proportionate increase of 9·34 per cent between the 1955–8 and 1963–6 time periods (Table 6.2). It is also a category that involves a high, and increasing, proportion of empirical studies. And the overriding majority of these have been conducted on school and college age-groups.[6] This suggests it has a high ranking because of an increasing devotion of sociological attention to youth. Thus the next subject-category which involved a majority of studies conducted on this age-range was that of the 'sociology of education', and this ranked fourth as a sub-category (Table 6.1) and also showed a percentage increase (of 2·2 per cent) over the two previously mentioned time-periods. Details of the empirical studies in this field are to be given later. For the moment we may indicate some possible reasons for this trend.

Firstly, it is a frequently cited characteristic of modern society that it is 'youth-centred' in terms of its publicly-expressed concerns, and our evidence suggests that sociological research is reflecting these concerns. Secondly, however, it seems that the particular factors which make youth a problem-area for the society at large serve also as rationales for studies of values in this area. Any discussion of these factors must, of course, take into account the rapidity of social

151

and technical change in modern societies. One aspect of this, in our view, is the fact that one, largely unintended, consequence of the rapid social and technological development that is taking place is that it is producing a 'new generation', with its own distinctive outlook and shared experiences, within increasingly shorter periods of time.[7] Their socialization is discontinuous partly in the sense that the moral language, and moral codes which are passed down to them are experienced as increasingly irrelevant or inadequate to the situations in which they find themselves.[8] Consider, for example, the Protestant Ethic of work in this light.[9] In such a context, it is understandable that the problems of youth, its education, its relation to the established society should rank highly in our sample. For it is not only the case that youth *par excellence* is the area in which value-conflict, and the necessity of generating new values, occurs, it is also a matter of importance to determine the pattern of choices which is emerging here, both in a simple prospective sense, and also as a means of apprehending the nature and consequences of such socio-technical change.[10]

A final reason, applicable to the empirical studies in this field, concerns the methodological advantages of selecting a sample within this age-group. Thus, the sector of youth most extensively researched is firstly that of undergraduate students at university, and secondly that of schoolchildren. The details of this will be discussed later.[11] For the present, one need hardly enumerate the advantages of such 'captive audiences', though in the case of university students they include not only the factor of articulateness, particularly significant in view of the emphasis on verbal methods of inquiry, but also that of a population already attuned to the values of scientific inquiry, and hence, among other things, unlikely to provide significant refusal rates, at least in those cases where the possibility of non-participation may be genuinely said to exist.[12] And the more sophisticated the methodology, the more salient such factors seem to become.[13]

We have discussed youth studies briefly as part of our consideration of those subject-categories which respectively ranked third and fourth in our sample: namely, those of 'the family and socialization' and 'social differentiation'. The next two categories in rank order are those of 'methodology and research techniques' and 'social change and economic development'. These four taken together account for the second quartile (28·8 per cent) of the total distribution (Table 6.1). The substantial number of references under the category of 'methodology' is accounted for largely by the continuing debate on the issue of value-freedom in sociology, upon which opinion is still divided. The majority of authors adopt a Weberian stance in favour of both the possibility, and desirability, of value-neutrality in social science, although an appreciable number continue to detract from it.

152

A somewhat predictable pattern emerges in which the more empirical the orientation of the author, and, in the case of articles, the journal, the more likely the value-free thesis will be defended. And the more philosophical the author's orientation and background the more likely it will be called into question, or subjected to qualification. What there is a lack of, however, are empirical studies of the social origins of choices of problem-area, type of inquiry, and utilization of results, and even of the general methodology adopted, in both the social and the natural sciences.[14] The latter would probably be classified as the sociology of science. It is perhaps noteworthy, therefore, that this was one of the least-represented areas in our sample, accounting for only 1·2 per cent of the total number of references.

'Social change and economic development' forms the next major category of content, and its sub-category of the same title ranks second, alongside 'methodology', in terms of number of references. This major category shows also the second highest percentage increase (+5·2 per cent) over the three four-year time periods given in Table 6.2. Confirmation of the perceived importance of this field of inquiry may be drawn from various sources. For example, in a recent study by a Yugoslav social scientist 30 sociologists drawn from seven universities in America were interviewed (during 1963 and 1964) about their discipline. One of the questions asked, 'Which problems are among the most important in contemporary sociology?' The answers, in order, were social change and economic development; the application of theoretical categories to empirical research; social integration; and the further elaboration of general sociological theory.[15]

This is also the field with the highest proportion of comparative— in the sense of cross-national and cross-cultural—approaches, and with a particular emphasis on the 'developing' countries.[16] Emphasis on this field reflects, at the most obvious level, the global significance of the process of industrialization, and of the fundamental change in values, and moral reasoning, which this both effects and presupposes.[17] However, it reflects also, we would argue, the concomitant tendency to make economic growth the primary national value, and particularly the value which informs the interests of those institutions, governmental and otherwise, which provide a major part of the sponsorship of social science research.[18] Such interests may also be said to be related to the increasing focus of attention upon the developing countries. For this arises, we would suggest, at least as much from strategic reasons, as from the more altruistic ones which derive from an ideology of egalitarianism. Put simply, it appears that the developed countries and, within the Western world, especially the United States, are increasingly aware of both their *inter*dependency with the developing countries, and also of the growing relative gap between them.[19] The latter is a potentially important source of tension because of the well-established fact that although the relative difference between developed and less developed nations is increasing in terms of GNP, it is narrowing in terms of more qualitative factors (literacy, education, health, participation in the mass media, etc.); and whilst the latter provide a social basis for rising expectations, the former denies them of realization. Several observers have argued, therefore, that the North-South division, between rich and poor countries, is becoming more salient than the ideologically defined East-West one.[20]

We have discussed above those categories which were particularly well represented in our sample. The categories we have cited account for about one half of the total distribution of references. To complete the picture, mention should be made also of the 'social psychology' category which ranks equally with that of 'social change and economic development'. Again, a substantial proportion of the studies in this field were empirical in character, and frequently they were conducted under broadly 'experimental' conditions. (Although, since these studies have tended to use 'experimental' formats merely as a *context* for the deployment of survey methods as the main instruments of data-collection they have been coded as such in the present study (see below).) However, discussion of some representative examples of these will be given in the next chapter. For the present, we may consider briefly a number of categories which were rather markedly under-represented.

One must be cautious about generalizing from the lacunae which are apparent in our results in view of the limited nature of our sample. However, in many cases our evidence is compatible with that from other sources, and so it may be afforded greater credence. It is to be acknowledged that in one instance, that of 'demography and human biology', the neglect is explicable in semantic terms: values are, perhaps *par excellence*, products of culture rather than nature.[21] Less explicable is the lack of attention given to the sociology of law, the sociology of the arts, and the previously-mentioned sociology of science.[22] It is less easy to explain these deficiencies, except in terms of the traditional types of inquiry which an academic discipline develops over time, and possibly also in terms of the structural determinants of these lines of inquiry.[23] In view of the subject of the present study, the neglect of the sociology of law in these terms is to be particularly noted, although it has been remarked upon by other authors,[24] as has also the lack of attention afforded in sociological theory and research to artistic and aesthetic traditions as component parts of the sociology of culture.[25] Attention might also be drawn to the undeveloped state of such fields as the sociology of leisure,

154

despite the growing importance of mass leisure in post-industrial society.[26] However, we would tend to view the latter as part of a more general pattern of interest which these studies exhibit, and one which entails very little attention being given to the requirements of a prospective sociology and to the broader questions of social choice and social planning which this would comprise. It is to be acknowledged, however, that the last few years have witnessed a new interest in the social sciences for issues of a prospective kind, and so this deficit may, in fact, be in the process of being remedied.[27]

*Summary*

We have observed in this section a distinct patterning in the distribution of our sample of references on values by subject-matter, and we have considered briefly some of the fields of inquiry which were particularly highly represented, as well as some of the ones with little representation. The main results of our study are presented in Tables 6.1 and 6.2. The first of these orders the information for the whole period under review according to a series of categories of content. Table 6.2, however, specifically relates content with time, by comparing the distribution of references by subject-matter over the three time-periods of 1955–8, 1959–62, and 1963–6. A chi-squared test was conducted on this table to examine our initial hypothesis of a significant relationship between time-period and the amount of emphasis given to particular subject-areas. This proved to be significant at the 0·05 level. We may say, therefore, that our sample of references indicates also the existence of definite trends over time with regard to subject-matter. The major percentage increases over the period in question were, as we have mentioned, in the fields of the 'family and socialization', 'social change and economic development', 'social psychology', and the 'sociology of education'. The areas of most marked percentage decrease, on the other hand, were the more general ones of 'sociology: history and theory', and 'methodology and research techniques', indicating, at the simplest level, an ongoing trend toward specialization in published sociological work. We turn now to the second stage of our analysis.

**Analysis of empirical studies**

To gain a more detailed view of the empirical studies carried out in this field, we selected the years 1954, 1957, 1960, 1963, and 1966 for closer examination. For background purposes, Table 6.3 presents the relative proportion of books and articles in the sample over these years, the overall ratio being, respectively, about 1:6. Similarly, Table 6.4 discriminates the references into commentaries, empirical studies, and theoretical studies. From this it can be seen that the first

155

two of these three categories accounted for over four-fifths of the references (84 per cent), with a slight excess of 'commentaries' (44 per cent). Empirical studies, however, were well-represented in the literature, accounting for exactly two-fifths of the total.

These empirical studies were examined firstly according to the research method which they employed. The results are contained in Table 6.5. From this, an overriding emphasis upon the verbal methods of the interview and questionnaire is apparent: together these accounted for 65 per cent of all the research methods employed. This becomes more significant in view of the fact that for each empirical study *all* the distinct methods employed were coded, and not merely the principal ones. Thus, in several of the cases in which alternative

TABLE 6.3  *Source of references: proportion of books and articles*

|          |     | 1954 | 1957 | 1960 | 1963 | 1966 | Total N. | % |
|----------|-----|------|------|------|------|------|------|------|
| Books    | no. | 1    | 1    | 8    | 2    | 26   | 38   | 14·9 |
|          | %   | 10   | 8    | 15   | 3    | 22   |      |      |
| Articles | no. | 9    | 11   | 44   | 61   | 92   | 217  | 85·1 |
|          | %   | 90   | 92   | 85   | 97   | 78   |      |      |

TABLE 6.4  *References according to type of content*

|       |     | Commentaries | Empirical studies* | Theoretical studies | Total |
|-------|-----|--------------|--------------------|--------------------|-------|
| 1954  | no. | 5            | 5                  | —                  | 10    |
|       | %   | (50)         | (50)               | —                  |       |
| 1957  | no. | 5            | 3                  | 4                  | 12    |
|       | %   | (42)         | (25)               | (33)               |       |
| 1960  | no. | 23           | 22                 | 7                  | 52    |
|       | %   | (44)         | (42)               | (14)               |       |
| 1963  | no. | 24           | 29                 | 10                 | 63    |
|       | %   | (38)         | (46)               | (16)               |       |
| 1966  | no. | 54           | 44                 | 20                 | 118   |
|       | %   | (46)         | (37)               | (17)               |       |
| Total | no. | 111          | 103                | 41                 | 255   |
|       | %   | 44           | 40                 | 16                 | 100   |

* 24 per cent (N=25) of the empirical studies were classed as 'empirical-theoretical' and 4 per cent (N=4) as 'empirical-methodological'; cf. page 168.

techniques were employed, their role was strictly supplementary to either interviews or questionnaires as the main instruments of data-collection. We may interpret this as evidence in favour of our earlier comments regarding the tendency of sociologists to overstress the importance of verbal culture. A variety of methods are in fact available for the empirical study of values, and moral codes generally, most of which are currently under-employed, and, as a result, insufficiently developed.[28]

TABLE 6.5  *Empirical studies according to research method employed*

| | | Interview | Questionnaire | Observation | Projective techniques | Content analysis | Q-sort | Experiment | Semantic differential | Total |
|---|---|---|---|---|---|---|---|---|---|---|
| 1954 | no. | 2 | 1 | 2 | — | — | — | — | — | 5 |
| | % | (40) | (20) | (40) | | | | | | |
| 1957 | no. | 2 | 1 | — | 1 | — | — | — | — | 4 |
| | % | (50) | (25) | | (25) | | | | | |
| 1960 | no. | 11 | 7 | 5 | 2 | 2 | — | 1 | — | 28 |
| | % | (39) | (25) | (18) | (7) | (7) | | (4) | | |
| 1963 | no. | 7 | 12 | 4 | 3 | 3 | 1 | 1 | 1 | 32 |
| | % | (22) | (38) | (13) | (9) | (9) | (3) | (3) | (3) | |
| 1966 | no. | 20 | 17 | 4 | 6 | 4 | 2 | — | — | 53 |
| | % | (38) | (32) | (7) | (11) | (7) | (4) | | | |
| Total | no. | 42 | 38 | 15 | 12 | 9 | 3 | 2 | 1 | 122* |
| | % | 34 | 31 | 12 | 10 | 7 | 2 | 2 | 1 | 100 |

* Where more than one principal method could be identified each was coded; hence this total exceeds that given in the previous table.

This practice of concentrating on only a few 'standard' methods, and typically utilizing only one method for the purpose of an inquiry, is to be criticized on other grounds. Thus, to follow up a given sociological theme—for instance, the relationship between education and values—by employing a number of different methods to test the validity of certain empirical propositions, comprising the hypotheses at stake, is to act in accordance with the principles of the scientific method. For one such principle is that we ascribe a greater degree of confidence to an hypothesis the more, and the more diverse, the situations in which it has been tested. And the method employed may itself be considered to be an important component of the testing situation.[29] Therefore, the more evidence we can bring to support an hypothesis from using different methods, the more confidence we can have in the validity of the hypothesis.

The second point is that, even within the confines of a single empirical study, the advantage of using more than one method of data-collection is that of making oneself more available to serendipitous, as well as confirming and disconfirming, information. Not only is the range of information so gained more complete, it is also gained under more controlled conditions. That is, by utilizing more than one method one allows, however partially, for the method itself to be treated as a variable, the effects of which can be empirically ascertained. Further, we would think that this strategy facilitates also the *generation* of theory (as opposed to its mere verification), as this process is outlined, for instance, in Glazer and Strauss's book, *The Discovery of Grounded Theory* (1968). Naturally this is partly a question of practicality: some questions will be phrased in terms to which, let us say, only interview or questionnaire methods are appropriate. But since the elaboration of more sophisticated research techniques and procedures has been focused principally upon the development of these two methods, it would seem that this has also tended to determine the kind of questions asked in empirical sociology, and arguably also the kind of theory proposed to answer them.

What is needed, then, is the development of reliability measures to establish comparability between different methods, rather than, as tends to be the case now, solely with reference to different applications of only one method at a time. It is indicated also, and more specifically, in Table 6.5 that there is a need for the development of standardized methods for collecting behavioural data, as well as information of a purely verbal type.[30] This is particularly relevant to a sociology of moral codes since it would allow us to pursue, in particular instances, the general issue, which is important in a pragmatic as well as a theoretical sense, of the empirical relationship between actions and attitudes.[31] That this question has received relatively little attention is, as we have suggested earlier, no doubt in part a function of the lack of appropriate behavioural indices of proven adequacy.[32]

The empirical studies in our sample were examined secondly according to certain general characteristics of the populations which they selected for investigation. Table 6.6 presents data on the national origins of the samples used for each of the five time-periods. From this we can see an expected concentration on populations drawn from the United States. These comprised almost two-thirds (62 per cent) of the overall total of samples, only 38 per cent being drawn from other countries. To gauge, however partially, some of the characteristics of those samples which were drawn from countries other than the United States (although often by sociologists based in America) we have provided firstly a list of the countries from which samples were chosen, together with the number of times (frequency) that samples were drawn from them. Secondly, we have ranked these countries according to their socio-economic level of development, as defined in the tables given by Russett et al., which we employed earlier (Chapter 4) in our discussion of pluralism.[33] The results of these analyses are presented, respectively, in Tables 6.6 (b) and 6.6 (c). From this we can observe an interesting concentration of attention upon 'developing' societies, namely those located in level 4, and to a lesser degree at level 3. These two stages of socio-economic development are respectively characterized by Bruce Russett as comprising Industrial Revolution societies and Transitional societies.[34] That the attention given to these types of society is disproportionate, at least with respect to the number of nations potentially available, can be established by comparing the histogram in Table 6.6 (c) with the results in Table 6.6 (d), which gives the percentage distribution of world nations according to socio-economic level.[35] From this it can be seen that, for example, although 49 per cent of the populations included in the empirical studies were drawn from stage 4 on the scale of development, this level accounted for only 34 per cent of the total number of nations.

If populations drawn from the United States are also included, then, of course, stage 5, the highest stage of development, comprising 'High mass-consumption' societies, will account for the overriding majority (60 per cent) of studies. The figures for this are given in Table 6.6 (d).

Such comparisons as the above, of course, rest upon the assumption that in empirical sociology of this kind every country should have an equal chance of being selected for research purposes. This is, we readily acknowledge, a considerable oversimplification, and in the majority of cases constitutes an unwarranted assumption, in large part because the factors of population-size and politics have both been excluded.[36] However, it is employed here as a heuristic device to underline the descriptive point we are making: namely, that of a concentration of attention, in research in this field, upon industrializing societies, such as (for the period under study) India and Brazil. This may be taken to supplement the comments offered earlier in this chapter on the high, and increasing, amount of interest being devoted to the subject of 'social change and economic development'.[37]

It has been mentioned earlier also that empirical inquiries into values, and moral codes generally, in sociology have focused principally upon populations of students and schoolchildren. Evidence for

159

this is contained in Table 6.7, which demonstrates that almost one-third of the studies under consideration involved samples of students, and that, taken together with samples of schoolchildren, these two social categories accounted for almost half (46 per cent) of the total number of samples under review, a pattern which shows no sign of decreasing over time.

The empirical research was lastly examined according to the type and extent of comparative approaches employed. The importance of a self-consciously comparative framework for the development of empirical and theoretical adequacy in the sociological analysis of moral codes has been emphasized throughout this study. However, it is difficult to specify a single, rigorous meaning to the notion of 'comparative research' since, at one level, virtually every sociological inquiry is of this kind. That is, any attempt to *analyse* data, however rudimentary, must involve comparison. For example, almost all the empirical studies we examined discriminated their populations according to one or more of the familiar sociological variables of age, sex, and socio-economic status. However, this discrimination was typically *post factum*; in what appeared to be only a minority of cases were samples employed which were stratified beforehand according to criteria such as these. And in only about 50 per cent of the cases in which this procedure was adopted were more than two groups designated for study.

More central to the usual notion of 'comparative research' is the study that is cross-cultural or cross-national. Inquiries of this kind,

TABLE 6.6  *Empirical studies: source of samples by national origin*

(a) Proportion of samples from the United States*

| Year | U.S.A.† N | U.S.A.† % | Other countries N | Other countries % |
|---|---|---|---|---|
| 1954 | 5 | (100) | — | |
| 1957 | 3 | (60) | 2 | (40) |
| 1960 | 15 | (68) | 7 | (32) |
| 1963 | 17 | (53) | 15 | (47) |
| 1966 | 27 | (61) | 17 | (39) |
| Totals | 67 | (62) | 41 | (38) |

* This table is restricted to samples of individuals and, e.g. content analyses of books, documents, etc., have been excluded, as have studies in which individual countries could not be identified, e.g. studies conducted with participants at international conferences. On the other hand, where samples were clearly drawn from more than one country, each country has been included.

† Studies of Amerindian groups have been excluded from this category.

160

### (b) Samples from other countries

| | Frequency | | |
|---|---|---|---|
| | 3 | 2 | 1 |
| | Japan | E. Africa | Brazil | Peru |

| Country | 3 | 2 | 1 | |
|---|---|---|---|---|
| | Japan | E. Africa | Brazil | Peru |
| | | Canada | Chile | Trinidad |
| | | India | Finland | Uganda |
| | | Israel | Germany | Uruguay |
| | | Korea | Haiti | U.S.S.R. |
| | | Mexico | Hong Kong | |
| | | Philippines | Iran | |
| | | Spain | Italy | |
| | | Turkey | Jamaica | |
| | | U.K. | Lebanon | |
| | | (Amerindian) | Norway | |

### (c) Samples from other countries by socio-economic levels of development

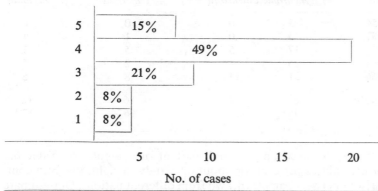

| 5 | 15% |
| 4 | 49% |
| 3 | 21% |
| 2 | 8% |
| 1 | 8% |

5    10    15    20

No. of cases

### (d) Empirical studies: total samples by socio-economic level (including U.S.A.)

| | Level | No. | % | Distribution of world nations at 1963† |
|---|---|---|---|---|
| Modern industrial society | 5 | 73 | 69 | 14 (14%) |
| | 4 | 19 | 18 | 36 (34%) |
| | 3 | 8 | 8 | 31 (29%) |
| | 2 | 3 | 3 | 15 (14%) |
| Traditional primitive society | 1 | 3 | 3 | 11 (10%) |
| | Sum | 106* | 100 | 107 (100%) |

\* The two studies of Amerindian groups were excluded from this table.
† From the full series of tables given in Russett *et al.* (1964), pp. 294–8.

161

TABLE 6.7   *Empirical studies: type of samples**

| Year | Students | Schoolchildren | Others |
|------|----------|----------------|--------|
| 1954 | 3 | 1 | 4 |
| 1957 | 1 | 0 | 3 |
| 1960 | 3 | 3 | 15 |
| 1963 | 11 | 3 | 16 |
| 1966 | 16 | 10 | 21 |
| Totals | 34 | 17 | 59 |
|        | 31% | 15% | 54% |

* Documentary analyses have been omitted from this table, but where more than one distinct type of sample was employed each was recorded.

TABLE 6.8   *Empirical studies: extent of comparative approaches*

| Year | Synchronic/diachronic | | More than 1 method | Cross-national |
|------|-----------------------|---|-------------------|----------------|
| 1954 | 5 | 0 | 0 | 0 |
| 1957 | 3 | 0 | 1 | 1 |
| 1960 | 17 | 5 | 5 | 1 |
| 1963 | 25 | 4 | 2 | 5 |
| 1966 | 31 | 13 | 8 | 5 |
| Totals | 81 | 22 | 16 | 12 |
|        | 79% | 21% | 16% | 12% |

however, occupied only a small part of our sample. As Table 6.8 shows, only 12 per cent, or about one study in eight, involved comparisons between samples drawn from different nations. Our estimate would be that the full range of cross-cultural studies amounts on average to only about one study in seven.[38] Table 6.8 also indicates the amount of comparison made with respect to time and method. Thus, the majority of studies examined were also synchronic, only about one in five involving research on values over time. Similarly, the proportion of studies utilizing more than one method of research averaged only 16 per cent.[39]

The overall impression one gains from these references, therefore, is that the empirical research which they encompass is comparative in only a limited sense of the term, typically involving, for example, comparisons between college students of different class backgrounds, and at different levels of education, or between schoolchildren of different ages and grades. What is rather markedly lacking is empirical research that is comparative in both a broader sense, and also one that would better express the distinctive perspective of sociology. The research design we refer to would involve controlled comparisons across groups and institutions that have been matched in a formal sense but which embody diverse cultural traditions. Usually this is best achieved by making comparisons between geographically separated societies. But this is not necessarily so. Considerable scope exists, for example, for diachronic analyses over more substantial periods of time. It is noteworthy that most of the analyses of this type in our sample (e.g. panel analyses) limited themselves to durations of less than one year. Research over extensive periods of time does, of course, face many practical problems. The difficulties of ensuring population stability over time and of controlling for extraneous changes in the environment are salient examples of this. On the other hand, exposure to the relativities of history can add considerably to our degree of confidence in a particular hypothesis. As Webb et al. (1968) observe in favour of time-series data:[40]

> If a research hypothesis, particularly for social behavior, can survive the assaults of changing times and conditions, its plausibility is far greater than if it were tested by a method which strips away alien threats and evaluates the hypothesis in an assumptive, one-time test. Validity can be inferred from a hypothesis' robustness. If the events of time are vacillating, as they usually are, then only the valid hypothesis has the intellectual robustness to be sustained, while rival hypotheses expire.

Particularly in need of further development here are not only more extensive panel and cohort analyses, but also the use of archival records of various kinds for longitudinal investigations. The latter have the additional advantage usually of low collection costs, and they avoid some of the problems of 'reactivity' inherent in the interview and questionnaire in the sense that they constitute data not initially produced for the purposes of social science research. Naroll (1962), however, has drawn our attention to the need for rigorous methods of representative sampling in the selection and use of archival data.[41] Thus, modern sampling theory and methods have focused almost exclusively upon locational sampling problems, particularly in the theory and practice of stratification, leaving the subject of sampling over time-periods relatively undeveloped.[42] In the context of modern bureaucratic societies, studies utilizing archival data become more feasible because of the many organizations, both governmental and private, which maintain continuous records. Direct use, for example, may be made of actuarial data. The study by Burchinal and Chancellor (1963) illustrates this.[43] They examined the complete governmental records on marriage and divorce for the state of Iowa for the years 1953 and 1959. On the basis of this marriages of same-religion and mixed-religion pairs were compared for longevity and, amongst other findings, mixed-religion marriages were found to be the significantly shorter-lived of the two types. Here, of course, shared religion might have reflected a broader range of value-homogeneity affecting the results.

For more complex studies, index-numbers can be constructed in an attempt to control for the effect of extraneous changes in the environment, a problem which any inquiry conducted over a substantial period of time is likely to encounter. Variations in the population size form a typical example of this. The use of index-numbers to correct for this is illustrated in an ingenious piece of research by DeCharms and Moeller (1962).[44] In this, information was collected on the number of patents issued by the U.S. Patent Office over the period 1800–1950. The resulting data were then systematically related to population statistics for this time-period to produce a 'patent production index' for 20-year intervals over the 150-year span. These indices were matched with findings from a content analysis of children's readers for the same period which focused principally upon the occurrence of achievement imagery. The matching revealed a strong correlation between the amount of achievement imagery and the number of patents per million population. It should also be mentioned here that the basic research of David McClelland (1961), which supplied the impetus for this study, itself forms an impressive example of the fruitful use of varied kinds of historical evidence.[45]

But in spite of the possibilities outlined above, most of the empirical research upon aspects of moral codes, at least on the evidence of our sample, might be validly described as 'ahistorical' in content and method. As such, this constitutes a second respect in which the research we have sampled exhibits a lack of comparative perspective. Modern sociology in general has been criticized for its lack of a historical consciousness.[46] But, particularly in the case of the present subject-matter, a sense of history in sociological methods and interpretations could serve to compensate for the lack of history in the self-interpretations of modern society. In fact, however, sociology, as a product of modern society, appears more to reflect this ahistoricity.

In drawing attention to the un-historical character of much available research in this field, we do not wish to imply that sociology should direct its attention to strictly historical subjects, but rather that contemporaneous facts and processes should, wherever feasible, be comprehended and examined within a more historical framework. As we have put it elsewhere, adoption of a comparative perspective involves viewing the present as history, as anthropology. But this implies looking forward as well as back, and so more attention needs

164

also to be given to the interests of a prospective sociology.[47] In our view, a strategy of this kind would permit both a more faithful application of the distinctive perspective of sociology, and also a closer articulation between, on the one hand, empirical research and, on the other, the comparative dimensions of sociology theory.

Aside from such longitudinal analysis, the principal connotation of 'cross-cultural' research involved, as we saw, a process of comparison between geographically separate societies. But although this is the usual connotation of the concept, it should not be treated as the only one. As was observed earlier, societies can be fruitfully characterized in terms of their degree of internal cultural pluralism.[48] And we saw that a highly pluralistic situation was characteristic of many less developed societies. In view of this, we should not allow models derived from the experience of relatively unitary modern industrial societies to bias our perception of the possibilities for substantial and fruitful intrasocietal comparisons between cultural groups. In the research we reviewed, however, little use was made of these comparative possibilities.

In addition, even modern industrial societies contain pluralistic elements which appropriate research designs could exploit. One important basis of such pluralism in America, for example, is the ethnic one.[49] Yet in our sample, despite the concentration of studies on the United States, only 6 per cent chose populations from different ethnic groups. Similarly, virtually no attention was given to the analysis of regional pluralism in modern society; almost the only study to include this as a major variable was one which examined North/South differences in America with regard to a number of civil rights issues.[50] In sum, insufficient attention was given to the possibilities of research which was cross-cultural by virtue of being conducted across different cultural segments of a society, including modern societies. This under-exploitation of the pluralistic features of various types of society may, of course, also reflect the underdevelopment of relevant theoretical treatments of the concept of cultural pluralism.

The tendency towards parochialism in empirical sociology of this kind has its methodological correlate in an emphasis upon standards of *internal* reliability and validity as the criteria of 'scientific' merit for a research design. As such, these were achieved at the cost of a low generalizability of the resultant findings. It is worth noting, then, that research designs which incorporate highly diverse situations, either in the form of inter- or intrasocietal comparisons, or of comparisons over time, tend to provide more rigorous tests of whatever hypothesis is under examination. They are also more likely to fulfil a serendipitous function; that is, to lead to unexpected insights into the subject under consideration, or phenomena closely related to it.

165

One descriptive feature of the methodology of those inquiries in our sample which were carried out across distinct cultural groups also deserves mention. Thus, studies of this kind are faced with a dilemma of sampling strategy: do they want representativeness within each community or equivalence across communities? This constitutes a dilemma because maximizing representativeness usually means minimizing equivalence, and vice versa. We may illustrate this with an example given by Osgood (1967) from the field of cross-national research.[51] Thus, as he notes, a representative sample in India, for example, would involve proportionate numbers of many castes, many religions, and many languages, and it would include many illiterates and persons in villages having minimal awareness of the outside world. Such a sample would hardly be comparable with one drawn, say, from the United States, using its usual criteria. On the other hand, a sample of Indian college students would obviously be much more highly selected (less represenative) than an equivalent sample of American college students. Whatever compromise is made between these two poles will depend primarily upon the purposes of the research. It is indicative, therefore, that almost all the cross-national (and cross-cultural) studies in our sample were designed to maximize equivalence before representativeness.

Equivalence permits more controlled and limited comparisons, so that the influence of factors such as language, culture, nationality can be examined under conditions in which other variables are held relatively constant. Representativeness, on the other hand, permits one to generalize with more confidence to the broader communities or cultures concerned. It is clear that much social research needs to meet both these criteria, and that a compromise is therefore usually necessary. For example, Lambert and Klineberg (1967) in their cross-national study wished to compare children's images of themselves and foreigners as a function of their nationality and age. Therefore they wanted both equivalence, in the sense of age-levels, sex ratios, intelligence, and so on, and representativeness, in the sense of socio-economic status and the like, so that differences could not be attributed, for example, to levels of parental education.[52] Their solution was a compromise in the form of a stratified sample (by age-group, status, etc.) within otherwise equivalent groups. It is apparent that the usage of more compromise strategies of this type will be necessary if we are to be able to generalize the findings of comparative research to each of the cultural groups involved.

But the parochialism of the empirical studies we have reviewed is not only to be considered in terms of its methodological implications. The theoretical value of a continuing sensitivity to the realities of cultural relativism is also evident, both as a means of becoming more self-aware of one's own preconceptions and also of thereby avoiding too limited and ethnocentric a view of the problem under study. This would appear particularly relevant to the present subject, in view of the pervasive tendency to 'objectify' and absolutize accepted moral codes and the modes of reasoning with which they are associated. And because of the emotional correlates surrounding moral attitudes and precepts, most evident at their transgression, it might appear particularly difficult to deal with them in a way that is free of bias and value-judgment. Rigorous research designs, in which every effort is made to control for ethnocentric projection and prejudgment, are needed to avoid these problems and thus to facilitate conceptual clarification and a more objective approach to the standards of one's own culture. But it is important too that these research designs be comparative: as Weber and Durkheim, in their different ways, were among the first to demonstrate, the social meanings which are particular to a given culture can only be explicated and understood by a systematic process of contrast and comparison with alternative sets of social meanings. Moreover, a sense of comparative standards, and of the range of possibilities inherent in social situations,[53] has also an evident pragmatic justification to the extent that sociology is conceived as a broadening intellectual discipline.

In summary, there appears to be a need, particularly in the case of the present subject, to develop more comparative research designs in social science. And this is required in various senses. Firstly, research is needed in which comparisons can be made between different methods, and multi-method formats need to be developed as the ideal research design. In our' sample, it will be recalled, only 16 per cent of the studies were of this type. Secondly, research is also needed which comprises content of a more cross-cultural kind. Thus, only 12 per cent of the studies in our sample were carried out on a cross-national basis, and the total of cross-cultural studies was estimated at only about 14 per cent. More attention needs to be given, then, to longitudinal analyses, to intersocietal surveys, and also to comparisons between distinct cultural sectors within single societies, and especially those that exhibit a high degree of pluralism in this respect.

### Further observations: towards a critique of research

By way of conclusion, some more qualitative observations, which are less amenable to statistical evidence, may be offered with regard to the empirical research we have examined above. Since we believe these remarks may be generalized to the broader field encompassed by the empirical sociology of moral codes, the following will serve as a critique of this aspect of sociology. However, we shall restrict ourselves to adumbrating only the more salient points, each of which could, of course, be pursued in greater detail than we provide.

167

## The lack of theory

The first, and perhaps most evident feature of this research concerns the absence of any generally-accepted theoretical framework which would lend coherence to the various empirical studies and permit them to have mutual implications. Only 24 per cent of the references were assessed as 'empirical-theoretical' in the sense that they constituted empirical tests of hypotheses explicitly derived from a broader set of propositions or a distinctive theoretical approach to the subject under review.[54] A further 4 per cent were classified as 'empirical-methodological' in the sense that they were designed almost exclusively to test the validity or reliability of a particular research instrument (e.g. a specific scale of values). The substantive research, however, had in general the characteristic of being non-cumulative; studies tended to proceed on independent, parallel lines rather than in an integrated form.[55]

Most of the research was of the information-gathering rather than hypothesis-testing sort, and most of the hypotheses that were tested tended to be relatively discrete and *ad hoc*. Few were derived from either explicit 'theories of the middle range' or provided tests of the central implications of more general theoretical perspectives. In such cases, even where the hypotheses tested were strongly confirmed, a great deal of ambiguity of interpretation remained, whether it was recognized as such or not. This is because a single hypothesis does not suggest a unique interpretation of itself: rather, there is in principle no limit to the number of theories from which a given set of hypotheses could be deduced. That is, there is no limit, apart from human ingenuity, to the variety one can obtain from specifying the higher-level hypotheses, and then combining them in all logically possible ways.

Thus a statement of theory is necessary for a clear-cut interpretation of the significance of research findings. Other grounds have, of course, been proposed for the value of theory in general and specifically for its application to sociology, and these arguments are relevant here too. For example, as Talcott Parsons has written:[56]

> The basic reason why general theory is so important is that the cumulative development of knowledge in a scientific field is a function of the degree of *generality of implications* by which it is possible to relate findings, interpretations, and hypotheses on different levels and in different specific empirical fields to each other. If there is to be a high degree of such generality there *must* on some level be a common conceptual scheme which makes the work of different investigators in a specific sub-field and those in different sub-fields commensurable.

168

In addition, empirical research which is deprived of theory and cross-cultural comparison is deprived also of any systematic means of comprehending the social reality encompassed by the *status quo* other than in terms of those descriptions already available within this social reality and partly constitutive of it. The consequence of this which we would draw attention to here is not so much the conservative nature of such research, in any ideological sense, although there may be some truth in this, but rather that such research militates against recognition of the *relativity* of the *status quo* and hence tends to exclude from its analyses that very type of critical realism which the sociological perspective is best equipped to bring to its subject-matter.

Such theories as were invoked in this research usually constituted either classificatory schemes or relatively informal sets of assumptions. Of the former, the Allport-Vernon and Kluckhohn-Strodbeck typologies, which we discussed earlier, were respectively the most frequently employed. What was perhaps particularly lacking, from our point of view, was the use of theories and hypotheses directed towards some of the central issues of ethical and cultural relativism: some of the issues we have in mind here will be considered in the next section of this inquiry. As it is, we may note merely that issues of this kind can only be properly considered within the context of a comparative empirical sociology, which, as we have observed, these studies matched only to a limited extent. In sum, the tendency exhibited by the studies we reviewed was in the direction of empirical research which, although more sophisticated in a methodological sense, is in general less significant to theory, or at any rate to a more limited order of theoretical concerns than seems desirable.

*Strategic studies*

The researcher might plausibly defend the above strategy by pointing to the limitations or unavailability of existing theory. But in so far as this is true, it serves only to underscore a second point. And this is to the effect that the research we have examined is also rarely strategic from a practical point of view, in relation to social needs as well as to theory. Most of these inquiries concerned themselves with limited facets of contemporary society, to the neglect of the larger social-political problems of the time. One index of this is the large proportion of studies (31 per cent) which sampled college students. Needless to say, these constitute an atypical social category, although one which will be more unrepresentative in some societies than in others.[57] In interpreting these findings, therefore, it is important to be aware of the usual correlates of higher education: urban origins, high parental status, more exposure to other cultures (and possibly less integration with their own), and so on. However, our main point here is that there seems to have been relatively little motivation in the selection of problem-areas and samples to ally academic criteria with considerations of a more practical kind. This, of course, has been a frequent criticism of social science in general, and particularly of its dominant American expressions, in contrast with the supposedly more committal attitudes of European scholars.[58] It is important then to recognize that the pursuit of these broader problems does not necessitate a lessening or abandonment of the interest in acquiring for sociology the status of an empirical science, with rigorous operational procedures and standards of validation. There may, however, be a psychological point here: namely, that empirical sociology is perhaps conservative because a 'respect for the facts' tends to inhibit the development of a critical attitude towards them.

Not all social research is as neutral and microsociological as this characterization might suggest, and even America has its advocates of sociology as one of the policy sciences.[59] But what we would emphasize here is that a conscious selection of ethically neutral problem-areas in research, possibly deriving from a misconception of the doctrine of *wertfrei* social science, can lead to a number of lacunae which comprise areas of substantive academic as well as practical interest. To cite but one example of this with regard to the present subject, it is noteworthy how little attention has been given to the application of a sociological analysis of values, beliefs, and moral reasoning in the field of population control, which is commonly regarded (with, say, conservation of the environment) as constituting one of the world's major contemporary problems.[60]

Demography is basically concerned with changes over time in the population structure. Most studies in sociology and anthropology, on the other hand, have tended to encompass static cross-sections of a society. Perhaps because of this, investigators have shown only a slight interest in demography. But in two of the few contributions to this field from a strictly sociological viewpoint, Mary Douglas (1966) and Paul Vieille (1967) have both demonstrated, within different contexts, the crucial importance of taking agent's *reasons* into account as well as considering purely material causes: that is, they have demonstrated the key role played by sets of values and beliefs regarding fertility, as distinct from purely economic (and medical) factors, in determining population control.[61] Equally important here also is the effect upon cultural values and beliefs of current demographic changes in developing countries which are radically changing life-expectations and experiences. The rigorous application of demographic methods to historical materials has advanced rapidly over the last decade and as such promises a great deal for a prospective, as well as historically-oriented, sociology of this type. But, in the last analysis, some impetus for research must surely also spring from the fact that the traditional model of a demographic transition, involving sharp consecutive decreases in death rates and birth rates, on present evidence does not appear to be, as was assumed, a necessary consequence of the processes of industrialization and social change. Thus, the social optimism which this model gave some grounds for would appear to have been misplaced.

## Conceptual analysis and justification

As we have said, sociological research has frequently been criticized for its insufficient attention to both theory and to social needs, and in this respect our sub-sample confirms a more general pattern. But almost equally apparent, and related to these points, is a third characteristic of our sample: namely, the pervasive tendency of the research under the rubric of values to eschew philosophical questions, and distinctions to be drawn from moral philosophy. Although the motivation for this may be understandable as a desire to interpret sociology as an autonomous, empirically-based discipline, its consequences have not been wholly desirable.

Thus, as has been indicated elsewhere in this study,[62] developments in the philosophical study of ethics, and particularly in contemporary analytic approaches, can supply a degree of conceptual clarification and sophistication which is greatly needed in sociology, both for the construction of theory, and also for more refined interpretations of data and for the development of research designs which avoid ethnocentric preconceptions and permit inquiry into processes of ethical reasoning. The conceptual assumptions made in many sociological accounts of moral codes often exhibit a naïvety that could be easily avoided: the frequent omission of a clear distinction between evaluations and prescriptions and the tendency to accept implicitly an approbationist view of their interrelationship exemplify this, as does the failure to examine relationships between cognitive assumptions and standards of evaluation and prescription.[63]

The above constitute only the most salient distinctions that need to be made and pursued. And the need for guidance from philosophy is indexed by the fact that virtually none of the studies we examined gave explicit attention either to modalities of ethical reasoning or to the question of the interrelationship between beliefs, values, and precepts of various kinds. At the least, then, moral philosophy could provide greater awareness of the centrality of these issues and could adumbrate some of the leading points for their analysis. Here use could be made not only of analytic ethics, but also of normative philosophy. Thus the latter could supply alternative models for the description and comparison of modes of reasoning in ethics.[64]

One needs to be aware of alternative ways of justifying principles and reasoning about moral codes in order to prevent culture-bound assumptions intruding in one's observations and descriptions. The neglect of consideration of these processes in the studies we reviewed forms perhaps the most important consequence of the assiduous avoidance of philosophical issues in this research. However, it is important to be clear here that, in drawing attention to the neglect of moral reasoning and justification in these inquiries, we do not wish to imply commitment to the view that sociological analysis should, as some writers have argued,[65] restrict itself to interpretations on the level of the reasons avowed by the agents under study or that causal explanations are logically inappropriate to the subject-matter of the social sciences. We would neither regard these presumptive alternatives as mutually exclusive approaches, nor reject the possibility of causal interpretation in sociology.[66] Thus causal analysis has been effectively applied to the explanation of the occurrence and persistence of moral codes under the aegis of the sociology of knowledge. But of the two approaches, an emphasis upon reasons has a programmatic primacy since it designates a significant part of the facts to be explained.

Thus the priority of reasons in sociological analysis derives from their status as part of the *explicanda*. As Isaiah Berlin states: 'The first step in the understanding of men is the bringing to consciousness of the model or models that dominate and penetrate their thought and action. . . . The second task is to analyse the model itself, and this commits the analyst to accepting or modifying or rejecting it, and, in the last case, to providing a more adequate one in its stead.'[67]

We may therefore rephrase our criticism of the research and say that the *explicanda* which it provides are inadequate from the point of view of causal analysis. And this is due principally to the omission of data on modalities of reasoning and justification in ethics, rather than merely on their end-products, whether in the form of sets of values or precepts. In consequence, the data we are normally provided with have a one-dimensional quality: the values and prescriptions for action associated with certain social groups are made to appear arbitrary and gratuitous, since little indication is given as to why they are held—that is, as to what reasons the respondents would adduce for them. The analyses move too readily from the empirical establishment of certain values and norms to the explanation of these in sociological terms. What is omitted is part of the *explicandum*: namely, the empirical establishment also of the reasons, the modes of justification and validation, which the subjects offer for the standards they avow. In short, we have a great deal of information from empirical research on the social background of moral codes, in terms of their distribution, origins, and consequences, but surprisingly little on their intellectual background. An adequate sociology of ethics, however, should surely attempt to fulfil both these requirements.

Inclusion in empirical studies of data on modes of ethical reasoning and justification would permit respondents' attitudes to be conceptualized in terms of the broader moral code to which they adhered. This would involve a more complete account of the context within which specific attitudes had meaning, and would supply a more reliable basis for the prediction of responses to novel situations for the subjects in question. It would also provide a more detailed basis of evidence for the articulation of theory in this field, since, as we have seen, typologies and generalizations abound, but their descriptive foundations are insecure.[68] Finally, as we saw in the previous chapter, analyses in terms of reasons are necessary for a fuller understanding of the relationship between expressed attitudes and overt actions.

In sum, in the sample of research which we assessed, values (and prescriptions) were in the main treated discretely and, as it were, *in vacuo*. Future research, therefore, should take respondents' moral codes as its objects of study and attempt to apply to them the kind of distinctions which have proven utility within the philosophy of ethics. If one is to consider the discursive structure of moral codes, then attention must also be directed to the so-called naturalistic aspects of these codes. That is, research must inquire into the descriptive foundations of particular moral outlooks. And although naturalistic arguments may be logically vulnerable, they are none the less clearly important to any adequate account of the grounds adduced for values and precepts. Investigation is needed, therefore, of the relationships between values and beliefs, or, more generally, between the analytically separable processes of cognition, evaluation, and prescription, which are characteristic of a given cultural tradition.

### Value-systems

The question of the interrelationships between values and beliefs was afforded little consideration in the studies we sampled. Indeed, in so far as value-systems were empirically characterized, and not merely treated in metaphorical terms, this characterization usually took the form not of the discursive structure involved but rather of a simple analysis of correlations between expressed values. In a sense, a correlation matrix of this type does constitute the simplest summary measure of the value-systems characteristic of particular social groups and as such it can have some heuristic value. Thus, clusters of highly significant correlations may be taken to indicate the presence of more general value-orientations. An example of such an analysis is contained in W. A. Scott's (1965) study of student attitudes, presented here as Table 6.9.

173

TABLE 6.9  *Intercorrelations among value scales*[69]

| | Independence | Intellectualism | Creativity | Academic achievement | Honesty | Religiousness | Self-control | Kindness | Loyalty | Social skills | Status | Physical development |
|---|---|---|---|---|---|---|---|---|---|---|---|---|
| Independence | (0·51) | | | | | | | | | | | |
| Intellectualism | 0·22 | (0·69) | | | | | | | | | | |
| Creativity | 0·21 | 0·51 | (0·54) | | | | | | | | | |
| Academic achievement | 0·07 | 0·34 | 0·31 | (0·63) | | | | | | | | |
| Honesty | 0·04 | 0·09 | 0·00 | 0·23 | (0·30) | | | | | | | |
| Religiousness | −0·22 | 0·18 | 0·13 | 0·15 | 0·17 | (0·76) | | | | | | |
| Self-control | −0·18 | 0·15 | 0·08 | 0·08 | 0·06 | 0·31 | (0·61) | | | | | |
| Kindness | −0·10 | 0·23 | 0·19 | 0·11 | 0·15 | 0·43 | 0·51 | (0·57) | | | | |
| Loyalty | −0·07 | 0·06 | 0·13 | 0·18 | −0·10 | 0·36 | 0·31 | 0·26 | (0·62) | | | |
| Social skills | −0·27 | 0·01 | 0·07 | 0·18 | −0·09 | 0·26 | 0·33 | 0·20 | 0·36 | (0·62) | | |
| Status | −0·10 | 0·13 | 0·12 | 0·28 | −0·01 | 0·14 | 0·12 | 0·07 | 0·35 | 0·42 | (0·47) | |
| Physical development | −0·12 | 0·04 | 0·15 | 0·30 | −0·06 | 0·25 | 0·11 | 0·11 | 0·41 | 0·25 | 0·41 | (0·71) |

From this table, Scott identifies two broad clusters of values, which he describes, after Reisman (1950),[70] as comprising 'inner-directed' and 'outer-directed' orientations. As he writes:[71]

The former group consists of the values of independence, intellectualism, and creativity, while the latter group includes loyalty, social skills, kindness, status, physical development, self-control, and religiousness. The average intercorrelation within the inner-directed cluster is ·33, while that within the outer-directed cluster is ·29; the average correlation between the two clusters is ·03. Thus, to the extent that this population of college students can be classified by these value scales into the two broad orientations, inner-directedness and other-directedness tend to be independent, rather than mutually exclusive dispositions. The value of honesty does not fit particularly well in either cluster, while academic achievement correlates substantially with both.

Table 6.9 represents also a statistical test of the independence of the various conceptually-defined scales. The appropriate test of independence here is that of determining whether or not the several items within a scale are more highly correlated with each other than they are with items from different scales; or, more efficiently, determining whether or not the scale reliabilities (internal consistencies) are higher than the intercorrelations between different scales. From the above table (based on a random cross-section of university students) we can see that this condition holds for each scale in relation to every other scale; that is, no correlation between scales exceeds the separate reliabilities of the two scales (in parentheses the diagonal). This indicates that the scales are measuring distinct, though correlated, values.

Analyses of value-systems through the examination of correlation patterns, like the above, may, of course, be supplemented by various forms of factor analysis. A number of studies of values (mainly of student groups) are available which employ this method.[72] However, although in some cases the factors that emerge can serve as relatively self-interpretive dimensions to differentiate clusters of attitudes, in other cases it is difficult to offer an unambiguous interpretation of the factors so produced.

But both the correlational approaches and their extensions in factor analysis are at best only heuristic means to the depiction of value-systems: they can indicate which items are closely associated in a statistical sense, and in some cases also the main dimensions of variation that account for the variance exhibited by these patterns of association. But this is only an initial, rather superficial notion of value-systems; although, to the extent that they include reference to

175

the interrelationship of value-items, it is usually here that most empirical studies effectively stop. In fact, however, analyses of this kind should lead us on to examine the way in which the values in question are justified. That is, attention needs to be given to the structure of reasoning which supplies the rationale for particular associations between values: it is this 'internal', discursive structure that comprises the primary sense in which particular sets of values can be said to constitute 'value-systems'.

An analogous observation is applicable to sets of precepts for action. However, if one wishes to examine the discursive aspects of moral codes, then it is to be noted that sets of values, unlike sets of prescriptions, are not amenable to relations of logical inference. The potential application of logic, and other formal languages, is thus much greater for the analysis of the structural aspects of the *prescriptive* components of moral codes. Indeed, as we shall see in Chapter 8, a number of analytic tools, including the use of multi-valued logic, are currently being developed to facilitate the rigorous description of these structures. It is, therefore, perhaps a result of the lack of a close relationship with developments in theoretical and conceptual sociology, as well as with moral philosophy, that questions of this type, concerning the structure of moral codes rather than their more immediate characteristics of content, have not normally been raised in the research literature. Also, we observed earlier that theories and empirical inquiries in sociology have focused upon values as the primary constituents of moral codes, at least for sociological purposes. A number of reservations have been expressed about this strategy. But one important deficit would appear to lie in the fact that the emphasis upon values, as distinct from precepts for action, has discouraged concern in theory and research with the 'logical' and deliberative aspects of moral codes, since the latter are both less easily, and also less significantly, applied to interrelationships among values.[73]

## Values and beliefs

We have seen, then, that issues regarding the structure of moral codes have been insufficiently considered in the empirical research, and that correlational analysis provides only a limited introduction to the systemic aspects of moral codes. None the less, it also seems that further use could be made of correlation methods in this field, and that a number of the available attitude surveys could be reinterpreted within the above terms. In particular, just as intercorrelations among values can have a heuristic function, so similar studies of the relations between cognitive and evaluative or prescriptive types of attitudes can also lead to insights. Also, as we have seen, the cognitive aspects in question here are not to be reduced to general beliefs and categories of perception (as in ethnoscience), but will include also factual assumptions and expectations.

A simple illustration of the latter is given in the recent '2000 Project', which surveyed a range of attitudes towards the future held by young people in a number of European countries.[74] Some of the findings of this survey indicate close correlations between, on the one hand, *hopes* for particular social and scientific developments in the future, and, on the other, factual *expectations* that these developments will occur within a certain time-period. One might assume a reciprocal causation here: that is, to some degree the individuals who most hope for a particular development are, by virtue of this, also most likely to predict its occurrence, and vice versa.

However, a full understanding of questions of this type will require the development of theoretical approaches to the analysis of moral codes and attitudes in general. To some extent, hypotheses (like the above) can be derived by extending existing theories of attitude organization to this area, the most obvious candidate here being that of balance theory in its various forms.[75] Interrelations among cognitions, evaluations, and prescriptions, however, are likely to be complexly patterned and correlations between attitude items will only serve to indicate some of the leading features of these patterns and thereby to raise some of the questions which will need to be answered. For the explication of moral codes, it is particularly important to investigate basic beliefs about the social world held by different sectors of society. We have noted already that the absence of adequate taxonomies of beliefs is to be viewed within the context of the difficulty of doing justice to the realities of cultural relativism in this field, and of the limitations inherent in the typological method —namely, its exclusion of the discursive aspects of attitudes. But even allowing for this, there are few approaches that are even suggestive for more limited comparisons, since the cognitive dimensions of moral codes were afforded little conscious scrutiny in the research we reviewed. Consequently, there exists little standardization between different surveys, and many omit questions regarding background preconceptions. Yet it is just these conceptions, often 'obvious' and taken-for-granted, and so unlikely to be volunteered, that allow us to make sense of particular moral stances. Important among these will be conceptions of 'human nature'. Often partial questions on this subject are included in surveys. Table 6.10, drawn from a nationwide sample in the United States, is fairly representative of the type of question we have in mind.

The reversal of the position of the majority expressing full agreement with the proposition (in 1958), from Whites in the North to Negroes in the South, is of some intrinsic interest here. However, our

177

main point in presenting this is to show that results of this kind are only suggestive, since further, more detailed questioning would be needed for an adequate interpretation. But at least a series of responses to questions of this type should help us to comprehend the rationales which lie behind, say, the interracial attitudes and behaviour of specific social groupings, just as they may permit more

TABLE 6.10 *Perceptions of equality*[76]

Question: Do you think that the Declaration of Independence was right, only half right, or not right at all when it stated that 'all men are created equal'?

| Response (1958) | Whites % | Negroes % |
|---|---|---|
| Northerners: | | |
| Right | 82 | 75 |
| Half right | 10 | 12 |
| Not right at all | 3 | 6 |
| No opinion | 5 | 7 |
| Southerners: | | |
| Right | 67 | 83 |
| Half right | 17 | 8 |
| Not right at all | 6 | 4 |
| No opinion | 10 | 5 |

adequate reconstructions of the moral codes operative in other spheres of life. In particular, they will provide information necessary to explicate the ways in which these codes are justified, as well as to suggest other features of their internal organization. Supplementary evidence could then be adduced on their modes of categorization, notions of ethical competence, and so on.

It is because specifically moral attitudes are characteristically justified, in part, by an appeal to the 'nature of things' that the cognitive/evaluative-prescriptive patterns are significant for their analysis. Obviously any attempt to explicate these relationships will have to begin with certain logical postulates, and in particular with the so-called naturalistic fallacy, but also with the fact that certain descriptive (or explanatory) parameters are logically presupposed by evaluations and prescriptions, and finally with the possibility of various non-deductive ties between 'is' and 'ought' propositions which will require careful exploration. But the main task here will be that of reconstructing the norms of rationality, or the culturally-specific patterns of reasoning, that are characteristic of a particular society or social group.

## The neglect of institutions

One final, and in our view important, criticism may be made of the empirical sociology of values (and moral codes generally). This concerns the general conception of the social world implicit in these studies. Thus, in general they have presented attitudinal data, usually in the form of personal preferences or choices, either of general cross-sections of the population (as in community studies) or of segments of it delineated according to such familiar variables as class, age, and sex. The information thus gained has then been statistically analysed, and proposed causal interpretations have centred about the correlations that are revealed between the attitudes in question and a limited number of background variables. The principal lesson which has emerged from such research has been to the effect that attitudes (values, beliefs, precepts, etc.) are not randomly distributed throughout a society, but rather are stratified according to a range of social variables, and thereby characteristics of the society. Thus, we now have cumulative evidence on the social *structuring* of attitudes, both moral and non-moral. Secondly, we have evidence also that these attitudes are distributed in a way that is amenable to sociological description and explanation. To a somewhat lesser degree, we have corresponding evidence that social behaviour is structured throughout society according to variables of the same type. And finally, some data exist to the effect that the discursive components of attitudes, and thus the more formal aspects of moral codes, are similarly patterned according to social criteria: in Britain, for example, the work of Bernstein and his associates has drawn attention to class differences in styles of reasoning.[77]

In addition, evidence for the stability of such structuring is provided by longitudinal analyses. A number of studies have shown that the direction and intensity of attitudes associated with particular social groupings can remain substantially the same at future points in time, and that such changes as do occur tend to exhibit an ordered variation that is itself explicable in sociological terms. However, it may also be noted, *en passant*, that different values have often been shown to exhibit different stabilities over time. Just as different attitudes have varying degrees of reliability as predictors of behaviour,[78] so they also differ as predictors of future attitudes. A simple illustration of this may again be taken from the study by W. A. Scott (1965) which was cited earlier. Here value scores for a class of college students were compared in post-tests at two intervals in time (Table 6.11).

Evidence for the pervasiveness and stability of the social structuring of attitudes is also gained by studies showing, for example, the same correlations between ethnicity and religious orientations even among the well educated in a society. This is relevant evidence in view of the popular conception of education as a means for the individual to free himself from the more obvious determinations of his social background. But as a result of this cumulative information, the social distribution of attitudes has, at least in social science circles, become so much taken for granted that inquiries are treated as especially noteworthy when, like Rose's (1969) study of racial attitudes,[80] no well-marked differences according to social categories are shown to exist.

TABLE 6.11 *Stabilities of value scores over a one-year interval and over a two-week interval*[79]

| | Intra-class correlations between test and retest | | |
|---|---|---|---|
| | (1) One year apart (N=462) | | (2) Two weeks apart (N=208) |
| Value | | | |
| Intellectualism | 0·55 | | 0·63 |
| Kindness | 0·43 | * | 0·68 |
| Social skills | 0·50 | * | 0·73 |
| Loyalty | 0·44 | † | 0·57 |
| Academic achievement | 0·45 | * | 0·67 |
| Physical development | 0·53 | * | 0·71 |
| Status | 0·41 | * | 0·70 |
| Honesty | 0·41 | * | 0·72 |
| Religiousness | 0·64 | * | 0·77 |
| Self-control | 0·53 | * | 0·72 |
| Creativity | 0·43 | * | 0·66 |
| Independence | 0·42 | * | 0·73 |

* Adjacent columns significantly different at $\propto$ <0·001.
† Adjacent columns significantly different at $\propto$ <0·05 (via $z$ transformations).

Information of this kind, gathered under controlled conditions, adds to our understanding of society by depicting the features of its, so to speak, social typography. Also, as well as augmenting our knowledge, this research has invalidated a number of common factual assumptions. For example, although it is frequently assumed that lower-working-class whites are the most prone to adopt racialist attitudes, recent evidence, at least in Britain and America, suggests that extreme prejudice is to be found more often among skilled manual workers and their wives in the lower middle class.[81] Finally, such information also serves as a basis for social planning, particularly in modern societies, and for the development of sociological theory, with regard to such issues as the role of group-identifications on attitude formation and change.

On the other hand, most research of this kind appears to be

premissed upon an individualistic approach and, by implication, upon an atomistic conception of social order. As such, it tends to neglect the central importance of social institutions, and of the process of institutionalization. The latter focus has, paradoxically, been emphasized in much sociological theory, particularly in accounts stressing the normative bases of social order, and in our view is needed to supplement the pervading style of empirical research. Thus, with respect to the present subject, for example, we need to know the moral ideologies associated with particular roles and institutions in society, and most especially with regard to those commanding power and influence. Ideally, such an analysis would also be sensitive to the operation of the 'politics of culture' in this field.[82]

To illustrate this, we may take the example of present-day managers. Several writers, including Burnham and Dahrendorf, have argued that modern industrial power is passing to salaried executives who do not own the companies they control. They have argued also that these managers adopt a professional ethic and code of conduct distinct from that of their capitalist predecessors; namely, one replacing short-term profit with long-term growth, with an awareness of the social responsibilities of industry, and so on. But although ideas such as these have led to various theoretical interpretations of the economic aspects of modern society, they have yet to be explicitly formulated as hypotheses and subjected to empirical test, preferably on a cross-national basis. At present, our reliable knowledge of the moral ideology and general conceptions of present-day managers, of the extent to which this ideology is homogeneous, and of the degree to which this social category may be said to constitute a social group, is very limited. Yet these are significant issues since they call into question the motivation of contemporary neo-capitalism.[83] And because, by virtue of its social location, this sector of society is in a position to implement its ideology (or ideologies) with far-reaching consequences, this is obviously also a question with important ramifications for the sociology of industry in general.

There are two related points we are concerned to establish here. In the first place, we need to know the nature and operation of clearly *institutionalized* moral codes, as these are associated with particular role-systems, institutions, etc., as well as of those moral codes that are only partially institutionalized and that find expression more in the form of individual 'preferences'. Yet it is the latter which constitutes the principal type of empirical information we have at present. But in the second place, we need a focus of research attention, not solely upon individuals, randomly sampled, as the units of analysis, but also upon supra-individual, higher-order collectivities. From an analytic point of view, a number of the latter may be defined according to the type and degree of internal structure that they exhibit.[84]

But perhaps the most intuitively evident example would be the organization as a unit of analysis.

Thus in organizations of various kinds one encounters the social process whereby 'knowledge' and opinions held only tentatively by individuals become crystallized into certainty, at times even dogma. As such, they may find concrete expression as the formal objectives and rules of procedure of the organization. This is the process of institutionalization. It is exemplified by the formalization of religious creeds in institutional settings of various types. But any organization, or coherent system of roles, will be premissed upon certain general ideological assumptions which provide the rationale for the behaviour that they enjoin.

The nature of institutionalization, which formal organizations embody in their normal procedures, renders the organization, at least *prima facie*, less refractory as a unit for the empirical analysis of moral codes in a society. Thus these codes will normally be more coherent, explicit, and stable within an institutional framework of this kind. Organizations, then, like other collectivities, are to be studied in terms of the ideological assumptions implicit in their operation and existence, and the question needs also to be asked: are their objectives in fact achieved?

The limited extent to which organizations have in fact been selected as units for analysis in the empirical research on moral codes, and generally in sociology, is surprising in view of the oft-mentioned increase in the salience of organizations, and organizational decisions, within the structure of modern society. The process of bureaucratization accounts in part for this, and it is a phenomenon that appears characteristic of modern societies almost irrespective of their ideological commitments. In the economic sphere, for example, Professor Galbraith has frequently emphasized the occurrence of parallel processes of this kind in both Eastern and Western industrial nations. He outlines the reasons for this as follows:[85]

Although the purists on both sides greatly resist the evidence, there can be no real doubt that the two systems [of America and Russia] have a broadly convergent tendency. This is not from choice, nor is it from the Soviets discovering the magic of the market in accordance with one simplistic western view, rather it is that both communities are subject to the common imperatives of large-scale industrial production with advanced technology. So both systems repose large responsibilities on the industrial firm, the one inescapable instrument of industrialism. In both, men are subject to its social and mental disciplines. The Soviets have had to make concessions to the autonomy that the firm, evolving from the market economy, has enjoyed as a matter of course in the western economies. . . . Industrialization also requires planning and here concessions have been made by the west. . . . And in both societies the guiding force is not the individual but the organization.

Galbraith goes on to note that both societies are characterized by a sense of individual helplessness and impotency before the power and influence of organizations. The primacy of collective decisions in modern society has also been commented on by Daniel Bell. As he states:[86]

More and more we are becoming a 'communal society' in which the public sector has a greater importance and in which the goods and services of the society—those affecting cities, education, medical care and the environment—will increasingly have to be purchased jointly. Hence, the problem of social choice and individual values—the question of how to reconcile conflicting individual desires through the political mechanism rather than the market—becomes a potential source of discord.

Yet, despite these features of modern society, the research we examined exhibited an individualistic, almost reductive perspective. This was so in the sense that it derived its awareness of the institutional, of social institutions and their effects, indirectly, through an examination of the social structuring of values and standards of conduct at the personal level, at the level of individuals. Knowledge of social structure was derived from the presumptive influences of the background variables used to characterize respondents. But social structure may be studied much more directly by selecting higher-level collectivities as the units of analysis. Insufficient attention, for instance, was given to the moral codes adopted and implemented by the major institutions of society, whether political, educational, economic, or social. Yet this, as we have seen, is especially relevant and practicable in modern society, where commentators seem agreed on the overriding importance of public institutions of various kinds, and particularly those of a bureaucratic type.[87] In a similar way, more inclusive units, such as nation-states in the international system, were also given scant attention as units for analysis.

This pattern of emphasis in the research is clearly related to methodological considerations. In particular, it will be recalled that the interview and questionnaire accounted for two-thirds (65 per cent) of the total number of methods used in our sample. Perhaps, then, a degree of individualism is in some sense endemic to traditional survey methods. This argument has been suggested by Galtung (1969). As he writes:[88]

183

Characteristic of the traditional survey is the tendency to treat the individual as the social unit. Only the individual can be interviewed and given questionnaires (even though he may express himself in the presence of others, as in the group interview). This individualism is further emphasized by building a probability model into the sampling procedure, so that the individual is literally torn out of his social context and made to appear in the sample as a society of one person to be compared with other societies of one person. In very heterogeneous societies like Mexico, Colombia, India such samples quickly lose any meaning.

His argument suggests that traditional survey analysis is most appropriate as an instrument for explanation and prediction within particular types of society: namely, those characterized by both a high degree of individual mobility (geographical, horizontal, vertical) and also a high degree of inner-directedness (i.e. where others are less salient as cues for behaviour). In societies low on these criteria the survey method generates too individualistic a model of the social order. However, he indicates two useful respects in which modern surveys can counter this excessive individualism:[89]

First of all, the sampling procedures can be revised in accordance with the advice of the Columbia tradition, i.e. more emphasis on purposive sampling where individuals are picked according to their position in the social structure, less on random procedures (tests of generalizability will then have to be done by means of replication methods). For instance, one may sample individuals together with some salient members of their role-set. And secondly, analysis can play down the importance of the manifest attitude and play up the importance of social position—as when the vote of the wife is predicted better from the voting intention of her husband than from the voting intention she herself expresses. The latter is a question of including the crucial information about the social position of the respondents in relevant subsystems, which is usually rather different from the superficial knowledge gained through the traditional 'background questions'. Sociometric questions have been used here with some success, as has contextual analysis and all kinds of analysis where properties of collectivities are brought into the picture.

This seems useful advice for future surveys to adopt, both for the analysis of moral codes and for sociological research in general. However, as we noted earlier, there is also a need to make further use of other available research techniques, again within the context

184

of the analysis of social structure and social institutions. The possibilities of more extensive and comparative content analyses of institutional documents, and of the construction of behavioural indices appropriate to organizational settings, both exemplify this. And there are other opportunities, some of which will be indicated in chapter 8.

Moreover, the further exploration and development of methods designed for the study of social collectivities of various kinds would appear to enhance the possibility of a more strategic and critical sociology, and also one that is more closely related to the central concerns of sociological theory. But such developments would need to begin with recognition of the fact that, as Galtung puts it: 'Neither theoretically nor methodologically has modern social science come to grips with what might be termed collective attitudes, as opposed to the individual attitudes of which we know a lot.'[90]


This completes our review of the research. We have outlined above a number of more qualitative criticisms of the empirical studies on values and moral codes. Our main points were concerned with the general lack of comparative approaches; the absence of a generally-accepted framework of theory; the selection of neutral, unstrategic areas for inquiry; the tendency also to avoid philosophical questions and distinctions, and, connected with this, to neglect the discursive aspects of moral codes; and finally, with the individualistic perspective implicit in most research designs, and, as we saw, related to the preponderance of survey methods.

As such, these considerations supplement the review of the research given in the earlier part of this chapter in which a series of characteristics of content and method were enumerated. Taken together, the various items mentioned interrelate to some degree to form a distinguishable style of research, with its characteristic virtues and deficits. For example, it is very much within the tradition of analytic, as opposed to holistic, sociology, and as such probably reveals its Western origins.[91] However, it is also a style that should benefit from more self-awareness and self-criticism, and it is to this end that the above assay in the sociology of sociology is principally directed.[92]

# 7  Empirical studies: I  Survey methods

## Introduction

In chapter 6 we reviewed a cross-section of the literature on the sociology of moral codes, principally with respect to those commentaries, theoretical and empirical studies concerned with social values. Particular attention was given to the empirical studies in this literature and our later comments and criticisms were directed mainly toward these. In this and the following chapter we shall discuss some representative examples of this research. In this way, we would hope to give more concrete specifications to some of the points already made, as well as to develop some further ones.

Attention was drawn in chapter 6 to the concentration of research initiative on interview and questionnaire methods and to the biases this may give rise to, and secondly to the lack of studies making use of more than one method of inquiry. In view of this, it seemed useful to indicate at least part of the broader range of research techniques that are available and applicable to the present subject. For, as we have observed, many of these are at present under-employed and could be further developed to serve the aims of this field of inquiry. The following discussion, therefore, has been organized according to distinct types of methodology, beginning, in the present chapter, with survey methods.

Naturally, a selective approach has been necessary, and we could not hope to exhaust the potential range of research instruments, let alone fully illustrate them. Rather, we have aimed to indicate some of the main alternatives available and to exemplify these with research projects of both a general interest and a particular relevance to the present subject.

For reasons of space, it similarly cannot be our concern here to

186

examine in detail the methodological and statistical properti each of these techniques. An extensive literature already exis these matters and, where relevant, reference has been made Clearly, any adequate summary of empirical research on the pr subject will entail a sizeable number of references. Wherever possible, therefore, the attempt has been made to restrict citations to some of the more significant or pertinent examples of research, rather than to present exhaustive lists for the category in question.

As was shown in chapter 6, the greater part of research in the present field has been carried out by means of either interviews or questionnaires, and occasionally by means of both. Our discussion, then, will begin with these methods. The two may be distinguished as involving, respectively, verbal (oral) responses to verbal stimuli, and written responses to written stimuli. Most of the literature on social science methodology has concentrated on the problems entailed by these two methods, and, since most of these issues are equally applicable to the study of moral attitudes, we need not repeat them here.[1]

### 'Open' v. 'closed' approaches

Attention need only be briefly drawn to one or two points that constantly recur in the present field, and that have relevance to some of our general arguments. Thus, discussions of these methods normally commence with an examination of the conditions under which questions (or stimuli in general) and responses should be structured. As might be expected, there is no invariant rule of procedure to be followed here. In general, the principal value of unstructured approaches is seen to reside in their greater *validity*, and that of structured approaches in their *reliability*. As a result, unstructured techniques are usually advised for use during the initial stages of research, during the period of delineating the problem-area more closely, of developing certain hypotheses about it, and carrying out the pilot survey. Whilst more structured techniques are favoured for the actual collection of data and verification of hypotheses. The majority of studies examined in the last chapter involved the use either of structured interview schedules, or of questionnaires that were relatively well-structured. Also, within any questionnaire or interview the tendency was for the 'open-ended' questions to occur at the beginning, to be followed by more structured items. It is generally useful to have at least some questions of the former kind, since, although they may not make for ease of coding and raise problems of standardization, they at least permit responses outside the conceptual framework one has, usually tacitly, adopted and hence may suggest novel lines of inquiry and interpretation.

This last point has particular relevance to the study of moral

187

attitudes, because of the tendency of social scientists to oversimplify, and thereby often distort, the respondent's viewpoint. Also, as Osgood (1967) states: 'The tendency of the human mind to project its own values and beliefs into others is now clearly recognized in the area of culture conflict; it is not so clearly recognized in the area of cross-national, social science research.'[2] But the distortion can occur in more subtle ways than this suggests. In particular, ethnocentric assumptions are likely to be made with regard to the discursive aspects of moral codes. For example, we discussed earlier an important distinction between intrinsic and extrinsic modes of justification. Yet in many studies it seems to be assumed that moral reasoning will concern itself exclusively with valued goals; as a result, justifications of an intrinsic kind are either ignored or treated as elliptical.[3]

The open-ended approach is perhaps particularly useful for cross-national and cross-cultural inquiries where it may act as a defence against ethnocentric preconception and bias. Indeed, an approach of this type would seem necessitated in the initial phases of research of this kind. A major limitation of open-ended methods, however, also concerns their possible suppression of the 'obvious', just as one of their advantages is the recognition they permit of novel attitudes and ways of reasoning. For example, Osgood (1967) cites the following problem encountered by Cantril's open-ended 'self-anchoring' device:[4]

'It should also be made clear that no claims are made that the Self-Anchoring Striving Scale gets at "everything" it is important to know about an individual . . . individuals do not mention aspects of life they take for granted—thus, for example, American college students tend not to mention a high standard of living, which they assume they will have, but on the other hand will talk about the place in society they want to attain or how they measure up to their own standards' (p. 25). In other words, the definition of 'good' and of 'bad' for self and country varies markedly with what one 'has' (or 'has-not') at the moment.

In a similar way, many moral attitudes have a normally 'taken-for-granted' status and so are unlikely to be volunteered in the absence of systematic questioning designed to elicit them. But this leads to a further consideration: namely, the fact that, in view of the conception of moral codes we proposed earlier, the cognitive assumptions which underlie these codes and the kind of justifications offered in support of them are important constituents for a full understanding of moral attitudes. A relatively unstructured approach is suggested for empirical inquiry into these in view of the, at least *a priori*, considerable difficulty implicit in the attempt to specify adequate response-categories for them.

In short, both the closed and the open-ended type of question have their own respective merits and demerits. The former establishes a common frame of reference and so generates results that are potentially more comparable. Thus, it is usually associated with higher degrees of reliability (both intrasubjective and intersubjective). In addition, structured questions offering explicit choices may encourage the inarticulate to reply, as well as avoiding the complexities and expenditure of time and money that coding responses to open questions can often entail. The merits of the unstructured approach, on the other hand, lie in its greater flexibility and lack of preconception on the part of the investigator (although this may be of more use for prediction than explanation). Hence, a greater degree of validity is often claimed for unstructured methods on these grounds. But this will depend in large part on the kind of response-categories that could be developed and in particular on the extent to which mutually exclusive and reasonably exhaustive categories can be provided for the particular items in question. This in turn will be a function of the subject-matter and purpose of the investigation and of the amount of information, theoretical and empirical, that one already possesses with regard to it. For example, if one is investigating the extent to which a particular community adhered to some of the well-defined tenets of Orthodox Judaism, a structured approach would seem quite feasible. If, on the other hand, one wishes to investigate a respondent's justifications for his expressed attitudes, then a set of pre-defined categories would seem likely to lead to bias and loss of information. An empirical illustration of the latter point has been provided by Achal (1958).[5]

To summarize: for inquiries confined to investigating specific values or precepts, no general *a priori* judgment can be made on the choice of open or closed instruments, except to note that the greater control offered by the structured approach seems to have been favoured by most studies in this field. On the other hand, for inquiries into the discursive aspects of moral codes, including the role of beliefs and cognitive assumptions, an open-ended approach would seem advisable in most cases, in part because of the lack of adequate theoretical treatments of these subjects and also because of the intrinsic difficulties they present for effective categorical treatment.

Cultural factors are, of course, also to be taken into account in any choice between these two polar types of instrument. For example, as Galtung observes:[6]

In some cultures, e.g. middle-class Mid-West USA, the population is so trained for social research, so well socialized as respondents, that it seems of no concern. But in other cultures, e.g. in the elite in developing countries, the difficulties in entering with social research are already considerable, and to add to them with excessive, and really unnecessary, pre-coding would be anti-methodological.

## The intensity of attitudes

Attitude measurement is usually distinguished from opinion-polling by the fact that the latter attempts merely to assess what proportion of the survey population verbally subscribe to a given opinion, whilst the former goes further and tries to measure the strength with which opinions are held or the more general attitude dimensions that they serve to indicate. Thus attitude measurement typically involves a range of questions bearing on a particular subject, the aggregate of replies being taken as the index of attitude. This procedure is subject to the usual principles of index construction, and so, given a certain level of semantic clarification, particular items may be differentially weighted as indicators of the attitude in question (e.g. 'achievement orientation', 'religiosity'). Although the latter is comparatively rarely carried out, it has obvious uses for the empirical study of moral codes, particularly in the case of those precepts and standards of evaluation that have a clear consensual definition.

In the second place, various values may be associated with the items. The most common type here is the two-valued question, in which statements, actions, etc. are evaluated in terms of such categories as true-false, right-wrong, agree-disagree. This is intended to duplicate the binary characteristics of judgment and decision-making in general. Thus, as Payne (1963) argues: 'whether we realize it or not, it is probably correct that even our complicated decisions are broken down into many separate two-way issues.'[7]

Dichotomous items also best satisfy the requirements of additivity and have the obvious advantage of simplicity. Their disadvantage is their inflexibility. Thus a trichotomy is required to allow for neutral and uncertain responses (including 'no answer's and 'don't know's). Such an approach is clearly necessary where there is a danger of forcing clear-cut responses upon subjects who in fact have no opinion either on the issue generally, or in terms of the alternatives portrayed. The dichotomous approach, on the other hand, is appropriate to situations in which a decision one way or the other has to be made (as in litigation) or for issues (e.g. capital punishment) that have polarized public opinion. In general, two-valued thinking appears most characteristic of those individuals with strong convictions on an issue, as well as of those with personalities that are 'intolerant of ambiguity', as in Adorno's model of the authoritarian personality and Rokeach's depiction of closed-mindedness.

But there is a further consideration here. Thus, it will be recalled that in our earlier discussion of the elements of a moral code (chapter 3) we observed that it is a common misconception to think of moralities in two- or three-valued terms: that is, as designating particular actions as simply prescribed or proscribed (or indifferent). Prescriptions are characterized by varying degrees of stringency. In a similar way, values may be rank-ordered, such that in certain situations (of value-conflict) a lesser value is sacrificed for the sake of realizing a higher-order one. It would appear necessary, therefore, to know wherever possible *how* positive or negative an evaluation is or *how* stringent a particular precept is thought to be. The number and kind of gradations recognized here will vary with the moral code in question. But for the study of moral prescriptions generally a 5-point scale would seem a minimal requirement, such as the following:

| (a) | (b) | (c) | (d) | (e) |
|---|---|---|---|---|
| absolutely must | preferably should | indifferent (may or may not) | preferably should not | absolutely must not |
| +2 | +1 | 0 | −1 | −2 |

Further gradations may be recognized, as in 7-point and 11-point scales. However, it becomes difficult in these cases to attach unambiguous verbal descriptions to each of the values, and so graphic presentations may be necessary (as in the semantic differential).[8] An interesting point which arises here, however, concerns the assumption of symmetry between the positive and negative halves of the scale. In fact, for many moral codes the evidence suggests that the notion of a continuum or of a number of gradations of stringency is more applicable to injunctions of various kinds than to proscriptions. Thus the former tend to be more vaguely defined and less absolutely stringent than the latter, reflecting the various connotations of 'ought' from actions that *must* be taken to others that are 'ideal' or simply 'preferable' in various senses. Hence in the above diagram we might expect the majority of responses to many characteristically moral issues to concentrate on categories (b) and (e).

Comparison is suggested at this point with some theoretical writings on attitude organization. For example, Rokeach (1960) emphasized the importance of examining the total belief-disbelief system and he characterized closed-mindedness primarily on the basis of the low differentiation of the disbelief system that it involved.[9] However, suffice it to say here that the relation between positive and negative prescriptions and evaluations, and the number and type of gradations recognized by each, as these vary with particular moral traditions, collectivities, and individuals, itself forms an important issue and one that is amenable to empirical investigation. And such

191

investigation would not only be of intrinsic value but would also aid the development of more informed and reliable principles of question design in attitude measurement.

To the extent that moral codes (informal and formal) are most validly characterized as comprising degrees of evaluation and gradations of moral preferableness, rather than a simple dichotomy between obligations and prohibitions, direct use can be made of the traditions of scale-construction in attitude research since one of the earliest concerns of this field has been the development of uni-dimensional scales from which the extremity or strength of attitudes could be estimated. The earliest scales of this kind derive from the work of Thurstone.[10] His technique involved listing a large number of opinion-statements considered to be relevant to the attitude under review, which were then ordered into 11 categories by a team of judges. These categories formed a scale ranging from extreme favourability to extreme unfavourability, such that the 'differences' between each category were judged to be equal. A number of criteria were then employed to ensure that the final scale, which was based on this ordering, matched the complete range of the original scale. Respondents were thus asked to indicate those statements with which they agreed and the individual's score was taken from the median scale value of the total number of the statements that he so indicated.

A modification on this technique was proposed by Likert.[11] In this version, a large number of statements were presented to a panel of judges who rated the strength of their agreement or disagreement with each item on a 5-point scale. The statements selected for the final scale were those whose scores showed the most consistency with the judges' own final scores for the original scale. A respondent's score on the final scale was assessed by the sum of his ratings of the strength of his agreement or disagreement with every item in the scale. One response to the problem of unidimensionality, i.e. of ensuring that all scale items measure the same attitude, has been the 'scalogram' technique of Guttman.[12] Scales developed by this method have a cumulative property such that if an individual were to agree with a statement at, say, the fourth position on a scale, he would almost certainly agree also with the items at the first three positions on the scale.

The techniques of Guttman, Likert, and Thurstone form the best-known methods of scale construction. However, other methods also exist and there is now a considerable literature on the subject.[13] Taken together, these methods have much potential value for the empirical study of moral attitudes, particularly since a number of inquiries have already indicated that 'moral' attitudes (and especially moral values) are amenable to measurement by techniques that yield similar degrees of reliability and validity to those attained by typical measures of other types of attitude.[14]

However, the ultimate test of the validity of an attitude scale remains that of whether it provides an accurate model of the social (or individual) reality that it purports to measure. And this raises questions of a general conceptual, as well as technical, nature. Thus, from our argument above it would seem that whichever of the available types of attitude scale is best suited for the analysis of at least relatively formalized moral codes will depend in part upon the nature of the code in question, the degrees of stringency it recognizes, and so on.

## Preliminary distinctions

Also to be drawn from the above argument is the general point that in attitude research on moral ideologies a number of preliminary philosophical distinctions need to be drawn in order to permit more valid descriptions of the data and a sounder basis for theory. The most basic requirement here is that of distinguishing explicitly between three types of response that are frequently confounded in attitude surveys: namely, cognitions, evaluations, and prescriptions. Each of these may be further discriminated according to degree of generality to yield the simple classification given in Table 7.1.

TABLE 7.1   *Categories of response to attitude questions*

|  | *Cognitive* | *Evaluative* | *Normative* |
| --- | --- | --- | --- |
| *General* | beliefs | values | general precepts[15] |
| *Specific* | knowledge | evaluations | prescriptions |

This is, of course, only a rudimentary typology. Yet it is important to discriminate between these basic analytic categories in attitude research, and also to investigate their interrelationships within particular moral ideologies. Further distinctions can also be drawn on this basis: for example, each category may be positively or negatively accented, and so on. But our main point here is that by making preliminary distinctions of this kind more systematic models can be developed of particular moral codes and of less complete sets of attitudinal data.

## Social desirability and response-sets

Another consideration may be introduced at this point. Thus, since the study of moral codes is, *per definitionem*, the study of what is most salient to the processes of evaluation and prescription associated with particular individuals, groups, and collectivities, and since moral standards frequently have significant affective components, it might seem that direct verbal methods of inquiry, whether by interview or questionnaire, are especially prone in this field to measure the respondent's wish for social approval. Indeed, to avoid this social desirability factor is a principal rationale for alternative techniques (e.g. observation) and for the use of indirect (and projective) questions.

But if this is a source of bias to which studies of moral attitudes are particularly susceptible, then it is also one that sophisticated research designs may incorporate for the purpose of measurement. Thus, the role of the social desirability factor in attitude research has been emphasized by Edwards (1957), but he also proposes an attitude scale for its assessment.[16] Subsequent measures of social desirability have focused upon different aspects of the problem, such as the scale constructed by Crowne and Marlowe (1960), which is intended to measure the need for social approval.[17] Taken together, these studies indicate that the principal dimensions of the social desirability response-set are themselves amenable to empirical measurement. In the second place, however, the research of Couch and Keniston (1960), Christie and Lindauer (1963), and Liberty et al. (1964) all suggests that social desirability is a factor independent of 'acquiescence' and that each is related to certain personality attributes.[18]

Acquiescence is the term normally used now to refer to the various forms of response-set: that is, of the tendency to give a certain type of response regardless of the stimulus. It is important to be able to distinguish this from genuine regularities of response: for example, a particular respondent might validly select the middle position on a broad range of issues. Thus, one should be able to estimate true response-set by, for example, noting the frequencies of certain response categories when questions are changed from positive to negative wording.

By the use of methods of this kind it has been shown that a great deal of response-set can be considered an artifact of the research instrument employed, and corrigible if the instrument is suitably adapted. In a classic statement of the issue, Cronbach (1946), for instance, found that acquiescence (in the sense of agreement with scale items, 'yes' responses, 'true' responses, etc.) occurred especially when the items were vague or ambiguous.[19] This was later confirmed by Banta (1961) and Peabody (1961) who both found that acquiescent response-set was virtually eliminated when scale items were free of ambiguity.[20]

However, in the case of studies of moral attitudes there is the particular problem of response-sets that are elicited by emotive words and phrases. For example, in certain contexts such a term as 'democracy' or 'communism' may evoke an automatic, unreflective type of response. Rephrasing items may solve this problem, but in some cases would entail cumbersome reformulations. Similarly, such emotive items could be excluded, but this is often at the price of triviality. Yet the problem does not seem ineradicable. In the first place, interviews and questionnaires may be redesigned in various ways to take account of it. Common strategies are to disperse questions of a similar type, or of similar linguistic content, so that they do not occur together in a schedule; to avoid simple response categories (e.g. by leaving certain questions open-ended); and (common in Likert scales) to formulate one half of the items negatively and the other half positively so that both positive and negative response-sets will finally concentrate in the middle category. Another method would be to request reason- or explanation-giving responses to certain items, rather than mere selections between different categories.

In the second place, however, we may assume that some cases in which emotive issues elicit automatic responses are not in fact artifacts of the method used but reflect a real tendency. Thus it has been shown in a number of studies that response-set is related to low education and social position generally, and so, as Frederiksen and Messick (1959) argue, it might often be validly interpreted as uncriticalness of judgment on the part of the respondent.[21] In addition, there is also a cultural factor to be taken into account: Jones (1963), for instance, has usefully drawn our attention to the operation of a 'courtesy bias' in surveys conducted in South-East Asia.[22] Matters of this kind will clearly need more investigation in order that valid surveys may be carried out in foreign cultures.

In sum, the problem of response-sets of various kinds is encountered by all types of attitude survey, including those concerned with moral attitudes. In so far as it does not represent a general, real-life tendency, however, the evidence suggests that response-set may be effectively controlled for by various modifications and refinements of research design.

## Emotional correlates

This still leaves the more general problem of data that is rendered biased and un-objective by virtue of the emotional correlates of moral views, and some comments may now be made on this. First of all, it should be noticed that affectivity does not equally characterize all types of response to moral issues. In our own culture at least, highly emotional reactions (guilt, shame, embarrassment, etc.) seem most frequently associated with negative rather than positive prescriptions, and also with prescriptions afforded a high degree of stringency. Combining these, we arrive at the classification shown in Figure 7.1.

195

FIGURE 7.1   *Emotional correlates of prescriptions*

|  |  | Type of prescription | |
| --- | --- | --- | --- |
|  |  | negative | positive |
| Degree of stringency | high | (i) | (ii) |
|  | low | (iii) | (iv) |

Key
(i) highest emotional saliency
(iv) lowest emotional saliency
(ii)/(iii) intermediate

Since both negative and highly stringent prescriptions tend also to be the most specific, the above ordering would seem to be in part a function of this degree of specificity and thereby of the relative 'visibility' (intra- and intersubjective) of violations and non-performances of precepts. Of course, research also indicates that emotional saliency is correlated with the general intensity of attitudes. This has been demonstrated in the field of race prejudice, for instance, by means of physiological measurements of emotional reactions (e.g. Cooper and Pollock, 1959).[23]

It is important to allow, therefore, for the influence of emotional variables in the measurement of moral attitudes. Various norms of procedure have relevance here. In the case of question sequence, for example, the complex, critical, or emotional part of the interview or questionnaire normally occurs in the middle phase, between the easier introductory items and concluding section. This sequence seems the most efficient for maintaining rapport, particularly in protracted studies.[24]

Similarly, a number of interview techniques are available for asking the 'embarrassing question'. As summed up by Barton (1958), these include (i) the casual approach, (ii) the numbered card, (iii) the 'everybody' approach, (iv) the 'other people' approach, (v) the sealed ballot technique, (vi) projective methods, (vii) the Kinsey technique, and (viii) putting the question at the close of the interview.[25] Although all these techniques may be used in interviews, some of them are perhaps better employed in the context of questionnaires. However, the greater flexibility of the interview provides a wider variety of means for establishing the necessary rapport. This same flexibility also means that it is possible to record emotional reactions in the interview situation. Since such reactions show interesting differences from individual to individual,[26] and from culture to culture (as in the relative saliency of 'guilt' and 'shame'),[27] this can provide valuable information on the dynamics of moral codes at the social and personal level.

## Question-wording

In view of the refinement of modern survey methods it is surprising how little systematic attention has been given to the important issue of question-wording. There are, of course, a number of familiar rules of thumb, such as the need to phrase questions simply, unambiguously, and in language familiar to the respondent. But few studies have examined the variations in response that may be produced by the alternation of apparently equivalent terms. As we have seen, this is particularly pertinent to our present concerns in view of the emotive connotations of much moral language. Often these connotations are subtle enough to demand investigation on their own behalf: for instance, through the use of a semantic differential format.[28] Certainly, we should not assume a priori that 'correct' translation within a language system, as well as between different languages,[29] is not sufficiently sensitive to generate by itself major differences in response. This problem is heightened in the case of relatively formalized moral codes because of the systemic, mutually coherent, nature of the attitudes which they encompass.[30] In these cases, then, one needs to know the broader matrix of values, precepts, and beliefs in order to comprehend adequately the specific attitudes that may be expressed.

As we have said, few studies have examined these issues. One inquiry which did so, however, is cited in Payne (1963) and may be mentioned here as an illustration. In this, an American sample was asked the question: 'Do you think the United States should allow public speeches against democracy?' A comparable sample was then questioned on what would appear formally to be the same issue, phrased as follows: 'Do you think the United States should forbid public speeches against democracy?' In theory, since one question is the opposite of the other we should expect the pattern of responses to be similarly reversed. In fact, however, the results were as shown in Table 7.2.[31]

It is evident here that the different connotations of the words 'forbid' and 'allow' served to elicit distinctive patterns of response. In this particular case, one might expect more valid results if the two alternatives implied by the question were both made explicit. What this example indicates more generally, however, is the need to tap attitudes through a series of items, rather than with only one formulation. This is particularly true where the attitudes concern 'sensitive'

197

issues. Thus, in the above example a number of different types and contexts of anti-democratic activity could have been specified and respondents asked to evaluate (or prescribe for) each of these in turn. An individual's overall attitude could then be assessed by some aggregate score of all his responses. Put otherwise, it would appear that the study of complex and/or emotion-laden attitudes, where the subject may not be able to assess, or even express, his own views objectively, particularly requires the development of suitable attitude scales, and not just opinion surveys. Of course, wherever possible it is also preferable that these techniques be supplemented by other methods, such as those of observation and, where relevant, content analysis.

TABLE 7.2  *An illustration of the effects of question-wording*

| Qn 1: Do you think the United States should allow public speeches against democracy? | | Qn 2: Do you think the United States should forbid public speeches against democracy? | |
|---|---|---|---|
| *Responses:* | % | | % |
| Should allow | 21 | Should not forbid | 39 |
| Should not allow | 62 | Should forbid | 46 |
| No opinion | 17 | No opinion | 15 |

However, in so far as direct verbal methods of data-collection are utilized the problem of the differential effects of formally equivalent expressions must be taken into account. Research will therefore usually be needed on the respondents' general semantic frame of reference and linguistic ability: these matters, of course, will enter at the stage of the pilot survey. Thus, as Payne (1963) states: 'If all the problems of question wording could be traced to a single source, their common origin would probably prove to be in taking too much for granted.'[32] The examination of what *is* 'taken for granted' in the structure and content of moral discourse is also central to the concerns of analytic moral philosophy and so this subject should provide us with various conceptual refinements and clarifications that have relevance here. One reason little attention has been given to these problems so far is that, at least with regard to studies of values and other aspects of moral codes, survey methods have directed much of their sampling towards student populations, where issues of this kind are less salient. It is therefore worth attending to the comment of Webb *et al.* (1968) to the effect that 'A considerable proportion of the populace is functionally illiterate for personality and attitude tests developed on college populations.'[33]

## Interviewer effects

Most of the issues of methodology we have considered above derive ultimately from the status of interviews and questionnaires as 'intrusive' measures. Each involves a process of two-way interaction, whether interpersonal, as in the interview, or symbolic, as in the questionnaire. In each case, the respondent manifests his attitude or reaction in response to a stimulus, either in the form of an interviewer's question or an item on a questionnaire. The problem arises, therefore, of the extent to which the nature of the instrument, and the conditions under which it is applied, either contaminate or even determine the responses so obtained. To some degree, the amount of distortion that is being introduced can be measured and controlled for. For example, there is a great deal of literature on the effect of the interviewer in terms of such attributes as social class, age, sex, race and appearance.[34] Biases from this source would seem at least as likely to occur in the study of moral attitudes, if not more so. Consider the possible effects of male and female interviewers in surveys of sexual attitudes and practices, or of the role of ethnicity in studies of prejudice. Less obvious examples might be the role of the age of the interviewer in gathering data on achievement-orientation, or religiosity. The most practical solution to problems of this kind is to include interviewer variables, wherever possible, in the final data so that an estimate can be made of their possible influences. But even here the remedy will only be a partial one. To quote Webb *et al.* again: 'Some of the major biases, such as race, are easily controllable; other biases, such as the interaction of age and sex, are less easily handled. If we heeded all the known biases, without considering our ignorance of major interactions, there could no longer be a simple survey.'[35]

## Questionnaires v. interviews

One solution to the problem of interviewer effects (which can never be fully identified with certainty) is to resort to questionnaires, for which reactivity problems in general are lessened. The question arises, therefore, as to whether a questionnaire format is generally preferable to the interview as a means of investigating moral views. It is difficult to assay a general answer to this question since much will depend on the nature of the study in question and its purposes. The primary advantage of the questionnaire is the standardization it permits. Questionnaires are normally received under 'anonymous', comparable conditions that are free of all interviewer effects. Thus the standards of reliability are usually higher for questionnaires than for interviews. On the other hand, the interview is clearly the more flexible instrument. Probes and follow-up questions can be more effectively introduced in it, and the influences of a wider range of stimuli can be assessed: e.g. interviewer status and manner, question-wording and sequence, and so on. Similarly, interviews better facilitate studies of attitudes in depth, and the recording (manually or on tape) of a broader range of responses, including emotional reactions, tone of voice, and other non-verbal indicators. In addition, questionnaires are obviously ruled out for countries and social strata characterized either by illiteracy or by very low degrees of literacy.[36]

In sum, the choice of method will be largely dictated by the type and conditions of inquiry. For example, where investigations into moral codes are (i) concerned with questions to which there is a common frame of reference and a limited, consensually-accepted range of possible answers or responses (as is the case with most factual questions); (ii) where the population sampled is relatively well-trained in the techniques of literacy and the manipulation of verbal symbols; and (iii) where the sample has a relatively homogeneous composition, the preferable method might well be considered to be the structured questionnaire. Studies of reactions to a number of recent 'liberal' issues (e.g. law reforms on capital punishment and abortion) among college students exemplify these conditions.

If, on the other hand, inquiry is being made into the *discursive* aspects of moral codes, into questions of moral reasoning and the justification of expressed views, and also if the items being examined are likely to be judged embarrassing, or to evoke low response-rates for other reasons, the greater flexibility of the interview recommends itself as the more appropriate method. In particular, for the investigation of reason-why and explanation-requesting questions a relatively unstructured format would seem advisable, at least for the initial studies of a specific population or issue. This, as we have seen, is in view of the lack of theoretical knowledge of these subjects, together with the intrinsic difficulties of providing adequate response categories for them, such that either loss or distortion of data will not ensue. Here relatively extended, 'depth' interviews can be employed, and responses tape-recorded if necessary, with a full use of probes and follow-up questions to clarify meanings at various points and to correct misunderstandings, whereas the same procedure by means of relatively open-ended questionnaires would presuppose comparatively high degrees of linguistic skill and so entail considerable population restrictions.

From this, three further points suggest themselves. First, in view of the requirements it makes on linguistic ability, the relative importance of the questionnaire method in this field, noted in the last chapter, would appear artificially enhanced by the disproportionate number of studies that have been conducted on student populations. Second, this emphasis on structured questionnaires in the literature may itself have acted to discourage empirical interest in the discursive aspects of moral codes in favour of more discrete attitudinal data. And finally, a useful research design that suggests itself for the present subject is to apply the methods of the interview and questionnaire in consort. Thus semi-structured interviews could be employed at the early stages of the research process to gather general background information. From this information relatively structured questionnaires could then be developed and used as a means for gaining controlled data on respondents' attitudes to a wide range of issues. After these results have been processed, relatively open interview techniques could then be utilized for more intensive follow-ups to the attitudes revealed, with regard to their conceptual interrelationships and the reasoning processes that underlie them. Where large samples are involved, of course, adequate realization of this last stage is likely to be both expensive and time-consuming. In such cases, therefore, it might be useful to focus research attention instead on sub-samples that are characterized by distinctive attitude profiles (e.g. after factorial analysis). It is best, then, not to view these two methods as mutually exclusive. By means of designs such as the one suggested, the flexibility of the interview and the standardization of the questionnaire can be used to enhance each other's value.

## The Q-sort

One answer to the problem of differential articulacy, encountered by both open-ended interview and questionnaire, is the *Q-sort* method. This consists of a series of cards containing ideas or statements, or, occasionally, pictures, that are presented to the respondent for rank-ordering in terms of their relative 'truth', 'desirability', etc. Often respondents are asked to provide different types of ordering: for example, a list of possible priorities may be given and the subject asked to indicate their actual order in his life, their ideal order, how his parents or colleagues would order them, and so on. Since the Q-sort is mainly used in conjunction with written statements it is essentially similar to the structured questionnaire, and so requires no special treatment here. Thus, there is still the need to eliminate overlapping items and to present mutually exclusive and balanced choices. Similarly, there is the problem of response-sets: respondents often tend to overselect the extremes. The order of presentation, therefore, needs to be alternated with different subjects. In addition, a large number of cards cannot normally be used since, for many individuals, this would assume too great a degree of discriminative ability.

The particular advantage of the Q-sort as a method of inquiry for our present subject lies in the uses to which it can be put for the investigation of embarrassing questions or sensitive issues for which a degree of confidentiality is preferable. For example, Dr Belson and associates (1969) employed a modified card-sorting procedure to derive information about the variety and extent of stealing among adolescent boys.[37] In this, 44 cards were used and on each of them was a description of one class of stealing (e.g. 'I have stolen from work'). Preparatory work had indicated that these tended to cover the full range of juvenile stealing. Each of the respondents was separated from the investigator by a sorting screen, through which the cards were individually passed. If the subject had ever done what was on the card, he was to put the card in the 'Yes' box and if never, in all his life, he was to put it in the 'Never' box. Anonymity of the respondents was maintained and the confidentiality and safety of the procedure for the boy stressed throughout. In a reliability test, in which one sample (146) was twice subjected to the procedure, with approximately a week between applications, an overall 88 per cent consistency was found in the way in which the cards were sorted into the 'Yes' and 'Never' boxes.

Further details of sorting techniques, and of interview and questionnaire methods generally, are to be found in a number of methodology texts. There is now an extensive literature on survey methods of inquiry and a substantial number of empirical studies into various points of methodology. However, although some progress has recently been made in this direction, many of these observations and norms of empirical procedure still tend to be somewhat discrete and *ad hoc*, and their value would be greatly enhanced if they could be brought together within a more inclusive theoretical interpretation of survey methodology. For example, there is still some validity in Moser's (1958) observation that: 'Surveys would be greatly strengthened if there were a more scientific basis to question design; if the choice between the alternative forms of a question could more often be based on theoretical principles or on firm empirical evidence.'[38] And also in the earlier comment of Cannell and Kahn (1953) that 'Unfortunately, social science has not yet provided us with a comprehensive, integrated theory which enables us to understand completely the communication process and the interaction between interviewer and respondent.'[39]

Some of the limitations of the survey method, however, such as its inherent 'reactivity', can only be resolved adequately by an appeal to other methods. A number of these will be examined in the next chapter. For the present, we may look at some of the characteristic features of the way in which survey methods are actually employed to gather data on values and other aspects of moral codes.

## Surveys of values: comments and examples

It will be recalled that in the last chapter it was shown that approximately two-thirds (65 per cent) of the empirical studies in our sample had adopted either the interview or the questionnaire as a means of data-collection. The main use to which these methods were put was that of providing information on the social structuring of values and other attitudes at the level of the individual. The conceptual model was essentially that of a series of background social variables (education, religion, ethnicity, etc.) exercising a (largely unconscious) 'causal' influence upon manifest attitudes. We introduce inverted commas here since correlation patterns, of course, however statistically significant, do not of themselves provide sufficient grounds for the imputation of causality. Rather, their function is an indicative one, although a great deal of the research tends to assume that what relations they do indicate must necessarily be of substantive import.

In addition, it needs to be recognized that most of these inquiries focus upon the explanation (or simply description) of attitudinal differences among individuals and groups. The aim is to *discriminate* responses according to variables characterizing the respondents. Thus, even at the stage of the pre-test or pilot survey highly consensual items are normally rejected on the grounds that they will have no function in the analysis, since analysis is based on *covariation* and covariation presupposes variation in both variables.[40] This is sound procedure given the avowed purposes of inquiry. But it can easily lead to a neglect of consensual items that may themselves constitute findings of considerable empirical and theoretical significance. Thus, the discriminative power of a variable (attitude-dimension, etc.) in correlation analysis is normally taken as an index of its theoretical and explanatory significance. The result is that such research may generate an artificial impression of dissensus in society.

We have noted in chapter 4 that the factor of consensus is central to the sociological concept of culture as a system of shared meanings, and thus to a number of its correlates in social science. The integral role of consensus, real and perceived, within microsociological processes (e.g. small-group dynamics) and for the depiction of total societies (cf. cultural pluralism) and higher-order collectivities should be apparent.[41] But this still seems to await recognition in the selection of topics and lines of analysis in social research. The need here, as elsewhere, is for a closer analytic *rapprochement* between theory and empirical research. For if the model of society implicit in social research is probably overly conflictful and atomistic, then this is in contrast with the image presented by much sociological theory, in which the extent of normative integration in society is equally overstated.

In fact, of course, the degree of consensus over a number of items or categories of individuals may not only be presented as a finding in its own right, but may itself be taken as a variable for analysis and systematically related to other social variables. This is rarely done in research. Inter-individual or inter-group agreement usually appears as a residual finding in the form of zero correlations, or correlations substantially below significance level. But the absence of correlations may have as much conceptual significance as their presence. As Galtung writes: 'First of all, analysts must try to overcome the bias in favor of correlations and the neglect of zero correlations. There is a tendency to see only correlations as problematic and worthy of being "explained" and to see absence of correlations as absence of "findings", and hence as unproblematical.'[42]

In few surveys, then, has the question of consensus formed one of the central objects of inquiry. A useful paper by Larson and Sutker (1966), however, illustrates some of the insights that may accrue from altering this strategy.[43] The authors report the results of interviewing a cross-section (N=142) of the population of a Mid-West American city concerning the ranking of fourteen occupations and fourteen general desiderata (i.e. owning a home, cleanliness, having children, being respected by people, etc.). Their findings indicated that respondents manifested greater agreement in ranking the occupations than the desiderata; that the upper socio-economic respondents differed in their values from the lower-level respondents, but with fewer differences in occupational rankings than in desiderata; and thirdly, that the amount of value-agreement, reflecting consensus, varied in direct relation to socio-economic status. This last finding is of particular interest since there are a number of theoretical principles, associated with rank theory, to suggest that degree of consensus will correlate positively with social class.[44] Further research, however, could facilitate more refined analyses by distinguishing between different types of consensus, rather than treating it as a single, homogeneous category. The exploration of the distinction between real and perceived consensus on the more microsociological level is perhaps the most obvious example here.[45]

In sum, we should not necessarily assume that the discriminative value of a variable in correlation analysis is the sole indicator of its theoretical significance in research. Rather, there is a need to supplement present research with more explicit analyses of patterns of agreement. In this way, perhaps the division that exists between the prevailing style of empirical research and theoretical approaches to 'cultural' phenomena (e.g. with regard to the process of 'objectivation') can be bridged, to the mutual benefit of each.

But, as we saw in the last chapter, closer ties with theoretical concerns require also that empirical research adopt a more structural frame of reference. And to some extent the very individualism of the survey method militates against this. We say 'to some extent' since various possibilities in the form of more purposive sampling also exist. Thus it would be useful to see more studies of the ideologies of individuals selected as *representatives* of various social institutions and role-systems. Inquiries of this kind, focusing upon particular role-incumbents in the government, education system, judiciary and so on, would seem to permit a more structural reference. Of course, such a procedure would require some revision of the usual sampling criteria, which so far have emphasized the need for random selections from the mass population. In particular, it would involve more élite-oriented uses of the survey method.

An annotated review of the full range of empirical studies into various aspects of moral codes that have made use of either the interview or the questionnaire is obviously beyond the scope of the present study. And any attempt to summarize the main findings is hampered by the lack of any overall theoretical integration of this research. Almost all that we can say is that certain foci of research initiative, in the form of recognizable clusters of subject-matter/method/type of population, do tend to occur, as a perusal of some of the data in chapter 6 will serve to suggest. More conceptual inter-coherence is to be found in these distinctive sub-fields of inquiry since, after a while, traditions of research and theoretical guidelines, however rudimentary, do begin to emerge.

For example, one such field of inquiry is that of the use of survey techniques to diagnose the influence of the process, and institutional context, of higher education upon the values and attitudes of college students. Some of the more notable studies here would include those by Goldsen (1960), Jacob (1962), and Turner (1964).[46] A useful summary and critique of this work is given in A. H. Barton's monograph, *Studying the Effects of College Education* (1965). Amongst other findings, most of this research has stressed the tendency of the educational environment to homogenize attitudes in the direction of the prevailing consensus, but has cast some doubt on the extent of direct change effected by the experience of education. This area of inquiry also merits mention on the grounds that it accounts for a high proportion of the available longitudinal studies of value- and attitude-change in individuals and groups. However, as elsewhere in the research, little indication is usually given of the possible behavioural manifestations of expressed attitudes. Naturally, the latter is outside the scope of survey methods. But it also appears that the research literature has considerably under-employed the possibilities that these methods do present for the investigation of reported behaviours, both with regard to the subject's account of others' actions and also of his own.

he aggregation of proto-theoretical traditions in specific sub-
such as the above, is the exception rather than the rule. As we
in the last chapter, taken as a whole, the empirical research on
s exhibits a generally 'atheoretical' character. Hypotheses tend
e developed *ad hoc* and almost the only common conceptual
frames of reference that cut across specific subjects are those provided
by a number of recurrent typologies. Of these, the schemes of Allport
and Vernon (1951) and Kluckhohn and Strodbeck (1961), which we
outlined earlier, were respectively the most frequently used.

In the study by Tagiuri (1965), for example, the Allport-Vernon
Scale of Values was applied in structured interviews to distinguish the
value-orientations of scientists and industrial managers during the
period of the Harvard Advanced Management Program in 1960–4.[47]
The differences between the two groups were, in fact, found to be
negligible, although exaggerated in each group's perception of the
other. A more comparative survey, which employed the Allport-
Vernon Scale in questionnaire form, was reported in *Sociological
Analysis* for the same year (1965).[48] In this the hypothesis was derived
from Oscar Lewis's observation that the 'culture of poverty' trans-
cends regional and national differences. A partial test of this was
provided by postulating a greater similarity of scores for students of
the same social class in two cities in North and South America (i.e.
Chicago and Lima, Peru) than for students in different classes within
each culture. 480 students (half from each city) were matched for
sex, religion, and social class and presented with the questionnaires
on personal values. The results showed that the consensus was intra-
class rather than intracultural, thus confirming the initial hypothesis.

An illustrative application of Kluckhohn and Strodbeck's questionnaire is provided by the research carried out by Liu (1966) in
Hong Kong.[49] In this study samples were drawn of adolescents in the
tenth and twelfth grades at three high schools, and their responses
to the various items were compared with those of their parents.
The findings indicated a shift in the attitudes of youth to individualism and an orientation to the future, but also evidenced considerable
ambivalence toward the 'traditional' outlook of their parents. Very
similar findings were also discovered in an earlier study of Japanese
youth by Caudill and Scarr (1962), which employed the same method,
derived from Kluckhohn and Strodbeck and adapted to the Japanese
context, and also involved comparisons with parental standards.[50]

## Class and values: Kohn's study

Despite the inherent individualism, and the other limitations of the
dominant style of social research, it is evident that studies of the
social structuring of moral attitudes by means of survey methods

could have a greater theoretical relevancy. Within these terms, one of the aspects of the social correlates of values and other moral attitudes which is of the most general theoretical interest to social science is surely that which concerns the moral codes associated with different social classes. Such work forms part of the study of the subjective correlates of social class and raises a number of familiar questions. How distinct are the classes in these terms? How valid is the thesis of a gradual process of *embourgeoisiement*? How applicable is the notion of 'false consciousness'?

In fact, in spite of the central and indeed protean status of both the concept of class and that of values in social science, there is still relatively little reliable data on their possible interrelationships. The empirical inquiries that have been carried out on this subject are limited in scope, both in respect of the nature of the samples and of the range of attitudes studied, and are rarely cross-cultural. And the danger here as elsewhere of non-comparative research is that of the implicitly partisan viewpoint, representative of a single nation, or ideology. However, accepting these limitations, mention may be made of the studies by Duvall (1946), Aberle and Naegele (1952), Hyman (1953), Kohn (1959), Sugarman (1966), and Swift (1967).[51]

Kohn's (1959) study is reasonably typical of the investigations of this kind and is also more broadly representative of the literature on the social structuring of values, sharing some of its characteristic merits and demerits. We may close the present chapter on survey methods, therefore, with a description of this particular inquiry.

Conducted in Washington D.C., Kohn's study aimed to sample approximately 200 representative white 'middle-class' and 'working-class' families, each with a child in the fifth grade (i.e. 10–11 years old). Each family's social class position was determined by the Hollingshead Index of Social Position, the father's occupational status (the most usual indicator of class) being assigned a weight of 7, and his educational status a weight of 4. Hollingshead's Classes I—III were operationally defined as middle class, and his Classes IV and V as working class.

The scope of the inquiry was restricted to those values parents would most like to see embodied in their children's behaviour. The procedure was that parents were asked to choose, from among a range of alternative attributes that might be judged desirable, those few which they considered most important for a child of the appropriate age (i.e. 10–11 years). Each parent was presented with a list of seventeen characteristics that had been suggested by other parents during the pre-test as highly desirable, the order in which they were given varying from interview to interview. They were then asked, 'Which three of the things listed on this card would you say are the *most* important in a boy (or girl) of (fifth-grade child's) age?' The

207

selection of a particular characteristic was taken as the index of value.

The main results are presented in Table 7.3. From this it can be seen that middle- and working-class mothers shared a broadly common set of values. Thus, it is evident that appreciable consensus exists in both social classes that happiness and such standards of conduct as honesty, consideration, obedience, dependability, manners, and self-control are highly desirable for both boys and girls at this age. Relatively few respondents, on the other hand, chose ambition, ability to defend oneself, affectionate responsiveness, being liked by adults, ability to play by one's self, or seriousness as highly desirable at this age, although these items might, of course, become more highly valued for children of other ages, or for adults.

Aside from this general agreement, however, some class-specific attitudes are also indicated in this Table. Thus, significantly fewer working-class mothers regarded happiness as highly desirable for *boys* of the present age category. Working-class respondents were also more likely to value obedience: they would have their children responsive to parental authority. This latter finding has also been confirmed by other studies and accounts of 'working-class culture'.[52] Middle-class mothers, on the other hand, were more likely to value consideration and self-control: they would have their children develop inner control and sympathetic concern for others. In addition, middle-class mothers were more likely to regard curiosity as a primary virtue. Whilst working-class mothers put the emphasis upon neatness and cleanliness, valuing the imaginative and exploring child relatively less than the socially presentable one.

In the second place, it is evident that middle-class respondents' conceptions of what is desirable for boys largely match their conceptions of what is desirable for girls. Working-class respondents, however, make a clear distinction between the sexes. They are more likely to regard dependability, being a good student, and ambition as desirable for boys, and to regard happiness, good manners, neatness, and cleanliness as desirable for girls.[53]

Kohn also examined some of the interrelationships among the values. Thus, significant differences were noted between middle- and working-class parents in the way in which their choice of any one characteristic is related to their choice of each of the others.[54] Information on this is given in Table 7.4. A number of observations may be made on this. For example, it can be seen that despite the consensus across the classes on the value of honesty, this value is quite differently related to the choice of other characteristics in the two classes. In this case, it is not so much the specific values as certain components of the presumptive value-*system* that are class-specific. Thus, middle-class respondents who chose honesty were more likely than other middle-class subjects to regard consideration,

TABLE 7.3 *Proportion of mothers who select each characteristic as one of three 'most desirable' in a 10- or 11-year-old child*

| CHARACTERISTICS | FOR BOYS | | FOR GIRLS | | COMBINED | |
|---|---|---|---|---|---|---|
| | Middle class | Working class | Middle class | Working class | Middle class | Working class |
| 1 That he is honest | 0·44 | 0·57 | 0·44 | 0·48 | 0·44 | 0·53 |
| 2 That he is happy | 0·44* | 0·27 | 0·48 | 0·45 | 0·46* | 0·36 |
| 3 That he is considerate of others | 0·40 | 0·30 | 0·38* | 0·24 | 0·39* | 0·27 |
| 4 That he obeys his parents well | 0·18* | 0·37 | 0·23 | 0·30 | 0·20* | 0·33 |
| 5 That he is dependable | 0·27 | 0·27 | 0·20 | 0·14 | 0·24 | 0·21 |
| 6 That he has good manners | 0·16 | 0·17 | 0·23 | 0·32 | 0·19 | 0·24 |
| 7 That he has self-control | 0·24 | 0·14 | 0·20 | 0·13 | 0·22* | 0·13 |
| 8 That he is popular with other children | 0·13 | 0·15 | 0·17 | 0·20 | 0·15 | 0·18 |
| 9 That he is a good student | 0·17 | 0·23 | 0·13 | 0·11 | 0·15 | 0·17 |
| 10 That he is neat and clean | 0·07 | 0·13 | 0·15* | 0·28 | 0·11* | 0·20 |
| 11 That he is curious about things | 0·20* | 0·06 | 0·15 | 0·07 | 0·18* | 0·06 |
| 12 That he is ambitious | 0·09 | 0·18 | 0·06 | 0·08 | 0·07 | 0·13 |
| 13 That he is able to defend himself | 0·13 | 0·05 | 0·06 | 0·08 | 0·10 | 0·06 |
| 14 That he is affectionate | 0·03 | 0·05 | 0·07 | 0·04 | 0·05 | 0·04 |
| 15 That he is liked by adults | 0·03 | 0·05 | 0·07 | 0·04 | 0·05 | 0·04 |
| 16 That he is able to play by himself | 0·01 | 0·02 | 0·00 | 0·03 | 0·01 | 0·02 |
| 17 That he acts in a serious way | 0·00 | 0·01 | 0·00 | 0·00 | 0·00 | 0·01 |
| N | (90) | (85) | (84) | (80) | (174) | (165) |

* Social-class differences statistically significant, 0·05 level or better, using chi-squared test.
From M. L. Kohn (1959), op. cit, p. 339.

manners, and (for boys) dependability as highly desirable; and, similarly, those respondents who regarded any of these as desirable were more likely to value honesty highly. Consideration, in turn, is positively related to self-control, and manners to neatness. Kohn summarizes this as follows: 'Honesty, then, is the core of a *set* of standards of conduct, a set consisting primarily of honesty, consideration, manners, and dependability, together with self-control and neatness. As such, it is to be seen as one among several, albeit the central, standards of conduct that middle-class mothers want their children to adopt.'

He observes further, however, that[55]

This is not the case for working-class mothers. Those who regard honesty as predominantly important are not especially likely to think of consideration, manners, or dependability as comparable in importance; nor are those who value any of these especially likely to value honesty. Instead the mothers who are most likely to attribute importance to honesty are those that are concerned that the child be happy, popular, and able to defend himself. It is not that the child should conduct himself in a considerate, mannerly, or dependable fashion but that he should *be* happy, *be* esteemed by his peers, and, if the necessity arise, *be* able to protect himself. It suggests that honesty is treated less as a standard of conduct and more as a quality of the person; the emphasis is on being a person of inherent honesty rather than on acting in an honest way.

To specify more closely the relationship of social class to values, Kohn further subdivided his class samples on the basis of other familiar social variables, including status, religious affiliation, educational attainment, and rural/urban background. Although each of these exercised an influence upon the choice of characteristics, and so permitted a more precise description of the relationship between social class and values, the original variable of class-position still seemed to provide the single most relevant line of demarcation. In addition, parents were questioned on their actions when their children behaved in disvalued ways. These self-reports indicated that parents were more likely to punish behaviour that seemed to violate those values for which they had professed high regard. However, the relative 'disinterestedness' of the parents' choice of values was also suggested by the fact that there appeared to be no relationship between the selection of a specific characteristic and the tendency to rate the behaviour of one's own child as either high or low on that characteristic.

TABLE 7.4 *All cases\* where mothers' choice of one characteristic as 'desirable' is significantly related to their choice of any other characteristic as 'desirable'.*

| | | MIDDLE-CLASS MOTHERS | | |
|---|---|---|---|---|
| | | | Proportion who choose B among those who: | |
| *Characteristic* | | | *Do Not* | |
| A | B | *Choose A* ($p_1$) | *Choose A* ($p_{11}$) | $p_1/p_{11}$ |
| *Positive relationships:* | | | | |
| 1 Honesty | Consideration | 0·42 | 0·37 | 1·14 |
| 2 Honesty | Manners | 0·22 | 0·16 | 1·38 |
| 3 Honesty | Dependability (boys) | 0·33 | 0·22 | 1·50 |
| 4 Consideration | Honesty | 0·47 | 0·42 | 1·12 |
| 5 Manners | Honesty | 0·52 | 0·43 | 1·21 |
| 6 Dependability | Honesty (boys) | 0·54 | 0·41 | 1·32 |
| 7 Consideration | Self-control | 0·24 | 0·22 | 1·09 |
| 8 Self-control | Consideration | 0·41 | 0·39 | 1·05 |
| 9 Manners | Neatness | 0·24 | 0·08 | 3·00 |
| 10 Neatness | Manners | 0·42 | 0·16 | 2·63 |
| 11 Curiosity | Happiness | 0·58 | 0·43 | 1·35 |
| 12 Happiness | Curiosity | 0·23 | 0·14 | 1·64 |
| 13 Happiness | Ambition (boys) | 0·13 | 0·06 | 2·17 |
| *Negative relationships:* | | | | |
| 1 Honesty | Popularity | 0·04 | 0·24 | 0·17 |
| 2 Popularity | Honesty | 0·12 | 0·50 | 0·24 |
| 3 Curiosity | Obedience | 0·03 | 0·24 | 0·13 |
| 4 Obedience | Consideration | 0·17 | 0·45 | 0·38 |
| | | WORKING-CLASS MOTHERS | | |
| *Positive relationships:* | | | | |
| 1 Happiness | Honesty | 0·51 | 0·55 | 0·93 |
| 2 Popularity | Honesty | 0·62 | 0·51 | 1·22 |
| 3 Honesty | Popularity | 0·20 | 0·14 | 1·43 |
| 4 Honesty | Defend self | 0·07 | 0·05 | 1·40 |
| 5 Consideration | Manners (girls) | 0·42 | 0·30 | 1·40 |
| 6 Manners | Consideration (girls) | 0·31 | 0·20 | 1·55 |
| 7 Consideration | Curiosity | 0·11 | 0·04 | 2·75 |
| 8 Ambition | Dependability | 0·29 | 0·19 | 1·53 |
| 9 Happiness | Consideration (boys) | 0·35 | 0·27 | 1·30 |
| 10 Consideration | Happiness (boys) | 0·32 | 0·25 | 1·28 |
| 11 Happiness | Popularity (girls) | 0·25 | 0·16 | 1·56 |
| *Negative relationships:* | | | | |
| 1 Obedience | Popularity | 0·05 | 0·24 | 0·21 |
| 2 Manners | Popularity | 0·00 | 0·23 | 0·00 |
| 3 Consideration | Popularity | 0·02 | 0·23 | 0·09 |
| 4 Popularity | Obedience | 0·10 | 0·38 | 0·26 |
| 5 Popularity | Manners | 0·00 | 0·29 | 0·00 |
| 6 Popularity | Consideration | 0·03 | 0·32 | 0·09 |
| 7 Manners | Dependability (girls) | 0·00 | 0·20 | 0·00 |

\* Where it is not specified whether the relationship holds for boys or for girls, it holds for both sexes. In each case, $p_1$ and $p_{11}$ are based on a minimum of 20 instances. *Source:* Kohn, op. cit., p. 343.

The main findings, then, are that (i) parents, whatever their social class, consider it very important that their children be honest, happy, considerate, obedient, and dependable; and (ii) parents' manifest values are related to their social position, and in particular to their class position.

The question arises, therefore, of how this relationship between parents' social position and their values is to be interpreted. In particular, what underlies the differences between the values of the middle- and working-class parents? In answer to this last question, Kohn acknowledges firstly that some parents may take for granted values that others hold dear. For example, middle-class parents may take 'neatness and cleanliness' for granted, while working-class parents treat it as highly desirable. But this, he argues, is to say in effect that middle-class parents value neatness and cleanliness as greatly as do working-class parents but not so greatly as they value other items, such as happiness and self-control. And, if this is true, then it can only indicate that in the circumstances of middle-class life neatness and cleanliness are easily enough attained to be of less immediate concern than are these other values.

Secondly, he notes the possibility that these value-concepts might possess different meanings for parents of different cultural backgrounds. For instance, one might argue that honesty is a central standard of conduct for middle-class parents because they see honesty as meaning truthfulness; and that it is more a quality of the person for working-class parents because they see it as meaning trustworthiness. But this, of course, is to raise the further problem of explaining this difference in meaning.

With respect to this issue, Kohn observes that 'It would be reasonable for working-class parents to be more likely to see honesty as trustworthiness. The working-class situation is one of less material security and less assured protection from the dishonesty of others. For these reasons, trustworthiness is more at issue for working-class than for middle-class parents.'[56]

Thus, both these considerations would appear to lead to the view that the different values of the classes reflect their different circumstances in life and, by implication, their conceptions of the effects that these circumstances may have on their children's future lives. Kohn's main conclusion is therefore that[57]

> Parents are most likely to accord high priority to those values that seem both *problematic*, in the sense that they are difficult of achievement, and *important*, in the sense that failure to achieve them would affect the child's future adversely. From this perspective it is reasonable that working-class parents cannot afford to take neatness and cleanliness as much for granted as can middle-class parents. It is reasonable too that working-class parents are more likely to see honesty as implying trustworthi-

ness and that this connotation of honesty is seen as problematic.

Thus, honesty and neatness are important to the child's future precisely because they assure him a respectable social position. The same holds for the value of obedience. Even in the way in which they delineate what is desirable for boys from what is desirable for girls, working-class respondents seem to show a clear appreciation of the qualities making for respectable social position.

However, the attributes that middle-class parents are more likely to value for their children comprise 'internal' standards for governing interpersonal relationships and, in the last analysis, one's relationship with one's self. And so it is not that middle-class parents are less concerned than are working-class parents about social position. The qualities of person that assure respectability may be taken for granted, but in a world where social relationships determine position, these standards are both more problematic and more important.

The middle-class stress on internal standards is apparent in various ways: in their selection of the cluster of characteristics centring about honesty; in their being less likely than working-class parents to value obedience and more likely to value self-control and consideration; and in their viewing obedience as inconsistent with both consideration and curiosity. In sum, these values place responsibility directly upon the individual, upon his inner control rather than conformity to authority.

The value of curiosity well exemplifies the close relation between parents' values and their circumstances of life and expectations. Thus, the proportion of mothers valuing curiosity rises slowly from status level to status level until we come to the wives of professionals and the more highly educated businessmen; then it increases rapidly. The value is afforded priority, it would seem, in exactly that portion of the middle class where it is most appropriate and where its importance for the child's future is most apparent.

This completes our summary of Kohn's study. We have described it in some detail since, as we indicated above, it is reasonably representative of the literature on the social structuring of values. Also it selects an issue—that of the correlates of social class—which enjoys a traditional importance in social science. A number of criticisms of research of this general type were given in the last chapter. We need not examine the applicability of each of these in turn to Kohn's study, although it should be apparent that several of them do have relevance here. However, a few leading points do suggest themselves.

## Comments on Kohn's study

First, one of the limitations of Kohn's technique of allowing respondents to select their values from amongst a list of summary descriptions is that it introduces an element of ambiguity. This may be taken as the price of its otherwise commendable simplicity. Thus, as he rightly notes, the value of 'honesty' may mean quite different things to working-class and middle-class subjects. To some extent, these different connotations can be determined by examining the other values that are normally chosen in conjunction with that of honesty. But this difficulty could probably have been avoided if a suitable multi-item instrument had been used to measure the attitudes in the first place.

This leads to a second consideration. Thus, although Kohn might be said to tap in some degree the 'structure' of certain sets of values by noting the ways in which the choice of one characteristic renders the choice of others more probable (Table 7.4), this provides only a limited depiction of the value-systems that are involved here. In fact, this approach, like that of comparable analyses of correlation patterns, supplies the kind of indicative information that could have been usefully employed to supplement and check data of a more discursive kind: that is data which derives from investigations of respondents' *reasons* for their professed choice of values and their broader conceptions of parenthood with which these choices are associated. This would make for a more inclusive and self-interpretive account of the value-systems that are associated with the different social classes.

Of course, *how* these discursive aspects are examined will depend both on the degree of detail required and on the results of the pre-test. Thus, while the settings and general procedures may remain relatively standardized throughout, the degree to which use is made of structured questions will depend essentially upon whether the pre-test indicated a high dispersion of responses or a low dispersion that may be reasonably classified according to a few modal categories.

Thirdly, although Kohn provides no direct behavioural evidence on the socialization practices associated with the different social classes, he at least includes some self-reports from the respondents. However, perhaps a more complete and symmetrical picture could have been attained if some evidence had also been drawn from a sample of the children involved, both in regard to their parents' priorities as they saw them and their behaviour. We mention this since social research seems rarely to take advantage of the possibilities of symmetrical, two-way observations that are inherent in many situations of inquiry. For instance, as Galtung points out,[58] there are any number of studies of attitudes towards and relations with minority groups, but virtually no corresponding inquiries into minorities' perceptions of the dominant group. Yet in many cases this would seem an obvious direction for social research to take in order to avoid implicit allegiances with any partisan or ideological

214

viewpoint. This is, of course, especially applicable to studies of conflict-situations, where it is important that the social scientist achieve a more complete and balanced account of the situation than that which may characterize the views of either side to the conflict.

Parenthetically, it may be noted that although Kohn does not relate his study to other inquiries of a similar kind, a number of his findings have, in fact, been confirmed by other investigators, both in the United States and other modern industrial societies. One of the more interesting of these confirmations concerns Kohn's observation of a linear relation between social position and the value of curiosity. This matches, for instance, the findings of the study by Robinson and Rackstraw (1967), which we cited earlier and in which middle- and working-class parents were questioned on how they would respond to a number of explanation-requesting questions from their children.[59] The middle class, it will be recalled, were far more likely to answer the actual questions, and the information they gave was more accurate and complete. Working-class respondents, on the other hand, were more likely to deny the basis of the question ('Why shouldn't they?'), appeal to authority ('It's the law'), or to the nature of things ('That's the way things are'), and so on. In other words, the middle-class subjects appeared more likely to respond to their children's curiosity as a valid characteristic, even one to be encouraged.

Finally, we may briefly indicate the more general context of Kohn's study. Essentially its role is to bring some factual information to bear on a subject—that of working-class and middle-class 'culture' —about which less empirically-inclined observers are all too ready to generalize. Thus, although it is evident that certain subjective correlates of social class, in the sense of the present study (i.e. mainly 'manual/non-manual'), may be said to exist, it is also clear that the differences of attitude between the classes are subtle ones, and that the values they characteristically promulgate exemplify this. In particular, it would appear that there are systematic differences between the classes in the way in which their values are interrelated: that is, in their value-systems.

But beyond describing these phenotypic differences of attitude, and possibly of reasoning, one assumes further, of course, that the characteristics selected are to some degree also put into practice. That is, that parents do not only hold these values with regard to children of a particular age-group, but also attempt to bring up their own children in accordance with them. In this way, a basis is laid for the perpetuation of social class differences in outlook.

The broader issue which the present study raises, then, is that of what might be termed the social definition of childhood, and the way this varies in different sectors of a society. But with a subject of this

215

kind it is best to introduce a more comparative approach: that is, one with a more historical and/or cross-cultural frame of reference. The reason is that recognition of the relativity of 'social definitions of childhood' not only facilitates the search for explanation and interpretation, but also brings into perspective those features that are most in need of explanation. That is, the principal modes of variation become apparent. In the present case, these will involve both cognitive and evaluative components.[60] And the utility of a comparative perspective here is illustrated, for example, by Philippe Ariès (1962) in his historical review of the changing social reality of childhood and of corresponding alterations in the conceptions of parenthood, and by Bronfenbrenner's (1972) recent cross-cultural analysis of Russia and America in these terms.[61]

Let us conclude, therefore, with a brief illustration of the possibilities of applying a more comparative perspective to Kohn's study. Thus, one of his findings, it will be recalled, concerned the fact that although middle-class respondents' conceptions of what was desirable for boys were largely congruent with their views of what was desirable for girls, this did not appear to be the case for working-class respondents. The latter drew a clear distinction between the sexes: dependability, being a good student, and ambition were more likely to be regarded as desirable for boys; and happiness, good manners, neatness, and cleanliness were more likely to be chosen as desirable for girls.

However, in both classes this was a matter of degree; in neither was a clear-cut dichotomy apparent. In this respect, Kohn's data is compatible with that, for instance, from some northern European nations. But although American culture as a whole, and especially its middle-class components, may draw no rigid distinction between the values deemed appropriate to the two sexes, this is in sharp contrast with the value-systems of such Mediterranean countries as Spain and Greece, with most Arab nations, and with, for instance, Latin America.[62] In societies such as these, the variable of sex, rather than socio-economic class, appears often to provide the principal basis for determining those values and forms of conduct that are appropriate to a given individual.[63]

Also it is important for the understanding of these societies to be aware of the systemic nature of their moral codes made possible by such polarities as these. For example, as Lison-Tolosana (1966) writes in respect of Spanish culture:[64]

> *Donjuanismo* is only possible in a society in which the supreme feminine *vigencia*—backed by a moral code, by religious beliefs, and by the structure of the family—is virginity or chastity. The Don Juan cannot exist without this *vigencia* and vice versa: the

*vigencia* which compels women to safeguard their virginity or chastity in every minute particular requires and is only possible through the existence of the *vigencia* which demands a *donjuanesque* behaviour from young men.

How are these differences to be explained? In most of the relevant ethnographies the main appeal seems to be to unique historical traditions in the countries concerned. But perhaps we can also recognize the presence here of more general sociological factors. Thus, as we have seen, moral codes, like other attitudinal complexes, are closely related to social activities, and thereby to social structure. And in this case, the main factor that differentiates those societies which vary markedly in the degree of congruency between the values deemed appropriate to each sex (in childhood and after) appears to be that of their level of modernization: in general, the more modern the society, the more compatible the values deemed appropriate to the two sexes.

We would suggest that the explanation of this lies in part with the nature of a modern economy, where the shift of emphasis towards the tertiary sector and the progressive mechanization of work create conditions in which men and women are required to perform increasingly similar work tasks. Naturally, there is more to it than this and other characteristics of modern societies, such as their distinctive family structures, would have a part to play in any full account of the differences. But at least the basic line of reasoning should have been established.

If so, then two of its immediate implications may be cited. In the first place, our general prediction would simply be that as societies modernize, so the saliency of sex-specific values and norms—such as those summed up by the concepts of *machismo* and *vergüenza* and their corresponding forms of *honra*—will begin to decrease. Indeed, there is some evidence that this process is already under way, as Michael Kenny's (1961) comparisons between social life in the *pueblo* and the city exemplifies.[65]

In the second place, we would expect that within modern society the working class will be more likely to draw a sharp distinction between the standards appropriate to each sex, because this sector of society is characterized by a greater dissimilarity in the work roles of men and women. In effect, of course, this prediction is exactly what Kohn's study bears out. More specifically, his findings indicate that these differences in valuation become apparent at an early age: that is, with regard to children ten to eleven years old.

This, then, may serve to briefly indicate some of the explanatory uses to which a more comparative perspective in studies of this kind may be put. As a matter of fact, Kohn (1969) has recently extended his own work on the relationship of values to social class to involve some comparisons with other social groups.[66] Thus, he has shown that (on the basis of a second study in Turin, Italy) the relationship between class and values is essentially similar in an appreciably different social and historical context and (as demonstrated by a third study of men employed in civilian occupations throughout the United States) that the class-values relationship is essentially the same for different segments of American society.

# 8 Empirical studies: II Other methods

In chapter 7 we considered the usage of the survey methods of the interview and questionnaire for the empirical study of moral codes. As we have seen, a considerable proportion of the empirical research that is available is accounted for by these methods of inquiry. Similarly, most methodology texts in social science are oriented towards discussion of survey techniques. But this concentration of research initiative upon survey methodology has not been wholly advantageous. Thus, it may well have served to hinder the further development and utilization of other methods of research. These methods are not only amenable for use in place of the traditional interview and questionnaire, but also may be combined with the latter as supplementary and cross-validating sources of data.

The arguments in favour of multi-method research designs have been alluded to earlier.[1] Essentially, they are summed up in the following observation:[2]

> Once a proposition has been confirmed by two or more independent measurement processes, the uncertainty of its interpretation is greatly reduced. The most persuasive evidence comes through a triangulation of measurement processes. If a proposition can survive the onslaught of a series of imperfect measures, with all their irrelevant error, confidence should be placed in it. Of course, this confidence is increased by minimizing error in each instrument and by a reasonable belief in the different and divergent effects of the sources of error.

Ideally, of course, different methods within a particular research programme would be differentially weighted in terms of (i) their centrality to the hypothesis or research objective at stake; and (ii) the degree of extraneous variation that each is known to possess.

219

In this way, and where appropriate, the focal position of survey methods could be maintained within the multi-method research design.

Survey methods will, of course, always form an integral part of the empirical sociology of moral codes because of the particular relevancy of data on ethical reasoning, which controlled verbal methods of inquiry would seem especially suited to elicit. However, they should not be treated as the exclusive means of inquiry. The sociology of moral codes, as other aspects of empirical sociology, stands to gain from further recognition of the diversity of available methodologies and from the more rigorous application in each case of the essentially shared criteria of validity and reliability. The current chapter, therefore, seeks to outline some of these alternative methods and to illustrate their use for the present subject.

## Observation

Some form of observation is contained in all methods of social inquiry. And even when it is interpreted as a distinct research technique in its own right—as in the sense of 'participant observation' —it is evident that many different types of social observation may be said to exist. However, it is also apparent that under certain circumstances observational methods of inquiry are, at least *prima facie*, preferable to survey techniques. Among the more salient of these circumstances are the following. First, some participant observation would seem necessary for large-scale studies of either whole societies or whole communities, or for essentially *contextual* analyses of social groups and organizations. Hence, for example, we find that participant observation is the traditional method of ethnography. Second, and closely related to this, observation has a particular value for the direct study of social processes (e.g. religious ceremonies, court trials, innovation). Here, of course, survey methods are restricted to specific cuts in time and by such factors as the unreliability of recall data.[3] Third, observation has a special applicability to those areas of content and population for which verbal reports are either of low reliability or simply unavailable. For example, many (though not all) moral questions are prone to unreliable patterns of response in view of their emotional correlates and the social sanctions which attend them. Similarly, verbal methods of inquiry encounter population restrictions which derive from the general fact that articulacy varies considerably with social position.[4] Hence, observational methods are often especially indicated for studies of the social periphery, as well as for the study of those actions that are not easily verbalized. Finally, non-participant forms of observation in particular may serve to avoid much of the 'reactivity' inherent in the interview and questionnaire, and thus to provide data that is less in danger of being an artifact of the methods used to gather it.

These advantages of observational methods of inquiry are reflected in the history of their use in social science. Thus, LePlay's study, *Les Ouvriers Européens* (1855) is often cited as the first example of the use of participant observation in sociology. This technique was further developed by the Chicago School in the 1920s and 30s, in which a more committal, social-problems orientation characterized the selection of subjects and directed research attention towards the more peripheral sectors of society. This process of selection is well exemplified in such works as Frederick Thrasher's *The Gang*, Clifford Shaw's *Brothers in Crime* and *The Jack Roller*, Harvey Zorbaugh's *The Gold Coast and the Slum*, Louis Wirth's *The Ghetto*, and William Whyte's *Street Corner Society*. Similarly, observational methods and informal interviews were used in a series of community studies, beginning with the Lynds's investigation of *Middletown* in the 1920s; and in industrial sociology techniques of the same kind were initiated by Roethlisberger and Dickson's *Management and the Worker*, published in 1930. In addition to these, of course, one must mention the continuing tradition of anthropological inquiries deriving first-hand data on alien cultures by means of extended periods of participant observation.

Taken together, these examples of social research tend to exhibit a less individualistic perspective than that characteristic of many representative applications of the survey method. Social groups and communities, for example, are chosen as the units of analysis and a more contextual understanding of the subtle interrelationships between social institutions of various kinds is provided. Thus, inquiries of this kind supplied much of the motivation for subsequent empirical sociology by opening up the investigation of sub-cultures of diverse kinds, conceived as having their own values, norms, and attendant social activities and as existing in complex relations of dependency with the wider society. In particular, these observational studies indicate many of the possibilities of determining how cultural categories (beliefs, values, precepts, etc.) can be studied in relation to 'social' categories (class, community, organization, etc.). This remains an important question in sociology that deserves much more attention than it has received.

On the debit side, however, these observational studies would not perhaps today be judged as having employed sufficiently rigorous and replicable procedures in their investigations. In this respect, they do not differ greatly from many inquiries using methods of social observation at the present time. And it is for reasons of this kind that techniques of observation cannot usually be considered systematic methods in the sense that one might apply this term to a great deal of

H*

survey research. In participant observation, for example, the general factor of experience still seems to count for more than the adherence to explicit and generally-accepted rules of procedure. As Bruyn (1966) observes, much observational research is 'marked more by a style than by any careful procedures, more by the observer's own sensitivity to what he sees than by what he believes others will ordinarily see, more by the observer's special interests in studying the social scene than by purely scientific interests'.[5] Of course, research of this kind has frequently demonstrated that it can be of considerable value, and in certain cases it might be advisable. In general, however, we would think that the goal of objectivity requires the further use and development of *structured* forms of observation.

## Objective observation

The general problem of 'objectivity' that is encountered in any form of social observation, and particularly in the case of participant observation, concerns the degree to which the process of observation itself can be considered to be free of bias and distortion. That is: to what extent can the (trained) observer record what he sees and hears without implicitly selecting, interpreting, and evaluating the material? This is properly an epistemological issue, upon which various positions may be taken. Unfortunately, in social research the actual position adopted tends to be assumed rather than made explicit and so a number of the questions which such research raises are effectively ignored. For example, cross-cultural studies at least presuppose rejection of the more extreme versions of epistemological relativism but rarely offer any grounds for this rejection.[6]

In modern social research a number of recurrent assumptions may be discerned. These include the following. First, most researchers would reject the idea that the social investigator, however well-trained, should be depicted in terms of the traditional Cartesian *tabula rasa*. Although every effort may be taken to ensure an open mind it is usually recognized that a certain degree of preconception is inescapable and hence a potential source of selective perception and interpretation. Furthermore, experimental evidence has been adduced to indicate that, as Bartlett expressed it, even our most elementary perceptions have an inferential character. Thus, attention has been given to our tendency to project our own values and categories of experience on to other groups for which they may be inappropriate. But second, however, it is also commonly thought that the distortions produced by these processes can in part be compensated for by a clear consciousness of them: hence researchers are often urged to state their assumptions and value premises in detail prior to conducting and describing their research in order to set both themselves

222

and their readers on guard. This, of course, presupposes that these factors are in fact amenable to reflective self-awareness and that they are communicable. Finally, in practice objectivity is usually conceived in relative terms: in particular, it is seen to centre upon attainment of a high degree of validity and reliability, both of these being conceived as continua.

Taken together, these considerations in our view indicate the need for more structured types of observational inquiry, both with respect to studies of moral codes and to empirical sociology in general. We mean by 'structured' here inquiries in which (i) research objectives and hypotheses are well-defined and fully stated; (ii) procedures adopted for gathering data are replicable and determined, wherever possible, by sampling criteria; and (iii) where standardized and explicit categories for the recording and classification of observations are used, with measures being taken, where appropriate, of intersubjective (and intrasubjective) reliability.

It might be noted at this point that the general relevancy of so-called value premises can easily be overstated, particularly since, as we have seen, much contemporary social research tends toward the examination of relatively neutral subjects. Perhaps more important are cognitive assumptions; for example, since any given range of phenomena can be classified according to an indefinite number of principles, it is clear that those features which are recorded will depend both upon the purposes of the inquiry and also upon the conceptual scheme already adopted. This is most clear in the case of competing theoretical accounts. Thus, it will be apparent, for example, that prior commitment to either a structural-functional or a Marxist frame of reference within, say, a community study project is likely to lead not only to diverse forms of analysis and interpretation, but also, and prior to this, to the selection of different aspects of the community as central, as the principal dimensions of variation, and possibly also to different classifications of the same phenomena. It is important, therefore, that assumptions of this kind be made explicit.

The problem of stressing, as many accounts do, the influence of values upon selective observation is that this approach tends to lead to neglect of the simple fact which we discussed in the first section of this study: namely, that the acceptance of a particular cognitive framework itself serves to restrict the range of value-positions that may be defensibly adopted. That is, an emphasis upon the role of value premises tends to focus the problem of objectivity on to the influence of the evaluative upon the cognitive, rather than—which is at least equally important—vice versa.[7]

Although unstructured observation is sometimes claimed to be more valid there is little evidence available to support this. In fact,

223

as we have seen, it seems likely that this approach will merely permit the introduction of biases from implicit sources that, at least to some degree, could either be avoided or made explicit in a more structured design. In general, then, we would tend to see the more structured approach as potentially the more valid form of observation, although the type and degree of structuring that is advisable will depend in part on the content and purposes of the research in question. The case of reliability is much clearer. Thus one central test of reliability is whether a replication of a particular study will produce the same results. Replicability in turn depends upon the extent to which the research problem, procedures, and categories of observation in the original study were standardized and made explicit. But even granting this, one must admit that survey techniques can usually attain higher levels of reliability, because of the greater flexibility of verbal categories and the finer degrees of standardization that they permit.

So far, relatively few structured, replicable studies have been carried out, although mention should be made of the work of Bales and Barker, both of whom have developed predefined sets of categories for recording behaviour and established reasonably high levels of intersubjective reliability in their research.[8] In the case of larger-scale research projects, partial replications have tended to produce different results, although, since the original study has usually employed a relatively unstructured approach, complete replication has not normally been possible. A classic example here is concerned with anthropological research in the Mexican village, Tepoztlán. This community was first investigated by Robert Redfield (1930) and then, seventeen years later, restudied by Oscar Lewis (1951).[9] And a number of Lewis's interpretations diverged from those of Redfield. In particular, while Redfield emphasized the presence of a coherent cultural *Gestalt* exhibited in the social patterns of the village, Lewis stressed the material poverty of Tepoztlán and the hostility, jealousy, and divisiveness in the lives of its inhabitants. In some respects the two accounts are incompatible; in others they supplement each other. And although the later study was not a full replication of the first one, since it involved the use of more complex techniques and the employment of projective devices such as the Rorschach test, these two studies at least testify to the pervasive effects of different (and largely implicit) selective factors on social observation.

So far we have directed our argument in favour of more structured types of observation and the development of more standardized rules of procedure as means of raising the levels of validity and reliability in this area of social science. But in so doing we do not wish to imply that the unstructured, informal type of observational inquiry has no place. Firstly, this kind of approach often has value at the initial, exploratory stages of research, where it may provide a general sense of reference, and also at the final stages, where possible interpretations of the findings are being sought. In each case, the more flexible, informal perspective is more likely to permit recognition of unanticipated findings which a more structured approach might inhibit. Secondly, the self-admittedly subjective report may allow us insight into the personal reactions of the investigator to his objects of study and the kind of mutual attachments that developed, both of these being features of research that are not normally reported on in any detail. This is perhaps particularly relevant in the case of anthropological investigations. Indeed, anthropologists often feel that much of the quality of their experiences cannot be satisfactorily expressed in objective terms or in the language of available theory, and that it is still worth communicating, even if in more inchoate and subjective forms. Three outstanding examples of this personal anthropology, which collectively may be taken as proof that it is not always without value in social science, are Lévi-Strauss's *Tristes Tropiques* (1955), Elenore Bowen's *Return to Laughter* (1964), and Kenneth Read's *The High Valley* (1966). One of the merits of these accounts is that they help us to see where some of the sources of bias in objective observation may enter, as well as indicating suggestive lines of inquiry in their own right and interpretations of data already established. As such, they provide useful insights into some of the phenomenological aspects of culture contact.

## Types of observation

So far we have distinguished broadly between two types of observation in social science, the structured and the unstructured. In so doing, we have held the position of the observer in relation to his subject-matter relatively constant. Yet it is clear that problems of maintaining objectivity will increase as the observer becomes more closely involved with the objects of his inquiry: that is, as he changes from playing an unobserved and unobtrusive role to being either a visible researcher-observer or a full participant-observer. Our basic classification of types of observation in social science, then, would be as Figure 8.1 shows.

By the term 'active' in this diagram we refer to more experimental designs in which the investigator takes an active role in either controlling or manipulating the behaviour under observation or where the behaviour takes place under artificial conditions supplied by the researchers. Some examples of this will be considered in our discussion of experimental research below.[10] In passive observation the emphasis is upon permitting entirely natural sequences to occur without any attempt to influence the occurrence or direction of the behaviour being observed. Naturally, the six variables above are polar types and actual investigations will match them to varying degrees. It may be noted, however, that the greater number of observational studies in social science would be most likely classified in cell (3); that is, as participant, at best semi-structured, and also largely passive in the present sense. A second major category, of course, would be laboratory experiments, falling in cell (2), as structured, non-participant, and active. These, however, will be considered later in this chapter.

So far, we have argued, in effect, for the further development of categories (1) and (2), and perhaps especially category (1), for the

FIGURE 8.1 *Polar types of observation*

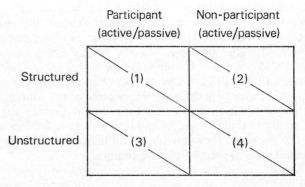

empirical study of moral codes. In short, it does not seem necessary to restrict systematic, structured forms of observation to laboratory experiments. Let us, therefore, give some brief consideration to more structured forms of participant and non-participant observation respectively.

*Participant observation*

First, participant observation. This method usually permits access to a broader, more varied, and more intimate range of information than non-participant observation. And in the second place, it tends to be particularly well suited for the study of social groups, organizations, and other higher-order collectivities. In this way, data may be gained on social processes on an inside basis, from which certain other types of data-collection are excluded. Thirdly, it offers the possibility of more continuous and natural observations than those permitted, for example, within the somewhat restricted (and temporally limited) stimulus-response framework of traditional survey methods.

On the other hand, the fact of participation introduces a possible element of reactivity. This is analogous to the similar problem faced

226

by the interview and questionnaire methods. That is, there are similar problems of observer (or, in some cases, interviewer) effects, of the subjects' awareness of being tested or observed (and so role-playing, etc.), and of the process of observation itself acting as an agent of change. One possible answer to this is to allow the observer contaminant to wear off, and to start analysis with data subsequent to the point at which the effect is negligible. This, of course, presupposes that the independent effect of observation can be reliably assessed. Measurements of this kind, however, are rarely given systematic attention in participant observation research. Instead, more or less intuitive criteria are employed to estimate the period of time over which such bias occurs, and this in anthropology as well as sociology.

A second defence against the problems of reactivity is the adoption of a more 'natural', and so less visible, social role: for example, a student of organizational behaviour might join a particular organization as an apparently *bona fide* member. Thus, in his study of *Street Corner Society*, Whyte became a full member of the gang he was observing, and in the study, *When Prophecy Fails* (1964) by Leon Festinger *et al.* a team of observers studied an apocalyptic social movement by posing as ordinary members who believed as the others did.[11] Naturally, this is not always practicable or possible, and is generally restricted to studies within the investigator's own culture, although in some anthropological studies, the researcher may be automatically assigned to a particular clan grouping, and is anyway normally associated with specific members of the community (e.g. the leading family, or with individuals with some cross-cultural experience). In addition, certain ethical, as well as practical, considerations are involved in the question as to how far the researcher should reveal his true purposes.[12] None the less, it is evident that to have one's role defined simply as that of an 'observer' or 'sociologist' may discourage spontaneity and lessen rapport, and that in general the degree of compatibility of the investigator's presumptive role with the cultural standards and specific expectations of those he studies will in part determine how well he can perform his tasks.

It is frequently the case, however, that the adoption of a specific social role, while it may facilitate access to some classes of information, will also preclude access to others. For example, as Severyn Bruyn (1966) states:[13]

The participant observer who studies a complex social organization must be aware of the fact that clearance at one level of organization does not insure clearance at another level. It is very important that the researcher takes into account the levels of power and decision-making extant in the group he studies before he makes his overture to become part of the group.

227

Thus, in conflict-situations a single observer tends to become confined to studying the group with which he is most identified (e.g. management v. unions, Protestants v. Catholics, gang-members v. public authorities, and so on). Where this is the case, team research may be called for, with different members of the team focusing upon different facets of the social reality under study, and possibly assuming different social roles. This will be particularly necessary for the study of rigidly stratified social systems (e.g. the caste-system) or collectivities (e.g. many public bureaucracies) where a tradition of information access and exchange is not well established.

The adoption of an effective social role is important in circumstances generally in which particular classes of information tend to be either concealed, distorted, or made available in only abridged forms. One important example of such information concerns processes of reasoning and justification. Thus, full and effective participation is likely to be necessary in the case of many organizations and social groups in order to record not only the decisions that are reached, and the policies adopted, but also, and equally important, the considerations which led to these decisions and the grounds on which they were justified. The need for access to data of this type indicates the particular value of participant forms of observation. Thus, barriers generally arise between social classes, racial groups, ethnic groups, religious, political, and business organizations, and so on, which censor information from the public or provide special interpretations for public consumption.[14] In consequence, a great deal of relevant data cannot be attained without effective entrée into these relatively closed groups. Of course, in less democratic societies the range of possibilities for participant observation of this kind will be lessened. However, this is not solely a question of different political arrangements. It needs also to be remembered that those classes of information and areas of behaviour that are normally closed to public access will vary generally as between different cultures, both within and between societies, often in quite subtle ways. This is most apparent in differing conceptions as to what is permitted and what is taboo in conversation, not only in general, but also in relation to specific categories of person (kin, friends, elders, etc.).

Allowing a 'cooling-off' period for observer effects and the adoption of a natural social role are both defences against the reactivity that is implicit in much participant observation. One general conclusion which may be drawn from the above is to the effect that social scientists should specify the way in which *they* were defined during their research, the social position they occupied within the milieu under study, and the changing images others developed of them whilst in this position. The latter can easily affect the range and quality of the information at their disposal. For instance, in developing countries visiting social scientists are commonly regarded by the members of a community at the initial stages of their research as Government emissaries, and this in spite of what they may claim to be themselves, and it is only later that their true function may become known and accepted.[15]

A second type of distortion may derive from the observer. Thus, although an investigator may succeed in becoming a natural part of the life of the observed, there arises thereafter the problem of maintaining scientific integrity whilst affectively involved with the objects of study. Just as too great a social distance between observer and observed may preclude access to the information required, so biases can also derive from over-rapport: that is, the observer may become too closely identified with his subjects to be able to report and interpret their behaviour objectively.[16] On the other hand, of course, the subjects may come to identify too closely with the observer.

The correct level of detachment is not always easy to achieve in participant observation, or to maintain constant, but it is necessary in order to safeguard objectivity. It is perhaps assisted simply by a more contextual awareness and understanding of the activities being observed than that which is held by the subjects themselves. Similarly, in cross-cultural inquiries the researcher can most usefully adopt a perspective of what might be termed an 'operational relativism'. This will be discussed in more detail in the next section of this study. In brief, however, it refers to the anthropologist's recognition of the fact that social reality is relative to man's definition of it, however apparently consensual particular definitions might be. Thus, although he is interested in adequately describing the reality of a particular community in its own terms, he is also interested in comparing this social reality with that exhibited by other cultures. And none of these is afforded any special priority. Unlike the subjects of his inquiry, therefore, he seeks to avoid any tendency to either absolutize or hypostatize the particular culture under review. This is an operational relativism since it is merely a means of securing objectivity, and so appropriate for the anthropologist *qua* scientific observer.

In some cases, however, the desire to avoid ethnocentric perceptions may lead to a kind of bias that is the reverse of the usual projective ones, namely, to the accentuation of differences and the neglect of similarities. Naroll and Naroll (1963) have argued that much anthropology has a tendency to be predisposed towards 'exotic data':[17] that is, that the observer is more likely to report on phenomena that are substantially different from those found in his own society or sub-culture than he is to report on phenomena common to both. Again, however, this would seem less likely to be encountered within systematic, structured forms of observation than within their more informal variants. In addition, the tendency to accentuate differences, although it may characterize some short-term studies, would appear to become less over longer periods of exposure. It is often noticeable in anthropological monographs, for instance, that this gradual process of familiarization with local values, beliefs, and social practices eventually permits a more balanced presentation of them.[18]

The question of whether the participant observer should exercise an active or passive role will depend upon the purposes of the investigation and the nature of the subject-matter. On the whole, participant observers usually attempt to gather information whilst assuming a passive role in which their own influence is rendered as negligible as possible. The major exception to this is, of course, the traditional laboratory experiment in which the research is normally designed in order to permit much easier control and measurement of those variables that are to be manipulated.

But sometimes the observer influences the behaviour he is studying by accident. We have already mentioned the problems of reactivity inherent in participant observation which derive from the subjects' awareness of being observed. Comparable effects may also arise when reactivity in its usual sense is minimized. A good example of this is described in *When Prophecy Fails* (1964) by Festinger, Riecken, and Schachter.[19] This involved a participant-observation study of an apocalyptic social movement. The main interest was in testing a number of hypotheses derived from balance theory regarding the effect upon belief systems of disconfirmation. The observation was carried out without either the knowledge or the consent of the members of the movement because their secrecy and general attitude towards non-believers had already indicated that a study could not be conducted openly. In this way, reactivity was effectively minimized. As the authors describe their aims:[20]

> Our basic problems were then obtaining entree for a sufficient number of observers to provide the needed coverage of the members' activities, and keeping at an absolute minimum any influence which these observers might have on the beliefs and actions of members of the group. We tried to be nondirective, sympathetic listeners, passive participants who were inquisitive and eager to learn whatever others might want to tell us.

However, as it turned out, the stories which were told in order to fit the beliefs of the group members for the sake of gaining entrance had the unintentional effect of reinforcing these beliefs, as indeed did the fact of a sudden increase in the movement's membership. None the less, whilst in the group, the observers made every effort to avoid proselytizing, or giving any indication of conviction, and no attempt

230

was made to affect the course of the movement. But even here the authors are led to admit that[21]

Actually, we were unable to achieve our goal of complete neutrality. At various points there arose situations in which the observers were forced to take some action and no matter what they might have done, their action would have had some effect on developments in the group. . . . In short, as members, the observers could not be neutral—any action had consequences.

In fact, this particular study encountered a number of relatively atypical difficulties and the very transience and unpredictability of the movement being studied meant that a comparatively unstructured observational format had to be adopted. But some of the problems it indicates are general ones: in particular, it exemplifies the possibility of observer effects even when the observation is covert and not recognized as such by the subjects. Factors of this kind, therefore, need to be accounted for in participant-observation designs.

*Non-participant observation*

We may turn now to non-participant forms of observation. The primary advantage of these is the lack of 'reactivity' that they permit. It was principally on these grounds that this class of measurements was advocated for use in social science by Webb *et al.* in their book, *Unobtrusive Measures* (1968). In this, various forms of observation—hidden observation, contrived observation, trace analysis, and secondary records—are discussed in which the individual is unaware of being tested, and where there is little danger that the act of measurement will serve as an agent of change in behaviour or elicit role-playing that confounds the data. There is also minimal risk in these forms of unobtrusive observation that biases sourcing from the status, physical appearance, manner, or other cues supplied by the investigator will contaminate the results. Yet, as the authors note, this class of measurements contains several of the most under-used resources in social science; in part, of course, because of the concentration of research initiative on survey methodology.

Various possibilities exist for the ingenious application of non-participant forms of observation in research designs. And a number of these have relevance to our present subject. For example, Cambell, Kruskal, and Wallace (1966) examined one behavioural facet of race relations by means of unobtrusive observations carried out under relatively standardized conditions.[22] In this, the mixing of negro and white children in a classroom setting was investigated. Since seating was entirely voluntary, the authors used the degree to which negroes and whites sat by themselves, rather than mixing randomly, as a

231

presumptive index of the degree to which acquaintance, friendship, and sociometric preference were strongly influenced by 'race', as opposed to being distributed without regard to racial considerations. Classes in four schools were studied, and significant aggregation by race was discovered, although this varied in degree between the individual schools. In this research design, as the authors make clear, the subjects were not aware that they were being observed and so the process of observation seems unlikely to have affected the findings.

Of course, this particular example also illustrates the greater content restrictions encountered by non-participant, as opposed to participant, forms of observation. Thus, although negro-white, male-female, even young-old relations might be observed in this way, it will be apparent, for instance, that Protestant-Catholic or Jewish-Christian relations cannot normally be studied by similar means. One solution to these limitations is to employ an informant who acts, as it were, as a substitute for a participant observer. Yet unless he is well-trained, the informant is likely to introduce a number of errors into this procedure. Hence it is usually necessary in such studies to have some independent means of checking the reliability of the informant's observations.[23] However, in those cases where usage of an informant is most called for, as in studies of closed groups, such as some sectarian religious organizations, the nature of the conditions often entails that this is virtually the only means of collecting data and alternative sources are simply unavailable. Here, then, one has to rely on careful selection of informants, and, wherever appropriate, some measure of intrasubjective (or even intersubjective) reliability.

Again, the question of whether the researcher should attempt to influence the behaviour under observation will depend upon the nature and purposes of the inquiry. One general argument in favour of taking an active role is in order to avoid an excess of irrelevant data. However, Webb *et al.* (1968), for instance, list a broad range of opportunistic uses of observation of events over which the investigator has no control—these are categorized as the recording of exterior physical signs (clothes, etc.), expressive behaviour (non-verbal communication), physical location (e.g. aggregation studies), language behaviour (e.g. conversation sampling), and time-duration behaviour (patterns of attention, etc.).[24]

Apart from the formal laboratory experiment, in which a range of variables are carefully controlled, there are various opportunities for less precise, and less easily regulated 'natural experiments'. One simple example of this is reported in the study by Milgram, Mann, and Harter (1965).[25] Their technique involved the dispersion in city streets of a large number of unmailed letters, enclosed in envelopes and stamped. The finder has the choice of mailing the letter, disregarding it, or actively destroying it. It was found that a return-rate may thus be obtained which is specific to the type of organization to which the letters are addressed. It was therefore suggested that this method constituted a useful non-intrusive technique for determining community orientations towards political groups and other institutions. Thus, in the first study (in New Haven, Conn.) it was found that 72 per cent of letters addressed to 'Medical Research Associates', 71 per cent of personal letters, and 25 per cent of letters addressed to 'Friends of the Communist Party', were returned. Of course, a measure of this kind still remains susceptible to various kinds of extraneous error and can only really serve an indicative role. Thus, it provides a rudimentary indication of a community's evaluations, but does not readily permit exploration of the reasons and explanations for these evaluations, whereas a laboratory experiment would.

Active and participant forms of observation are perhaps generally more useful for explanatory purposes. For the sake of prediction, however, it may well be best to utilize that method which least interferes with natural sequences of behaviour, and so passive and non-participant types of observation may be preferable.

In sum, however, we may say that although non-participant observation removes some of the errors that derive from the problem of reactivity, it imposes new limitations on content. Also, it does not eradicate the possibility of errors deriving from the observer. Thus, the observer's efficiency may vary over time: for example, his coding may become more standardized (i.e. reliable), or his attentiveness may decrease, and so on. All these could lead to spurious differences in comparisons. However, some attempt can usually be made to assess errors of this type and thus to correct for them in observational studies.[26] Rosenthal (1963, 1964), for example, has carried out a number of investigations of experimenter effects in laboratory settings.[27] In particular, he has demonstrated that the experimenter's hypothesis can act as an unintended determinant of research findings, and that varying degrees of training can have considerable influence upon the relative efficiency of observers. One important conclusion to be drawn from his work concerns the value of employing observers who are unaware of those classes of behavioural outcomes that are compatible with the hypothesis at stake. The more general point here, however, is that since social psychology has established the presence of various sources of selective perception and recall (in terms of familiarity, compatibility with existing values and beliefs, etc.) experimenters should be fully cognizant of the reflexive character of these findings. That is, they should pay more concern to the possible influence of such variables upon their own observations.

*Sampling procedures*

Both participant and non-participant forms of observation are, as we have seen, amenable to more structured research designs than many of those which are currently employed. That is, more rigorous delineation of research problems, more explicit and standardized procedures of observation, and more systematic coding of results are all required. But what is also involved here is the need for more frequent use, wherever applicable, of sampling criteria in order to achieve more representative series of observations. One aspect of this concerns the further development of time-sampling procedures in observational research. Thus, as Webb *et al.* (1968) comment:[28]

> The power of the questionnaire and interview has been enormously enhanced, as have all methods, by the development of sensitive sampling procedures. With the early impetus provided by the Census Bureau to locational sampling, particularly to the theory and practice of stratification, concern about the population restrictions of a research sample has been radically diminished. Less well developed is the random sampling of time units—either over long periods such as months, or within a shorter period such as a day. There is no theoretical reason why time sampling is scarce, for it is a simple question of substituting time for location in a sampling design. Time sampling is of interest not only for its control over population fluctuations which might confound comparisons, but also because it permits control over the possibility of variable content at different times of the day or different months of the year.

Because of the risks of error and the danger of unknown biases, the need for careful and representative data sampling in social research will be apparent. But this is much more frequently achieved in survey research than in studies using observational methods. Yet it is usually necessary in observational research to study subjects in a variety of social settings. For one thing, this normally enhances the observer's ability to accurately interpret the subject's behaviour. But it is also often the case that comparisons will have to be made concerning the relative validity of different response patterns that are characteristic of different social situations. Howard Becker (1958) encountered this problem in his participant-observation study of medical education. As he writes:[29]

> Thus, students in their clinical years may express deeply 'idealistic' sentiments about medicine when alone with the observer, but behave and talk in a very 'cynical' way when surrounded by fellow students. An alternative to judging one or the other of these situations as more reliable is to view each

datum as valuable in itself, but with respect to different conclusions. In the example above, we might conclude that group norms may not sanction expression.

But although random sampling procedures might help guarantee the representativeness of the material gained, they will still run the risk of producing a great deal of information that is largely irrelevant to the concerns of a given study, and of omitting some critical observations. Thus, as in the case of survey methods, there is often a justification here for purposive sampling, and *focused* observation. For studies of aspects of moral codes, for instance, it is frequently useful to have strategic observations on subjects' reactions to 'crisis-situations': that is, those situations which involve conflict or dilemma and so serve to highlight competing principles of action and actual priorities followed. Etzioni (1961) makes a point analogous to this when, in his discussion of interview and observation methods for the study of organizational 'compliance structures', he comments:[30]

Finally, incidents of conflict, such as strikes, riots, or assault on an officer, when competently analyzed, may serve as X-rays revealing the real control structure of the organization. Priorities camouflaged by verbal agreements and the ideology of cooperation during the regular round of activities come to the fore in cases of internal conflict over methods of control, scarce means, personnel, power positions, and the like. The winners are likely to represent the predominant pattern.

Many verbal methods of studying values, both within the usual survey format and also in more projective approaches, effectively focus upon responses to this type of situation at the level of the individual. That is, they present in symbolic (oral or written) form certain hypothetical or real moral dilemmas faced by the respondent, who usually indicates which of the available courses of action he would adopt. This, for instance, is the normal basis of question-construction in the Allport-Vernon and Kluckhohn-Strodbeck scales. What is also needed, of course, is the selection of collectivities of various kinds as the units of analysis in this type of research. But secondly, exclusive reliance should not be placed on purely symbolic responses. These need to be supplemented by behavioural data. Hence, more use should be made of this type of crisis-situation in observational studies, both on the individual and organizational levels.

*Other forms of observation*

In the foregoing discussion we have conceptualized observation, in its participant and non-participant forms, in terms of the surveillance

235

by individuals of overt behaviour. This has an obvious application to the study of moral codes in view of the practical functions of the latter. Of course, certain familiar philosophical problems arise when attempts are made to relate non-verbal behaviour to expressed attitudes. Since such behaviour can only be properly identified as constituting 'action' in so far as it is premissed upon certain attitudes and dispositions, a general problem of inference emerges. That is, in the absence of specific assurances from the agent under observation (which may, of course, be forthcoming and form part of the evidence), we are obliged to say of a particular individual that he acted *as if* he held certain purposes and beliefs which we identified. Or, put otherwise, an acceptance of these purposes and beliefs is a necessary condition for the intelligibility of the agent's overt behaviour. Naturally, in many cases attributions of this kind will, at least *prima facie*, be relatively simple: some forms of behaviour are unambiguously classified within a society. For instance, some forms of behaviour will constitute clear-cut violations or performances (especially the former) of particular moral precepts. In other cases, the identification may be less easy, and so an appeal to the agent becomes necessary. However, this general issue has been raised earlier in this study, and need not be pursued further here.[31]

What we may note now, for the sake of completion, is that the simple equation of human observer/observed behaviour does not completely exhaust the category of observational methods in social science. In fact, either side of the equation may be modified. In the first place, the human observer may be supplanted by various mechanical means of observation, such as tape-recorders and film cameras. These tend to be employed when (i) it is required to record one class of behaviour in full detail (e.g. complete conversations or non-verbal reactions to a stimulus); (ii) where observation is required over substantial periods of time without the varying reliability (and high cost) of individual observers; and (iii) where the privacy or inaccessibility of the behaviour renders it impracticable for individual observation. The latter indicates the ethical problems involved in the use of concealed recording devices. But however valid these objections might be, it remains true that techniques of this type can often yield valuable data that would otherwise either be unavailable or available only in an unreliable form (e.g. recalled behaviour, etc.). This is well illustrated by the work of Strodbeck and his associates (1956, 1957), who obtained full permission from the court in order to use concealed microphones as a means of recording selected jury deliberations.[32]

Tape-recorders are now frequently employed in open-ended interviewing and generally serve to avoid individual recording errors. Although, unless concealed, such devices may generate some biases in the respondent that will need to be accounted for. In the second place, of course, errors can arise in the classification and analysis of the recorded material. Even when no elaborate interpretation is attempted, some prior editing is normally required before the data is presented and this may reflect the editor's selective perceptions, value-biases, and so on. This problem arises, for instance, in the assessment of several of Oscar Lewis's works, such as *The Children of Sánchez* (1961) and *La Vida* (1967), since, although the evidence these contain is given entirely in the form of first-person narratives, the accounts were based on very extensive interviews and so considerable selection and editing of material would have been necessary. The problem arises, then, as to how representative the final version is of the original evidence. Again, it is advisable for researchers to state clearly the criteria according to which selections of this type are made.

The use of tape-recorders in open-ended interviewing is matched by the use of photography in anthropological studies. Thus, as Collier (1967) states in his review of the subject:[33]

In line with the culture of anthropology, which places considerable value on intensive firsthand experiences, it is in the initial phase of field research that photography has had its most enthusiastic use. This appreciation is realistic, as the foremost characteristic of the camera is its ability to record material that the camera operator himself cannot recognize or yet understand. Photography offers the stranger in the field a means of recording large areas authentically, rapidly and with great detail, and a means of storing away complex descriptions for future analysis.

Mechanical means of observation, then, have mainly been used at the initial, exploratory stages of research, or for broadly interpretive purposes. There are, of course, some exceptions to this, and mention needs to be made not only of the research of Lewis, but also of the use of photography in the classic study of *Balinese Character* (1942) by Bateson and Mead. On the whole, however, technical means of data-collection have been most commonly and integrally employed in small-scale laboratory experiments by social psychologists, particularly with regard to learning studies. Settings of this kind can also permit useful methodological comparisons between different research instruments. This type of inquiry is illustrated by the study of Siersted and Hansen (1951).[34] They reported on three independent measures of children's reactions to a particular film. These included the use, during the film, of infra-red photography, and hidden tape-recorders to record verbal comments, and the deployment after the film had been shown of individual interviews. The authors' findings indicate that in this case at least the evidence of the interview responses did not well match that gained by either of the other two methods.

Finally, although we have restricted our discussion to first-hand observations of behaviour, observational methods might arguably be extended to include also the study of cultural artifacts and secondary sources of various kinds. Thus, many possibilities exist for documentary analysis, some of the more systematic examples of which will be considered below in our discussion of content analysis. Similarly, physical and archival data of various kinds may be included within observational research, as the ingenious employment of economic records, children's books, and even archaeological evidence in David McClelland's (1961) cross-national study of achievement motivation exemplifies.[35] This study also illustrates the fact that secondary materials also often permit the development of more longitudinal analyses.

In general, physical evidence and documentary records have the advantage of being relatively free of problems of reactivity. That is, the material examined was not originally produced for the purposes of social science research, unlike survey data, and so the fact and process of measurement is unlikely of itself to generate bias. However, since such material was produced for other purposes, various types of error (from the social scientist's point of view) may have entered into its creation. Thus, there may be changes in archival recording standards over time, either due to varying degrees of efficiency, or to variations in procedure, definitions of key terms, and so on.[36] Secondly, of course, there is the possibility of selective biases in the initial recording and subsequent preservation of the material. Thirdly, in so far as the records are themselves based on external sources of evidence they may reflect various forms of error present in these originals: for example, an apparent rise in crime might be due simply to a greater readiness on the part of the public to report crimes. Finally, since archival and documentary evidence often extends over appreciable periods of time, materials of this kind are particularly susceptible to extraneous changes in the environment that serve to confound comparisons. For instance, an increasing divorce rate may simply reflect a growth in the underlying population (or a change in its age-profile).

It is for this last reason that the construction of indices is particularly appropriate to this type of data.[37] In the second place, wherever sufficient data allows this, the researcher should employ careful sampling criteria.[38] But perhaps the need for the systematic use of secondary materials is rendered most salient by their sheer availability as sources of information. Thus, in modern, bureaucratic societies a wide range of records of various kinds are maintained by organizations and public authorities. Also, reasonably accurate inventories are available for use in social science. Hence, it is indispensable for current sociological inquiry to have national data on such topics as GNPs, income distributions (e.g. *Gini* indices), crime rates, membership figures of organizations, and so on. These tend to be used as direct indicators of certain social phenomena: for example, relative GNP breakdowns may be used to compare budgetary priorities in different countries. But more uses could be made of index-constructions here and, in the Durkheimian tradition, such data could be employed for more inferential purposes, as indirect indicators of attitudes and behaviour patterns.

For instance, Christensen (1960) conducted a cross-cultural analysis of marriage and birth records in order to assess the relative incidence of premarital sex relations in different societies.[39] As an indicator of this, he simply recorded the time-interval between marriage and the birth of the first child—a procedure which indicated significant differences in premarital conception, if not in activity, between different cultures. His final index was corrected by information on premarital births of later-born children. This, of course, does not rule out the possibility of errors due to a selective recording of births and marriages in the individual societies.

Errors of this last kind may be avoided when an observer is able to make inventories of his own. Perhaps the best-known example of this is the use of personal possessions (including type of house and neighbourhood) as objective indicators of social status, which derives much of its original impetus from the work of Lloyd Warner and his associates (1949).[40] But of more relevance to our present subject is a study of the poor in these terms by Oscar Lewis (1969).[41] The scene of this research was a small *vecindad* (tenement), one of the poorest in Mexico City, that housed 14 families, totalling 83 people, or an average of about 6 persons per family. The study involved a systematic inventory of all the possessions of these families, the various items being classified into 13 categories (see Figure 8.2). The total value of all the assets was approximately 4,730 dollars (or an average of about $338 per household), about 60 per cent of which was accounted for by furniture and clothing. Several further details of the type, frequency, and origins of the possessions are provided. And the author concludes as follows:[42]

> For one thing, I was struck by the truly remarkable differences within this group of families, all of whom might seem to a casual observer to be living at the same level of poverty. Moreover, the differences in the value of their possessions were greater than differences in their income. If we compare the possessions of the three 'wealthiest' families with those of the three poorest families, we see that the top three owned a total

239

of $1,754.46 worth of purchased goods, whereas the bottom three owned a total of $250.55—only a seventh as much.

A second interesting finding was that the only category in which the poorer families had spent more than the better-off was that of religious objects. The absolute difference in amount here was small, but in its proportion to the families' total investment in material goods the contrast was great. Whereas the better-off families had invested only slightly more than 1 per cent of their money in religious items, the poorer families had invested nearly 14 per cent. This is reflected in Figure 8.2, in which the relative possessions of the 'wealthiest' and the poorest family in the *vecindad* are compared.

The relative preponderance of religious items among the poorest families was an unexpected finding and presumably has some relationship to the greater insecurity of the conditions of life encountered by these families. Thus, it is also noteworthy that the investment in religious objects by the *vecindad* as a whole was remarkably large: for example, each household possessed an average of more than ten religious pictures. Moreover, as Lewis points out:[44]

The fact that the tenement dwellers had held on to religious objects longer than most of their other possessions attests to the crucial role of religion in the lives of the poor. It appears also that religious objects may be the only things they own long enough to establish a real identification with. Yet even these are held for a fairly brief period, an average of about five years. The brevity of possession, and the singular absence of heirlooms passed down from generation to generation, suggest that the life of the very poor is weak in tradition and is oriented almost exclusively to day-to-day concerns.

Lewis further observes that, although it is usually assumed that the mobility of poor people is highly restricted, the analysis of the families' possessions revealed that the objects came from 43 different markets or localities, some of them at considerable distances from Mexico City. As he writes: 'It therefore appears that at least some of the Mexican urban poor may move about more widely than has been supposed.'[45]

In sum, Lewis's study shows that a systematic, objective inventory of this kind, supplemented by some interview data, can serve as a concrete expression of the lives led by these people. That is, inferences can be made from their possessions to their patterns of evaluation and to other aspects of their local 'culture'. The objectivity (and non-reactivity) of observations of this nature needs to be emphasized since much sociological work on the culture of poverty has been criticized on the grounds that it embodies tacit middle-class value-judgments.[46]

The present study may be judged largely free of such biases. And what it indicates also, of course, is the need to avoid treating the 'culture of poverty' as an entirely homogeneous phenomenon: in fact, as this inventory demonstrates, a number of significant variations are comprised within it.

FIGURE 8.2   *The relative possessions of the poor*[43]

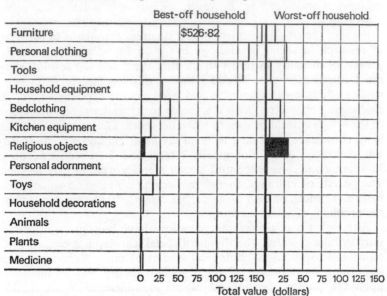

| | Best-off household | Worst-off household |
|---|---|---|
| Furniture | $526·82 | |
| Personal clothing | | |
| Tools | | |
| Household equipment | | |
| Bedclothing | | |
| Kitchen equipment | | |
| Religious objects | | |
| Personal adornment | | |
| Toys | | |
| Household decorations | | |
| Animals | | |
| Plants | | |
| Medicine | | |

O   25   50   75   100   125   150      25   50   75   100   125   150
Total value   (dollars)

## Experiments

When social observation involves the use of formal settings and the careful manipulation of independent variables the method being employed is better described as experimentation. As is well known, the 'pure' experiment involves controlling the values of all variables in the situation other than those whose interrelationships are being investigated. This is a condition more closely approximated within the natural sciences than the social sciences, in part because of the multiplicity, and immeasurability, of the factors that are potentially operative in social situations.

However, if the term is not restricted to this *cas pur*, we may say that a wide range of at least quasi-experimental evidence is available in the social sciences on various aspects of moral behaviour. This evidence has been mainly gathered by social psychologists, focusing principally on the moral behaviour and judgments of children.

241

Perhaps for this reason, it has been afforded relatively little attention in the sociological literature. None the less, its relevance, direct and indirect, for the sociology of ethics is considerable. Indeed, many of the best-validated theories of moral behaviour and development have been established by this method. Further, certain traditions of research have become crystallized over time, allowing particular studies to have a greater mutual relevancy. Since the available evidence is wide-ranging, however, we can only indicate but a few aspects of it.

Perhaps the single most important theoretical impetus to this type of research in social psychology has been Freud's account of the genesis of morality in terms of identification and the resolution of the Oedipus Complex. Freud's theory derived largely from case-studies of his own experience and need not be explained here. Its challenging character, however, needs to be understood in relation to the beliefs current in society when he wrote. Thus, in the Victorian view, conscience was taken to be of divine origin and sexual identity was conceived of as biologically established. In Freud's account, however, *both* conscience and sexual identity were largely learned. The genesis of morality, therefore, became no longer a question of natural instincts, or their absence, but essentially a problem, perhaps *the* problem, of social learning.

Although Freud's own interpretations have been given little support by later research, the theme of social learning has continued to be central to social-psychological studies of moral behaviour. One important shortcoming of the Freudian theory was its insistence upon the paramouncy of emotional identification in the child's internalization of moral precepts, to the neglect of the more 'intellectual', or cognitive aspects of moral codes. Recognition of the latter, however, does appear in the work of a number of non-Freudian researchers, and most notably in the studies of Jean Piaget, most of whose research has been conducted under broadly experimental conditions.

## Piaget

In *The Moral Judgement of the Child* (1932) Piaget investigated children's understanding of moral concepts by telling them short stories, with small variations in content, under standardized conditions, and then asking the children which of the actions described they thought to be the worst one. Two such stories were the following:[47]

> There was once a little girl who was called Marie. She wanted to give her mother a nice surprise, and cut out a piece of

sewing for her. But she didn't know how to use the scissors properly and cut a big hole in her dress.

A little girl called Margaret went and took her mother's scissors one day that her mother was out. She played with them for a bit. Then as she didn't know how to use them properly she made a little hole in her dress.

Piaget found that younger children tended to think the first story involved the naughtiest action, whilst older children chose the second. This appeared to result from a difference in moral reasoning: children from approximately four to eight years reasoned in terms of *consequences*, the worst action being the one that involved the greater damage; whilst children more than eight years old reasoned in terms of *intentions*, the better action being the one involving the worthier motive.

The results of a variety of experiments like this were summarized by Piaget in two theoretical models of morality. The first, associated with children between four and eight, he termed heteronomous, and the second, associated with older children, autonomous. These, in turn, were interpreted within his general theory of cognitive development ('genetic epistemology'). The first designates a moral code that is essentially subject to adult authority. Adult norms are perceived as immutable facts, and moral wrongness is defined in terms of adult sanctions, wrong acts being simply those which adults punish. Duty is understood as obedience to authority and the intellectual limitations of the younger child, together with his respect for authority, cause him to conceive of wrongdoing in highly literal, objective terms, without regard to context or intentions. He perceives moral values as absolute and universal, and thinks that justice is best served by severe arbitrary punishment, rather than by restitution to the person wronged.

Autonomous morality, on the other hand, is largely the reverse of this. Thus, it is said to comprise moral concepts that are subjective rather than objective, and relative rather than absolute. Norms of conduct are perceived as artifacts of group agreement, and subject to change by such agreement. Essentially they become identified as instruments of co-operative action. Similarly, emphasis is now put on the restitutive aspects of justice, which is viewed as a matter of reciprocal rights and obligations.

Piaget's theory is that this process of moral development derives principally from the child's continuing, and spontaneous, attempt to comprehend within one system his total moral experience, rather than, as Freud suggested, simply from the internalization of adult standards. The process, then, becomes as much cognitive as emotive. Some of the main aspects of Piaget's account have been given

243

cross cultural support, as in the experimental study by Bandura and McDonald (1963), although others have been disputed, such as his conception of a transition from respect for authority to a respect for peers (Kohlberg, 1963).[48] However, the point we would wish to question concerns the basic idea of a *dichotomy* between an objective, absolutized conception of morality and one which is both subjective and relativist. Expressed in this way, this seems to understate the degree to which the moral codes characteristic of social groups and societies are normally apprehended in reified and universalized terms, even by mature adults.[49] Indeed, maturity itself is often defined in terms of the acceptance and internalization of the objectivity and absolute status of cultural standards. If anything, social theories have tended historically to be anti-relativistic: that is, they have claimed to be true for all men.[50]

In sum, the transition from heteronomous to autonomous types of morality can perhaps be more validly conceived as a matter of degree, and as appropriate to some standards more than others. It is undoubtedly true that, at least within certain cultures, some aspects of moral codes do become perceived as mutable and open to collective (or individual) choice, and that they tend also to be applied in a relativistic manner. But it seems unrealistic to generalize from this to all aspects of such codes. Put otherwise, we do not doubt that the possibility of apprehending moral standards in Piaget's autonomic terms arises at the age he estimates it to, but this is not to say that this then becomes adopted as a typifying attribute of individual or social consciousness. It would seem that it does not. And it is precisely those institutional arrangements, and the process of institutionalization itself, which militate against this that are excluded from Piaget's account.

### Experiments: limitations and advantages

Our argument, therefore, would be that this aspect of Piaget's work, apart from its intrinsic interest, serves also to exemplify two limitations of experimental designs. Thus, in the first place, experiments, by their very nature, tend to focus upon individuals as the units of analysis. Social factors may, of course, be introduced; but, in practice, these tend to be restricted either to microsociological studies of the dynamics of small groups, or (more commonly) to studies of the effect of small groups upon individual behaviour (e.g. the influence of group norms on individual judgments). And in each case the groups in question are normally created *ad hoc* (according to certain criteria) for the purposes of the experiment. What experiments become less appropriate for is the study of higher-order collectivities and of individual behaviour within institutional contexts.

In the second place, and related to this, experiments tend to achieve what might be termed an 'internal' validity, but at the price of low generalizability of the findings (or external validity). The difficulty in generalizing to populations (and measures) beyond those immediately studied derives from two principal sources: namely, (i) the small samples that are characteristic of experimental designs; and (ii) the artificiality of experimental settings, and particularly their exclusion of institutional factors present in the wider society.

On the other hand, experimental designs permit more control over the variables being examined and finer discriminations within both stimuli and effects: for instance, in studies of the influence of personal values on word-recognition thresholds, the amount of time elapsing prior to correct recognition can be precisely calculated for each item and for various states of the environment. Similarly, experimental situations permit more focused, and critical observations, with less risk of data irrelevant to the hypothesis. Thirdly, experiments usually allow more complex, multivariate assessments of the interaction amongst variables, which ordinary observations might be closed to, and which survey methods might only be able to identify *post factum*, during analysis. Fourthly, the standardized setting of the experiment makes it the most feasible method for subsequent replications. And finally, although problems of reactivity are certainly present, the greater control of the experiment means that several of these can be more readily assessed and accounted for.

But despite the diagnostic value of the experiment, there remains the problem of the artificial nature of its usual context. In addition, the formal experiment may generate expectations in its subjects that add to this artificiality. Thus, as Orne (1962) states:[51]

> The experimental situation is one which takes place within context of an explicit agreement of the subject to participate in a special form of social interaction known as 'taking part in an experiment'. Within the context of our culture the roles of subject and experimenter are well understood and carry with them well-defined mutual role expectations.

It should be recognized, however, that the artificiality inherent in experimental designs is appropriate for some research purposes, if not for others. For example, as Galtung observes in his discussion of the problem of formal v. informal settings:[52]

> It may well be that the 'natural', unmanipulated, setting is better for prediction studies and the manipulated, formal setting for explanatory studies. A partial reason for this is that systematic variation of stimuli may permit the researcher to see

his unit from many angles and not only under the limited range of variation provided by the natural setting.

And he continues:

The physicist does this, but also one thing more to learn more about his material: *expose it to the extremes of the range of variation.* The structure of a compound is revealed by such methods as extreme pressure, temperature, bombardment by various particles, etc. A car is tested not under natural conditions but under extreme and artificial conditions. Correspondingly, the social scientist can learn more about the structure of a society, its strong and weak points, by observing it under crisis. And here the systematic stimuli of the formal setting enter: they can be regarded as some kind of bombardment to make the individuals reveal what is ordinarily not revealed.

We may find this last point illustrated in a number of otherwise quite diverse experimental studies of moral behaviour: they are united in their focus upon subjects' responses to rather extreme and atypical situations. And the responses to these are used as means of highlighting otherwise concealed or abstruse aspects of more familiar behaviour and reasoning. Two examples may be briefly given: those of Kohlberg and Milgram.

### Kohlberg

Various social psychologists have pursued methods of inquiry similar to those of Piaget, but special interest lies with the studies of moral development by L. Kohlberg.[53] In discussion of his work, Roger Brown (1967) comments that:[54] 'In psychology, the study of morality is often regarded as equivalent to the study of values. ... Among psychologists who study morality only one, Kohlberg, seems to have made a serious effort to separate moral values from other kinds and to invent techniques of investigation aimed at the specifically moral.'

In fact, Kohlberg's concern is with precepts for action rather than values. And he distinguishes the 'specifically moral' simply by appealing to the notion of obligatoriness contained in such terms as 'ought' and 'should', as distinct from mere statements of preference. To apply this distinction within the context of experimental research, he has developed a number of stories that describe situations of basic moral decision. To this extent his method approximates to Piaget's. Unlike Piaget, however, Kohlberg's stories are sufficiently complex to be applicable to adults: typically, they permit the articulation of moral precepts which, in the situations depicted, would contradict the *prima facie* demands of law and authority.

246

His aim is to render explicit the largely tacit moral codes which his subjects have internalized, both in respect of the general principles that are invoked to resolve moral dilemmas and also of the type of reasoning used to justify these principles. Although his methods are applicable to the study of adults, his own research has been largely conducted on children between the ages of seven and seventeen. One of the problem-situations which he presents, for example, is that of whether a man in a civilian air-defence post should, after a heavy bombing raid that may have endangered his family, stay at his position and help others or go to his family.

As an illustration, we may cite the response of a sixteen-year-old boy to this dilemma. He reasoned as follows: 'If he leaves, he is putting the safety of the few over the safety of the many. I don't think it matters that it's his loved ones, because people in the burning buildings are someone's loved ones too. Even though maybe he'd be miserable the rest of his life he shouldn't put the few over the many.'[55]

The specific reply here is of less interest than the general mode of reasoning that it embodies. In more analytic terms, this respondent can be taken as stating the following principles: first, the man should take the roles of all the people involved—('people in the burning buildings are someone's loved ones too'); second, all persons are to be considered of equal value—('I don't think it matters that it's his loved ones'); and third, the utilitarian principle of the greatest good for the greatest number—('he shouldn't put the few over the many') —is invoked to resolve the dilemma.

Problems of this kind were presented to a sample of 100 boys aged between 7 and 17 and matched for class and other background variables. Age was selected as the main interpretive variable and a series of six developmental stages with respect to changing moral concepts was postulated. These resemble Piaget's theory in several respects, although a somewhat more complex and gradual process of development, extending over a longer period of time, is proposed.

Like most inquiries of similar design, Kohlberg's procedures and interpretations are more psychological than sociological. Social factors, as the formal setting itself, are introduced as factors to be controlled for (i.e. by standardization or randomization), in order to prevent extraneous variations deriving from these sources. The primary interest is in individual psychological dynamics, *within* certain social co-ordinates. A more sociological focus could, of course, be achieved by selecting social factors as the main independent variables: for example, investigations could be made of the different styles of moral reasoning associated with different social classes. But this still involves a rather individualistic perspective. A more structural reference might be attained if the focus were upon subjects chosen as representatives of certain social institutions and

247

role-systems, rather than of purely aggregated social categories. But the problem of the formal, experimental setting, of course, still remains.

### Milgram

One response to this problem is to conduct the experiment under façade conditions. This is exemplified in the study of obedience by Milgram (1963, 1965).[56] In this, the subjects were told that they were helping to study the effects of punishment on learning, and were instructed that when another person (actually a confederate of the experimenter) made a wrong response, they were to give him an electric shock, increasing its intensity each time. The shock was ostensibly administered by a realistic-looking machine with 30 voltage switches classed in groups from 'slight shock' to 'danger—severe shock'.

About halfway up the supposed shock intensity scale, the experimenter's colleague stopped responding, and occasionally banged on the sides of the cubicle where he was sitting. The subjects were told to treat this as a wrong response, and to continue giving stronger shocks. The aim of the experiment was to find out for how long the subjects would continue to obey, if assured that although the shocks were extremely painful, they would cause no permanent damage. In fact, of the 40 subjects tested, 14 stopped giving shocks at various points, but 26 obeyed to the full. However, many of these revealed characteristic signs of nervous tension, such as trembling, profuse sweating, and outbursts of nervous laughter. The most interesting finding, then, was the sheer strength of obedience, despite the subjects having been trained from childhood to avoid giving pain to others against their will.

Milgram's study well exemplified the use of experimental conditions to investigate 'extremes of variation' in phenomena, and, unlike Kohlberg's research, his results are in the form of overt acts rather than purely symbolic, verbal responses. However, the question still arises of the manner and degree of confidence with which we may generalize from these findings. The author himself allows that some special factors might have encouraged obedience in the circumstances: the prestige of Yale University, the apparently worthy purpose of the experiment, the fact that the victim was also a volunteer, and that subjects had been paid to participate. But even if all these factors were operative, the findings are still of interest. Thus, Milgram suggests that the resultant psychological conflict manifested by many of the subjects was caused by the opposing demands of the experimenter and the victim, of advancing scientific knowledge as against personal suffering, and of obedience versus early training.

It might be noted, in passing, that the results obtained by Milgram could also be interpreted as lending support to the strength and pervasiveness of the 'Hawthorne effect' in experiments in the social sciences. The phrase derives from the famous studies in industrial sociology reported in Roethlisberger and Dickson's *Management and the Worker* (1930). It refers to those biases which arise from the tendency of subjects, who are aware of their participation in an experiment, either to over-co-operate, or to adopt too passive a role. This crucial condition of awareness held in both the original Hawthorne studies and in Milgram's research. Although, as we saw, Milgram did attempt to mislead his subjects as to the exact focus of his inquiry. On the one hand, such passivistic tendencies perhaps impose special responsibilities upon the investigator, in view of the degree of implicit trust typically ascribed to him. On the other hand, and together with unintended experimenter effects, they provide a constant source of potential error with regard to the external validity of experiments.

*Hartshorne and May*

One possible solution to the limited generalizability of laboratory experiments is the use of quasi-experimental designs, conducted in a series of different settings, and with the aid of larger samples. The classic example of this in research on moral behaviour is the series of experiments carried out by Hartshorne and May (1928–30), in which some 12,000 children were involved.[57] For their volume, *Studies in Deceit* (1928), a variety of tests were devised, including tests where it was easy to cheat, tests which the children marked themselves, coin problems with the opportunity to steal the coins, and so on. These were applied in a variety of settings: in classrooms, at home, in athletic contests, and in party games of various kinds. A principal finding of this research concerned the marked specificity of moral conduct, and of honesty in particular. The setting of the experiments, which varied in degree of naturalness, proved to be a crucial variable, and the mean correlation between bad conduct in one setting and bad conduct in another was only 0·34.

Similar results were recorded in their other two volumes, *Studies in Service and Self-Control* (1929) and *Studies in the Organization of Character* (1930). In one test of service in the former of these, for example, the schoolchildren could put pictures, stories, etc. in envelopes to give to hospitalized children, could promise to do so, or not do so. In another, the children were given a choice of whether they would work for themselves or for the class in a spelling contest. Hartshorne and May concluded, therefore, that moral behaviour, at least in children, appears largely a function of the particular situation in which it occurs. Although they also noted that tests of moral attitudes and knowledge reveal greater degrees of consistency. Some later researchers, however, have argued that Hartshorne and May somewhat overstated the specificity of moral conduct, and that their findings do indicate some generality, for instance with regard to honesty.[58] Of course, in evaluating their results, attention needs also to be given to the possibility of the operation of social desirability response-sets, and other extraneous sources of error, which may have varied with the particular settings. However, it is also arguable that the fact that the research was carried out in a broadly educational context, with the roles of the experimenters not radically dissimilar from those usually performed by teachers, means that the administration of a series of tests was a much more 'natural', familiar, and hence less reactive, process for the subjects involved.

## Other studies

Hartshorne and May's research has given rise to many subsequent experimental studies of children's moral behaviour by the use of various combinations of constraints, temptations, and rewards. But despite the ingenuity of many of these, few have been able to match the scope of the original series. Apart from this tradition of work on moral behaviour, the greater part of experimental research within the terms of the present subject appears to have been focused upon attitudinal data regarding processes of evaluation. Such processes become most amenable to experimental designs when they can be related to relatively 'constant' variables, such as the dynamics of perception. This last point is well illustrated by studies of the influence of personal values on word-recognition thresholds. The first experiment in this particular field was conducted by Postman, Bruner, and McGinnies (1948).[59] Their general hypothesis was that 'personal values are demonstrable determinants of what the individual selects perceptually from his environment.' To test this, 25 subjects were shown 36 words, one at a time, in a modified tachistoscope. The tachistoscope allowed the observations to be expressed in fundamental units (i.e. varying durations of time). The words used were chosen to represent the six values measured by the Allport-Vernon Scale of Values, which was also administered to each subject, either before or after the experiment. The results indicated a marked tendency for high-value words to be recognized at shorter time exposures than low-value words. A subsequent study by Howes and Solomon (1951), however, suggested that much of the variance in duration-thresholds could be accounted for in terms of the relative familiarity of the words to the subjects.[60]

Other studies within this general field of evaluative attitudes have examined a range of topics: for instance, the effect of group standards on individual judgments, stereotyping, dissonance and cognitive/ evaluative consistency, attitude-change, open- and closed-mindedness, and so on.[61] The majority of these findings, however, are still tentative, as the Postman study illustrates, and await further confirmations or disconfirmations. Also, taken together, they demonstrate the fact that the central problem encountered by this method—that of generalizing from the experimental microcosm to broader social and psychological processes—can only be satisfactorily resolved within the interpretative framework of empirically-based social scientific theory. And, at least within the present subject, this is still at relatively rudimentary stages of development.

In conclusion, there are, of course, many other facets of our present field of inquiry that may well prove amenable to experimental investigation. Also, there is the need to design, and utilize, experimental formats for more strictly sociological, as opposed to social-psychological, purposes. This will require both a degree of methodological insight and imagination, and also further initiative in the selection and formulation of appropriate research problems. It will also require careful attention to the problem of biases deriving either unintendedly from the experimenter himself, or from certain characteristics of the experimental situation.[62]

## Content analysis

Whereas experimental research designs permit the analysis of behavioural data gained at first hand, content analysis as a method of inquiry is restricted to secondary sources in the form of cultural artifacts (books, journals, pictures) or to *post hoc* analyses of responses to open-ended interviews and questionnaires. It differs from more informal documentary analyses by the adoption of an explicit, and standardized, coding frame, the purpose of which is to classify particular items of content into meaningful categories so as to express their essential pattern in quantitative form. The most immediate advantages of using such a coding scheme are that (i) precise replications of particular analyses can be made; and so (ii) tests can be carried out to estimate intra- and intersubjective reliabilities.

Related to this question of reliability between coders, the presence of an explicit coding scheme provides also a defence against those perceptual biases which, as social psychology has well demonstrated, tend to vitiate the objectivity of less formal types of analysis, and ways of monitoring communications. Furthermore, explicit coding schemes open up the possibility of precise, quantifiable results and the introduction of statistical measures of significance and of the covariation of two or more attributes of content.

Thus in Berelson's definition content analysis is 'a research

251

technique for the objective, systematic, and quantitative description of the manifest content of communication'.[63] Since Berelson wrote this, however, the tendency of subsequent research has been to favour a more catholic definition of the method with regard to its inclusion of both more qualitative approaches and more 'latent' interpretations of content.[64] Since, as we saw earlier in our discussion of non-verbal 'languages', communications need not employ the vehicle of words (written or spoken) in order to convey meaning, so content analysis is not necessarily restricted to written forms of communication, and hence to the literate aspects of culture. Pictorial and graphic data, where it is reasonably comparable, may also be used. Indeed, a few studies have been carried out into the values expressed in material of this kind. Wayne (1956), for instance, examined the respective content patterns of pictures appearing in the American magazine *Life* and in the analogous Russian publication *Ogonek*.[65] His analysis indicated similar profiles, but also some significant differences in detail. The pictures were classified according to a modified version of the Allport-Vernon Scale of Values, and both magazines were shown to devote a very small part of their space to theoretical, religious, and educational subjects. Each devoted somewhat over 20 per cent of their pictures to politics. The significant differences, however, were to be found in the greater weight attached to economic subjects by the Soviet publication (27·6 per cent v. 16 per cent) and in the much lower importance attached to 'tension-management' (18 per cent v. 30·8 per cent). In the latter case, the Soviet publication also differed from the American one in showing only posed, organized forms of recreation.

Although various possibilities exist for analyses of this type, particularly in view of the extensive visual and graphic records kept by the mass media, relatively few studies have so far been carried out. Of course, verbal language is usually a more precise instrument of communication, permitting finer gradations of meaning and less ambiguity than visual material. Thus, we may expect that it will permit higher levels of reliability and validity for research purposes. It is no doubt for reasons of this type, together with the sheer availability of data, that most content analyses have been conducted on written materials, either in the form of serial publications (journals, magazines, newspapers) or of books organized into distinct genres (e.g. religious literature, Cold War studies, and so on). These have been mainly used as sources of systematic data on popular culture within the general context of 'mass society'. Thus studies within the present subject have been directed principally towards identifying the relatively consensual values that are expressed in popular publications, particularly serial publications. An early example of this is the research by Johns-Heine and Hans H. Gerth (1949), who conducted a content analysis of mass periodical fiction in America between the years 1921 and 1940 in order to single out some of the dominant evaluative themes.[66] A more recent example is provided by the study by Ginglinger (1955).[67] He used a summary version of R. K. White's (1951) catalogue of values as a basis for examining the content of three popular digest-type publications in France, again in terms of their dominant orientations.[68]

The more critical uses to which analyses of this kind can be put is illustrated in the early study of American magazine fiction by Berelson and Salter (1946).[69] In this, a sample of short stories from a range of popular magazines was examined. And by accumulating data over an appreciable period of time, it was shown that these stories revealed a tacit, but pervasive ethnocentrism of outlook, which was expressed in subtle stereotyping and discrimination against non-Anglo-Saxon characters. The authors also showed that the minority problems of the United States, despite the country's ethnic heterogeneity, received very little attention in the literature.

This particular study serves to suggest some of the more constructive uses to which content analysis could be put as a means of elucidating a society's culture and the ideologies of particular groups within it. We note this since there is some tendency for content analysis in general to be employed rather mechanically and uncritically, producing enumerations of items of content that have little practical or theoretical import, and so border on the gratuitous and self-evident. To combat this a number of considerations are in order. In the first place, content analysis should be employed for more broadly comparative purposes. Second, it needs to be applied within a more institutional framework. And third, account should be taken of the discursive content of communications. In addition, it is important to be fully aware of the various assumptions that are made at different stages of this procedure. And finally, wherever possible, the leading ideas that are embodied within the coding scheme should have some explicit relationship to theoretical concerns. Brief illustration of each of these points may be given.

## Comparative approaches

First, the comparative aspect. It needs to be recognized initially here that a genuine problem of choice is encountered by many analyses of this kind that have only limited resources available (including time). It is a problem of choosing between (i) extending the number or scope of the units of analysis (whether books, papers, journals, etc.); or (ii) increasing the specificity and detail of the analysis (e.g. by studying a whole issue of a newspaper rather than merely the editorials, examining books by paragraph rather than 'globally', and so on). The

I*

particular way in which this problem is resolved in research will depend on the nature of the source material and the specific theoretical or practical purposes of the study under consideration. What we wish to point out here, however, is the general value of more comparative uses of source materials as a means of avoiding outcomes that are theoretically uninteresting or practically gratuitous.

More comparative elements can be introduced into content analysis in various ways: by sampling a broader range of materials so as to be able to compare different publications etc.; by sampling similar publications within different societies for cross-cultural purposes; by matching results attained by content analysis with those produced by other methods; by comparing findings with some standard of adequacy (e.g., of 'unbiased' news reporting); and so on. But the main advantage of content analysis over other techniques of inquiry lies in its greater suitability for longitudinal analyses. In comparison, other methods of data-collection, and survey methods in particular, are relatively present-bound. Thus, subtle changes over time in values and other attitudes can be detected by content analysis which would not normally be apparent, and which other techniques of inquiry would find either very difficult or impossible to record reliably. As a result, content analysis, imaginatively used, opens up the possibility of a more historically-oriented sociology, as well as of comparisons over more limited time-spans.[70]

This is illustrated in a few available studies. For example, De-Charms and Moeller (1962) examined the values expressed in children's readers over the time period 1800 to 1950.[71] A whole page was adopted as the unit of analysis within each reader, and the results indicated a general increase in achievement orientation up to 1900 and then a subsequent decline. They also suggested a general decline in the specifically moral content of these books. A second example would be the survey, by Schneider and Dornbusch (1958), of popular religious literature in the United States published over the years 1875–1955.[72] The source material here consisted of 46 best-sellers. All of these were analysed 'globally' (i.e. the entire book was coded for main themes) and 31 of them were further analysed by paragraph. This allowed the separate reliabilities of the two procedures to be checked against each other (indicating 74 per cent agreement on the identification of main themes). In the light of our discussion of the problem of specificity v. scope, it is of interest to note their conclusion here that 'The paragraph analysis performs most useful fine-grained operations. For general themes, however, we could discern little loss from use of the more rapid global scoring method.'[73]

Content analysis can also be of greater potential theoretical and practical significance if carried out cross-culturally, since again similarities and differences of outlook may be diagnosed which might not otherwise be apparent, or amenable to investigation. However, cross-cultural applications of this method are relatively infrequent, and it is clear that many possibilities exist here which await exploitation. As one of the few relevant examples, citation may be made of the resourceful study by Robert Angell *et al.* (1964) of élite media in Russia and America in terms of their professed social values, particularly with regard to foreign policy.[74] In this, periodicals were chosen at standardized intervals of time, representative of various matched élite-groups (political, military, scientific, cultural, etc.), and the content analysis was usually applied either to the entire contents of the publications or restricted to the editorials. Angell's study is of particular interest in that it illustrates some of the sampling problems that are involved in attempting to meet the often incompatible criteria of representativeness and equivalence in cross-cultural analyses of this kind.[75] Also it exemplifies the kind of problem—i.e. the analysis of Soviet élite values—for which content analysis (of 'élite articulations') is virtually the only systematic means of data-collection available.

A good example of a study which combined two dimensions of comparison in its design, the historical and the cross-national, is reported by Pool (1952).[76] This content analysis was conducted upon editorials drawn from prestige newspapers representing each of five countries—the United States, Britain, France, Germany, and the Soviet Union—for the period 1890–1949. Editorials published on the first and fifteenth day of each month were coded for the presence of some 416 key symbols, which included 206 geographical terms, such as names of countries, international organizations, and minority groups, and 210 major ideological and doctrinal symbols. Frequency counts were based upon the number of editorials in which particular symbols appeared and attitudes toward the symbol (e.g. 'democracy') were coded in terms of approval, disapproval, or neutrality. In this way some attempt was made to chart major changes in attitudes, values, and general foci of attention over a 60-year period covering the first half of the twentieth century. Amongst a variety of interesting findings were the following:[77]

> Symbols of representative government are used where the practice is under dispute, not where it is an accepted part of the traditions.

> Two main trends in the modern world are: (1) a shift in the center of attention, in which traditional liberalism is being replaced by proletarian doctrines, and (2) a growing threat of war and a corresponding increase of nationalism and militarism.

Mention should, of course, also be made in the present context of

255

the cross-national studies of achievement values by David McClelland (1961).[78] This work has provided motivation for a number of subsequent applications of content analysis, and well illustrates the theoretical value to be gained by applying this method within an historical and cross-cultural perspective.

From the foregoing, it will be evident that content analysis can have particular utility as a means of charting social processes *post hoc*. The eventual outcome of these processes may be well known, but the exact details of the developments which led up to them may be more obscure. This is perhaps of particular interest to conflict studies, where materials might be drawn from each of the protagonists to a situation of conflict and the complex interplay of attitudes and actions reconstructed. An outstanding example of the use of content analysis for this type of inquiry is provided by the research of Robert North *et al.* on the immediate origins of the First World War and the Cuban missile crisis of 1962.[79] In the first of these, the authors emphasized the role played by misperception and misinterpretation among the various protagonists. More recent, and on the same theme, is the study by Baum (1968), who gathered data on the values of German society before the First World War from popular novels for the period 1871 to 1914.[80] His study indicates some of the more ingenious uses to which content analysis may be put. Thus, the author adapted a questionnaire from the theoretical work of Parsons and Shils, and then completed this from the point of view of 170 fictional characters in 39 popular novels over the 33-year period mentioned. To assess reliability, a control reader completed questionnaires for 53 fictional characters in the sample, indicating an overall agreement of 78 per cent. On the basis of this data the author draws a contrast between the Prussian ethic (duty, obedience, order) and that of South Germany (traditionalism, security of custom, etc.). Such value heterogeneity, he argues, provided a social climate particularly disadvantageous to the development of democracy in a socially mobile industrial society. Where there is no consensus over basic values, he suggests, the nation-state may break apart and the very principle of majority rule itself will remain unacceptable. He concludes by noting that further research is needed on regional groups in pre-1914 Germany, and that class variation should be taken into account as a possible integrative element across the regional differences.

### Institutional reference

One important feature that is characteristic of most applications of content analysis is the absence of any institutional frame of reference. This is most apparent in the studies of 'mass culture', where the

256

analyses are conducted upon communications (papers, magazines, etc.) that, by virtue of their popularity, are taken to reflect (and determine) the attitudes of broad sections of the population. The result is a somewhat individualistic perspective analogous to that exhibited by survey methods: society is conceived as consisting of aggregates of individuals, distinguished according to a number of 'background' variables (class, age, sex, etc.). This model has an obvious utility for certain types of inquiry, but it also means that little attention is given to the major institutions in society and their organizing influence on the life of its members.

In particular, adequate use has not yet been made of content analysis for the study of social organizations. This would facilitate a more structural perspective, and its neglect is somewhat surprising in view of the unprecedented growth in modern society of large-scale formal organizations. Furthermore, the emphasis in these organizations upon accountability, the adherence to formalized rules, and decision-making by committee, together often with their sheer internal complexity, means that the more important processes occurring within them are almost invariably accompanied by written materials—statements of policy, records of decisions, and *procès-verbaux* of various kinds. This offers a rich source of data for the social scientist, and also one that largely awaits exploitation.

Of course, content analysis applied to such records is likely to provide only a selective view of any given organization: in particular, it will tend to be biased toward the activities of the élite and towards the more formal aspects of the organization. But this would seem less detrimental if the focus is upon the organization *per se* as the unit of analysis, as opposed to being on its internal structure. For this purpose at least, many of the matters that are expressed in documentary form may not otherwise be reliably ascertainable. And secondly, where required, other techniques of inquiry, such as participant observation and survey methods, can be used to study the informal and non-élite aspects of an organization, supplementing the content analysis. Again, as in the use of these other methods, special attention can be given in content analyses to the reactions of organizations, and institutions generally, to situations of crisis and conflict as a means of highlighting assumptions and priorities that might otherwise remain implicit.

The point about the élite-bias of content analysis has a more general significance. Thus, content analysis as a research technique has a special utility for studies of élite groups. This is for two main reasons. Firstly, this sector of society tends to be over-represented in many documentary materials (books, records of speeches, policy statements, etc.) simply by virtue of its position. Secondly, élite groups are often closed to other means of investigation, such as the

257

interview or questionnaire, or observation. This may be due to refusal or unavailability, but the result is that social research tends to overselect the middle ranges of society, and so content analysis offers the possibility of a valuable corrective to this.

More generally, content analysis can have a particular value where there are problems of access to data. Circumstances often exclude more direct means of inquiry and one is frequently restricted to messages produced by individuals. As we have seen, this is commonly the case in the study of élite groups. It is also often true of groups engaged in conflict-situations (e.g. in studies of enemy propaganda or, say, of the goals of proscribed political organizations, such as guerilla movements). Thirdly, it is a situation encountered also, of course, in the study of historical data. It is not surprising, therefore, that a substantial proportion of available content analyses have been carried out within these three broad categories of data.

*Rationales*

However, it is important here, as elsewhere, to realize that content analysis as a method of inquiry in social science is not restricted solely to the recording and enumeration of particular items of attitude, such as a pro or con attitude towards further immigration, or towards the espousal of achievement values. It can also be used for the study of the type of rationales offered for the attitudes adopted. This will no doubt entail more refined and complex coding schemes in many cases, and will involve less mechanical procedures than the usual additive analyses. But it offers considerable promise as a tool in social research, and one with particular relevance for the analysis of moral codes. Thus, its use in content analyses should permit this method to encompass more efficiently and inclusively the overt meaning of particular communications. Further, one would in general expect particular modes of justification and forms of reasoning to exhibit greater stabilities over time, and be less subject to extraneous sources of variation, than specific items of attitude. As such, they should afford a firmer empirical basis for generalizations and predictions.

We know of no full-scale inquiry of this type that is within the terms of our present subject. However, a few partial examples of analyses of rationales are available, and these are suggestive of some of the further research that could be carried out. For instance, in Schneider and Dornbusch's (1958) study, cited earlier, some allowance was made in their coding scheme for data on the type of justifications offered for religiosity in the literature they sampled: that it will have social value, that it will bring material prosperity, and so on. And the authors' findings suggest that perceptible changes in

258

styles of reasoning can be diagnosed over the seventy-year period of their study.[81]

Content analysis of modalities of reasoning and justification can also be conducted on survey materials: that is, on responses to open-ended interviews or questionnaires, particularly the former. Yet again this is rarely done in social research. One application of this general type of inquiry which may be cited, however, is given in Richard Brandt's book, *Hopi Ethics* (1954). Part of this study involved an interview session with 26 Hopi subjects in which they were asked to express their views about the rightness or wrongness of some thirty types of conduct, selected partly for probable interest in cross-cultural comparison and partly for supposed simplicity and familiarity to the Hopi. The informants were then asked to explain *why* they held the views they had expressed. Their responses were recorded, and Brandt provides a summary classification of some of the most frequently cited reasons, which include those given in Table 8.1.

TABLE 8.1 *Hopi rationales of conduct*[82]

| | |
|---|---|
| 1 Injury of somebody: public, the victim, the agent himself | 59* |
| 2 Need of money and food: the family needs it, you can't afford it, food is hard to get | 57 |
| 3 It makes trouble, enemies, friction | 39 |
| 4 It's his business, their business | 33 |
| 5 Upsetting psychologically: hurts someone's feelings, makes one sad, etc. | 26 |
| 6 You must support your family | 23 |
| 7 This is futile, does no good | 21 |
| 8 This is your child; you should love it; it is your responsibility to your child | 21 |
| 9 You shouldn't condemn it, because it can't be helped; e.g. children don't know any better than to fight | 21 |
| 10 This is treatment justified by the wrongdoing of its victim | 20 |

* This represents a simple additive index arrived at from the sum of (i) the number of times a reason was mentioned in connection with some type of behaviour, and (ii) the number of different types of behaviour in connection with which that reason was mentioned.

Of course, this is only a rudimentary analysis, and the results might have been different had other forms of behaviour been inquired into. But at least it serves to suggest that this type of analysis is possible on a cross-cultural basis, even with relatively refractory materials, such as those drawn from preliterate communities. Thus further analyses of the above kind might, in certain cases, lead to coding schemes that could be applied to such a community's myths, traditional stories, etc. in a manner analogous to the tradition of structural anthropology.[83]

It could, of course, be argued that one limitation of a content analysis of rationales for attitudes and actions, as indeed of specific attitudinal items, is that some of the most common types of reasons, as some of the most basic attitudes, are also largely taken for granted and so remain implicit. Thus, their elucidation might seem to require the use of a more 'intrusive' method, such as the interview or question-naire, which would permit specific probes to be made. There is probably often a great deal of truth in this, and it is a possible limitation of many content analyses of which we should be aware. However, the most immediate answer to the problem is that content analysis may itself be applied in more intrusive ways. Thus it is somewhat misleading to state, as Galtung does, that 'In practice, it looks as if the real characteristic of the data that content analysis makes use of is that the data are printed and not produced for the purpose of investigation.'[84]

In fact, of course, neither of these conditions need be fulfilled. One example where the second requirement is not met is in the use of content analysis as a supplementary method to the open-ended inter-view or questionnaire. A fuller instance is in the application of content analysis to topic essays (e.g. future autobiographies) that have been set by the investigator. A number of variations on this basic procedure are available. For instance, as part of his studies of achievement motivation, McClelland (1953, 1961) presented his subjects with a number of pictures relevant to this theme and asked them to write short, five-minute stories about them, which were then subject to content analysis.[85] This technique, of course, unites content analysis with a projective approach. In a similar way, content analysis may also be applied to 'topic drawings': that is, drawings made (usually by young children) on a specific subject or theme laid down by the investigator. This is demonstrated by the cross-national research of Peter Cooper *et al.* on children's conceptions of 'war' and 'peace' as expressed in their paintings on these topics.[86]

Techniques of this kind, then, do allow some specific probing of taken-for-granted attitudes and modes of reasoning. However, their utility for this purpose is limited. Thus, procedures like the topic essay are largely restricted to studies of children (and possibly stu-dents) or to individuals willing to participate in experimental situations. Secondly, since (as in the postcoded survey) this data *is* produced for the social scientist, potentially reactive elements enter from which content analysis as a whole is usually relatively free. Thirdly, these intrusive forms of content analysis tend only to lead to the explication of 'obvious' and taken-for-granted items if the investigator already has some idea of their nature. Finally, within the constraints of content analysis, even these procedures will not wholly absolve the necessity for a degree of inference with respect to the identification of modes of reasoning, if not specific attitudes, simply because these will be frequently manifested in elliptical forms. It is here that we can see the special advantage for this purpose conferred by the greater flexibility of survey methods.

Nevertheless, a second response to this problem of implicit and taken-for-granted reasons is to give special attention to those situations—which may range from 'real-life' strikes and international conflicts to simulated debates—in which the presumptive 'obviousness' of certain attitudes or actions is called into question. Clearly, it is in situations of this type, and in the communications that may be derived from them, that basic justifications are most likely to be elicited. A further strategy is to focus upon the more formal, and less substantive, aspects of reasoning. In Chapter 3 we considered some examples of this. For instance, we contrasted extrinsic with intrinsic modes of justification. Further conceptual analysis of this kind should supply models which could be applied in content analysis research. As yet few inquiries have been carried out along these lines. However, an interesting analysis of political rhetoric by Shneidman (1963) does attend to styles of reasoning in order to infer personality traits of the speaker.[87] As Holsti (1970) sums up this method:[88]

> The text is first coded into two category sets. *Idiosyncrasies of reasoning* include 32 categories consisting of idiosyncrasies of relevance, idiosyncrasies of meaning, arguments containing suppressed premises or conclusions, idiosyncrasies of logical structure, and idiosyncrasies of logical interrelations. *Cognitive maneuvers* consist of 65 styles of thought development; for example, to switch from normative to descriptive mode, or to render another's argument weaker or stronger by paraphrase.

After this, the logical conditions under which each idiosyncrasy is controverted are worked out and the psychological assessment is based upon this. Such a method for analysing logical styles, within a content-analysis framework, is plainly suggestive for our own concerns. None the less, in Shneidman's particular usage one must recognize that the psychological inferences are heavily dependent upon theoretical assumptions.

### Assumptions and theory

And this leads to our final point: namely, that, however reliable a particular coding frame might prove, content analysis as a research method does not guarantee access either to the author's intentions or to the effects of a given communication. Without additional empirical data, generalization to either of these must take the form of imputation. These, then, are the main interpretative problems raised by

261

content analysis. They may be expressed in simple diagrammatic form as in Figure 8.3.

FIGURE 8.3 *Intentions, content and effects in content analysis*

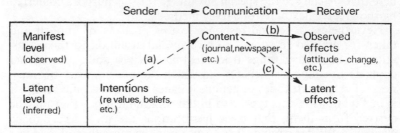

Most of the available literature on content analysis has focused upon relation (a) in the above diagram: namely, the problem of inferring from manifest to latent content. Relations (b) and (c), concerning inferences between overt content and manifest and latent effects, have been treated only secondarily.[89]

Even less frequently have attempts been made to go beyond presentation of the problems to an empirical investigation of these relationships in content analysis. Obviously, there are practical limitations here: one cannot, for instance, constantly check one's coding of a newspaper's editorials by interviews with the editor. But one can do so occasionally. Similarly, it is often practicable to test the results of one's analysis of a given communication against (i) the perceptions of content by a sample of the recipients; and (ii) against the observed effects of the communication (or series of communications) on such a sample, in terms of attitude-change, attitude-acquisition, subsequent behaviour, etc.

The problem with using ordinary recipients to make assessments of content is that coding frames are frequently too complex for this purpose, unless radically simplified. And such simplification may raise problems of comparability. Thus, as Schneider and Dornbusch (1958) note with respect to their study,[90]

> The persons who did the paragraph and global analyses of the forty-six works are all professionals in the field of social research or publishing. . . . It is a valid question, therefore, whether their apprehension of meanings and that of ordinary readers are congruent. To meet the challenge of this question, it would be desirable to have a panel of untutored laymen read these books and record their findings. Unfortunately, this is not practicable, for the very act of training these people to analyze the books in a manner permitting direct comparisons would prove self-defeating. Our coding scheme is too complex to be taught

without introducing a new element of sophistication into the act of reading.

But this is not always impossible; and even simplified tests of recipients' perceptions of the main themes of a communication, when compared with one's own, more complex analysis, can be of considerable value. In a similar way, tests can usually be carried out on the manifest effects of communications. There are, of course, many studies of the effects of communications already available in social science. Aside from numerous marketing surveys, and surveys on such topics as the effects of television, there are a number of well-controlled inquiries into this subject in social psychology which make use of panel analysis. But few of these have been systematically related to independent content analyses of the communications.

Empirical inquiries into these relationships in any particular study would not simply constitute tests of validity, and discoveries of incongruencies between intentions, apparent content, and effects should not of themselves warrant rejection of the results of the content analysis. Rather, these may be taken as findings in their own right, and possibly ones of substantial empirical and theoretical interest. For instance, they may lead us to discern pressures upon authors which restrict accurate expression of their intentions. By collecting data over extended periods of time 'intervening variables' operative between author and communication may be diagnosed of which the author himself is largely unaware. Or the presence of incongruencies may suggest observations regarding the differential efficacies of varying types of communication upon their audiences. In short, they may allow us to develop more complex and more complete models of particular processes of communication; models which would elucidate the complex interplay of intentions, communications, effects, and intervening variables of various kinds. And again interest should be directed not solely upon the transmission of specific values, precepts, opinions, etc., but also, and perhaps more importantly, upon the communication of their justification and the reasoning which supports them. It is important to distinguish these two aspects of the content of a communication, and one might expect, for instance, that many communication processes effectively transmit particular precepts or even values, but fail to convey adequately their respective justifications. As a result, the recipient might either accept, or at least be aware of, the particular 'point' of the message, but be unaware of the reasoning that attends it. It is perhaps by accepting conclusions whilst rejecting their rationales in this way that individuals can use communications for their own purposes, and to reinforce quite different attitudes from those intended by the communicator.

263

Thus, in so far as the discursive aspects of moral codes, as distinct from their specific content, can be communicated, the effects are likely to be more pervasive and enduring, and in this sense the communication may be described as more 'efficient'. To give a simple illustration: a race-relations programme will be more successful to the extent that it can communicate not merely specific prescriptions that are anti-discriminatory, but also a mode of reasoning about race relations that invalidates attitudes of prejudice and acts of discrimination in general.

To summarize: content analysis, rather than being used entirely in isolation, can be usefully related to attitudinal (or behavioural) measures from either the initiators or the receivers of the communication under study. Such an approach would have a general theoretical and empirical interest, apart from being a means of indicating the adequacy of the content analysis itself. Thus, it would allow content analysis to be related to more social and contextual concerns, rather than (as at present) involving treatments of communications, so to speak, *in vacuo*. The only short-coming of such complementary investigations into intentions and effects is that these might introduce reactivity effects. But under sufficiently controlled conditions it might also be possible to estimate and make allowances for these.

The more general point to be derived from these considerations is that content analysis can often be most valuably employed in consort with other measures and techniques of inquiry. Often quite simple combinations can enhance the theoretical significance of content analyses, as is demonstrated by the study of Middleton (1960).[91] In this, the author conducted a longitudinal analysis of the fertility values expressed in magazine fiction and related these to actuarial fertility figures for the same period. The time-periods 1916, 1936, and 1956 were selected, and fertility values were assessed by recording the size of fictional families in eight popular American magazines. Comparison with the population statistics indicated that changes in the size of the fictional families closely matched changes in the true national fertility levels. Thus, the author suggests that the media, if carefully sampled, can serve as a mirror of society's changing values—or at least of some selective elements within society.[92]

But content analysis used on its own can have a wider sociological significance if its coding frame is constructed with some reference to theoretical concerns or to relevant conceptual distinctions. For instance, in studies of moral codes it is often best to go beyond simple dichotomous or trichotomous codings (i.e. recording attitudes towards a particular subject in terms of being positive, negative, indifferent, etc.). That is, wherever possible, allowance should be made for the provision of graded information of *how* positive or

264

negative an evaluation is, or *how* stringent a prescription. The amount of detail which is to be included will, of course, depend on the nature of the source material and the type of analysis envisaged. But it is often best to err on the side of excess here, since, if required, some of the categories can be subsequently collapsed. On the other hand, we do recognize that coding for intensity can easily become very complex, in large part because of the variety of linguistic devices that are available to denote degrees of intensity.

The design of the coding scheme is important precisely because it forms, in effect, the concrete, operational expression of the researcher's hypotheses and theoretical assumptions. Hence, as Berelson observed, any particular content analysis stands or falls by its categories.

One further point. Content analysis as a method suffers at present from a lack of standardized coding categories. The introduction of these would have two clear advantages. First, it would mean that the findings of different studies could be directly compared and that traditions of cumulative research could be initiated. Second, it would permit the development of *content norms* for particular classes of communications. This, in turn, would allow one to assess whether the findings of any given content analysis marked any significant deviation from general standards for this class of communications. For instance, one could ask whether a particular newspaper was unusually objective in its presentation of the news. Or whether a particular magazine was atypical in its treatment of religious subjects. And so on. A further advantage of standard categories concerns the encouragement they would give to comparisons of content across different media. So far few such comparisons have been made. But research of this kind has an immediate theoretical importance in that it questions the extent to which we may validly generalize about the 'mass media'. To what degree do they in fact exhibit the moral homogeneity so commonly ascribed to them? The answers to such questions should permit much more refined models of mass society to be developed.

Coding schemes are usually to be judged in terms of both their inductive and deductive adequacy. That is, we ask whether they do justice both to the empirical materials under examination and also to the theoretical expectations being tested, although the one or the other will receive differential emphasis depending on the nature of the research. In a similar way, standard categories may be derived in either a primarily inductive or deductive manner. Essentially inductive categories, for example, have been developed for descriptive studies of newspaper content.[93] But what is particularly needed is the development of theoretically-derived schemes. Among the most obvious of such schemes are those providing operational definition of typologies of values. Thus, the previously-cited studies by Wayne (1956) and Ginglinger (1955) made use, respectively, of the typologies of Allport and Vernon and R. K. White. The further development of such typologies, therefore, and particularly the inclusion within them of the discursive elements of moral codes, is an important prerequisite for the more extensive application of content analysis to the present subject-area.

Naturally, some degree of individual judgment will enter into any but the most rudimentary forms of coding, and so tests of intra- and intersubjective reliability will be necessary. For this purpose it is usually preferable to supplement judgmental items with quantitative indices: e.g. the number of lines, paragraphs, or minutes devoted to a given subject, or a particular point of view. However, it is important here to be fully aware of the procedural assumptions that are being made. The most familiar simplifying assumption is that the frequency of mention, or the amount of time or space devoted to, a particular subject or point of view can be taken to indicate its perceived importance and centrality in the communication. It should be evident that this assumption is not invariably a valid one.

Against the pervasive idea of a necessary relationship between frequency and importance, for example, it has been argued that this draws attention away from the crucial role of the context in which statements occur, and in which they may be under- or over-emphasized. In addition, the single appearance or omission of an attribute in a communication may possess greater significance than the relative frequency of other characteristics.[94] Since selectivity in the treatment of facts is the hallmark of propaganda, the latter is particularly true if one wishes to analyse communications designed to manipulate existing attitudes or beliefs.[95] It is important, therefore, that implicit premisses such as these be spelled out and, wherever possible, subjected to some test of their validity. This need for explicitness applies as much to procedural assumptions as to more general inferences concerning the antecedents or effects of a communication.

Until recently, content analysis has been treated as a cheap, but often laborious method, and one that is largely secondary to other techniques of investigation, such as the traditional survey. There are now indications that this method has become a more systematic and rigorous instrument of research in its own right.[96] For one thing, explicit sampling criteria seem to be increasingly employed in content analyses, and, of course, the further development of methods of time-sampling should prove particularly fruitful here. Also to be encouraged is the greater use of multi-stage designs, involving sampling of *sources* of communication, of *units* of communication (e.g. documents), and also *within units* of communication (e.g. randomly selected pages).

## Computer applications

In the second place, computer applications of content analysis have been developed. These can reduce much of the tedium of this method. In general, the introduction of computer-based content analysis designs should allow more elaborate coding frames, more extended use of source materials, more rapid and complex data analysis, and also the capability for reanalysing data stored on punched cards according to strictly novel specifications. A full description of available programs is beyond our immediate needs here. Suffice it to note that beyond simple frequency-count programs, there are also dictionary-type systems available. These enable text words to be looked up and automatically coded with information representing the researcher's frame of reference and theoretical assumptions. The coded text may then be manipulated and categorized according to whatever type of information is required. The best-known of these programs is the 'General Inquirer' system developed at Harvard.[97] There are now several 'dictionaries' within the General Inquirer format and these are based upon a variety of theoretical assumptions. For example, one follows the procedures developed by McClelland for the manual scoring of 'need achievement' imagery in projective test materials. The dictionary classifies about 1,200 entries into 25 tag categories representing, in operational form, McClelland's basic theoretical assumptions. A second type of dictionary tags words according to the semantic differential system, which is to be described below. And so on. The result is that one can, for instance, quickly examine expressed attitudes toward specific topics and also interrelate various attributes of the text. Furthermore, the same data can be analysed by a series of dictionaries for different theoretical purposes.

The future will no doubt see the development of more adequate and versatile programs along these lines. These should certainly aid the analysis of systems of values and rules, and also, at least potentially, of the distinctive modes of justification associated with them. In conclusion, we would agree with Holsti's (1970) judgment that: 'The computer, like any tool properly used, can enhance the creativity of the scholar by freeing more of his time for those indispensable ingredients of significant research—the original idea, the creative hunch, the insight which is necessary to make "facts" meaningful.'[98] The only proviso to be added is that in order to make use of these possibilities theoretical assumptions will need to be defined much less ambiguously than at present, and operational hypotheses specified with a new rigour and precision.

## Projective techniques

The extensive use of projective techniques, such as the Rorschach and the Thematic Apperception Test, in the study of personality dynamics has suggested the possibility of their application to the study of attitudes as well, particularly when it seems desirable not to question the respondent directly, but to arrive at an indirect expression of the attitude.

### Uses

Thus, the motivation for this class of measures in social science derives mainly from psychology. In psychology, projection, like displacement, is treated primarily as a mechanism of defence, its function being to enable the subject to remain unaware of something he does not wish to face directly. Similarly, in attitude investigations projective tests attempt to tap otherwise inaccessible attitudes by indirect means. The advantage of projective techniques, then, is that by virtue of being indirect and relatively impersonal, a degree of validity can be achieved by them that would, at least in certain situations, not be attainable by direct methods, such as the interview or questionnaire. That is, they are thought to have a special applicability to controversial items (e.g. attitudes towards race in a recently integrated area), or to 'sensitive' issues upon which the respondent is likely to be evasive, to rationalize, or to conceal the views he holds. In the second place, projective tests are often used as a means of investigating issues that are outside an individual's usual self-awareness, and so which direct questioning might fail to elicit. Thirdly, projective methods are often justified as a means of overcoming problems of inarticulacy and limited reasoning ability. Thus, an individual may not be able to express adequately his attitudes towards a particular subject, perhaps because of their complexity, and so it may be necessary to approach these in an indirect manner. This is a problem particularly encountered in research on children, preliterates, and highly peripheral and deprived groups in a society. However, account must be taken here not only of inability to express one's views about relatively complex or subtle issues, but also of social groups, either on the local or more societal level, that are simply unaccustomed, and hence untrained, to do so. This may not be a salient difficulty in highly educated, socially complex societies, such as those in which most social research is carried out. But it becomes much more frequently encountered in undeveloped, highly unitary societies that are closed in Popper's sense of the term.[99] Further, it is perhaps a problem particularly associated with many ethical questions, in view both of their emotional connotations and of their cognitive grounding in the 'nature of things'. Thus, such taken-for-granted attitudes might often appear best explicated indirectly, through the use of projective techniques.

In sum: methods of investigation, such as the interview and questionnaire, which depend on the subject's own report of his behaviour, attitudes, feelings, and beliefs presuppose that he is willing and also qualified to give such information about himself. But individuals are often unwilling to discuss certain topics, particularly when they have a significant evaluative, or emotional, content. And in other cases they may not be aware of their real feelings or they may have made convenient rationalizations. Finally, even when they are aware of their attitudes, they may be unable to convey them adequately in response to direct questions.

*Types of projective tests*

To surmount these difficulties, a number of projective approaches are available that are considered to be more or less independent of the subject's degree of self-insight, or of his willingness to state his views explicitly. However, since these projective measures vary considerably, and since the nature of the response obtained will be closely related to the type of instrument used, it is necessary to give some preliminary indication of the range of projective methods that are available. For this purpose, the classification in Table 8.2 may be of use.

TABLE 8.2 *Types of projective tests*

| | Non-directive ———————————→ Directive | | | |
|---|---|---|---|---|
| Visual: | Rorschach | T.A.T. | Drawings | Photographs |
| Verbal: | Word-association | | Sentence-completion | Indirect (e.g. 'Other people') questions |

With regard to the directive/non-directive distinction, the essential point is that in the more directive forms of projective testing the stimulus to which the subject responds is more specifically defined by the investigator; that is, it is more structured. In the Rorschach and word-association tests, on the other hand, and particularly the former, the stimulus is unstructured; the meaning, or interpretation, is supplied entirely by the respondent. This meaning is 'projected' on to the ostensible subject-matter of the test.

It may be noted here that one difference between the visual and verbal methods is that the former can generally be less directive and more symbolic than the latter. Further, the non-verbal presentation can help overcome problems of illiteracy and facilitate questioning across the language barrier in cross-cultural inquiries. On the other hand, verbal methods generally offer the possibility of more specifically-focused stimuli, and hence in some cases less irrelevant information.

However, in our above classification both the visual and the verbal methods of inquiry are intended to elicit primarily verbal (written or spoken) responses from the subject. In addition to this, then, it may be noted that there are also a number of behavioural projective tests, such as those of doll-play and figure-drawing of various kinds. These, however, are mainly designed for use with children.

Aside from the visual/verbal distinction, projective tests also differ, as we have seen, according to the degree of directiveness of the stimuli. Since all the types cited in the diagram may be applied in studies of an individual's values and precepts, particularly the former, some of these may now be illustrated in terms of the present subject.

In the first place, highly unstructured, abstract tests, like the Rorschach, are, at least in sociology, used for mainly exploratory purposes. They are designed to encourage the subject to reveal himself without being aware of the fact that he is doing so. Hence, they are sometimes employed in anthropology as a means of determining a community's main concerns, which other, possibly more ethnocentric methods might have failed to discern. Or they may be used as a means of validating one's prior conceptions of these concerns. Oscar Lewis (1958) uses the Rorschach for this last purpose in his study of the village of Tepoztlán, which we cited earlier. His intention here was to give some confirmation to his findings derived from other sources, including interviews and participant observation, especially with regard to the emotional reactions of the villagers. Similarly, Cora DuBois (1961), for instance, in her well-known study of the Alor used Rorschach tests in order to gauge some of the main preoccupations of the people, and to test some of her predictions, deriving from knowledge of the social structure, of consequent emotional problems and expected responses.[100] In other studies, the same method has been applied to suggest insights into subjects which respondents would not normally discuss: such as intra-family problems, or questions of magic and supernatural belief.

The main value of the Rorschach is its non-directiveness. It is not necessarily free of response-sets, or of problems of reactivity, but it involves the presentation of a stimulus which does not in itself predetermine the subject's categories of response: he is free to see in the Rorschach whatever he wishes. Thus, a special validity is claimed for it in much the same way that this is claimed for unstructured methods generally in social research. Like the latter, however, it raises several analytic problems. Scoring of Rorschach data is becoming fairly well standardized. Thus, particular responses are scored usually in terms of the number of items seen, whether the items involve the whole of the ink blot or only parts, the qualities perceived (form, colour, movement), and the type of things reported (persons, plants, animals, etc.). But the interpretative problem remains, it seems, one that is to be largely solved in terms of subjective judgment.

Similar comments apply to word-association tests. These, however, have been largely restricted to use in individual diagnostic psychology. The only variant of this procedure that is used fairly frequently in sociology, and has some relevance to the present subject, is Osgood's semantic differential test, and this is to be considered later in this chapter.

Thematic Apperception Tests, and sentence-completion procedures, provide more structured stimuli for the subject to respond to. Also, each permits the degree of definition, or structure, of the stimulus to be varied. Thus, the TAT, like the Rorschach, is intended to reveal the subject's main concerns, but in a way that requires less imaginative effort on his behalf. Hence, it is often useful as a means of eliciting semi-conscious and half-concealed attitudes. Similarly, it can have a special applicability to controversial subjects, and to emotion-laden attitudes, which may be highly salient to an individual, but which he is unprepared to verbalize directly. This is illustrated by the study of De Vos et al. (1961), in which the TAT was used in two villages in South-West Japan in order to investigate women's attitudes towards their marriage roles.[101] The projective test was used as an indicator of attitudes towards arranged v. love marriages, with regard to sex relations, self-expression, and conflict between the wife and the husband's mother, subjects that would have been concealed from direct questioning. Thus, the authors were able to validate their hypothesis that differences in the socio-economic status and role of women would be reflected in the projective psychological materials.

The more comparative uses to which this test may be put are illustrated in Banfield's (1958) study of a village in Southern Italy.[102] He found that in most of the stories told by sixteen peasants who were given the TAT, the central character was explicitly defined as a father or mother, son, or daughter, thus indicating the overriding centrality of the nuclear family in their lives. And as Banfield continues:[103]

The adult individual, then, is thought of as a parent bringing up children. In Montegrano this is viewed as—and is in fact— a hard and unremitting struggle. Parents must work desperately merely to keep the family alive. But they have an obligation also to 'set the children on the right road,' i.e., to put them in a position to marry and have children of their own. This necessitates continued 'sacrifices' for the sake of the children. ('There was a poor man who had many children and who made many sacrifices to set them on the right road. . . .' TAT stories characteristically begin.) Children are naturally lazy and wayward; all the homilies, scoldings, and beatings an indulgent parent gives them may not suffice to set them on the right road. . . . No matter how hard the parents struggle, the family may suddenly be destroyed or reduced to beggary. The peasant expects some dreadful calamity to befall it at any moment.

These preoccupations are revealed in the peasants' responses to the TAT test, where stories of misadventure predominate. But to show that this predominance is atypical, as opposed to being, say, characteristic of peasants or farm labourers generally, some comparative evidence is needed. Banfield provides this by conducting comparable tests on farm labourers in Northern Italy and on farm owners in rural Kansas. Although these three groups are not perfectly matched, the results do confirm his interpretation (see Table 8.3).

TABLE 8.3   *TAT stories having themes of calamity or misfortune*[104]

|  | (i) Southern Italy | (ii) Northern Italy | (iii) Rural Kansas |
|---|---|---|---|
| Story ends in: | | | |
| (a) Calamity (death, etc.) | 44 | 13 | 9 |
| (b) Misfortune (injury, loss of money, etc.) | 20 | 11 | 7 |
| (c) Calamity or misfortune averted or mitigated | 26 | 38 | 26 |
| (d) Safety (no theme of peril) | 7 | 29 | 50 |
| (e) Unclassifiable | 3 | 9 | 8 |
| Total | 100 | 100 | 100 |

(i) 320 stories by 16 persons; complete Murray test of each respondent. (ii) 200 stories by 10 persons; complete Murray test of each respondent. (iii) 386 stories by 30 persons; incomplete Murray test.

Like the TAT, sentence-completion tests may be more or less directive according to the amount of detail given in the stimulus. One application of this method was cited in chapter 5 (in the section on 'Attitudes and actions'), namely, the study by Getzels and Walsh (1958), which used both direct and indirect (i.e. sentence-completion) questions in order to examine the relationship between children's expressed, or manifest, and 'real', or latent, attitudes towards a number of subjects, such as honesty, religion, race, and helping others.[105] It will be recalled that consistent differences according to age, sex, and socio-economic status were found in the degree of discrepancy between responses to projective and direct items, and that this was taken as a preliminary indicator of the kind of social factors affecting veracity and expression in children.

Sentence-completion tests have also a particular value as a means of overcoming problems of differential articulacy. These are problems especially associated with research on children and the social periphery. But they may also be encountered in more typical interviewing situations. Thus, the problem of inarticulacy was one justification for the use of sentence-completion tests by E. M. and M. Eppel (1967) in their study of adolescent morality.[106] This research investigated the attitudes of fifteen- to eighteen-year-olds attending day-release colleges in central and east London. Various projective measures were employed, although in some the specifically projective element was minimized. One of the questions, for instance, asked respondents to complete the sentence 'It's wrong to . . .'. The responses to this were coded, and the largest number of replies were shown to fall into the category of 'unfairness to people'. In other cases, however, the problems of inarticulacy and limited reasoning ability are much more apparent: as is illustrated in the study by Green (1965).[107] She wanted to compare the cultural attitudes of East Indian and negro children in Trinidad. For this purpose, samples of twelve-year-old children from low-income families representative of each racial group were drawn from a number of primary schools. In view of the nature of the population, the attitudinal material was gathered by means of incomplete sentence blanks, which were directed towards three main topics: social reference and self-adequacy; extra-family involvement; and free expression. The results indicated a clear difference between the negro and East Indian groups. The negroes were oriented towards the present; the East Indians to the past and their cultural heritage, and towards the future in respect of material prosperity. Further, the negroes valued self-expression and had a wider range of social interaction; the East Indians, on the other hand, valued self-control and their interaction was restricted, usually at the level of the family. In this way, some insight was gained into the nature of a 'plural society'.

Drawings and photographs of various kinds can also be employed in more directive projective tests, and respondents asked to describe, evaluate, prescribe for, etc. the scenes that are depicted. This has the advantage of being likely to enlist the interest of the subject, and also of being able to present situations of particular local significance.

273

Thus, they can be used in place of the Rorschach and TAT in cultures in which these fail to produce any significant responses (see Adcock and Ritchie, infra).

Goldschmidt and Edgerton (1961) report upon a technique for studying values that involves presentation of a series of drawings which present value-choices.[108] Respondents are asked what specified actors will, and should, do in the situations depicted. In the first study, the pictures were applied to an Amerindian population, for whom a graduated range of degrees of acculturation had been previously established. Five of the eleven pictures used elicited significant differences in response between the acculturated and the un-acculturated respondents. Similar techniques were also employed by the authors in the Culture and Ecology Project: this involved the use of survey research methods (together with the projective items) to investigate values, attitudes, and personality characteristics among both the herding and farming sectors of four tribes in East Africa (the Kamba, Hehe, Pokot, and Sebei) and attempted to determine the degree to which differences in these subjective factors were due to differences in ecology (Edgerton, 1971).[109]

Picture cards having some plausible reference to achievement values have also been utilized by McClelland (1953, 1961).[110] The usual procedure followed here is that subjects are presented with four such cards and asked to write short, 5-minute stories about each of them. These stories are then content-analysed according to the frequency with which the subject mentions 'doing things better', this being taken as an index of achievement motivation. Unlike many investigators using this type of method, however, McClelland is aware that extraneous cues might be drawn from the type of context in which the test is taken. Thus he varies the application of the tests according to three types of situations: conditions that are evocative of the motivation to achieve; neutral conditions; and 'relaxed' conditions. In this way, an attempt is made to hold the effects of the situation constant, in order to measure the 'inner drive' to achieve.

For inquiries into more substantive and specific attitudes, the same type of procedure may be adopted, although with the use of more directive pictures. In an early study of this kind, Proshansky (1943) studied class attitudes towards labour as these were expressed in the responses of subjects to pictures which showed working people in various conflict situations.[111] The use of locally-significant photographs in anthropological interviewing has also been discussed by Collier (1967), who gives a number of illustrations[112]—although, as he suggests, the use of clear photographs of familiar situations, though it certainly *can* have projective value, is none the less perhaps best suited to eliciting more factual descriptions and explanations regarding a community and its culture.

In some cases of the use of these visual methods, subjects need not be asked to tell a story based on the picture presented, but, less demanding, simply to indicate what an individual depicted is likely to be thinking or saying. Alternatively, they may be afforded a series of possible responses and asked to select the most appropriate one from these. As part of his research on socialization, Bernstein (1968), for example, has reported on the responses of young children to a picture showing a burglar encountering a man whilst leaving a house.[113] The children were asked simply what they thought the burglar would say. The results indicated a clear difference in the attitudes towards authority of the middle-class and working-class children: in the first group, expressions of remorse were most common; in the second, expressions of defiance.

Finally, the use of indirect questions has become a familiar part of survey research. The majority of studies which have utilized these techniques have been concentrated on the investigation of racial or ethnic attitudes. For instance, subjects might be asked how they think certain other people (with varying degrees of specification) would react if negro families moved into their neighbourhood. Their reply would then be taken as indicative of their own attitudes towards negroes. It is important to be careful here, however, to avoid indirect questions to which the respondent might plausibly be able to supply an objective answer. To give a simple example: if asked the question 'How do you think most people feel about the issue of capital punishment?' at a time when the issue is being publicly aired, a respondent might well base his reply upon opinion figures remembered from his newspaper. In such a case, his response would bear no necessary relationship to his own attitudes and so would be quite ineffective as a projective measure.

There are, of course, other forms of indirect questions, and the example given above could be variously rephrased (e.g. 'What do you think a regular churchgoer will feel about the issue of capital punishment?'; or 'What do you think those who really know about the subject feel about the issue of capital punishment?' and so on). Or, even better, it could form part of a series of indirect (and possibly direct) items tapping the attitude in question. An ingenious example of this type of approach is reported by Carter (1956).[114] He adopts what he terms a 'Platonic dialogue' technique to measure the importance of certain value-concepts to three groups: namely, 42 Indian nationals, 79 Filipinos, and 60 university students. The technique involved discussion of a fictional newly-discovered country in terms of various issues. These included its type of government, race relations, birth-control, religion, and family structure. Each paragraph of the dialogue was written so that it contained only one value-concept. Subjects were asked to place $+ +$, $+$, $-$, $- -$, beside each argument with which they would agree or disagree if they were discussing the national goals of the country. No mark indicated uncertainty of agreement or disagreement and this approach was considered superior to calling for a 'no opinion' or 'DK' response. The author notes that among the technique's advantages for measuring values in a cross-cultural study are the interest and motivation on the part of the subjects that it permits. Also, it allows a relatively wide range of interrelated issues to be examined, and calls for the valuation of types of justification as well as the expression of specific attitudes. However, techniques of this general type will also encounter population restrictions: as Daniel Lerner (1964) has shown, the ability to project one's attitudes into entirely novel contexts is largely a function of the degree of modernization of a society and of the development of mass media within it.[115]

In sum, indirect questioning is a flexible procedure, with many possible variants, and one easily introduced into standard survey practice. It is also frequently employed in market research: a common type of question, for instance, asks the respondent to describe the kind of person who would own or purchase a particular product, as a means of assessing the respondent's 'image' of this product.

### Limitations of projective tests

We have outlined above some of the special uses of projective measures, and illustrated some of their main types, as far as possible in terms of our present subject. By way of conclusion, recognition needs also to be given to some of the limitations of these means of data-collection. Thus, in the first place, there appear to be limitations on the cross-cultural uses to which tests of this type can be put. This is particularly true for non-directive projective tests, such as the Rorschach and the TAT. Adcock and Ritchie (1958), for example, question the cross-cultural validity of the Rorschach in many cases.[116] To estimate this validity, they suggest the use of factor analysis, the finding of similar factors in two cultures being evidence that the test is measuring similar dimensions in both. They applied this method to responses drawn from samples of 203 Maoris and 122 Europeans who had been tested with the Rorschach. The findings indicated little comparability between the two sets of respondents. The authors were led to conclude, therefore, that the Rorschach was of limited value for testing purposes in 'non-literary' and 'imagination-deficient' non-Western cultures, and so should be employed in such contexts only with caution.

However, even in cultures that are not markedly 'imagination-deficient' projective measures encounter difficulties. Firstly, low intra- and intersubjective reliability coefficients are frequently characteristic of at least the less structured projective tests, again particularly the Rorschach. This, of course, is a problem faced by unstructured methods in general. But this does not alter the fact that it lessens their value as viable instruments of social research. All that one can observe in reply is that relatively low reliability scores may, in the circumstances, be none the less of some significance. For example, Roger Brown (1967) writes in respect of McClelland's use of thematic apperception testing as follows:[117]

> Scores on McClelland's measure are far from having the perfect stability one would like in an index of a presumably enduring personality characteristic. However, the weight of the evidence is in favor of a small positive relationship over periods as long as six years. This is a rather remarkable outcome. The measure is a twenty-minute sample of the contents of consciousness, a tiny spinal tap from the lifetime stream. It is remarkable that an assay of so small a quantity of material should yield results having any stability at all.

But, aside from problems of reliability, there is the basic question of validity. Essentially the difficulty here is that responses to projective stimuli, particularly of the unstructured type, are open to a number of interpretations. Thus, in general the use of projective tests is premissed upon the assumption that when no clear, objectively verifiable basis exists for selecting between alternative responses to a stimulus, then an individual's responses will tend to reflect his predispositions. This means that projective testing is more compatible with certain types of psychological theory than with others. In particular, it appears most compatible—and certainly is most frequently associated—with what might be termed psychological theories of passivity. That is, those theories which emphasize the role of involuntary and unintentional factors in the determination of consciousness and cognitive activity. Freudianism is a good example of this, as are other theories which emphasize the role of the unconscious in the formation of attitudes.[118] More generally, projective approaches are compatible with theories which stress the emotional bases of many attitudes. The essential idea here is that certain attitudes, even if not ultimately involuntary, are emotionally salient to an individual, and yet are often prevented from being expressed by the presence of emotional barriers and defence-mechanisms. Thus, the projective stimulus is supposed to facilitate expression by being indirect and no longer ego-threatening.

This is to simplify greatly. But the point can perhaps be better appreciated if we consider alternative psychological approaches. One could argue, for example, that responses to a Rorschach card may be entirely spontaneous, without being indicative of any strongly-held attitudes. That is, the response could be conceived as a purely *ad hoc* creation, having no privileged status, and liable to be changed on subsequent occasions. Naturally, this is to go to the other extreme: some midway position seems the most reasonable. However, we may note that theories emphasizing rationality and choice in attitude-formation would presumably be more likely to allow arbitrary responses of this last kind, rather than would theories emphasizing the involuntary, and perhaps irrational, character of many attitudes. According to the latter type of theory, an individual's spontaneous responses would become significant indicators of his main concerns almost of necessity, at least in so far as motivation for defence, rationalization, etc., had been minimized.

The problem is, then, how to interpret projective responses without committing oneself to any particular type of psychological theory.[119] However, these difficulties seem less severe in the case of more structured forms of projective testing, and so for this, and other, reasons it is these which appear to have the greater validity for purely sociological purposes. On the other hand, problems of reactivity inhere in all these forms of measurement. These are perhaps most evident in the case of older and better-educated respondents, who are also most likely to diagnose the true purpose of the tests. In general, projective attitude tests seem particularly applicable to children, and to studies of the less educated, and less self-analytic.

*Summary and conclusions*

More evidence regarding the validity of specific projective measures is needed in order to be confident about their use in sociological inquiry. The evidence to date is inconclusive, and frequently disconfirmatory. But also too few systematic tests of projective measures have been carried out. The validity of such measures can be assessed in various ways, including in terms of their efficiency in predicting overt behaviour. The most frequent test is simply to match their results against those attained by other, consensually-accepted measures. In one form, this is the 'known groups' technique. It is exemplified by the study of Goldschmidt and Edgerton (1961), cited earlier, in which their picture test was applied to an Amerindian group distributed over certain known categories of acculturation. Five out of the eleven pictures, it will be recalled, successfully discriminated between acculturated and unacculturated respondents. On this basis, the authors concluded that their technique showed promise not only as a stimulus for helping people to talk about their values, but also as a means of eliciting evaluative and non-evaluative responses that can be quantified and compared on an intra- and inter-group basis.

But much more work of this kind needs to be done on the problem of validation, and on that of establishing reasonable coefficients of reliability, before such techniques can be granted a central place in objective attitude research. However, it is recognized that this criticism has less application to those projective tests which employ relatively structured stimuli, as in the various forms of indirect questioning. Also, these measures as a whole, and perhaps particularly their more structured variants, do have a clear utility for the study of some attitudes, held by certain types of respondents, that are not accessible to direct questioning. Indeed, in particular cases, their function here may be an indispensable one.

However, granting these considerations, there is no reason why (i) projective items of different types should not be used together; and (ii) projective tests should not be used in consort with other methods. Thus, in the first case, in view of the greater specificity and reliability of the more structured or directive techniques, it would be useful to employ them in the sequence: non-directive→directive→non-directive. That is, the non-directive measures (e.g. the Rorschach) could be used for initial, exploratory purposes and also for later, interpretative work, whilst the more directive techniques (e.g. sentence-completion) are utilized at the main stage of data-collection and hypothesis-testing. In the second case, projective measures as a whole can be introduced at the exploratory and interpretative phases of the research process as supplementary to other means of gathering data, such as the standard interview or questionnaire. The design, then, would be: projective→non-projective→projective. In this way, it might be possible to make use of some of the main advantages of projective methods, whilst minimizing the effects of their disadvantages.

### Semantic differential

The importance of linguistic analysis to the sociology of moral codes has been alluded to at various points in this study. In the present section we shall consider the relevance of some psycholinguistic research. Psychological studies of the use of language—especially evaluative and prescriptive language—have an obvious *prima facie* importance for the understanding of moral codes in sociology. Although this field is not to be restricted to the work we shall examine, our discussion will be centred on one aspect of this research which shows promise for the analysis of processes of evaluation.

The particular example of psycholinguistic research we shall consider concerns the comparative use of the semantic differential technique developed by Charles Osgood and his associates.[120] This method focuses upon the 'affective' or connotative aspects of the terms used in different language/culture communities in order to elicit their relevant similarities and differences of meaning. Over a period of two decades, this research has accumulated evidence for the existence of a universal framework underlying the semantic aspects of language. This, in turn, suggests the possibility of constructing instruments for measuring these features of subjective culture comparably in diverse societies—in effect, of circumventing the barrier of language. Osgood sums up the practical relevance of his research as follows:[121] 'Since the affective reactions people make to symbols and events are important determiners of their overt behaviours with respect to these symbols and events, having comparable means of measuring affective meanings assumes some importance in a world that is rapidly shrinking psychologically, socially, and politically.'

*Principles*

Although his method has become associated with detailed technical research procedures, its basic principle is a simple one. The theory presupposed by the semantic differential interprets each substantive (or noun) in a language as occupying a distinctive 'semantic space'. The connotative meaning of the term for the users of the language is determined by the position, on a 7-point scale, assigned to various qualifiers (adjectives) in the form of verbal opposites. That is: the respondent judges a series of concepts (e.g. Money, Progress, Peace) against a series of bipolar, 7-step scales defined by verbal opposites (e.g. good-bad, strong-weak, fair-unfair, etc.), by marking the appropriate position on the scale: for instance, +3 extremely good, +2 quite good, +1 slightly good, 0 equally good and bad or neither, −1 slightly bad, −2 quite bad, and −3 extremely bad.[122]

When a group of respondents judge a set of concepts against such a set of adjectival scales, representing a semantic differential, the resulting matrix of data can be analysed in a variety of ways, depending on the purposes of the research. The main procedure which has been adopted by Osgood and his co-workers has been to employ correlational methods to generate a scale-by-scale matrix of intercorrelations and then subject this matrix to factor analysis. Results of such analyses conducted on American samples are given in his book, *The Measurement of Meaning* (1957). In this it is shown that although the sampling of both scales, concepts, and subjects was deliberately and independently varied, three dominant and independent factors constantly recurred: namely, an *evalautive* factor (represented by such scales as good-bad, pleasant-unpleasant, and positive-negative), a *potency* factor (e.g. strong-weak, heavy-light, and hard-soft), and an *activity* factor (e.g. fast-slow, active-passive, and excitable-calm). As Osgood writes:[123]

> What this means is that there are at least three 'directions' in the semantic space which are regions of relatively high density, in the sense of many closely related modes of qualifying, and that these 'directions' tend to be orthogonal to each other, in the sense of being independently variable dimensions of meaning.

*Applications*

Research conducted since 1960 has attempted to validate this conclusion cross-culturally. To avoid ethnocentric assumptions, the principal danger in this type of research, each language/culture group selected its own qualifying scales, and the methodology employed was carefully standardized. The research was initially carried out among sixteen distinct language communities: the United States, Finland, Japan, India (on both Kannada and Hindi language-groups), the Netherlands, Belgium, France, Lebanon, Sweden, Hong Kong (Cantonese), Iran, Afghanistan (Farsi and Pashto language-groups), Yugoslavia, and Poland. Other communities were added to this list as the research progressed.

The procedures adopted in testing the hypothesis and developing comparable semantic differentials for use in these separate communities were detailed and complex. However, their essential stages are summed up in the following statement by Osgood:[124]

> Our own research imposed standardization upon both stimuli and responses in all phases. It also required representative sampling among both stimuli and responses in its several stages. *Qualifier elicitation.* A diverse sample of 100 culture-common and (roughly) translation-equivalent substantives (nouns) were given as stimuli to 100 young boys in each community and they were instructed to give the first qualifier (adjective) that occurred to them for each. *Qualifier sampling.* The 10,000 responses obtained were analyzed (by computer) so as to generate a set of qualifiers for each community ordered according to three criteria—overall frequency of usage, diversity of usage across the 100 nouns, and independence of usage across the nouns (to avoid redundant dimensions). *Opposites elicitation.* Small numbers of sophisticated subjects generated opposites for the ordered list of qualifiers (e.g., good-*bad*, strong-*weak*, etc.), items lacking agreed-upon opposites (e.g., sympathetic—??) being

281

eliminated, until a set of 50 pairs was obtained. *Conception-scale differentiation.* The original set of 100 substantives were each rated against the entire set of 50 scales (now seven-step: *good* : : : : : : *bad*) by a new group of 200 young boys, dividing the total concepts into 10 manageable subsets. *Scale sampling.* Utilizing factor analytic procedures on our computers—a bit of modern technology without which this type of project would be impossible—the relations among the qualifying scales when used in judging concepts were determined and the major factors extracted. The first three factors proved to be the same in every case. The scales most purely and highly representative of each factor in each language (three or four for each) were assembled as a measuring instrument—a semantic differential which can be shown to be comparable with others despite differences in language.

A number of these procedures have a direct relevance to our present subject. In particular, the stage of qualifier sampling deserves our attention. This, as noted above, involved the ordering of the original set of qualifiers according to their frequency, diversity, and independence. The purpose was thus to derive, for each language/ culture community, a set of terms that would comprise its most characteristic modes of qualifying experience. In fact, when frequency and diversity of usage are combined into a single index and the qualifier-types are ranked for each community according to this index a number of significant comparisons become evident. Table 8.4 presents the rank correlations (here, separately for the frequency and diversity indices) of the 40 highest-ranking qualifiers for some of the communities, as translated into English in each case.

Despite the difficulties of mapping one language on to another in translation, all the correlations in the above table are positive and highly significant. The relative importance, in terms of frequency and diversity of usage, of various modes of qualifying experience appear, therefore, to be shared, in spite of substantial differences in both language and culture. This is a significant outcome, and it might be taken to provide some grounds for the possibility of valid communication and mutual understanding between these apparently diverse language communities. It is also, of course, an encouraging result from the viewpoint of cross-cultural research.

It may be observed further that the correlation patterns for both frequency (F) and diversity (D) parallel each other closely in the above table. The highest correlations, as one might expect, are between Flemish and Dutch (F=0·95, D=0·89); and secondly, between English and Finnish (F=0·78, D=0·68) and, less obviously, between English and Kannada (F=0·76, D=0·70). The lowest

TABLE 8.4  Intercorrelations among translated qualifiers[125]

| | Frequency | | | | | | | | Diversity | | | | | | | |
|---|---|---|---|---|---|---|---|---|---|---|---|---|---|---|---|---|
| | English | Arabic | Dutch | Finnish | Kannada | Japanese | French | Flemish | English | Arabic | Dutch | Finnish | Kannada | Japanese | French | Flemish |
| English | 1·00 | 0·53 | 0·66 | 0·78 | 0·76 | 0·43 | 0·58 | 0·65 | 1·00 | 0·64 | 0·56 | 0·68 | 0·70 | 0·60 | 0·53 | 0·56 |
| Arabic | | 1·00 | 0·29 | 0·35 | 0·31 | 0·39 | 0·37 | 0·34 | | 1·00 | 0·37 | 0·58 | 0·49 | 0·46 | 0·50 | 0·40 |
| Dutch | | | 1·00 | 0·73 | 0·59 | 0·29 | 0·53 | 0·95 | | | 1·00 | 0·49 | 0·48 | 0·33 | 0·41 | 0·89 |
| Finnish | | | | 1·00 | 0·66 | 0·39 | 0·62 | 0·71 | | | | 1·00 | 0·54 | 0·56 | 0·64 | 0·55 |
| Kannada | | | | | 1·00 | 0·33 | 0·45 | 0·56 | | | | | 1·00 | 0·39 | 0·46 | 0·52 |
| Japanese | | | | | | 1·00 | 0·33 | 0·34 | | | | | | 1·00 | 0·46 | 0·36 |
| French | | | | | | | 1·00 | 0·55 | | | | | | | 1·00 | 0·42 |
| Flemish | | | | | | | | 1·00 | | | | | | | | 1·00 |

correlations are found between Arabic and Dutch (F=0·29, D=0·37), between Dutch and Japanese (F=0·29, D=0·33), and, for diversity, Japanese and Flemish (D=0·36).[126]

Secondly, the final phase of scale sampling, as a basis for constructing comparable semantic differentials for measuring the meaning of certain concepts in the different communities, has a particular relevance for our subject. Here, the factor analysis of the qualifiers yielded three principal factors and these proved to be the same in every case. Osgood interprets these, in order of magnitude (percentage variance extracted), as Evaluation, Potency, and Activity. In other words, the same semantic pattern was found cross-culturally as was derived from the samples of American English speakers reported in *The Measurement of Meaning* (1957). He interprets this similar factorial structure as confirmative of the basic hypothesis of this research: namely, that 'regardless of language or culture, human beings utilize the same qualifying (descriptive) framework in allocating the meanings of concepts.'[127] In illustration of this basic finding, we present, in Table 8.5, the highest loading scales (as translated) for a sub-sample of six of the language/culture communities studied.

Table 8.5 suggests a great deal of comparability between different cultures in the use of qualifying terms. Our own interest is particularly with those qualifiers which have a primarily *evaluative* function (i.e. Factor I): here, again, there is much similarity between the communities, although together with some intriguing differences, which comparative anthropology might be able to throw some light on. However, there is the familiar problem of loss of information through translation here, and this needs to be taken account of in interpretation of the table. The Spanish *simpático*, for example, as a key term of evaluation, is not perfectly translated by the English 'sympathetic'. None the less, a sense of universality in the basic structure of these various qualifiers is apparent.

Of even greater interest to us, however, is the cross-cultural application of these qualifier-scales to a series of culture-common concepts. Thus, the motivation for generating the kind of information that is given in the above table was not only that of testing the initial hypothesis concerning the presence of a general semantic structure; given verification of this hypothesis, the intention was also to apply this data in the construction of efficient and comparable linguistic instruments (i.e. semantic differentials) in each language-culture community for measuring concept meanings, or, at least, their connotative meanings. This stage of research is currently being carried out. One aspect of it will be the development of an 'Atlas' of some 500 translation-equivalent concepts in terms of comparative semantic-differential responses. This should provide some insight into the similarities and dissimilarities of the subjective culture of

TABLE 8.5    *Pan-cultural factor scales for six language culture communities (four highest loading scales for each pan-cultural factor arranged by culture)*[128]

| Factor I | | Factor II | | Factor III | |
|---|---|---|---|---|---|
| *American–English* | | | | | |
| nice—awful | 0·94 | big—little | 0·70 | fast—slow | 0·61 |
| good—bad | 0·92 | powerful—powerless | 0·69 | alive—dead | 0·53 |
| sweet—sour | 0·90 | strong—weak | 0·59 | noisy—quiet | 0·42 |
| helpful—unhelpful | 0·89 | deep—shallow | 0·58 | young—old | 0·42 |
| *Arabic* | | | | | |
| good—bad | 0·90 | large—small | 0·53 | light—heavy | 0·34 |
| sound—dangerous | 0·90 | strong—weak | 0·43 | infirm (loose)—solid | 0·33 |
| beautiful—ugly | 0·89 | long—short | 0·43 | fast—slow | 0·32 |
| merciful—cruel | 0·89 | high—low | 0·36 | emotional—rational | 0·32 |
| *French* | | | | | |
| pleasant—unpleasant | 0·90 | large—little | 0·70 | lively—indolent | 0·64 |
| good—bad | 0·89 | strong—weak | 0·61 | fast—slow | 0·57 |
| nice—wicked | 0·89 | huge—tiny | 0·59 | living—dead | 0·56 |
| proud—frightened | 0·87 | heavy—light | 0·52 | young—old | 0·42 |
| *Japanese* | | | | | |
| pleasant—unpleasant | 0·92 | heavy—light | 0·67 | colourful—plain | 0·48 |
| good—bad | 0·92 | big—small | 0·65 | active—inactive | 0·47 |
| comfortable— | | difficult—easy | 0·57 | noisy—quiet | 0·46 |
| uncomfortable | 0·91 | brave—cowardly | 0·57 | soft—hard | 0·45 |
| happy—sad | 0·90 | | | | |
| *Kannada* | | | | | |
| merciful—cruel | 0·79 | big—small | 0·44 | active—dull | 0·45 |
| good—bad | 0·77 | wonderful—ordinary | 0·44 | unstable—stable | 0·37 |
| calm—frightful | 0·74 | huge—small | 0·43 | loose—tight | 0·35 |
| delicate—rough | 0·74 | great—little | 0·37 | fast—slow | 0·34 |
| *Spanish* | | | | | |
| good—bad | 0·93 | giant—dwarf | 0·61 | active—passive | 0·55 |
| admirable— | | big—small | 0·59 | rapid—slow | 0·43 |
| contemptible | 0·93 | greater—small | 0·55 | young—old | 0·43 |
| agreeable— | | strong—weak | 0·55 | bland—hard | 0·36 |
| disagreeable | 0·93 | | | | |
| sympathetic— | | | | | |
| antipathetic | 0·92 | | | | |

diverse communities, and as such would supplement similar information drawn from English-American samples which is already available.[129] Preliminary results indicate an appreciable degree of comparability in the connotational significance of several concepts in the communities studied, although also some interesting differences. For instance, as Osgood writes:[130]

> Some of the differences in concept allocation are suggestive of real culture differences; for example: *progress* is *good-strong-active* for all except Finnish, where it is *passive*; similarly,

K*

*future* is *good-strong-active* for all except Finnish, where it is *good*, but *weak* and *passive*; ... *mother* and *father* are both *good-strong-passive* for Americans and Flemish and are both *good-strong-active* for Japanese, but *father* is *good-strong-active* and *mother good-weak-active* for the Finns; the concept of *power* is *good-strong-active* for both Americans and Flemish speakers; but it becomes *passive* for Finns and turns both *bad* and *weak* (but still *active*) for Japanese.

These particular comparisons should be taken more as illustrations of the kind of differences that may be determined when the full sample of communities and concepts have been examined and appropriate statistical tests of significance carried out. Nevertheless, they do illustrate that the project has a clear relevance to the comparative understanding of moral assumptions and patterns of evaluation. Thus, insight should be permitted into the connotative meanings of such concepts as *nation, freedom, future, life*, etc. both within and between different communities, and also into the degree of consensus that exists over the ascription of these meanings. In addition, specific classes of concepts (e.g. kinship terms) may be analysed in this fashion, as may the presence of stereotyping with reference to particular national and ethnic groups, and human collectivities generally.

Aside from its intrinsic interest, and its possible use in improving cross-cultural communication, two main applications of such data in social research may be indicated. Firstly, this information can make a direct contribution to the theoretical and empirical study of universals in the lexical and semantic components of language, and this in turn could have various repercussions for social science. And secondly, in view of the preponderance of verbal methods in social research, this data might be put to use in refining many of these instruments of inquiry. For example, it may provide a sounder basis for preparing semantically equivalent interview schedules in cross-cultural research. This would be a significant contribution since problems of translation arise at all stages of comparative inquiries, and are perhaps particularly acute when moral attitudes are being examined. Moreover, this is not only true of research across different languages; it may also apply to studies within a language community. For instance, in attitude surveys across different classes within a society a given question might possess quite different connotations to each class. In such a case, if the stimulus is to be kept constant, the question would have to be rephrased. But problems of this kind (which may, of course, not always be successfully diagnosed in research) could be averted were prior information available on the connotations of the terms used, and the way these varied, if at all, with social position.

286

Of course, the problem of keeping all stimuli (verbal and non-verbal) constant is much greater in cross-cultural inquiries. Indeed, this constitutes the main difficulty encountered by Osgood's research: thus, even slight changes in the denotative significance of a term, owing to inefficient translation, could have marked effects on the results of the semantic differential. One response to this is to search for patterned differences between communities, this being an indicator that the comparison being made is in fact a valid one.

One caveat with respect to this research, however, does deserve mention. Thus, although Osgood's main concern is to demonstrate the presence of certain presumptive universalia with respect to the semantic aspects of language, and although his evidence favours this hypothesis, it is also true that several of his procedures actually presuppose rejection of a linguistic relativism. For example, he excludes those substantives (nouns) at the earliest stages of his inquiry that encounter translation difficulties. But the linguistic relativist (in the Sapir-Whorf tradition) might argue at this point that this is precisely to exclude from one's analysis those items which are the most salient (because the most unique) in the cultures concerned. Of course, it is also true that Osgood could appeal to pragmatic considerations here: namely, that his assumptions have proved their utility in research and are vindicated on the available evidence. Also, he could note that some assumptions of this kind, and the selection of data they give rise to, had to be made since in any extreme form of linguistic relativism cross-cultural linguistic inquiries of the present type would be ruled out *a priori*. However, it would have been preferable to have had these anti-relativist assumptions stated in more explicit form, and to have seen more recognition paid to the type of position from which they detract. Our own discussion of this doctrine will be given in part three of this book.

Osgood's research is, in fact, of significance in large part precisely because it raises these broader questions of absolutism and relativism with regard to language and semantic systems. As such, it is complementary to other recent research on the subject of linguistic universals, which has mainly been concerned with the syntactic aspects of language.

*Research on values*

However, these questions do not arise, at least in such a form, when the semantic differential is used for research within the confines of a single language community. Of the studies which exist of this kind, a few may be singled out as particularly relevant, since they have concerned themselves specifically with the empirical investigation of values. Gordon *et al.* (1963), for instance, utilized the semantic differential in order to test some hypotheses concerning the role of distinctive values as an important link in the causal chain leading from social status to delinquent behaviour.[131] The hypotheses were derived from the work of Cohen, Miller, and Cloward and Ohlin.[132] Although based on quite different premises, each of these theories leads to the expectation that gang boys will evaluate deviant or illegitimate images of behaviour higher than do middle-class boys.[133] To test this, the authors sampled negro and white youths in gangs, and also from the lower and middle classes. The subjects were asked to rate a series of verbal descriptions on the semantic-differential scales. The descriptions to be rated were chosen to represent, in the authors' words, 'salient examples of instrumental or dominant goal activity, leisure-time activity, and ethical orientation for each of five theoretically significant subcultures—middle class, lower class, conflict, criminal, and retreatist'.[134] For example, the description of 'Someone who works for good grades at school', and 'Someone who shares his money with his friends' were classified respectively as 'middle class, dominant goal activity' and 'lower class, ethical orientation'. The semantic scales against which such images were judged were:

| Evaluation | Potency |
|---|---|
| clean—dirty | hard—soft |
| good—bad | large—small |
| kind—cruel | strong—weak |
| fair—unfair | brave—cowardly |
| pleasant—unpleasant | rugged—delicate |

Three additional scales, derived from Miller's 'focal concerns' of lower-class culture, were also included. These were 'smart—sucker', 'lucky—unlucky', and 'exciting life—boring life'. Each scale had seven points and was applied to seventeen descriptive images, the resultant scores being analysed in terms of the initial six social variables. The main findings indicated that the middle-class images were evaluated significantly higher by all the samples than almost all other subcultural images, especially those which were unquestionably illegitimate. In view of this general consensus, the authors rejected, in its present form, the hypothesis concerning the existence of a distinct delinquent value-system.

In another study, by Osgood, Ware, and Morris (1961), the semantic-differential technique was employed to investigate the connotations that Morris's various 'ways to live' had for a sample of American college students.[135] Standard statements of Morris's Ways to Live were judged against a 26-scale form of the semantic differential by 55 students, who indicated their preferences between them. The mean ranking of preferences for the group was almost identical with

288

that for other American student samples studied by Morris. Factor analysis of these connotative meanings yielded a reasonably clear 4-factor system: dynamism, control, socialization, and perhaps venturousness. Factor analysis of the semantic scale relations yielded three clear factors that accounted for large portions of the total variance: successfulness, predictability, and kindness. Of other inquiries, mention might be made, for example, of the research reported in Mary Goodman's *Race Awareness in Young Children* (1964), which examined the concept of 'race' held by Negro and white children, and involved utilization of the semantic differential together with other techniques.[136]

## Summary and conclusions

In conclusion, the semantic differential as a method of attitudinal research consists essentially of a structured word-association test, although one which has been developed on the basis of extensive empirical experience. As such, it can provide comparable data on the 'intensional', or connotative meanings of certain concepts and statements. The stimulus need not always be a verbal one, and pictorial (non-verbal) forms of the semantic differential have also been developed, mainly for the purpose of inquiring into such issues as synaesthesia and the use of metaphor.[137]

As a specific method of eliciting a subject's values, however, it is, like the standard survey methods, susceptible to reactivity effects, and to response-set tendencies.[138] In the second place, it has the limitation of excluding from its concerns the question of the subject's justification of his attitudes; instead, only their immediate impressions of certain concepts and images are recorded. And finally, by excluding the denotative aspects of meaning, it is open to the criticism that it neglects the more integral aspects of language in favour of their more peripheral dimensions. On the other hand, it is, of course apparent that no general, comparative measure of the denotative significance of terms is yet available for use in the social sciences, and perhaps never will be. Osgood, however, is fully aware of the potential utility of such a measure; as he writes: 'The development of a satisfactory quantitative measure of denotative meaning appears to me to be one of the most important problems for contemporary psycholinguistics.'[139]

And as he observes further:[140]

An adequate measure should reflect the multidimensional nature of meaning, should yield a quantitative measure of degrees of denotative similarity, should be completely general for all pairs of terms measured, and should meet the usual

289

criteria of reliability, validity, and comparability across subjects and concepts. . . . Linguistic componential analysis, as applied to restricted semantic domains like kin-terms, provides only a partial answer—precisely because the components appropriate to one area (e.g., male-female, older-younger, blood-marital relation, etc., as applied to kinship) prove to be completely irrelevant to another (e.g. utensils or foodstuffs or modes of transportation). The semantic differential, as usually applied, reflects affective or connotative similarities, but clearly fails to reflect denotative similarities in any consistent fashion (e.g. pairs of terms like *nurse* and *sincerity* or *rabbit* and *melody* or *fate* and *quicksand* may have almost identical locations in affective space).

In view of this shortcoming, the way in which the semantic differential is judged will depend largely upon the type of context in which it is applied. On the one hand, used as a central technique of data-collection and hypothesis-testing regarding respondents' evaluations *within* a particular language community, its applicability seems limited. Other methods available in social science would appear to offer the opportunity of gaining more reliable and valid information, with less risk of irrelevancy, and under more controlled conditions. For such purposes, then, the semantic differential as it currently stands seems best suited to the initial, exploratory stages of research and for later, interpretative purposes. Although, with less articulate and self-analytic respondents, and for those subjects which exist in respondents' minds more in the form of vague associations than of clear ideas, the method might assume a more central role: studies of children's concepts of race well illustrates this.

On the other hand, for cross-cultural and cross-linguistic inquiries its potential seems greater. Thus, on the evidence attained so far, it shows promise both as a means of 'measuring' the connotative (and thereby also evaluative) meanings of significant concepts in comparable fashion, and also for providing insights into the universal and relative aspects of the language of evaluation generally. As such, it has a clear relevance to comparative studies of moral codes.

### Simulation and game theory

Game theory is a branch of mathematics which attempts the formal analysis of certain problems of conflict and decision-making by abstracting common strategic features for study in theoretical models —termed 'games' because they are patterned on actual games such as bridge or poker. Following the work of Émile Borel, the theory of games of strategy, in which outcomes are a function of the participants' decisions, was classically applied to competitive economic behaviour by John von Neumann and Oscar Morgenstern (1944).[141] Since this work, and deriving its theoretical impetus from it, increasing attention has been given to the application of the mathematics of game theory to a broader range of problems in the social sciences, particularly in political science and sociology.[142]

Although most actual games, and game-like situations, elude full analysis because of the highly complex, and interrelated, character of the variables which enter into them, many can be reduced to essentials and analysed in a simplified or minimal form. Simulation, in the present context, refers to the use of such simplifications for the development and use of methodologies appropriate to the study of conflict behaviour and strategic situations. Many of the models implicit in these simulations, particularly the simpler ones, derive the logic of their construction from the findings of game theory. And despite their considerable variety, all these types of simulation are best conceived as a sub-class of the general category of experiments. They are given some consideration here partly because of the lack of attention which they have been afforded as valid means for sociological investigations of moral codes. Special mention might be made, however, of the lecture by R. B. Braithwaite (1955), which relates game theory and moral philosophy. The conclusion to this lecture, although it now appears over-sanguine, at least bears repetition; as he writes:[143]

No one today will doubt the intensity, though he may dislike the colour, of the (shall I say) sodium light cast by statistical mathematics, direct descendant of theory of games of chance, upon the social sciences. Perhaps in another three hundred years' time economic and political and other branches of moral philosophy will bask in radiation from a source—theory of games of strategy—whose prototype was kindled round the poker tables of Princeton.

So far, simulation techniques have been perhaps most frequently, and most fruitfully, employed as teaching devices, particularly in business schools, but increasingly in the classroom as well.[144] As a research technique its principal application has been within political science, and particularly with respect to international relations: the standard text currently available concentrates mainly on this field (Guetzkow, 1963).[145] However, its relevance extends to more general sociological concerns, including a number of those comprised within the present study. We may briefly illustrate this by considering one of the simplest, and most commonly employed games: the so-called 'Prisoner's Dilemma'.

## Prisoner's Dilemma

Prisoner's Dilemma is one example of a $2 \times 2$ game; that is, a game which involves two players, each with two choices open to them, and in which the outcome of the game is determined by their joint decisions.[146] A basic distinction within games of this type is that between those in which the possibility of a compromise beneficial to both players exists, and those in which it does not. Games of diametrical opposition—what one gains, the other loses—where no compromise is possible are termed zero-sum games (e.g. chess). Games in which such compromise is possible, with varying degrees of benefit, are termed mixed-motive games, and since they permit inclusion of conflict-resolution and *rapprochement*, and the element of threat as well as co-operation, these tend to reflect more situations encountered in the real world and so are more fruitful for research purposes. The Prisoner's Dilemma is an example of this last type of game, and its basic rationale has been summed up as involving 'an attempt to capture the essential feature of a deadlock in which two potential partners are unable to co-operate with each other for lack of mutual trust'.[147] The kind of matrix of choices which subjects confront in this game is illustrated by Figure 8.4.

FIGURE 8.4  *Prisoner's Dilemma: an example*

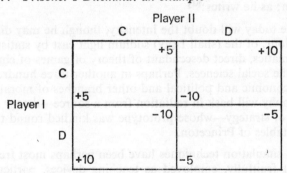

The numerals in the four cells represent the outcomes ('pay offs') of the joint choices of the two players. The situation involves the following strategic elements: (i) both players gain most by co-operating (i.e. selecting C); (ii) each player is tempted to defect (i.e. to select D) in order to get more; (iii) if one defects, the non-defecting player is 'punished'; and (iv) if both defect, both are punished.

A number of experiments have been carried out using the Prisoner's Dilemma as a probing technique to find out what people will actually do in this type of situation. In this way, it is intended empirically to investigate responses (and their determinants) to at least one important element in many situations that engender conflict and strategic choice: namely, that involving a basic dilemma between individual and joint or collective interests. As such, it has the advantage of being simple, easily and fully replicable, and of supplying quantified data for analysis. Various components of the game-situation may themselves be treated as independent variables: namely (within certain limits) the pay-off values, the length of sequences of choices, and (if one player is given appropriate instructions) of responses to certain types of sequence.

For strictly sociological purposes, however, our main interest will be with the characteristics of the population from which the players have been drawn. Few investigations of this kind have been carried out so far, and the ones which do exist have mainly used psychological variables to discriminate their populations. Thus, Deutsch (1960) distinguished between high scorers on a scale of Authoritarianism (including the F scale) and those with more liberal attitudes and found that, rather consistently, the 'authoritarians' co-operated less frequently than the others.[148] Studies involving more socially-oriented attitude scales are also available. For instance, Lutzker (1960) divided his sample into high and low scorers on an Internationalism scale and observed that the former group exhibited a higher mean level of co-operation than the latter, and one that was also less likely to decline over a sequence.[149] In another study, by Terhune (1965), three populations were tested: those motivated by McClelland's 'need for achievement', those motivated by a 'need for affiliation', and those motivated by a 'need for power'.[150] The results indicated that the highest co-operation scores were attained by the achievement-oriented group, followed by the 'need for affiliation' group, the 'need for power' group gaining the lowest scores (cf. Deutsch, supra).

Of the few studies in which the results for this experiment were explicitly structured according to social variables, mention should be made of the research by Lumsden (1967).[151] In this, 30 psychology students played 100 trials of Prisoner's Dilemma, and frequencies of co-operative strategies were related to Galtung's 'index of social position'. Other studies include the one by Oskamp and Perlman (1965), who found that students from a large university co-operated less frequently than students from a small college.[152] Also, in an unpublished paper by Dencik and Wiberg (1966) data is presented which shows clear differences of behaviour between younger and older children, and between children of lower and higher socio-economic status.[153] Finally, mention might also be made of the result, found on a number of occasions, that more co-operation is exhibited by men than women in the Prisoner's Dilemma game.[154]

293

Many of these findings should be treated as tentative, in view of the limited samples that are frequently used (e.g. 30–50) and of the limited duration of sequences (e.g. 30). Although this may matter less in other types of experiments, it is particularly important here because sufficiently large populations are required in order to render statistical fluctuations negligible. And the more differentiated the population (by age, sex, status, etc.) the larger the sample-size will have to be. As Rapoport (1967) writes of this game: 'Clearly, the answers will provide no information about how particular *individuals* will behave, but only how the "average" individual will tend to behave. Thus, any relevance of these answers to real life would be in the context of gross trends, involving great numbers of individuals in identical situations.'[155]

But however statistically insecure the results attained so far they at least appear to indicate that game strategies, and particularly the relative incidence of co-operative choices, can be consistently and significantly related to social variables characterizing the players. As such, the technique shows promise as a valid instrument of sociological inquiry.

Prisoner's Dilemma is but one example of a number of $2 \times 2$ games, which are themselves a sub-class of a much broader range of types of games. The appeal of the $2 \times 2$ games is the simplicity of the data which they generate. Sequences of choices (or protocols) are naturally quantifiable and both internal and external factors in the situation are manipulable as independent variables. By 'internal' here we refer to the factors comprising part of the definition of the game, such as the pay-off values, the number of plays already made in a sequence, or the strategy adopted by a particular player under instructions from the experimenter. Taken on their own, these factors permit empirical inquiry into various aspects of the logic of strategy, particularly with regard to the rationality of certain strategies, and the conditions under which these tend to be adopted.[156] By 'external' factors, we refer to psychological and social variables defining the participants. The controlled manipulation of these may permit us to develop and test certain hypotheses concerning the socio-psychological correlates of co-operative, and other, strategies. If the manipulation of internal factors is added to this, perhaps even more refined analyses can be made.

Other forms of the basic $2 \times 2$ game schema permit the introduction of new variables. Some of the games, for instance, simulate the components of 'threat' and 'force', or provide a system of rules which entail that defection is only worth while in the event of the other player's co-operation.[157] However, so far research concerned with the influence of particular social and psychological variables has been conducted almost exclusively within the context of the Prisoner's

Dilemma game, and even here the focus of interest has been largely a psychological one. Considerable scope exists, therefore, for the exploration of these types of games from a sociological point of view. It is to be acknowledged, however, that in any instance of research utilizing these techniques considerable caution must be maintained with regard to generalizing whatever results are attained to the real world. As is true in varying degrees of all simulated and experimental contexts, the complexities of social reality have been drastically simplified.[158]

*Simulation methods*

Closer approximations to social reality are attempted by the more realistic simulations, such as those concerned to depict particular international conflict-situations. These tend to be less derivative from game theory and more dependent upon the abstraction of salient characteristics of the 'real world'. Thus, they often involve the abstraction of certain boundary conditions from the real world (e.g. the objectives of a given national government, the strength of its forces, etc.). And then, on this basis, an event is introduced (e.g. the breaking of a treaty) which will serve to initiate a sequence of decisions on both sides in response to constantly varying conditions. In this way, an attempt is made to simulate some of the dynamic features of particular social processes. The main application of these so far has been as teaching devices and in studies of war and international conflict. In the latter case, the main rationale for them has tended to be a predictive one: that is, as a means of extending our knowledge of the kind of decisions likely to be taken in certain circumstances, and also of the particular conditions which appear to facilitate certain sequences of choice (e.g. increasing co-operation) and to constrain others (e.g. an escalation of aggression). However, the development of predictions that are transposable to real-life situations may not be the main value to be gained from such studies. For the more realistic the simulation, the greater the number, and so the less manageable, are the variables one has to introduce. In particular, there is the problem of systemic effects. As Rapoport (1967) writes of this type of simulation:[159]

> If the purpose of an experiment is to find out how imposed conditions determine or influence observed outcomes, excessive 'realism' defeats this purpose. To analyse the effects of changes in the various components separately is not practical, since there not only are too many components, but they all interact with one another. A change in one may affect the functional dependence of others on the remaining ones, even

295

though everything else remains constant. . . . This may, of course, be typically the case in real life. However, recognizing the fact does not help us find the dependence even in the laboratory. The problem becomes simply too big to handle.

Put otherwise, the more 'realistic' the simulation, the less experimental the simulation. The price of realism is a set of variables which are less amenable to discrimination and manipulation, and a set of outcomes that are complex and ambiguous from the point of view of interpretation and explanation. Further, these outcomes become much more difficult to replicate.[160]

As a result, the realistic simulation involves two distinct types of problems. The first concerns the relevance of the sequences and outcomes observed to the real world. How valid are these as predictions? The second concerns the difficulty of analysing and interpreting the data produced by the simulation. How are the results to be explained? In principle, the latter of these two problems is most serious in the more realistic simulations, and the former in the context of more artificial, simplified games, such as the Prisoner's Dilemma. But where simulations attempted to represent highly complex social processes, such as inter-nation interactions, their degree of realism will always fall far short of the ideal, and as a result the predictions they generate will be at best in the form of counterfactuals rather than historical assertions.

In view of this, perhaps the main value to be gained from the more realistic types of simulation is a heuristic one. That is, they facilitate the formulation of questions and hypotheses, rather than the provision of answers. Their role is more indicative than probative. Thus, simulation methods may be applied to social processes that are closed to other forms of social investigation, either by virtue of their infrequency or for other reasons. In addition, simulations may be made of hypothetical processes and ones that have not yet occurred. Here, as elsewhere, the simulation may be conducted with the aid of computers. That is, a series of probabilistic rules can be fed into the computer and the outcomes of the complex interplay of different decision-makers determined. But we shall reserve further discussion of this technique for the end of the chapter.

However, for our own purposes, perhaps the most valuable heuristic use to which the more realistic simulations may be put is that of explicating assumptions and priorities that would otherwise remain implicit. Furthermore, attention can be given to processes of reasoning and the justifications offered for the particular decisions taken and lines of conduct adopted. Here, for example, interaction may be recorded by introducing written, as well as verbal, communications. The focus of research attention in such studies may be

296

either upon investigating the principles, and available choices, that are implicit in particular types of situation encountered in the real world, or upon gaining insight into the assumptions and priorities of given classes of individuals by putting them in hypothetical situations of—to use the terminology adopted in the Introduction—perceived crisis, in which basic choices are called for. In other words, the emphasis may be placed either upon the participants or upon the type of situation depicted. In either case, it need not be the particular outcomes which form the centre of interest, but rather the processes whereby these outcomes are attained. And here, for instance, attention can be given to the limits of strategic action, that is, what kind of considerations enter to limit a purely instrumental pursuit of one's objectives?

In a similar vein, Rapoport (1967) writes in respect of highly complex inter-nation simulations:[161]

In short, one cannot expect the 'realistic game' to become a convenient experimental tool by means of which one obtains well established results with well defined regions of validity. One will do better to view such games as means of inducing *experiences* rather than as a method for designing experiments. Once this is clear, one may remain content to confine oneself to the 'case study method', each case being potentially unique. Then one need no longer economize on design. One can introduce into the game everything one can think of, hoping thereby to enrich the 'experience' to the extent that one acquires a feeling for these simulated case histories of inter-nation interaction.

*Conclusions*

In conclusion, we do not wish either to overstate the importance and relevancy of these procedures, nor to understate the precariousness of generalizations transposed from the experimental situation to the real world. On the other hand, any definitive judgment would be inappropriate at this stage: their potential, with regard to our present subject, and for social science generally, cannot be adequately assessed without evidence from many more studies than are currently available.

Suffice it to say here, then, that two broad types of games may be distinguished, each with its own characteristic uses. First, there is the small-scale, highly simplified game, such as the Prisoner's Dilemma. This usually abstracts certain features from conflict-of-interest situations encountered in the real world and expresses them in a way that is logically determinate and easily replicable. Their main

297

interest for us is as a means of providing experimental formats for studies of the social structuring of moral conduct of various kinds, particularly with regard to co-operation. Thus, their essential simplicity facilitates the manipulation of both internal and external factors, and permits specific dependent/independent variable relations to be elucidated.

Second, there are the larger-scale, more complex simulations, which attempt to represent social processes with a greater degree of realism and completeness. In principle, these have more predictive power, although at the cost of lessened control over the situation and so less utility for explanatory purposes. In practice, their main value is often a heuristic one: that is, they give some sense of the complexity, and systemic character, of many real-life situations, and may permit some of the assumptions and priorities which normally underlie these to be explicated and examined.

In each case, however, a more complete judgment must await further exploration, both of abstract game formats (in relation to game theory) and also of concrete simulation designs. Certainly, the results that have been attained so far are sufficiently interesting to warrant further investigation.

## Formal techniques

The formal techniques we will review here differ from the previous research devices in that they are not primary means of data-collection, or, as in the case of simulation, of data-creation. Rather, they involve a secondary stage in research in which artificial languages are employed for the description of empirically available (or hypothetical) moral codes in a manner that permits a greater degree of precision, rigour, and determinacy than can be obtained by means of natural languages alone. As such, they are not, of course, themselves means of data-collection, although they may influence the kind of data which is collected, and hence, indirectly, the methods employed.

The principal function of the present techniques is to provide an efficient means of analysing the structural attributes of data in social science which can both improve its precision and completeness and also serve as a precursor to theory. Such analysis is effected by translating, or mapping, the empirical information into a formal language. Various such languages are available, and some of the main types may be briefly considered.

### Propositional logic

The first, and most obvious, candidate of a formal language is propositional logic. Since the time of Aristotle, and until relatively recently, studies in the field of logic have been devoted mainly to the development and exploration of the familiar two-valued propositional calculus. And the fruits of this work can be usefully applied to our present subject. As an illustration of this we may consider a recent analysis by Hans Hoffmann (1959) of the Pawnee kinship system, which followed Lounsbury's (1956) refinement of the ethnographic data.[162] The basic defining attributes used in Lounsbury's account of Pawnee kinship rules are those of sex, agnatic and uterine consanguinity, and generational differences between kinsmen. Hoffmann adopts these and demonstrates that a number of very intricate kinship relationships can be abstracted by the rules of symbolic logic. He applies the formal approach also to the residence rules of the tribe (matrilocality, patrilocality, and neolocality), and then to these according to the three age-grades for each of which a different residence rule applies. Hoffmann finally uses logical analysis to represent the class-inclusion rules of lineage membership in the Pawnee system. Thus far, however, Hoffman demonstrates merely that aspects of the Pawnee kinship rules may be treated as propositions and rendered in the notational form of symbolic logic, the greater concision and consistency of which may, in certain cases, prove advantageous, whilst in others it is unnecessary. That is, symbolic logic has functioned so far merely as 'an ideographic shorthand for recording empirical data', and also for describing relationships within this data.

More interesting, however, is the use of symbolic logic for purposes of inference. Thus, in this way it can also be shown to have a predictive, as well as descriptive, function. The present study illustrates this usage, although some of the predictions Hoffmann draws are intuitively obvious: for instance, that a mother is in the same uterine lineage as her son. He notes also, however, that conclusions may be derived by means of symbolic logic which are not explicitly stated in the ethnographic records. He exemplifies this by proving that the preferential marriage rule—viz: 'A Pawnee's marriage partner must be the granddaughter of the sister of ego's father's father'—is also a theorem of the system, although we have no ethnographic reference to this effect. Thus he shows that symbolic logic, can lead to the generation of data, in the form of a reconstruction of an otherwise unrecorded aspect of Pawnee culture. Whether or not this particular rule is actually followed is, of course, an empirical question. But if it is not, then we know that there is an inconsistency within the system of kinship rules, a finding which much recent anthropology would suggest to be unlikely, but which would anyway be of interest in its own right.

*Deontic logic*

Kinship systems are treated above as systems of rules, and the same kind of analysis is applicable, in principle, to other areas of social life that are rule-governed. The main limitation on the use of propositional logic here, however, is its failure to give adequate account of the prescriptive, and not merely descriptive and explanatory (as, e.g., in ethnoscience), character of rule-systems. However, recent developments in logic hold promise for the analysis of these aspects of normative systems as well. In particular, the development of *deontic* logics, which include such normative concepts as obligation, prohibition, permission, and commitment, has a particular relevance here.

Modern logics such as these have found relatively little application in the behavioural sciences as yet, but their potential may well prove considerable. Thus a number of systems of deontic logic have been constructed, and this work has become particularly associated with such scholars as von Wright and the late A. N. Prior.[163] Formal systems of imperatival logic have also been proposed by, amongst others, Hofstadter and McKinsey (1939), Menger (1939), and Bohnert (1945).[164] Omar K. Moore and Alan R. Anderson (e.g. 1957, 1962) have been particularly responsible for the advocacy, and limited application, of the deontic systems in the social sciences.[165] Further, although formal systems of deontic logic (i.e. the logic of obligation and permission) and imperatival logic were previously considered autonomous, requiring special assumptions of their own, distinct from the axioms of either truth-functional or alethic modal systems (i.e. logics of possibility and necessity), Anderson (1958, 1967) has shown that they require no specifically deontic assumptions, but may be regarded simply as a branch of modal logic.[166] Naturally, such a reduction facilitates the further development of deontic logics, in that a normal deontic logic can, as a result, be constructed merely by adding appropriate definitions to *any* normal alethic modal logic, and there are many logics of the latter kind. Indeed, the fecundity of the modal systems has frequently been commented on by modern logicians.[167]

The principal advantage to be gained from translating empirical (or, for that matter, hypothetical) prescriptive systems into deontic terms is the formalization of the notion of proof that such a translation permits. The point of the formal approach is to display in a clear and rigorous manner the logical relations among groups of sentences (prescriptions, prohibitions, etc.), irrespective of their empirical content. For this purpose, an unambiguous statement of the three basic elements in any system of symbolic logic is essential: namely, the 'well-formed formulas', or sentences; the axioms (from which other theorems are deducible); and the principles of inference (i.e. the principles which will count as valid in deducing new theorems from old ones).

Such a formal system has a number of distinct advantages apart from its formalization of the notion of proof. In the first place, it permits the ideas of the consistency and completeness of a set of norms to be given a clear and comparable explication. The first of these notions, as we have observed elsewhere, has been particularly central to many theoretical accounts of normative systems in sociology, and especially to those emphasizing the presumptive tendency towards 'balance' in such systems. The examination of a system for completeness allows also, of course, the possible derivation of unexpected hypotheses and relationships. Examples of the application of these two concepts are given in the paper by Anderson and Moore (1957), and the notion of completeness is in part illustrated by Hoffmann's (1959) study, discussed above.[168]

In the second place, the process of translating normative language from informal English (for example) into a logical notation itself leads to a degree of conceptual clarification, and to the exposure of ambiguities and indeterminacies present in the natural language. As a result, it is often misleading to describe the formal interpretation as a translation from the natural language, since this suggests a semantic equivalence that is frequently not present. As Anderson (1967) writes:[169]

> The logical structure of English (and natural languages generally) is vague, ambiguous, and in many respects confusing, whereas the logical structure of the formal systems is precise and clear. The point of 'translating' ordinary English expressions into the formalism is *not*, therefore, simply to write familiar things in funny notation. It is rather to exhibit our ideas within a framework which has a well-defined and clearly specified logical structure, and which enables us to say accurately and in a way that minimizes the chance of disagreement, just what follows logically from what. It is only by considering theories formally that their deductive and explanatory power (or lack thereof) can be made manifest.

Thirdly, then, the development of such formalisms, capable of handling normative concepts, should also permit greater insight into the operation and mutual relations of these concepts in our natural language. Although their principal function will, of course, be that of supplying adequate rational reconstructions of existing moral codes in society, and also of artificial moral codes drawn from the history of moral philosophy. The latter would not only be of intrinsic interest, but could also serve as analytic models for comparative

301

purposes. Finally, such formalisms should also permit the creation of hypothetical moral codes (e.g. as algorithms in simulation exercises) for heuristic purposes, the logical consequences of which could be easily derived and examined.[170] In each case, a closer, and mutually beneficial, relationship could be established between developments in logical analysis and in the understanding of society.

However, this is to stress only the possible benefits which may accrue. To this, certain qualifications should be added. In general, the very precision involved in logical formalization is also the main source of its problems, at least in the present context. These problems occur both at the stage of translating from the natural language into the terms of the chosen logical system, and also at that of translating the results of the formalism back into the natural language. These two stages might be termed, respectively, those of mapping and of interpretation. To some extent, of course, they form merely the reverse sides of the same coin. It will be convenient, however, to discuss them separately. Having briefly considered these, we will then mention some of the possibilities of relating deontic systems to other types of modal logic, and finally cite some of the other formal languages available for the analysis of normative systems.

## Mapping and interpretation

The conceptual analysis of empirically available moral codes for the purpose of constructing (if it is possible consistently to do so) deontic systems which accurately reflect the distinctions made in these structures has yet to be systematically attempted. Such comment, however, may be offered on the deontic systems presently available, some of which may prove to reflect at least certain aspects of empirically available codes. In general, the precision of these logical systems, in comparison with the type of codes they seek to describe, is gained at the price of considerable oversimplification. Wherever possible, further developments will be required in order to permit inclusion of a number of other significant empirical distinctions. Normal alethic modal logic, for instance, fails to provide a characterization of the concept of possibility which discriminates between the logical, theoretical, and practical senses of this term. In a similar way, available deontic systems fail to give wholly adequate characterizations of the terms 'obligatory' and 'permitted'. In particular, in the systems proposed by von Wright, who has been mainly responsible for initiating the development of this branch of logic, acts (or act-types) are trichotomized into those which are defined as 'obligatory', 'forbidden', or 'indifferent'.[171] But this is to exclude the conception of a continuum of moral 'preferableness', including notions of the ideal and other degrees of stringency over prescriptions, which, as we have argued earlier, seems to provide a more valid interpretation or model of many ethical systems.[172]

None the less, whatever the limitations of existing systems, there are many possible ways to strengthen these by the addition of intuitively plausible axioms and rules. Anderson (1967), for example, has expressed his belief that: 'Techniques of symbolic logic are sufficiently flexible and general to allow for the construction of formal systems of virtually any complexity.'[173] His own work in part exemplifies this flexibility. Thus, he demonstrates the possibility of constructing deontic systems by a technique which, in comparison with von Wright's work, has the merit of reducing the number of new primitive constants to be added to the alethic modal logic from two to one, and also of reducing the number of new axioms from two to one. His method appeals to the centrality of *sanctions* in normative systems and involves a definition of the deontic notions of 'obligation', etc. as follows:[174]

A state-of-affairs p is obligatory if the falsity of p entails the sanction S; p is forbidden if p entails the sanction S; and p is permitted if it is possible that p is true without the sanction S being true. It develops that formalization of these suggestions within a sufficiently strong alethic modal logic *does* lead to a system of deontic logic, provided an assumption is made concerning the sanction S, namely, that it is possibly false. The rationale for such an additional assumption is that if the sanction were not possibly false (i.e. if it were necessary), then *no* behavior designed to avoid it could be successful. The point of choosing penalties in drafting laws (as well as the point of such penalties or sanctions as come to be associated with non-observance of unwritten social norms), is that the hope of avoiding the penalty might serve as a motivating factor in human behavior; a 'sanction' would serve no such purpose if it were not avoidable (i.e. possibly false).

This particular example may be taken to illustrate also, however, the importance of prior analysis of a purely philosophical and, in this case, sociological kind. Thus, in spite of the *prima facie* validity and simplicity of this account, and despite the flexibility of interpretation which the formal category 'sanction' permits here, we have provided evidence earlier against the use of this concept as the most fruitful means for the analysis of moral codes, and, in particular, for regarding it as entailing a degree of ethnocentrism.[175] This is not, of course, necessarily to discount its applicability for the analysis of some moral codes. But we would question its universality. Indeed, from the viewpoint of analysing those systems of norms which could be plausibly described as entailing specifically moral prescriptions,

303

we would consider that the formal approach could be more validly directed towards examining the criteria of superiority and legitimacy proposed in the first section of this study.

None the less, it is to be allowed that in some cases the gain achieved in realism by incorporating analytic, or empirically available, distinctions such as these, even if it is possible to do so consistently, may still be outweighed by the complexity which ensues. For instance, one problem which the development of deontic systems has raised concerns the deontic status of necessary and impossible propositions. Counter-intuitive results have been achieved by the inclusion of necessities and impossibilities among the objects of prescriptions and imperatives. One method of circumventing these problems, which Anderson proposes, is to restrict the notions of 'obligation', 'permission', etc. to contingent propositions. It is clear that such a restriction should allow more realistic models of empirical codes to be developed. In Anderson's view, however, 'it is doubtful whether these gains are adequate compensation for the additional complications which ensue' and which make 'it considerably less easy to get an intuitive insight into the formal relations', as well as leading to some intuitively unacceptable results. In this case, therefore, he suggests that it be carefully borne in mind that the notation for 'obligation', for example, has the meaning 'obligatory for normative or logical reasons', and that, pending future investigations, this procedure be retained.[176]

Translating the intuitive intent of certain empirically available moral codes will involve a number of decisions regarding intended meaning. Moreover, it will be likely to involve not merely the transcription of empirical data into formal terms, but also, to a degree, the creation of such data. After the construction of an apparently adequate formalism, the problem then re-emerges with the need to translate this back into the natural language, such as English. For certain theoretical purposes this requirement will be less stringent than for others. However, we would in general agree with Anderson (1967) when he writes, 'the indefiniteness of natural languages cannot be entirely eliminated. For one thing, every formal system ever described has been discussed in some natural language. But it is to be hoped that the study of formal systems will illuminate the enormously complex structure of the natural languages in which they are discussed.'[177] The problem is not specific to logic, but is shared by other available formal languages, some of which will be cited below. However, it is a problem with which logicians have been perhaps particularly familiar, since logic was among the first of the formal languages developed to improve upon the precision and clarity of the natural language. Like many other formal languages, though, the formalization that is involved in the logical method has the property of being *self-contained*, in the sense that several of its terms can only be given precise definition by an appeal to other terms available within the formalism. That is, its definitions are inter-coherent.[178] Even the briefest experience of logic will indicate, for example, that the constants of the familiar two-valued propositional calculus do not always permit unambiguous interpretation in a natural language such as English and can only be satisfactorily defined in terms of the truth-table.[179] A similar comment is even more applicable to multi-valued logics, such as the deontic systems.

The main difficulty this gives rise to in the present context is that of the empirical verification of a proposed formalization of an ethical system. Often, in view of the inadequacies of the natural language, the evidence for the adequacy of such reconstructions will be at best persuasive, since the intuitive, common-sense ideas to be explicated, not being clearly and unambiguously defined, do not admit of rigorous handling. Where possible, one test would be a predictive one. For instance, where such a formalism generates a novel prescription, for which no evidence previously existed, the subsequent confirmation that this rule is in fact accepted by the community in question would provide some evidence in favour of the formalism. But if it were not confirmed, this could be evidence either for the inadequacy of the reconstruction, or for the presence of an inconsistency or incompleteness in the moral code, or (more likely) in its practice. Thus, the evidence from such predictions has only a limited value, particularly since the same prediction could be derived from different formalisms, just as any given hypothesis may be derived from an infinite variety of theories. In view of this, it appears that we should talk of 'degrees of confirmation' for given formalisms, as for theories, at least in so far as the axioms of the system cannot be directly validated. None the less, the heuristic function still remains; for instance, such formalisms can clearly serve as means of indicating unsuspected inconsistencies within a particular code and unexpected implications of it.

*Some possible applications*

The interpretive difficulties derive from the fact that formal systems proper are purely syntactical. They are designed simply to demon-strate the logical relations among propositions, but not to tell us which empirical propositions are in fact true. Nothing whatever in the formalism dictates the particular choice of an interpretation for the relata. However, the flexibility of interpretation of a formal system from this point of view has distinct advantages as well. Two aspects of this may be cited. In the first place, most of the applied research using logical systems in sociology has so far focused upon the analysis of kinship norms. This is in part due to the presence of exceptional ethnographic data on this subject, particularly with regard to kinship terminologies. However, there is no compelling reason to restrict the use of logic to this area of application. In principle, the deontic, and other, logical approaches are applicable to *any* normative system for which reasonable data exists. For instance, Anderson and Moore's work has been directed towards the development of normative systems by small groups, mainly under experimental conditions; similarly, Hoffmann, as we saw, has applied symbolic logic to residence rules; other applications have been made in the field of jurisprudence; and so on.[180] Many other possibilities are evident, and the exploration of these should in turn permit direct comparisons to be made of the structure of normative systems between different societies and between different segments of the social life of any particular society, a procedure that is compatible with the aims and assumptions of intellectual traditions as diverse as structural anthropology and general systems theory.

In the second place, the possibility exists of relating the logical approach to other formal languages, and also of interrelating different branches of logic. McKinsey, for example, has suggested the interpretation of modal logic as an algebra of topology.[181] Of more immediate interest, however, is the exploitation of the close formal connections between the deontic concepts and other logical concepts, particularly those encompassed within the various systems of modal logic. Recognition of some of these connections has led von Wright, for example, to present the principal modal categories in the schema given in Table 8.6.

TABLE 8.6 *Modal categories*[182]

|     | Alethic | Existential | Epistemic | Deontic |
| --- | --- | --- | --- | --- |
| (a) | necessary | universal | verified | obligatory |
| (b) | possible | existing | unfalsified | permitted |
| (c) | contingent | partial | undecided | indifferent |
| (d) | impossible | empty | falsified | forbidden |

Among the formal similarities which von Wright notes are the following: 'Whatever is "a" is "b", whatever is "b" is not "d", and whatever is "c" is neither "a" nor "d".'[183] Our point here, however, is that more powerful and inclusive conceptual tools for the analysis of normative systems may be gained by the judicious combination of a number of these modal categories. The development of more adequate reconstructions along these lines can be both guided by, and itself help to represent and clarify, certain fundamental distinctions derived from moral philosophy. Some of these are fairly obvious, and have been mentioned already. For example, Anderson's restriction of his deontic system of contingent propositions permitted the derivation of the two theorems that 'Whatever is obligatory is possible' and 'Whatever is permitted is possible', which embody the familiar dictum from moral philosophy that 'ought implies can'.

Similarly, a consideration of Anderson's proposed systems of deontic logic will reveal a basic similarity of structure between the deontic modalities and the alethic modalities, except for the lack of connection between deontic modalities and truth or falsity. Here, the absence of implications between proper deontic modalities and truth or falsity reflects the lack of (deductive) connection between 'is' and 'ought', which has been plausibly termed the most important distinction in moral philosophy.[184] However, having noted this, Anderson adds: 'It is no doubt true that a sharp distinction is made by most normative systems between what *is* the case and what *ought* to be the case, but it is doubtful whether the distinction need drive us to the view that normative statements and factual statements are somehow irreducibly different in kind, having no logical connection whatever.'[185]

Our view is similar. In particular, two points made earlier in this study may now be recalled. In the first place, we argued that there *are* logical relations between these two classes of statements in the minimal sense that every 'ought' proposition presupposes an 'is' proposition—or, alternatively, every expression of value (i.e. every evaluation) implies a corresponding set of beliefs—although not vice versa. In the second place, we argued that specifically moral values and prescriptions claim, *inter alia*, a special 'legitimacy', and that part of this legitimacy consists in their being well grounded, that is, in some sense founded on the perceived nature of things, or upon basic *beliefs*.[186] In consequence of these views, the individual development, and mutual interrelating, of especially the deontic and existential modes, (the latter being handled by the theory of quantification), seems particularly promising for our purposes. Quantificational extensions of deontic logic would permit the development of more inclusive formalisms. For example, it would then be possible to formalize statements mentioning individual agents (role-incumbents, institutions, etc.) in a society and characterizing their moral (and, e.g., legal) relations to each other. Similarly, closer relations between deontic and alethic logic would permit clarification of such important concepts as those of possibility, necessity, and contingency as applied to aspects of human action and ethical systems. In these various ways, perhaps further light can be shed on the analytic relations between the existential and the prescriptive, between notions of what 'is' the case (including notions of possibility, etc.) and what 'ought' to be the case.

Developments such as these would constitute part of the general exploration of modal logic. So far the investigation of this type of logic has been particularly productive, and there is good reason to expect that new discoveries will have relevance to our present subject. The development of *tense-logic*, as a branch of modal logic, in recent years might serve to illustrate this, for, as von Wright (1969) has noted: 'The need for a logic which studies the conceptual frame of a *dynamic* world, a world of change and flux, has, somewhat surprisingly perhaps, largely grown out of the interest which (analytic) philosophers recently have come to take in concepts relating to human action. To act, one can say, is to bring about or to prevent changes in nature—and to forbear action is to let things change or leave them unchanged.'[187] Advances such as these testify to the potential of modal logic in the future for supplying more extensive, and so more insightful, formalisms of normative systems.

## *Other formal languages*

Although our discussion has been concentrated upon types of symbolic logic up to this point, this is not, in fact, the only formal language available for the description of normative systems. Mathematics provides a number of conceptual tools appropriate to our present subject since these too are concerned with the description and analysis of structures. Particular mention might be given here of the work of H. C. White, as reported in his *An Anatomy of Kinship* (1963).[188] In this, White re-examines a number of normative systems specifying prescribed (and permitted) marriage arrangements by means of algebraic group theory. Within these kinship systems the individuals are conceived as divided into disjoint segments such that, for each segment, the men can select their wives from only one distinct segment and, similarly, their children belong to only one distinct segment. The rules which govern these two types of relationship are expressed, respectively, by the permutation matrices W and C, a particular product of which supplies the marriage relationship M. Each distinguishable type of kinship system is characterized by a distinct algebraic group, and is classified in terms of this group. In this way, a cross-cultural typology of kinship systems is provided on the basis of the type of marriages that they enjoin.

We can anticipate many more sophisticated analyses along the lines of White's study in the near future, in view of the vigorous attention being given to group theory in contemporary mathematics. There is every reason to suppose that as new formalisms are developed

308

for dealing with group concepts in mathematics, these will eventually be transposed to the social sciences as means of describing rule-systems, and indeed social structures, of various kinds.

Linguistic analysis, deriving its terms and much of its rationale from works such as Chomsky's *Syntactic Structures* (1957), has also been applied to the examination of, again, kinship grammars, perhaps most outstandingly Floyd Lounsbury (1964).[189] Other, semi-formal presentations are also available, such as Smith's (1956) approach to the 'structure of value', which introduces a mathematical model based on the theory of stochastic processes to facilitate the analysis.[190] (Use of computer simulation to examine stochastic models is discussed later in this chapter on pp. 310f.) Smith's account is intended to be little more than suggestive, and as such it is similar to many other heuristic applications within the general field of systems theory. Most of these approaches are relatively novel and tentative; their utility has yet to be proven. Also, in relatively few cases are systematic comparisons made between the structure of different normative systems, although this would appear to be one of the primary advantages offered by the present approaches. Similarly, there has been little attempt to translate rule-systems from one formal language into another for the sake of comparison. However, there is some evidence that this situation will improve. A recent paper by Boyd (1969), for instance, follows up White's analysis of kinship norms by means of algebraic group theory, although this time he selects the permutation matrices based on the relationships of father-hood and motherhood.[191] Boyd uses sophisticated algebraic methods and as a result is able to include within his formulation the analysis of kinship grammars by Floyd Lounsbury, and others. His work also goes some way towards meeting the criticisms of White, and of linguistic approaches such as Lounsbury's, for focusing exclusively upon kinship terminology, and ignoring ethnographic data on the actual operation of kinship systems.

## Summary

In sum, we have examined, albeit briefly, a number of formal approaches to the analysis of normative systems, although with particular attention to the one which seems to hold the most potential for use in social science, namely, deontic logic, and other branches of modal logic.[192] Several of these different 'languages' may prove effective as ideographic shorthands for the description and, equally important, comparison of rule-systems of various kinds (legal, ethical, informal, etc.). But the privileged position of logical systems in this regard lies in the fact that they permit us to understand such matters as processes of ethical reasoning in a more intimate, flexible, and dynamic manner. The fact that we do reason about prescriptive concepts, and that we also attempt to justify them as reasonable, indicates the general possibility of a formal logic of norms. And, in turn, the development of this aspect of logic, and its application to sociology, should permit a refocusing of research attention upon processes of ethical argumentation, and so supply the motivation for supplementing the 'one-dimensional' evidence that is currently provided by most available research techniques.

## Computer simulation

Having discussed formal approaches and simulations, we may add a few general comments about a technique which partakes of the characteristics of both methods; namely, computer simulation. This has become increasingly popular as a methodology in both the pure and applied sciences. It is to be found in studies of systems in industry, commerce, engineering, military affairs, and the public services. Particular uses range from the optimization of systems of air-traffic control to the analysis of mathematical models concerning the formation and dissociation of molecules.[193] Its application within the social sciences has been less common, although this application is increasing.

The main reasons for the use of computer simulations closely parallel the justification for simulations in general and are essentially similar in the case of both the natural and social sciences. Principal among these reasons is the fact that computer simulations allow the investigator to explore unanticipated consequences implicit in his theoretical models. The type of model utilized is thus taken to be sufficiently complex that a number of its implications cannot be readily analysed by other methods. This may be due to various characteristics of the model: to the complexity of the quantitative data it comprises, for instance, or to the uncertainty arising from synergistic effects and the complex interplay of forces within it, and so on. It is also, of course, in circumstances where it is either impracticable or prohibitively expensive to study the behaviour of the real situation, particularly over a wide range of conditions, that the behaviour of a model is analysed instead.

Once a reasonably reliable model, in either a theoretical or empirical sense, has been developed it may be manipulated in a variety of ways by altering particular specifications. In this way, one can explore many characteristics of the model, regarding critical variables, lacunae in the underlying theory, cumulative effects, and so on. Similarly, as we shall see, one can bring out the practical consequences of given systems of values or rules (which may be broadly ethical in character) by examining their implications within the con-

310

text of certain hypothetical or simplified social situations (or scenarios). Also this potentially systemic character of simulation designs, and of computer simulations in particular, can help militate against an excessive individualism in social research, which we commented on earlier in this section.

But if computer simulations confer these advantages, they also impose certain requirements. In the main these requirements centre upon the need for precision, detailed description, and lack of ambiguity in the models that are to be simulated. Thus, independent and dependent variables, and the dynamic relationships that hold between them (i.e. over time), must be carefully specified. Similarly, the overall model must form a closed system; that is, there must be no undefined circumstances in the theoretical description. Although some concession to the familiar *ceteris paribus* clause can be made by the admission of probabilistic events. Furthermore, dummy variables and 'empty' processes can be included in order to permit additional variables to be incorporated at later stages as necessary.

When all these criteria are met the model is written up in the form of a computer program. This often entails new difficulties which need not be entered into here. However, we may note that the ability to specify various rule-systems in either logical or mathematical formalisms may well render them more tractable for inclusion in computer simulations. None the less, most of the possibilities here largely await exploration.

As noted above, even though it is gradually gaining ground as an acceptable research technique, computer simulation is still in its earliest stages in social science. Hence there is no dearth of immediately relevant examples which we may cite. However, those studies which, either directly or indirectly, do have most relevance to our present concerns may be broadly divided into two main types according to whether their research focus is primarily psychological or sociological. Each may be given some brief consideration.

*Psychological models*

The research that pioneered the use of computer simulations in psychology was reported by Newell, Shaw, and Simon in 1957.[194] They wished to simulate the elementary logical operations of an individual's thinking and, in order to describe this, initiated the development of list-processing languages, which have been much used in subsequent work of this kind.[195] The most influential feature of their work, however, lay in the theoretical assumption upon which it was based. This was simply to the effect that a functional analogy could reasonably be drawn between 'thinking' processes of various kinds and the operation of a computer program. And it was, of course, this central idea that their own research was designed to both test and illustrate.

This analogy, between the operation of a program sequence and thinking, has proved particularly heuristic to subsequent inquiries in psychology and it has stimulated an increasing number of further attempts to simulate cognitive processes by means of the computer. To illustrate the potential applicability of this work to our own interest brief summary may be given of the study by Abelson and Carroll (1965), since this is fairly typical of the genre, in form if not content.[196] Abelson and Carroll's aim was to simulate some of the basic cognitive mechanisms whereby accepted and taken-for-granted belief systems are defended against the intrusion of statements which either contradict or undermine them. The simulation thus incorporated a set of beliefs (i.e. stored statements within the computer), together with a set of evaluations upon certain of these beliefs. It was then possible to introduce input assertions which, from the viewpoint of the simulated individual's memory, expressed apparent inconsistencies (e.g. a 'good' actor carrying out 'bad' actions). In such circumstances, the system had to respond by either accepting or rejecting the input assertion, at the same time giving its reasons for so doing. Thus if, for example, the system was to deny the assertion, it would have to search its memory for appropriate evidence to support the negation of the input assertion. A similar procedure applied to other defence mechanisms. In this way, some attempt, albeit at a very elementary level, was made to explore the ways in which dissonant cognitive states are avoided.

This particular model is at present only at the rudimentary stages of development. But it does indicate one area in which further refinements can reasonably be expected. Thus, by further simulations along these lines we may learn much more of the detailed microprocesses whereby individuals (and indeed groups) maintain their value- and belief-systems intact even in the face of contrary evidence. Then hypotheses regarding such analytic topics as dissonance reduction could be explored in terms of the specific cognitive procedures and stratagems that comprise them. Ideally, we would expect this kind of knowledge to be closely paralleled by successive theoretical refinements.

Several attempts have been made to simulate other types of cognitive processes. These include models of decision-making in elementary circumstances, of individual problem-solving, of concept-learning, hypothesis-testing, and so on. There is no need for us to enumerate all these here. Useful bibliographies, and examples, are to be found in Simmons and Simmons (1962), Feigenbaum and Feldman (1963), Sass and Wilkinson (1965), and Abelson (1968).[197] Suffice it to say that all these models are at present highly simplified and tentative and permit only limited analogy with the real world. However, many of them also show promise for further development in the future.

Aside from these psychological inquiries, other investigators making use of computer simulations have focused more upon social processes and systems in the construction of their models. Although a number of these do possess an essentially reductionist character, in the sense that they conceptualize social collectivities merely as aggregates of discrete individuals each pursuing his own goals. In these, the individual is the locus of explanation and different individuals are chosen in turn to initiate the simulation. Examples of this level of analysis are contained, for instance, in reports by Loehlin (1969) and Pool and Kessler (1965).[198]

## Sociological models

But more systemic simulations of a variety of social scenarios are also available and these possess more immediate sociological interest. To help fix ideas, we may consider a fairly straightforward example of this kind. Thus, Pool, Abelson, and Popkin (1964) developed a computer simulation model with predictive intent, in order to investigate the behaviour of the American electorate in the 1960 Presidential election.[199] The study required the use of a computer simply by virtue of the enormous quantity of data involved. One of the authors, Abelson (1968) has given a succinct description of their basic procedure as follows:[200]

> The opinions of some 100,000 survey respondents served as the basis for the characterization of the political orientations of 480 voter types arising from cross classifications of occupation, race, religion, sex, region, and party. The relative prevalence of these various types was laboriously estimated from a combination of census and survey data. The sensitivity of individual voter types to appeals based on 'issues' such as Kennedy's Catholicism was estimated via careful interpretations of the survey data. Prognoses of total gain and loss for each candidate were generated by assuming simplified campaigns consisting of only one or two issues.

And as he continues:

> The method rather successfully prognosticated state-by-state election returns by assuming that Kennedy's Catholicism was the dominant theme of the campaign. Simulation runs omitting or minimizing this factor were markedly less successful. Reasonably precise quantitative estimates of the effects of the 'Catholic issue' in fact became available through a series of

313

goodness-of-fit tests. These estimates were extremely valuable because they brought precision into an area which had been rife with rather loose speculation.

However, despite its success, their model cannot be applied automatically to any election situation. Thus a new set of appropriate assumptions had to be included for simulation of the 1964 Presidential election.[201] None the less, as it was based upon survey and census data their research does demonstrate how the present technique can be used in conjunction with other methods of data-collection so as to augment the utility of their findings. Other kinds of social processes have proved similarly amenable to computer simulation. For example, successful models have been developed to describe the diffusion of innovations via local processes of social influence.[202] Interesting attempts have also been made to simulate community controversies over such 'moral' issues as school segregation and fluoridation of the water supply.[203] These models have attempted to be realistic, rather than parsimonious, by incorporating a wide range of complex and mutually related socio-psychological variables into their specification. There is a continuing debate here, as in the field of simulation generally, upon the relative virtues of simplicity and realism in simulation designs.[204] The merits and demerits of the latter strategy are well illustrated in attempts which have been made to simulate national economies and patterns of economic growth. Such studies on the British economy have been particularly associated with the work of Professor Richard Stone and his colleagues at the University of Cambridge. This research has always had a more than academic interest and has indeed been conducted with the ultimate aim of aiding national policy-making, both by exposing weak points in the developing economy and also by exploring the detailed implications of alternative policies, without having to suffer their consequences in real life. However, this work has been limited so far both by a lack of theoretical knowledge in certain areas of economics and also by limitations in the capacity of available computers to store all the potentially relevant information. Both of these problems, however, should be at least ameliorated within the near future. These, then, are some examples of computer simulations at the level of social systems.

Simplifying considerably, we may say that moral codes, as defined within the present study, may be introduced into computer simulations in two main forms. In the first place, they may be taken to designate sets of evaluations, which specify certain actions or outcomes as desirable or as preferable on some ranking scale. Here decision-making models may be constructed for certain problems, real or hypothetical, in order to analyse the full ramifications for any given system (e.g. the economy, the social services, etc.) of particular options. As we have seen, computer models of the economy incorporate in part this kind of reasoning. In the second place, such codes may be conceived as *rule*-systems, perhaps described with the aid of formal languages. Here again a computer simulation would, in principle, allow one to explore the implications of such rules, operating over a certain period of time, for the state of other given socio-psychological variables. Depending upon the theoretical intent of the research, various possible scenarios could provide the context for such investigations.

A suggestive illustration of this last type of inquiry, and one of the few of its kind, is described by Gilbert and Hammel (1966).[205] They designated a number of groups of families living in small villages. The culture of this purely hypothetical 'society' was then specified to include certain prohibitions against various types of cousin marriages. By simulating many generations of mate selection and the production of new offspring, the authors were able to make detailed assessments of the implications of various marriage rules for population survival. Further, a version of the simulation in which mate selection was permitted to cross over village boundaries allowed deductions also to be made about the dependence of migration rates on marriage rules.

The Gilbert–Hammel study has certain limitations, but it is also surely suggestive of what may be achieved in the future by this method. Furthermore, the study of the implications of marriage rules for tribal population stability, and the possibility of analogous inquiries in other subject-areas, indicates that this methodology may well acquire much practical—as well as purely academic—significance. Their study also illustrates a fundamental feature of computer simulations; namely, that having set up the simulation model, one can always change the 'rules of the game' and explore the consequences which flow from this. The flexibility necessary to do this will be more or less limited according to how the model has been originally specified. In general, it is most important to write programs in a way that permits the maximum feasible flexibility.[206] For the ability to run several versions of a general model in order to assess their relative validity has an important role in the empirical validation of simulations.

One way to isolate the decision rules that may be operative in particular social processes is to make use of simplified experimental designs which attempt to capture some of the leading features of such processes. Because of its amenability to precise analysis, game theory, as briefly outlined earlier in this chapter, can supply the basis for several such designs. The recent study by Emshoff (1970) is an example in point.[207] He attempted to develop a simulation model

315

capable of reproducing the observed behaviour of actual players in a Prisoner's Dilemma game. The model was based upon hypotheses— or proposed decision rules—that were descriptive of a player's response to moves (past and present) made by the other subject. These hypotheses were difficult to test individually, but their consequences, in terms of observable game behaviour, could be tested against actual games. In this way, an experimental game format was used in conjunction with a computer simulation both to suggest relevant parameters (the hypotheses were in fact derived from interviews with players) and then to provide a basis for validating these parameters by comparing simulated outcomes with real game behaviour.

If it is the case, then, that various kinds of normative systems can be incorporated within computer simulations, then further attention ought to be given to the conceptual analysis of these systems as a source of more refined models of them. Of course, some of these refinements may prove relatively easy to state analytically but difficult to specify for computer purposes. Nevertheless, there must be several possibilities here. For example, perhaps the notion of degrees of stringency qualifying certain rules could be incorporated by specifying such rules in probabilistic terms; thus, expressed verbally, a rule or precept of only moderate stringency would in effect be designated as 'occasionally operative', and so on. Certainly, this field would seem to invite close collaboration between hitherto disparate aspects of conceptual analysis and simulation methodology.

Also, as we have seen, simulations can be made of the consequences of different types of priorities for other desiderata, assuming our knowledge of the system involved permits the necessary level of detailed specification. This should acquire growing importance within the context of social policy decision-making. For instance, models might be constructed for urban planning problems where, say, the effects of a proposed highway programme could be estimated in terms of its effects upon traffic flow, noise and air pollution levels, access to service and welfare facilities, land available for other needs, and so on. In this way, and even though some quantities must necessarily remain approximate, a more thorough knowledge may be achieved of the consequences—and, one might say, value implications—of various possible planning priorities. The simulation cannot, of course, determine these priorities. Rather, as a method it is more likely to heighten awareness of the need for conscious choice amongst alternatives.

## Validation and other problems

As we have emphasized, computer simulations in social science, as indeed in natural science, are at the exploratory stages only. They are certainly not immune from criticism. A major problem concerns the selection of appropriate means of validation. This is crucial if computer simulations are to be more than mere heuristic devices. Yet it is a particularly refractory problem in the case of larger-scale, social simulations. Abelson (1968) has outlined a number of validational strategies: namely, response matching; sequential dependency tests; Turing Tests; and experimental tests of simulation predictions.[208] The last-named is perhaps the most obvious among these. But even this procedure is not without its difficulties.

Thus, a general problem with computer simulations is that the accuracy of the outcomes does not guarantee the validity of the simulated processes which led up to these outcomes. Indeed, as Abelson (1968) comments, 'If a simulation could be "right for the wrong reason," that is, fit the data by virtue of compensating errors, then in what sense can a good fit be regarded as support for the theory underlying the simulation model? Can one ever "prove" a simulation theory by displaying good imitations of particular outcomes?' However, we would share his view that this problem is generally less severe in the case of cognitive simulations, simply because: 'Most cognitive simulations are so rich in qualitative detail that it is very easy for them to fail, particularly when the most frail validating technique, response matching, is used. Because it is so hard to obtain good data fits, anything which comes close is impressive, and any cognitive model yielding an apparently perfect fit to a wide range of data would indeed deserve serious theoretical recognition.'[209]

On the other hand, with social simulations the problem may be more severe, since[210]

> If the outcome variables of the model are few while the
> number of parameters to be juggled is great, there can always
> be the lingering suspicion that a good fit was too easy to
> achieve and thus not strongly supportive of the model. One
> remedy is to show, if possible, that the fit was not so easy by
> changing the model in various ways and demonstrating
> consistent lack of fit. Another remedy is to design the simulation
> so as to generate as large a number of outcome variables as
> possible. . . . In this light, the philosophical context surrounding
> simulation is not fundamentally different from that of any other
> type of scientific theorizing. No theory can ever be 'proved',
> only rendered more plausible by virtue of accounting well for
> more phenomena.

One consequence of the above concerns firstly, the importance of testing variations of the model to be validated on different runs of the simulation using the same data. This in turn requires, as indicated earlier, a sufficiently flexible program of instructions. Second is the

L*                                                                317 need for closer collaboration between computer simulations and other methods of social research. We have already seen that simulation models are frequently based upon data from these other methods. The point here is that they need to be introduced for purposes of cross-validation as well. As yet too few simulations have taken adequate account of the need to validate their models empirically, with the result that many of the ones available have a largely heuristic or demonstrative, rather than genuinely theoretical, status.

Another series of problems derive from the difficulties of describing the detailed specifications contained in most computer programs into the easily comprehensible terms of ordinary language. This is particularly acute in the case of many cognitive simulations, which typically include 'microprocesses which do not have standardized programming recipes, as common mathematical processes do' and so where the programmer 'will usually develop idiosyncratic private notations and methods in coping with various programming problems' (Abelson, 1968).[211] This was a problem we encountered also in dealing with formal languages. In both cases it is a product of the special needs for precision which these methods impose, and as such it is a problem that may prove difficult to eradicate even in the future. However, it is to be hoped that subsequent developments of this method in social science will also bring with them much more standardization in programming procedures.

A final problem-area concerns the existence and extent of possible fundamental limitations upon the construction of programs for solving certain problems. For example, one ideal goal, put simply, would be to discover the rules according to which real decision-makers are guided in making their decisions. But the actual extent to which such rules may both be said to exist and to be also capable of expression in the form of specific procedures, or *algorithms*, is a very debatable question. It is also a question that invites comparison with the problems faced by current research on machine intelligence in computers. Here the logical analysis into deductive sequences of even the simplest tasks requiring human intelligence has been found to be forbiddingly complex. As one investigator notes, 'The difficulty lies not in the shortage of computing power, but of the needed insights into mathematical logic and programming theory to enable us fully to harness it.'[212]

Thus it may be true, as one text puts it, that 'Any sequence of tasks that follows a specific regimen, or a problem solution that relies on definable and routinizable approaches, can be automated (at least in concept) through computers or computer-controlled instrumentation.'[213] But the important question for social science concerns the degree to which the undoubted uniformities of social phenomena

318

may prove amenable to description in the form of machine-implementable procedures of this kind. Of course, here, as elsewhere, the ability to find algorithms for solving problems can be expanded appreciably once we are willing to accept approximate solutions.

But this whole question needs also to be put in proper perspective. And here there are, so to speak, some historical grounds for optimism. Thus the speed with which computer science has evolved can hardly be overstated. Computers presently enjoy a unique industrial growth rate of above 20 per cent per annum, and the mean lifetime of a computer generation is estimated at a mere six years, after which a fundamentally new technology is introduced.[214] In the light of this, any general evaluation at this stage is likely to be premature. We cannot yet perceive adequately where the limitations upon programming will lie, or how extensive these will be.[215] What we can be reasonably confident of is that the use and general methodology of computer simulation will continue to advance, both within the natural and social sciences, and in relation to practical problems of planning and system design. In this way, its role, both as a distinct method of research to complement the traditional methodological tools of the natural and social sciences, and also as a practical aid to decision-making, should continue to grow in importance. The actual extent of this expansion would appear to be largely contingent upon technical factors; in particular, upon advances in computer capacity and programming technique. In social science specifically, more versatile languages could arise from novel ways of describing the uniformities and interrelationships among social phenomena. And here the lead, certainly within our present subject-area, may well come from the formal approaches discussed in the previous section.


This completes chapter 8, and also part two, on methods of data-collection. In so far as a summary statement may be ventured it would be in favour of exploiting the full range of methods of research, rather than concentrating exclusively upon survey techniques. And secondly, it would draw attention to the fact that greater use can, and should, be made of the many opportunities that arise for judicious combinations of research methods within the context of particular studies. Although each of these procedures is limited in itself, their skilled combination may bring the researcher closer to gathering data in a manner that is relatively free of biases and limitations deriving from the method used.

In part three we return to more philosophical concerns. In this, we examine a question that has remained implicit in much of the conceptual discussion in part one, and that is tacitly raised at many points in our consideration of the empirical research and means of data-collection in part two. It is the question of ethical and cultural relativism, and of their interrelationship. Since we have now examined the sociological analysis of moral codes, broadly defined, in many of its empirical and conceptual aspects, it seems appropriate to give our final attention to this general question which pervades so much of the subject-matter of sociology and, indeed, of modern ethics.

# part three

# Ethical relativism

# 9  Types of relativism

If one were to select *the* issue which the practice of sociology both raises and is relevant to, one might well choose the issue of ethical relativism. But in so doing one would be selecting an issue notable also for its lack of clarity. Indeed, as one author concludes of the absolutist-relativist controversy: 'There is hardly another field of inquiry to be found in which vagueness and ambiguity (and consequently, talking at cross-purposes) is more prevalent than in this subject.'[1]

Part three, then, is an attempt at clarification. We shall suggest that these ambiguities arise largely because a number of distinctions need to be made which usually remain obscured in relativist arguments. In outlining these points, and the relevance of sociological data to them, we shall be concerned not so much with adjudicating the relativist issue, as with providing a framework within which discussions of the issue might be more fruitfully conducted.[2]

*In nuce*, our main contention will be that to talk of *the* issue of ethical relativism, in the singular, is itself misleading, since this subject comprises a number of distinct issues, and it is best to consider them separately. And secondly, we shall argue that with respect to any one of these issues positions of varying degrees of extremeness are available, depending in part upon the kind of justification offered for them.

### Relativism in ethics

Historically, the question of absolutism and relativism in ethics dates back to the origins of moral philosophy, at least within the tradition of Western thought. As long as the universal validity of the established customs was not seriously questioned, there was no social need for a reasoned theory of conduct. But when societies come into closer contact with one another, whether through processes of commerce or conflict, people's horizons widen to include awareness of new cultures and this presumed universal validity comes under threat. Hence when, in fifth-century Greece, the force of customs was weakened, by processes such as these, and ethical dogmatism was attacked by the sophists, a new foundation for moral action and judgment was sought. It was then that the philosophical ethics of Socrates came into being. Thus, ethical theory arose out of the discussion as to the natural ($\phi\acute{v}\sigma\iota\varsigma$) or merely conventional ($\nu\acute{o}\mu o\varsigma$) character of morality. Not only ethics, but the whole philosophical system of Socrates and Plato was profoundly influenced by the desire to meet the challenge of ethical relativism.

This illustrates a more general point. Namely, that most novel directions in moral thinking, at least throughout Western history, have been taken when formerly unified social forms began, for one reason or another, to break down, and thus where the established moral vocabulary became incongruent with social reality. The emergence of moral philosophy in ancient Greece and the development of ethical rationales for modern capitalism form perhaps the paradigm examples of this in the West.[3] But they are not the only examples. And the exploration, cross-culturally, of analogous social processes would seem to form an integral part of the sociology of ethics.

The question of the relationship between the problem of relativism and the social-historical situation of a society is properly an issue for the sociology of knowledge. But one overall point is clear. The problem of relativism arises most acutely in times of transition and change, and the practical implications of taking one side or the other in the controversy are especially relevant in such times. Like Greece in the fifth century, our own century is an epoch of change, although on a vastly wider scale. Now all societies participate in a world-wide transition. And the revolution in transportation and communications entails a new interdependence; each society is to a greater or lesser extent influenced by the changes occurring in the others. There can be little doubt, therefore, that in our time the issue of relativism is of great practical importance.

Ethical relativism is often associated with ethical nihilism, and, in fact, the significance of the issue does rest upon the extent to which it leads to a conception of moral codes as arbitrary. Moral principles do acquire this character precisely if it is held that a society's mores, no matter how accidental their origin, are the ultimate standard of morality.[4] They are arbitrary in the sense that in their justification no appeal is made to considerations likely to compel the assent of an outsider who does not happen to have been conditioned by the cultural biases and *idées reçues* of the society whose mores provide the standard. And to regard moral principles as arbitrary is to treat them with scepticism.

Secondly, such a relativistic doctrine weakens also, to use Ginsberg's phrase, 'the moral unity of mankind'. This is so not in the factual sense of sharing common moral principles, but with regard to the universal validity of such principles. If the mores are the ultimate source of moral value for a particular society, then societies not only differ in their moral principles, but these differences are legitimate ones and no standard exists to unite these societies morally. In an important sense, they live in different moral worlds.

A third reason for the significance of the issue concerns the ethical implications of sociology itself, and in particular the common view that anthropology demonstrates the validity of ethical relativism. It does not seem unlikely that social scientists are more sympathetic to relativist arguments than their peers, but to what extent do the disciplines themselves dictate this conclusion?

One cannot attempt to evaluate these issues without first recognizing that the problem at stake is a complex one. Ethical relativism may be interpreted in a variety of ways, and, in the absence of those distinctions which would make one's meaning clear, it is not difficult to back up a particular viewpoint with equivocal arguments. For instance, in the literature relativism is usually presented in an all-or-nothing form. One is either for it, or against it. Whereas a more realistic formulation would ask which kind of relativism one was prepared to accept, and to what extent.

The context of relativist arguments is usually a cultural one. That is, it is taken to refer not to the relativity of value to the individual as such, whether as moral agent or evaluating spectator, but to cultures and whole societies. Although the individualistic thesis has been espoused, for instance, by particular versions of existentialism and finds expression in the popular idioms of various languages. Put crudely, it is the thesis of *chacun sa verité*, and it tends to be characteristic of those societies in which a premium is put upon individualism and tolerance.

With respect to the cultural thesis, however, it is clear that various bases are available for classifying cultures and societies. Some are more broad-ranging than others: for instance, we can speak in a sense of the Western world as one culture, or we can distinguish particular national cultures within this context, and so on. Similarly, there is no reason why societies and cultures should coincide, unless they do so by definition. For example, if we define societies politically, we must often recognize the presence of intrasocietal cultural differences. South Africa is a salient example here.

But how are such sub-cultures to be delineated? We demonstrated in chapter 4 that the concept of cultural pluralism may be operationally defined and, as such, can possess considerable predictive value. Of course, that particular operational definition encompassed only part of what we intend by the concept here. But the inquiry in chapter 4 also indicated that the question of pluralism is usually one of degree. Some nations—like South Africa, Nigeria, India—are highly plural in the present sense. Others—such as the U.K., Portugal, and the Scandinavian countries—considerably less so.

From a practical point of view, it seem unnecessary to attempt definitive answers to these operational questions here. The usual framework for the discussion of ethical relativism is a simplified one of cultures and societies where ways of life, and basic beliefs, are far apart. Hence the examples used in relativist discussions are most frequently drawn from preliterate communities and societies of antiquity. None the less, we do recognize that such a practice might result in—if not itself reflect—an overly academic notion of the significance of these questions. Extreme examples like these serve to highlight relativist issues, but they are by no means the only relevant ones. In practice, one is often faced with questions involving relativism to which only very particular, and much less clear-cut, aspects of culture are relevant. One has then to decide whether on the single issue in question two communities are in fact sufficiently far apart to be considered to have distinct cultural traditions. It is here that operational approaches to culture acquire their relevance. Although, as we shall see, this is not the only kind of sociological data which has a central role to play in the present subject.

On the other hand, although the questions of individual relativism and cultural relativism are usually treated entirely separately, they are not unrelated. Thus, several of the points to be made could be applied, *mutatis mutandis*, to ethical diversity among individuals. And this, as we saw in chapter 1, is a problem not without relevance to our own society.

Given this, the first distinction to be made is that between ethical relativism as a descriptive or evaluative thesis. The two are frequently confused. This is partly because several writers—such as Sumner, Herskovits, and Ruth Benedict—who have popularized the former view have also espoused the latter one. Descriptive relativism, however, merely asserts the factual diversity of customs, of moral beliefs and practices. It may also, of course, try to explain these in terms of the more general nature of the cultures and societies under review. The thesis itself, however, is a purely factual one. It may be termed, therefore, *cultural relativism*, of which strictly it is a special case. Ethical relativism proper, on the other hand, is an evaluative thesis, affirming that the value of actions and the validity of moral judgments are dependent upon their socio-cultural context. The two theses are logically distinct, though not unrelated. But before we can consider the way in which they may be related, it is necessary to distinguish various versions of the thesis of ethical relativism. We shall then see that each relates to cultural relativism in a distinctive way.

## Types of ethical relativism

'Traditionally,' as Nowell-Smith observes, 'moral philosophy has always been regarded as a practical science . . . because the goal was practical knowledge, knowledge what to do.'[5] Moral philosophy was a source of advice. During the present century, however, ethical philosophy has turned increasingly away from this normative role to an analytical one. In place of making moral judgments, the principal concern has become that of analysing their nature. To distinguish it from practical ethics, the latter activity has been termed, as we noted in the Introduction, analytic ethics. In practice, it is often difficult to distinguish the two since philosophy texts typically contain elements of both.

These two levels of ethical inquiry, however, provide a useful basis for classifying types of ethical relativism. On the one hand, we have views containing commitments to a certain conception of moral knowledge and justification in ethics, and on the other hand, views which are non-committal in this matter. Although historically relativism, viewed as involving a conception of values as arbitrary, has been opposed by views justifying moral beliefs in terms of the nature of reality, i.e. ontologically, we shall argue that this is not necessarily applicable to all kinds of relativism. That is, at least two kinds of relativism are compatible with the view that certain moral standards have universal validity. Nor does the view that there are universal standards commit one to an ontological (or intuitionist) view of ethics. Utilitarianism, for instance, in Bentham's or Mill's sense did not involve ontological premises about the structure of reality or intuitions, but still intended the principle of utility or of harmonious happiness to apply to all cultures under all circumstances.

A further distinction is evident in discussions of ethical relativism. It is that between two objects of evaluation, agents or actions. Some arguments are concerned with ascribing praise or blame to particular agents, others with assessing the rightness or wrongness of particular actions, or the principles behind these actions.

If we add this distinction to the previous one, we arrive at a tentative classification of types of ethical relativism, as in Table 9.1, which will serve as the basis for our discussion.

The two types of normative relativism above are less fundamental

327

TABLE 9.1  *Types of ethical relativism*

| | | Object of Moral Judgment | |
|---|---|---|---|
| | | Agents | Actions (*or principles*) |
| **Level of Inquiry** | Normative (applied) | **Evaluative relativism** Allows possibility of evil actions which are not *blameworthy* in particular societies  1 | **Relativism of rightness** Allows possibility of evil actions which are not *wrong* in certain societies  2 |
| | Analytic (meta-ethical) | 3 **Epistemological relativism** Denies validity of cross-cultural moral judgments by virtue of limitations upon our possible knowledge | 4 **Axiological relativism** Denies the cross-cultural validity of values; the intrinsically good and evil are culturally specific |

versions of relativism than the analytic types. The latter are concerned with the very premises of ethical inquiry. Also, as one moves from 1 to 4, one is taking up a moral radical form of relativism at each stage. We will begin our discussion with the normative theses, which are relevant in so far as they involve a relativistic application of moral judgments rather than, as in the analytic cases, a relativistic conception of moral judgments as such.

Evaluative relativism, or 'relativism of desert' (Moser), calls into question the universalizability of praiseworthiness and blame-worthiness. The problem here is that of applying given moral standards to the assessment of agents in other cultures. For instance, it is the practice of certain African communities to put newborn twins to death because they fear the supernatural consequences of allowing them to live. The evaluative relativist might hold in this case the view that infanticide is an evil action wherever it occurs, but that these people were not to be blamed for their practice of it. Whereas, if it occurred in our society, it would not only be evil, but obviously blameworthy too. This ethical discrimination might be justified in the following way. Firstly, it could be pointed out that, however objectively wrong the action might be, given the Africans' cultural beliefs, their actions were subjectively right. And secondly, given the level of their culture and the degree of development of their society, they could not be expected to discover that their beliefs were wrong.

The beliefs in question may be moral or factual. We would generally expect them to be a mixture of both. It is evident, however, that here, as elsewhere, when we relate these two elements together

328

we are interested in factual beliefs that are relevant in a psychological, rather than a logical, sense. We cannot, therefore, expect to be able to work out which the relevant beliefs are by purely analytic techniques, even though the latter might in cases provide useful clues. To illustrate this, we may take a simple prescription, such as 'Do not lie'. One may then work out what this entails in a logical sense—the existence of the speaker, the possibility of lying and not lying, and so forth. Yet the essential background belief is likely to be one which is not logically entailed: it may be, for instance, the idea that to lie is to incur supernatural punishment.

This type of relativism, then, exonerates the agent from his evil actions by drawing attention to cultural motives beyond his responsibility. The practice is evaluated, but not the practitioners. The evaluation may be positive or negative. Thus it could also refer to a type of conduct that is *per se* morally desirable but does not deserve praise when practised in certain societies. Further the judgment need not be comparative, it could also be historical. It might be applied, for instance, to historical notions of justice and punishment; indeed, some future civilization might well examine our own practices in just these terms. The problem of assessing the degree of blameworthiness becomes a practical one when dealing, for example, with present-day 'primitive' societies. The literature on millenarian movements, and the outbreaks of violence and looting which they involve, is a case in point.[6]

Relativistic statements of this kind in effect stress a point we noted earlier (see chapter 3, pp. 49–57); that is, the importance of the *contexts* in which actions occur for their evaluation. Such statements are frequently encountered, and often confused with assertions of the relativity of intrinsic worth or of rightness. As a general thesis it is usually held in a qualified form, though it could also be held unconditionally. Thus the extreme version would maintain that there has never been a practice, no matter how intrinsically evil, from which certain societies engaging in it could not be exonerated from blame. The qualified version would hold that this is true of certain practices only, either because there are some practices so self-evidently wrong or evil that no society could regard them as right, or that if they did so their error was inexcusable.

The plausibility of the moderate version is gained at the price of indeterminacy, for one has then the problem of specifying these self-evidently evil actions and justifying one's choice. It is also often difficult to determine to what extent people are responsible for their ignorance, that is, for their wrong factual and moral beliefs. Were the members of the Spanish Inquisition blameworthy for their actions, given the cultural environment in which they lived? Evidently, as in this case, it is often a matter of degree: put otherwise, the criteria of ethical competence may be easy to state, but difficult to apply. And extremist versions easily become facile, as Robert Redfield aptly illustrates when he talks of the absurdity involved in 'anthropologizing the Nazis'.[7]

Relativism of moral rightness is a second type of relativism which also draws attention to the overall contexts in which actions are performed. But since it is now the actions themselves, or the principles they embody, which are being evaluated, the relevant context is more that of their social consequences than of the cultural motives which may lie behind them.

The essential thesis of this type of relativism is that there may be intrinsically good practices which are wrong in certain societies, and intrinsically evil types of actions which are right in certain societies. A pair of examples will illustrate the kind of reasoning involved.

At certain periods of time, traditional Tikopian society sent out groups of its young men on canoe expeditions, from which none were allowed to return, and on which, except in the unlikely eventuality of another island being reached, it was expected that all would eventually die. In addition to this, during the same periods infanticide was sometimes practised.[8] As a second example, it has been held that, although all men have a self-evident right to freedom, slavery as practised throughout the Greek city-states was an acceptable social institution.

In fact, a relativist of the present kind might well argue that both practices are to be regarded not only as subjectively right, but as objectively right also, and for similar reasons. In the Tikopian instance he would draw attention to the fact that the canoe journeys and infanticide took place only when there was a real danger of the growth of population out-running the supply of food. As precautions against overpopulation, these practices, though intrinsically undesirable, would be regarded as necessary evils. Similarly, in the case of Greece, it might be argued that the evil of the institution of slavery was outweighed by its positive consequence of making possible the development of a leisure class, which in turn was a necessary condition for the development of Greek culture, itself one of the sources of Western civilization.

The structure of the argument involved here is a comparatively simple one. The intrinsic justification of a particular practice is seen to be outweighed in certain cases by the extrinsic justification of its opposite. The social context is relevant in so far as it supplies this extrinsic justification. Ultimately, of course, even an extrinsic justification must rest upon some notion of the desirable *per se*. In the last analysis, therefore, the issue at stake is one of priorities among values. It is for this reason that research questions which pose some form of the intrinsic v. extrinsic dilemma can serve a useful role in the study of people's moral priorities (of which, of course, they may be largely unaware). More detailed attention was given to these two types of ethical justification earlier in our inquiry (cf. chapter 3, pp. 75–88).

Relativism of moral rightness, then, draws attention to the consequences of social practices. Institutions are to be seen within their structural context, and are to be evaluated with regard to their implications for this context. This is similar to the functionalist viewpoint that institutions should be examined in terms of their functions, positive and negative, latent and manifest, for other institutions or for the whole society. Functionalism draws attention to the interconnectedness of social practices; to change part of the system is to risk undermining the whole.

Given these views, it is not surprising that functionalists have themselves often professed ethical relativism in the present sense. In the 1930s and 1940s the colonial situation was commonly examined in these terms. Here, ethical relativism and the politics of culture became a joint issue. And the issue at stake was whether enlightened interference with native customs was justified. For instance, in *The Argonauts of the Western Pacific* (1922), Malinowski wrote: 'The rapid dying out of native races is, I am deeply convinced, due more to wanton interference with their pleasures and normal occupations, to the marring of their joy of life as they conceive it, than to any other cause.'

As a more specific example, a number of anthropologists, such as Rivers,[9] argued that the abolition, by the British Government, of headhunting in New Guinea was the major cause of the rapid decline of the birth rate in that region. This was, they claimed, because this institution, although very infrequently practised, none the less permeated almost all aspects of the culture. Thus, without it the natives lost all 'interest in life'.[10]

A more extreme type of relativism of rightness, which functionalism might encourage, is what Moser terms conformity relativism.[11] This makes the value of social conformity and cohesion paramount, with the result that one has only to know whether a given institution, however contradictory it is to one's other values, is established in a certain society in order to evaluate the rightness of the institution in that society. This argument is often used to supplement relativist positions, but as a main thesis it is rare. Certainly, this thesis has been more commonly ascribed to the early functionalists, such as Malinowski, and the modern structural-functionalists, such as Parsons, by their critics, than explicitly adopted by these authors.[12]

To return to the overall thesis of relativism of moral rightness, we may again distinguish an extreme version from a more moderate one. The extreme form would hold that no type of conduct may be found that would be right in all societies or wrong in all societies. The moderate form, on the other hand, would affirm merely that, either occasionally or frequently, practices and institutions which are intrinsically good are wrong in certain societies, and intrinsically wrong or evil types of actions are right in certain societies. The problem with this, more common, version lies in specifying the conditions, external or psychological, that would justify these different practices. Since the idea of permanent psychological characteristics attached to racial groups, which Pitt-Rivers,[13] for instance, used to back up his relativism, has been largely rejected by the scientific world, the question rests mainly with the external conditions. The problem arises, for instance, of deciding the necessity of slavery for the development of Greek culture. Here, a functionalist search for structural alternatives might lead one against this kind of relativism.

The doctrine of relativism of rightness is more heterogeneous than that of evaluative relativism since various reasons may be given for holding it. But it is also more fundamental. Thus, a relativistic standard of rightness implies exoneration from blame, but not vice versa; that is, factual or moral ignorance do not by themselves make a practice right. In so far as this doctrine undermines belief in universal standards, it comes close to the two more basic types of relativism that we shall now consider.

## Epistemological and value-relativism

Since the types of relativism we have so far examined seek merely to impose limitations upon the application of moral codes, they are usually in the form of specific statements about individual cases. The next two types of relativism are about the general conception of moral standards as such and hence normally take the form of general theses, from which particular applications may be deduced.

First, epistemological moral relativism. As the name suggests, this deals with the competence of people in one culture to pass judgments on the conduct of people in other cultures. By drawing attention to the inaccessibility or complexity of the information potentially relevant to evaluations across the dividing lines of culture, it denies that judgments of this type can be well-grounded. Broad comparative generalizations would remain essentially speculative in this view.

In its main form it stresses our incompetence to judge whether the practices of other societies deserve praise or blame. Thus, the motives, and degree of responsibility, of the agents concerned, it is claimed, can only be understood by those who participate in the same culture. For example, it might be argued that we, as members of a distinct culture, could never feel ourselves into the motives of the primitive

332

who commits infanticide, and therefore could never know whether he deserves to be blamed or not. Logical limits are set upon the scope of our understanding. A similar type of argument in sociology asserts, for example, that to understand the world of religion, the observer must himself be religious, or, again, to understand the position of the Negro in the United States it is necessary to see social reality through their eyes, that is, to be a Negro oneself. And so on.[14]

However, although the above version of epistemological moral relativism can be argued to be both the most basic and empirically the most common one, it is not necessarily restricted to this type; and in this sense our original typology (p. 328) is an oversimplification. The same viewpoint may also be applied to positions 2 and 4 in the diagram, to relativism of rightness and axiological relativism. With regard to relativism of rightness, it may be argued that an outsider cannot possess knowledge of all the facts relevant to such evaluations. For instance, it might be pointed out that it is difficult for us to determine, say, whether Eskimo widowers who killed their infants had any other choices available to them, or whether slavery was a necessary condition for the development of culture in some ancient Greek city-states,[15] and so on. Often subtle psychological factors are involved which are relevant not only to judgments of praise and blame but also to judgments of rightness and wrongness, and these factors may not reveal themselves to outsiders.

*Vis-à-vis* axiological relativism, the epistemological relativist may deny also that we are competent to pass judgment upon the *per se* morally desirable in other cultures. For example, if it is held that the latter cannot be understood without reference to the most generalized assumptions and beliefs of the culture in question, then the epistemological relativist could maintain that since we cannot have adequate knowledge of these presuppositions and the structure of motives and goals that they give rise to, then we similarly cannot judge with any confidence what is intrinsically good or evil, in the moral sense, for these societies.

A viewpoint of this kind has, of course, been put forward in the first part of the present study. Thus, we have argued for such an intimate relationship between cognitive assumptions and moral codes, and for the need to take the former fully into account in any attempt adequately to comprehend such moral codes. Needless to say, such a viewpoint does not commit us to any form of epistemological relativism: there is no necessary relationship between the two theses. Indeed, it could be argued that some of the more facile forms of relativism have exaggerated the exotic and incomprehensible character of certain alien practices and principles precisely because they have given insufficient attention to the structure of beliefs which lie behind them.

To summarize, then, all the above epistemological theses have the common property of stressing that what we know, and understand, of other cultures is limited. The extreme view would maintain that, however abhorrent certain practices might appear, they may still be both subjectively right in certain cultures and comprehensible only in terms of psychological and external conditions that we can never fully appreciate. As a result, the cross-cultural evaluation of moral codes is always unjustified. A more moderate view would, whilst recognizing that this is true in some cases, none the less recognize other situations which were so clearly right or wrong that cross-cultural judgments could be passed on them with the same certainty as judgments within a culture.

In general, it seems that we may take one of two overall positions with regard to this doctrine. On the one hand, we may take it merely as a warning against over-confident generalization. In this sense, it would involve taking care, when assessments are about to be made, or prescriptions about to be offered, to get full information about the overall contexts in which events occur, and it would involve recognizing that the contexts in question may be radically different from those of our normal experience. However, it might also be argued that in some cases coming to a decision is a practical necessity, irrespective of whatever doubts we may have about the grounds upon which our decision rests.[16] On the other hand, it is possible to go further and maintain that all, or at least many, judgments of this kind are to be ruled out as invalid. This involves a general philosophical position which asserts, even more than that our information on other cultures is limited, that our thinking in general is culture-bound, and that we cannot therefore regard other cultures impartially.

It is often held that this is not only true of ethics, but of the social sciences, and even of the natural sciences, as well. In other words, a more general cultural epistemological relativism is involved. Thus, for example, 'objective' anthropology becomes a mere exercise in disguised ethnocentrism. With regard to history, Benedetto Croce expressed this view when he said that all history is contemporary history and that all history is philosophy.[17] The fact that this type of relativism involves an incisive re-evaluation of social science often leads to an inconsistency between theory and practice. Thus Lévi-Strauss has argued for a qualified epistemological relativism, to the effect that we can only comprehend cultures which are not radically dissimilar to our own. His own practice of anthropology, however, seems hardly in accord with this view.[18]

This type of relativism usually points to some overall determinant of culture, including styles of science, to justify its views. Various such factors are historically available. The best known is perhaps the thesis of economic determination as formulated by Marx and Engels. The Chinese leader Mao Tse-Tung expresses a radical version of this when he writes: 'In class society everyone lives as a member of a particular class, and every kind of thinking, without exception, is stamped with the brand of a class.'[19] Other theories have specified other factors as major determinants, such as linguistic structures (Sapir, Whorf), geographic factors (Huntington), dominant media (McLuhan), and so on.

If one gives some credence to the view (especially from psychology) that 'awareness of determination ends it', then one might hold that the sociologist has a privileged position on this matter. But the question remains of the extent to which he can become aware of his own conditioning. This is again an epistemological issue, upon which various positions are available.[20] A different approach is suggested by Johan Galtung. Recognizing that distinct styles of social science exist as a result of different ideological bases, and citing the traditions of Columbia, Louvain, and the University of Moscow as examples of this, he argues that this is an advantage rather than a threat to social science. He accepts the idea of three or more ways of explaining the human condition, and suggests that we relax the criterion of 'intersubjective validity' so that it involves 'requesting as a minimum intersubjectivity within, if not between the camps'.[21] He discusses the consequences as follows:[22]

> This has the advantage of making for a more pluralistic world, if we accept that as a value. For the final consequence of intersubjectivity is a unitary world where science is concerned, which is a considerable value-choice as a consequence of a doctrine of value-neutrality. Today there is little doubt that there is a basic correspondence between the social matrix and the kind of social science it produces, and it is probably also true that styles of scientific pursuit will converge as the social matrices converge. It may well be that a doctrine of value-neutrality, i.e. invariance of value-orientation, will speed up this process. In the meantime, maximum openness between camps to learn other perspectives, and maximum intersubjectivity within camps seem to be the best one can make of the situation.

He goes on to suggest that the present situation of competition between the different camps, and reasonable consensus within them, may be historically the optimum one for progress in the social sciences.

Thus, there are many different types of relativism with regard to epistemology, and the significance of epistemological moral relativism will depend upon the version chosen. If it refers only to

335

judgments of praise and blame, or rightness and wrongness, then it will be similar in its consequences to the doctrines of, respectively, evaluative relativism and relativism of rightness. On the other hand, if it is maintained that we are not competent to pass judgments on what is intrinsically good and bad in other cultures, and especially if it is held that our moral thinking is incapable of transcending cultural (or class) biases, then epistemological moral relativism becomes a doctrine conducive to moral scepticism and arbitrariness, and is detrimental to the belief in the 'moral unity of mankind'.[23]

The final type of relativism, which we have termed axiological relativism, may be looked upon as value-relativism proper. It is a fairly straightforward doctrine which asserts that values and dis-values, or the intrinsically good and evil, are always relative to a given socio-cultural system and that no moral standards have cross-cultural, universal validity. It is termed axiological relativism since it refers to the morally valuable in itself.

As a general thesis, this is more exclusively in the domain of ethical philosophy than the other types of relativism. It is also the most fundamental type. Thus, with regard to epistemological relativism, one can still make, without self-contradiction, judgments on other cultures of the type which say 'Such-and-such a practice is wrong, but our judgment that it is wrong is not valid (i.e. well-founded).'

Various ethical philosophies are available to justify this kind of relativism. We can briefly indicate a few of these. One of the best-known of these viewpoints is that of A. J. Ayer.[24] He denied that what we call moral judgments are in fact capable of any rational or objectively valid justification. Instead, they were merely expressions of emotion. Frankena classifies this among non-cognitivist theories of ethics, and observes that many existentialists, including religious ones, likewise regard basic value-judgments as arbitrary commitments or decisions for which no justification can be given.[25] Similarly, moral judgments have been analysed as merely expressing commands, which again are ultimately arbitrary. A second view makes such judgments synonymous with descriptive assertions about the person making them; thus 'X is good' is interpreted to mean simply 'I like X' or 'Most people like X'. Sumner exemplifies a third approach, which argues, in effect, that moral standards are constituted ultimately by a society's customs. Thus in his *Folkways* (1940) he wrote, 'The notion of right is in the folkways. It is not outside of them, of independent origin, and brought to them to test them. In the folkways, whatever is, is right. When we come to the folkways we are at the end of our analysis.'[26] Other philosophical positions are available to justify value-relativism but the above examples will suffice for our present purposes.

# 10    Relativism and sociology

The question of the relevance of the data made available by the social sciences to the various types of relativism outlined in the last chapter raises in special form the Humean problem of the relationship which factual propositions bear to evaluative or prescriptive ones. In this case, the relevant facts are ethnological ones, and the question is: What does comparative sociology and anthropology commit us to in an evaluative sense? What are the ethical implications of cultural relativism?

Our procedure will be to discuss this issue first, and then to offer some observations on research on relativist attitudes and, finally, upon the nature of the sociological perspective in these terms.

## Cultural diversity

The facts of cultural relativism will be familiar to the social scientist. Examples abound both of widely divergent practices in different societies and of radically different interpretations of the same practices. Writers such as Margaret Mead and Ruth Benedict have been especially influential in popularizing data of this kind. And, despite disputed interpretations of individual cases, the empirical evidence has accumulated with the extension of the anthropological enterprise.[1] Thus, the overriding consensus in social science would appear to accept cultural relativism. It has, indeed, become a basic premiss in anthropological inquiry. Those who have disputed this view have been concerned mainly with the question of emphasis, rather than with a fundamental reinterpretation of the facts, or with individual cases rather than the general thesis. Thus, the structuralist approach of Lévi-Strauss, and the linguistic approaches of such writers as Chomsky supplement rather than contradict the thesis of cultural relativism. With regard to the present subject, two principal types of anti-relativist arguments have been advanced. On the one hand, attention has been drawn to certain presumptive functional prerequisites, or cultural universals, claimed to be inherent (either causally or logically) in the nature of man in society. In different ways David Aberle, Talcott Parsons, and G. P. Murdock exemplify this approach.[2] The general agreement would be, however, that such factors impose limits upon the variability of moral codes: they do not directly determine their content.

The second type of argument holds that cultural relativism applies to the derived, rather than basic, values and precepts of different societies. Ralph Linton and S. E. Asch have at times espoused this view, and Frankena (1963) has drawn our attention to it when he states in regard to the thesis of descriptive relativism that:[3]

> It does not say merely that the ethical and value judgments of different people and societies are different. For this would be true even if people and societies agreed in their basic ethical and value judgments and differed only in their *derivative* ones. What descriptive relativism says is that the *basic* ethical beliefs and value judgments of different people and societies are different and even conflicting. I stress this because the fact that in some primitive societies children believe they should put their parents to death before they get old, whereas we do not, does not prove descriptive relativism. These primitive peoples may believe this because they think their parents will be better off in the hereafter if they enter it while they are still able-bodied; if this is the case, their ethics and ours are both alike in that they include the precept that children should do the best they can for their parents. The divergence, then, would be in factual, rather than in ethical beliefs.

The consensus here seems to be that, although this may be the case in certain instances, and perhaps in more than we have yet recognized, in many others the divergent value-judgments can be genuinely considered to be basic ones. Also, there is a particular danger of overplaying this argument, which the academicism of much modern sociology encourages; that is, there is a tendency to try to subsume whichever particular value-judgments appear to us to be alien under more general categories of value that are compatible with the traditions of Western culture, and from which the former are then alleged to be derived. It would appear that this is only warranted in those cases where there is clear and reliable evidence that the respondents themselves think in these terms. In the absence of such supporting evidence, this thesis must always remain in the nature of an hypothesis.

We still lack a systematic compilation of the anthropological data on cultural relativism. The future will probably see steps taken in this direction. At present, the nearest approximation is perhaps the Human Relations Area Files at Yale University.[4] A limitation of these, however, is that the cross-cultural data refers principally to aspects of social structure, such as kinship systems, rather than to the beliefs and values which underlie these institutions. Although the work of David McClelland and, using the method of factor analysis, Raymond Cattell might also be mentioned in this category, together, of course, with the development of cross-national attitude and opinion surveys.[5]

The facts of cultural relativism have been somewhat neglected by moral philosophy. In many cases this has been intentional: the argument has been limited to individuals sharing certain given cultural assumptions, including a common language and a more or less shared interpretation of the vocabulary. But in many other cases an anthropological perspective of this type would have enhanced the argument.

One of the first works of moral philosophy to give systematic attention to these facts was Westermarck's *Ethical Relativity* (1932). To illustrate the relativity of morals he cited widely different attitudes that various societies had taken towards killing the old, infanticide, suicide, sacrifice, sexual practices, the treatment of animals, and towards members of other societies.[6] His examples were mainly historical, and, despite some impressionistic anthropology, he brought to the subject a wide-ranging scholarship. On the social meaning of suicide, for instance, he cites its honourable connotations in many circumstances in traditional China and Japan; its acceptance as a religious rite among Hindus; and the absence of censure in the Old Testament, in contrast to the position the Church, following the teaching of St Augustine and Thomas Aquinas, was later to adopt.[7] Although his own ethical relativism rested more upon an emotivist theory of ethics than upon cultural relativism as such, his book anticipated many of the views to be later adopted.

We are fortunate today, of course, in having more reliable and systematic data on the various issues he raised, as well as on other aspects of cultural relativism. And we can turn now to consider the relevance of such knowledge for the various types of relativism in ethics that were outlined in the last chapter.

### Facts and values: cultural and ethical relativism

Firstly, it will be evident that the two theses—cultural and ethical relativism—are not wholly independent of each other. In fact cultural relativism is related to each version of ethical relativism, but not to all in the same way. The overall relationship is that the facts of cultural diversity form a *necessary*, but not sufficient, condition for ethical relativism in its various senses. Were there no such diversity, there would be no need for relativist arguments. But, on the other hand, such evaluative or prescriptive propositions are not directly deducible from purely descriptive ones without committing the naturalistic fallacy. However, to specify the relationship in more detail it will be necessary to consider each form of relativism in turn.

First, evaluative relativism. This, it will be recalled, concerns the assessment of agents in other cultures. Here, statements of descriptive relativism provide one reason for the corresponding statements of evaluative relativism. These evaluative statements require also, however, the assumption that the society which holds the wrong moral opinion in question had no opportunity to correct it; and secondly, that the practice in question is held to be right in that society. The latter will involve some appeal to the notion of consensus. Thus, we may say that the evidence must demonstrate a reasonable degree of consensus concerning the rightness of the given practice, for the presence of dissensus is itself an index of the opportunity to correct it.

Rhodesia, South Africa, and the southern states of America provide convenient illustrations. Racialists in these societies are condemned precisely because, as part of Western culture, they have access to a body of moral and scientific evidence which invalidates rather than supports their actions. In short, descriptive relativism is a necessary but not sufficient condition of evaluative relativism.

In the case of relativism of rightness the difference between the descriptive and normative theses is a greater one. Apart from conformity relativism, a relativist statement of rightness does not appeal principally to the fact of the difference in the evaluated moral codes, but rather to the facts which justify this difference. The factual appeal, like the moral one, is to the context within which the practices in question occur.

For example, where it is maintained that infanticide, though intrinsically evil everywhere, is right in certain societies, the reason for this lies not in the fact that certain societies regard infanticide as right, but in the circumstance that the practice is a necessary evil.

Thus, although the practice might be condoned as a necessary evil in such societies as those of traditional Tikopia and the Eskimos at certain times, elsewhere, where there was no evidence of its fulfilling a necessary function, it would not be so condoned. There are a number of examples of this. In the Murray Islands of the Torres Straits, for instance, it was considered proper to have the same number of boys and girls in the family, and if there were too many of

340

the same sex, some were put to death. In this case, there was no evidence of consequences which provided an overriding justification. Even clearer is the example of the Arioi, in Tahiti, among whom special privileges were acquired by membership, but who had a rule, enforced without exception, that all their children should be immediately put to death. A woman who failed to kill her child was known as a 'bearer of children', which was a term of reproach, and she was expelled from the society.[8]

Even in Melanesia, the argument against overpopulation is not always a relevant one. Otto Klineberg (1954) writes: 'So great is the objection to any degree of intimacy between brother and sister that there are parts of Melanesia where one of twin siblings of different sex may be put to death immediately on account of their objectionable contacts before birth.'[9]

This well illustrates the distinction between evaluative relativism and relativism of rightness, since one might reject the practice here, yet exculpate the practitioners as incapable of seeing through their erroneous beliefs. The notion of necessary evil, however, is also relative to the people's available knowledge. Thus, the introduction of modern birth-control methods in Melanesia rendered the justification of infanticide in societies like Tikopia obsolete.[10]

This is not to claim that evidence on the subjective rightness of conduct is irrelevant to a relativism of rightness. First, it is a necessary element in our proposed conception of morality. Second, it is highly relevant to the question of social changes introduced from outside. *Ceteris paribus*, it is clearly preferable to introduce changes to a community which accepts them than to one which does not. Third, the fact that a practice is perceived to be right by the participants themselves is often an indication of the fact that it *is* right in terms of the present type of relativism.

The relationship between descriptive relativism and conventionalism, or conformity relativism, is comparable to the relationship between the former and evaluative relativism. The conformity relativist fears social disruption as a consequence of changes which he admits to be morally desirable in themselves. But the social cohesion which he values so highly is usually taken to be dependent upon commonly accepted values and norms.[11] Hence the thesis of relativism of rightness, when based on the value of conformity, is closely related to the facts affirmed by descriptive relativism.

The decisive facts, however, concern differences in the established customs between the compared societies, rather than differences in moral opinion. Unlike evaluative relativism the main interest is not in the subjective rightness of the evaluated conduct, but in the fact that following established practices furthers the cohesiveness of a society and helps avoid conflicts within it. The usual model of the society is to the effect that it is a system of interdependent parts held in more or less precarious equilibrium. On the basis of the evidence, it has often been held that this is a more valid model of certain primitive societies than of their modern counterparts.[12] Functionalists, who proposed this model of the social system to replace the 'trait atomism' of historiography, have thus not infrequently been accused of generalizing their experience of selected preliterate societies, usually with a finely balanced ecology, to all societies.[13]

By recognizing the presence of dysfunctions, asymmetrical relationships, and degrees of interdependency, contemporary functionalists such as Gouldner[14] to some extent escape this charge. And although several classical (as well as modern) conservatives—Burke, Bonald, de Maistre—have used functionalist arguments to justify their positions, Merton has made the point that functionalism could equally be used to justify a policy of total revolution. For, if all the features of social life are completely interdependent, then the only hope for social reform is a total transformation of society; to change only some parts would be impossible, for these changes would be ineffective, unless linked with a totally different system.[15]

Of course, this argument would have no relevance to a conformity relativist who valued social cohesion literally above all else. It might, however, be argued that, given the intricate interdependencies of a social system, to change radically any part of it would involve such a potentially wide range of consequences, that many of them could not be predicted or, in the short term, even recognized. Such change would be irresponsible in that one would be in no position to judge whether social cohesion would be maintained or not.

Arguments of this type are embodied in the political philosophy of such writers as Michael Oakeshott,[16] and come close to epistemological relativism, which we may now consider.

Epistemological moral relativism stresses the limitations, logical or practical, imposed on our understanding of other cultures. The facts of moral diversity tend to make us sceptical of our competence to pass judgment on the conduct of people in alien cultures, and this scepticism is, in essence, epistemological moral relativism. Again, a holistic approach to cultures encourages this viewpoint: if it is argued that particular moral opinions and practices can only be understood with reference to the broader moral *code* of which they form part, and that this code in turn cannot be understood without reference to the general ontology which underlies it, and the structure of motives and perceptions which both give rise to, then it might well be held that our knowledge of such cultures must necessarily be limited. As one writer has put it, 'We have imprisoned our own conceptions, by the lines which we have drawn in order to exclude the conceptions of others.'[17]

One possible basis for the present kind of relativism is the thesis of linguistic relativity, particularly associated with Sapir and Whorf. This hypothesis about the effects of language on cognition has been summarized by one of its proponents as follows:[18]

> The background linguistic system (in other words, the grammar) of each language is not merely a reproducing instrument for voicing ideas but rather is itself the shaper of ideas, the program and guide for the individual's mental activity, for his analysis of impressions, for his synthesis of his mental stock in trade. Formulation of ideas is not an independent process, strictly rational in the old sense, but is part of a particular grammar and differs, from slightly to greatly, as between different grammars.

The cultural world-view associated with a particular language community thus becomes, on this account, principally an artifact of syntax. The hypothesis is an intriguing one: for, if it were true, then such cultural communities might well become closed to anything but a purely internal understanding, carried out by their own members. The sociologist could presumably only achieve such an understanding after a lengthy process of socialization into the language and into the ways of thought it presented, and even then he might be able only to communicate this insight to the members of his own language-community in an atrophied and distorted form. To be at all empirically testable, however, this thesis needs to be more specifically defined; and observations regarding linguistic structures alone, aside from any corroborative attitudinal or behavioural data, are insufficient to validate it.[19]

It raises, secondly, the psychological paradox that, again if it were true that we can perceive or conceive only that which can be codified in our language, then a child could hardly learn this language, for how could he learn the conceptions basic to a language which would itself be prerequisite to the learning of those conceptions? Linguistic codification, whatever its significance, could hardly be expected to operate prior to perception.

A more plausible model of the effects of language upon cognitive processes is, as one linguist terms it, the 'lattice theory'.[20] This states, in brief, that a language is like a lattice or screen through which we see our world of experience: the learned categories of our language simply inhibit certain distinctions (or discriminations) and facilitate others, and hence predispose us to reason, recognize, remember, etc. along certain distinctive and shared lines. But this does not imply that we cannot choose to recode radically our experience in ways more useful to the attainment of our goals: the development of technical languages, including that of sociology, well

343

illustrates this process. Finally, the present model has also the virtue of being compatible with available experimental evidence on language behaviour.

The question as to *how* selective languages are with reference to the total range of discriminations that could be made, and as to how comparable they are to each other in this respect, are properly empirical issues. Presumably our evaluations, for instance, both partly reflect and partly affect the range of discriminations at our disposal. Needless to say, some languages have richer vocabularies than others and languages vary in the richness of their vocabularies in certain semantic domains in ways that rather obviously reflect the interests of their users. That Arabic has some 6,000 names associated with 'camel', and that the Eskimos have a comparable range of terms for describing varieties of snow, are by now standard examples.

Finally, it should be mentioned that some of the most influential lines of inquiry being developed in modern language studies are profoundly anti-relativistic, concerned with universals of categorization, structure, etc. The work of Noam Chomsky on syntax posits some aspects of the 'deep structure' rules of languages to be universal, even though the evidence for such structures is at present inferential; whilst that of Charles Osgood, on semantics, has provided (as we saw in part two) cross-cultural data to show that the modes of qualification employed in different language-communities are highly comparable, particularly in their factorial structure.[21] Inquiries of these kinds, both of the mainly theoretical and the mainly empirical types, do have relevance to arguments concerning moral relativism, especially in its epistemological version. Hence our brief discursus on them would appear justified.

The fact of moral variability is one of the principal props of axiological relativism, that is, of value-relativism proper. Again, however, there is no logical implication between descriptive and axiological relativism, as often seems mistakenly assumed.[22] Thus the evidence made available by the social sciences in general, and comparative anthropology in particular, does not as such commit one to a relativism of basic values.

The relationship between the two is a more indirect one. And in this respect, it may be taken to exemplify non-deductive ties between fact- and value-statements: the two *are* related, but not in a simple deductive form. The tendency has been to say that they are therefore unrelated, both in this case and in cases of the same logical type. The implausibility of this assumption, however, has been one *leitmotiv* of the present study; hence the 'cognitivist' definition of morality presented in part one.[23]

We may say broadly that profound divergences in moral attitude, which are institutionalized in different societies, and which therefore seem often to be impervious to rational argument, have a tendency to evoke scepticism concerning the universalizability of certain values and precepts. This scepticism is likely to be expressed in the form of axiological moral relativism. In some cases, the related meta-ethical views may themselves be more a result of this moral scepticism than of independent epistemological or philosophical considerations. But in other cases, such as those of logical positivism and other emotivist accounts of ethics, the relationship may be reversed: that is, the epistemological or philosophical assumptions lead to a certain conception of ethics, which in turn entails a relativism of values.

Differences in moral opinion alone are not sufficient to justify a relativism of values. This is most evident in the case of those moral systems, such as Christianity and other major religious traditions, which give grounds for claiming a privileged status for their moral precepts which are independent of any appeals to the *consensus gentium*.[24] But even if the latter appeal is made, for example where the ethics in question are considered to be in some sense self-evident, certain criteria of ethical competency are usually also available. Thus, one could still argue that if all the different communities were equally factually informed, and were all taking the 'moral point of view' (i.e. viewing issues clearly, disinterestedly, with due respect for the evidence, etc.), then there might well be a general, if not universal, consensus on moral opinions.[25] And this, of course, although an hypothetical empirical proposition, must remain largely undecidable.

Since we have noted the empirical connection between value-relativism and social scientists, as distinct from the logical relation discussed above, we might consider some of the implications of the present relativist doctrine.

## Implications of value-relativism

The possibility of comparative evaluation, whilst adhering to value-relativism, exists to a degree perhaps not at first recognized. Thus although the fact of moral diversity might be claimed to be the main source of axiological moral relativism, the latter is quite consistent with rejecting many of the moral opinions which are commonly accepted in certain societies. In such cases, attention can be drawn to some of the more formal aspects of a society's ethics.

Firstly, the radical axiological moral relativist lacks any standard for evaluating the *basic* moral principles of a culture, but he can still apply the principle of consistency. That is, he can criticize some of a society's attitudes or actions as being incompatible with its basic principles. A great deal of social criticism, in Western societies at least, is in fact of this kind, as public debates about issues from prosthetic surgery to the ethics of capital punishment exemplify. And such criticism can be effectively applied within the framework of a social-scientific perspective, as Gunnar Myrdal's classic study of race relations in America, *An American Dilemma* (1944), well illustrates.[26]

It might, of course, be argued that consistency, between different attitudes, and between attitudes and actions, is itself a value. But, if so, then there is every evidence of its generality. And, where it is accepted, it seems that the value-relativist may employ it as a formal criterion for evaluating the society's practices.

Similarly, the value-relativist can make judgments with regard to the efficacy of certain practices, where these are viewed as ethically neutral in themselves, and justified solely as efficient means to desired ends. For example, if the sole justification of a given form of punishment in a certain society is in terms of its deterrence and corrective value, then the relativist is still at liberty to produce factual evidence to contradict these claims of efficacy, and so to criticize the practice on these grounds. A great deal of empirical social science can be employed in this way.

Thirdly, the value-relativist may apply a concept of justice to societies other than his own. Thus, in *The Concept of Law* (1961), H. L. A. Hart treats this as a formal, rather than substantive principle and sums up its meaning as the precept to: 'Treat like cases alike, and different cases differently.'[27] The main application of the concept of justice is, therefore, not with regard to a single individual's conduct, but with the way in which classes of individuals are treated when some burden or benefits falls to be distributed among them. But the principle will remain indeterminate until there is a criterion for specifying when, for any given purpose, cases are in fact alike or different. And these criteria vary from society to society, and as between different historical periods of the same society.[28] For instance, in South Africa there are laws which prohibit coloureds from using various civic amenities that are available to the white population. The law here considers race to be a relevant category for distinguishing between individuals; and, given this, in so far as it is just, the law is applied impartially to all coloured, or, in some cases, to all Bantu, non-Bantu coloureds, and whites respectively.[29] Indeed, as Hart states, it might be said that to apply a law justly to different cases is simply to take seriously the assertion that what is to be applied in different cases is the same general rule, without prejudice, interest, or caprice.

This, of course, is not to suggest that South Africa's practices are to be judged just according to some less technical, more substantive definition of the term. Thus, in the modern world it is generally recognized that all human beings share certain qualities to which the

346

law ought to attend. And it is thought that both criminal and civil law would be unjust if, in the distribution of burdens and benefits, they discriminated between people on the grounds of such characteristics as colour, race, or religious creed. This attitude finds expression in the first principle of the United Nation's Declaration of Human Rights, although for many societies it remains more of an ideal than a reality.[30]

However, if we restrict ourselves to the formal usage of the term, it would seem that the value-relativist can assess societies with regard to the justice of their practices in terms of their own standards. In a sense, this is to apply a combination of the principles of consistency and completeness. And it is also in this sense that he could adopt a notion of moral progress. That is, he could compare the same society at different periods of time with regard to whether: (i) its moral principles were applied with a greater or lesser degree of consistency; (ii) its non-moral means to certain desired ends were clearly recognized as such and were more or less efficacious *vis-à-vis* attainment of these ends; and (iii) its moral code were applied with a greater or lesser degree of completeness (e.g. in extending the value of tolerance to all those classes of persons for which no grounds for intolerance could be provided).

## Research

With regard to empirical research on relativist attitudes, the extent to which individuals hold relativist views, and the social and psychological correlates of this, has not, to our knowledge, been the subject of any major study. Such data as there is derives from subsidiary questions on relativism from research projects in which the main interest was elsewhere. We have seen that 'ethical relativism' as such is a general concept, usually vaguely defined. This renders the empirical results of many such surveys equivocal, and also supplies one reason for the lack of research. A more refined concept of ethical relativism should make for more refined and rigorous research designs. Thus, the kind of distinctions we have drawn above should both help to clarify the issues at stake and provide a conceptual basis for such research.

At the simplest level, we would expect that associations could be reliably established between commitment to the various types of relativism and a series of familiar socio-psychological variables. For instance, on the basis of general sociological knowledge, one might broadly hypothesize that acceptance of relativist attitudes will correlate positively with social position,[31] knowledge, and degree of open-mindedness, and with the societal factor of degree of modernization.

Naturally this is a *ceteris paribus* statement, holding constant, for

347

instance, the content of the moral code in question. However, research on the empirical consequences of the adoption of certain moral codes for relativist attitudes could form an important contribution to the sociology of ethics.

Since it is likely to be difficult to get many respondents to appreciate absolutism and relativism as general concepts, except perhaps in the case of the well-educated, a multi-item instrument would be necessary for research purposes, with particular opinion-statements involving situations that are relatively familiar and, taken together, serve to tap the type of relativism being studied. Each form of relativism could be studied in this way, and one might find, for instance, interesting differences between evaluative relativism and relativism of rightness among respondents (such as Catholics) who express clear adherence to universalist standards. Also, in this way one might be better able to determine the sense and degree to which modern societies can be said to be characterized by universalistic attitudes.

One of the few studies along these lines that we know of is reported in a paper by Putney and Middleton (1962).[32] In this, ethical relativists and ethical absolutists were compared with regard to their acceptance and observance of certain social norms. The findings indicated that the relativists did not appear to exhibit any greater degree of *anomie* than the absolutists in terms of any of the following indicators: difficulty in evaluating actions; a sense of making too many exceptions to principles; failure to live up to verbally expressed precepts; or general rejection of the norms. However, the relativists were less likely to accept ascetic norms which stemmed directly from an absolutistic religious tradition. But the authors concluded that there was a core of generally-accepted social norms which governed the behaviour of both the relativists and the absolutists, and that at least among educated and predominantly middle-class American young people, ethical absolutism does not seem essential to the efficacy of social norms.

Of the other available psychological scales relating at least indirectly to relativist attitudes, one of the best-known is the Ethnocentrism Scale developed by the authors of the classic study of prejudice, *The Authoritarian Personality* (1950).[33] In this, a mean correlation of 0·75 was found between responses to the scales measuring ethnocentrism and fascism. Later research has produced further evidence for this association, often by means of more refined measures of ethnocentricity.[34] Such research has also confirmed their finding of a negative correlation between education and ethnocentrism.[35] One of their tables which provided evidence for this relationship is based on a sample of male students at a maritime school (see Table 10.1).

TABLE 10.1    *Mean ethnocentrism scores for groups having various years of education*

| Years' education | Form 45 $(E_{a+b})$* N | Mean | Form 40 $(E_a)$ N | Mean | Total Group N | Mean |
|---|---|---|---|---|---|---|
| Less than 12 | 36 | 4·38 | 60 | 5·21 | 96 | 4·90 |
| 12 years | 104 | 4·28 | 91 | 5·04 | 195 | 4·63 |
| 13 years | 13 | 4·75 | 7 | 4·40 | 20 | 4·63 |
| 14 years | 18 | 4·34 | 6 | 5·17 | 24 | 4·55 |
| Blank | 7 | 4·63 | 0 | — | 7 | 4·63 |
| Overall | 178 | 4·36 | 164 | 5·08 | 342 | 4·68 |

* Two versions of the Ethnocentrism Scale were used, the first of these being an extended version of the second (i.e. Form 40).

Apart from the studies of ethnocentrism which have followed from the authoritarian personality research, some indirect evidence on relativist attitudes is also to be gained from other attitude studies concerned with the investigation of subjects' values. One such study is W. A. Scott's *Values and Organizations* (1965), an analysis of student attitudes, and their organizational correlates, in ten sororities and fraternities at the University of Colorado. Here, relativism is given operational definition as the degree of correlation between the individual's expressed values and the values he prescribes for others. Table 10.2, taken from Scott's study, summarizes the extent to which his sample of students prescribed their personal values for others.

Scott interprets these findings as follows:[37]

> Taken together, these results indicate that values, as measured by the present instrument, are indeed concepts that these subjects tend to regard as absolutes and universals. Though it might have been expected that relatively sophisticated college students, amply exposed to doctrines of cultural relativism, would disclaim any professions of universal 'oughts', such relativist tendencies did not appear in any substantial proportion of these samples. Whenever a subject claimed to admire a personal trait himself, he was very likely to regard it as 'right' and to think that other people should admire it also.

Other studies have borne out this conclusion: namely that, at least in Western society, individuals tend to hold their moral opinions in a rather absolutist manner. Scott, however, did not discriminate between students according to their field of study; had he done so, we might have expected social science students to exhibit slightly more relativist attitudes than their peers in the natural sciences. At least, the limited data available would seem to suggest this conclusion.[38]

M*

TABLE 10.2 *Correlations between personal values and (a) conceptions of 'right' and 'wrong'; (b) prescribed values for others* $(N = 208)$[36]

| Value | 'Right' and 'wrong' | | Prescribed for others | |
|---|---|---|---|---|
| | r | r$_{cor}$* | r | r$_{cor}$* |
| Intellectualism | 0·63 | 0·95 | 0·44 | 0·67 |
| Kindness | 0·72 | 1·00 | 0·61 | 0·95 |
| Social skills | 0·74 | 1·00 | 0·54 | 0·90 |
| Loyalty | 0·69 | 0·96 | 0·46 | 0·75 |
| Academic achievement | 0·52 | 0·74 | 0·48 | 0·72 |
| Physical development | 0·69 | 0·88 | 0·63 | 0·88 |
| Status | 0·64 | 1·00 | 0·54 | 0·93 |
| Honesty | 0·69 | 1·00 | 0·57 | 1·00 |
| Religiousness | 0·78 | 0·98 | 0·53 | 0·67 |
| Self-control | 0·69 | 0·96 | 0·58 | 0·83 |
| Creativity | 0·57 | 0·86 | 0·47 | 0·77 |
| Independence | 0·74 | 1·00 | 0·56 | 1·00 |
| Median | 0·69 | 0·97 | 0·54 | 0·86 |

* *rs corrected for attenuation; when computed values exceed 1·00, they are reported as 1·00.*

We should emphasize that this study, and the previous ones we have mentioned, consist at best of rather rudimentary and indirect investigations of relativist attitudes. They are cited merely to indicate some of the possibilities for research on this subject. Although they also serve to indicate that such research, if it is to be adequate, will need to be grounded on much more clear and rigorous conceptual assumptions. Some of the main distinctions that need to be drawn here have been proposed earlier in this section. These may help to clarify the complex issues involved, although it is evident that a full treatment would require devotion of a whole book to this question alone.

However, the issue of relativism has also the advantage of illustrating two other points that have recurred throughout this study. First, it serves to exemplify the complex interrelationships that may hold between beliefs (descriptive and explanatory), values, and precepts.[39] And in particular, it demonstrates the possibility of non-deductive ties between fact- and value-propositions. Second, it indicates the need to go beyond a mere recording of attitudinal data to an investigation of the *justifications* that are proffered for these attitudes. The two questions are, of course, interrelated. That is, inquiry into the justifications for avowed attitudes will permit us also to investigate the empirical relationships between factual assumptions and valuations. This would have a clear theoretical relevance, for models of attitude organization, and also some practical significance, in terms of the insights it could permit into the processes of attitude formation and change.[40]

## Relativism and the critical perspective

We turn now, briefly, to the relationship between the intellectual perspective of sociology—the so-called 'sociological imagination'—and relativism. But before introducing this, let us firstly notice that relativist ideologies can have distinct political implications. Thus, it would appear that the extension of relativist attitudes, at least among the élite in society, is likely to encourage a continuous reassessment of institutions, and of the values and beliefs which underlie them. Such attitudes can provide an enduring intellectual basis for both tolerance and reform. And if it is the case, as we suggested at the beginning of part three, that relativism has its social origins in periods of rapid social change, then our own times, in which such change is contingent principally upon our continuing technological development, should bear ample witness to the causes and consequences of ethical relativism.

If one accepts this critical function that we have ascribed to relativist doctrines, it will come as no surprise that the most fundamental critique of modern society, namely Marxism, involved also a relativism of values. In this case, such relativism derived principally from the materialist conception of history. Thus, as Eugene Kamenka (1969) states:[41]

If we leave aside the Marxist commitment to an ultimate morality, or an ultimate moral end, we might treat the materialist interpretation of history (especially in Engels's hands) as saying that there are no ethical truths—there are only moral outlooks. Such outlooks are produced historically—they are the outlooks, interests, demands of specific social groups (classes) in specific periods. It makes no sense to ask whether they are true or false. We can only ask what conditions produced them, what makes people subscribe to them, what conditions militate against their continued importance in society.

But the materialistic critique has had comparatively few concrete applications in the history of ideas, and, as the above passage suggests, it has tended to be advocated in a way that glosses over the logical distinction between explanation and justification.[42] Beyond this, however, the foregoing passage also points to a basic inconsistency in the Marxist tradition, an incompatibility between, on the one

351

hand, espousing a relativist view of all historically available moral codes, and on the other hand asserting socialism as having an objective moral superiority over all other types of society. This inconsistency becomes more apparent in some of the later Marxists than in Marx himself,[43] and, from a practical point of view, it has also been a fruitful contradiction for socialist societies—providing grounds both for negating other societies, whilst preserving a confidence in the direction and goals of one's own.

In fact, Marxist thought has a central importance for our present subject because it demonstrates, almost paradigmatically, the kind of problems to be encountered by a basically relativist approach to moral codes. It demonstrates, for instance, the *reflexive* character of certain relativist arguments. Thus, Marxism classed not only moral codes as ideological but also a range of other intellectual products, such as a society's law, its political philosophy, and in modern societies perhaps also their social science.[44] But a doctrine which emphasizes the relativity of factual judgments, and belief systems, might be claimed to be self-defeating, since the doctrine itself could be taken as an instance of the very theory it is proposing. Thus, by implication, Marxism might itself be treated as essentially ideological in character.

However, such *tu quoque* arguments are far from conclusive and involve the logical paradox that their own validity would appear to depend upon the validity of the theory under criticism. In addition to which, various accounts may be given to justify the privileged epistemological position that is claimed for the original theory. A clear example of this is contained in Mannheim's conception of the epistemologically privileged status of the intelligentsia, as a social stratum with minimal involvement in the vested interests of society.[45] Similarly, in the case of Marxism, MacIntyre (1971), for instance, argues that Marx resolved the contradiction between relativism and absolutism in his work by his practical notion of truth, expressed in the concept of *praxis*. As he writes:[46]

It is this conception of truth that enables Marx both to affirm a historical relativism concerning all philosophies and also to deny that his own philosophy is merely a product of the time, since it is in Marx's own thought that philosophy has for the first time become conscious of its historical basis in seeking to transform that basis and has therefore passed beyond the limitations of earlier philosophy.

This may be found a more or less satisfactory solution according to personal viewpoint. From our own point of view, we would observe merely that Marxism has not notably respected the autonomy of ethics, and would tend to agree with Kamenka that, in the field of ethics, Marx was more of a social critic than a moral philosopher, and that his followers have on the whole maintained the habit of confusing problems of moral philosophy with problems of social reform: as he puts it, 'They claim as a virtue, instead of recognizing as a theoretical defect, that they devote their attention to conditions that stand in the way of human happiness instead of asking precisely what "happiness" means.'[47]

None the less, as Kamenka (1969) adds:[48]

All this is not to say that Marx has made no contribution whatever to the discussion of ethics in modern philosophy. It was he who pointed the way to a sociology of morals, to the recognition of moral codes and moral principles as social products, formed in specific social contexts, derived from human activities and human and social demands. He has thus greatly increased our sophistication in talking about morals and he has enabled others—sociologists, anthropologists and psychologists—to increase it still further.

In sum, Marx's main contribution for our present purposes has been to bring a sociological perspective to the study of ethics, and to relate specific moral codes to the human activity that produced them and to the broader social structures within which such activity occurred. Our question now will be concerned with the ethical implications of this overall perspective, and particularly with the sense (if any) in which it can be said to involve a relativization of ethics.

## Relativism and the sociological perspective

The main theme of this chapter has been to examine the conceptual links between, on the one hand, comparative evidence from sociology and anthropology concerning the relativity of cultural standards in the realm of ethics, and, on the other, the philosophical doctrines of ethical relativism. Our intention was to make clear that, although the two of these are related, the latter cannot be directly inferred from the former. And to demonstrate further that certain forms of ethical relativism presuppose additional factual assumptions, apart from those concerning the mere variability of moral standards.

However, sociology does not consist solely of sets of empirical facts, but also of a distinctive way of looking at these facts, a particular mode of reasoning that C. Wright Mills summed up as the 'sociological imagination'. And although the *facts* of sociology and anthropology may not logically commit one to a relativism of values, it does seem arguable that the sociological perspective involves, at the least, a relativist outlook. For, as we have suggested earlier, this perspective is necessarily a comparative one, providing thereby a functional analogue to the experimental method in the natural sciences. And the principle of holding any evaluation of other forms of social life to be inadmissible to a science of society entails also treating them as of equal potential significance, despite their evident differences. And this in turn involves viewing the social reality encompassed by the *status quo* as neither necessary nor inevitable; in this sense it robs it of its universal validity. Instead, the sociologist, *qua* sociologist, adopts a relativist viewpoint: he sees the present, so to speak, as history, as anthropology.

This is to be contrasted with the broad tendency—classically recognized by Durkheim—of societies to absolutize and hypostatize their cultures. To put this a little differently, we may say that whilst sociology distinguishes sharply between nature and culture, and tries to record faithfully the diversity of the latter, the tendency of 'social theories' is to translate the latter into the former, ascribing to both domains essentially similar attributes.[49] Culture thus appears to its participants, to common sense, as independent of human activity and volition and as sharing in the inert 'objectivity' of nature. Sociology, however, stresses the nature of culture as artifact, as social product. It *may* be more than this, but this is its exclusive status within the concern of the sociologist. Thus sociology may be said to unmask what cultures seek to hide: namely, the contingency, the empirical nature of the present social arrangements.

We may sum all this up by saying that the sociological awareness is relativizing and, *eo ipso*, dereifying. As such, it serves as a corrective to the reifying propensities of discursive thought in general, and of ethical systems in particular. With reference to such systems, although not exclusively so, the processes of objectivation and reification are most evident, and most pervasive, in the conceptualizations of human nature that are put forward in different societies. These, as we have seen, are central to both the understanding and justification of the moral codes that are operative in these societies. We 'make sense' of a society's practices, moral and otherwise, by appealing to such social constructs precisely because they exist not merely as 'ideas' in these societies, but are also actualized, or institutionalized, in the normal activities of the society. And to understand these activities is to understand the concepts which they embody.[50] To make intelligible the Western educational system, for instance, at any period of time, we must refer back to the historical conception of man's 'nature', as well as of his proper pursuits and values. Transformations in such conceptions resulted in corresponding transformations of the educational system. The revolution in education at the end of the nineteenth century, for example, involved such a transformation, together with the development and application to education of a new set of causal principles relevant to the teaching process;[51] as indeed does the contemporary emphasis upon pre-school education, the only difference being that this last change is less different in kind and based upon more reliable empirical data.[52]

The anthropologist, or comparative sociologist, would elucidate such philosophical anthropologies by appealing to cross-cultural data, the social historian by viewing them strictly *sub specie temporis*. In each case, the kind of intellectual awareness involved is relativizing in character. What remains constant, at least in so far as we are dealing with social science, is the commitment to shared standards of rigour in empirical inquiry, and so the adoption of standardized research procedures designed to maximize reliability, objectivity, and validity.

But this relativist perspective is adopted for purely instrumental purposes. It is a methodological convenience. Hence, we might speak more accurately of the social sciences adopting a methodological relativism. Similarly, to say (for instance) that moral codes are cultural products is not to say they are thereby false, or 'all equally valid', as one viewpoint would have it. The sociologist, *qua* sociologist, puts such ontological and evaluative questions strictly in parentheses, at least in so far as such codes do not posit empirical assumptions that are directly contradicted by the evidence of sociology.

Indeed, to translate the methodological relativism of social science into a more substantive form of relativism, might be interpreted as an instance of *mauvaise foi*. Peter Berger (1966), for instance, gives the following example in point:[53]

Cross-cultural comparisons of sexual conduct bring home to us powerfully the near-infinite flexibility that men are capable of in organizing their lives in this area. What is normality and maturity in one culture, is pathology and regression in another. This relativization in the understanding of sexual roles does not, of course, free the individual from finding his own way morally. *That* would be another instance of 'bad faith', with the objective fact of relativity being taken as an alibi for the subjective necessity of finding those single decisive points at which one engages one's whole being. For instance, it is possible to be fully aware of the relativity and the precariousness of the ways by which men organize their sexuality, and yet commit oneself absolutely to one's own marriage. Such commitment, however, does not require any ontological underpinnings. It dares to choose and to act, refusing to push the burden of decision on nature or necessity.

355

But social scientists, and perhaps particularly anthropologists, do frequently go beyond a mere methodological relativism to more prescriptive and evaluative statements of this thesis. Roughly two views may be taken on this *de facto* tendency. On the one hand, it may be taken to express a genuine tolerance and indeed respect for the integrity of alien cultures, and perhaps, more generally, as a positive valuation of a culturally plural world. This attitude is well exemplified in the statement issued by the American Anthropological Association to the United Nations Commission on Human Rights, in which the central precept was expressed in the view that a respect for the differences between cultures is as important as a respect for the personality of the individual as such.

Thus, anthropologists have been particularly prone to express opposition to planned cultural change, and to oppose all aspects of colonialism, missionary work, and agricultural and educational reform. With regard to this, however, Shelton (1965) has argued to the effect that such criticism has its base in the false notion that cultures are static, and includes the ideas (i) that outsiders, as Europeans, have no right to induce culture change, even with the consent of the community; (ii) that outsiders involved in such culture change 'play God' among 'simple' villagers; and (iii) that they spoil the villagers for the real anthropologists.[54] Such arguments, he says, are based upon the assumption that anthropologists have special rights to contact unspoiled villagers, whereas proper anthropological inquiry is of the culture as it exists, and prescriptiveness has no place in this science.

Other observers have come to similar conclusions on the matter of relativism v. culture change. Thus, Moser (1963) sums up the data from a series of anthropological studies of attitudes towards change, and concludes that 'the prevalent attitudes of primitive peoples towards cultural change do not lend support to the view that the best that can be done for such peoples is to leave their status quo intact, as far as possible, because this is their paramount desire.'[55] Similarly, Lévi-Strauss has pointed to the irony in the fact that whilst anthropologists argue on relativist grounds for the preservation of native cultures, the majority of native communities effectively reject such relativist doctrines themselves, and desire to change their cultures in the direction of modernization.[56]

On the other hand, one might argue, in more *ad hominem* terms, that the relativist predilections of anthropologists and sociologists are to be understood as more in the nature of an ideology. That is, in parallel with Gouldner's comments concerning the ideological uses of a *wertfrei* conception of social science, an ethical relativist doctrine might similarly operate as a kind of intellectual anodyne to the political impotency of social scientists. There is probably some truth in this notion, as in the fact that relativist beliefs are often held in rather inchoate and uncritical forms, without serious examination of the grounds upon which they are credible. On the other hand, it would be invidious to deny that some such views may be held sincerely. Thus, comparative anthropology has provided reliable data (particularly within the modern ethnoscientific tradition) to show that primitive communities exhibit a coherence not only in their social life, but in their cultures as well. Such data has emancipated us from the older, essentially evolutionist, conception of primitive thought, and primitive social forms, as mere precursors to modern culture and society. As such, the evidence of cultural relativism does militate against any over-confident absolutism that bases itself upon a simple evolutionary conception of society (or of race). This latter conception did, of course, inform much of nineteenth-century anthropological thought and colonial practice.[57] And, indeed, a number of subsequent attempts have been made, often with disastrous consequences, to resurrect systems of evolutionist ethics.[58]

In sum, it might reasonably be thought that the evidence of cultural relativism invites us to treat undeveloped societies in less cavalier, or exploitative, a fashion than was once common, and which in certain areas still persists, and to recognize that these societies comprise distinct ways of life, and ways of thought, *sui generis*, and not merely inferior versions of our own. However, it is to be acknowledged that recognition of this had as much intellectual, as moral, significance, for it provided a rationale for potentially much more rigorous and objective anthropological studies.

To round off our account, two further points may be made about the relativizing motif in the sociological perspective. First, it would seem true to say that sociology, like moral philosophy before it, emerged under conditions in which awareness of the relativity of the *status quo* was facilitated by certain structural changes occurring in the society at large. We do not wish to involve ourselves in a detailed intellectual history here. The relationship between the fundamental transformations of society, since the eighteenth century, and the emergence of the social sciences is one that has been repeatedly charted, although perhaps without due emphasis being paid to the role played by the emergent awareness of cultural relativism, and of the artifactual nature of the *status quo*, which these transformations permitted. Suffice it to note in this connection, for instance, that Salomon (1955) has observed that the very concept of society, in its modern, sociological sense, could only emerge as the normative structures of Christendom, and later of the *ancien régime*, were collapsing.[59] It is interesting to compare this with the history of other concepts in social science; in particular, the growing awareness of the relativity of social reality finds expression in the changing meanings, and increasing centrality, of the term 'culture' as Levin (1965) has shown.[60]

Second, sociology may be said to prosper as an intellectual discipline where the conditions of the society in which it occurs serve to encourage a continuing awareness of the relativity of the *status quo*. Modern Western societies are of this general type, and perhaps increasingly so. Thus, the presence in these societies of comparatively high rates of social mobility and (to a lesser degree) geographical mobility permit some first-hand awareness of alternative forms of social life and modes of understanding, even if these differ only marginally from each other. Similarly, the very flexibility of modern technology may in some degree militate against the tendency to absolutize the *status quo*.[61] And more directly, scientific epistemology and the sheer rapidity of scientific progress generates a suspicion of *idées reçues* and a conception of all knowledge as ultimately tentative. In addition, of course, the mass media in modern society at once foster participation, albeit a vicarious participation, in alternative ways of life and different cultures, whilst at the same time acting as a culturally homogenizing influence.

Finally, the very pervasiveness of utilitarian culture, and of the extrinsic standard of utility in modern society involves a relativizing tendency essentially because it leaves the question of 'utility for *what*?' in parentheses and so the answer to it becomes a matter of historical contingency. Gouldner (1971) expresses the point as follows:[62]

> Since the useful is judged in terms of the consequences of actions the useful is a contingent thing, that might vary with, or be relative to, time and place. Again, that which is useful is so only relative to that *for* which it is useful. Things are useful only in relation to something else, to an 'end'. There was a drift toward relativism in utilitarianism.

However, the sense of relativity in modern societies can easily be overstated. Relativist perspectives may be taken for granted among the better-educated echelons of such societies, may even be *de rigueur* for certain groups, but all this is to be seen in the context of a much more absolutized, reifying form of consciousness among the majority of people. Again, the point we are making here can only be established in comparative terms; and we can think here, for instance, of the villagers depicted in Lerner's study of the contemporary Middle East (in *The Passing of Traditional Society*), who were unable to project themselves into any roles, or situations, substantially different from those they already occupied.[63] Whereas the sociologist might take all socially assigned identities with a grain of salt, and whereas the individual in a modern society can at least imaginatively project himself into some radically different social role or form of life, for these peasants their positions in life were part of their inexorable fate, and alternatives were not only closed to objective attainment, they could not even be conceived of. In sum, in modern societies, unlike traditional societies, various elements combine to produce a form of consciousness that is compatible with the relativizing motif that characterizes the sociological perspective.[64]

# Notes and references

Cross-references are to chapter and note number, e.g. 'n.10.27' refers to chapter 10, reference 27.

## Introduction

1 The distinction between positive and negative freedom is discussed in Isaiah Berlin, *Two Concepts of Liberty* (Oxford: Clarendon Press, 1958) and reprinted, with an extended Introduction dealing with criticisms, in his *Four Essays on Liberty* (Oxford University Press, 1969).

2 Cf. chapter 2. In view of the multiple connotations of the term 'moral', one is constantly tempted to reassure the reader that it is being employed *faute de mieux*. However, we can think of no adequate substitute to denote the particular legitimacy and precedency that, as we shall argue, are embodied in the notion of moral standards and behaviour. To avoid the term's restrictive connotations would involve cumbersome periphrasis. However, in noting this we are also drawing attention to the fact that we shall be employing the term more neutrally and less committally, than is common in ordinary usage. It is to be noted also that although the term 'ethics' is sometimes used to refer to the broader pattern of reasoning associated with particular moral views it is used here interchangeably with the term 'morality'.

3 Cf. especially chapters 3 and 8. Above all, analytic philosophy can serve the interests of theory in sociology by elucidating the *discursive* aspects of moral codes.

4 From J. Ladd, *The Structure of a Moral Code* (Harvard University Press, 1957), p. 2.

5 From D. Braybrooke, *Philosophical Problems of the Social Sciences* (London: Collier-Macmillan, 1965), p. 2.

6 Cf. chapter 5. Recent philosophical analyses of action include S. Hampshire, *Thought and Action* (London: Chatto & Windus, 1959); A. I. Melden, *Free Action* (London: Routledge & Kegan Paul, 1961); A. R. Louch, *Explanation and Human Action* (Oxford University Press, 1966); and A. R. White (ed.), *The Philosophy of Action* (Oxford University Press, 1968).

7 Gouldner and Peterson's work also illustrates very clearly, however, the precariousness of generalizing from correlations to causes, and the

361

danger of misconstruing the philosophical question of the relationship of attitudes to actions. On the latter, see chapter 5.

8 Of most immediate interest here is the kind of sociology (empirical
and theoretical) that is being produced in totalitarian and ideologically
closed societies, and also in the third world countries. On this, see, for
instance, H. Hartmann, 'Sociology in Cuba', *American Sociological
Review*, 1963, 4, 28, pp. 624–8 and E. Veron, 'Sociologia, ideologia y
subdesarrollo', *Cuestiones de Filosofia*, 1962, pp. 13–40. Cf. too nn.
1.4 and 6.91 infra. On this overall question, cf. R. W. Friedrichs, *A
Sociology of Sociology* (London: Free Press, 1970).

9 Hence the frequent criticisms of scholasticism in theoretical sociology.
For a rather intemperate statement of this view see C. Wright Mills,
*The Sociological Imagination* (Harmondsworth: Penguin, 1970 edn;
first pub. 1959). Cf. too Barrington Moore, 'Strategy in social science',
in M. Stein and A. Vidich (eds), *Sociology on Trial* (Englewood Cliffs,
N. J.: Prentice-Hall, 1963), pp. 66–95. One of the themes of the present
work will be that sociological theories have operated with considerably
oversimplified accounts of the data to be explained, in part because
adequate use has not been made of the full range of research techniques available.

10 See L. Baritz, *The Servants of Power* (New York: Wiley, 1960);
L. Bramson, *The Political Context of Sociology* (Princeton University
Press, 1961); I. L. Horowitz (ed.), *The Rise and Fall of Project Camelot*
(M.I.T. Press, 1967); G. Sjoberg (ed.), *Ethics, Politics and Social
Research* (London: Routledge & Kegan Paul, 1969); and G. Boalt,
*The Sociology of Research* (Southern Illinois University Press, 1969).
See, too, N. Glazer, 'The ideological uses of sociology', in P. F.
Lazarsfeld *et al.* (eds), *The Uses of Sociology* (London: Weidenfeld
& Nicolson, 1968); and on the relationship between sociology and
social policy: G. Winter, *Elements for a Social Ethic: The Role of
Social Science in Public Policy* (New York: Collier-Macmillan, 1969).
For a complementary analysis of the sponsorship of research in the
natural sciences, cf. D. S. Greenberg, *The Politics of American Science*
(Harmondsworth: Penguin, 1969).

11 The possible social factors influencing methodological decisions have
so far been afforded little systematic attention in sociology. However,
the general possibility of such a programme of inquiry, and the relevance of the philosophy of social science to it, has been noted, for
instance, by Alasdair MacIntyre in a recent review of the anthology,
*Readings in the Philosophy of the Social Sciences* (ed. May Brodbeck,
1968). As he writes

> looked at from a completely different point of view such an
> anthology may guide us not only, as it professes to do, to the
> appropriate *form* for theorizing in the social sciences, but to a
> certain *content and subject-matter* for theorizing in the sociology
> of science, including the sociology of social science. Accounts of
> the logical structures of theory and of explanation, of the
> relationship of falsifiability to theorizing, of the relationship
> between prediction and explanation, and so on are and must be

accounts of norms and ideals which, implicitly or explicitly, characteristically and for the most part guide the behaviour of scientists. Many of the papers in this anthology characterize at one level the alternatives confronting a scientist whose theorizing confronts either empirical or conceptual difficulties. Now such a characterization is a prerequisite for an enquiry into why particular types of scientists in such situations adopt one strategy or attitude rather than another. It is also a prerequisite for distinguishing those norms guiding the activity of scientists which arise from the logical character of scientific enquiry from those which arise from the particular social situation, status and role of particular sorts of scientists at particular times and places (e.g. norms concerning publication and other forms of collaboration or norms, if any, dictating choice of subject-matter). It is also the case that philosophy of science may yield essential clues to the sociologist who wishes to study the relationship between role and belief outside science.
Extracted from 'On the relevance of the philosophy of the social sciences: Review symposium', *British Journal of Sociology*, 1969, 20, 2, pp. 225–6.

12  J. E. Curtis and J. W. Petras (eds), *The Sociology of Knowledge* (London: Duckworth, 1970), Introduction, p. 56.
13  It is, for instance, related to the question of whether we can describe social action without imposing our own norms of rationality, and also, and more generally, to the issue of 'epistemological relativism', discussed in part three.
14  See A. W. Gouldner, 'Anti-Minotaur: the myth of a value-free sociology', *Social Problems*, 1962, 9, 3, pp. 199–213.
15  On this question, cf. chapter 3.
16  Alternatively, a degree of reification appears a necessary component to any institutional social reality. For a lucid exposition, see Peter L. Berger and Stanley Pullberg, 'Reification and the sociological critique of consciousness', *History and Theory*, 1965, IV, 2, pp. 198f. The term *mauvaise foi* is, of course, from Sartre and consists essentially in the abdication of one's freedom in favour of an illusory determinacy. The process is classically typified by Sartre in his description of the waiter in the cafe in *L'Être et le néant*. Thus, in principle, existentialism replaces any kind of theoretical morality with a thoroughgoing particularism in these matters. In practice, however, some commitment to general rules and standards may be inescapable. And so it is noteworthy that the impossibility of producing a coherent ethical system within the confines of existentialism has been proposed as one factor which led the later Sartre (in the *Critique de la raison dialectique*) to espouse instead a more Marxist form of doctrine: cf., for example, M. Warnock, *Existentialist Ethics* (London: Macmillan, 1967).
17  See J. Piaget, *The Child's Construction of Reality* (London: Routledge & Kegan Paul, 1955) and idem, *The Child's Conception of Geometry* (London: Routledge & Kegan Paul, 1960).
18  For instance, by scholars such as Noam Chomsky and Lévi-Strauss.

19 On this, cf. especially the brief discussion in chapter 5, pp. 142–4.

20 Cf. part two for a criticism of the individualistic perspective implicit in much social research.

21 On the institutional aspects of this process, compare, for instance:

> One may say . . . that the facticity of the social world or of any part of it suffices for self-legitimation as long as there is no challenge. When a challenge appears, in whatever form, the facticity can no longer be taken for granted. The validity of the social order must then be explicated, both for the sake of the challengers and of those meeting the challenge. . . . The wrongdoers must be convincingly condemned, but this condemnation must also serve to justify their judges. The seriousness of the challenge will determine the degree of elaborateness of the answering legitimations.

From Peter Berger, *The Social Reality of Religion* (London: Faber & Faber, 1969), p. 31.

22 An accessible historical introduction is R. M. Smith, *Spain: A Modern History* (Ann Arbor: University of Michigan Press, 1965).

23 Of course, this encyclical has also a special sociological interest in so far as it resulted in a series of further ideological dilemmas and confrontations, during which the whole concept of *magisterium* in the Church was called into question.

24 For empirical studies of situations of role-conflict, see, for instance, S. A. Stouffer, 'An analysis of conflicting social norms', *American Sociological Review*, 1949, 14, pp. 707–17; R. L. Kahn *et al.*, *Organizational Stress: Studies In Role Conflict And Ambiguity* (New York: Wiley, 1964); and J. R. Rizzo *et al.*, 'Role conflict and ambiguity in complex organizations', *Administrative Science Quarterly*, 1970, 15, 2, pp. 150–63.

25 We are thinking here of the break-up of the traditional social order, and the experience of culture contact, in post-Homeric Greece, at the time of the transition to the city-state. The intellectual significance of this is noted, for instance, in A. C. MacIntyre, *A Short History of Ethics* (London: Routledge & Kegan Paul, 1967), especially chs 2 and 8.

26 Modern Protestantism is analysed in these terms in Peter Berger and Thomas Luckman, 'Secularization and pluralism', *International Yearbook for the Sociology of Religion*, 1966, p. 73f. The concept of cultural pluralism is examined in chapter 4 of the present study.

27 In part, dilemmas of this kind serve also to draw attention to the fact that the typical normative theory, religious or otherwise, contains premisses of a descriptive, empirical nature. The findings of sociology, therefore, will be of importance to religion (and other normative doctrines) in so far as the latter makes claims of an empirical, social-historical kind. Such claims, are of course, to be found within the Judaeo-Christian tradition. On this general question, cf. especially chapters 2 and 3 infra.

28 For depiction of these social and psychological mechanisms, see respectively, for example, P. Berger and T. Luckman, *The Social Construction of Reality* (London: Allen Lane, 1967), especially pp.

122–46 and L. Festinger, *A Theory of Cognitive Dissonance* (Evanston: Row-Peterson, 1957).

29 I. Berlin, 'Does political theory still exist?' in P. Laslett and W. G. Runciman (eds), *Philosophy, Politics and Society* (Oxford: Blackwell, 1964), p. 17.

30 Cf. especially T. S. Kuhn, *The Structure of Scientific Revolutions* (University of Chicago Press, 1970 edn.).

31 For instance, a number of the specifications of the term proposed, explicitly or implicitly, in recent years by liberal philosophers would appear to restrict the domain of morality, *per definitionem*, to a kind of utilitarian humanism. This is apparent, for example, in J. Wilson *et al.*, *Introduction to Moral Education* (Harmondsworth: Penguin, 1967), especially Part I. For a further example of *a priori* restrictions on the possible content of moral codes, see infra p. 40 and cf. also chapter 3. To avoid restrictions of this kind, the definition proposed in part one of this study is more formal than substantive. Thus, under its aegis the actual *content* of moral values and precepts is theoretically unlimited. However, such a definition is proposed for strictly sociological purposes. It is not claimed as an ideal formulation for all types of inquiry.

PART ONE: ETHICS AND SOCIOLOGY

## Chapter 1

1 For a similar view, with respect to urban sociology, see Lewis Mumford, *The Culture of Cities*, (London: Secker & Warburg, 1938) and, more recently *The Myth of the Machine* (London: Secker & Warburg, 1967).

2 Edmund Leach, *A Runaway World?* (London: BBC Publications, 1968).

3 See, for example, J. Galtung, 'Foreign policy opinion as a function of social position', *Journal of Peace Research*, 1964, pp. 206–31.

4 Cf. A. K. Saran, 'Indian social thought as sociology', *Indian Journal of Social Research*, 1961, 2, 1, pp. 22–8 and M. B. Clinard and J. W. Elder, 'Sociology in India: A study in the sociology of knowledge', *American Sociological Review*, 1965, 30, 4, pp. 581–7. See also, for instance, J. Galtung, 'Socio-cultural factors and the development of sociology in Latin America', *Social Science Information*, 1967, pp. 7–33 and the discussion in P. F. Lazarsfeld and E. Leeds, 'International sociology as a sociological problem', *ASR*, 1962, 27, 5, pp. 732–41.

5 A. C. MacIntyre, *A Short History of Ethics* (London: Routledge & Kegan Paul, 1967) pp. 266–8.

6 See chapter 8, pp. 298–310.

7 Since survey methods tend to focus on discrete attitudes, the systemic nature of moral codes is often neglected in social research, if not in social theory. Cf. especially chapters 6 and 7.

8 See, for example, T. Parsons, *The Social System* (London: Routledge & Kegan Paul, 1951).

9 Two well-known examples are David Lockwood, 'Some remarks on "The Social System"', *British Journal of Sociology*, 1956, 7, 2, pp. 134–46, and C. Wright Mills, *The Sociological Imagination* (Oxford University Press, 1959).

10 Put otherwise: any prescriptive or evaluative proposition entails a descriptive proposition, but not vice versa.

11 In fact, the *Bhagavad Gita* presents three principal 'paths of life': aside from the 'path' of religious devotion, there is the classic distinction between the 'way of knowledge' (*jnana-marga*) and the 'way of action' (*karma-marga*). These tenets are, of course, related to a broader belief-system which determines the structure of Hindu ethics. This includes, for instance, the belief in reincarnation, the depreciation of the empirical world as *maya*, and explanatory beliefs about pollution and purity. On this, cf. A. Chandhuri, *The Doctrine of Maya* (Calcutta: Das Gupta, 1950) and H. Orenstein, 'The structure of Hindu caste values: A preliminary study of hierarchy and ritual defilement', *Ethnology*, 1965, 4, 1, pp. 1–15, which brings out the cognitive assumptions behind Hindu precepts very clearly. For an empirical study of modern attitudes towards this last topic, indicating that conservatism is most prevalent among the lower castes, see R. Rath and N. R. Sircar, 'The cognitive background of six Hindu caste groups regarding the low caste untouchables', *Journal of Social Psychology*, 1960, 5, pp. 295–306.

12 As a result, there are many more typologies and scales for values than for beliefs; representative examples are discussed in chapter 3.

13 Thus it is common for preliterate communities to restrict the domain of their moral codes to their own society, and to class individuals outside it, and not related to them in kin terms, as sub-human. For examples, see p. 34f.

14 The application of sociology to such a programme is discussed in Peter I. Rose, *The Subject Is Race: Traditional Ideologies and the Teaching of Race Relations* (Oxford University Press, 1968). See too, for example, M. Banton, 'What do we mean by "racism"?', *New Society*, 1969, pp. 551–4. Banton argues that racism is increasingly being justified by appeals to cultural differences, rather than to alleged biological differences. But this position is clearly a weaker one than the first because of the obvious susceptibility of cultures to change, whether from internal or external pressures. However, some empirical evidence that this shift in type of justification is in fact occurring is given in the study of E. J. B. Rose *et al.* on race relations in England: *Colour and Citizenship* (Oxford University Press, 1969). As such, it is matched by a similar process occurring in non-white forms of racialism, where the cult of *négritude*, especially in the United States, becomes stripped of strictly racial beliefs, and constitutes instead a search for a distinctive cultural and intellectual pedigree.

15 See W. H. R. Rivers (ed.), *Essays On The Depopulation of Melanesia* (Harvard University Press, 1922).

16 One of the most frequently cited definitions of 'values' in sociology is that of Clyde Kluckhohn: 'A value is a conception, explicit or implicit, distinctive of an individual or characteristic of a group, of the desirable which influences the selection from available modes, means, and ends of action.' ('Values and value orientations', in T. Parsons and E. A. Shils (eds), *Toward A General Theory of Action* (Harvard University Press, 1951), p. 395. A definition like this, however, prejudges the relation between values and actions. For a review of other conceptions, from a positivist point of view, see F. Adler, 'The value concept in sociology', *American Journal of Sociology*, 1956, 62, 3, pp. 272–9.

17 A recent account is D. J. O'Connor, *Aquinas and Natural Law* (London: Macmillan, 1967).

18 E. R. Service, *The Hunters* (Englewood Cliffs, N. J.: Prentice-Hall, 1966), excerpts from pp. 64–7.

19 G. Warnock, *Contemporary Moral Philosophy* (London: Macmillan, 1967), pp. 52–5.

20 R. Brandt, *Hopi Ethics: A Theoretical Analysis* (University of Chicago Press, 1954).

21 C. von Furer-Haimendorf, *Morals and Merit, A Study of Values and Social Controls in South Asian Societies* (London: Weidenfeld & Nicolson, 1967), p. 9.

## Chapter 2

1 For a functionalist approach, see A. MacBeath, *Experiments in Living* (London: Macmillan, 1952). Evidence of the kind of circularity which such an approach can lead to is found in many functionalist accounts of 'religion'. And a comparable criticism of circularity in functionalist definitions is given in the discussion of Davis and Moore's well-known paper on stratification by Melvin Tumin, 'Some principles of stratification: A critical analysis', *ASR*, 1953, 18, 4, pp. 387–94.

A common psychological approach is to define moral codes in terms of the degree of guilt associated with their transgression. This, however, is very misleading. Not only is it a function of the individual and his social class (depending largely on socialization practices in each case) but it is also ethnocentric in a broader, cultural sense. In many cultures guilt is relatively unimportant. For instance, one experimental study showed that American children in Hawaii cheated less and yet showed more guilt than Samoan children at the same school: R. E. Grinder and R. E. McMichael, 'Cultural influence on conscience development: resistance to temptation and guilt among Samoans and American caucasians', *Journal of Abnormal and Social Psychology*, 1963, 66, pp. 503–7. Similarly, it should be remembered that the evidence of social psychology suggests that it is the people with the strongest 'superegos', who tend to behave the best, who are most prone to guilt feelings in everyday life. On this, see Roger Brown, *Social Psychology* (London: Collier-Macmillan, 1967).

2 As, for instance, in the work of Talcott Parsons.

3 On the other hand, the term can easily be applied in too restrictive a fashion. For instance, in everyday language morality is still sometimes taken to denote, almost exclusively, Victorian teachings about sex. Such a conception is, of course, much too narrow for our present purposes, and in the light of the comments offered earlier (in chapter 1) we would also view it as very misleading.

4 This is only one of the more obvious respects in which moral codes posit general conceptions of human nature. Thus, within the voluntarist tradition, different limitations have, at different times, been placed upon man's freedom of action, with the immediate consequence of either expanding or contracting the domain to which moral standards were potentially applicable. An example from the history of social science would be the redefinition of poverty which resulted from the research of Rowntree and Booth. By seeing this condition, not solely as a result of the individual's choices and 'character', but as socially determined, poverty necessarily lost some of its moral opprobrium. This idea, of course, also supplied one of the intellectual foundations of the Welfare State. It is thus somewhat ironic that today determinist interpretations of the conditions of the poor are being utilized (especially in America) to justify essentially conservative political policies: see C. A. Valentine, *Culture and Poverty* (University of Chicago Press, 1968) and P. Townsend (ed.), *The Concept of Poverty* (London: Heinemann, 1970), particularly chapter 8.

A more contemporary illustration of this dilemma—between, respectively, more or less deterministic conceptions of man—is provided by the contrasting attitudes of social scientists and psychologists on the one hand, and those of the legal profession on the other, supplying, no doubt, one reason for the lack of interaction between these two groups. On this, see H. Schoeck and J. W. Wiggins, *Psychiatry and Responsibility* (Princeton: Van Nostrand, 1962) and B. Wootton, *Social Science and Social Pathology* (London: Allen & Unwin, 1959), especially chapter 8. For discussion of the concepts of punishment and treatment in these terms, see infra, chapter 3, p. 87f.

5 Von Furer-Haimendorf, op. cit., p. 216.

6 Projections of determinism of this type might be said to exemplify an alienated false consciousness as defined by Peter Berger and Stanley Pullberg in their article 'Reification and the sociological critique of consciousness', *History and Theory*, 1965, IV, 2, p. 196f.

7 It should be mentioned here that the normal practice of social science is to leave ultimate questions concerning the extent of particular agents' free will in parenthesis, and to proceed on the assumption that their behaviour is causally determined. However, it is also to be noted that a demonstration of causal determination does not necessarily invalidate the (agent's) assumption of free will. That is, the notions of causal explicability and unavoidability, which are often subsumed under the concept of determinism, need to be distinguished. On this complex question, see, for example, D. F. Pears (ed.), *Freedom and the Will* (London: Macmillan, 1963); P. F. Strawson, *Freedom and Resent-*

*ment* (London: Oxford University Press, 1962) and J. R. Lucas, *The Freedom of the Will* (Oxford University Press, 1970).

8 E.g., Raymond Firth, *Elements of Social Organization* (London: Watts, 1951), especially ch. 6. and *Essays on Social Organization and Values* (London School of Economics Monographs on Social Anthropology: Athlone Press, 1964), especially ch. 9. Despite the extensive application of the 'spectator approach' in the social sciences, John Ladd has suggested that it may not be applicable to all cultures. Specifically, he argues that it was not to be found in Greek culture, nor does it reflect Navaho ethics, where actions are evaluated from the point of view of the patient—the person who is actually or who may be affected—rather than from the viewpoint of the disinterested spectator. See his *The Structure of a Moral Code* (Harvard University Press, 1957), p. 70 and pp. 304–5. The discussion in the present chapter, and that in the first part of chapter 3, is much indebted to Ladd's analysis and presentation of these issues.

9 For a representative discussion of the moral point of view, which includes impartiality as a criterion, see Kurt Baier, *The Moral Point of View: A Rational Basis of Ethics* (Cornell University Press, 1958—or abbreviated, Random House, 1965). For the idea of society as the 'objective' source of obligation, see Durkheim's *The Elementary Forms of the Religious Life* (Chicago: Free Press, 1947). Durkheim's argument, however, rested on a possibly hypostatized conception of society.

10 One example is the Navaho: cf. John Ladd, op. cit., p. 67.

11 See, for instance, the debate between Roderick Firth and Richard Brandt on the definition of the ideal observer, in *Philosophy and Phenomenological Research*, 1952, XII, 3 and 1955, XV, 3.

12 See later comments on the concept of culture in chapter 4. This problem is, of course, especially applicable to pluralistic societies, elements of which are shared by all modern industrial societies: cf. the discussion of pluralism infra, p. 93f.

13 Examples are given in A. MacBeath, op. cit., pp. 161–2. In a similar vein, Lévi-Strauss writes: 'Men are not all alike, and even in primitive tribes, which sociologists have portrayed as crushed by all-powerful tradition, the differences between one man and another are noted as exactly, and exploited with as much pertinacity, as in what we call our "individualist" society.' From *A World On The Wane* (New York: John Russell, 1961), p. 310. Awareness of this is also found in the work of Paul Radin. Cf. too n. 3.31.

14 Op. cit., p. 67.

15 Ibid., pp. 73–4.

16 See Ladd's criticisms of MacBeath's *Experiments in Living* in the *Journal of Philosophy*, 1952, 49, no. 19.

17 Cf. David Aberle, A. K. Davis, M. J. Levy, and F. X. Sutton, 'The functional prerequisites of a society', *Ethics*, 1950, vol. LX.

18 E. Gellner, *Words and Things* (Harmondsworth: Penguin, 1966). A similar criticism has been made by other philosophers, including Herbert Marcuse, *One Dimensional Man* (London: Routledge & Kegan Paul, 1964), especially ch. 7.

19 Kant's 'categorical imperative' is one of the best-known formulations.
20 Douglas Oliver, *A Solomon Islands Society* (Harvard University Press, 1955), pp. 454–5.
21 See, for instance, M. D. Sahlins, *Tribesmen* (Englewood Cliffs, N. J.: Prentice-Hall, 1968), especially pp. 19–20, where he writes:

> A contrast between tribal and civilized moral orders is suggested —between relative and situational norms as opposed to universal imperatives. In the tribal framework, a given act is not in itself good or bad whomever it may concern; it depends on exactly whom it does concern. Stealing another man's goods or his woman is a crime in one's own community, but the same act if perpetrated against an outsider can be a deed of merit. The suggested contrast with the absolute injunctions of modern law may be overdrawn. No moral scheme is strictly absolute— especially in a time of war, when thou *shalt* kill some people— and maybe none is strictly contextual. Still, universalist injunctions are singularly required in state (civilized) societies confronting the emergent problem of keeping the peace of a heterogeneous domain within which conflict of interest is a condition of organization. In tribal circumstances, free reign is given to homebred ideas of right and wrong—and charity begins at home. A sectoral morality thus prevails among tribesmen, and in sufficient contrast to ourselves to draw repeated ethnographic comment.

The principles of the Welfare State are, of course, universalistic in character and as such contrast with the particularistic, and especially familistic, ethics of pre-industrial societies. But it remains common for some groups even within modern societies to maintain a strict code of co-operation or honour for within-group relations, which is reversed in dealings with the wider society. Criminology provides a number of case-studies of this: vide, for example, Norman Lewis, *The Honoured Society* (London: Collins, 1964) and Lewis Yablonsky, *The Violent Gang* (Harmondsworth: Penguin, 1967, first pub. 1962).
22 E. C. Banfield, *The Moral Basis of a Backward Society* (New York: Free Press, 1958), pp. 110–11. For a critique of Banfield's data, which argues that the Montegrano ethos is a consequence rather than a cause of the prevailing social structure, see S. F. Silverman, 'Agricultural organization, social structure, and values in Italy: Amoral familism reconsidered', *American Anthropologist*, 1968, 70, 1, pp. 1–20.
23 Cf. J. A. Pitt-Rivers, *The People of the Sierra* (University of Chicago Press, 1961) and C. Lison-Tolosana, *Belmonte de los Caballeros* (Oxford: Clarendon Press, 1966).
24 Ladd, op. cit., pp. 94–5.
25 See, respectively, Pitt-Rivers, op. cit., especially ch. 12, p. 178f, and J. G. Peristiany, 'Honour and shame in a Cypriot highland village', in J. G. Peristiany (ed.), *Honour and Shame: The Values of Mediterranean Society* (London: Weidenfeld & Nicolson, 1965), pp. 173–90. Both *sinvergüenza* and *adiantropos* mean, literally, 'without shame'. Mention should also be made of those cases where an élite group is

defined as 'beyond the moral law' by virtue of its superiority rather than inferiority, as among the Brahmans, where the *ngana yogin* claims freedom from all the rules of caste.

26 A. C. MacIntyre, op. cit., pp. 94–5.
27 One instance would be the Zuni, as described in Ruth Benedict, *Patterns of Culture* (London: Routledge & Kegan Paul, 1935). Cf. also Cora Du Bois, *The People of Alor* (Harvard University Press, 1961 edn, first published 1944).
28 Ladd, op. cit., p. 52f.
29 Ibid., p. 53.
30 Von Furer-Haimendorf, op. cit., p. 216.
31 John Ladd, op. cit., p. 53.
32 C. Lévi-Strauss, *Tristes Tropiques* (Paris: Plon, 1955). Translated in an abridged edition as *A World On The Wane* (New York: Russell, 1961), pp. 386–7. Cf. also Karl Menninger, *The Crime of Punishment* (New York: Viking Press, 1968).
33 M. Mead, *Cooperation and Competition Among Primitive Peoples* (New York: McGraw-Hill 1937), p. 33.
34 In *The Chrysanthemum and the Sword* (Boston: Houghton Mifflin, 1946), pp. 222–4, Ruth Benedict draws the distinction between 'shame' and 'guilt' cultures as follows:

A society that inculcates absolute standards of morality and relies on man's developing a conscience is a guilt culture. . . . Shame cultures rely on external sanctions for good behavior, not, as true guilt cultures do, on an internalized conviction of sin. Shame is a reaction to other people's criticism . . . by being openly ridiculed and rejected or by fantasying to himself that he has been made ridiculous. . . . In either case it is a potent sanction. But it requires an audience or at least a man's fantasy of an audience. Guilt does not. . . . [For example] Shame has the same place of authority in Japanese ethics that a 'clear conscience', 'being right with God', and the avoidance of sin have in Western ethics. Logically enough, therefore, a man will not be punished in the afterlife. The Japanese—except for priests who know the Indian *sutras*—are quite unacquainted with the idea of reincarnation dependent upon one's merit in this life, and—except for some well-instructed Christian converts—they do not recognize post-death reward and punishment or a heaven and a hell.

Again the Navaho provide an example of a culture in which guilt has minimal importance: cf. Ladd, op. cit., p. 272. See also n. 2.1 supra.
35 Cf. Peristiany, op. cit., in which illustrations are given from communities in Spain, Cyprus, Greece, Algeria, and Egypt. More detailed case-studies in the context of Spain are available in Pitt-Rivers, op. cit. and Lison-Tolosana, op. cit. M. Kenny, in *A Spanish Tapestry: Town and Country in Castile* (London: Cohen & West, 1961) contrasts the ethos of the traditional *pueblo* with that of the capital city, and finds that within the urban environment, loyalty to the community becomes

a matter of choice and so the saliency of shame as an effective sanction is diminished. An extended discussion of a Greek mountain community in these terms is given in J. K. Cambell, *Honour, Family and Patronage* (Oxford: Clarendon Press, 1964). Cf., too, P. Walcot, *Greek Peasants, Ancient and Modern: A Comparison of Social and Moral Values* (Manchester University Press, 1970). In all the societies mentioned above the centrality of shame is correlated with the value of honour. Both concepts ascribe overall importance to social evaluation. Thus, Pierre Bourdieu observes ('The sentiment of honour in Kabyle society', in J. G. Peristiany, op. cit., p. 212) that:

> The important position accorded to the sentiment of honour is a characteristic of 'primary' societies in which the relationship with others, through its intensity, intimacy and continuity, takes precedence over the relationship one has with oneself; in which the individual learns the truth about himself through the intermediary of others; and in which the being and the truth about a person are identical with the being and truth that others acknowledge in him.

36 G. J. Warnock, op. cit., p. 54.

37 John Ladd, op. cit., pp. 101–8.

38 Von Wright's 'deontic logic' operates with the primitive concept of 'permission' and allows the three categories of 'obligatory', 'forbidden', and 'indifferent' to be defined in terms of it. Thus, account cannot be taken by it of *degrees* of moral preferableness. Cf. G. H. von Wright, *Norm and Action* (London: Routledge & Kegan Paul, 1963). Prescriptive logics will be discussed in chapter 8, pp. 298–308.

39 Cf. Mary Warnock, *Existentialist Ethics* (London: Macmillan, 1967).

40 For a description of this process, see Peter Berger and Thomas Luckman, *The Social Construction of Reality* (London: Allen Lane, 1967), especially pp. 65–109.

41 A description of the utility of projective tests to check the validity of direct methods is given on p. 120f. Projective measures are also discussed in chapter 8, p. 268f.

## Chapter 3

1 Contrast this with Hare's thesis that moral evaluations are universalized prescriptions: *The Language of Morals* (Oxford: Clarendon Press, 1961) and *Freedom and Reason* (Oxford: Clarendon Press, 1963). General introductions to evaluative and prescriptive discourse, relevant to the first part of this chapter, are available in Paul Edwards, *The Logic of Moral Discourse* (Chicago: Free Press, 1955) and Paul W. Taylor, *Normative Discourse* (Englewood Cliffs, N. J.: Prentice-Hall, 1961). See too W. D. Lamont, *The Value Judgement* (University of Edinburgh Press, 1955).

2 A clear example of this is provided by Smelser's typology of 'components of social action' in his *Theory of Collective Behaviour* (London: Routledge & Kegan Paul, 1962).

3 In English jurisprudence *obsolute offences* refer to a range of forbidden acts which are so defined by Parliament that the very doing of them, or permitting them to be done, is punishable, even though the accused neither intended the act nor could have avoided it by exercising reasonable care. Examples include the possession of an altered passport, selling adulterated milk, and dangerous driving.

4 Compare      The last temptation is the greatest
                   treason:
                   To do the right deed for the wrong
                   reason.
               T. S. Eliot, *Murder in the Cathedral*, Pt I.
   However, although the importance of good motives is integral to both Roman jurisprudence and the Judaeo-Christian tradition, we should take care not to universalize this.

5 This point is made by H. A. Pritchard, *Moral Obligation* (Oxford University Press, 1968; first published 1949).

6 Some examples are given in MacBeath, op. cit., p. 161.

7 Ladd, op. cit., pp. 69–70.

8 Ibid., p. 70.

9 For a table illustrating the relationship between students' expressed values and overt behaviour, see p. 119. Chapter 5 examines the issue of attitudes vs. actions in general.

10 Cf. G. Lagos, *International Stratification and Underdeveloped Countries* (University of North Carolina Press, 1963). The theory of rank dimensions, and especially of asymmetries between ranks, has been well developed in recent years. Its application, however, has been largely restricted to studies of social groups and individuals *within* particular societies. Little work has been conducted using societies as the main units of analysis.

11 See J. O. Urmson, 'Saints and heroes', in J. Feinberg (ed.), *Moral Concepts* (Oxford University Press, 1969) and F. H. Bradley, *Ethical Studies* (Oxford University Press, 1962; first published 1958).

12 A detailed historical account of Soviet ethics with regard to labour, dealing mainly with the period 1917–1920, is given in F. I. Kaplan, *Bolshevik Ideology and the Ethics of Soviet Labour* (New York: Philosophical Library, 1968). This includes discussion of the sanctions employed by the Bolshevik Party and of the type of attitudes they attempted to foster in the workers of the Soviet Union.

13 W. Goldschmidt, 'Values and the field of comparative sociology', *ASR*, 1959, 18, pp. 287–93.

14 Ruth Benedict (1935), op. cit.

15 The difference in attitudes towards individuality here is commonly generalized to the conceptions that are typical of the East and West respectively. In the case of the West, attention is drawn to the distinctive Judaeo-Christian conception of selfhood, which has its modern origins in the philosophy of Renaissance individualism, and involves a self-actualizing, self-fulfilling conception of man. Whereas in the East, it is argued, philosophies such as Hinduism and Buddhism advocate the elimination of selfhood and all the desires associated

with it. Expressed thus, the contrast is, of course, somewhat over-simplified, and would anyway require some qualification today. However, it is important to be aware of the distinctive elements in the tradition of Western individualism, whether religious or secular, and to recognize the multiple sociological consequences of this tradition. For examination of some of the less familar of these consequences, see, for instance, H. G. Beigel, 'Romantic love', *ASR*, 1951, 5, 16, pp. 326–34 and Z. Barbu, ' "Chosisme:" A socio-psychological interpretation,' *European Journal of Sociology*, 1963.

16 Ian Watt, *The Rise of the Novel* (London: Chatto & Windus, 1957).
17 Particularly in his *Pour une Sociologie du roman* (Paris: Gallimard, 1964). It is interesting to compare Goldmann's thesis on this subject with that of George Steiner in *The Death of Tragedy* (London: Faber & Faber, 1968; first published 1961).
18 See John Sturrock, *The French New Novel* (Oxford University Press, 1969) and Barbu, op. cit.
19 Cf., for instance, Leach, op. cit.
20 H. L. A. Hart, *The Concept of Law* (Oxford University Press, 1961).
21 A. C. MacIntyre, *Secularization and Moral Change* (Oxford University Press, 1967).
22 G. Sjoberg and L. D. Cain, 'Negative values and social action', *Alpha Kappa Deltan*, 1959, 29, 1, pp. 63–70.
23 Milton Rokeach, *The Open and Closed Mind* (New York: Basic Books, 1960).
24 R. C. Johnson, C. W. Thompson, and G. Frincke, 'Word values, word frequency, and visual duration thresholds', *Psychological Review*, 1960, 67, pp. 332–42.
25 W. E. Lambert and O. Klineberg, *Children's Views of Foreign Peoples: A Cross-national Study* (New York: Appleton-Century-Crofts, 1967).
26 H. Cantril, *The Pattern of Human Concerns* (New Brunswick, N. J.: Rutgers University Press, 1965).
27 For this distinction cf. Ladd, op. cit., p. 123f.
28 Cf. P. Huby, *Greek Ethics* (London: Macmillan, 1967).
29 The work of such writers as Bonhoeffer, Tillich, and Robinson illustrate this.
30 Judaism is, of course, undergoing a number of changes in modern society, and some of its more reformist versions draw closer to being an 'ethics of direction'. For a discussion of this in the American context, see Marshall Sklare, *Conservative Judaism* (Chicago: Free Press, 1955) and idem, *America's Jews* (New York: Random House, 1971).
31 As analysed by Ladd, op. cit.
32 For methods of investigating modes of argumentation, see the discussion of formal approaches in chapter 8.
33 First proposed in 'Values, motives and systems of action' in T. Parsons and E. A. Shils (eds), *Toward a General Theory of Action* (Harvard University Press, 1951).
34 See, for instance, T. Parsons, 'A revised analytical approach to the theory of social stratification' in his *Essays in Sociological Theory* (New York: Free Press, 1964 rev. edn).

35 See, for instance, R. Dubin, 'Parsons' Actor: Continuities in social theory', *ASR*, 1960, 25 and Parsons' reply: 'Pattern variables revisited: A response to R. Dubin', Ibid. Cf. also the contributions to Max Black (ed.) *The Social Theories of Talcott Parsons* (Englewood Cliffs, N. J.: Prentice-Hall, 1961).

36 Peter M. Blau, 'Operationalizing a conceptual scheme: The Universalism-Particularism pattern variable', *ASR*, 1962, 27, 2, pp. 159–69; Harry A. Scarr, 'Measure of Particularism', *Sociometry*, 1964, 27, pp. 413–32; Peter Park, 'Measurement of the pattern variables', *Sociometry* 1967, 30, pp. 187–98.

37 Op. cit.

38 See, for example, Parsons (1964), op. cit.

39 Cf. R. K. Merton and E. Barber, 'Sociological ambivalence', in E. A. Tiryakian (ed.), *Sociological Theory, Values and Sociocultural-Change* (London: Collier-Macmillan, 1963).

40 Kingsley Davis, *Human Society* (New York: Macmillan, 1949), ch. 3; A. H. Barton, 'The concept of property-space in social research' in P. F. Lazarsfeld and M. Rosenberg (eds), *The Language of Social Research* (Chicago: Free Press, 1955); R. T. Morris, 'A typology of norms', *ASR*, 1956, 21, pp. 610–13; and J. P. Gibbs, 'Norms: The problem of definition and classification', *AJS*, 1965, 70.

41 See p. 37f. supra.

42 G. W. Allport, P. E. Vernon and G. Lindzey, *A Study of Values* (Boston: Houghton Mifflin, 1951 rev. edn); F. R. Kluckhohn and F. L. Strodbeck, *Variations in Value Orientations* (London: Harper & Row, 1961).

43 Reported in Kluckhohn and Strodbeck, op. cit.

44 Vide W. T. Liu, 'Chinese value orientations in Hong Kong', *Sociological Analysis*, 1966, 27, 2, pp. 53–66 and W. T. Caudill and H. A. Scarr, 'Japanese value orientations and culture change', *Ethnology*, 1962, 1, 1. These studies are briefly described on p. 206 infra.

45 This characterization is suggested in Kluckhohn and Strodbeck, op. cit.

46 Ibid.

47 Joseph Needham, 'Time and knowledge in China and the West', in J. T. Fraser (ed.), *The Voices of Time* (London: Allen Lane, 1968). Excerpt from pp. 128–9.

48 Cf. especially Norman Cohn, *The Pursuit of the Millennium* (London: Secker & Warburg, 1957).

49 See the classic study by J. B. Bury, *The Idea of Progress* (London: Macmillan, 1920). More recently, see L. Sklair, *The Sociology of Progress* (London: Routledge & Kegan Paul, 1970).

50 Cf., for instance, the symposium by F. d'Arcais *et al.*, 'Progresso scientifico e contesto culturale', *Civiltà delle Macchine*, 1963, 11, 3, p. 19f. Cited in Needham, op. cit.

51 This is to some extent implicit in Weber's thesis: *The Protestant Ethic and the Spirit of Capitalism* (London: Allen & Unwin, 1962; first published 1930). As such, it is also to be found in a number of the studies that have followed Weber's pioneering work. Two of the best

overviews of these later studies are Ephriam Fischoff, 'The Protestant Ethic and the Spirit of Capitalism: The history of a controversy', *Social Research*, 1944, 11, pp. 53–77 and Samuel N. Eisenstadt, 'The Protestant Ethic thesis in analytical and comparative context', *Diogenes*, 1967, 59, pp. 25–46. It is also of interest here to note that some experimental research has indicated significant correlations between time imagery and judgment, achievement motivation, and interest in the physical sciences: see R. H. Knapp, 'Time imagery and the achievement motive', *Journal of Personality*, 1958, 26, p. 426f., and Idem, 'Attitudes toward time and aesthetic choice', *Journal of Social Psychology*, 1962, 56, p. 79f. Knapp himself observes (Knapp, 1958, op. cit.) that

> The rise of time measurement as a serious concern, the development of time pieces themselves, the first establishment of time-monitored industrialism occurred in exactly those Northern European cultures . . . (which) fostered entrepreneurship, the rise of capitalism, and strong emphasis upon achievement motivation.

52 As Needham (op. cit., p. 622) writes: 'Roman thought was rather different, as witness the "linear" epic of Virgil, the metrical chronicles that preceded it, and the theory of the *urbs aeterna*.' See also M. Eliade, *The Myth of the Eternal Return* (London: Routledge & Kegan Paul, 1955).

53 This conception of time in Indian thought is, of course, most clearly illustrated by the doctrine of *karma-samsara*. See, for example, H. Nakamura, 'Time in Indian and Japanese thought', in Fraser (ed.), op. cit., pp. 92–135.

54 Cf. M. Eliade, op. cit.

55 Op. cit., p. 129.

56 Ibid., p. 132. Of course, the presence of a linear time-consciousness does not appear sufficient in itself to lead to the development of modern science. Thus, Needham's main contention in his essay is that, in spite of impressionistic judgments to the contrary, China's attitude to time was more of the Judaeo-Christian type than the Indo-Hellenic; and yet China did not spontaneously develop modern natural science as Western Europe did.

57 As Needham observes, one can see this, for instance, in the Spenglerian view of history.

58 See particularly chapter 9.

59 Cf. D. F. Aberle *et al.* (1950), op. cit.; and also M. J. Levy, *The Structure of Society* (Princeton University Press, 1952).

60 For a review of some of the implications of a cultural relativist position, see part three of this study.

61 This is not to imply that modes of ethical reasoning are themselves necessarily closed to typological analysis; see, for instance, p. 62f. infra.

62 C. Morris, *Varieties of Human Value* (University of Chicago Press, 1956).

63 Ibid. See too C. Morris and L. V. Jones, 'Value scales and dimensions', *Journal of Abnormal and Social Psychology*, 1955, 51, pp. 523–35.

64 F. Fearing, Review of Morris (1956), *Contemporary Psychology*, 1957, 2, pp. 157–9.
65 In fact, Morris's 'Philosophical Beliefs' questionnaire, although it includes a number of items on cognitive assumptions (e.g. the belief that the course of history is purposive) also comprises items that primarily designate prescriptions (e.g., that a person ought to follow his conscience). As we shall see, social research in general has given little empirical attention to the interrelationship of cognitive, evaluative, and prescriptive attitudes; cf. chapter 6.
66 See, for example, Smelser, op. cit.
67 C. E. Birdwell, 'Values, norms and the integration of complex social systems', *Sociological Quarterly*, 1966, 7, 2, pp. 119–36.
68 See chapter 8, pp. 298–310.
69 Ladd, op. cit., p. 153.
70 For instance: mode (2) might involve some kind of rank ordering of basic prescriptions, or some designation of the kind of conditions under which each is applicable.
71 Ladd, op. cit., 153f.
72 See chapter 8.
73 Symmes C. Oliver, 'Individuality, freedom of choice and cultural flexibility of the Kamba', *American Anthropologist*, 1965, 67, 2, pp. 421–8.
74 See pp. 49–52 supra.
75 See p. 22f.
76 Cf. p. 45f.
77 Cf. the discussion of different branches of modal logic, and their possible combinations, in chapter 8, pp. 298–310.
78 A. Edel, 'Social science and value: A study in interrelations', in I. L. Horowitz (ed.), *The New Sociology* (New York: Oxford University Press, 1966).
79 See *From Max Weber: Essays in Sociology*, trans. by H. H. Gerth and C. Wright Mills (New York: Oxford University Press 1946), pp. 196–244; and Max Weber, *The Theory of Social and Economic Organization*, trans. by A. M. Henderson and Talcott Parsons, (New York: Oxford University Press, 1947), pp. 329–41.
80 W. K. Frankena, *Ethics* (Englewood Cliffs, N. J.: Prentice-Hall, 1963), pp. 13–14. First italics in each case ours.
81 Ibid., p. 15.
82 Cf. Mary Warnock, *Existentialist Ethics* (London: Macmillan, 1967).
83 Frankena, op. cit., p. 15.
84 On p. 70. 'Act-deontological' theories, for instance, match the 'mode of extreme particularism' in this account.
85 The hostility of medieval Catholicism to scientific activity is well known. However, its disvaluation of curiosity about the natural world is to be found also in the late nineteenth century, and even today certain aspects of science—and particularly recent developments in biochemistry—are treated by the Catholic Church with opprobrium. The Protestant tradition, of course, proved generally more favourable to the development of modern science: cf. R. K. Merton, *Science*,

377

*Technology, and Society in Seventeenth-Century England* (New York: Fertig, 1970; first published 1938).

86 See, for instance, John Vyvyan, *In Pity and in Anger* (London: Michael Joseph, 1969). Cf., too, Paul Ramsey, *The Patient as Person: Explorations in Medical Ethics* (Yale University Press, 1971).

87 See, for instance, E. A. Shils, 'Social inquiry and the autonomy of the individual', in D. Lerner (ed.), *The Human Meaning of the Social Sciences* (Cleveland: Meridian, 1959), pp. 114–57. Shils rejects all forms of social investigation in which the subjects under study are not fully informed of the purposes and intentions of the research. Such a practice would, of course, greatly increase the problems of reactivity in social research. On this, cf. chapters 7 and 8 infra.

88 F. Fanon, *The Wretched of the Earth* (London: McGibbon & Kee, 1965).

89 The ideology of Black Power is well discussed in Stokeley Carmichael and C. V. Hamilton, *Black Power: The Politics of Liberation in America* (Harmondsworth: Penguin, 1969).

90 An interesting analysis is Arne Naess, 'A systemisation of Gandhian ethics of conflict resolution', *Journal of Conflict Resolution*, 1958, 2, pp. 140–55. See too the theoretical exposition of non-violent forms of action in Johan Galtung, 'On the meaning of non-violence', *Journal of Peace Research*, 1965, 2, 3, pp. 228–57 and idem, 'Pacificism from a sociological point of view', *J. Conflict Resoln.*, March 1969. An interesting, although arguably over-extended, reformulation of the concept of 'violence' is offered by Galtung in his 'Violence, peace, and peace research', *J. Peace Research*, 1969, 3, pp. 167–91.

91 The way in which questions of this type are resolved will, of course, depend upon the degree of stringency associated with the precepts in question; and here advocates of (for instance) violent action can often point out that society does not absolutely proscribe violence, and in some cases (e.g. in times of war) actually prescribes it.

92 'Violence, peace, and peace research', loc. cit., p. 184.

93 'Does political theory still exist?', in Peter Laslett and W. G. Runciman (eds), *Philosophy, Politics and Society*, 2nd Series (Oxford: Blackwell, 1964), p. 11.

94 G. Myrdal, *Asian Drama: An Enquiry into the Poverty of Nations*, 3 vols. (London: Allen Lane, 1968).

95 E. J. Mishan, *The Costs of Economic Growth* (Harmondsworth: Penguin, 1969).

96 T. Wilson, 'The contradiction in our attitudes to freedom', *New Society*, 1968, pp. 223–8.

97 The views expressed in Mill's classic *Essay on Liberty* (1859) may be fruitfully compared with regard to the present issue with those of a modern liberal such as H. L. A. Hart in his *Law, Liberty, and Morality* (Oxford University Press, 1968).

98 Op. cit., p. 41. The emergence of the pollution issue as a consensual *cause célèbre* in recent times might hopefully encourage this awareness.

99 See M. Weber, *The Theory of Social and Economic Organization* (1947), p. 115.

100 For a critical review of the development of Parsons' theory, see J. F. Scott, 'The changing foundations of the Parsonian action scheme', *ASR*, 1963, 28.

101 This is noted in C. Morse, 'The functional imperatives', in Max Black (ed.), op. cit. and in R. Dubin (1960), op. cit.

102 On this general issue in social science, see W. S. Robinson, 'Ecological correlations and the behavior of individuals, *ASR*, 1950, 15, pp. 351–7 and H. Menzel, 'Comment', loc. cit., p. 674. Also P. F. Lazarsfeld and H. Menzel, 'On the relation between individual and collective properties' in A. Etzioni (ed.), *Complex Organizations* (New York: Holt, 1961), pp. 422–40.

103 Parsons also employs the term 'norms' at times to refer to specific standards of evaluation; like many social theorists, he gives comparatively little attention to the basic distinction between processes of prescription and evaluation.

104 Op. cit.

105 R. K. Merton, 'Social structure and anomie'. In his *Social Theory and Social Structure* (Chicago: Free Press. 1968 edn.). His paper was first published in 1938, and then revised in 1949. A useful summary of the debate his typology gave rise to is given in H. Johnson, *Sociology* (London: Routledge & Kegan Paul, 1961), pp. 557–62.

106 J. Rawls, 'Two concepts of rules', *Philosophical Review*, 1955, 64, 3–32 and idem, 'Justice as fairness', *Philosophical Review*, 1958, 67, pp. 164–94; J. O. Urmson, 'The interpretation of the moral philosophy of J. S. Mill', *Philosophical Quarterly*, 1953, 3, pp. 33–9. The papers by Rawls (1955) and Urmson are also reprinted in Philippa Foot (ed.), *Theories of Ethics* (Oxford University Press, 1967). A number of the essays in this collection are concerned with the problems raised by utilitarian theory, and among other things they indicate the type of response that may be made to the criticisms given in the present chapter: namely, the endorsement of a qualified form of *rule*-utilitarianism, in which the utility test is applied not to individual actions, but to *types* of actions. This parallels the distinction cited earlier between 'act-deontologists' and 'rule-deontologists' (p. 76). And although it limits the utilitarian claim, it does not fundamentally alter the type of reasoning and justification involved; except that now, of course, the utilitarian may allow that a different kind of reasoning would, in particular cases, be appropriate to the justification of *specific* actions.

After the present chapter was completed a most perceptive critique of the relationship between sociology and utilitarianism appeared, namely, Alvin W. Gouldner's *The Coming Crisis in Western Sociology* (London: Heinemann, 1971), especially ch. 3. His argument is essentially that Western sociology emerged in large part as a response to the utilitarian culture of the industrial middle class. Hence he observes, for example, that: 'The successful appeal of Functionalism has rested, in part, on its ability to resonate congenially the practical utilitarian sentiments of men socialized into a dominant middle-class culture, men who feel that things and people must be, and are, legitimated by their ongoing usefulness' (p. 121).

107 Cited in A. C. MacIntyre (1967), op. cit., p. 240.

108 Cf. T. Sellin (ed.), *Capital Punishment* (London: Harper & Row, 1967) and T. Honderich, *Punishment: The Supposed Justifications* (Harmondsworth: Penguin, 1971).

109 See especially the discussion of survey methodology in chapters 6 and 7.

110 Op. cit., p. 244.

111 For examples, see H. L. A. Hart (1961), op. cit., ch. 8.

112 Op. cit., p. 243.

113 Eric D'Arcy, *Human Acts: An Essay in their Moral Evaluation* (Oxford University Press, 1963).

114 The centrality of intentions to evaluative judgments, for instance, although basic to Roman jurisprudence and the Judaeo-Christian tradition, is not common to all cultures.

115 See R. S. Peters, *Education as Initiation* (London: Evans, 1963) and idem, *Ethics and Education* (London: Allen & Unwin, 1966).

116 R. S. Peters (1966), op. cit., p. 27.

117 Cf. n. 2. 4.

118 In addition, of course, the law has modified its conceptions of responsibility, giving more consideration to extenuating circumstances and even defects of will. One response to the consequent difficulties involved in establishing *mens rea* has been the advocacy of the extension of the range of absolute offences, for which proof of intentionality is not necessary: for this, see H. L. A. Hart, 'Prolegomenon to the principles of punishment', *Proceedings of the Aristotelian Society*, 1959–60, LX, p. 19f; and cf. n. 3.3.

119 See, for instance, Karl Menninger, *The Crime of Punishment* (New York: Viking Press, 1968).

120 The voluntaristic criterion applies to most laws, but not to those designated as absolute offences, where strict liability applies.

## Chapter 4

1 E. B. Tylor, *Primitive Culture* (London: Murrow, 1873), vol. 1, p. 1. There is a useful review of Kluckhohn and Kroeber's book, *Culture, A Critical Review of Concepts and Definitions* (Papers of the Peabody Museum, Harvard University, 1952), by Leslie White, in the *American Anthropologist*, 1954, 56, pp. 461–8. This author has also provided a detailed discussion of the issue in his 'The concept of culture', *American Anthropologist*, 1959, 61, 2, pp. 227–51.

2 An alternative formulation would be that social structure is institutionalized culture. This is not, of course, to imply an idealistic determination of social reality. Rather, we would conceive the relation between ideas and activities in more dialectical terms: that is, the social meanings men produce in their joint activities, once established, acquire a degree of 'objectivity' and, so to speak, autonomy from these activities, which indeed they may then serve to change. The relation-

ship between capitalist activity and the Protestant Ethic, for instance, may be seen in this light. However, this should not lead us to think of beliefs and actions as related in purely external, contingent terms. Clearly, there are conceptual, or logical, relations between the two: for discussion of this, see A. C. MacIntyre, 'A mistake about causality in social science', in P. Laslett and W. G. Runciman (1964), op. cit., pp. 48–70, and chapter 5 infra., espec. p. 142f.

3 Cf. Berger and Pullberg, op. cit. In general, language and religion form paradigmatic examples of this reification. But for an illuminating account of religion (Christianity) as a de-reifying agency, see Peter Berger, *The Social Reality of Religion* (London: Faber & Faber, 1969), p. 96f. Cf. also the discussion of 'operational relativism' in social science in chapter 10 infra.

4 Elizabeth Herzog, 'Some assumptions about the poor', *The Social Service Review*, 1963, 37, 4, pp. 389–402.

5 Cf. D. F. Aberle *et al.* (1950), op. cit.

6 This is too brief. However, it does seem that sociology could give more attention to the genesis and development of *nomoi*, rather than treating them in purely static terms. For an excellent discussion of the institution of marriage from this point of view, see Peter Berger and Hansfried Kellner, 'Marriage and the construction of reality', *Diogenes*, 1964, 46, pp. 1–24. This article also draws attention to the integral role of language in the process of 'nomization'. As Berger has written elsewhere (1969, op. cit., p. 20):

The fact of language, even if taken by itself, can readily be seen as the imposition of order upon experience. Language nomizes by imposing differentiation and structure upon the ongoing flux of experience. As an item of experience is named, it is *ipso facto*, taken out of this flux and given stability *as* the entity so named. Language further provides a fundamental order of relationships by the addition of syntax and grammar to vocabulary. It is impossible to use language without participating in its order. Every empirical language may be said to constitute a nomos in the making, or, with equal validity, as the historical consequence of the nomizing activity of generations of men.

However, although language is an important instrumentality in this process, its determinative influence can be over-stated, as in the linguistic relativity thesis of Sapir and Whorf (cf. p. 343f. infra.). The development of culture may also be viewed in more historical terms, as when, for instance, a particular social group gradually acquires a self-consciously common 'identity'; an example of this would be the development of working-class consciousness in England, as described by E. P. Thompson, *The Making of the English Working Class* (Harmondsworth: Penguin, 1968).

7 Cf. T. Scheff, 'Toward a sociological model of consensus', *ASR*, 1967, 32, 1, pp. 32–46; see, too, the 'Comment' by van den Berghe, loc. cit., pp. 1001–2, and Scheff's 'Reply', loc. cit., pp. 1002–3. Cf. also, O. E. Klapp, 'The concept of consensus and its importance', *Sociology and Social Research*, 1957, 41, pp. 336–42. Game theory supplies a number

of simplified, experimental formats for the study of consensus; vide T. Scheff, 'A theory of social coordination applicable to mixed motive games', *Sociometry*, 1967, 30, pp. 215–34; and see our discussion in chapter 8, pp. 290–8, infra.

8 The South African case is perceptively examined in Pierre van den Berghe, *South Africa: A Study in Conflict* (Middletown, Conn: Wesleyan University Press, 1965).

9 The process of polarization is discussed in James S. Coleman, *Community Conflict* (Chicago: Free Press, 1957). From an analytic point of view, one may distinguish polarization of interaction, and of affective orientations, from cultural polarization proper—i.e. polarization of basic attitudes and beliefs. The three aspects, however, are usually empirically correlated.

10 The 'classic' text on this subject, examining the plural aspects of the colonial situation, is that of J. S. Furnival, *Colonial Policy and Practice* (London: Cambridge University Press, 1948).

11 M. Haug, 'Social and cultural pluralism as a concept in social system analysis', *AJS*, 1967, 73, pp. 294–304; see also: M. G. Smith, 'Social and cultural pluralism', *Annals of the New York Academy of Sciences*, 1957, 83, pp. 763–77. The present sense of the term 'pluralism' should be distinguished carefully from the concept of 'political' pluralism.

12 Haug, op. cit., pp. 302–3. Significant horizontal power distribution is defined by Banks and Textor as the 'effective allocation of power to functionally autonomous legislative, executive and judicial organs'. Generalizing from this finding, together with the previous one, we may say that cultural pluralism is negatively correlated with political pluralism.

13 Haug, op. cit., p. 304.

14 Bruce M. Russett, H. R. Alker, K. W. Deutsch, and H. D. Lasswell, *World Handbook of Political and Social Indicators* (Yale University Press, 1964), pp. 293–303. The information on national GNPs per capita is matched with data on: (i) percentage urban (in cities over 20,000); (ii) percentage adult literacy; (iii) higher education per 100,000; (iv) Inhabitants per physician; (v) radios per 1,000; (vi) percentage voting; (vii) percentage military (of ages 15–64); and (viii) percentage expenditure of the central government. High correlations were found between GNP figures and the first six of these indices, and less marked correlations for the two political variables.

The main criticism to be made of the GNP/capita index is, of course, the fact that it is an aggregate measure and so one that obscures qualitative differences *within* nations (i.e. degree of equality in GNP distribution, etc.). However, this does not seem a serious short-coming for our investigation, the intention of which is to make broad international comparisons. For this purpose, the GNP per capita measure is one of the few accessible economic indices.

In addition to the main study presented in the text, we also compared the data on levels of pluralism with selected geographic and political variables. Among these studies, the following may be cited: First, mean levels of pluralism were calculated for each of nine major geographic regions; the results are given in Table N4.1. Second, we compared levels of pluralism with two indices of political instability contained in Russett *et al.*, op. cit., pp. 95–104. These were: (i) no. of deaths from domestic group violence per 1,000,000 population; and (ii) the rate of turnover in office of the legally designated chief executive (e.g. president) of the country. The results of this are given in Table N4.2.

TABLE N4.1. *Geographical regions according to levels of pluralism*

| Region | Mean Level | S.D. | Rank Order ($\bar{x}$) | (S.D.) | No. of cases |
|---|---|---|---|---|---|
| North America | 4·5 | 1·5 | 2 | 6 | 2 |
| Central America | 2·1 | 1·4 | 7 | 8 | 7 |
| Caribbean | 2·6 | 1·4 | 4* | 7 | 5 |
| South America | 2·6 | 2·6 | 4* | 1 | 10 |
| Africa | 5·0 | 1·9 | 1 | 3 | 31 |
| Australasia | 1·5 | 0·5 | 8 | 9 | 2 |
| West Europe | 1·4 | 1·8 | 9 | 4 | 17 |
| East Europe | 2·6 | 2·0 | 4* | 2 | 10 |
| Asia | 4·4 | 1·7 | 3 | 5 | 30 |

\* Indicates tied position.

In Table N4.1 it can be seen that Africa is the continent with the highest mean level of pluralism per nation, whereas West Europe has the lowest. Particularly interesting are comparisons between regions which comprise predominantly developing countries: thus, Africa, for example, exhibits a mean level of pluralism that is twice that of South America. However, South America exhibits a higher standard deviation. We would expect that facts such as these will have relevance to our understanding of such matters as the possibilities of intracontinental alliances, and relations between states generally. In these respects, however, our data can only claim to be suggestive. A fuller analysis of these questions would require the development of a more refined index of pluralism, and the use of a broader range of national statistics.

In the case of Table N4.2, we hypothesized that the degree of political instability for nations would be positively associated with their level of pluralism. As can be seen, the table does not support our expectation. Of course, the indices here tap only a limited aspect of political stability, and other dimensions could be proposed which might discriminate more effectively for our present purposes.

For a review of studies using *World Handbook* data, see Bruce M. Russett, 'The *World Handbook* as a tool in current research', *Social Science Information*, 1967, 6, 6, pp. 17–33. Inquiries particularly relevant to our present concerns include the study by Gregg (1966), which involved the use of GNP/capita and other indices to analyse the

383

TABLE N4.2. *Indices of political stability related to levels of pluralism*

Executive stability: No. of Years
Independent/No. of chief Executives
1945–1961

| | | HIGH* | MIDDLE | LOW |
|---|---|---|---|---|
| Deaths from domestic group violence per 1m population: (1950–62) | HIGH | 4·1† | 1 | – |
| | MIDDLE | 4·0 | 3·6 | 6·5 |
| | LOW | 2·1 | 2·4 | 3·2 |

*Natural cut-off points for each of the two sets of categories were chosen from the relevant tables in Russett *et al.*, op. cit., pp. 95–104.
†The figure in each cell represents the mean level of pluralism for this category.

degree of within-region homogeneity, and thereby the prospects for political integration, in each of the major geographical areas of the 'Third World'. Also, the study by Fishman (1966) examines the interrelationships between linguistic homogeneity (one aspect of our index of pluralism) and a broad range of economic, demographic, and political variables. For these, see R. Gregg, 'The UN Regional Economic Commissions and integration in the underdeveloped regions', *International Organization*, 1966, 10, 2, pp. 208–32 and J. A. Fishman, 'Some contrasts between linguistically homogeneous and linguistically heterogeneous polities', *Sociological Inquiry*, 1966, 36, 2, pp. 146–58. Taken together, these studies indicate some of the further possibilities of investigating the issue of pluralism with the aid of cross-national statistics.

15 Cf. 'The ideas of the ruling class are in every epoch the ruling ideas; i.e. the class which is the ruling material force of society is at the same time its ruling intellectual force.' K. Marx, *The German Ideology*.

16 Berger and Luckman (1967), op. cit., p. 134.

17 S. Carmichael, 'Black power', in *The Dialectics of Liberation*, ed. by David Cooper (Harmondsworth: Penguin, 1968), pp. 157–8. The psychological consequences of this have also been examined by Franz Fanon; see, for instance, his *Black Skins and White Masks* (London: MacGibbon & Kee, 1968).

18 Cf., for example, Peter J. Fleiss, *International Relations in the Bipolar World* (New York: Random House, 1968).

19 The expression is the late President Kennedy's, cited in Fleiss, op. cit., p. 68. For the common strategies of the two superpowers, cf. especially chapter 5 of this book.

20 Berger and Luckman, op. cit., p. 141.

21 Aesthetic patterns have been granted little attention in sociological theories of culture. For an account emphasizing their relevancy, see

G. Jaeger and P. Selznick, 'A normative theory of culture', *ASR*, 1964, 29, 5, pp. 653–69. One attempt to integrate artistic styles within general sociological theory is contained in the work of V. Kavolis: see his *Artistic Expression: A Sociological Analysis* (Cornell University Press, 1968).

22 E. Shils, 'Primordial, personal, sacred, and civil ties', *British Journal of Sociology*, 1957, 8, 2.

23 Johan Galtung, *Theory and Methods of Social Research* (London: Allen & Unwin, 1969).

24 The phrase is from H. Garfinkel, 'Studies of the routine grounds of everyday activities', in his *Studies in Ethnomethodology* (Englewood Cliffs, N. J.: Prentice-Hall, 1967), ch. 2, pp. 35–75.

25 C. Lévi-Strauss, *The Savage Mind* (London: Weidenfeld & Nicolson, 1966), p. 268.

26 Berger and Luckman, op. cit., pp. 26–7.

27 Impressive evidence on the institutional aspects of this is provided by Peter Drucker, *The Age of Discontinuity* (London: Heinemann, 1969), when he writes:

> The 'knowledge industries', which produce and distribute ideas and information rather than goods and services, accounted in 1955 for one quarter of the US gross national product. This was already three times the proportion of the national product that the country had spent on the 'knowledge sector' in 1900. Yet by 1965, ten years later, the knowledge sector was taking one third of a much bigger national product. In the late 1970s it will account for one half of the total national product. Every other dollar earned and spent in the American economy will be earned by producing and distributing ideas and information or will be spent on procuring ideas and information.

For application of the idea of the 'informed society' to political science, see R. E. Lane, 'The decline of politics and ideology in a knowledgeable society', *ASR*, 1966, 31. The pioneering work which has stimulated much subsequent research on the growth rate of the natural sciences is D. J. de Solla Price, *Little Science, Big Science* (Columbia University Press, 1963); cf. also Alvin M. Weinberg, *Reflections on Big Science* (Cambridge, Mass.: MIT Press, 1967). The principles of the measurability of scientific development, and of its characteristic exponential growth rate were established in de Solla Price's study. However, the rate of expansion of the social sciences, since the late nineteenth century, has surely been similarly exponential, although we know of no exact data on this topic. On the present general topic, cf. also D. N. Chorafas, *The Knowledge Revolution* (London: Allen & Unwin, 1970).

28 Thus, national survey data of this kind can serve as one indicator of the efficacy of socialist policies in particular countries.

29 It is, of course, often very difficult to test the degree to which this is so directly, i.e. by the use of survey methods. This is mainly because of the problems involved in constructing culture-fair knowledge questions. A recent cross-national survey in Europe, for instance—reported in

*Images of the World 2000* (Hague: Mouton, 1971)—found that the countries which were apparently best informed about issues such as the membership of NATO and similar organizations were not those which were most economically (and educationally) advanced, but rather were the ones whose national defence systems were most dependent upon the existence of these organizations.

30 Cf. J. Galtung, 'After Camelot', in I. L. Horowitz (ed.) *The Rise and Fall of Project Camelot* (Cambridge, Mass.: M.I.T. Press, 1967), pp. 281–312.

31 E. J. B. Rose *et al.*, *Colour and Citizenship* (Oxford University Press, 1969).

32 Cf. the distinction (p. 92 supra) between real and perceived consensus.

33 J. Galtung, *Theory and Methods of Social Research* (1969), pp. 152–3. Alternative methods of inquiry to the traditional survey are discussed in chapter 8 infra.

34 Examples which come to mind are Zola's *Germinal*, London's *Children of the Abyss*, possibly Steinbeck's *Grapes of Wrath*. Occupying an almost intermediate position between 'realistic' literature and social science are some of the studies of Oscar Lewis on the culture of poverty. Here the literary element enters at the stage of editing and organizing the recorded interviews: see especially *The Children of Sánchez* (Harmondsworth: Penguin, 1964, first pub. 1961) and *La Vida* (London: Secker & Warburg, 1967).

35 See, for instance, B. Bernstein, 'A socio-linguistic approach to socialisation: with some reference to educability', in J. Gumperz and Dell Hymes (eds), *Directions in Sociolinguistics* (New York: Holt, Rinehart & Winston, 1970).

36 Cf. P. R. Hawkins, 'Social class, the national group and reference', *Language and Speech*, 1969, 12, 2, p. 125f. Much of the factual data on this topic has been generated from research carried out at the University of London Institute of Education. See, e.g., W. Brandis and D. Henderson, *Social Class, Language and Communication* (London: Routledge & Kegan Paul, 1970) and G. J. Turner and B. A. Mohan, *A Linguistic Description and Computer Program for Children's Speech* (London: Routledge & Kegan Paul, 1970).

37 W. P. Robinson and S. J. Rackstraw, 'Variations in mothers' answers to children's questions, as a function of social class, verbal intelligence test scores and sex', *Sociology*, 1967, 1, 3, pp. 259–76.

38 Put otherwise, language is characteristically apprehended in the same absolutized and reified terms as other cultural artifacts, and this holds also for its metalinguistic aspects.

39 Ray L. Birdwhistell, *Introduction to Kinesics* (University of Louisville Press, 1952), and *Kinesics and Context* (London: Allen Lane, 1971).

40 E. T. Hall, *The Silent Language* (New York: Doubleday, 1959) and idem, *The Hidden Dimension* (London: Bodley Head, 1969). Cf. also his articles, 'The anthropology of manners', *Scientific American*, 1955, 192, pp. 84–90 and 'A system for the notation of proxemic behavior', *American Anthropologist*, 1963, 65, pp. 1003–26. Hall uses rather impressionistic examples often to 'confirm' his arguments, but

his work is suggestive, and may eventually lend itself to more precise, analytic treatment.

41 The importance of everyday language for sociology and psychology has been stressed by R. S. Peters in *The Concept of Motivation* (London: Routledge & Kegan Paul, 1960). As he writes, 'ordinary language enshrines all sorts of distinctions, the fine shades of which often elude the clumsiness of a highly general theory.' And again, 'We know *so much* about human beings, and our knowledge is incorporated implicitly in our language. Making it explicit could be a more fruitful preliminary to developing a theory than gaping at rats or grey geese' (pp. 49, 50). This is very much in line with some modern analytic philosophy, one influential school of which has emphasized the wisdom implicit in everyday utterances.

The psychologist, Peter Madison, adopts a similar view and argues that 'distinctions made in our everyday language are far richer and more complex than those made in psychological theory today, and that, consequently, common sense is not to be dismissed as lightly as psychology tends to do. In fact, it should be regarded as our principal source of theoretical knowledge about man, to which psychology has only added in modest ways as yet.' From T. Mischel (ed.), *Human Action: Conceptual and Empirical Issues* (London: Academic Press, 1969), p. 253.

42 Hall (1959), op. cit., p. 171.

43 See Hall (1969) and (1963), both op. cit. An experimental test of some of Hall's hypotheses regarding the different proxemic behaviour of Arab and American students is given in O. M. Watson and T. D. Graves, 'Quantitative research in proxemic behavior', *American Anthropologist*, 1966, 68, 1, pp. 971–85.

44 See M. Argyle, *The Psychology of Interpersonal Behaviour* (Harmondsworth: Penguin, 1967) and idem, *Social Interaction* (London: Methuen, 1969). Argyle's research has been mainly conducted under a series of controlled experimental conditions, and so his interpretations tend to be more firmly grounded in empirical evidence. Other references on the present subject include J. Ruesch and W. Kees, *Non-Verbal Communication: Notes on the Visual Perception of Human Relations* (University of California Press, 1956) and T. Burns, 'Non-verbal communication', *Discovery*, 1964, 25, 10, pp. 30–7.

45 W. G. Runciman, 'What is structuralism?' *British Journal of Sociology*, 1969, 20, pp. 253–65.

46 As one author states, 'The term "ethnoscience" is unfortunate for two reasons—first, because it suggests that other kinds of ethnography are *not* science, and second because it suggests that folk classifications and folk taxonomies *are* science.' (W. P. Spaulding, Unpublished paper (1963). Cited in W. C. Sturtevant, 'Studies in ethnoscience', *American Anthropologist*, 1964, 66, 3, pt II, Special Publication: 'Transcultural Studies in Cognition', pp. 99–131.) However, usage of the term might be justified on the grounds that repeated studies have demonstrated 'primitive' classificatory systems to be *analogous* to modern science in their degree of rigour and consistency.

47 H. C. Conklin, 'Lexicographical treatment of folk taxonomies', *International Journal of American Linguistics*, 1962, 28, 2, pp. 119–41; C. O. Frake, 'The ethnographic study of cognitive systems' in T. Gladwin and W. C. Sturtevant (eds), *Anthropology and Human Behavior* (Anthropological Society of Washingon, 1962), pp. 72–85, 91–3; and W. C. Sturtevant, op. cit. (1964).

48 Emile Durkheim and M. Mauss, *Primitive Classification* (London: Cohen, 1963).

49 W. H. Goodenough, 'Property, kin, and community on Truk', *Yale University Publications in Anthropology*, 1951, 46 and idem, 'Componential analysis and the study of meaning', *Language*, 1956, 32, 2, pp. 195–216; F. G. Lounsbury, 'A semantic analysis of the Pawnee kinship usage', *Language*, 1956, 32, 1, pp. 158–94. For a logical formalization of Lounsbury's account, see chapter 8, pp. 299ff. infra.

50 Op. cit., p. 75.

51 See, for instance, H. C. Conklin, 'Hanunóo color categories', *Southwestern Journal of Anthropology*, 1955, 11, 4, pp. 339–44 and H. J. Landar, S. M. Ervin, and A. E. Horowitz, 'Navaho color categories', *Language*, 1960, 36, 3, pp. 368–82.

52 See C. O. Frake, 'The diagnosis of disease among the Subanun of Mindanao', *American Anthropologist*, 1961, 63, 1, pp. 113–32.

53 Runciman (1969), op. cit., suggests that one might view Lévi-Strauss's 'structuralism' 'less as a doctrine of what societies are and how their workings are to be explained than as a fresh attempt to resolve for social science as a whole the perennial conflict between idealism and empiricism' (p. 261).

54 This is implicit, for instance, in his remark that 'If and when we solve the problem of the origin of language we shall understand how culture can appear within nature and how the transition from one category to the other was able to occur.' G. Charbonnier, *Conversations with Lévi-Strauss* (London: Cape, 1969), p. 154.

55 C. Lévi-Strauss, *The Savage Mind* (1966), p. 75.

56 E. Leach, 'The legitimacy of Solomon', *European Journal of Sociology*, 1966, 7, p. 80.
Lévi-Strauss takes up the question of whether his accounts of particular myths can claim any epistemologically privileged status in *The Raw and the Cooked: Introduction to a Science of Mythology*, vol. 1 (New York: Harper & Row, 1969; first published (in French) 1964).

57 See, for instance, J. Dollard *et al.*, *Frustration and Aggression* (Yale University Press, 1939) and L. Berkowitz, *Aggression: A Social Psychological Analysis* (New York: McGraw-Hill, 1962).

58 R. A. Hinde, 'The nature of aggression', *New Society*, March 1967, p. 304.

59 In England, L. T. Hogben and J. B. S. Haldane were the first to reject the idea of a *general* solution to the problem of estimating the size of the contribution made by nature and nurture to overt (phenotypic) behaviour patterns. This was essentially because the relative contribution made by nature is itself a function of nurture (environment, learning, etc.).

60 Roger Brown, *Social Psychology* (London: Collier-Macmillan, 1967), pp. 394–5.
61 See F. Fraser Darling, *Wilderness and Plenty* (London: BBC Publications, 1970), in which it is suggested that man should begin to assume an attitude of *noblesse oblige* towards nature.
62 K. Watt *et al.*, 'A model of society', *Simulation*, 1970, 14, 4, p. 153.
63 For a recent summary, see 'Scientific American' (eds), *The Biosphere* (San Francisco: Freeman, 1971).
64 One method likely to be further developed for this purpose is computer simulation. The method is described in chapter 8. It was used, for example, by Watt *et al.* (1970), op. cit., in order to investigate the multiple consequences to society and to the 'human ecosystem' which result from rapidly rising population densities.

PART TWO: REVIEW OF RESEARCH

Chapter 5

1 Cf. Lévi-Strauss (1966, 1969), op. cit.
2 See the references to ethnoscience in chapter 4. And for a brief example of this consistency and completeness in a preliterate system of 'natural science', see also L. B. Glick, 'Categories and relations in Gini natural science', *American Anthropologist*, 1964, 66, Special Publication, 'New Guinea: The Central Highlands', pp. 273–80.
3 Relevant here is the argument that the existence of language in society necessarily entails that norms of truth-telling be established. For this, cf. particularly Peter Winch, 'Nature and convention', *Proceedings of the Aristotelian Society*, 1959–60, LX. See also A. C. MacIntyre, *A Short History of Ethics* (1967), p. 77.
4 The first example was suggested to me by Professor MacIntyre and invites comparison with Banfield's (1958) study of 'amoral familism' in Southern Italy, which we cited earlier. The second example is drawn from John Ladd (1957), op. cit.; Ladd also presents the rationale for this practice in terms of Navaho beliefs. As in the case of the Bantu, these involve ideas regarding supernatural threats, and witchcraft.
5 Adapted from J. Galtung, *Theory and Methods of Social Research* (1969), p. 91.
6 Ibid., p. 124.
7 If true, this is probably related to Spanish values of individualism and assertion, especially for the male: the term *arrogante*, for instance, often has positive connotations. Thus, it may be that a greater margin of disbelief is ascribed to an individual's assertions, whilst he is also expected to exaggerate more. On this, see espec. C. Lison-Tolosana (1966), op. cit. and cf. pp. 216f. infra.
8 Galtung (1969), op. cit., p. 126.
9 From W. A. Scott, *Values and Organizations* (Chicago: Rand McNally,

1965), p. 37. This indicates that the values of intellectualism and religiousness are the best predictors of overt behaviour, and those of kindness and independence the least so. *Why* this should be the case, Scott does not examine, although it is a question which might itself prove amenable to sociological explanation. This assumes, of course, that the results are not artifacts of the indices chosen. In the case of the value of loyalty, for instance, the behavioural index was based on responses to questions concerning the frequency of attendance at meetings and the amount of time devoted to organizations of which the subject was a member. But other, possibly more valid, measures might also have been used. For instance, using a revised version of the original value scales, Scott later examined the relation between verbal responses to these scales and behaviour as judged by friends of the subject. The results are given in Table N5.1.

TABLE N5.1  *Correlations between professed values
and behaviour as judged by friends*
(N=259)

| Value | r |
|-------|---|
| Intellectualism | 0·07 |
| Kindness | 0·32† |
| Social skills | 0·33† |
| Loyalty | 0·27† |
| Academic achievement | 0·11* |
| Physical development | 0·14* |
| Status | 0·04 |
| Honesty | 0·23† |
| Religiousness | 0·52† |
| Self-control | 0·12* |
| Creativity | 0·17** |
| Independence | 0·27* |

\* $\propto 0\cdot05$          Source: Scott, ibid.,
\*\* $\propto 0\cdot01$         p. 259
† $\propto 0\cdot001$

Again, Table N5.1 indicates that, at least for ten of the twelve values, there is a significant correlation between subjects' verbal responses to the value-scales and the way in which their friends judge their behaviour. To this, Scott adds (pp. 259–60):

The two exceptions to this general trend occur for the values of intellectualism and status. Either these two values were not well manifest in overt behaviour or else the raters judged them by cues different from those referred to in the scale items. By contrast the correlation between judged religiousness and score on the religious value was .52 (95 % confidence interval between .43 and .60), which indicates a considerable degree of consensus in the culture concerning the meaning and behavioral manifestations of this value.

But although Scott does not spell this out, the above may also be taken to indicate that the method of using friends' reports, or even self-reports, as an index of behaviour will vary in efficiency depending on the particular value at stake. That this is so can be clearly seen if we think of the values of religiousness and, say, self-control and honesty in these terms. As a result, it would seem that, at least in the case of some values, more experimental and direct observational data will be needed in order to permit adequate inquiries into the interrelationships between attitudes and actions. A number of the available studies of this type are discussed in the present chapter, on p. 131f.

10 A classic example of the use of panel analysis in political science is the study by P. F. Lazarsfeld, B. Berelson, and H. Gaudet, *The People's Choice* (New York: Columbia University Press, 1948).

11 One simple respect in which knowledge can affect the attitude/action relationship is summed up by the fact that some people do not put their expressed values into practice largely because they do not know how to; for an empirical study which raises this issue, see the discussion of Kreitler and Kreitler's research, p. 123f.

12 This table, and the study it is part of, are described in J. W. Getzels and J. J. Walsh, 'The method of paired direct and projective questionnaires in the study of attitude structure and socialization', *Psychological Monographs*, 1958, 72, 1, 1; for discussion of the significance of the J-curve, see F. Fearing and E. M. Krise, 'Conforming behaviour and the J-curve hypothesis', *Journal of Social Psychology*, 1941, 14, 1.

13 Getzels and Walsh, op. cit.

14 Most of the longitudinal studies in this field, however, have been concerned with testing the expectations to be derived 'balance theory' with respect to relationships among attitudes. A good example of this is provided by M. J. Rosenberg and R. P. Abelson, 'An analysis of cognitive balancing', in C. I. Hovland and M. J. Rosenberg (eds), *Attitude Organization and Change* (Yale University Press, 1960), pp. 112–63. However, essentially similar theoretical ideas could be tested in terms of consistencies between attitudes and actions over time. On this, cf., for instance, H. J. Erlich, 'Attitudes, behaviour, and the intervening variables', *American Sociologist*, 1969, 4, 1, pp. 29–34 which proposes a paradigm for the analysis of the relations of attitudes to behaviour, particularly with respect to prejudice and discrimination.

15 H. Kreitler and S. Kreitler, 'Crucial dimensions of the attitude towards national and supra-national ideals: A study of Israeli youth', *Journal of Peace Research*, 1967, 2, pp. 107–24.

16 Both tables have been adapted from those given in Kreitler and Kreitler, op. cit.

17 Ibid.

18 See, for instance, A. Cambell, *The American Voter* (New York: Wiley, 1960), pp. 104–5

19 Cf. A. Cambell *et al.*, 'Sense of political efficacy and political participation', in H. Eulau *et al.* (eds), *Political Behavior* (Chicago: Free Press, 1956), pp. 172–3.

391

20 On this, cf. chapter 3 supra.

21 See p. 140 infra.

22 Cf. the examples on p. 116.

23 Goffman uses the term 'role distance' to denote those cases in which particular social roles are self-consciously 'acted out': see Erving Goffman, *Encounters* (Englewood Cliffs, N. J.: Prentice-Hall, 1961). Such purely presentational roles are particularly likely to be encountered in coercive environments, or in situations clearly structured in subordinate-superordinate terms. For instance, Bantu in South Africa may self-consciously attempt to match certain white expectations, and thereby exercise also a covert form of protest. That is, they may derive some satisfaction from a role which allows them, for example, to 'go slow' at work, and to commit a variety of errors and omissions, particularly since other avenues of expression are barred.

However, although an element of role-distance may be inherent in many social situations, particularly in modern society, this should not lead us to understate the degree to which individuals may come to identify with their roles, and with the typified attitudes and actions which they encompass. As Berger and Luckman (1967) state: 'To learn a role it is not enough to acquire the routines immediately necessary for its "outward" performance. One must also be initiated into the various cognitive and even affective layers of the body of knowledge that is directly *and* indirectly appropriate to this role.' Hence, it is perhaps more commonly the case that 'the actor identifies with the socially objectivated typifications of conduct *in actu*, but re-establishes distance from them as he reflects about his conduct afterwards.' (Excerpts from Berger and Luckman, 1967 op. cit. pp. 94, 91). The element of *mauvaise foi*, of course, enters where the individual denies his choice between available courses of action on the basis of his identification with a given social role.

24 E. T. Hall (1959), op. cit., pp. 83–4.

25 R. LaPiere, 'Attitudes vs. actions', *Social Forces*, 1934, 13, pp. 230–7.

26 Ibid., p. 233.

27 M. L. DeFleur and F. R. Westie, 'Verbal attitudes and overt acts: An experiment on the salience of attitudes', *ASR*, 1958, 23, pp. 667–73.

28 Viz. age, sex (half of each group was male), marital status, religion, social class, social mobility experience, residential history, and previous contact with negroes.

29 In brief, the autonomic measures consisted of galvanic skin responses and changes in finger blood volume in relation to the stimuli. These measures were shown to effectively discriminate between subjects classified as prejudiced and unprejudiced. Other studies have supported this finding: see, for instance, J. B. Cooper and D. Pollock, 'The identification of prejudicial attitudes by the galvanic skin response', *Journal of Social Psychology*, 1959, 50, pp. 241–5. The advantage of these measures for the study of attitudes, and especially as means of checking verbal responses, is of course, their presumed 'objectivity'. That is, they are usually taken to be beyond the subject's control. Current research indicates that such measures may in the future be-

come more effectively related to important social-psychological variables and as such may become common as the dependent variables in this type of research. On this, cf. D. Shapiro and A. Crider, 'Psychophysiological approaches in social psychology' in G. Lindzey and E. Aronson (eds), *Handbook of Social Psychology* (London: Addison-Wesley, 1968), vol. 3, ch. 19.

30 J. D. Lohman and D. C. Reitzes, 'Deliberately organized groups and racial behavior', *ASR*, 1954, 19, pp. 342–8.

31 Cf. the discussion of observational methods in chapter 8 infra.

32 The term was introduced by E. H. Sutherland, 'White collar criminality', *ASR*, 1940, 5, pp. 1–12. See also idem, 'Is "white collar crime" crime?', *ASR*, 1945, 10, 2, pp. 132–9; and V. Aubert, 'White-collar crime and social structure', *AJS*, 1952, 58, 3, pp. 263–71.

33 LaPiere, op. cit., p. 236. The use of survey methods in the study of moral codes is discussed in chapter 7 infra.

34 C. R. Tittle and R. J. Hill, 'Attitude measurement and prediction of behavior: An evaluation of conditions and measurement techniques', *Sociometry*, 1967, 30, pp. 199–213.

35 Tittle and Hill, op. cit., p. 203 (modified version of their Table 1).

36 Ibid., p. 202.

37 Cf. H. J. Parry and H. M. Crossley, 'Validity of responses to survey questions', *Public Opinion Quarterly*, 1950, 14, pp. 61–80.

38 Tittle and Hill, op. cit., pp. 210–11.

39 Ibid., p. 213.

40 Cf. chapter 3.

41 Cf. p. 50 supra, and the distinction between the evaluation of *actions* and *agents* with regard to ethical relativism in chapter 9.

42 For a brief introduction, cf. K. M. Sen, *Hinduism* (Harmondsworth: Penguin, 1970 edn), especially Pt I.

43 Cf. M. Watt, *Islam and the Integration of Society* (Evanston: Northwestern University Press, 1961) and R. Levy, *The Social Structure of Islam* (Cambridge University Press, 1957).

44 V. Steinitz, 'Cognitive imbalance: A considered response to a complicated situation', *Human Relations*, 1969, 22, 4, pp. 287–308. Cf. also F. Heider, 'Attitudes and cognitive organization', *Journal of Psychology*, 1946, 21, pp. 107–112 and idem, *The Psychology of Interpersonal Relations* (New York: Wiley, 1958); L. Festinger, *A Theory of Cognitive Dissonance* (Evanston: Row-Peterson, 1957); R. P. Abelson and M. J. Rosenberg, 'Symbolic psycho-logic: a model of attitudinal cognition', *Behavioural Science*, 1958, 3, pp. 1–13; and M. J. Rosenberg and R. P. Abelson (1960) op. cit. See, too, R. P. Abelson *et al.*, *Theories of Cognitive Consistency: A Source Book* (Chicago: Rand McNally, 1968).

45 The 'drive towards consistency' theory of attitude organization has been mainly interpreted in terms of psychological dynamics that is, evidence has been adduced to show that individuals prefer 'balanced' states, feel uncomfortable when presented with imbalance, and strive to change their attitudes in ways that will restore balance. However, these processes may also be approached in more sociological terms:

that is, recognition could be given to the *social* factors which demand consistency within systems of attitudes, and to the ways in which existing inconsistencies may be successfully disguised or rationalized. A good example of the latter would be the redefinition of Christianity in South Africa in order to match the realities of *apartheid*. In this way, the findings of balance theory could be applied within a more institutional, less individualistic, context.

46 Steinitz, op. cit., p. 288.

47 One of the main virtues of simulation procedures of this kind is that they allow for the relatively 'spontaneous' elicitation of justifications for expressed attitudes. For further discussion of these techniques, see chapter 8, p. 290f.

48 Cf. especially A. C. MacIntyre, 'A mistake about causality in social science', in P. Laslett and W. G. Runciman, *Philosophy, Politics, and Society* (Oxford: Blackwell, 1964), 2nd Series, pp. 48–70, in which this is very clearly spelled out. Compare also idem, 'The idea of a social science', *Proceedings of the Aristotelian Society*, 1967, pp. 95–114, where the original formulation of a basic incompatibility of explanation in terms of reasons and causes is qualified and it is argued that one may speak, without logical impropriety, of an agent's 'possessing a reason' as a cause of his action. On this, see too the following paper by D. R. Bell, loc. cit., pp. 115–32. Both of these articles, of course, are concerned mainly with the epistemological views of Peter Winch, q.v. *The Idea of a Social Science* (London: Routledge & Kegan Paul, 1958). Cf. also A. C. MacIntyre, *Against the Self-Images of the Age* (London: Duckworth, 1971) pt 2.

49 Op. cit., p. 52.

50 Cf. C. G. A. Bryant, 'In defence of sociology: a reply to some contemporary philosophical criticisms', *BJS*, 1970, 21, 1, pp. 95–107. Bryant argues that certain philosophical critics of sociology (namely, Winch, Louch, and MacIntyre) have over-emphasized the sociologist's concern with accounting for *action*, and thereby have failed to appreciate the diversity of sociological explanations.

## Chapter 6

1 Cf. p. 22f. and 49f. for criticisms of this practice.

2 For discussion of the distinction between precepts and values and for the tendency of sociologists to take an approbationist view of their interrelationships, cf. chapter 3 supra.

3 These major journals include, for instance, the *American Sociological Review*, the *British Journal of Sociology*, the *European Journal of Sociology*, and the *American Journal of Sociology*

4 Cf. Table 6.3, p. 156 infra.

5 The work of the normative functionalists, of course, most clearly illustrates this.

6 Cf. Table 6.7, p. 162 infra.

7 Cf., for example, F. Musgrove, *Youth and the Social Order* (Indiana University Press, 1965).

8 The comment by MacIntyre cited on p. 19 above is, therefore, particularly relevant to this section of society.

9 Cf. Joffre Dumazedier, *Toward a Society of Leisure* (New York: Free Press, 1967; first published (French edn) 1962). The decline of the traditional Protestant virtues in Western society in favour of a more materialistic, other-directed ethic has become, of course, a familiar thesis in social science; for an influential account, see David Riesman, *The Lonely Crowd* (Yale University Press, 1950).

10 On this question, see K. Baier and N. Rescher (eds), *Values and the Future* (New York: Collier-Macmillan, 1969).

11 See Table 6.7.

12 As is well known, it is common to use social science and psychology students in social research, particularly of the experimental type, and so their participation might often appear to be considered part of their coursework.

13 We noted, though have not measured, an increase over time in the use of *analytic* statistics, as distinct from statistics of the purely descriptive kind. For confirmation of this trend, cf. J. Galtung, *Theory and Methods of Social Research* (1969), pp. 500–4.

14 For available studies, see n.10 to the Introduction.

15 M. Popovich, 'What the American sociologists think about their science and its problems', *American Sociologist*, 1966, 1, 3, pp. 133–5.

16 Cf. Tables 6.6 and 6.8.

17 Thus the role of Weber's Protestant Ethic, and of its secular variants (e.g. achievement orientation) and possible ideological surrogates (e.g. nationalism), provides a common theoretical reference point for many of these studies. For a bibliography on this subject, see John Brode, *The Process of Modernization* (Oxford University Press, 1969).

18 Cf. the discussion of 'instrumentalism' in chapter 3.

19 In the case of the two major powers, Russia and the United States, together with China, this interdependency is arguably more political than economic in nature; thus, Galtung has shown that these powers are among those with the smallest parts of their economies devoted to international commerce, and so comparatively unsusceptible to economic sanctions: see his 'On the effects of international economic sanctions, with examples from the case of Rhodesia', *World Politics*, 1967, 19, 3, pp. 378–416.

20 Cf. J. Galtung, 'On the future of the international system', in Robert Jungk and J. Galtung (eds), *Mankind 2000* (London: Allen and Unwin, 1969), pp. 12–41. This, of course, assumes the validity of the relative deprivation thesis in international affairs. But this seems an eminently reasonable, if simplifying, assumption. Given this, we may note that there is every evidence that the relative gap between North and South will grow over the next few decades: see, for instance, the economic extrapolations in Herman Kahn and A. J. Wiener, *The Year 2000: A Framework for Speculation on the Next Thirty-Three Years* (London: Collier-Macmillan, 1967). The inequality is already very considerable: as one estimate of it states, 'At present, the gap between percapita income in developed and less-developed countries is $1,540; at the

present rate of growth it will be $5,450 by the end of the century'—
(Lester Pearson, *Peace in the Family of Man*, BBC Publications, 1969).
Some empirical confirmation of the relative saliency of North/South
relations may be obtained, for example, from an analysis of trends in
United Nations debates and their attendant voting patterns. On this,
cf. Bruce M. Russett, *Trends in World Politics* (New York: Macmillan,
1965) and K. Jacobsen, 'Some aspects of UN voting patterns', in
*Proceedings of IPRA Second Conference*, vol. 1 (Assen: Van Gorcum,
1968).

21 Although this does not mean that value analysis bears no relationship
to demographic studies; cf. p. 170f. infra.

22 Whatever its limitations, one of the few accounts in sociology of the
values that are conducive to, and implicit in, the scientific enterprise is
Bernard Barber's *Science and the Social Order* (Chicago: Free Press,
1952). From an historical point of view, the interrelationships between
Protestantism and scientific activity have particular interest for social
science: on this, cf. ref. 3.85 and also 3.51 above. See too I. Thorner,
'Ascetic Protestantism and the development of science and technology',
*AJS*, 1953, 58. For a recent empirical study of the values of scientists
in industry, cf. S. Cotgrove and S. Box, *Science, Industry and Society*
(London: Allen & Unwin, 1970). This demonstrates that differential
socialization and occupational choice are important mechanisms
which moderate the potential conflict of values between science and
industry.

23 Cf. n.10 to the Introduction. We acknowledge that some sources of
bias here may be due to the categorization of studies. For instance,
some items included under the sociology of occupations could be
classed as part of the sociology of science (e.g. Cotgrove and Box,
1970, op. cit.).

24 E.g., by J. P. Gibbs, 'The sociology of law and normative phenomena',
*ASR*, 1966, 31.

25 See Jaeger and Selznick (1964), op. cit.

26 Almost the only general study is Dumazedier (1967), op. cit., in which
the need for adequate planning for leisure activities is emphasized,
particularly within the context of French society.

The question of leisure grows in importance in modern society, of
course, as the saliency of work diminishes; and this is the case both in
the sense of a gradual decrease in the amount of time spent at work,
and also in terms of changing orientations to work. Thus, as a result
of familar socio-technical processes—job specialization, bureaucratization, automation—work activities as such become less of a focus for
an individual's values and aspirations, and a sense of autonomy and
achievement is increasingly realized in the non-work areas of life.
Robert Dubin, for instance, found in his study of several hundred
industrial workers that work was a central life interest for only a small
minority: cf. his 'Industrial workers' worlds: A study of the "central
life interests," of industrial workers' *Social Problems*, 1956, 4, pp.
131–42.

This, of course, is less applicable to professional and executive workers, where greater possibilities of self-determination and creativity generally exist, and may indeed in some cases compensate for monetary losses: cf. J. J. Marsh and F. P. Stafford, 'The effects of values on pecuniary behavior: the case of academics', *AJS*, 1967, 32, 5, pp. 740–54; see too M. Rosenberg, *Occupations and Values* (Chicago: Free Press, 1957).

But for both groups the problem remains of the kind of influence that is exercised by the nature of work itself on other, non-work areas of life. Aside from a few suggestive community studies—such as Dennis *et al.*, *Coal is Our Life* (London: Eyre & Spottiswoode, 1956) and possibly W. H. Whyte's *The Organization Man* (New York: Simon & Schuster, 1956)—this question largely awaits systematic investigation.

And such research, by throwing light on patterns of leisure activity, would not only be of theoretical interest to social science, but would also have a practical value. It has been estimated, for instance, that there will be a fortyfold increase in the patronage of vacation and resort areas in the United States by the year 2000. And similar developments will, no doubt, characterize other industrial societies. To make adequate provision for these coming recreational needs, then, we shall need much more information than we have at present as to the nature of these needs, and as to the likely consequences of their fulfilment. However, there is some evidence that leisure is gradually becoming accepted as a legitimate subject for research. Indicative of this change, for instance, is the publication, in America, of a *Journal of Leisure Research*.

27 It is noteworthy that *Sociological Abstracts* introduced a new coding category in 1969 for studies devoted to futurology. Illustrative of this development are the studies by Kahn and Wiener (1967), op. cit. and Jungk and Galtung (1969), op. cit. See too D. Bell (ed.), 'The year 2000: Work in progress', *Daedalus*, Summer, 1967. An influential statement on the character of 'post-industrial' society is contained in D. Bell, 'Notes on the post-industrial society', *The Public Interest*, 1967, nos 6 and 7. Preferable, in our view, would be the development, alongside such analyses of possible and probable (e.g. Kahn's 'surprise-free' projections) futures, of more public debate on criteria for *desirable* futures, with a continuing exchange of ideas between these two enterprises. Perhaps the emergence of publications such as the journal, *Futures*, can help stimulate such debate.

28 Alternative methods to the standard survey are discussed in chapter 8 infra.

29 Cf. D. T. Cambell and D. W. Fiske, 'Convergent and discriminant validation by the multitrait-multimethod matrix', *Psychological Bulletin*, 1959, 56, pp. 81–105, in which some of the merits of a multimethod design are spelled out. The case for such designs is also argued in N. K. Denzin, *The Research Act in Sociology* (London: Butterworth, 1971).

30 For discussion of such methods, see chapter 8. It should be noted in this connection that the studies coded under the category of 'Observation'

exhibited varying degrees of rigour in the procedures used. Since it was difficult to draw any hard and fast line here as to which studies should be included, we admitted a number of inquiries in which the methods of observation were relatively informal. Thus, if anything we have understated the degree of emphasis upon information of a purely verbal kind.

31 See chapter 5.
32 Cf. also chapter 8 infra.
33 Russett *et al.* (1964), op. cit., pp. 293–303.
34 These stages comprise GNPs per capita (in $ U.S.) of 262–794 and 108–239 respectively.
35 Calculated from Russett, loc. cit.
36 In fact, the distribution of population per stage of development is as shown in Table N6.1.

TABLE N6.1.  *Population size and stages of development\**

| Stage | % of Total Population |
|-------|-----------------------|
| I     | 3·8                   |
| II    | 53·5†                 |
| III   | 13·8                  |
| IV    | 12·7                  |
| V     | 16·2                  |

\*Calculated from Russett *et al.*, loc. cit.
†This high proportion is, of course, accounted for by the presence of Mainland China and India at this stage.

37 Cf. pp. 153–4 supra.
38 Based on our own assessment and that of a colleague who independently coded a sample (about 50 per cent) of the references.
39 And the majority of studies which did employ more than one method of inquiry still restricted themselves to verbal techniques.
40 E. J. Webb, D. T. Cambell, R. D. Schwartz, and L. Sechrest, *Unobtrusive Measures: Nonreactive Research in the Social Sciences* (Chicago: Rand McNally, 1968), p. 84. On this general topic, cf. also W. D. Wall and H. L. Williams, *Longitudinal Studies and the Social Sciences* (London: Heinemann, 1970).
41 R. Naroll, *Data Quality Control* (New York: Free Press, 1962).
42 Cf. L. A. Brookover and K. W. Back, 'Time sampling as a field technique', *Human Organization*, 1965, XII and R. Arrington, 'Time sampling in studies of social behavior: a critical review of techniques and results with research suggestions', *Psychological Bulletin*, 1943, 40, pp. 81–124.
43 L. G. Burchinal and L. E. Chancellor, 'Survival rates among religiously homogamous and interreligious marriages', *Social Forces*, 1963, 41, pp. 353–62.
44 R. DeCharms and G. Moeller, 'Values expressed in American

children's readers: 1800–1950', *Journal of Abnormal and Social Psychology*, 1962, 64, pp. 136–42.

45 *The Achieving Society* (Princeton: Van Nostrand, 1961).

46 See, for example, the contributions of Barrington Moore and Gerth and Landau to M. Stein and A. Vidich (eds), *Sociology on Trial* (Englewood Cliffs, N. J.: Prentice-Hall, 1963), pp. 26–34 and 66–95.

47 Cf. n. 6.27.

48 Chapter 4, p. 92f.

49 Hence the 'melting pot' thesis. For a useful discussion, see J. S. Roucek, 'The quest for the ramifications of the "cultural pluralism" concept', *Sociol. Int.*, 1965, 3, 2, pp. 129–68.

50 Yet although the ecological pluralism of, for instance, the United States has been given little recognition in its sociology, it has found expression in its literature: with such writers as Faulkner and Penn Warren analysing the culture of the South, Marquand the North-East, Steinbeck the Mid-West and West Coast, and so on. Perhaps too much attention has been afforded to the concept of the 'mass society', and too little to regional differences. One of the few discussions of pluralism in the present context is John Gillin, 'National and regional cultural values in the U.S.', *Social Forces*, 1955, 34, 2, pp. 107–13. Although see, too, H. J. Gans, 'Popular cultures in America: social problems in a mass society or social asset in a pluralist society?', in H. Becker (ed.), *Social Problems: A Modern Approach* (New York: Wiley, 1966). A similar criticism of a lack of ecologically-based studies in empirical political science has been made by Henry Pelling. However, his own work forms a useful exception to this; see his *Social Geography of British Elections* (London: Heinemann, 1968).

51 C. Osgood, 'On the strategy of cross-national research into subjective culture', *Social Science Information*, 1967, 6, 1, pp. 5–37.

52 Cf. W. E. Lambert and Otto Klineberg, *Children's Views of Foreign Peoples: A Cross-national Study* (New York: Appleton-Century-Crofts, 1967).

53 Compare Galtung's idea of sociology as the 'science of the socially possible' in his 'Rank and social integration: A multi-dimensional approach', in M. Berger *et al.*, *Sociological Theories in Progress* (Boston: Houghton Mifflin, 1966), pp. 145–98.

54 Based on our own assessment and on the independent coding of a sample of references (about 50 per cent) by a colleague.

55 For a similar observation on social research in Britain over the 1950s and 60s, see E. Krausz, *Sociology in Britain* (London: Batsford, 1969).

56 T. Parsons, 'The prospects of sociological theory', in his *Essays in Sociological Theory* (New York: Free Press, 1964 edn), p. 352.

57 In the United States, for instance, they represent a substantial proportion of the relevant age-group. Indeed, here the rapid expansion of higher education has, as one author states, 'produced a belief that college attendance is a part of the experience of coming of age in America': F. H. Bowles, 'Changing educational values', in R. M. MacIver (ed.), *Dilemmas of Youth in America Today* (New York: Harper, 1961).

58 See, for instance, Karl Mannheim, 'American sociology', in Stein and Vidich (1963), op. cit., pp. 3–11.
59 Cf., for instance, D. Lerner and H. D. Lasswell (eds), *The Policy Sciences* (Stanford University Press, 1951).
60 See, for instance, Fraser Darling (1970), op. cit.
61 M. Douglas, 'Population control in primitive groups', *British Journal of Sociology*, 1966, 17, 3, P. Vieille, 'Birth and death in an Islamic society', *Diogenes*, 1967, 57, pp. 101–27.
62 Cf. chapters 1–3.
63 Cf. chapter 3.
64 Cf. p. 70f. supra and chapter 8, p. 298f.
65 Cf. Peter Winch, *The Idea of a Social Science* (1958).
66 Cf. A. C. MacIntyre, 'The idea of a social science' (1967), loc. cit. and R. S. Peters, *The Concept of Motivation* (1960).
67 I. Berlin (1964), op. cit., p. 19.
68 Cf. chapter 3.
69 Op. cit., p. 28.
70 *The Lonely Crowd* (1950).
71 Op. cit., pp. 29–30.
72 See especially S. Rettig and B. Pasamanick, 'Changes in moral values among college students: A factorial study', *ASR*, 1959, 24; idem, 'Differences in the structure of moral values of students and alumni', *ASR*, 1960, 25, 4, pp. 550–5; idem, 'Moral value structure and social class', *Sociometry*, 1961, 24, 1, pp. 21–35; and B. Pasamanick, 'Invariance in factor structure of moral value judgements from U.S. and Korean college students', *Sociometry*, 1962, 25, 1, pp. 73–84. Cf. also Charles Morris (1956), op. cit. and L. V. Jones and R. D. Brock, 'Multiple discriminant analysis applied to "Ways to Live" ratings from six cultural groups', *Sociometry*, 1960, 23, 2, pp. 162–76.
73 Cf. the discussion of 'deontic logic' in chapter 8.
74 Reported in *Images of the World 2000* (Hague: Mouton, 1971).
75 See n. 5.44.
76 From Hazel Erskine, 'The polls: Negro philosophies of life', *Public Opinion Quarterly*, 1969, 33, 1, pp. 147–58.
77 See Bernstein (1970), op. cit., and Hawkins (1969) and Robinson and Rackstraw (1967), both op. cit.
78 See p. 119 supra and n. 5.9.
79 Op cit., p. 80.
80 Op. cit. A good example of the social structuring of attitudes among the well-educated, concerning the influence of ethnic differences upon attitudes within the Jewish, Catholic, and Protestant traditions, is the study by A. M. Greeley, reported in *Sociology of Education*, 1969, 42, 1, p. 98f.
81 This was one finding of Rose *et al.* (1969), op. cit.
82 For brief discussion of this, see p. 97f. supra.
83 For a useful discussion, see T. Nichols, *Ownership, Control and Ideology* (London: Allen & Unwin, 1969). Any attempt to account for managerial ideologies must, of course, view these within terms of the broader economic structure. One perceptive, if contentious, analysis of the

latter is provided by Paul Baran and Paul Sweezy, *Monopoly Capital* (Harmondsworth: Penguin, 1968).

84 Cf. J. Galtung, *Theory and Methods of Social Research* (1969), ch. 2. This subject, of course, raises important theoretical questions, and as such deserves far more attention than it has so far been given. See too n. 3.102.

85 J. K. Galbraith, 'The limits of super-power', *The Times*, 8 October, 1969.

86 D. Bell (1967), op. cit.

87 Modern sociological analysis of formal organizations begins, of course, with the work of Weber on the characteristics of 'bureaucracy' (see n. 3.79). Subsequent research has focused mainly on the structural attributes of organizations, and on the psychological consequences of these (cf. the well-known paper by Robert Merton, 'Bureaucratic structure and personality', *Social Forces*, 1940, 17, pp. 560–8). Less attention has been given to the more ideological characteristics of organizations and social institutions. One aspect of this, as we have seen above, concerns what might be termed the 'corporation ethic'; for which, cf. F. X. Sutton, S. E. Harris, C. Kaysen, and J. Tobin, *The American Business Creed* (Harvard University Press, 1956). But it also involves studying the ideologies associated with a much broader range of institutions and role-systems; to take two such examples, see, for instance, F. A. R. Bennion, *Professional Ethics* (London: Allen & Unwin, 1969), and E. Freidson, *Profession of Medicine* (New York: Dodd, Mead, 1970).

88 *Theory and Methods of Social Research* (1969), p. 150.

89 Ibid., pp. 150–1.

90 Ibid., pp. 151–2.

91 Cf. Raymond Aron, *Main Currents in Sociological Thought*, vol. I (London: Weidenfeld & Nicolson, 1965), Introduction, for a brief characterization of Soviet and American styles of sociology; cf., too, n. 1.4. The question of the interrelationships between social structure and styles of social research is one that largely awaits systematic exploration and aside from contributing to the sociology of science such an enterprise should also permit insight into the conditions that facilitate (or discourage) objectivity in social science.

92 See also the comments on reflexive sociology in A. W. Gouldner, *The Coming Crisis in Western Sociology* (London: Heinemann, 1971). It should be noted that a number of the defining characteristics of the prevailing style of social research, as of changes in this style, that have been observed in the present chapter have been independently corroborated by other studies, giving us greater confidence in the generality of our findings. On this, cf. particularly J. S. Brown and B. G. Gilmartin, 'Sociology today: lacunae, emphases, and surfeits', *American Sociologist*, 1969, 4, 4, pp. 283–91 and J. L. McCartney, 'On being scientific: changing styles of presentation of sociological research', *American Sociologist*, 1970, 5, 1, pp. 30–5.

**Chapter 7**

1 Among the standard texts on interview and questionnaire procedure are H. Hyman *et al.*, *Interviewing in Social Research* (University of Chicago Press, 1954); idem, *Survey Design and Analysis* (London: Collier-Macmillan, 1955); C. Sellitz *et al.*, *Research Methods in Social Relations* (New York: Holt, Rinehart, & Winston, 1964 edn); F. J. Stephan and P. J. McCarthy, *Sampling Opinions* (New York: Wiley, 1963); G. Lindzey and E. Aronson (eds), *Handbook of Social Psychology*, vol. II: 'Research methods' (London: Addison-Wesley, 1968), especially chs 15, 11, 10; and C. A. Moser and G. Kalton, *Survey Methods in Social Investigation* (London: Heinemann, 1971; first edition 1958). See too R. L. Gorden, *Interviewing: Strategy, Techniques, and Tactics* (Homewood, Ill.: Dorsey 1969); Morris Rosenberg, *The Logic of Survey Analysis* (London: Basic Books, 1969); and D. L. Phillips, *Knowledge From What? Theories and Methods in Social Research* (Chicago: Rand McNally, 1971).
2 'On the strategy of cross-national research into subjective culture' (1967), loc. cit., p. 9.
3 Cf. the discussion of these two modes of justification in chapter 3 supra.
4 Ibid., pp. 34–5; the study referred to is H. Cantril's, *The Pattern of Human Concerns* (1965).
5 See A. P. Achal, 'Relative value of poll-end and open-end questions in search for reasons of a problem', *Educ. and Psychol.*, 1958, pp. 55–60. Achal found that the kind of choice made by the respondents was clearly biased by the alternatives presented, although this effect was to some degree off-set by age and education.
6 *Theory and Methods of Social Research* (1969), p. 137.
7 S. Payne, *The Art of Asking Questions* (Princeton University Press, 1963; first published 1951), p. 55.
8 The semantic differential technique is discussed in chapter 8, pp. 279–90.
9 Cf. *The Open and Closed Mind* (1960).
10 See L. L. Thurstone and E. J. Chave, *The Measurement of Attitudes* (University of Chicago Press, 1929).
11 Described in G. Murphy and R. Likert, *Public Opinion and the Individual* (New York: Harper, 1938).
12 See L. Guttman, 'A basis for scaling qualitative data', *ASR*, 1944, pp. 139–50 and idem, 'The basis for scalogram analysis', in S. A. Stouffer *et al.*, *The American Soldier*, vol. IV (Princeton University Press, 1950), pp. 60–90. Cf., too, W. Torgerson, *Theory and Methods of Scaling* (New York: Wiley, 1958), espec. ch. 12.
13 See, for instance, Torgerson, op. cit. and W. A. Scott, 'Attitude measurement', in Lindzey and Aronson (1968), op. cit., vol. II, ch. 11.
14 Relevant studies here include W. R. Catton, 'Exploring techniques for measuring human values', *ASR*, 1954, 19, 1, pp. 49–55; idem, 'A retest of the measurability of certain human values', *ASR*, 1956, 21, 3, pp. 357–9; and W. A. Scott, 'Empirical assessment of values and

ideologies', *ASR*, 1959, 24, 3, pp. 299–309, and idem, *Values and Organizations* (1965). See, too, for instance, R. K. White, *Value-analysis: The nature and use of the method* (Ann Arbor: Society for the Psychological Study of Social Issues, 1951).

15 In particularistic moral codes the category of general precepts is, *per definitionem*, inappropriate. However, such codes are likely to be far more common in philosophical theory (e.g. existentialism) than in empirical practice. None the less, the question of the relationship between general precepts and specific prescriptions remains to be determined for any given case. Thus, an introductory typology is given on p. 70 supra.

16 A. L. Edwards, *The Social Desirability Variable in Personality Assessment and Research* (New York: Holt, Rinehart & Winston, 1957).

17 D. P. Crowne and D. Marlowe, 'A new scale of social desirability independent of psychopathology', *Journal of Consulting Psychology*, 1960, 24, pp. 349–54.

18 See A. Couch and K. Keniston, 'Yea sayers and nay sayers: Agreeing response set as a personality variable', *Journal of Abnormal and Social Psychology*, 1960, 60, p. 151f.; R. Christie and F. Lindauer, 'Personality structure', *American Review of Psychology*, 1963, 15, pp. 201–30; and P. G. Liberty, C. E. Lunnenborg, and G. C. Atkinson, 'Perceptual defense, dissimulation, and response styles', *Journal of Consulting Psychology*, 1964, 28, 6, pp. 529–37.

19 L. J. Cronbach, 'Response-set and test validity', *Educational and Psychological Measurement*, 1946, 6, pp. 475–94.

20 See T. J. Banta, 'Social attitudes and response styles', *Educ. and Psychol. Meast.*, 1961, 21, pp. 543–57 and D. Peabody, 'Attitude content and agreement set in scales of authoritarianism, dogmatism, anti-Semitism, and economic conservatism', *Journal of Abnormal and Social Psychology*, 1961, 61, pp. 1–11. Cf. also the discussion in P. A. Hare, 'Interview responses: Personality or conformity?', *Public Opinion Quarterly*, 1960, pp. 679–85.

21 N. Frederiksen and S. Messick, 'Response set as a measure of personality', *Educ. and Psychol. Meast.*, 1959, 19, pp. 137–59.

22 E. L. Jones, 'The courtesy bias in South-East Asian surveys', *International Social Science Journal*, 1963, pp. 70–6. A large part of this volume is devoted to the question of 'Opinion Surveys in Developing Countries' and so has relevance to the present chapter.

23 J. B. Cooper and D. Pollock, 'The identification of prejudicial attitudes by the galvanic skin response', *Journal of Social Psychology*, 1959, 50, pp. 241–5. See also M. L. DeFleur and F. R. Westie (1958), op. cit. (discussed in chapter 5).

24 Cf. the discussion of interviewing procedure in N. Gross, W. Mason, and A. W. McEachern, *Explorations in Role Analysis* (New York: Wiley, 1958).

25 A. H. Barton, 'Asking the embarrassing question', *Public Opinion Quarterly*, 1958, pp. 67–8. Cited in Galtung, *Theory and Methods* (1969), p. 510.

26 One of the early studies on this subject, which established an inverse

relationship between guilt feelings and degree of wrongdoing, was D. W. MacKinnon's research, reported in his 'Violations and prohibitions', in H. A. Murray, *Explorations in Personality* (New York: Oxford University Press, 1938).

27 Cf. nn. 2.34 and 2.1 supra. See, too, G. Piers and M. B. Singer, *Shame and Guilt* (Springfield, Ill: Thomas, 1953).

28 See the discussion of this technique in chapter 8 infra.

29 For examples of translation difficulties, see pp. 20 and 68 supra.

30 Hence some knowledge of the broader structure of the code under study is necessary for adequate 'translations' in many instances, such as that of Hinduism as described earlier by K. Sen (p. 20). However, it is important also in this connection to be aware of the fact that codes may differ widely in their degree of determinacy (cf. Oliver 1965, op. cit.).

31 D. Rugg, 'Experiments in wording questions: II', *Public Opinion Quarterly*, 1941, 5, 1, pp. 91–2. Cited in S. Payne (1963), op. cit., p. 57.

32 Ibid., p. 16. Although it is only an introductory text, and one that eschews the *esprit de serieux* common to most discussions in methodology, Payne's book is one of the few concerned with problems of phraseology in survey research, and as such it provides useful advice on some of the more common, and yet often unnoticed, errors in attitude studies.

33 E. J. Webb, *et al.* (1968), op. cit. p. 25. The authors state this as one reason in favour of the further development of observational measures in social science. To which we may add that the latter has been retarded perhaps as a direct consequence of the preponderance (31 per cent in our sample) of studies conducted on college populations.

34 See the discussion in Hyman *et al.* (1954), op. cit. Relevant studies, on the effect of class, age, and race respectively, include D. Riesman, 'Orbits of tolerance, interviewers and elites', *Public Opinion Quarterly*, 1956, 20, pp. 49–73 and G. E. Lenski and J. C. Leggett, 'Caste, class, and deference in the research interview', *AJS*, 1960, 65, pp. 463–7; D. Riesman and J. Ehrlich, 'Age and authority in the interview', *Public Opinion Quarterly*, 1961, 25, pp. 39–56, and M. Benney, D. Riesman, and S. Star, 'Age and sex in the interview', *AJS*, 1956, 62, pp. 143–52; and K. R. Athey, J. E. Coleman, A. P. Reitman, and J. Tang' Two experiments showing the effect of the interviewer's racial background on responses to questionnaires concerning racial issues', *Journal of Applied Psychology*, 1960, 44, pp. 244–6.

35 Webb *et al.* (1968), op. cit., pp. 21–2.

36 This, of course, becomes a very real problem in many cross-national surveys. For data on the extent of literacy by nation (mean = 52 per cent), see Russett *et al.* (1964), op. cit., pp. 221–6.

37 W. A. Belson, 'The extent of stealing by London boys and some of its origins', *Survey Research Centre*, Reprint Series, 1969, no. 39.

38 C. A. Moser (1958), op. cit., ch. 12.

39 C. F. Cannell and R. L. Kahn, 'Collection of data by interviewing', in L. Festinger and D. Katz (eds), *Research Methods in the Behavioral Sciences* (New York: Holt, Rinehart, 1953).

40 Cf. Galtung, *Theory and Methods of Social Research* (1969), pp. 139–40.

41 Cf. pp. 92–7 supra. For a more historical approach, see E. Rose, 'Uniformities in culture: Ideas with histories', in N. F. Washburne (ed.), *Decisions, Values and Groups* (New York: Pergamon, 1962). Rose states that 'The notion that an idea can be shared by a number of people is plausible; we all subscribe to it and find it indispensable for human involvement. And yet it is a proposition rarely tested, and when tested never clearly established' (p. 155). See too E. Rose and W. Felton, 'Experimental histories of culture', *ASR*, 1955, 20, 4, pp. 383–92 and R. W. Gerard, C. Kluckhohn, and A. Rapoport, 'Biological and cultural evolution: Some analogies and explorations', *Behavioral Science*, 1956, 1, 1, pp. 6–34.

42 Galtung, *Theory and Methods*, op. cit., p. 396.

43 R. F. Larson and S. S. Sutker, 'Value differences and value consensus by socioeconomic levels', *Social Forces*, 1966, 44, 4, pp. 563–9.

44 Cf. J. Galtung, 'A structural theory of aggression', *Journal of Peace Research*, 1964, 1, 2, pp. 95–119 and idem, 'A structural theory of integration', *Journal of Peace Research*, 1968, 5, pp. 375–95. Thus, one presumptive reason for differences in degree of consensus by social position concerns the positive relation between rank and social interaction. This is most apparent when the units of analysis are nations or other social collectivities, rather than individuals: cf., for instance, J. Galtung, 'East-West interaction patterns', *Journal of Peace Research*, 1966, 3, 2, pp. 146–77.

45 Cf. T. Sheff (1967), op. cit. One inquiry which compares interview and questionnaire approaches to this subject is reported in J. N. Morgan, 'Some pilot studies of communication and consensus in the family', *POQ*, 1968, 32, 1, pp. 113–21.

46 R. K. Goldsen *et al.*, *What College Students Think* (Princeton: Van Nostrand, 1960); P. E. Jacob, *Changing Values in College* (University of California Press, 1962); and R. H. Turner, *The Social Context of Ambition: A Study of High School Seniors in Los Angeles* (San Francisco: Chandler, 1964). See too, for instance, W. A. Scott (1965), op. cit. and R. N. Sanford (ed.), *The American College* (New York: Wiley, 1962).

47 R. Tagiuri, 'Value orientations and relations of managers and scientists', *American Sociological Quarterly*, 1965, 10, 1, pp. 39–51.

48 M. Theresita, 'An inter-class cross-cultural comparison of values', *Sociol. Analysis*, 1965, 26, 4, pp. 217–23. Other studies employing the Allport-Vernon Scale, and illustrating some of its possible applications include L. Postman *et al.*, 'Personal values as selective factors in perception', *J. Abn. & Soc. Psychol.*, 1948, 43, pp. 142–54; H. Fensterheim and M. E. Tresselt, 'The influence of value systems on the perception of people', *J. Abn. & Soc. Psychol.*, 1953, 48, pp. 93–8; J. R. Warren and P. A. Heist, 'Personality attributes of gifted college students', *Science*, 1960, 132, 5, pp. 330–7; L. B. Costin, 'Values in social work education', *Social Service Review*, 1964, 38, 3, pp. 271–80; and S. Yourglich, 'A four phase study of value homophily, friendship,

social participation, and college dropouts', *Sociological Analysis*, 1966, 27, 1, pp. 19–26. As the first two of these studies exemplify, the All-port-Vernon Scale has been most commonly used in the context of social-psychology experiments, to which, as we suggested earlier (chapter 3), it is perhaps best suited.

49 W. T. Liu, 'Chinese value orientations in Hong Kong', *Sociol. Analysis*, 1966, 27, 2, pp. 53–66.

50 W. Caudill and H. A. Scarr, 'Japanese value orientations and culture change', *Ethnology*, 1962, 1, 1. For a more practically-oriented inquiry using the Kluckhohn-Strodbeck Scale, see too F. Turner, 'A comparison of procedures in the treatment of clients with two different value orientations', *Social Casework*, 1964, 54, 5, pp. 273–7. An interesting study, which utilizes the same schema to demonstrate the presence of value pluralism in Salamanca, Spain, is F. Sanchez Lopez, 'Orientaciones valorativas de una region espanola', *Revista Internacional de Sociologia*, 1966, 24, 93–4, pp. 23–50.

51 See E. M. Duvall, 'Conceptions of parenthood', *AJS*, 1946, 52, pp. 193–203; D. Aberle and K. D. Naegele, 'Middle class father's role and attitudes toward children', *American Journal of Orthopsychiatry*, 1952, 22, pp. 366–78; H. H. Hyman, 'The value systems of different classes' in R. Bendix and S. M. Lipset (eds), *Class, Status, and Power* (Chicago: Free Press, 1953), pp. 426–42; Melvin L. Kohn, 'Social class and parental values', *AJS*, 1959, 64, 4, pp. 337–51; B. N. Sugarman, 'Social class and values as related to achievement and conduct in school', *Sociological Review*, 1966, 14, 3, pp. 287–301; and D. F. Swift, 'Social class and achievement motivation', *Educational Research*, 1967. Cf. also the previously-cited studies by Rettig and Pasamanick (1961), Theresita (1965), and Robinson and Rackstraw (1967).

52 See, for instance, J. Newson and E. Newson, *Patterns of Infant Care in an Urban Community* (London: Allen & Unwin, 1963); R. R. Sears, E. Maccoby and H. Levin, *Patterns of Child Rearing* (New York: Row, Peterson, 1957); M. Paneth, *Branch Street* (London: Allen & Unwin, 1944); and B. Jackson, *Working Class Community* (London: Routledge & Kegan Paul, 1968).

53 A sub-sample of 82 fathers was also selected and their rating of the values appropriate to either sex was found to be highly compatible with that of the mothers. See M. Kohn (1959), op. cit., p. 340.

54 For the statistical logic behind this procedure, see Kohn, p. 341.

55 Ibid., p. 342.

56 Ibid., p. 349–50.

57 Ibid., p. 350.

58 *Theory and Methods*, p. 158.

59 W. P. Robinson and S. J. Rackstraw (1967), op. cit.

60 One aspect of this, for instance, will be the way aggressive behaviour is conceptualized: on this, cf. pp. 108–9 supra. Similarly, the *duration* of childhood may be said to be socially defined, although within the context of certain biological constraints regarding the process of maturation. However, the cultural component in the latter process

can be seen if we think, for instance, of different conceptions, found in different societies or different segments of a single society, of the learning capacities of children of given ages, of their natural emotional attributes, and of their degree of moral, or legal, accountability (ethical competency).

61 P. Ariès, *Centuries of Childhood* (London: Cape, 1962); U. Bronfenbrenner, *Two Worlds of Childhood* (London: Allen & Unwin, 1972).

62 See, for example, J. G. Peristiany (ed.), *Honour and Shame: The Values of Mediterranean Society* (London: Weidenfeld & Nicolson, 1965) and Pitt-Rivers (1961), Lison-Tolosana (1966), and J. K. Cambell (1964), all op. cit. For a discussion of the diffusion of Spanish culture to Latin America, and its political consequences, see E. Vivas, 'The Spanish heritage', *ASR*, 1945, 10, 2, pp. 184–91.

63 Cf. John Gillin, 'Ethos components in modern Latin American culture', *American Anthropologist*, 1955, 57, 3, pp. 488–500, in which it is suggested that the value of *machismo* is more important as a determinant of behaviour and interpersonal evaluation than middle-class identification.

64 *Belmonte de los Caballeros* (1966), p. 333.

65 *A Spanish Tapestry* (1961).

66 See Melvin Kohn, *Class and Conformity: A Study in Values* (Homewood, Ill.: Dorsey, 1969). Cf. too M. Kohn and E. E. Carroll, 'Social class and the allocation of parental responsibilities', *Sociometry*, 1960, 23, pp. 372–92.

# Chapter 8

1 Cf. pp. 157–8 supra. It will be recalled here that only 16 per cent of the studies within our sample utilized more than one method of data-collection.

2 E. J. Webb *et al.* (1968), op. cit., p. 3.

3 Cf. H. J. Parry and H. M. Crossley, 'Validity of responses to survey questions', *Public Opinion Quarterly*, 1950, 14, pp. 61–80.

4 See, for instance, P. R. Hawkins (1969), op. cit.

5 Severyn T. Bruyn, *The Human Perspective in Sociology: The Methodology of Participant Observation* (Englewood Cliffs, N. J.: Prentice-Hall, 1966), p. 201.

6 This, and other forms of relativist arguments will be examined in the next chapter.

7 Cf. Part One, particularly chapter 3. Good illustrations of the mutual interplay of cognitive and evaluative conceptions can be drawn from the intellectual history of the social sciences. A salient example here, of course, is the diverse interpretations, and valuations, of the capitalist social order that are to be found in the works of Max Weber and Karl Marx. A useful summary is given in N. Birnbaum, 'Conflicting interpretations of the rise of capitalism: Marx and Weber', *British Journal of Sociology*, 1953, IV, pp. 125–41. There have been various analyses of more recent competing theoretical paradigms in social

407

science, such as systems theory v. action theory, or order theories v. conflict theories. Most of these accounts have sought to underscore the irreconcilability of the respective cognitive assumptions involved in these divergent approaches. Then, in the final paragraph, as it were, cognitive assumptions are in turn 'explained' as the product of radically different *values*, these values being perhaps embodied in separate political historical traditions. Rarely has the epistemological primacy thus granted to values been called into question. Cf. J. Horton, 'Order and conflict theories of social problems as competing ideologies', in J. E. Curtis and J. W. Petras, (eds), *The Sociology of Knowledge* (London: Duckworth, 1970), pp. 605–24 and A. Dawe, 'The two sociologies', *BJS*, 1970, 21, 2, pp. 207–18. A valuable discussion of a number of recent texts in political science, most notably Lipset's *Political Man*, which brings out the influence of authors' cognitive frameworks upon subsequent evaluations is C. Taylor, 'Neutrality in political science', in P. Laslett and W. G. Runciman (eds), *Philosophy, Politics and Society*, 3rd Series (Oxford: Blackwell, 1967), pp. 25–57.

8  R. F. Bales, *Interaction Process Analysis* (Reading, Mass.: Addison-Wesley, 1950) and R. G. Barker, 'Behavior units for the comparative study of cultures', in B. Kaplan (ed.), *Studying Personality Cross-culturally* (New York: Row, Peterson, 1961), pp. 457–76. Relevant also to the question of the reliability of observational data are E. F. Borgatta and R. F. Bales, 'The consistency of subject behavior and the reliability of scoring in interaction process analysis', *ASR*, 1958, 23, pp. 566–8; A. J. Vidich and G. A. Shapiro, 'A comparison of participant observation and survey data', *ASR*, 1955, 20, pp. 28–33; and also F. J. Davis and R. Hagedorn, 'Testing the reliability of systematic field observations', *ASR*, 1954, 19, pp. 345–8. See also the useful discussion, and extensive bibliography, given in K. E. Weick, 'Systematic observational methods', in G. Lindzey and E. Aronson (eds), *Handbook of Social Psychology* (1968), pp. 357–451.

9  See R. Redfield, *Tepoztlán: A Mexican Village* (University of Chicago Press, 1930) and O. Lewis, *Life in a Mexican Village: Tepoztlán Restudied* (Urbana, Ill.: University of Illinois Press, 1951). It would, of course, be desirable to see more restudies of this kind, if not complete replications, in anthropological fieldwork.

10  On p. 241f.

11  L. Festinger, H. W. Riecken, and S. Schachter, *When Prophecy Fails* (New York: Harper & Row, 1964). On the general question of role-playing in order to avert reactivity effects, see A. H. Stanton, K. Black, and E. Litwak, 'Role-playing in social research', *AJS*, 1956–7, pp. 172–6.

12  On this issue, cf. E. Shils, 'Social inquiry and the autonomy of the individual', in D. Lerner (ed.), *The Human Meaning of the Social Sciences* (Cleveland: Meridian, 1959), pp. 114–57.

13  Bruyn (1966), op. cit., p. 204.

14  Cf. Goffman's discussion of 'impression management' in his *The Presentation of Self in Everyday Life* (New York: Doubleday, 1959). See, too, his *Strategic Interaction* (London: Blackwell, 1971).

15 Cf. R. W. Janes, 'A note on phases of the community role of the participant observer', *ASR*, 1961, 26, pp. 446–50. The problem of being defined as Government representatives has been encountered in our own fieldwork in a 'developing' society. One result is that respondents' orientations to the present Government may enter as a possible source of response bias.

16 Cf. S. M. Miller, 'The participant observer and over-rapport', in G. J. McCall and J. L. Simmons (eds), *Issues in Participant Observation* (Reading, Mass.: Addison-Wesley, 1969), p. 87f.

17 R. Naroll and F. Naroll, 'On bias of exotic data', *Man*, 1963, 25, pp. 24–6.

18 See, for instance, R. Firth's *We, The Tikopia* (London: Allen & Unwin, 1957; first edn 1936).

19 Op. cit. See particularly the 'Methodological Appendix', pp. 234–49.

20 Ibid., p. 234.

21 Ibid., p. 241.

22 See D. T. Cambell, W. H. Kruskal, and W. P. Wallace, 'Seating aggregation as an index of attitude', *Sociometry*, 1966, 29, pp. 1–15.

23 Cf. K. W. Back, 'The well-informed informant', in R. N. Adams and J. J. Preiss (eds), *Human Organization Research* (1960), pp. 179–87.

24 Op. cit., ch. 5, pp. 112–41.

25 S. Milgram, L. Mann, and S. Harter, 'The lost-letter technique: A tool of social research', *Public Opinion Quarterly*, 1965, 29, 3, pp. 437–8. Cf. too S. Milgram, *Science*, 1970, 167, pp. 1461–8.

26 Cf. D. T. Cambell, 'Systematic error on the part of human links in communication systems', *Information and Control*, 1959, 1, pp. 334–69. See too n. 8.8.

27 See R. Rosenthal, 'On social psychology of the psychological experiment: the experimenter's hypothesis as unintended determinant of experimental results', *American Scientist*, 1963, 51, pp. 268–83; R. Rosenthal and K. L. Fode, 'Psychology of the scientist: V. three experiments in experimenter bias', *Psychological Reports*, 1963, 12, pp. 491–511; and R. Rosenthal, 'Experimenter outcome-orientation and the results of the psychological experiment', *Psychological Bulletin*, 1964, 61, pp. 405–12.

It is salutary to consider also here the classic study by Robert Rosenthal and L. Jacobson, *Pygmalion in the Classroom* (New York: Holt, Rinehart & Winston, 1969), which demonstrates in a quite different context the integral, self-confirming role that expectations, often imperceptibly conveyed, can play in the determination of another's performances. In this case, their experimental study showed some of the ways in which teachers' expectations of schoolchildren's 'ability' and intellectual performances can, in fact, come to determine these performances. Social science is not immune from biases of this kind, and evidence such as this should encourage us to develop more systematic and, where feasible, replicable, observational procedures in social research. On this general question, cf. E. D. Oliver and A. W. Landfield, 'Reflexivity: an unfaced issue of psychology', *Journal of Individual Psychology*, 1969, 20, 187.

28 Op. cit., p. 173.
29 H. Becker, 'Problems of inference and proof in participant observation', *ASR*, 1958, 23, p. 655.
30 A. Etzioni, *A Comparative Analysis of Complex Organizations* (New York: Free Press, 1961), p. 300.
31 See especially chapter 5, pp. 142–4.
32 See F. L. Strodbeck and R. D. Mann, 'Sex role differentiation in jury deliberations', *Sociometry*, 1956, 19, pp. 3–11 and F. L. Strodbeck, R. M. James, and C. Hawkins, 'Social status in jury deliberations', *ASR*, 1957, 22, pp. 713–19. On the general question of threats to privacy in modern society, owing to new techniques of surveillance, see A. F. Westin, *Privacy and Freedom* (London: Bodley Head, 1970).
33 J. Collier, *Visual Anthropology: Photography as a Research Method* (New York: Holt, Rinehart & Winston, 1967), pp. 7–8.
34 E. Siersted and H. L. Hansen, 'Réaction des petits enfants au cinema: resumé d'une serie d'observations faites au Danemark', *Revue Internationale de Filmologie*, 1951, 2, pp. 241–5. Cited in Webb *et al.*, op. cit.
35 *The Achieving Society* (Princeton: Van Nostrand, 1961).
36 Cf. J. I. Kitsuse and A. V. Cicourel, 'A note on the uses of official statistics', *Social Problems*, 1963, 11, pp. 131–9.
37 See, for instance, B. D. Mudgett, *Index Numbers* (New York: Wiley, 1961).
38 Cf. R. Naroll, *Data Quality Control* (Collier-Macmillan, 1962).
39 H. T. Christensen, 'Cultural relativism and premarital sex norms', *ASR*, 1960, 25, pp. 31–9.
40 See especially W. L. Warner *et al.*, *Social Class in America: A Manual of Procedure for the Measurement of Social Status* (New York: Harper, 1960; first published 1949). Other studies using 'objective', observational indices of social status include: D. Chapman, *The Home and Social Status* (London: Routledge & Kegan Paul, 1955) and R. Centers, *The Psychology of Social Classes* (Princeton University Press, 1949).
41 Reported in Oscar Lewis, 'The possessions of the poor', *Scientific American*, 1969, 221, 4, pp. 114–24.
42 Op. cit., p. 124.
43 Adapted from Lewis, op. cit., p. 118.
44 Ibid., p. 124.
45 Ibid., p. 124.
46 This criticism is made, for instance, by C. A. Valentine, *Culture and Poverty: Critique and Counter-Proposals* (University of Chicago Press, 1969). Thus, he expresses the view that 'an important underlying source of bias in these writings [about the poor] is an unexamined and strongly negative value-judgement about the culture of the lower-class poor', and he argues for more objective studies.
47 J. Piaget, *'The Moral Judgement of the Child* (Chicago: Free Press, 1948; first published 1932), p. 118.
48 See A. Bandura and F. J. McDonald, 'The influence of social reinforcement and the behavior of models in shaping children's moral judgements', *Journal of Abnormal and Social Psychology*, 1963, 67, pp.

274–81 and L. Kohlberg, 'Moral development and identification', in National Society for the Study of Education: 62nd Yearbook, *Child Psychology* (University of Chicago Press, 1963), pp. 277–332. Cf., too, for instance, R. C. Johnson, 'A study of children's moral judgements', *Child Development*, 1962, 33, pp. 327–54.

49 On this point, compare, for instance, Berger and Luckman (1967) op. cit.

50 This has typically been achieved (at least in part) by positing a *general* philosophical anthropology, involving a notion of man's basic needs, or his 'nature', which have supplied a rationale for the imperatives contained within the code, and to which the latter have been directed. It is to be noted, however, that this does not operate in a purely negative sense; that is, the precepts are characteristically justified, and made plausible, not only as means of constraining man's nature but also of facilitating its 'true' expression.

51 M. T. Orne, 'On the social psychology of the psychological experiment: with particular reference to demand characteristics and their implications', *American Psychologist*, 1962, 17, pp. 776–83. See too M. T. Orne and F. J. Evans, 'Social control in the psychological experiment: antisocial behavior and hypnosis', *Journal of Personality and Social Psychology*, 1965, 1, pp. 189–200.

52 *Theory and Methods*, p. 119.

53 See L. Kohlberg, 'The development of children's orientations toward a moral order: I. Sequence in the development of moral thought', *Vita Humana* (Basel), 1963; idem, 'Moral development and identification', loc. cit., 1963; and idem, 'The development of children's orientations toward a moral order: II. Social experience, social conduct, and the development of moral thought', *Vita Humana* (Basel), 1964.

54 R. Brown, *Social Psychology* (London: Collier-Macmillan, 1967), pp. 404–5. His chapter 8 on 'The Acquisition of Morality', provides a good introduction to some of the experimental evidence in this field.

55 Kohlberg, 'The development of children's orientations . . .' (1963), p. 28. Described in Brown (1967), op. cit., p. 405.

56 See S. Milgram, 'Some conditions of obedience and disobedience to authority', *Human Relations*, 1965, 18, pp. 57–75. See too, his report in the *Journal of Abnormal and Social Psychology*, 1963, 67, 4. For debate on the ethical questions raised by Milgram's experiments, see D. Baumrind, 'Some thoughts on ethics of research', *Amer. Psychologist*, 1964, 19, pp. 421–3. Milgram's reply is given on pp. 848–52 of this volume of the journal.

57 H. Hartshorne and M. A. May, *Studies in the Nature of Character* (New York: Macmillan, 1928–1930), 3 vols: Vol. I: *Studies in Deceit* (1928); Vol. II: (with J. B. Maller) *Studies in Service and Self Control* (1929); Vol III: (with F. K. Shuttleworth) *Studies in the Organization of Character* (1930). On the general question of 'quasi-experiments', see D. T. Cambell, 'Quasi-experimental design', in D. L. Sills (ed.), *International Encyclopaedia of the Social Sciences* (New York: Collier-Macmillan, 1968).

58 See R. V. Burton, 'The generality of honesty reconsidered', *Psychological Review*, 1963, 70, pp. 481–99. For an overview of some of the studies which followed on from Hartshorne and May's pioneering research, cf. V. Jones, 'Character development in children: an objective approach', in L. Carmichael (ed.), *Manual of Child Psychology* (New York: Wiley, 1946), pp. 707–51.

59 L. Postman, J. S. Bruner, and E. McGinnies, 'Personal values as selective factors in perception', *Journal of Abnormal and Social Psychology*, 1948, 53, pp. 142–54.

60 R. L. Solomon and D. H. Howes, 'Word frequency, personal values, and visual duration thresholds', *Psychological Review*, 1951, 58, pp. 255–70; and D. H. Howes and R. L. Solomon, 'Visual duration threshold as a function of word probability', *J. Exper. Psychol.*, 1951, 41, pp. 401–10.

61 For a review, see W. F. Dukes, 'Psychological studies of values', *Psychol. Bulletin*, 1955, 52, pp. 24–50 and D. Wright, *The Psychology of Moral Behaviour* (Harmondsworth: Penguin, 1971).

62 On the first of these problems, see R. Rosenthal, *Experimenter Effects in Behavioral Research* (New York: Appleton-Century-Crofts, 1966). Cf., too, Rosenthal (1963, 1964), op. cit. and Rosenthal and Fode (1963), op. cit. On the second problem, see, for instance, M. T. Orne (1962), op. cit., M. T. Orne and F. J. Evans (1956), op. cit., and M. J. Rosenberg, 'When dissonance fails: on eliminating evaluation apprehension from attitude measurement', *J. Pers. Soc. Psychol.*, 1965, 1, pp. 28–42. For a general review of experimental procedure, which considers some solutions to these problems and provides a full bibliography, see: E. Aronson and J. M. Carlsmith, 'Experimentation in social psychology', in G. Lindzey and E. Aronson (eds), *Handbook of Social Psychology* (1968), vol. 2, pp. 1–79. The *locus classicus* on the subject of experimental rationales is, of course, Sir Donald Fisher, *The Design of Experiments* (London: Oliver & Boyd, 8th edn 1966).

63 B. Berelson, 'Content analysis', in G. Lindzey (ed.), *Handbook of Social Psychology* (Cambridge: Addison-Wesley, 1954), vol. 1, p. 489.

64 For an excellent review, see O. R. Holsti, *Content Analysis for the Social Sciences and Humanities* (London: Addison-Wesley, 1970).

65 I. Wayne, 'American and Soviet themes and values: a content analysis of pictures in popular magazines', *Public Opinion Quarterly*, 1956, 20, 1, pp. 314–20.

66 P. Johns-Heine and H. H. Gerth, 'Values in mass periodical fiction, 1921–1940', *Public Opinion Quarterly*, 1949, 13, pp. 105–13.

67 G. Ginglinger, 'Basic values in "Reader's Digest", "Selection", and "Constellation"', *Journalism Quarterly*, 1955, 32, 1, pp. 56–61. Cf. too M. C. Albrecht, 'Does literature reflect common values?', *ASR* 1956, 21, pp. 272–9.

68 Cf. R. K. White, *Value-Analysis: the nature and use of the method* (1951).

69 B. Berelson and P. J. Salter, 'Majority and minority Americans: An analysis of magazine fiction', *Public Opinion Quarterly*, 1946, 10, pp. 168–90. For a study which adopts a similar methodology, relating con-

tent analysis findings to census data, again with some critical intent, cf. M. L. De Fleur, 'Occupational roles as portrayed on television', *Public Opinion Quarterly*, 1964, 28, pp. 57–74. However, the Berelson-Salter study deserves to serve as a model for many more inquiries of this kind.

70 For the absence of an historical perspective in the available research, cf. our review in chapter 6 supra.

71 R. DeCharms and G. Moeller, 'Values expressed in American children's readers: 1800–1950', *Journal of Abnormal and Social Psychology*, 1962, 64, 2, pp. 136–42.

72 L. Schneider and S. N. Dornbusch, *Popular Religion* (University of Chicago Press, 1958). The coding scheme adopted is given in Appendix B, p. 148f.

73 Op. cit., p. 167.

74 R. Angell, V. Dunham, and J. Singer, 'Social values and the foreign policy attitudes of Soviet and American elites', *Journal of Conflict Resolution*, 1964, 8, 4.

75 Cf. C. Osgood, 'On the strategy of cross-national research into subjective culture' (1967), loc. cit.

76 I. de Solla Pool, *The 'Prestige Papers': A Survey of their Editorials* (Stanford University Press, 1952a).

77 From, respectively, I. de Solla Pool, *Symbols of Democracy* (Stanford University Press, 1952b), p. 72 (cited in Holsti, 1970, op. cit.), and I. de Solla Pool (1952a), op. cit., p. 84.

78 *The Achieving Society* (1961). McClelland's research has been criticized by Merritt on the grounds that bias enters into his sampling of nations. Using Russett's data on national indicators, Merritt shows that McClelland's sample of nations for his content analyses exhibits some bias in favour of those countries that have experienced rapid development. As such, his paper well illustrates the importance of correct sampling procedures to content analysis, as to other methods to social research. Cf. his 'The representational model in cross-national content analysis', in J. Bernd (ed.), *Mathematical Applications in Political Science* (Dallas: Southern Methodist University Press, 1966), pp. 44–71.

79 See R. C. North, O. R. Holsti, M. G. Zaninovich, and D. A. Zinnes, *Content Analysis: A handbook with applications for the study of international crisis* (Evanston, Ill.: Northwestern University Press, 1963) and R. A. Brody, O. R. Holsti, and R. C. North, 'Measuring affect and action in international reaction models: Empirical materials from the 1962 Cuba crisis', *Journal of Peace Research*, 1964, 1, nos 3–4.

80 R. C. Baum, 'Values and democracy in Imperial Germany', *Sociological Inquiry*, 1968, 38, 2, pp. 179–96.

81 See L. Schneider and S. N. Dornbusch, op. cit., Appendix B. and ch. 2.

82 Adapted from R. Brandt, op. cit., p. 170.

83 Such an analysis would, of course, be mainly designed to elucidate the 'phenotypic' content, whereas the work of Lévi-Strauss, for instance, is

more concerned with determining the underlying, or genotypic, structure of the communication. However, the former would seem a necessary precursor to the latter, and as Galtung states: 'The force of content analysis lies precisely in its possibilities as a technique for analysis of manifest content *before* one jumps to conclusions most people are willing to jump to right away' (*Theory and Methods*, p. 70).

84 Op. cit., p. 68.

85 In D. McClelland *et al.*, *The Achievement Motive* (New York: Apple. ton-Century-Crofts, 1953) and idem, *The Achieving Society* (Princeton: Van Nostrand, 1961). This method was used particularly in the early stages of McClelland's research.

86 The report on this is forthcoming. For earlier studies on this line of inquiry, which were particularly influenced by the maturational models of Piaget, see P. Cooper, 'The development of the concept of war', *Journal of Peace Research*, 1965, 2, p. 1–17 and L. Rosell, 'Children's views on war and peace', *Journal of Peace Research*, 1965, 2, pp. 268–76.

87 E. S. Shneidman, 'Plan 11. The logic of politics', in L. Arons and M. A. May (eds), *Television and Human Behavior* (New York: Appleton-Century-Crofts, 1963), pp. 177–99.

88 Op. cit., p. 628.

89 See, for instance, the discussion of manifest and latent content in B. Berelson, *Content Analysis in Communication Research* (Glencoe: Free Press, 1952). The relationship between content attributes and the effects of communications has been most rigorously examined within the context of readability studies; for one method, see W. L. Taylor, ' "Cloze Procedure": a new tool for measuring readability', *Journalism Quart.*, 1953, 30, pp. 415–33. Particularly lacking has been any systematic inquiry into the relative effects of different propaganda formats.

90 Op. cit., pp. 156–7.

91 R. Middleton, 'Fertility values in American magazine fiction: 1916–1956', *Public Opinion Quarterly*, 1960, 24, pp. 139–43. Another piece of research which illustrates the same point is reported by S. A. Rudin in *Science*, 1968, 160, p. 901f. In this intriguing study the author examined the relationship between achievement scores (after McClelland) for several countries and statistics for the same countries on 'psychomorbidity'. The latter was assessed by checking death rates due largely to psychological factors—including suicide and alcoholism, and deaths due to cirrhosis of the liver, ulcers, and high blood pressure. This data was collected for the year 1950. Achievement orientation, on the other hand, was determined by content analysis of the values expressed in children's readers for each country for the year 1925. The time period between 1925 and 1950 was taken as approximating a generation. Rudin's chief findings were that for sixteen of the countries (mainly modern and Western) the 1925 achievement scores correlated positively with the 1950 data on 'deaths due to inhibition', i.e. due to ulcers and hypertension. In addition, he found that the 1925 'need for power' scores correlated positively with 1950 statistics on 'deaths due to aggressiveness', i.e. due to murder, suicide, or

alcoholism. His study suggests some of the insights to be gained from the development of research into 'sociosmatics', a term suggested by Peter Berger in his 'Identity as a problem in the sociology of knowledge', *European Journal of Sociology*, 1966, 7, pp. 105–15. For studies combining content analysis with projective measures, see McClelland (1953, 1961), op. cit. and Cooper (forthcoming), op. cit. For a comparison of content analysis and simulation data, which utilizes material from the 1914 study, see D. A. Zinnes, 'A comparison of hostile behavior of decision makers in simulated and historical data', *World Politics*, 1966, 28, p. 474f.

92 For an interesting discussion of this thesis with respect to literature, see M. C. Albrecht, 'Does literature reflect common values?' (1965), op. cit. and idem 'The relationship of literature and society', *AJS*, 1953–4, 59.

93 See, e.g., C. R. Bush, 'A system of categories for general news content', *Journalism Quart.*, 1961, 38, pp. 312–22.

94 Cf. A. L. George, 'Quantitative and qualitative approaches to content analysis' in I. de Solla Pool (ed.), *Trends in Content Analysis* (Urbana: University of Illinois Press, 1959), pp. 7–32.

95 For such an analysis, see B. Ohlstrom, 'Information and propaganda', *Journal of Peace Research*, 1966, 1, pp. 75–88.

96 A sense of the increasing sophistication of content analysis as a method of social research is best gained by a perusal of the principal texts on this method over a period of time: viz. B. Berelson, *Content Analysis in Communication Research* (1952); I. de Solla Pool (ed.), *Trends in Content Analysis* (1959); R. C. North *et al.*, *Content Analysis* (1963); R. W. Budd *et al.*, *Content Analysis of Communications* (London: Collier-Macmillan, 1967); and O. R. Holsti, *Content Analysis for the Social Sciences and Humanities* (1970). One of the continuing technical problems of content analysis, as we have seen, is that of maintaining high coefficients of reliability, whilst at the same time using flexible, non-mechanical coding procedures. Two useful discussions are G. H. Stempel, 'Increasing reliability in content analysis', *Journalism Quart.*, 1955, 32, pp. 449–55 and W. A. Scott, 'Reliability of content analysis: the case of nominal scale coding', *Public Opinion Quarterly*, 1955, 19, pp. 321–5. Scott develops a coefficient of agreement, originally for nominal coding, but applicable also to ordinal and interval data, which is corrected for the amount of agreement that would be expected on the basis of chance. This measure is utilized in his paper, 'Empirical assessment of values and ideologies' (1959), op. cit., p. 302f.

97 See P. J. Stone *et al.*, *The General Inquirer: A Computer Approach to Content Analysis in the Behavioral Sciences* (Cambridge: M.I.T. Press 1966) and idem, *User's Manual for the General Inquirer*, ed. J. Kirsch (M.I.T. Press, 1968). See too G. Gerbner *et al.* (eds), *The Analysis of Communication Content: Developments in Scientific Theories and Computer Techniques* (New York: Wiley, 1969).

98 Op. cit.

99 Cf. K. Popper, *The Open Society and its Enemies*, 2 vols. (London:

Routledge & Kegan Paul, 1962 edn). Useful introductions to projective methods include L. E. Abt and L. Bellack, *Projective Psychology* (New York: Knopf, 1950); H. H. Anderson and G. L. Anderson (eds), *An Introduction to Projective Techniques* (New York: Prentice-Hall, 1951); and B. I. Murstein (ed.), *Handbook of Projective Techniques* (New York: Basic Books, 1965). Relevant articles include D. T. Cambell, 'The indirect assessment of social attitudes', *Psychological Bulletin*, 1950, 47; L. K. Frank, 'Projective methods for the study of personality', *Journal of Psychology*, 1950, 47; and W. G. Cobliner, 'On the place of projective tests in opinion and attitude surveys', *International Journal of Opinion and Attitude Research*, 1951, 5, pp. 480–90.

100 See C. DuBois, *The People of Alor* (Harvard University Press, 1961; first published 1944).

101 G. De Vos *et al.*, 'Value attitudes towards role behavior of women in two Japanese villages', *American Anthropologist*, 1961, 63, 6, pp. 1204–30.

102 E. C. Banfield, *The Moral Basis of a Backward Society* (1958).

103 Ibid., pp. 104–5.

104 Adapted from Banfield, op. cit., p. 105.

105 Cf. chapter 5, pp. 120–3.

106 E. M. and M. Eppel, *Adolescents and Morality* (London: Routledge & Kegan Paul, 1967).

107 H. B. Green, 'Values of Negro and East Indian schoolchildren in Trinidad', *Soc. Econ. Studies*, 1965, 14, 2, pp. 204–24.

108 W. Goldschmidt and R. B. Edgerton, 'A picture technique for the study of values', *American Anthropologist*, 1961, 63, pp. 26–47.

109 R. B. Edgerton, *The Individual in Cultural Adaptation* (Univ. of California Press, 1971). See too, idem, ' "Cultural" vs. "ecological" factors in the expression of values, attitudes, and personality characteristics', *Amer. Anthrop.*, 1965, 67, 2, pp. 442–7 and W. Goldschmidt, loc. cit., pp. 400–8.

110 In *The Achievement Motive* (1953) and *The Achieving Society* (1961).

111 See H. M. Proshansky, 'A projective method for the study of attitudes', *Journal of Abnormal and Social Psychology*, 1943, 38, pp. 393–5. A not dissimilar projective method was employed also by Stoetzel in his study of Japan to elicit modern Japanese conceptions of *giri*: see J. Stoetzel, *Without the Chrysanthemum and the Sword* (London: Heinemann, 1955), pp. 190–200.

112 See J. Collier (1967), op. cit.

113 B. Bernstein, 'Socialization and linguistic codes', Talk given at Essex University, 1968. A similar technique was used to study the priorities of a team of social scientists carrying out research for the U.S. Government: see W. G. Bennis, 'Values and organization in a university social research group', *ASR*, 1956, 21, 5, pp. 555–63.

114 R. E. Carter, 'An experiment in value measurement', *ASR*, 1956, 21, 2, pp. 156–63.

115 Cf. D. Lerner, *The Passing of Traditional Society* (New York: Free Press, 1964).

116 C. J. Adcock and J. E. Ritchie, 'Intercultural use of Rorschach', *American Anthropologist*, 1958, 60, 5, pp. 881-92. On this, cf. also B. Klopfer *et al.*, *Developments in the Rorschach Technique* (New York: Harcourt, Brace, 1971).

117 R. Brown, *Social Psychology* (1967), p. 434.

118 Cf., for instance, R. S. Peters, 'Emotions, passivity and the place of Freud's theory in psychology', in B. Wolman and E. Nagel (eds), *Scientific Psychology* (New York: Basic Books, 1965).

119 All methods of social inquiry, of course, presuppose certain minimal psychological premisses. However, other things being equal, one would assess a particular class of measurements as preferable to another to the degree to which it was neutral *vis-à-vis* competing psychological theories: that is, one test of the value of a given method of data-collection concerns the range of theories that it can be used to validate without prejudice, i.e. without itself implying any truth-claims regarding these theories. In short, a method is preferable to the extent that it is theory-independent.

120 Most of this research has been based at the Institute of Communications Research at the University of Illinois.

121 C. Osgood, 'Semantic differential technique in the comparative study of cultures', *American Anthropologist*, 1964, 66, Supplement, p. 171.

122 Osgood (1964, loc. cit.) has observed that psychological evidence is available to demonstrate that these particular qualifiers yield approximately equal gradations of intensity: see N. Cliff, 'Adverbs as multipliers', *Psychological Review*, 1959, 66, pp. 27-44. The 7-step scale is, of course, best known in sociology through the work of Osgood. However, some questions still arise concerning the general relevancy of this procedure. As in the case of research into values, the number of scale items of perceived relevance to respondents may be specific to the concept under review, to say nothing of possible cultural and linguistic relativity on this issue.

123 Osgood, 1964, op. cit., p. 173.

124 C. E. Osgood, 'On the strategy of cross-national research into subjective culture', *Social Science Information*, 1967, 6, 1, pp. 24-5.

125 From Osgood (1964), op. cit., p. 179.

126 One of the results of Osgood's research has been to bring out the distinctiveness of Japanese culture, particularly within the context of other modern industrial societies. Thus the evidence suggests the presence of a more *aesthetic* motif in Japanese modes of qualifying experience.

127 Osgood (1967), op. cit., p. 8.

128 Adapted from Osgood (1967), op. cit., pp. 32-3.

129 See J. J. Jenkins, W. A. Russell, and G. J. Suci, 'An atlas of semantic profiles for 360 words', *American Journal of Psychology*, 1958, 71, pp. 688-99 and idem, 'A table of distances for the semantic atlas', *American Journal of Psychology*, 1959, 72, pp. 623-5.

130 Osgood (1964), p. 195.

131 R. A. Gordon, J. F. Short, D. S. Cartwright, and F. L. Strodbeck, 'Values and gang delinquency: A study of street-corner groups', *AJS*, 1963, 69, 2, pp. 109-28.

132 The theoretical statements are contained in A. K. Cohen, *Delinquent Boys* (Chicago: Free Press, 1955); W. B. Miller, 'Lower class culture as a generating milieu of gang delinquency', *Journal of Social Issues*, 1958, 14, 3, pp. 5–19; and R. A. Cloward and L. E. Ohlin, *Delinquency and Opportunity* (New York: Free Press, 1960).

133 The respective reasons proposed for this are: because of reaction formation (Cohen), because these images correspond to the focal concerns of lower-class culture (Miller), and because the images represent adaptations to the relative unavailability of legitimate opportunities for members of the lower class (Coward and Ohlin). However, only Cohen's theory carries the stronger implication that gang boys will value deviant images even higher than the middle-class images.

134 Gordon *et al.*, op. cit., pp. 111–12.

135 C. E. Osgood, E. E. Ware, and C. Morris, 'Analysis of the connotative meaning of a variety of human values as expressed by American college students', *Journal of Abnormal and Social Psychol.* 1961, 62, 1, pp. 62–73.

136 M. E. Goodman, *Race Awareness in Young Children* (New York: Collier-Macmillan, 1964).

137 See C. E. Osgood, 'The cross-cultural generality of visual-verbal synesthetic tendencies', *Behavioral Science*, 1960, 5, pp. 146–69.

138 The response-set problem was encountered, for instance, in the attitude/actions study by C. R. Tittle and R. J. Hill (1967), op. cit., which we discussed in chapter 5. The authors note (op. cit., pp. 212–13) that subjects

> Observe that 'desirable' things appear on one side of a continuum and 'undesirable' things appear on the other. The discriminal process then apparently becomes a matter of self-evaluating overall attitude and marking the scale accordingly, with little distinction between the various adjectival pairs. Interspersing reversed continua probably only serves to make the respondent's task more difficult without fundamentally altering the problem.

In this instance, the tendency for subjects to adopt a response set probably accounts for the fact that the semantic differential procedure resulted in a measure having high reliability but low predictive validity.

139 Osgood (1964), p. 198.

140 Ibid. As a final incidental point, it is perhaps worth noting that the semantic differential was used by political advisers during the 1968 American Presidential campaign; see Joe McGinniss, *The Selling of the President* (Harmondsworth: Penguin, 1970), p. 72f.

141 See J. von Neumann and O. Morgenstern, *Theory of Games and Economic Behavior* (New York: Wiley, 1944).

142 One of the most useful introductions for the sociologist is R. D. Luce and H. Raiffa, *Games and Decisions* (New York: Wiley, 1957); see too M. Shubik, *Game Theory and Related Approaches to Social Behavior* (New York: Wiley, 1964); M. D. Davis, *Game Theory: A Non-technical Introduction* (New York: Basic Books, 1970) and A.

Rapoport, *N-person Game Theory* (Ann Arbor: University of Michigan Press, 1970).

143 R. B. Braithwaite, *The Theory of Games as a Tool for the Moral Philosopher* (University of Cambridge Press, 1955), pp. 54–5.

144 See P. J. Tansey and D. Unwin, *Simulation and Gaming in Education* (London: Methuen, 1969).

145 H. Guetzkow, *Simulation in International Relations* (Englewood Cliffs, N. J.: Prentice-Hall, 1963). Cf. also H. Guetzkow (ed.), *Simulation in Social Science* (Englewood Cliffs, N. J.: Prentice-Hall, 1962).

146 The standard text on this subject is A. Rapoport and A. M. Chammah, *Prisoner's Dilemma: A Study in Conflict and Cooperation* (Ann Arbor: University of Michigan Press, 1965).

147 A. Rapoport, 'Games which Simulate Deterrence and Disarmament" *Peace Research Review*, 1967, I, 4 (Clarkson, Ontario: Canadian Peace Research Institute), p. 7. Cf. too, R. P. Wolff, 'Reflections on game theory and the nature of value', *Ethics*, 1962, 73, 3, pp. 171ff.; G. Thompson, 'Game theory and "social value" states', *Ethics*, 1964, 75, 1, p. 36f.; V. Held, 'Rationality and social value in game theoretical analysis', *Ethics*, 1966, 76, 3, p. 215f.; and G. Tullock, 'The Prisoner's Dilemma and mutual trust', *Ethics*, 1967, 77, 3, pp. 229–30. In the last of these articles, Tullock argues that contrary to the statements of the previous authors (and so *pace* Rapoport) the essential problem of Prisoner's Dilemma is *not* one of mutual trust. As he writes (op. cit., p. 229):

> The problem raised by the dilemma is simply that if both parties make the same decision, they are better off if that double decision is 'don't squeal' than if it is 'squeal'. For the little society of the two prisoners, the individually rational decisions of the prisoners are socially irrational. It is clearly highly desirable that the philosophers join the game theorists in research in this area.

However, Tullock seems here to be taking the nomenclature—Prisoner's Dilemma—rather literally. Hence, for him, the problem becomes largely one of the individual v. social value states. This problem is not raised by the formal, experimental designs we shall consider, where, over extended sequences of play, the central issue does seem to be that of mutual trust. None the less, the individual/social values formulation is also of interest and on this the discussions in Tullock, and the articles preceding his, deserve attention.

148 M. Deutsch, 'Trust, trustworthiness, and the F scale', *Journal of Abnormal and Social Psychology*, 1960, 61, pp. 138–40.

149 D. R. Lutzker, 'Internationalism as a predictor of co-operative behavior', *Journal of Conflict Resolution*, 1960, 4, pp. 426–35.

150 K. H. Terhune, 'Psychological studies of social interaction and motives: I. Two-person gaming study', *Internal Research* No. 86–145, 1965, Cornell Aeronautical Laboratories, Buffalo, N.Y. Cited in Rapoport (1967), op. cit., p. 18.

151 M. Lumsden, 'Social position and cognitive style in strategic thinking', *Journal of Peace Research*, 1967, 3, pp. 289–303.

152 S. Oskamp and D. Perlman, 'Factors affecting co-operation in a

Prisoner's Dilemma game', *Journal of Conflict Resolution*, 1965, pp. 357–74.

153 L. Dencik and H. Wiberg, *Strategic thinking as a function of social attitudes: An experiment with the Prisoner's Dilemma* (University of Lund, 1966, mimeo.).

154 See A. Rapoport and A. M. Chammah (1965), op. cit. and M. Lumsden, 'Perception and information in strategic thinking', *Journal of Peace Research*, 1966, 3, pp. 256–77. Cf. also L. Lave, 'Factors affecting cooperation in the Prisoner's Dilemma', *Behavioral Science*, 1965, 10, 1 and for a review of the literature (to 1963) on this class of games, see P. S. Gallo and C. McClintock, 'Cooperative and competitive behavior in mixed motive games', *Journal of Conflict Resolution*, 1965, p. 68f.

155 Rapoport (1967), op. cit., p. 13.

156 Cf. von Neumann and Morgenstern (1944), op. cit., and Rapoport and Chammah (1965), op. cit.

157 Examples of these are discussed in Rapoport (1965, 1967), op. cit.

158 Hence the repeated use of simulations by the military in strategic research (e.g. by the Americans in Vietnam) has been considered by some to be tantamount to an evasion of reality and part of a growing, yet misleading, 'technicization' of questions of principle. For a popular treatment, see Andrew Wilson, *War Gaming* (Harmondsworth: Penguin, 1970).

159 Op. cit., p. 62.

160 Such interpretations as are made from games of this sort, therefore, tend often to be rather speculative, despite the apparent rigour of their presentation. For an example, see the discussion in R. A. Brody, 'Some systemic effects of the spread of nuclear weapons technology: A study through simulation of a multi-nuclear future', *Journal of Conflict Resolution*, 1964, 7, pp. 663–753.

161 Op. cit., p. 62. Comparison is invited with such techniques as those of the sociodrama and the psychodrama, which are also designed to elicit assumptions, social and individual, implicit in everyday conduct. In addition, of course, a number of experiments not normally classified as simulations none the less fulfil a similar function: the study of obedience by Milgram (1965: op. cit.) is a case in point here.

162 See H. Hoffmann, 'Symbolic logic and the analysis of social organization', *Behavioral Science*, 1959, pp. 288–98; and F. G. Lounsbury, 'A semantic analysis of the Pawnee kinship usage', *Language*, 1956, 32, pp. 158–94. This may be taken to exemplify some of the possibilities for rigorous *post hoc* analyses of ethnographic data collected within the ethnoscientific tradition; cf. our discussion of the latter on p. 105f. supra.

163 See especially G. H. von Wright, *Norm and Action* (London: Routledge & Kegan Paul, 1963). Cf. too idem, 'Deontic logic', *Mind*, 1951, 60, pp. 1–15.

164 A. Hofstadter and J. C. C. McKinsey, 'On the logic of imperatives', *Philosophy of Science*, 1939, 6, pp. 446–57; K. Menger, 'A logic of the doubtful: an optative and imperative logic', *Reports of a Mathematical*

*Colloquium* (Notre Dame), 2nd series vol. 1 (1939), pp. 53–64, H. G. Bohnert, 'The semiotic status of commands', *Philosophy of Science*, 1945, 12, pp. 302–15.

165 See O. K. Moore and S. B. Anderson, 'Modern logic and tasks for experiments on problem solving behavior', *Journal of Psychology*, 1954, 38, pp. 151–60; A. R. Anderson and O. K. Moore, 'The formal analysis of normative concepts', *ASR*, 1957, 22, pp. 9–17, reprinted in I. M. Copi and J. A. Gould (eds), *Contemporary Readings in Logical Theory* (New York: Macmillan, 1967); and A. R. Anderson, 'Logic, norms and roles', *Ratio*, 1962, 4, pp. 36–49.

166 See A. R. Anderson, 'A reduction of deontic logic to alethic modal logic', *Mind*, 1958, 67, pp. 100–3 and idem, 'The formal analysis of normative systems', in N. Rescher (ed.), *The Logic of Decision and Action* (University of Pittsburgh Press, 1967), pp. 147–213.

167 See, for instance, G. H. von Wright, *Time Change and Contradiction* (Cambridge University Press, 1969), p. 32.

168 Both op. cit.

169 A. R. Anderson (1967), op. cit.

170 Cf. 'computer simulation', below, p. 310f. Also compare Galtung's idea of sociology as the science of the 'socially possible': J. Galtung, 'Rank and social integration: A multi-dimensional approach', in Berger, Zelditch, and Anderson, *Sociological Theories in Progress* (1966), pp. 145–98.

171 See von Wright (1951, 1963), op. cit.

172 See part one, particularly chapter 3. Perhaps an analogy may be permitted here with scientific epistemology, since this was surely advanced when the familiar logical dichotomy of 'true–false' was rejected in favour of a more continuum-like conception of truth-value, expressed in the idea of 'degrees of confirmation'.

173 Op. cit.

174 Ibid.

175 See chapter 2, especially p. 37f. Cf. too M. Barkun, *Law Without Sanctions* (Yale University Press, 1968), in which the thesis is developed (and perhaps somewhat overstated) that sanctions are unimportant in all legal systems, whether primitive, municipal, or international.

176 Anderson (1967), op. cit.

177 Ibid.

178 This is an ideal which sociological theory strives for, but seldom attains. For an attempt to specify role-theory in these terms, which well illustrates the difficulties involved and the analytic advantages to be gained, see N. Gross, W. Mason, and A. W. McEachern, *Explorations in Role Analysis* (New York: Wiley, 1958).

179 The interpretations of the truth-functional constants are discussed in most introductory texts on logic; see, for instance, P. F. Strawson, *Introduction to Logical Theory* (London: Oxford University Press, 1952); or, more recently, R. J. Ackerman, *Modern Deductive Logic* (London: Macmillan, 1970).

180 Cf. R. Hilpinen (ed.), *Deontic Logic: Introductory and Systematic Readings* (Dordrecht: Reidel, 1971).

181 See J. C. C. McKinsey, 'A solution to the decision problem for the Lewis systems S2 and S4, with an application to topology', *Journal of Symbolic Logic*, 1941, 6, pp. 117–34.

182 Cf. von Wright (1963), op. cit. Cited in Anderson and Moore (1957), op. cit.

183 Ibid.

184 Cf. W. D. Hudson (ed.), *Controversies in Philosophy: The Is-Ought Question* (London: Macmillan, 1969).

185 Anderson (1967), op. cit., p. 71.

186 See part one, and particularly pp. 45f. and 88f.

187 *Time, Change and Contradiction* (1969), p. 5. The development of tense-logic has mainly derived from the work of A. N. Prior; see his *Time and Modality* (Oxford University Press, 1957) and idem, *Past, Present and Future* (Oxford University Press, 1967).

188 H. C. White, *An Anatomy of Kinship* (Englewood Cliffs, N. J.: Prentice-Hall, 1963).

189 See, for instance, his 'A formal account of the Crow and Omaha-type kinship terminologies', in L. W. Goodenough (ed.), *Explorations in Cultural Anthropology* (New York: McGraw-Hill, 1964), pp. 351–93.

190 N. M. Smith, 'A calculus for ethics: A theory of the structure of value. Parts I and II', *Behavioral Science*, 1956, pp. 111–42 and 186–211. On the general question of the applicability of stochastic models in social science, see D. J. Bartholomew, *Stochastic Models of Social Processes* (New York: Wiley, 1968).

191 See J. P. Boyd, 'The algebra of group kinship', *J. Math. Psychol.*, 1969, 6, 1, pp. 139–67.

192 Such formalizations should, of course, facilitate more systematic and rigorous analyses of social science data, but they will not provide an instant solution to all the problems that any given inquiry might raise. It is important, therefore, to be sensitive also to some of the limitations of formalizations. On this, cf. C. Politis, 'Limitations of formalizations', *Philosophy of Science*, 1965, vol. 32.

On the other hand, there are certain other questions within our present field of inquiry that are amenable to elucidation by formal methods, but which have remained unconsidered. We are thinking particularly here of questions concerning the transitivity of preferences (and related issues) and of the relationship between individual and collective preferences, a problem that has some political as well as academic significance. The first of these issues is particularly relevant to sociology as a means of throwing light on the question of the social determinants (e.g. role-conflict) of intransitive choices. On this, see espec. J. M. Davis, 'The transitivity of preferences', *Behavioral Science*, 1958, which provides a competent review of the experimental evidence, and also A. M. Rose, 'Conditions for irrational choices', *Social Research*, 1963, 30, which sums up the social and psychological conditions conducive to individual or group intransitivity.

On the question of the relationship between individual and collective preferences—i.e. of how one aggregates the multiplicity of individual preference scales about alternative social actions—the *locus classicus* has become K. J. Arrow, *Social Choice and Individual Values* (Yale Univ. Press, 1970 edn), q.v. A shortened form of Arrow's central proof is given in his 'Values and collective decision-making', in Laslett and Runciman, *Philosophy, Politics and Society* (1967), 3rd Series, pp. 215–32.

193 See, for example, A. C. Wahl, 'Chemistry by computer', *Scientific American*, 1970, 222, 4, p. 54f. and J. R. Emshoff and R. L. Sisson, *Design and Use of Computer Simulation Models* (New York: Macmillan, 1970). F. P. Wyman, *Simulation Modeling* (New York: Wiley, 1970) discusses the simulation language SIMSCRIPT. For ongoing developments in this field, the interested reader should consult also the monthly journal *Simulation*, published by Simulation Councils, Inc. of America. The latter is the principal technical society at present devoted to the advancement of simulation through the use of computers.

194 A. Newell, J. C. Shaw, and H. A. Simon, 'Empirical explorations of the logic theory machine: a case study in heuristics', *Proc. Western Joint Computer Conf.*, 1957, 11, pp. 218–30.

195 A later version of this language is described in A. Newell *et al.*, *Information Processing Language—V. Manual* (Englewood Cliffs, N. J.: Prentice-Hall, 1964). One of the studies using the IPL language is R. P. Abelson and J. D. Carroll, 'Computer simulation of individual belief systems', *Amer. Behav. Scientist*, 1965, 8, pp. 24–30.

196 See Abelson and Carroll (1965), op. cit.

197 See P. L. Simmons and R. F. Simmons, 'The simulation of cognitive processes: II. An annotated bibliography', *IRE Trans. on Electronic Computers*, 1962, EC-11, pp. 535–52; E. A. Feigenbaum and J. Feldman (eds), *Computers and Thought* (New York: McGraw-Hill, 1963); M. Sass and W. D. Wilkinson (eds), *Computer Augmentation of Human Reasoning* (Washington, D.C.: Spartan Books, 1965); and R. P. Abelson, 'Simulation of social behavior', in G. Lindzey and E. Aronson (eds), *Handbook of Social Psychology* (1968), vol. 2, pp. 274–356.

198 See J. C. Loehlin, *Computer Models of Personality* (New York: Random House, 1969) and I. Pool and A. Kessler, 'The Kaiser, the Tsar, and the computer: information processing in a crisis', *Amer. Behav. Scientist*, 1965, 8, pp. 31–8.

199 I. Pool, R. P. Abelson, and S. Popkin, *Candidates, Issues, and Strategies: A Computer Simulation of the 1960 Presidential Election* (Cambridge: M.I.T. Press, 1964).

200 From R. P. Abelson (1968), op. cit., p. 334.

201 Cf. I. Pool, R. P. Abelson, and S. Popkin, 'A postscript on the 1964 election', *Amer. Behav. Scientist*, 1965, 8, pp. 39–44.

202 Cf., for instance, T. Hägerstrand, 'A Monte Carlo approach to diffusion', *European Journal of Sociology*, 1965, 6, pp. 43–67.

203 Cf. R. P. Abelson and A. Bernstein, 'A computer simulation model of community referendum controversies', *Public Opinion Quarterly*, 1963, 27, pp. 93–122.

204 See, e.g., R. Boudon, 'Réflexions sur la logique des modèles simulés', *European Journal of Sociology*, 1965, 6, pp. 3–20.

423

205 J. P. Gilbert and E. A. Hammel, 'Computer simulation and analysis of problems in kinship and social structure', *Amer. Anthropologist*, 1966, 68, pp. 71–93.

206 Thus Abelson (1968) offers the following advice: 'Wherever there are "degrees of freedom" clearly available to the programmer in his choice of programming options, he should try to write the program so as not to foreclose them; as many options as feasible should be put into the input specifications or made readily accessible through easily altered subroutines'. (Op. cit., p. 307. Italics omitted).

207 J. R. Emshoff, 'A computer simulation of the Prisoner's Dilemma', *Behavioral Science*, 1970, 15, 4, pp. 304–17.

208 Op. cit.

209 Ibid., p. 343.

210 Ibid., p. 344

211 Ibid., p. 320.

212 D. Mitchie, 'The intelligent machine', *Science Journal*, 1970, 6, 10.

213 T. D. Sterling and S. V. Pollack, *Computing and Computer Science* (London: Collier-Macmillan, 1970), p. 84.

214 Cf., for instance, E. Joseph, 'Towards a fifth generation', *Science Journal*, 1970, 6, 10, pp. 101–4. This whole issue is devoted to the subject of 'Computers in the 70s'.

215 For two contrasting views, with reference to social science possibilities, cf. U. Neisser, 'The imitation of man by machine', *Science*, 1963, 139, 193 and W. R. Reitman, 'Information processing models in psychology', *Science*, 1964, 144, 1192.

PART THREE:   ETHICAL RELATIVISM

Chapter 9

1 Shia Moser, *Absolutism and Relativism in Ethics* (Springfield, Ill.: Thomas, 1963), p. 4. This proved a valuable introduction to several of the issues at stake. Other useful sources are A. Edel, *Anthropology and Ethics* (Oxford: Blackwell, 1959); Morris Ginsberg, *Essays in Sociology and Social Philosophy*, vol. I (London: Heinemann, 1956), especially ch. 7, pp. 97–129; H. Shoeck and J. W. Wiggins, *Relativism and the Study of Man* (Princeton: Van Nostrand, 1961); and A. MacBeath, *Experiments in Living* (London: Macmillan, 1952), which discusses some of the ethical implications of comparative functionalism. Relevant articles include Ralph Linton, 'Universal ethical principles: an anthropological view', in R. N. Anshen (ed.), *Moral Principles of Action* (New York: Harper, 1952); D. Bidney, 'The philosophical presuppositions of cultural relativism and cultural absolutism', in L. B. Ward (ed.), *Ethics and the Social Sciences* (University of Notre Dame Press, 1959); M. J. Herskovits, 'Some further comments on cultural relativism', *Amer. Anthropologist*, 1959, 60, p. 267f.; and P. F. Schmidt, 'Some criticisms of cultural relativism', in R. A. Manners and David

Kaplan (eds), *Theory in Anthropology: A Source Book* (London: Routledge & Kegan Paul, 1968).

2 The typology outlined below is particularly indebted to the discussion in Moser (1963) op. cit.

3 The former is discussed briefly in A. MacIntyre, *A Short History of Ethics* (1967), especially chs 2 and 8. The *locus classicus* for the latter is of course, Max Weber's essay on the role of the Protestant Ethic in the genesis of modern capitalism—viz. *The Protestant Ethic and the Spirit of Capitalism* (London: Allen & Unwin, 1930). Relevant also, however, is C. B. MacPherson's perceptive interpretation of the political theories of Hobbes and Locke in terms of the industrial revolution and the development of a social order increasingly centred upon a market economy: see his *The Political Theory of Possessive Individualism* (Oxford University Press, 1962).

4 This was, of course, the position adopted by W. G. Sumner in his *Folkways* (Boston: Ginn, 1940; first published 1906).

5 P. H. Nowell-Smith, *Ethics* (Harmondsworth: Penguin 1954), p. 11.

6 Accounts are given in Peter Worsley, *The Trumpet Shall Sound* (London: MacGibbon & Kee, 1968; first published 1957); E. J. Hobsbawm, *Primitive Rebels* (Manchester University Press, 1959); and G. Cochrane, *Big Men and Cargo Cults* (Oxford University Press, 1970). A useful review is Y. Talmon, 'The pursuit of the millennium', *European Journal of Sociology*, 1962, 3, pp. 125–48.

7 R. Redfield, *The Primitive World and Its Transformations* (Cornell University Press, 1953), p. 145f.

8 See R. Firth, *We, The Tikopia* (London: Allen & Unwin, 1936). This has become the standard ethnography, but for a discussion cf. idem, 'Suicide and risk-taking in Tikopia society', *Psychiatry*, 1961, 24, pp. 1–17.

9 W. H. R. Rivers (ed.), *Essays on the Depopulation of Melanesia* (Harvard University Press, 1922), especially p. 96f.

10 This was a *cause célèbre* in anthropological circles at the time, although later opinion was to cast doubt upon this particular explanation.

11 S. Moser (1963), op. cit.

12 Such *ad hominem* criticisms of moral positivism in the writings of functionalists such as Parsons can be seriously misleading in so far as they direct attention away from certain *intellectual* failings in the theories in question that might seem to lead to this type of moral conclusion. In the case of the Parsonian tradition, this is most apparent in the idea of a general 'problem of social order' as the essential starting point for any theory of social systems. Thus, Mac-Intyre has argued that the reality of such a *general* problem of social order or disorder has not been convincingly demonstrated, and that the existence of such a problem (as, e.g., in the work of Durkheim) is compatible only with a Hobbesian view of human nature and with a conception of social norms as necessarily repressive or constraining, both of these being views that the available evidence does not support (A. C. MacIntyre: personal communication). On this, cf. too pp. 341–2 infra.

13 G. H. Pitt-Rivers, *The Clash of Culture and the Contact of Races* (London: Routledge, 1927). In the modern world, of course, this argument is sometimes reversed, and cultural differences are invoked as grounds for ignoring the biological unity of man. Such a change of thought, for instance, from the biological to the cultural, seems to have characterized recent justifications for *apartheid*, as issued by the South African Government. On this issue, cf. also n. 1.14 supra. One of the best of recent symposia on the concept of race in modern science is contained in M. Mead *et al.* (eds), *Science and the Concept of Race* (Columbia University Press, 1968).

14 An interesting illustration here is Peter Berger's *The Noise of Solemn Assemblies* (New York: Doubleday, 1961), since this analysis of modern Protestantism in America is written in the first half from the 'objective' position of a sociologist, and in the second half from the subjective, committed position of a practising Christian.

On this issue in general, justifications can be provided for both sides—the one stressing the importance of an internal understanding in the *Verstehen* tradition, the other stressing the need for objectivity and a measure of detachment from the object of study.

However, in relatively few cases is the choice one between total detachment and total identification with the subjects under study. As we saw in chapter 8, many possibilities exist for role-playing in participant observation, and in forms for which reasonable degrees of reliability can be attained. In addition to which, the kind of 'depth', subjectivistic knowledge of the motives and feelings associated with, say, a particular social movement that total identification may provide is likely to be of more interest to the concerns of the *littérateur* than to those of the sociologist. It might perhaps be noted further in this connection that the best informants (and respondents generally) are frequently those who combine full identification with a particular social category or group with a measure of detachment from it. In our own field work, for example, in a relatively traditional society, it was clear that those who had been away from their home community, even if for only short periods of time, were consistently better able to describe their communities to an outsider than those who had spent their whole lives there. Similarly, it has been commented in studies of unemployment that the most articulate about the condition of being unemployed are not those currently unemployed, but almost invariably the *previously* unemployed.

15 That is, in sociological terms, one would have to determine whether the same function could be fulfilled by any plausible structural alternatives; cf. D. Aberle *et al.* (1950), op. cit.

16 It is, of course, a general fact that however well we may seek to inform ourselves, we can never be wholly sure of the total consequences of our major decisions. But these have to be taken none the less.

17 B. Croce, *History: Its Theory and Practice* (New York: Russell, 1960; first published 1916), translated by D. Ainslie. Croce's attitude towards relativism in fact always contained elements of ambivalence, and is, of course, to be understood within the context of his idealistic

conception of history. A useful discussion is given in H. S. Hughes, *Consciousness and Society* (London: MacGibbon & Kee, 1959), espec. ch. 3 and 6.

18 Cf., for instance, the studies in *Tristes Tropiques* (1955) and *La Pensée Sauvage* (1966).

19 Mao Tse-Tung, *Selected Works*, vol. I (Peking: Foreign Languages Press, n.d.), p. 296.

20 Cf., for example, J. R. Lucas, *The Freedom of the Will* (Oxford University Press, 1970).

21 J. Galtung, *Theory and Methods of Social Research* (1969), p. 485.

22 Ibid., p. 485.

23 The phrase is from Morris Ginsberg (1956), op. cit., who expressed this very criticism of relativist doctrines.

24 Cf. his *Language, Truth and Logic* (Harmondsworth: Penguin, 1971 edn).

25 W. K. Frankena, *Ethics* (1963), pp. 88–92.

26 W. G. Sumner, *Folkways* (1940). For a discussion of Sumner's position, see R. Notestein, 'W. G. Sumner: An essay in the sociology of knowledge', *A. J. Econ. Sociol.*, 1959, 18, 4, pp. 397–413.

## Chapter 10

1 The well-known books by these authors include M. Mead, *Coming of Age in Samoa* and *Growing Up in New Guinea* (both Harmondsworth: Penguin; first published, respectively, 1928 & 1930); idem, *Sex and Temperament in Three Primitive Societies* (New York: Morrow, 1935); and idem, *New Lives for Old: A Cultural Transformation, Manus, 1928–1953* (New York: Morrow, 1956). Ruth Benedict's best-known work is *Patterns of Culture* (London: Routledge & Kegan Paul, 1963; first published 1935), which reviews and contrasts the cultures of the Dobuans, the Kwakiutl, and Zuni (Pueblo Indians). Some of her interpretations of these cultures have been disputed; see, for instance, L. An-Chi, 'Zuni: some observations and queries', *American Anthropologist*, 1937, 39, p. 63f. Cf. too: S. C. Oliver (1965), op. cit. It should be added here that in part one of this study it was pointed out that cultural relativism applies not only to the overt content of moral codes, to the distinctive precepts and values which they enjoin, but also, and less obviously, to their more discursive aspects (e.g. modes of justification) and more formal elements (e.g. criteria of ethical competency, scope, focus on intentions v. consequences, etc.).

2 See D. Aberle *et al.* (1950), op. cit.; G. P. Murdock, *Social Structure* (New York: Macmillan, 1949); and, for instance, T. Parsons, *Societies: Evolutionary and Comparative Perspectives* (Englewood Cliffs, N.J.: Prentice-Hall, 1966), especially pp. 21–5.

3 W. K. Frankena, *Ethics* (1963), p. 92.

4 For the code used in classifying this information, see G. P. Murdock *et al.*, *An Outline of Cultural Materials* (Yale University Press, 1961), and for the list of societies, idem, *An Outline of World Cultures* (Yale

University Press, 1963). Also, R. Textor (ed.), *A Cross-Cultural Summary* (New Haven: HRAF Press, 1967) lists a wide range of significant correlations between different aspects of this sample of cultures.

5 See McClelland's *The Achieving Society* (1961) and R. B. Cattell, 'The dimensions of culture patterns of factorization of national characters', *Journal of Abnormal and Social Psychology*, 1949, 44, pp. 215–53. See too R. B. Cattell *et al.*, 'An attempt at more refined definition of the cultural dimensions of syntality of modern nations', *ASR*, 1951, 17, pp. 408–21.

6 E. Westermarck, *Ethical Relativity* (London: Kegan Paul, 1932), ch. VII.

7 Ibid., pp. 189–91. For a good modern approach to this subject, see J. Douglas, *The Social Meaning of Suicide* (Oxford University Press 1968). Cf., too, idem (ed.), *Deviance and Respectability: The Social Construction of Moral Meanings* (New York: Basic Books, 1970).

8 Cited in O. Klineberg, *Social Psychology* (New York: Holt, Rinehart, & Winston, 1954), p. 83.

9 Ibid., p. 83.

10 Cf. M. Mead, *New Lives for Old* (1956) and C. Belshaw, *Changing Melanesia* (Melbourne: Oxford University Press, 1954). See too: R. Firth, *Social Change in Tikopia* (New York: Humanities Press, 1959).

11 This type of principle, for instance, often comes up in contemporary discussions of the legitimacy of 'direct action' (with, at least in some cases, its proven efficacy) as opposed to adherence to established democratic procedures.

12 On this, cf. also n. 9.12 supra.

13 See, for instance, C. Wright Mills, *The Sociological Imagination* (1959).

14 Cf. A. W. Gouldner, 'Reciprocity and autonomy in functional theory', in N. Gross (ed.), *Symposium on Sociological Theory* (New York: Harper & Row, 1959), pp. 241–70. See, too, the collection by N. J. Demerath and R. A. Peterson (eds), *System, Change, and Conflict* (New York: Free Press, 1967).

15 Cf. R. K. Merton, *Social Theory and Social Structure* (Chicago: Free Press, 1957), ch. 1.

16 Cf. M. Oakeshott, *Rationalism in Politics and Other Essays* (London: Methuen, 1962). The kind of political attitude we are depicting here is well exemplified in the following passage from Edmund Burke, *Reflections on the Revolution in France*, ed. by W. B. Todd (New York: Holt, Rinehart, & Winston, 1969):

> The science of constructing a commonwealth, or renovating it, or reforming it, is, like every other experimental science, not to be taught *a priori*. Nor is it a short experience that can instruct us in that practical science; because the real effects of moral causes are not always immediate; but that which in the first instance is prejudicial may be excellent in its remoter operation; and its excellence may arise even from the ill effects it produces in the beginning. The reverse also happens; and very plausible schemes with very pleasing commencements have often shameful

and lamentable conclusions. In states there are often some obscure
and almost latent causes, things which appear at first view of
little moment, on which a very great part of its prosperity or
adversity may most essentially depend. The science of government
being therefore so practical in itself, and intended for such
practical purposes, a matter which requires experience, and even
more experience than any person can gain in his whole life,
however sagacious and observing he may be, it is with infinite
caution that any man ought to venture upon pulling down an
edifice which has answered in any tolerable degree for ages the
common purposes of society, or on building it up again,
without having models and patterns of approved utility before
his eyes.

This, of course, was written before the social sciences, and empirical
sociology in particular, were to make the structure of society less
opaque than Burke's depiction of it. Also, more reliable comparative
societal data now provide a source for 'models of approved utility'
when social changes are contemplated.

17 S. T. Coleridge, *Biographia Literaria*; quoted in G. Leinhardt, *Social
Anthropology* (Oxford University Press, 1966), p. 115.

18 Benjamin Lee Whorf, *Language, Thought, and Reality*, ed. by J.
Carroll (New York: Wiley, 1956), p. 212f. See, too, for instance, E.
Sapir, 'The status of linguistics as a science', *Language*, 1929, 5, pp.
207–14.

19 Observations about cultures which rest solely on linguistic evidence
are always of questionable status. This is in part because the number
of concepts people possess, and their type, never accurately matches,
and indeed invariably exceeds, the range of words at their disposal.
The fact that members of a particular language-community do not
have a word to translate directly what to us is a key concept (e.g.
'history') does not permit us to conclude that this concept is therefore
unimportant to them. Instead, it may be signified indirectly, or by a
combination of words (e.g. 'my parents' childhood'). One article
which presents the example we have given, concerning time-perceptions,
and illustrates the error of interpretation we have outlined is Dorothy
Lee's discussion of Tikopian culture in 'Linear and nonlinear codi-
fications of reality', *Psychosomatic Medicine*, 1950, 12, pp. 89–97.

20 J. B. Carroll, 'Some psychological effects of language structure' in
P. H. Hoch and J. Zubin (eds), *Psychopathology of Communication*
(New York: Grune & Stratton, 1958) pp. 28–36. For confirmative
experimental evidence, see, e.g., R. Brown and E. H. Lennenberg, 'A
study in language and cognition', *Journal of Abnormal and Social
Psychology*, 1954, 49, pp. 454–62. This study indicated that a subject's
recognition memory for colours was a function of the degree to which
he had available appropriate names for these colours. Cf. too, R. L.
Solomon and D. H. Howes (1951), op. cit.

21 See N. Chomsky, *Aspects of the Theory of Syntax* (Cambridge, Mass.:
M.I.T. Press, 1965) and chapter 8 supra, in which Osgood's research
is discussed.

22 Cf. V. Howard, 'Do anthropologists become moral relativists by mistake?', *Inquiry*, 1968, pp. 175–89.

23 Cf. chapter 2, pp. 41–8.

24 These grounds, of course, usually rest upon particular cognitive premisses: the most apparent example being the belief, as in Judaism and Christianity, in a supreme God, from whom the basic moral precepts are derived in the form of commands.

25 Cf. K. Baier (1958), op. cit.

26 G. Myrdal, *An American Dilemma: The Negro Problem and Modern Democracy*, 2 vols (New York: Harper, 1944).

27 H. L. A. Hart, *The Concept of Law* (1961), ch. 8.

28 In modern societies this is true over relatively short periods of time since the laws are constantly being changed or amended and so the public are constantly being re-classified in legal terms. A recent example of this in England was the lowering of the age of legal majority from 21 to 18.

29 For a perceptive sociological analysis, see especially P. van den Berghe, *South Africa: A Study in Conflict* (Middletown, Conn.: Wesleyan University Press, 1965).

30 For discussion of some of the issues raised by the idea of human rights, see A. I. Melden, *Human Rights* (London: Wadsworth, 1970). On the application of this idea, cf. A. H. Robertson (ed.), *Human Rights in National and International Law* (Manchester University Press, 1970).

31 We are thinking here of social position in the composite sense suggested by Galtung in his paper 'Foreign policy opinion as a function of social position', *Journal of Peace Research*, 1964, pp. 206–31. In brief, society is conceived as a series of concentric circles, having a centre and a periphery. The 'centre' is characterized by such things as living in a city; living in the central area of the country; being between the ages of 30 and 50; having more than primary education; having an occupation in the secondary or tertiary economic sectors; having a skilled or professional occupation; being a man. The social periphery implies a lack of these attributes. An additive index can then be simply constructed with a theoretical range from 0 (periphery) to 8 (centre) by giving each item a value of 1 or 0. Cross-national evidence so far indicates systematic relationships between this summary index and a range of socio-political attitudes. Galtung has summarized these differences by noting that the periphery is characterized by absolutistic and moralistic views, and a tendency either to totally accept or totally reject certain attitudes; whilst the centre is characterized by gradualism pragmatism, and partial acceptance or rejection of the *status quo*. These results are broadly compatible with our hypothesis. We should not expect, however, that each attribute of status will correlate with relativist views to the same degree. In any research on this subject, then, it would be useful to see the relationship broken down per item of the centre-periphery dimension.

32 S. Putney and R. Middleton, 'Ethical relativism and anomia', *AJS*, 1962, 67, 4, pp. 430–8.

33 T. W. Adorno, E. Frenkel-Brunswick, D. J. Levinson, and R. N.

Sanford, *The Authoritarian Personality* (New York: Wiley, 1950).
34 Cf., for example, D. T. Cambell and R. A. LeVine, 'A proposal for cooperative cross-cultural research on ethnocentrism', *Journal of Conflict Resolution*, 1961, 5, 1, pp. 82–108 which takes up some of the methodological problems inherent in studies of ethnocentrism and suggests some solutions to them. The disparate nature of the items on the Ethnocentrism Scale of Adorno *et al.* is discussed in R. Christie and M. Jahoda (eds), *Studies in the Scope and Method of 'The Authoritarian Personality* (Chicago: Free Press, 1954).

For studies confirming the relation between ethnocentrism and fascist/authoritarian attitudes, see, for instance, H. G. Gough, 'Studies of social intolerance', *Journal of Social Psychology*, 1951, 333, pp. 237–69; D. J. Levinson, 'Authoritarian personality and foreign policy', *Journal of Conflict Resolution*, 1957, 1, pp. 37–47; and Milton Rokeach, *The Open and Closed Mind* (New York: Basic Books, 1960). In the last study, closed-mindedness is defined in formal, ideology-free terms, and the findings showed that authoritarian left-of-centre groups (communists and religious non-believers) and authoritarian right-of-centre groups (Catholics) both scored relatively high on the Dogmatism and Opinionation Scales, but only the authoritarian groups to right-of-centre scored high on the California F and Ethnocentrism Scales.

35 See, for example, H. Gleitman and J. J. Greenbaum, 'Attitudes and personality patterns of Hungarian refugees', *Public Opinion Quarterly*, 1961, 25, pp. 351–65.
36 From W. A. Scott, *Values and Organizations* (1965) p. 31.
37 Ibid., p. 32.
38 See, for example, L. F. Douglas, 'Types of Students and Their Outlook on University Education: A comparative study of students in the physical and social sciences' (Unpublished Ph.D. dissertation, London School of Economics Library, 1964).
39 To avoid excessive complexity here, we have not pursued in depth the consequences of the logical distinction between evaluation and prescription for the various relativist doctrines.
40 Programmes of education designed to change prejudicial attitudes towards other races and ethnic groups come to mind as an example here; cf. especially P. I. Rose, *The Subject Is Race* (1968).
41 E. Kamenka, *Marxism and Ethics* (London: Macmillan, 1969), pp. 36–7. Cf. also idem, *The Ethical Foundations of Marxism* (London: Routledge & Kegan Paul, 1962), espec. pt. IV.
42 This is particularly so in the work of Engels and his later followers, who, as Kamenka (1962, 1969) points out, tended to restate Marx's often complex and elusive ideas on this subject, as on others, in much cruder, more black-and-white terms. Thus, it is Engels who puts the relativist critique of moralities in its starkest terms. As he writes (*Anti-Dühring*, p. 109):

> We maintain . . . that all former moral theories are the product, in the last analysis, of the economic stage which society had reached at that particular epoch. And as society has hitherto moved in

431

class antagonisms, morality was always a class morality; it has either justified the domination and the interests of the ruling class, or, as soon as the oppressed class has become powerful enough, it has represented the revolt against this domination and the future interests of the oppressed.

43 In particular, the tension between relativism and absolutism is most apparent in the history of Soviet interpretations of Marxism. It is noteworthy, for instance, that especially since the Second World War, and comparative social stability, the Soviet Union has increasingly adhered to an absolutized conception of morality, and one that invokes such 'bourgeois' notions as the importance of conscience, a sense of duty, and so on. On this, cf. Kamenka (1962), pt V and idem (1969), ch. VI. It is, of course, recognized that these ideological vacillations may themselves be amenable to comprehension within a sociology-of-knowledge framework which relates them systematically to changing conditions in Russian society, material and otherwise.

44 Cf., for example (*The Communist Manifesto*):
Does it require deep intuition to comprehend that man's ideas, views and conceptions, in a word, man's consciousness, changes with every change in the conditions of his material existence, in his social relations, and in his social life? What else does the history of ideas prove, than that intellectual production changes its character in proportion as material production is changed? The ruling ideas of each age have ever been the ideas of its ruling class.

45 See K. Mannheim, *Ideology and Utopia* (New York: Harcourt, Brace, 1936).

46 A. C. MacIntyre, *Marxism and Christianity* (Harmondsworth: Penguin, 1971), p. 500.

47 E. Kamenka (1969), pp. 66–7.

48 Ibid., p. 67.

49 Social theories are being referred to here in the sense in which this expression is used in chapter 5 supra.

50 For the conceptual relation between beliefs and actions, cf. pp. 142–4 and n. 5.48 supra.

51 Cf. the contributions by L. R. Perry and R. S. Peters to R. D. Archambault (ed.), *Philosophical Analysis and Education* (London: Routledge & Kegan Paul, 1965) and L. Cremin, *The Transformation of the School* (New York: Knopf, 1961). Cf. too, for a historical treatment of anthropological conceptions in education, P. Nash, *Models of Man: Explorations in the Western Educational Tradition* (New York: Wiley, 1968). This involves a 'portrayal of the most influential models of the educated person that have been created as part of the Western cultural tradition'.

52 For a popular treatment, see Maya Pines, *Revolution in Learning: the years from birth to five* (London: Allen Lane, 1969). On the 'social definition of childhood', cf. also P. Ariès, *Centuries of Childhood* (1962) and Bronfenbrenner (1972), op. cit.

53 P. L. Berger, *Invitation to Sociology: A Humanistic Perspective* (Harmondsworth: Penguin, 1966), p. 180.
54 See: J. A. Shelton, 'Anthropological "values" and culture: a note', *American Anthropologist*, 1965, 67, 1, pp. 103-7.
55 S. Moser (1963), op. cit., p. 98.
56 For empirical examples, see, for instance, W. R. Bascom and M. J. Herskovits (eds), *Continuity and Change in African Cultures* (University of Chicago Press, 1959).
57 Cf. V. G. Kiernan, *The Lords of Human Kind* (London: Weidenfeld & Nicolson, 1969).
58 For a good discussion, see A. G. N. Flew, *Evolutionary Ethics* (London: Macmillan, 1967). The *exemplum horribile* of this type of doctrine in politics was the Social Darwinism associated with certain elements of the German Nazi Party. However, the analytic questions which derive from the relationship between ethical and evolutionary theory raise in interesting form the problem of the mutual implications of descriptive and normative discourse, and as such have been too summarily dismissed by philosophers on the grounds of their presumptive entailment of the 'naturalistic fallacy'. As Flew (op. cit.) states in regard to the latter: 'This has certainly been central in much which has been called evolutionary ethics; so much so that it has often, but wrongly, been thought to be the essential and polymorphous error which must both constitute and vitiate everything so labelled' (p. 31).
59 A. Salomon, *The Tyranny of Progress* (New York: Noonday, 1955).
60 See H. Levin, 'Semantics of culture', *Daedalus*, 1965, 94, 1, p. 1f.
61 The dereifying consequences of modern technology are alluded to in Herbert Marcuse, *An Essay on Liberation* (London: Allen Lane, 1969), p. 50f. et passim. The relativistic aspects of contemporary consciousness are discussed briefly in P. Berger (1966), op. cit., ch. 2.
62 *The Coming Crisis in Western Sociology* (London: Heinemann, 1971), p. 66.
63 See D. Lerner, *The Passing of Traditional Society* (London: Collier-Macmillan, 1964). Lerner ascribed much of this lack of empathy to the undevelopment of the mass media in these societies.
64 Hence, by implication, totalitarian and ideologically closed societies are much less conducive to the establishment, and maintenance, of a viable social scientific tradition.

# Name index

Abelson, R. P., 141, 312, 313, 317, 318, 391n
Aberle, D. F., 207, 338, 369n, 376n, 381n, 426n
Abt, L. E., 416n
Achal, A. P., 189
Ackerman, R. J., 421n
Adcock, C. J., 274, 276
Adler, F., 367n
Adorno, T. W., 190, 430n, 431n
Albrecht, M. C., 412n, 415n
Allport, G. W., 58, 59, 67, 169, 206, 235, 250, 252, 266, 405n, 406n
An-Chi, L., 427n
Anderson, A. R., 300, 301, 303, 304, 306, 307, 422n
Anderson, G. L., 416n
Anderson, H. H., 416n
Angell, Robert, 255
Arcais, F. d', 375n
Argyle, M., 104
Ariès, P., 216, 432n
Aristotle, 57, 298
Aron, R., 401n
Arrington, R., 398n
Arrow, K. J., 423n
Asch, S. E., 338
Athey, K. R., 404n
Aubert, V., 393n
Ayer, A. J., 336

Back, K. W., 398n, 409n
Baier, K., 369n, 395n, 430n
Bales, R. F., 224, 408n
Bandura, A., 244
Banfield, E. C., 34, 271, 272, 389n
Banks, A. S., 93, 382n
Banta, T. J., 194
Banton, M., 366n
Baran, P., 401n
Barber, B., 396n
Barbu, Z., 374n
Baritz, L., 6
Barker, R. G., 224
Barkun, M., 421n
Bartholomew, D. J., 422n
Bartlett, F. C., 222
Barton, A. H., 58, 196, 205
Bascom, W. R., 433n
Bateson, G., 237
Baum, R. C., 256
Baumrind, D., 411n
Becker, Howard, 234, 399n
Beigel, H. G., 374n
Bell, Daniel, 183, 397n
Bellack, L., 416n
Belshaw, C., 428n
Belson, W. A., 202
Bendix, R., 406n
Benedict, Ruth, 326, 337, 371n, 373n

435

# International Library of Sociology

Edited by
## John Rex
*University of Warwick*

Founded by
## Karl Mannheim

as The International Library of Sociology
and Social Reconstruction

*This Catalogue also contains other Social Science
series published by Routledge*

Routledge & Kegan Paul    London and Boston

68-74 Carter Lane  London EC4V 5EL
9 Park Street  Boston  Mass 02108

# Contents

● *Books so marked are available in paperback*
*All books are in Metric Demy 8vo format (216 × 138mm approx.)*

## GENERAL SOCIOLOGY

**Belshaw, Cyril.** The Conditions of Social Performance. *An Exploratory Theory. 144 pp.*

**Brown, Robert.** Explanation in Social Science. *208 pp.*

**Cain, Maureen E.** Society and the Policeman's Role. *About 300 pp.*

**Gibson, Quentin.** The Logic of Social Enquiry. *240 pp.*

**Homans, George C.** Sentiments and Activities: *Essays in Social Science. 336 pp.*

**Isajiw, Wsevold W.** Causation and Functionalism in Sociology. *165 pp.*

**Johnson, Harry M.** Sociology: *a Systematic Introduction. Foreword by Robert K. Merton. 710 pp.*

**Mannheim, Karl.** Essays on Sociology and Social Psychology. *Edited by Paul Keckskemeti. With Editorial Note by Adolph Lowe. 344 pp.*
Systematic Sociology: *An Introduction to the Study of Society. Edited by J. S. Erös and Professor W. A. C. Stewart. 220 pp.*

**Martindale, Don.** The Nature and Types of Sociological Theory. *292 pp.*

● **Maus, Heinz.** A Short History of Sociology. *234 pp.*

**Mey, Harald.** Field-Theory. *A Study of its Application in the Social Sciences. 352 pp.*

**Myrdal, Gunnar.** Value in Social Theory: *A Collection of Essays on Methodology. Edited by Paul Streeten. 332 pp.*

**Ogburn, William F.,** and **Nimkoff, Meyer F.** A Handbook of Sociology. *Preface by Karl Mannheim. 656 pp. 46 figures. 35 tables.*

**Parsons, Talcott,** and **Smelser, Neil J.** Economy and Society: *A Study in the Integration of Economic and Social Theory. 362 pp.*

● **Rex, John.** Key Problems of Sociological Theory. *220 pp.*

**Stark, Werner.** The Fundamental Forms of Social Thought. *280 pp.*


## FOREIGN CLASSICS OF SOCIOLOGY

● **Durkheim, Emile.** Suicide. *A Study in Sociology. Edited and with an Introduction by George Simpson. 404 pp.*
Professional Ethics and Civic Morals. *Translated by Cornelia Brookfield. 288 pp.*

● **Gerth, H. H.,** and **Mills, C. Wright.** From Max Weber: *Essays in Sociology. 502 pp.*

**Tönnies, Ferdinand.** Community and Association. *(Gemeinschaft und Gesellschaft.) Translated and Supplemented by Charles P. Loomis. Foreword by Pitirim A. Sorokin. 334 pp.*


## SOCIAL STRUCTURE

**Andreski, Stanislav.** Military Organization and Society. *Foreword by Professor A. R. Radcliffe-Brown. 226 pp. 1 folder.*

● **Cole, G. D. H.** Studies in Class Structure. *220 p.*

**Coontz, Sydney H.** Population Theories and the Economic Interpretation. *202 pp.*

**Coser, Lewis.** The Functions of Social Conflict. *204 pp.*

**Dickie-Clark, H. F.** Marginal Situation: *A Sociological Study of a Coloured Group. 240 pp. 11 tables.*

**Glass, D. V.** (Ed.). Social Mobility in Britain. *Contributions by J. Berent, T. Bottomore, R. C. Chambers, J. Floud, D. V. Glass, J. R. Hall, H. T. Himmelweit, R. K. Kelsall, F. M. Martin, C. A. Moser, R. Mukherjee, and W. Ziegel. 420 pp.*

**Glaser, Barney,** and **Strauss, Anselm L.** Status Passage. *A Formal Theory. 208 pp.*

**Jones, Garth N.** Planned Organizational Change: *An Exploratory Study Using an Empirical Approach. 268 pp.*

**Kelsall, R. K.** Higher Civil Servants in Britain: *From 1870 to the Present Day. 268 pp. 31 tables.*

**König, René.** The Community. *232 pp. Illustrated.*

● **Lawton, Denis.** Social Class, Language and Education. *192 pp.*

**McLeish, John.** The Theory of Social Change: *Four Views Considered. 128 pp.*

**Marsh, David C.** The Changing Social Structure in England and Wales, 1871-1961. *272 pp.*

**Mouzelis, Nicos.** Organization and Bureaucracy. *An Analysis of Modern Theories. 240 pp.*

**Mulkay, M. J.** Functionalism, Exchange and Theoretical Strategy. *272 pp.*

**Ossowski, Stanislaw.** Class Structure in the Social Consciousness. *210 pp.*

## SOCIOLOGY AND POLITICS

**Crick, Bernard.** The American Science of Politics: *Its Origins and Conditions. 284 pp.*

**Hertz, Frederick.** Nationality in History and Politics: *A Psychology and Sociology of National Sentiment and Nationalism. 432 pp.*

**Kornhauser, William.** The Politics of Mass Society. *272 pp. 20 tables.*

**Laidler, Harry W.** History of Socialism. *Social-Economic Movements: An Historical and Comparative Survey of Socialism, Communism, Co-operation, Utopianism; and other Systems of Reform and Reconstruction. 992 pp.*

**Mannheim, Karl.** Freedom, Power and Democratic Planning. *Edited by Hans Gerth and Ernest K. Bramstedt. 424 pp.*

**Mansur, Fatma.** Process of Independence. *Foreword by A. H. Hanson. 208 pp.*

**Martin, David A.** Pacificism: *an Historical and Sociological Study. 262 pp.*

**Myrdal, Gunnar.** The Political Element in the Development of Economic Theory. *Translated from the German by Paul Streeten. 282 pp.*

**Verney, Douglas V.** The Analysis of Political Systems. *264 pp.*

**Wootton, Graham.** Workers, Unions and the State. *188 pp.*

## FOREIGN AFFAIRS: THEIR SOCIAL, POLITICAL AND ECONOMIC FOUNDATIONS

**Bonné, Alfred.** State and Economics in the Middle East: *A Society in Transition. 482 pp.*
  Studies in Economic Development: *with special reference to Conditions in the Under-developed Areas of Western Asia and India. 322 pp. 84 tables.*
**Mayer, J. P.** Political Thought in France from the Revolution to the Fifth Republic. *164 pp.*

## CRIMINOLOGY

**Ancel, Marc.** Social Defence: *A Modern Approach to Criminal Problems. Foreword by Leon Radzinowicz. 240 pp.*
**Cloward, Richard A.,** and **Ohlin, Lloyd E.** Delinquency and Opportunity: *A Theory of Delinquent Gangs. 248 pp.*
**Downes, David M.** The Delinquent Solution. *A Study in Subcultural Theory. 296 pp.*
**Dunlop, A. B.,** and **McCabe, S.** Young Men in Detention Centres. *192 pp.*
**Friedlander, Kate.** The Psycho-Analytical Approach to Juvenile Delinquency: *Theory, Case Studies, Treatment. 320 pp.*
**Glueck, Sheldon,** and **Eleanor.** Family Environment and Delinquency. *With the statistical assistance of Rose W. Kneznek. 340 pp.*
**Lopez-Rey, Manuel.** Crime. *An Analytical Appraisal. 288 pp.*
**Mannheim, Hermann.** Comparative Criminology: *a Text Book. Two volumes. 442 pp. and 380 pp.*
**Morris, Terence.** The Criminal Area: *A Study in Social Ecology. Foreword by Hermann Mannheim. 232 pp. 25 tables. 4 maps.*
**Trasler, Gordon.** The Explanation of Criminality. *144 pp.*

## SOCIAL PSYCHOLOGY

**Bagley, Christopher.** The Social Psychology of the Child with Epilepsy. *320 pp.*
**Barbu, Zevedei.** Problems of Historical Psychology. *248 pp.*
**Blackburn, Julian.** Psychology and the Social Pattern. *184 pp.*
● **Fleming, C. M.** Adolescence: *Its Social Psychology: With an Introduction to recent findings from the fields of Anthropology, Physiology, Medicine, Psychometrics and Sociometry. 288 pp.*
●   The Social Psychology of Education: *An Introduction and Guide to Its Study. 136 pp.*
**Homans, George C.** The Human Group. *Foreword by Bernard DeVoto. Introduction by Robert K. Merton. 526 pp.*
  Social Behaviour: *its Elementary Forms. 416 pp.*

**Klein, Josephine.** The Study of Groups. *226 pp. 31 figures. 5 tables.*
**Linton, Ralph.** The Cultural Background of Personality. *132 pp.*
**Mayo, Elton.** The Social Problems of an Industrial Civilization. *With an appendix on the Political Problem. 180 pp.*
**Ottaway, A. K. C.** Learning Through Group Experience. *176 pp.*
**Ridder, J. C. de.** The Personality of the Urban African in South Africa. *A Thematic Apperception Test Study. 196 pp. 12 plates.*
● **Rose, Arnold M.** (Ed.). Human Behaviour and Social Processes: *an Interactionist Approach. Contributions by Arnold M. Rose, Ralph H. Turner, Anselm Strauss, Everett C. Hughes, E. Franklin Frazier, Howard S. Becker, et al. 696 pp.*
**Smelser, Neil J.** Theory of Collective Behaviour. *448 pp.*
**Stephenson, Geoffrey M.** The Development of Conscience. *128 pp.*
**Young, Kimball.** Handbook of Social Psychology. *658 pp. 16 figures. 10 tables.*

## SOCIOLOGY OF THE FAMILY

**Banks, J. A.** Prosperity and Parenthood: *A Study of Family Planning among The Victorian Middle Classes. 262 pp.*
**Bell, Colin R.** Middle Class Families: *Social and Geographical Mobility. 224 pp.*
**Burton, Lindy.** Vulnerable Children. *272 pp.*
**Gavron, Hannah.** The Captive Wife: *Conflicts of Household Mothers. 190 pp.*
**George, Victor,** and **Wilding, Paul.** Motherless Families. *220 pp.*
**Klein, Josephine.** Samples from English Cultures.
    1. Three Preliminary Studies and Aspects of Adult Life in England. *447 pp.*
    2. Child-Rearing Practices and Index. *247 pp.*
**Klein, Viola.** Britain's Married Women Workers. *180 pp.*
    The Feminine Character. *History of an Ideology. 244 pp.*
**McWhinnie, Alexina M.** Adopted Children. *How They Grow Up. 304 pp.*
**Myrdal, Alva,** and **Klein, Viola.** Women's Two Roles: *Home and Work. 238 pp. 27 tables.*
**Parsons, Talcott,** and **Bales, Robert F.** Family: *Socialization and Interaction Process. In collaboration with James Olds, Morris Zelditch and Philip E. Slater. 456 pp. 50 figures and tables.*

## SOCIAL SERVICES

**Bastide, Roger.** The Sociology of Mental Disorder. *Translated from the French by Jean McNeil. 264 pp.*
**Carlebach, Julius.** Caring For Children in Trouble. *266 pp.*
**Forder, R. A.** (Ed.). Penelope Hall's Social Services of Modern England. *352 pp.*
**George, Victor.** Foster Care. *Theory and Practice. 234 pp.*
    Social Security: *Beveridge and After. 258 pp.*

● **Goetschius, George W.** Working with Community Groups. *256 pp.*

**Goetschius, George W.,** and **Tash, Joan.** Working with Unattached Youth. *416 pp.*

**Hall, M. P.,** and **Howes, I. V.** The Church in Social Work. *A Study of Moral Welfare Work undertaken by the Church of England. 320 pp.*

**Heywood, Jean S.** Children in Care: *the Development of the Service for the Deprived Child. 264 pp.*

**Hoenig, J.,** and **Hamilton, Marian W.** The De-Segration of the Mentally Ill. *284 pp.*

**Jones, Kathleen.** Lunacy, Law and Conscience, *1744-1845: the Social History of the Care of the Insane. 268 pp.*

Mental Health and Social Policy, 1845-1959. *264 pp.*

**King, Roy D., Raynes, Norma V.,** and **Tizard, Jack.** Patterns of Residential Care. *356 pp.*

**Leigh, John.** Young People and Leisure. *256 pp.*

**Morris, Pauline.** Put Away: *A Sociological Study of Institutions for the Mentally Retarded. 364 pp.*

**Nokes, P. L.** The Professional Task in Welfare Practice. *152 pp.*

**Timms, Noel.** Psychiatric Social Work in Great Britain (1939-1962). *280 pp.*

● Social Casework: *Principles and Practice. 256 pp.*

**Trasler, Gordon.** In Place of Parents: *A Study in Foster Care. 272 pp.*

**Young, A. F.,** and **Ashton, E. T.** British Social Work in the Nineteenth Century. *288 pp.*

**Young, A. F.** Social Services in British Industry. *272 pp.*


## SOCIOLOGY OF EDUCATION

**Banks, Olive.** Parity and Prestige in English Secondary Education: a Study in Educational Sociology. *272 pp.*

**Bentwich, Joseph.** Education in Israel. *224 pp. 8 pp. plates.*

● **Blyth, W. A. L.** English Primary Education. *A Sociological Description.*
1. Schools. *232 pp.*
2. Background. *168 pp.*

**Collier, K. G.** The Social Purposes of Education: *Personal and Social Values in Education. 268 pp.*

**Dale, R. R.,** and **Griffith, S.** Down Stream: *Failure in the Grammar School. 108 pp.*

**Dore, R. P.** Education in Tokugawa Japan. *356 pp. 9 pp. plates*

**Evans, K. M.** Sociometry and Education. *158 pp.*

**Foster, P. J.** Education and Social Change in Ghana. *336 pp. 3 maps.*

**Fraser, W. R.** Education and Society in Modern France. *150 pp.*

**Grace, Gerald R.** Role Conflict and the Teacher. *About 200 pp.*

**Hans, Nicholas.** New Trends in Education in the Eighteenth Century. *278 pp. 19 tables.*

● Comparative Education: *A Study of Educational Factors and Traditions. 360 pp.*

7

**Hargreaves, David.** Interpersonal Relations and Education. *432 pp.*
- Social Relations in a Secondary School. *240 pp.*
**Holmes, Brian.** Problems in Education. *A Comparative Approach. 336 pp.*
**King, Ronald.** Values and Involvement in a Grammar School. *164 pp.*
● **Mannheim, Karl,** and **Stewart, W. A. C.** An Introduction to the Sociology of Education. *206 pp.*
**Morris, Raymond N.** The Sixth Form and College Entrance. *231 pp.*
● **Musgrove, F.** Youth and the Social Order. *176 pp.*
● **Ottaway, A. K. C.** Education and Society: *An Introduction to the Sociology of Education. With an Introduction by W. O. Lester Smith. 212 pp.*
**Peers, Robert.** Adult Education: *A Comparative Study. 398 pp.*
**Pritchard, D. G.** Education and the Handicapped: *1760 to 1960. 258 pp.*
**Richardson, Helen.** Adolescent Girls in Approved Schools. *308 pp.*
**Simon, Brian,** and **Joan** (Eds.). Educational Psychology in the U.S.S.R. *Introduction by Brian and Joan Simon. Translation by Joan Simon. Papers by D. N. Bogoiavlenski and N. A. Menchinskaia, D. B. Elkonin, E. A. Fleshner, Z. I. Kalmykova, G. S. Kostiuk, V. A. Krutetski, A. N. Leontiev, A. R. Luria, E. A. Milerian, R. G. Natadze, B. M. Teplov, L. S. Vygotski, L. V. Zankov. 296 pp.*
**Stratta, Erica.** The Education of Borstal Boys. *A Study of their Educational Experiences prior to, and during Borstal Training. 256 pp.*

## SOCIOLOGY OF CULTURE

**Eppel, E. M.,** and **M.** Adolescents and Morality: *A Study of some Moral Values and Dilemmas of Working Adolescents in the Context of a changing Climate of Opinion. Foreword by W. J. H. Sprott. 268 pp. 39 tables.*
● **Fromm, Erich.** The Fear of Freedom. *286 pp.*
The Sane Society. *400 pp.*
● **Mannheim, Karl.** Diagnosis of Our Time: *Wartime Essays of a Sociologist. 208 pp.*
Essays on the Sociology of Culture. *Edited by Ernst Mannheim in co-operation with Paul Kecskemeti. Editorial Note by Adolph Lowe. 280 pp.*
**Weber, Alfred.** Farewell to European History: *or The Conquest of Nihilism. Translated from the German by R. F. C. Hull. 224 pp.*

## SOCIOLOGY OF RELIGION

**Argyle, Michael.** Religious Behaviour. *224 pp. 8 figures. 41 tables.*
**Nelson, G. K.** Spiritualism and Society. *313 pp.*

**Stark, Werner.** The Sociology of Religion. *A Study of Christendom.*
  Volume I. *Established Religion. 248 pp.*
  Volume II. *Sectarian Religion. 368 pp.*
  Volume III. *The Universal Church. 464 pp.*
  Volume IV. *Types of Religious Man. 352 pp.*
  Volume V. *Types of Religious Culture. 464 pp.*
**Watt, W. Montgomery.** Islam and the Integration of Society. *320 pp.*


## SOCIOLOGY OF ART AND LITERATURE

**Beljame, Alexandre.** Men of Letters and the English Public in the Eighteenth
  Century: *1660-1744, Dryden, Addison, Pope. Edited with an Introduction
  and Notes by Bonamy Dobrée. Translated by E. O. Lorimer. 532 pp.*
**Jarvie, Ian C.** Towards a Sociology of the Cinema. *A Comparative Essay
  on the Structure and Functioning of a Major Entertainment Industry.
  405 pp.*
**Rust, Frances S.** Dance in Society. *An Analysis of the Relationships between
  the Social Dance and Society in England from the Middle Ages to the
  Present Day. 256 pp. 8 pp. of plates.*
**Schücking, L. L.** The Sociology of Literary Taste. *112 pp.*
**Silbermann, Alphons.** The Sociology of Music. *Translated from the German
  by Corbet Stewart. 222 pp.*


## SOCIOLOGY OF KNOWLEDGE

**Mannheim, Karl.** Essays on the Sociology of Knowledge. *Edited by Paul
  Kecskemeti. Editorial note by Adolph Lowe. 353 pp.*
**Stark, Werner.** The Sociology of Knowledge: *An Essay in Aid of a Deeper
  Understanding of the History of Ideas. 384 pp.*


## URBAN SOCIOLOGY

**Ashworth, William.** The Genesis of Modern British Town Planning: *A Study
  in Economic and Social History of the Nineteenth and Twentieth Centuries.
  288 pp.*
**Cullingworth, J. B.** Housing Needs and Planning Policy: *A Restatement of
  the Problems of Housing Need and 'Overspill' in England and Wales.
  232 pp. 44 tables. 8 maps.*
**Dickinson, Robert E.** City and Region: *A Geographical Interpretation.
  608 pp. 125 figures.*
  The West European City: *A Geographical Interpretation. 600 pp. 129 maps.
  29 plates.*
● The City Region in Western Europe. *320 pp. Maps.*

**Humphreys, Alexander J.** New Dubliners: *Urbanization and the Irish Family. Foreword by George C. Homans. 304 pp.*
**Jackson, Brian.** Working Class Community: *Some General Notions raised by a Series of Studies in Northern England. 192 pp.*
**Jennings, Hilda.** Societies in the Making: *a Study of Development and Re-development within a County Borough. Foreword by D. A. Clark. 286 pp.*
**Kerr, Madeline.** The People of Ship Street. *240 pp.*
● **Mann, P. H.** An Approach to Urban Sociology. *240 pp.*
**Morris, R. N.,** and **Mogey, J.** The Sociology of Housing. *Studies at Berinsfield. 232 pp. 4 pp. plates.*
**Rosser, C.,** and **Harris, C.** The Family and Social Change. *A Study of Family and Kinship in a South Wales Town. 352 pp. 8 maps.*

## RURAL SOCIOLOGY

**Chambers, R. J. H.** Settlement Schemes in Africa: *A Selective Study. 268 pp.*
**Haswell, M. R.** The Economics of Development in Village India. *120 pp.*
**Littlejohn, James.** Westrigg: *the Sociology of a Cheviot Parish. 172 pp. 5 figures.*
**Williams, W. M.** The Country Craftsman: *A Study of Some Rural Crafts and the Rural Industries Organization in England. 248 pp. 9 figures. (Dartington Hall Studies in Rural Sociology.)*
The Sociology of an English Village: *Gosforth. 272 pp. 12 figures. 13 tables.*

## SOCIOLOGY OF INDUSTRY AND DISTRIBUTION

**Anderson, Nels.** Work and Leisure. *280 pp.*
● **Blau, Peter M.,** and **Scott, W. Richard.** Formal Organizations: *a Comparative approach. Introduction and Additional Bibliography by J. H. Smith. 326 pp.*
**Eldridge, J. E. T.** Industrial Disputes. *Essays in the Sociology of Industrial Relations. 288 pp.*
**Hetzler, Stanley.** Technological Growth and Social Change. *Achieving Modernization. 269 pp.*
**Hollowell, Peter G.** The Lorry Driver. *272 pp.*
**Jefferys, Margot,** *with the assistance of Winifred Moss.* Mobility in the Labour Market: *Employment Changes in Battersea and Dagenham. Preface by Barbara Wootton. 186 pp. 51 tables.*
**Millerson, Geoffrey.** The Qualifying Associations: *a Study in Professionalization. 320 pp.*
**Smelser, Neil J.** Social Change in the Industrial Revolution: *An Application of Theory to the Lancashire Cotton Industry, 1770-1840. 468 pp. 12 figures. 14 tables.*
**Williams, Gertrude.** Recruitment to Skilled Trades. *240 pp.*

**Young, A. F.** Industrial Injuries Insurance: *an Examination of British Policy. 192 pp.*

## ANTHROPOLOGY

**Ammar, Hamed.** Growing up in an Egyptian Village: *Silwa, Province of Aswan. 336 pp.*

**Brandel-Syrier, Mia.** Reeftown Elite. *A Study of Social Mobility in a Modern African Community on the Reef. 376 pp.*

**Crook, David,** and **Isabel.** Revolution in a Chinese Village: *Ten Mile Inn. 230 pp. 8 plates. 1 map.*

The First Years of Yangyi Commune. *302 pp. 12 plates.*

**Dickie-Clark, H. F.** The Marginal Situation. *A Sociological Study of a Coloured Group. 236 pp.*

**Dube, S. C.** Indian Village. *Foreword by Morris Edward Opler. 276 pp. 4 plates.*

India's Changing Villages: *Human Factors in Community Development. 260 pp. 8 plates. 1 map.*

**Firth, Raymond.** Malay Fishermen. *Their Peasant Economy. 420 pp. 17 pp. plates.*

**Gulliver, P. H.** Social Control in an African Society: a Study of the Arusha, Agricultural Masai of Northern Tanganyika. *320 pp. 8 plates. 10 figures.*

**Ishwaran, K.** Shivapur. *A South Indian Village. 216 pp.*

Tradition and Economy in Village India: *An Interactionist Approach. Foreword by Conrad Arensburg. 176 pp.*

**Jarvie, Ian C.** The Revolution in Anthropology. *268 pp.*

**Jarvie, Ian C.,** and **Agassi, Joseph.** Hong Kong. *A Society in Transition. 396 pp. Illustrated with plates and maps.*

**Little, Kenneth L.** Mende of Sierra Leone. *308 pp. and folder.*

Negroes in Britain. *With a New Introduction and Contemporary Study by Leonard Bloom. 320 pp.*

**Lowie, Robert H.** Social Organization. *494 pp.*

**Mayer, Adrian C.** Caste and Kinship in Central India: *A Village and its Region. 328 pp. 16 plates. 15 figures. 16 tables.*

**Smith, Raymond T.** The Negro Family in British Guiana: *Family Structure and Social Status in the Villages. With a Foreword by Meyer Fortes. 314 pp. 8 plates. 1 figure. 4 maps.*

## DOCUMENTARY

**Meek, Dorothea L.** (Ed.). Soviet Youth: *Some Achievements and Problems. Excerpts from the Soviet Press, translated by the editor. 280 pp.*

**Schlesinger, Rudolf** (Ed.). Changing Attitudes in Soviet Russia.

2. *The Nationalities Problem and Soviet Administration. Selected Readings on the Development of Soviet Nationalities Policies. Introduced by the editor. Translated by W. W. Gottlieb. 324 pp.*

## SOCIOLOGY AND PHILOSOPHY

**Barnsley, John H.** The Social Reality of Ethics. *A Comparative Analysis of Moral Codes. 448 pp.*

**Douglas, Jack D.** (Ed.). Understanding Everyday Life. *Toward the Reconstruction of Sociological Knowledge. Contributions by Alan F. Blum. Aaron W. Cicourel, Norman K. Denzin, Jack D. Douglas, John Heeren, Peter McHugh, Peter K. Manning, Melvin Power, Matthew Speier, Roy Turner, D. Lawrence Wieder, Thomas P. Wilson and Don H. Zimmerman. 358 pp.*

**Jarvie, Ian C.** Concepts and Society. *216 pp.*

**Roche, Maurice.** Phenomenology, Language and the Social Sciences. *About 400 pp.*

**Sklair, Leslie.** The Sociology of Progress. *320 pp.*

# International Library of Social Policy

*General Editor* Kathleen Janes

**Jones, Kathleen.** Mental Health Services. *A history, 1744-1971. About 500 pp.*

**Thomas, J. E.** The English Prison Officer since 1850: *A Study in Conflict. 258 pp.*

# Primary Socialization, Language and Education

*General Editor* Basil Bernstein

**Bernstein, Basil.** Class, Codes and Control. *2 volumes.*
1. *Theoretical Studies Towards a Sociology of Language. 254 pp.*
2. *Applied Studies Towards a Sociology of Language. About 400 pp.*

**Brandis, Walter,** and **Henderson, Dorothy.** Social Class, Language and Communication. *288 pp.*

**Cook, Jenny.** Socialization and Social Control. *About 300 pp.*

**Gahagan, D. M.,** and **G. A.** Talk Reform. *Exploration in Language for Infant School Children. 160 pp.*

**Robinson, W. P.,** and **Rackstraw, Susan, D. A.** A Question of Answers. *2 volumes. 192 pp. and 180 pp.*

**Turner, Geoffrey, J.,** and **Mohan, Bernard, A.** A Linguistic Description and Computer Programme for Children's Speech. *208 pp.*

12

# Reports of the Institute of Community Studies and the Institute of Social Studies in Medical Care

**Cartwright, Ann.** Human Relations and Hospital Care. *272 pp.*
  Parents and Family Planning Services. *306 pp.*
  Patients and their Doctors. *A Study of General Practice. 304 pp.*
**Dunnell, Karen,** and **Cartwright, Ann.** Medicine Takers, Prescribers and Hoarders. *About 140 pp.*
● **Jackson, Brian.** Streaming: *an Education System in Miniature. 168 pp.*
**Jackson, Brian,** and **Marsden, Dennis.** Education and the Working Class: *Some General Themes raised by a Study of 88 Working-class Children in a Northern Industrial City. 268 pp. 2 folders.*
**Marris, Peter.** Widows and their Families. *Foreword by Dr. John Bowlby. 184 pp. 18 tables. Statistical Summary.*
  Family and Social Change in an African City. *A Study of Rehousing in Lagos. 196 pp. 1 map. 4 plates. 53 tables.*
  The Experience of Higher Education. *232 pp. 27 tables.*
**Marris, Peter,** and **Rein, Martin.** Dilemmas of Social Reform. *Poverty and Community Action in the United States. 256 pp.*
**Marris, Peter,** and **Somerset, Anthony.** African Businessmen. *A Study of Entrepreneurship and Development in Kenya. 256 pp.*
**Runciman, W. G.** Relative Deprivation and Social Justice. *A Study of Attitudes to Social Inequality in Twentieth Century England. 352 pp.*
**Townsend, Peter.** The Family Life of Old People: *An Inquiry in East London. Foreword by J. H. Sheldon. 300 pp. 3 figures. 63 tables.*
**Willmott, Peter.** Adolescent Boys in East London. *230 pp.*
  The Evolution of a Community: *a study of Dagenham after forty years. 168 pp. 2 maps.*
**Willmott, Peter,** and **Young, Michael.** Family and Class in a London Suburb. *202 pp. 47 tables.*
**Young, Michael.** Innovation and Research in Education. *192 pp.*
● **Young, Michael,** and **McGeeney, Patrick.** Learning Begins at Home. *A Study of a Junior School and its Parents. 128 pp.*
**Young, Michael,** and **Willmott, Peter.** Family and Kinship in East London. *Foreword by Richard M. Titmuss. 252 pp. 39 tables.*

# Medicine, Illness and Society
*General Editor* W. M. Williams

**Robinson, David.** The Process of Becoming Ill.
**Stacey, Margaret.** *et al.* Hospitals, Children and Their Families. *The Report of a Pilot Study. 202 pp.*

# Routledge Social Science Journals

**The British Journal of Sociology.** *Edited by Terence P. Morris. Vol. 1, No. 1, March 1950 and Quarterly. Roy. 8vo. Back numbers available. An international journal with articles on all aspects of sociology.*

**Economy and Society.** *Vol. 1, No. 1. February 1972 and Quarterly. Metric Roy. 8vo. A journal for all social scientists covering sociology, philosophy, anthropology, economics and history.*

Printed in Great Britain by Lewis Reprints Limited
Brown Knight & Truscott Group, London and Tonbridge          21972